OPEN JUSTICE: A CRITIQUE OF THE

Open Justice:
A Critique of the Public Trial

by
Joseph Jaconelli

OXFORD
UNIVERSITY PRESS

OXFORD

UNIVERSITY PRESS

Great Clarendon Street, Oxford OX2 6DP

Oxford University Press is a department of the University of Oxford.
It furthers the University's objective of excellence in research, scholarship,
and education by publishing worldwide in

Oxford New York

Auckland Bangkok Buenos Aires Cape Town Chennai
Dar es Salaam Delhi Hong Kong Istanbul Karachi Kolkata
Kuala Lumpur Madrid Melbourne Mexico City Mumbai Nairobi
São Paulo Shanghai Singapore Taipei Tokyo Toronto

with an associated company in Berlin

Oxford is a registered trade mark of Oxford University Press
in the UK and in certain other countries

Published in the United States
by Oxford University Press Inc., New York

British Library Cataloguing in Publication Data

Data available

Library of Congress Cataloging in Publication Data

Jaconelli, Joseph.
Open Justice: A Critique of the Public Trial/by Joseph Jaconelli.
p. cm.
Includes bibliographical references and index.
1. Conduct of court proceedings—Great Britain. 2. Publicity (Law)—
Great Britain. 3. Privacy, Right of—Great Britain. I. Title.
KD7117.J33 2002 345.42'05—dc21 2002020005
ISBN 0–19–825258–7

1 3 5 7 9 10 8 6 4 2

Typeset by Hope Services (Abingdon) Ltd.
Printed in Great Britain
on acid-free paper by
T. J. International Ltd., Padstow, Cornwall

Preface

Some initial observations are necessary on the aims and structure of this book.

That law suits in general, and criminal trials in particular, are required to be heard in public is a standard that has been observed in legal systems of very different eras and types. With the arrival of, first, the print media and, then, radio and television the means came into existence for conveying the trial events to a much larger audience than could be accommodated in the courtroom itself. Yet, whatever the extent and nature of the coverage, the norm that trials are open to the public merits systematic examination. A principal aim of this work is to consider critically the reasons for the near universal rule of open justice.

Equally, the general rule is subject to a range of exceptions. Sometimes, as with matters of national security, the exception is justified on the basis of considerations extraneous to the trial itself. More often, the reason for departure from the standard of open justice is to be found within court procedures themselves. Many witnesses, for example, feel daunted by the prospect of testifying in public, and all that is entailed by this. Here it is open justice itself that is, at least in part, responsible for creating the difficulties, and there is consequently reason for considering departure from the ideal. Whatever their basis, the scope of these exceptions forms another of the main themes of this work.

Attention will be focused on general issues of principle in preference to rendering a detailed account of the relevant aspects of English law. This approach is necessitated by the range and volume of material, encompassing not only the traditional sources of case law and statute but also newspaper reports of trials in which some element of secrecy has figured. In some areas, for example, the provisions of the recently enacted Youth Justice and Criminal Evidence Act 1999, a detailed rehearsal would be prohibitively long and would be at the expense of the clarity of the overall picture. The emphasis on general principle has necessitated the examination of some procedures which are scarcely used today but which cast a degree of light on open justice that is disproportionate to the amount of their use in the modern legal system. For example, contested divorce cases are but seldom encountered nowadays, yet in their time they have provided an illuminating perspective on several of the themes of the public administration of justice. Again, committal proceedings, though they have all but disappeared from contemporary criminal procedure, provide an instructive variation on some of the themes of this book.

The structure of the book is as follows. Chapter 1 is a preliminary piece in which several of the central concepts that will be used throughout are introduced and analysed. Chapter 2 then examines the rationale of public trial in the context both of different types of legal proceeding and of various procedures ancillary to trial. The emphasis shifts, in Chapter 3, to secrecy in the conduct of trials, both the possible methods of enforcing it and the control of its improper use. The theme of the following part of the book is that of departure from the standard of openness, whether for reasons of security (Chapter 4), for the protection of private or family life (Chapter 5), or with a view to maintaining commercial secrecy (Chapter 6). The subject matter of Chapter 7 stands somewhat apart in concentrating on the decision-making stage of the trial, in particular jury deliberations. The final two chapters are devoted to the reporting of trials to those persons who were not present in the courtroom, both generally (Chapter 8) and in the specific context of radio and television coverage of the proceedings (Chapter 9). In a short coda a brief conspectus is offered of the themes that have been covered.

Reference will be made to a number of cases, many of which are not reported in the usual way in a regular series of law reports. The facts and the issues involved in some of these cases will already be known to many readers. In order to assist those who are not familiar with them, and in order to avoid disruption of the narrative, a brief summary of the cases is given in the Appendix.

Account has been taken of significant developments in the subject up until February 2002.

Acknowledgements

A book that has had a gestation period as long as this one inevitably results in its author incurring numerous debts of gratitude. Particular thanks are due to the Press for their patience in the face of what must have seemed to be interminable delays. Mick Belson, John Louth, and Michael Watson provided much appreciated encouragement and support in the final stages. Geraldine Mangley handled with exemplary efficiency the day-to-day task of managing the book through the production process.

For assistance on particular points thanks are due to Cathy Deering, Mark James, Colin Reid, Hugh Wagner, and Robin White. The burden of writing on aspects of law far removed from my usual interests has been lightened by John Murphy and Mandy Burton, who readily agreed to comment on material relating to family law, tort, and criminal procedure. Sue Bate, law librarian at the John Rylands Library of the University of Manchester, was unstintingly helpful, as ever. I was kindly supplied with photocopies of material by Tony Oakley, Alessandro Pace, and the staff of the Kathrine R. Everett Library of the Law School of the University of North Carolina at Chapel Hill.

Use has been made, with adaptations and (I hope) improvements, of material that I have already published: 'Some Thoughts on Jury Secrecy', *Legal Studies* (1990) 91, and 'Rights Theories and Public Trial', *Journal of Applied Philosophy* (1997) 169.

Jackie Gandy, Laura Short, and Sarah Tiffany-Dodman did a substantial amount of the typing. Laura Short and Susan Lee assisted with running off the typescript. My own first faltering steps into word processing were taken in connection with the book and owe much to the instruction and support of Philip Bull, Tom Gibbons, and Ellen Lee.

The process of checking took on the character of a family event. Thanks are due to Gail, Rebecca, James, and, not least, to Laura, who was keen to help and wanted to know when she would be old enough to do so.

My greatest debts of gratitude are owed to two people.

Without my colleague, David Milman, the book would not have started. It was a chance conversation between us, on the practice of anonymously reporting petitions brought by disgruntled shareholders, that led to the realization that there was need for a monograph on the whole subject of open justice. I am very grateful to him, not only for providing initial stimulus for the project, but also for writing Chapter 6. Throughout, his support and interest in the project have been unflagging, whether in commenting on drafts or in tracking down far more material than it has been possible to incorporate in the text.

Without my wife, Anne, the book would not have been completed. Her help and support took many forms: discussing ideas, typing, cajoling, providing reassurance that the task was achievable, furnishing critical comment on drafts, and leading me back when I have been distracted by other research projects. It is a wholly inadequate recompense that the book is dedicated with love to her.

Law School   Joseph Jaconelli
University of Manchester

Contents

Table of Cases

EUROPEAN CONVENTION ON HUMAN RIGHTS

EUROPEAN UNION

ITALY

NEW ZEALAND

UNITED STATES OF AMERICA

Table of Legislation

CANADA

Table of Statutory Instruments

Table of Treaties

1

The Elements of Open Justice

1. INTRODUCTION

The subject matter of this book is the legal rule which requires courts and other bodies which discharge functions of a judicial nature to conduct their proceedings in public. While it covers civil and criminal proceedings alike, the demands imposed by the rule are generally viewed as particularly insistent in regard to the latter. The rule is also, quite properly, subject to a number of exceptions. Although many legal systems, both past and present, have subscribed to the norm as embodying a clear standard of civilized procedure, this account is confined to giving a critical statement of the English law on the subject. From time to time material will be drawn upon from other jurisdictions either to provide guidance where English law is uncertain or by way of suggestion of ideas for possible law reform.

A concern which permeates this work is the question of what values or interests are served by conducting trials in public. (The word 'trial', it should be noted, will be used to denote criminal and civil cases alike, unless the context indicates otherwise.) The secret trial, the trial conducted behind closed doors, has so often been used to advance the purposes of tyrannical government that it is rightly regarded with suspicion. But publicity, in itself, is not an unalloyed benefit in the administration of justice. The proceedings that are attended by excessive public attention may degenerate into a 'show trial' or, even if they do not do so, may invade important interests of participants in the trial.[1] One thesis of the present work, indeed, is that in this area there exists a golden mean that lies between the one extreme of secrecy and the other extreme of excessive exposure of judicial proceedings to the public gaze.

The subject of administrative secrecy in British government has formed the theme of a number of studies. Those who come to the present work from any of those studies will be struck immediately by a sharp contrast: the overriding importance that has traditionally been attached to the open conduct of judicial proceedings, by comparison with the indifference with which the practice of secrecy has been allowed to pervade the executive branch of government.

[1] Especially noteworthy are the various perversions of civilized standards of criminal procedure practised by the Soviet authorities, as recounted by Alexander Solzhenitsyn in *The Gulag Archipelago 1918–1956* (1974), chs 8–10. Secret trials, public trials, and trials attended only by carefully selected spectators, were all used at different times as means of enforcing obedience to Soviet rule.

Nothing points up this contrast more vividly than the fact that the fountain-head of the present study, the judgment of the House of Lords in *Scott v Scott*[2] which pronounced in ringing terms the supreme importance of the open conduct of trials, came a mere two years after Parliament, in the form of the Official Secrets Act 1911, had set the legal seal on secrecy in central government.[3]

A comparison of the judicial with the legislative branch of government is likely to prove more fruitful.[4] Parliament, it should be recalled, is a court—the High Court of Parliament. Parliamentary business, like judicial business, is conducted in full view of the public gallery although, in both spheres, exceptional circumstances may require the exclusion of the public. Similar privileges in the law of defamation attach to reports of the proceedings of both institutions. Also, in time, the courts may be permitted to follow the lead taken by Parliament in allowing transmission of its sittings, first by radio and then by television. The analogy, however, should not be pressed too far. The requirement of openness in the legislature is shaped by the demands of democratic accountability.[5] Such considerations do not figure—or, at any rate, they do not figure in exactly the same way—in regard to parallel issues in the courts.

2. THE IDEAL OF OPEN JUSTICE

The term 'open justice' is used throughout his book. It is suggested that the concept of open justice comprises the following presumptive elements.

It consists, in the first place, of the provision of adequate facilities for the attendance of members of the public at the trial. It also encompasses the provision of similar facilities for the representatives of the media—the print media, at least. Admission, whether of the public or the press, is to the trial as a live event. This first element constitutes the very core of the idea of open justice.

Secondly, there is a derivative aspect which guarantees the right of those in attendance—typically, one is speaking here of the representatives of the media—to report the proceedings to those who either could not gain admission to the trial or were simply not inclined to attend. This aspect finds expression in the freedom to recount aspects of the trial proceedings without running the risk of incurring

---

[2] [1913] AC 417.

[3] Trials were, of course, held in public long before the ruling in *Scott v Scott*. So, too, there was legislation on official secrecy—the Official Secrets Act 1889—which preceded the 1911 statute.

[4] See C. Parry, 'Legislatures and Secrecy' (1953–54) 67 *Harvard Law Review* 737. On the specific subject of voting see A. Reeve and A. Ware, *Electoral Systems: A Comparative and Theoretical Introduction* (1992), ch 5 ('Secret and open voting').

[5] In this regard the Council of Ministers of the European Union, the legislative organ of the Union, is particularly open to criticism. The public are not allowed to attend meetings of the Council, and its proceedings are confidential. Recently, however, there has been increased willingness to release the documents of the Council to interested parties.

the various forms of liability—most usually defamation or contempt of court—that might otherwise be incurred in this activity.

Thirdly, when documents have come into existence for the purposes of the trial—by way of pleadings, for example—these should presumptively be available for inspection by any member of the public. The procedures of the court systems of the world vary considerably. Some require as much material as possible (by way of pleadings and argument) to be committed to paper and read in advance of the hearing by the trial participants. At the other extreme, some legal systems permit a complete picture of the issues to emerge at the hearing itself by requiring the oral recital of the contents of all documents. Clearly, the more closely the legal system approximates to the first extreme, the greater the importance that this third element of open justice assumes.

Fourthly, the names should be openly available of the personnel of the trial: the accused (in a criminal case), the parties (in a civil case), judge, jurors and witnesses. This element is often, though not invariably, an aspect of the right to communicate a full report of the trial. In some instances the identity of the person—most usually, a witness—will be made known to the people present in the courtroom, but the judge makes an order enjoining secrecy beyond the confines of the court. In other instances the identity will be withheld even from other participants in the trial and hence, also, from all others in attendance at the proceedings.

All the above elements of 'open justice' are aspects of the right of the public to be informed and the corresponding right of the media to inform them. The remaining elements stand on a different footing, in that they identify the analogous rights of the accused in criminal proceedings.

Fifthly, then, the trial is to take place in the presence of the accused.[6] A few words are necessary to qualify this statement. It is quite clear that, although the accused possesses a right to attend his own trial, this is a right that is capable of waiver, whether wholly or in part, by him.[7] The court then has a discretion whether or not to proceed in his absence.[8] Of course, a defendant who absents himself and does not instruct counsel is denying himself the opportunity to learn the case against him and to contest the allegations. Moreover, in exceptional circumstances of personal fault (most typically unruly behaviour),[9] the accused, like any member of the public who does wish to remain present, may be ordered to be

---

[6] This is the subject of a specific guarantee in the International Covenant on Civil and Political Rights, Article 14(3): 'In the determination of any criminal charge against him, everyone shall be entitled to the following minimum guarantees, in full equality: . . . (d) To be tried in his presence, and to defend himself in person or through legal assistance of his own choosing; . . .'

[7] For a full review, see *R v Hayward, R v Jones (Anthony), R v Purvis* [2001] QB 862.

[8] It is possible, of course, to stage the trial of a suspect who has not even been apprehended. Quite apart from objections of principle to such a procedure, the trial will turn out to have had only a moot or speculative aspect if the suspect is never made subject to legal process.

[9] *R v Morley* [1988] QB 601.

removed from the courtroom.[10] In both situations the court is required to weigh carefully the question of fairness to the accused if the trial is to continue in his absence.

Sixthly, the accused is presumptively entitled to confront his accusers. This element, which is not assured simply by reason of his presence in the courtroom, comprises two aspects: the right to know the identity of the witnesses who testify against him and the right to confront them face to face. The guarantee of the one aspect will, in most circumstances, entail the assurance of the other. However there will be circumstances in which it does not. In the case of testimony given by an especially vulnerable witness—the typical instance is that of the child who has allegedly been the victim of sexual abuse at the hands of the accused—the identity of the witness will be known only too well. The aspect of face-to-face confrontation between the two persons, on the other hand, is eliminated by such means as the erection of a screen between them, or the interposing of a video link between the witness and the courtroom.

A word of explanation, finally, is necessary as to why this last element is to be included in a work on open justice. Any consideration that requires the anonymity of a witness vis-à-vis the accused will likewise require that the anonymity be safeguarded as regards the public gallery. Otherwise the information that has been denied in direct terms to the accused could reach him indirectly by way of his associates present in the courtroom. Moreover, even where there is no issue of anonymity, the sensitive witness who is protected from direct confrontation with the accused may, in addition, have to be spared the ordeal of giving testimony before a substantial number of members of the public.

3. CONSTITUTIONAL GUARANTEES

Many of the elements which we have sketched as constituents of the ideal of 'open justice' are guaranteed in the Sixth Amendment to the Constitution of the United States of America:

---

[10] An important point needs to be made here. In some instances a plea that an accused has not been permitted to be present at his own trial is based, not on his absence from the courtroom, but rather on the argument that an essential element of the trial (which the accused attended in the normal way) was held 'off stage'. See, for example, *R v Preston* [1994] AC 130, in which Lord Mustill described as held *'in camera'* (at 159) a phase in the trial—lasting some thirty working hours—in which the judge and counsel were secluded in the judge's chambers, to the exclusion of the accused and his solicitors (not to mention the jury and the public).

A case which similarly compounded secret proceedings with the exclusion of the accused was reviewed in *Lawrence v R* [1933] AC 699. The trial judge, among other faults, had altered the sentence while in chambers and in the absence of the accused. The Judicial Committee of the Privy Council pronounced, at 708: 'It is an essential principle of our criminal law that the trial for an indictable offence has to be conducted in the presence of the accused; and for this purpose trial means the whole of the proceedings, including sentence . . .'.

In all criminal prosecutions, the accused shall enjoy the right to a speedy and public trial, by an impartial jury of the State and district wherein the crime shall have been committed, . . . and to be informed of the nature and cause of the accusation; to be confronted with the witnesses against him; to have compulsory process for obtaining witnesses in his favor, and to have the assistance of counsel for his defence.

That trials are to be held in public, in particular, is a principle that has long been formally recognized in constitutional and human rights texts, whether national or international, contemporary or historical. While lacking the seniority of inscription in the Magna Carta or the Bill of Rights 1689, the right to a public trial is of sufficiently ancient vintage to appear—as in the case of the Sixth Amendment—in constitutional documents of the late eighteenth century. In some texts the guarantee of open justice is drafted quite generally. For example, Article 34.1 of the Irish Constitution 1937: 'Justice . . . save in such special and limited cases as may be prescribed by law, shall be administered in public.'

Article 6 of the European Convention on Human Rights states: 'In the determination of his civil rights and obligations or of any criminal charge against him, everyone is entitled to a fair and public hearing within a reasonable time by an independent and impartial tribunal established by law. . .'[11]

In the case of other texts the guarantee is limited to criminal proceedings only. Thus, section 11 of the Canadian Charter of Rights and Freedoms states: 'Any person charged with an offence has the right . . . (d) to be presumed innocent until proven guilty according to law in a fair and public hearing by an independent and impartial tribunal. . .'

Also Article 8(5) of the Inter-American Convention on Human Rights provides: 'Criminal procedure shall be public, except in so far as may be necessary to protect the interests of justice.'[12]

Two points emerge from a brief survey of this kind. Openness, while being of general importance to the conduct of trials, takes on heightened importance in the case of criminal proceedings. However, that quality is not exhaustive of the procedural prerequisites of a fair trial. It occupies but one space in a constellation of requirements: that the trial be speedy (though consistent with the right of the

---

[11] Article 6 appears to take its cue from the equivalent provision, Art 14(1), of the International Covenant on Civil and Political Rights. A person's entitlement to a public hearing under Article 14(1) arises '[i]n the determination of any criminal charge against him, or of his rights and obligations in a suit at law . . .'. The third paragraph of both provisions goes on to list additional minimum guarantees for those charged with a criminal offence.

[12] See also the Domestic and Appellate Proceedings (Restriction of Publicity) Act 1968, section 1(3), which recognizes the particular importance of openness in criminal procedure: 'Where the decision of any of the courts mentioned in subsection (4) below against which an appeal is brought—(a) is a conviction, or a sentence or other order made on conviction, or (b) was given in the exercise of jurisdiction to punish for contempt of court, the court hearing the appeal or any further appeal arising out of the same proceedings shall, notwithstanding that it sat in private during the whole or any part of the proceedings on the appeal state in open court the order made by it on the appeal.'

Subsection (3) is a qualification to s 1(1), which conferred a general power to hear an appeal in private where the court from which the appeal is being heard could sit in private.

accused to have adequate time to prepare his defence);[13] that there should be adequate opportunity to examine or cross-examine witnesses; that (if need be) the free services of an interpreter be provided;[14] that the tribunal be unbiased, and so on.

4. *SCOTT V SCOTT*

In English law there is no fundamental constitutional text embodying the right to an open trial or to any of the above-mentioned procedural safeguards. The nearest equivalent is to be found in the Human Rights Act 1998. This statute embodies, among other rights, the guarantees of Article 6 of the European Human Rights Convention. It does so, however, in the form of a principle of construction which must yield before the express wording of any Act of Parliament which overrides the right.[15] Even in the absence of such a formal guarantee, it was in these terms that the judgment of Lord Shaw in *Scott v Scott* extolled the open conduct of trials as 'a sound and very sacred part of the constitution of the country and the administration of justice'.[16] Since this is a case to which we must frequently return as the principal source of English law on the subject, it is appropriate to set out the facts and reasoning of that case as soon as possible.

In January 1911 Mrs Annie Maria Scott filed a petition in the Probate, Divorce and Admiralty Division of the High Court requesting that the marriage into which she had entered some dozen years earlier with Mr Kenneth MacKenzie Scott be declared void on the grounds of his impotence. The petition was heard in June of the same year by the President of the Division, Sir Samuel Evans, who granted a decree nisi. In accordance with an order of the registrar the case was heard in private—technically, *in camera*. In January 1912 the decree was made absolute, the husband choosing not to contest the proceedings. The course of events, in these respects, had proceeded like any other matrimonial cause of that type. However, in August 1911, Mrs Scott had asked her solicitor, a Mr Braby, to obtain from the court a transcript of the proceedings. She had three copies made, two of which were sent to Mr Scott's father and sister, the third to another person. Her reason for doing so was to refute certain allegations that had been made about her in these quarters by her estranged husband. The latter's response was to issue a notice of motion asking that Mrs Scott and Mr Braby be committed to prison for contempt of court for having published copies of the transcript of the official shorthand writer's notes of the proceedings.

---

[13] European Convention on Human Rights, Art 6(3)(b).

[14] European Convention on Human Rights, Art 6(3)(e).

[15] Human Rights Act 1998, in particular, s 1 (containing the definition of 'Convention Rights') and s 3 (1): 'So far as it is possible to do so, primary legislation and subordinate legislation must be read and given effect in a way which is compatible with the Convention rights.' The Act came into effect in October 2000.

[16] [1913] AC 417, 473.

Such were the facts. As has happened so very often, the initiation of legal proceedings with a view to punishing an act of publication has served to bring the background of the dispute to the notice of a far wider audience than would otherwise have been the case. Ironically, throughout its various stages the litigation was reported in the full names of the parties.

The case was heard at first instance by Bargrave Deane J,[17] who pronounced it a 'gross contempt of Court to report anything heard in camera'.[18] The reporting of summonses heard in chambers,[19] he added, would be viewed in the same light. In the circumstances, however, he accepted the apologies tendered by Mrs Scott and Mr Braby (though the conduct of the latter, as 'an officer of the Court', was rather less excusable). The only order made against them was an order as to costs. They appealed nevertheless.

The importance of the points of law in issue was marked, at the next stage, by the hearing of the case by a full Court of Appeal of six judges.[20] Their extensive analyses stand in marked contrast to Bargrave Deane J's one-page judgment. The dispute at this level turned on a mixture of procedural and substantive points. A preliminary objection was taken to the jurisdiction of the Court of Appeal, since it was precluded by section 47 of the Judicature Act 1873 from entertaining any appeal from the High Court 'in any criminal cause or matter, save for some error of law apparent upon the record'. The Court of Appeal, by a majority of four to two, ruled that the matter was indeed a 'criminal cause or matter' within the meaning of section 47 and the order made by Bargrave Deane J was not appealable.

The most detailed analyses of the issues are to be found in the dissenting judgments of Vaughan Williams and Fletcher Moulton LJJ. Not only would they hear the appeal, they would also allow it. The latter, in particular, concluded a lengthy historical excursus with some forcefully pronounced opinions on the scope and effect of a direction that a trial be heard *in camera*.

... the public are excluded from the hearing ... and the order is then entirely complied with and is exhausted. In the cases in which the Court can make such an order it is nothing more than an extreme exercise of its power to control its own proceedings, ... But the Court has nothing to do with the action of the individual parties when the suit is over ...' [21]

Their Lordships were much exercised by the problem of defining the exact effects of an *in camera* direction. Several of his colleagues could not agree with Fletcher Moulton LJ in his view of the direction as nothing more than an order to exclude members of the public from the hearing. Cozens-Hardy MR thought that '[i]t would be futile to say that although the public are not to be present at the hearing they may, when the hearing is over, be informed of all that has taken place'.[22]

---

[17] [1912] P 4.   [18] ibid. 6.

[19] For an account of the difference see Chapter 3, section 1, C–D, below.

[20] [1912] P 241. It was argued, at first, before Cozens-Hardy MR and Buckley and Fletcher Moulton LJJ. Only subsequently was it directed to be re-argued before the full Court of Appeal.

[21] See n 20 above, 284.   [22] See n 20 above, 247.

The clear implication behind this point of view was that disclosure was absolutely forbidden beyond the restricted circle of those who had been permitted to attend the hearing. However, Farwell LJ stressed the discretionary power retained in these matters by the trial judge: in his view, an *in camera* order amounted to a ban on 'the publication at any time without the leave of the judge of every detail that has passed in camera except the result'.[23] And Buckley LJ thought that publication within a limited circle and for 'proper purposes' might not be a contempt:

> A communication of the whole of the proceedings with every detail to those who professionally act for either party upon an appeal would of course be no contempt . . . A communication, for instance, made by a young wife to her mother of that which has taken place might well be no offence at all.[24]

In any event, it was apparent by now that the *Scott* case raised a number of important points that transcended those in issue between the estranged couple. When, therefore, Mrs Scott and Mr Braby appealed to the House of Lords special arrangements were made for the hearing. The Solicitor-General, Sir John Simon, argued the case for the respondent side by side with Mr Scott's counsel from the hearing in the Court of Appeal.

The five judgments in the House of Lords[25] are rich in statements on the subject of open justice in general: on its importance, the permissible exceptions to the rule, and the standard required to be met before an exception could be made. On the specific issues of the case their Lordships reversed the judgment of the Court of Appeal and decreed that the order made by Bargrave Deane J be discharged. The matter had been appealable: Bargrave Deane J's order as to costs was not a judgment 'in any criminal cause or matter' within the meaning of section 47 of the Judicature Act 1873. Their Lordships' view on the merits was that there had been no jurisdiction to make the *in camera* direction, even if (as had happened) the parties had concurred in its making. Viscount Haldane LC, in particular, emphasized the 'brief and simple character' of the evidence, adding that 'it might without difficulty have been tendered in open Court'.[26]

An alternative ground for the decision, advanced by certain of their Lordships, was that the *in camera* order—even if properly made in the circumstances—did not restrain subsequent publication of the proceedings. In this regard the judgment of Fletcher Moulton LJ in the court below was endorsed, whether with or without qualification. Earl Loreburn stressed the particular circumstances of the

---

[23] See n 20 above, 289. To like effect Cozens-Hardy MR said, at 247: 'the meaning and intent of the order is that the evidence should not be made public at any time without the leave of the Court'.

[24] See n 20 above, 294. This example, though, comes perilously close to describing the very limited disclosure which occasioned the actual dispute in the *Scott* case. Two of the people who were sent a transcript of the hearing, Mr Scott's father and sister, might well have been persons whose presence at the trial Mr Scott might have called for by way of emotional support had he chosen to contest the proceedings.

[25] [1913] AC 417.   [26] ibid. 439.

case. The disclosure by Mrs Scott 'in good faith of the true evidence in justifiable defence of her own reputation and happiness'[27] was not a contempt of court. Lord Atkinson, in contrast, stated:

I think the order in its true interpretation means what on its face it plainly says, and nothing more, namely, this, that the place where the case is to be heard shall be a private chamber, not a public Court . . . The order was, I think, spent when the case terminated, and had no further operation beyond that date.[28]

What, then, was the *ratio decidendi* of *Scott v Scott*? Notwithstanding the wide-ranging pronouncements on the subject of open trial, it should be noted that the case did not raise in a direct way the central elements of that subject: the right of access to the courtroom on the part of members of the public. The dispute did not concern, say, the right of an individual member of the public to remain seated in the gallery—tested, perhaps, in the form of an action in tort against the official who was instructed to remove him.[29] Nor was the issue one in which the losing party in a case, to the hearing of which the public had been denied access, was seeking on that account to impugn the validity of the proceedings. Strictly, *Scott v Scott* was authority only on the lack of power, at common law, and even with the consent of the parties, to direct the trial *in camera* of a nullity suit in the interests of public decency.[30] An additional basis for the decision—though, as we have seen, the judgments differed somewhat on this point—was the extremely limited scope of an *in camera* direction in curtailing the freedom of the parties to disclose details of the trial.

Although the various pronouncements in the House of Lords place the highest importance on the open conduct of trials, they differ from the majority of human rights documents in not assigning special weight to the value of open justice so far as criminal proceedings are concerned. The only respect in which the differential between criminal and civil law figured in the litigation was in the context of the procedural provision that lay at the centre of the appellate stages: section 47 of the Judicature Act 1873. One could argue from principle that the norm of open justice, invested with so much importance by the House of Lords in the context of a civil case, a suit for nullity of marriage, must surely apply with even greater force in criminal trials. In due course, particularly in Chapter 2, it will be necessary to address in more detail the distinction between the civil and the criminal law in so far as it bears on the subject matter of this book.

---

[27] ibid. 444.   [28] ibid. 453.

[29] Compare contractual licence cases such as *Wood v Leadbitter* (1845) 13 M&W 838, 153 ER 351, and *Hurst v Picture Theatres Ltd* [1915] 1 KB 1, where the legality of removal from property was tested in actions for assault and false imprisonment.

[30] This is the countervailing interest to that of open justice that is mentioned in the headnote to the case at [1913] AC 417, and also by Earl Loreburn at 447: 'Some passages in various judgments in this and other cases indicate that the Court has a right to close its doors in the interests of public decency. Apart from some Act of Parliament authorizing such a course in particular cases, I regret that I cannot find warrant for this opinion.'

Finally, by way of conclusion to this initial examination of *Scott v Scott*, it must be pointed out that several of the issues in that case have subsequently been addressed by statute. A brief mention of the relevant provisions will suffice for the moment. Nullity suits are still required to be heard in open court, but any evidence on the question of sexual capacity 'shall be heard in camera unless in any case the judge is satisfied that in the interests of justice any such evidence ought to be heard in open court'.[31] It is impossible to be exactly sure what point Mrs Scott was seeking to impress on her erstwhile father-in-law and sister-in-law (or, indeed, the third person) in sending them copies of the transcript of the proceedings. In doing so, arguably she went beyond the confines of the protection that would have been afforded to her if the above-quoted provision had been in effect. Nevertheless, it puts beyond doubt the legal propriety of part (at least) of a nullity suit being held *in camera*. Furthermore, to turn to the alternative ground upon which *Scott v Scott* was decided, it is now stated in section 12(1) of the Administration of Justice Act 1960 that the 'publication of information relating to proceedings before any court sitting in private shall not of itself be contempt of court' except in five listed situations.[32] Since the hearing of issues of sexual capacity in nullity suits does not figure in the list, the point remains to be resolved at common law in such circumstances.

This is an opportune point at which to take stock of the structure of this chapter. So far we have sketched the contents of open justice as an ideal and have identified the two possible forms of guarantee, as a constitutional right or at common law (as in *Scott v Scott*). In section 2 above the core element of open justice was identified as the confrontation—or, to be more precise, the provision of facilities for the confrontation—between the public and the press on the one side and the participants in the trial on the other. Both sides of this divide will require detailed examination in turn (in particular, see section 6, below). It is the latter which is considered in the immediately following section, where the three basic elements in the trial are isolated. Briefly, a trial is a type of function (section 5, C) which is discharged through the participation of various persons over a period of time (section 5, B) and in a particular location or locations (section 5, A). Of the three elements, it is that of function which is of overriding importance. For it is the characterization of a function as 'judicial' in nature which brings into play a presumptive requirement that it be performed in public. The consideration of this element in the present chapter will necessarily be preliminary in character. A more detailed examination in Chapter 2 will take us into an analysis of the ambit and rationale of open justice.

---

[31] Matrimonial Causes Act 1973, s 48(2). What, incidentally, is the criterion of 'justice' in this context? Note, also, the possible relevance of the Judicial Proceedings (Regulation of Reports) Act 1926, s 1(1)(b), whereby it is unlawful 'to print or publish . . . in relation to any judicial proceedings . . . for nullity of marriage' any particulars other than such outline information as the names of the parties, a concise statement of the charges, etc.

[32] For a detailed consideration of this provision, see Chapter 3, section 1, F, below.

5. THE ELEMENTS OF A TRIAL

A. Place

Historically, the idea of what constitutes a 'court' has not been free of difficulty.[33] Even today the concept is not entirely clear despite its central importance in designing the limits of offences that are concerned with maintaining order and decorum in the place of trial. In some contexts the word is used merely as a synonym for the judge or judges ('this court takes a dim view of your conduct') or in a general metaphorical sense (as, for example, in the designation of solicitors as 'officers of the court'). Our concern in this section, clearly, is with the concept of a court in a physical sense.

The overriding point to be made, in this context, is that no trial depends for its validity on its having been staged in a purpose-built courtroom (with its specifically designated press seats and public gallery).[34] The peculiar demands of some cases are such that any suitable building, irrespective of the nature of its regular use, may be designated as the trial venue. In some instances, it is the complexity of the case or the security aspects that surround it which are the decisive factors. In other cases, the reason for an unusual venue has been nothing more than the lack of availability of a regular courtroom.[35] Indeed, legal provisions that regulate the place of trial are quite sparse. A rare instance is provided by those which regulate the place (and time) of trial of young offenders. Defined in purely negative terms, by reference to the time and place of other types of proceeding,[36] their aim is to preserve the distinctiveness and seclusion of juvenile proceedings entirely apart from the trial of adult offenders.

The overwhelming majority of trials, nevertheless, are held in a purpose-built court. It is against the physical background of such a construction that the limits of the court, in a spatial sense, have been explored. A provision that is very much in point here is section 41 of the Criminal Justice Act 1925. Section 41 prohibits the drawing of sketches and the taking of photographs, not only in the 'court-room'

[33] See J. H. Baker, *The Legal Profession and the Common Law: Historical Essays* (1986) ch 10 ('The Changing Concept of a Court').

[34] The site of a trial becomes a matter of dispute in cases where, on account of the possibility of local prejudice, it is argued that the trial should not be held in the most natural location. It has been held that the decision where to hold a trial lies within the discretion of the trial judge, and the exercise of the discretion will not be readily reviewed: *R v Scott* [1994] Crim LR 947.

[35] In keeping with the notion that a regular courtroom is not essential for the proper conduct of a trial, it was held in *R v Norwich Crown Court, ex p Stiller* [1992] Crim LR 501 that the lack of such a courtroom (and of a judge) did not in general amount to a good and sufficient reason to extend the custody time limits under the Prosecution of Offences (Custody Time Limits) Regulations 1987, SI 1987/299.

[36] In this way the Children and Young Persons Act 1933, s 47(2), stipulates: '[a] juvenile court shall . . . sit either in a different building or room from that in which sittings of courts other than juvenile courts are held, or on different days from those on which sittings of such other courts are held . . .'. The juvenile court has since been superseded by the youth court.

itself but also in 'the building or . . . the precincts of the building in which the court is held.'[37] Instances have occurred of convictions for the taking of photographs of persons—in one case, that of a police marksman—outside the court building.[38] The spatial dimension is also of some importance in determining the boundaries of the jurisdiction to punish for contempt that has been committed 'in the face of the court'. This offence, of common law provenance, was given a measure of translation into statutory terms in section 12 of the Contempt of Court Act 1981, a provision which invests magistrates' courts with the power to deal with any person who, among other things, 'wilfully interrupts the proceedings of the court or otherwise misbehaves in court'. A rather extensive view has been taken, in these several contexts, of the ambit of the court. Disruptive conduct has been penalized, whether taking place in the public gallery,[39] on the roof of the court building,[40] or in the street outside the building.[41]

The physical layout of the courtroom itself rarely presents itself for legal comment. The features of the room are very familiar: the raised bench for the judiciary; a dock (in the case of many courts); a witness stand; a jury box; and seats for the press and members of the public. Traditionally, the concept of the 'Bar' is derived from the physical obstacle which prevented crowds intruding into the enclosure where judicial business was in progress. In this way it provided a rough and ready form of demarcation, to be explored in section 6 (below), between ordinary members of the public and those involved in the proceedings. On occasion, however, where the physical arrangements of the courtroom have been used as a basis for the contention that the accused has been denied a fair trial, such arrangements have been the subject of minute analysis.[42]

These familiar landmarks of the courtroom and the building in which it is housed are lost in those unusual instances where the court removes temporarily from its regular building: for example, in order to conduct a 'view' of the scene of an incident that is relevant to the case or in order to receive the testimony of a witness who is too ill to attend the courtroom in the usual way.[43] The issue of whether adequate (if any) provision has been made for the attendance of the public and the press in such temporary, makeshift courtrooms has not been the

---

[37] Criminal Justice Act 1925, s 41(2)(c). The provision is examined in detail in Chapter 9, section 2, below.

[38] In a ruling of December 1987 the Recorder of London, Sir James Miskin, held that photographs taken in this location fell within the scope of s 41: see the feature in The Independent, 29 January 1988, 3 ('Police Ban on Photos Taken Outside Court'). Note, however, the definition of 'precincts' given in the *Shorter Oxford English Dictionary*: 'the space enclosed by the walls or other boundaries of a particular place or building, or by an imaginary line drawn around it'.

[39] *R v Powell* The Times, 3 June 1993.   [40] *Balogh v Crown Court at St Albans* [1975] QB 73.

[41] *Bodden v Commissioner of Police of the Metropolis* [1990] 2 QB 397.

[42] *Sheppard v Maxwell* 384 US 333 (1966), 343.

[43] At least in such circumstances there exists no doubt as to the precise location of the court, even when transferred temporarily from its usual seat. Modern technology, in the form of video links, permits situations in which the location of a witness is far removed from the seat of the trial to which he is giving his testimony. For further consideration of the ensuing issues see Chapter 3, section 2, E, below.

subject of litigation. Nevertheless, it is very clear that the standards of propriety that are insisted on in the regular courtroom are also required to be observed in such other locations where the court sits. Therefore a 'view' from which the accused was excluded,[44] or which took place in the absence of one party to a civil suit,[45] has been held sufficient to vitiate the whole trial.

The spatial element in trials merits exploration in a further respect. The public and the press are admitted, for the purpose of observing trial proceedings, to property that belongs to another. What is their status, in terms of land law, while they are present in the courtroom, or even in the court building at large? Since they are not trespassers, they would appear to be present by virtue of some form of licence.[46] Yet it is difficult to slot their status within the established categories of licences. A bare licence would be inconsistent with their right to remain in the courtroom in the absence of special factors (for example, disruptive conduct on their part, or a decision of the court to go into private session). A contractual licence is not possible in the absence of payment of consideration. Nor is a licence by estoppel in the absence of factors giving rise to such an estoppel. As for a licence coupled with an interest, the qualifying interest must rank as a recognized property right.[47] The status of the trial spectator either must derive from a wholly distinct kind of licence or is to be found elsewhere in land law. It may rank as a 'public right', akin to the right of the public to pass and repass along the highway.[48] Alternatively, it may be possible to draw on American case law which requires reasonable access to—or, at any rate, no arbitrary exclusion from—premises designated as 'quasi-public'.[49]

B. Time

Just as there are typical locations in which trials are held, so too there are standard hours during which the courts sit in order to hear business.[50] As will be seen in Chapter 3, section 1, B, departures from the norm—especially in regard to time—have been used in an attempt to keep proceedings secret. An irregularity of

---

[44] *R v Ely JJ, ex p Burgess* [1992] Crim LR 888.   [45] *Goold v Evans & Co* [1951] 2 TLR 1189.

[46] See generally K. Gray and S. F. Gray, *Elements of Land Law* (3rd edn, 2001) 138–88.

[47] ibid. 186, where Gray and Gray criticize authorities which appear to cast in these terms the right to attend a creditors' meeting or to see a cinema performance.

[48] See Gray and Gray (n 46 above) 119–29.

[49] See K. Gray and S. F. Gray in S. Bright and J. Dewar (ed), *Land Law: Themes and Perspectives* (1998) 38–9. This categorization may be more appropriate for presence in the court building without being in attendance at any particular trial. The norm of open justice, while requiring strict scrutiny of reasons for exclusion from trial proceedings, does not protect presence in the wider court building other than for the purpose of attending trials and for purposes reasonably incidental thereto.

[50] Although magistrates' courts are local authority buildings, and subject to the supervision of the relevant magistrates' court committee, it has been held that the committee does not possess jurisdiction to direct the justices on the question whether or not to hold court sittings on Saturdays or public holidays within their own petty sessional areas: *R v Avon Magistrates' Courts Committee, ex p Broome* [1988] 1 WLR 1246. Decisions by local magistrates as to when they will sit form part of their judicial functions, on which they could not be directed by others.

this kind does not, in itself, furnish grounds for the invalidation of the trial in question. Such legislation as regulates the place and time of trial is, typically, quite open-ended. Consider, for example, the provision that regulates the manner in which an election court is to be held: 'An election petition shall be tried in open court . . . and notice of the time and place of trial shall be given in the prescribed manner.'[51]

A failure to hold the trial of an election petition 'in open court' would vitiate the outcome. The same result could not be so confidently attributed to a failure to comply with the provisions regulating the place and time of the hearing—even if a violation of such general directions could first be established.

The elements of place and time of trial, then, stand on the same, largely unregulated, footing. The latter is different only in the occasional stipulation of a time limit within which proceedings in respect of certain offences must be commenced.[52]

C. Function

Of the three elements, that of function is fundamental. A court is to be defined primarily by reference to the nature of the functions which it discharges: namely, judicial functions. This may appear simply tautologous. However, there are facets of the judge's role that are not judicial in character. And, by the same token, judicial functions may be discharged by persons other than 'judges' in the strict sense of that term. Without further delay, therefore, it is necessary to analyse the concept of a judicial function. The analysis given here is preliminary, further consideration being given to this issue in Chapter 2.

An extensive treatment of the subject, conducted for the purposes of administrative law, propounded three guidelines.[53] One of the three is characterized by matters of appearance. Does the body that is under consideration determine issues presented by the parties before it? May it compel the attendance of witnesses, who are examined on oath and whose testimony is governed by the law of evidence? In short, does the body *look* like a court? The other two guidelines are substantive in content. Is the decision of the body constrained by legal standards? And do its deliberations culminate in an order that has conclusive effect? Moreover, alongside judicial functions in the narrow sense there exists an awkward category of 'judicial discretions'[54] that are exercised in the course of such diverse activities as the awarding of costs, the variation of trusts and the sentencing of offenders.

Such guidelines, it should be pointed out, will be of only limited use in the context of the present study. There is an inconclusive, even a circular, element in

---

[51] Representation of the People Act 1983, s 139(1).

[52] See, however, *R v Governor of Spring Hill Prison, ex p Sohi* [1988] 1 WLR 596.

[53] S. A. de Smith, H. Woolf, and J. Jowell, *Judicial Review of Administrative Action* (5th edn, 1995), 1011–19.

[54] ibid. 1017.

their application to particular instances. A strictly logical sequence of reasoning would run as follows: 'Is this body, on this occasion, performing a judicial task? If so, and in the absence of any pressing reason to the contrary, it is required to sit in public.' So pervasive, however, is the association of judicial procedures with public access that this process of reasoning is capable of being inverted. That is to say, it is the requirement that a body sit in public, perhaps taken together with other indicia, which indicates that its functions are to be characterized as judicial in nature.[55]

There are additional difficulties that must be mentioned at this stage. To classify any matter as not judicial is usually sufficient to refute any suggestion that it is to be open to public access. However, sometimes an area of litigation is closed to the public merely by categorizing the proceedings as administrative, rather than judicial, in character. Consider, for example, the manner in which Viscount Haldane in *Scott v Scott* described two forms of proceedings from which members of the public have traditionally been excluded:

In the two cases of wards of Court and of lunatics the Court is really sitting primarily to guard the interests of the ward or the lunatic. Its jurisdiction is in this respect parental and *administrative*, and the disposal of controverted questions is an incident only in the jurisdiction.[56] (Emphasis added.)

It is submitted that the two instances in question are better categorized as *exceptions* to the norm of open justice. The reasons behind this preference will be explained in due course.[57]

Equally, that a body is undoubtedly judicial in character does not suffice, in itself, to subject each and every part of its proceedings to public scrutiny. The stage of reaching a verdict or arriving at a judgment in a trial at common law has traditionally been marked by secrecy. Of course, in one instance—civil trial before a single judge—it would be meaningless to grant public access since the process of arriving at a decision is a purely introspective event. However, in the case of a collegiate forum—a panel of magistrates, the members of the jury, or an appellate bench—there will inevitably be an exchange of views and process of argument which could, in a meaningful way, be opened up to public scrutiny. Yet the public is excluded from a stage that forms part, and in many ways the most critical part, of a procedure which is unquestionably judicial. This practice, which is sanctioned by long historical usage, has been placed on an explicit statutory footing in regard to certain courts. An example in point is that of the court martial. The Army Act 1955 required a court martial to sit not only 'in open court' but also 'in the presence of the accused',[58] subject to a power to sit *in camera* in certain defined circumstances. On the other hand, it was required to sit 'in

---

[55] See *Copartnership Farms v Harvey-Smith* [1918] 2 KB 405.
[57] See Chapter 5, section 1, below.

[56] [1913] AC 417, 437.
[58] Army Act 1955, s 94(1).

closed court while deliberating on [its] finding or sentence on any charge',[59] and could do so 'on any other deliberation amongst the members'.[60]

The process of deliberation on the verdict or judgment of the court, then, has long been conducted in secret. As this example demonstrates, the concepts of 'court' and 'judicial function' are of limited value as guides to the occasions on which business should (presumptively, at least) be conducted in the open. A more detailed treatment in the following chapter will consider the practices of English legal procedure in the light of the possible rationales of open justice.

6. *PERSONAE* AND PUBLIC

There is an important distinction to be drawn between the two different capacities in which attendance at a trial may take place. To take the example of a theatre, one might be present as a member of the cast or production team or, alternatively, as part of the audience. In the same way, a person's presence in the courtroom may be as one of the *dramatis personae* of the trial, or simply as a spectator. It is the latter category which forms the focus of interest of this book. For most purposes the *personae* of the trial can be clearly and uncontroversially identified: the judge, the parties, their legal representatives, witnesses and jurors, and the personnel of the court building.[61] Nevertheless, the line of demarcation is important for certain purposes.

For example, one of the authorities which is usually cited in support of the right to attend trials is *Daubney v Cooper*.[62] Summary proceedings had been brought against a man called Preston. Instead of attending in person, Preston chose to send Daubney to act as his attorney. The magistrates refused to allow Daubney to appear before them. When he refused to withdraw Cooper, one of the magistrates, ordered a constable to remove him from the courtroom. In the ensuing action for battery brought by Daubney the court was required to examine, as an integral element of the case, the legality of his forcible removal from the earlier proceedings. In the absence of any compelling reason for his exclusion from the courtroom the issue was resolved by reference to general principle:

... it is one of the essential qualities of a Court of Justice that its proceedings should be public, and that all parties who may be desirous of hearing what is going on ... provided they do not interrupt the proceedings, and provided there is no specific reason why they should be removed ... have a right to be present for the purpose of hearing what is going on.[63]

---

[59] Army Act 1955, s 94(3).

[60] Army Act 1955, s 94(4). The terms of section 94(5), indeed, appear wide enough to permit the exclusion of the accused and his legal representatives: 'Where a court-martial sits in closed court no person shall be present except the members of the court and such other persons as may be prescribed.'

[61] A note of caution needs to be sounded in regard to the last group. Despite their continuous presence in the various court buildings, members of the Witness Support or Victim Support Schemes undoubtedly rank as members of the public. They are independent of the court service though they derive some financial support from the Home Office.

[62] (1829) 10 B&C 237, 109 ER 438.   [63] (1829) 10 B&C 237, at 240; 109 ER 438, 440.

On the basis of such reasoning the plaintiff's claim for damages succeeded. The line of reasoning, however, appears to be defective in that it conflates the right to attend a trial *qua* member of the public with the right to attend *qua* advocate or representative of the accused. Although Daubney had presented himself in the latter role, his right to do so was justified by reference to the former. Indeed, the tone of the judgment in the civil case is cast in terms of safeguarding the interests of the accused, Preston, in the earlier proceedings: '[the accused] might be desirous of knowing what evidence there was to support the case, and . . . it might be of great importance [to him] . . . if there should be misconduct on the part of the witnesses, and if [they] should state more than the facts warranted. . .'[64] A closer examination, therefore, of the facts of *Daubney v Cooper* reveals that it is no authority on the subject of open justice and that the pronouncements on the rights of the public are mere obiter statements. Clearly, a member of the public who chooses to listen to the proceedings in the public gallery could not descend, in virtue of that right, to the well of the court to act as advocate for one of the parties, even with the party's consent. The right of audience, while an important matter of acute contention between the two branches of the English legal profession, is not an aspect of open justice. Its essence is the right to be heard as an advocate, rather than the right to hear (and see) proceedings in court as a spectator.

The confusion between the (unlimited in principle) right of the public to attend trials and the (limited) right of members of the particular legal professions to plead causes on behalf of others is but one instance of the failure to distinguish between the general public and the *dramatis personae* of the trial. The distinction between the two categories is one which has been largely assumed rather than consciously articulated. It has been deployed in a number of contexts. For example, a decision to hold a hearing *in camera* results in the exclusion of members of the public only.[65] Again, a trial which is held in open court but made subject to severe reporting restrictions—for instance, matrimonial suits for divorce and nullity, which are subject to the control of the Judicial Proceedings (Regulation of Reports) Act 1926—may well exempt (as that statute does),[66] the communication of material 'to persons concerned in the proceedings'.

In fact, it was the failure to draw the distinction between *personae* and public which occasioned Lord Atkinson some needless worries in *Scott v Scott*. His Lordship, it will be recalled, expressed general agreement with Fletcher Moulton LJ's view of the scope of an *in camera* direction. On this view, the order merely stipulated the mode of trial of the suit in question and was 'spent when the case

---

[64] ibid.

[65] In *Re a Debtor (No 28 of 1976), ex p The Debtor v Carr* [1977] 1 WLR 261 Foster and Fox JJ made a number of observations on the manner in which bankruptcy proceedings should be heard. Apart from the court officials, only the debtor, the petitioning creditor and their legal advisers should 'normally be present': ibid. 262. In this case the public had been allowed 'full access to the registrar's room during the hearing'.

[66] Judicial Proceedings (Regulation of Reports) Act 1926, s 1(4).

terminated'.[67] For, if the order enjoined perpetual or long-term secrecy on the parties to the suit, how could an aggrieved litigant ever lodge on appeal? It could be done only on the basis that he 'should consent to become a criminal and render himself liable . . . for criminal contempt of Court. . .'[68] As may now be appreciated, however, such an order would forbid the litigant from making disclosures to members of the public, but would not extend to those made to his legal advisers for the purpose of conducting an appeal.

The issue of whether any particular individual is to be classified as a *persona* of the trial or as a member of the public is to be determined by reference to the proceedings in hand.[69] As regards a hearing *in camera*, it is quite clear that a member of the Bar who is not engaged in the case ranks, in that context, as a mere member of the public and enjoys no greater right to attend the trial in virtue of his professional status than any other person.[70]

Finally, there can occur problematic cases on the *personae*—public divide. In which capacity, for example, does a person attend the court if he comes as an informal adviser or friend to one of the parties?[71] During an *in camera* examination of the affairs of a firm, does a clerk employed by the firm have a right to attend?[72] If a tribunal is required to hear a case 'in private', is the spouse of the complainant to be denied access?[73] Even if the terms '*in camera*' and 'in private' are to be taken as synonymous, would the deployment of the latter term to regulate the proceedings of an employment tribunal (with the greater informality attendant on tribunal procedure) allow a greater degree of flexibility?[74] As these examples show, on which side of the *personae*–public line an individual falls is important for his continued presence in the courtroom.

[67] [1913] AC 417, 453.   [68] ibid. 463–464.

[69] It should be emphasized that the text at this point is addressing itself exclusively to the position of adults. The rights of children to be present in court are limited by statute. Even if a child ranks as the central *persona* of the trial, he might (for paternalistic reasons) be denied the right to attend: see *re W (a Minor) (Secure accommodation order: Attendance at Court)* The Times, 13 July 1994.

[70] W. W. Boulton, *Conduct and Etiquette at the Bar* (6th edn, 1975) 84. This is perhaps borne out by *Malan v Young* (1889) 6 TLR 38, in which a barrister objected to leaving the court after Denman J had made an *in camera* direction in a libel case between the headmaster and an assistant master at Sherborne School. He asserted his right to remain, not as a member of the Bar, but as 'a member of the public and the father of sons at [*sc.* the] school', but was nevertheless ordered to withdraw.

[71] As with the so-called 'McKenzie man': *McKenzie v McKenzie* [1971] P 33.

[72] *In re Western of Canada Oil, Lands, and Works Company* (1877) 6 Ch D 109, 110, Jessel MR stated that the place where the examiner sits 'is not a public Court, but a mere office'. The dispute had arisen because the clerk had been ordered to leave the room. The firm objected on the ground that his presence was necessary for the proper instruction of its legal representatives. The relevant statutory provision did not in terms require the examination to take place *in camera*, stating only that it was to take place in the presence of 'the parties, their counsel, solicitors, or agents'. Jessel MR ruled that the clerk did not rank as an 'agent' for this purpose.

[73] *Fry v Foreign and Commonwealth Office* [1997] ICR 512.

[74] ibid. 517, where the Employment Appeal Tribunal stated: 'It is unnecessary to determine the definitive interpretation of the expression "in private". On one side, it can be said that "in private" means "not in public", thereby excluding the press and the general public, but not people connected with the case. . . . In our judgment "in private" is a question of fact and degree. Our decision is that . . . the tribunal will be sitting "in private", even though the applicant's husband is permitted to attend.'

On occasion the critical issue is the opposite to that which we have just con-sidered: namely, whether a person may temporarily be excluded from an open trial, rather than admitted to one that is being held *in camera*. This issue is posed by the position of the witness prior to the giving of his testimony.[75] Earl Loreburn in *Scott v Scott* categorized this situation as an exception to the rule of open just-ice: '. . . witnesses may be ordered to withdraw, lest they trim their evidence by hearing the evidence of others'.[76] The exclusion of witnesses from the courtroom is better viewed, not as an exception to open justice, but as not forming an aspect of the subject at all. Witnesses are predominantly *personae* of the trial—actors in, rather than spectators of, the courtroom scene. Their enforced absence from the place of trial until they are called in to give evidence is simply one aspect of a gen-eral concern about the pre-trial exchange of views between potential witnesses.[77] Once they have testified, their right to remain in the courtroom derives from their status simply as members of the public.

7. THE CONCEPT OF AN 'OPEN COURT'

The core of the idea of open justice is that the *personae* of the trial should play their various parts 'in open court'.[78] This phrase is encountered in a wide variety of statutory and other contexts.[79] Under what conditions are its requirements satisfied? In pursuing this inquiry we are moving away from a consideration of the actors in the drama to an examination of the composition of the audience.

The auditorium itself, it should first be noted, has come under scrutiny in the light of the standards set by the critical phrase. This was the issue that was raised in *Kenyon v Eastwood*.[80] Section 5 of the Debtors Act 1869 stipulated that orders for committal were to be made 'in open court'. The order that had been made in the proceedings in question was successfully challenged because it had not been

[75] An additional ground of the decision in *Re Western of Canada Oil, Lands, and Works Co* was that the clerk would probably be called as a witness, and the official liquidator did not wish him to hear the testimony of his principals: (1877) 6 Ch D 109, 111.

[76] [1913] AC 417, 446. See also at 448: 'The authority of the Court to treat disobedience in this mat-ter as a contempt rests on the same basis as its authority to treat as a contempt the wilful intrusion of a witness after an order has been made that all witnesses shall leave the Court.'

[77] *R v Arif* The Times, 17 June 1993, and *R v Dye and Williamson* [1992] Crim LR 449.

[78] Compare the similar, but distinct, concept of 'access to the courts', which is characteristically deployed in situations where a person is prevented from bringing proceedings in the courts, whether by formal rules or by reason of lack of financial resources. See the extended discussion of the phrase in *R v Lord Chancellor, ex p Witham* [1997] 2 All ER 779.

[79] It is to be found, for example, in provisions as diverse as: the Backing of Warrants (Republic of Ireland) Act 1965, Sch, para 2; Rules of the Supreme Court, Order 38, r. 1; Rules of the Supreme Court, Order 82, r. 5; Scotland Act 1998, s 103(1).

The expression is to be found as early as the time of Shakespeare. In the trial scene in *The Merchant of Venice* Portia refers to Shylock's earlier refusal of the outstanding loan in the following words: ' He hath refus'd it in the open court'. (Act IV, scene I, line 338)

[80] (1888) 57 LJ QB 455.

made in accordance with this requirement. The seat of judgment in the case, it was held, did not qualify as a court, defined (somewhat circuitously) by Lord Coleridge CJ as comprising 'all those external signs which people are accustomed to suppose necessary for it to be a Court [such as] the jury-box, the witness-box, the Judge's seat, and seats for solicitors and counsel and others'.[81] The area in dispute consisted of two rooms, one larger and one smaller. Only the former possessed the above-listed insignia of a courtroom. There was a connecting door, which it was the practice to keep open during the hearing of judgment summonses in the smaller room, the judge's private library. The order for committal had been made in the smaller room. It might have appeared that a plea based simply on that point would lack substantive merit. For there was no doubt that the proceedings had been 'open', in the sense to be examined shortly. The affidavit filed by the court registrar stated categorically: 'The public and the reporters for the local press are invariably admitted to both rooms.' Nevertheless, the order for committal was invalidated because it was 'not unimportant that orders affecting the liberty of the subject should be made in open Court'.[82]

On the authority of *Kenyon v Eastwood* there would appear to be scope for challenging the validity of judgments or verdicts emanating from proceedings that have not been held, contrary to the dictates of statute, 'in . . . court'. This, of course, is a ground of challenge based solely on the physical location of the trial. More usually—though even here the authorities are sparse—the burden of complaint is that proceedings were not held in open court in the sense that the court was not 'open' to 'the public'. Here the physical constraints of the courtroom (there is no doubt that it ranks as a 'court') combine with other elements, most usually the number of would-be spectators who are turned away.

The case of *R v Inner North London Coroner, ex p Chambers*[83] provides a rare instance of a challenge (in the event, unsuccessful) directed at the choice of location of a judicial hearing (a coroner's inquest, in this case) on the ground that the location of the proceedings was not commensurate with the interest in the case that had been shown by the public. Representations had been made, in view of the measure of that interest, to have the hearing moved from the coroner's court to the local town hall, which could accommodate a greater amount of public seating. The coroner declined to make the move, whereupon the Greater London Council[84] together with the parents of the deceased applied for judicial review of his decision. Woolf J ruled that the choice of the location of the inquest was a matter within the coroner's discretion, though the discretion must be exercised judicially. The coroner had divided up the available space in his courtroom so

---

[81] (1888) 57 LJ QB 455, 456. The words 'and others' are noteworthy and could be taken as referring to those who are spectators at the trial.
[82] ibid. 457.   [83] (1983) 127 Sol J 445.
[84] The Greater London Council came to have a role in the matter because it shared the view that the coroner's court was not sufficiently spacious. It had written to the coroner in such terms, offering the local town hall as an alternative venue.

that eighteen seats would be reserved for members of the deceased's family and twenty-two requests for press accreditation had been granted, which left between ten and twenty seats available for members of the public. Even on 'the lowest estimate of the number of people able to attend' the proceedings, Woolf J concluded, would be held in public.

That proceedings are to be held 'in open court' or 'in public' would appear to be requirements that are largely synonymous.[85] Locational factors were decisive in *Kenyon v Eastwood* and formed an aspect in *Ex p Chambers*. Most usually, the question whether either requirement has been satisfied turns on the issue of whether certain persons or categories of person were able to gain access to the courtroom—or rather, in view of the fact that standing is impermissible, to the seats set aside for members of the public within the courtroom. To this question issues of location have been, at most, of only subsidiary concern. A trio of cases, *McPherson v McPherson*,[86] *R v Lewes Prison (Governor), ex p Doyle*,[87] and *R v Denbigh JJ, ex p Williams*,[88] are of particular value in arriving at the meaning of the critical requirements and, hence, in helping to elucidate the rationale of open justice.

It was clearly established in the *Doyle* case that a trial is not held 'in open court' merely because the accused and his legal representatives are permitted to be present. The respondent prison governor's argument to the contrary rested—to use our terminology—on a confusion between the *personae* of the trial and the members of the public.[89] The words, 'in open court', meant 'a Court to which the public have a right to be admitted'.[90] This pronouncement, though sound, was strictly delivered obiter in the context of the dispute. The proceedings had been brought by way of challenge to the validity of a conviction by a court martial after a hearing from which the public and the press had been excluded. The application was rejected on the ground that every court, including a field-general court martial, had an inherent jurisdiction to exclude the public if such a step was necessary for the administration of justice.[91]

To satisfy the requirement that a trial be held 'in open court' or 'in public', paradoxically, does not require that any member of the public actually be present. This important point was implicit in the above-quoted extract from the judgment in *Ex p Doyle*. It was emphasized—though, again, in a context which rendered the pronouncement obiter—by the Judicial Committee of the Privy Council in *McPherson v McPherson*:

---

[85] The former, of course, contains the element of a 'court', which is not present in the latter.
[86] [1936] AC 177.   [87] [1917] 2 KB 254.   [88] [1974] QB 759.
[89] The confusion was probably accentuated by the loose drafting of the relevant provision, r 119(c) of the Rules of Procedure 1907, made under the Army Act 1881: 'The proceedings shall be held in open court, in the presence of the accused, except on any deliberation among the members, when the court may be closed.'
[90] [1917] 2 KB 254, 271.
[91] It was so deemed in the present case, the order that the proceedings be held *in camera* having been made by the Commander-in-Chief of the forces in Ireland.

The actual presence of the public is never of course necessary . . . the Court must be open to any who may present themselves for admission. The remoteness of the possibility of any public attendance must never by judicial action be reduced to the certainty that there will be none.[92]

Two points, then, are quite clear: the *personae* of the trial do not count as members of the public; and the public must be granted the opportunity of being present at the trial, without the additional necessity that any member of the public should actually take advantage of the opportunity. In addition, there exists an unexplored area—that was only touched on in *Ex p Chambers*—which considers the limited physical capacity of the courtroom in comparison with the numbers of those seeking to gain admission to the trial or (which may amount to the same thing) the public interest that has been aroused by the case.

It is now necessary to give a detailed account of *R v Denbigh JJ, ex p Williams*. The background to the case was the prosecution of two members of the Welsh Language Society who, for political reasons, had not obtained licences for their television sets. The trial was conducted at the magistrates' court, where the defendants arrived with a large entourage of friends and supporters. Conditions in the courtroom being rather cramped, the defendants were reduced to selecting only five of their group to occupy the public seats. In the course of the trial all five left, whether voluntarily or on the direction of the magistrates. The defendants were convicted and fined. The validity of the proceedings was then challenged, by way of certiorari, on the ground that the hearing had not been conducted 'in open court' as required by section 98(4) of the Magistrates' Courts Act 1952.[93] The basis of the application was the denial to the supporters waiting outside of the right of access to the seats vacated by the original five. There was some disagreement as to whether the defendants' supporters had been refused access to the vacant seats or whether they had simply failed to request it. The Divisional Court, following its usual practice, would not investigate disputed issues of fact on the affidavits. The case would be decided on the footing that no request to enter the courtroom had been made. On that basis the application failed.

The judgment of Lord Widgery CJ is full of observations—of necessity, rendered obiter—as to the meaning of the concept of an 'open court'. The opportunity for the press to attend, it would appear, is a necessary condition ('I find it difficult to imagine a case which can be said to be held publicly if the press have been actively excluded')[94] but not a sufficient condition of satisfying the standard ('one must not overlook the other factor of an open and public proceeding,

---

[92] [1936] AC 177, 200. For the facts of the case see Chapter 3, section 1, B, below.

[93] Section 98(4) reads: 'Subject to the provisions of any enactment to the contrary, where a magistrates' court is required by this section to sit in a petty-sessional or occasional court-house, it shall sit in open court.' The precursor of s 98(4) was s 12 of the Summary Jurisdiction Act 1848, which appears to define the critical phrase: 'and the Room and Place in which such Justice or Justices shall sit to hear and try any such Complaint or Information shall be deemed an open and public Court, to which the Public generally may have Access, so far as the same can conveniently contain them.'

[94] [1974] QB 759, 765.

namely, one to which individual members of the public can come if they have sufficient interest in the proceedings to make it worth their while so to do').[95] The judgment, moreover, clearly acknowledges that the *personae*–public divide is a distinction that is specific to the individual case ('there was also incidentally a defendant and his solicitor concerned in a later case who happened to be in court waiting their turn, and who I suppose for present purposes were members of the public').[96]

It was agreed on all sides that the initial stages of the proceedings were held in open court notwithstanding the fact that the facilities were insufficient to accommodate all those who wished to attend the trial. No adverse comment was passed by the Divisional Court on the decision to stage the trial in the smaller of the two courtrooms that were available.[97] Nevertheless, that decision had the effect of aggravating, at the very least, the problem of the disparity between the numbers seeking to gain entry and the space that was available. This type of situation could give rise to a number of issues. However, there exist only scant dicta to assist in their resolution. In particular, might the level of accommodation for members of the public be so low—whether in absolute terms or in comparison to the interest aroused by the case—that the particular proceedings may be deemed not to have taken place in public? There is a suggestion, in Woolf J's judgment in *Ex p Chambers*, that in sufficiently extreme circumstances such an argument might prove well founded. It is strange, therefore, that the Civil Procedure Rules 1998—for the drafting of which Lord Woolf was responsible—should state clearly that a requirement that a hearing should take place in public 'does not require the court to make special arrangements for accommodating members of the public'.[98]

One matter, at any rate, is beyond doubt. The failure of even a considerable number of members of the public to gain ingress to the courtroom because the public seating is already occupied does not, in itself, deprive the proceedings of their 'public' or 'open' character.[99] As we have seen, such was the initial position in the *Williams* case. It is a state of affairs commonly encountered throughout the

---

[95] ibid. 765.   [96] ibid. 765.   [97] ibid. 762.

[98] Civil Procedure Rules 1998, SI 1998/3132, r 39.2(2).

[99] It is quite clear that, in such circumstances, as many members of the public as may be accommodated in the seating area of the courtroom set aside for the public must be admitted. Contrast the situation of local authority meetings where the number of those wishing to attend exceeds the number of available seats. This occurred in *R v Liverpool City Council, ex p Liverpool Taxi Fleet Operators' Association* [1975] 1 WLR 701. There were over 40 members of the public seeking entry to the relevant committee room. Yet there were only 14 places left after the allocation to members and officials of the local authority. The chairman felt that he could not choose who was to occupy the 14 seats. A resolution was therefore passed under the Public Bodies (Admission to Meetings) Act 1960, s 1(2), excluding all members of the public. Two reasons were given, one of which was 'the limitations of available space'. According to the Divisional Court, provided that a reasonable amount of accommodation had been set aside, the authority was entitled to exclude all members of the public in the circumstances of the case. The circumstances amounted to a 'special reason' for the purposes of the Public Bodies (Admission to Meetings) Act 1960, s 1(2).

whole of the more sensational trials.[100] It may be worthwhile to illuminate the point by analogy with a comparable issue in a very different area of the law. In order to qualify as a charitable trust, a trust must not only promote a purpose that is recognized in law as charitable (the advancement of religion or education, for example), it must also benefit the public at large or a sufficient section of the public. It is well established that a trust is not disqualified in the latter regard simply because a limited number of persons is all that may be expected—or, indeed, may be able—to benefit from its provisions.[101]

However, purely numerical considerations aside, there are said to have been instances where arrangements have been made for the public gallery at certain trials to be packed with probationer constables in plain clothes.[102] In such circumstances there exists the basis for a submission that the trial has not been conducted in open court—at any rate where, as a result, it could be shown that casual members of the public were unable to gain admission.[103]

Finally, the standard of public access does not demand that the members of the public present in the courtroom have an unobstructed view of all that transpires there. The requirement that a coroner's inquest be held in public has been held not to have been violated by the erection of a screen between a witness and the public seats.[104] The device was needed in the circumstances to protect the anonymity of a police marksman, and the public interest in investigating the circumstances of the death could adequately be served by the ability of those present to hear the proceedings.

8. PUBLIC, PRESS, AND OTHERS

Now that the distinction has been drawn between *personae* and public, it is necessary to advert to several distinctions within the latter group.

There is a fundamental difference between a trial that, wholly or partly, takes place in private and one that is open to the public. The line of division, which exists clearly as a matter of common law, is blurred in some instances by the occasional statutory provision. Thus, although a hearing may take place in closed

---

[100] Note, however, the extraordinary circumstances of the trial of Francis Gary Powers, the American pilot who was shot down over the USSR while on a spying mission. The proceedings, held in August 1960 in the House of Trade Unions in Moscow, were attended by nearly a thousand persons: D. Wise and T. B. Ross, *The U-2 Affair* (1996) 197.

[101] P. H. Pettit, *Equity and the Law of Trusts* (9th edn, 2001) 264–70.

[102] C. H. Rolph, 'Open Court and the consumer' NLJ (10 May 1991) 654.

[103] To push the analogy with charitable trusts a little further, it has been held that even an appreciable number of potential beneficiaries will not qualify as a section of the public if they share a relationship (most usually, by way of employment) to a single person or body. See *Oppenheim v Tobacco Securities Trust Co Ltd* [1951] AC 297, 306, per Lord Simonds: 'A group of persons may be numerous but, if the nexus between them is their personal relationship to a single propositus or to several propositi, they are neither the community nor a section of the community for charitable purposes.'

[104] *R v Newcastle upon Tyne Coroner, ex p A* The Times, 19 January 1998.

session, a particular category of person whose professional interest (whether in an individual case or in the general standard of competence displayed by the tribunal in question) transcends that of the casual member of the public may be permitted to attend the proceedings. For example, when the Friendly Societies Appeal Tribunal goes into secret session, this state of affairs shall not 'prevent a member of the Council on Tribunals from attending the hearing, and (with the consent of the parties to the appeal) any deliberations of the Tribunal, in his capacity as such'.[105] An example on the other side of the line, as shaped by the circumstances of particular cases, is furnished by section 47(2) of the Children and Young Persons Act 1933, which gave an exhaustive list of the persons permitted to be present at the sitting of juvenile courts (as they were then called)—a list which includes persons who are 'directly concerned in that case'.[106]

The existence, and interpretation, of statutory provisions stipulating who may, and who may not, enter the courtroom in the course of a trial is clearly of decisive importance in a legal system that is characterized by parliamentary sovereignty. Occasionally statute differentiates in this regard between the press and members of the public at large. For instance, in the course of certain proceedings when a child or young person is giving evidence, the court is empowered to order the exclusion of everyone except the *personae* of the trial and 'bona fide representatives of a newspaper or news agency'.[107] More remarkable, and more restrictive still, is the situation where only a single representative of the media interest is permitted to remain in court. This position could arise under the Youth Justice and Criminal Evidence Act 1999. In certain circumstances defined by the Act, an order may be made directing the exclusion from the court (subject to some limited exceptions) of classes of individual. In the event of the order extending to 'representatives of news gathering or reporting organisations' such organizations shall be empowered to nominate one of their number who is to be permitted to remain in court as their sole representative.[108] Characteristically, however, such provisions are accompanied by reporting restrictions, which detract from the value of the privilege enjoyed by the press.

In the absence of an express statutory directive there exists some scope for ventilating the general issue of principle: under what circumstances, if any, should the rights of access of the press and public be different? In *Re Crook*[109] the applicant, a freelance journalist,[110] challenged the validity of two decisions by two separate judges at the Central Criminal Court to sit in chambers,[111] and thereby

---

[105] The Friendly Societies Appeal Tribunals Regulations 1993, SI 1993/2002, reg 13(5).

[106] Section 47(2)(b). The meaning of the phrase was put to the test in *R v Southwark Juvenile Court, ex p J* [1973] 1 WLR 1300, as a result of the exclusion, which the court ruled to have been improper, of the juvenile defendant's social worker.

[107] Children and Young Persons Act 1933, s 37.

[108] Youth Justice and Criminal Evidence Act 1999, s 25 (3).   [109] [1992] 2 All ER 687.

[110] And, therefore, a journalist who would not strictly qualify under those statutory exceptions that encompass 'representatives of a newspaper or news agency'.

[111] On the subject of proceedings in chambers see Chapter 3, section 1, D, below.

exclude both press and public, while they dealt with certain matters relating to the jury in each case.[112] While it was entirely proper to exclude the public, the journalist submitted, the press should not have been treated on the same footing since an order could have been made in reference to them restraining publication under section 4(2) of the Contempt of Court Act 1981. The Court of Appeal, Criminal Division, rejected the application. The press and public should be treated in the same manner,[113] not least because '[t]here will often be other members of the public, such as the family of a defendant, victims of the alleged crime and others having a direct concern in the case with as much interest in the proceedings and as good a claim to be present as the press. It could cause a real sense of grievance if they were excluded while representatives of the press were allowed to be present'.[114]

The application in *Re Crook* could be seen as an attempt to arrive at a position identical to that embodied in several statutory provisions, whereby the public are excluded from the courtroom but free access (subject to reporting restrictions) is granted to the press. The existence of the power to impose reporting restrictions was central to the applicant's case, furnishing a pragmatic reason for seeking to distinguish the legal positions of press and public. Pragmatic reasoning was also advanced, and rejected, in *R v Secretary of State for the Home Department, ex p Westminster Press Ltd*.[115] In this case it was the exposure of the press to potential liability for contempt of court which was unsuccessfully advanced as the basis of a claim to be informed of the names of persons who were under investigation by the police or were already subject to criminal charges.[116] The Divisional Court confined itself to dismissing as 'fanciful' the possibility that, in the absence of the information, the press might well blunder into the prejudicial naming of a person who was already in police custody. In short, the legal position of the press and the general public was exactly the same: neither was entitled to the information.

To debate the issue at this level leaves unaddressed the question of principle as to why, if at all, the press should be entitled to preferential treatment. The answer is clearly to be found in the institutional role performed by the media in informing the general public on matters of topical concern. A statement by the US Supreme Court puts the matter very succinctly: 'in a society in which each individual has but limited time and resources with which to observe at first hand the operations of his government, he relies necessarily upon the press to bring to him in convenient form the facts of those operations'.[117]

---

[112] The challenge was brought under the Criminal Justice Act 1988, s 159: as to which, see Chapter 3, section 3, C, below.

[113] [1992] 2 All ER 687, 694.   [114] ibid. 694–695.   [115] The Times, 18 December 1991.

[116] The case took the form of an application for judicial review of Home Office Circular No 115/82, which contained guidance to the police on the statements that they might make to the press in the aftermath of the enactment of the Contempt of Court Act 1981.

[117] *Cox Broadcasting Corporation v Cohn* 420 US 469 (1975), 491.

Such a conclusion is, perhaps, easier to reach in legal systems that are endowed with constitutional guarantees of 'freedom of the press'.[118]

[118] It is not, however, impossible to reach this conclusion in the absence of such a constitutional backdrop. See, for example, *R v Waterfield* [1975] 1 WLR 711, in which the trial judge had excluded the public from the courtroom while certain allegedly indecent films, the subject of the prosecution, were shown to the jury. The Court of Appeal, recognizing the role of the press as a general source of information, said: '... normally when a film is being shown to a jury and the judge, in the exercise of his discretion, decides that it should be done in a closed courtroom or in a cinema, he should allow representatives of the press to be present' (at 715).

2

The Rationale and Reach of Open Justice

1. OPEN JUSTICE AND NATURAL JUSTICE

In the Hamlyn lectures for 1986, published as *The Fabric of English Civil Justice*, Master Jacob identified the principle of publicity, together with those of 'orality' and 'immediacy', as the three traditional facets—from the point of view of the proceduralist—of the English civil trial. For these purposes he could equally have been speaking of the criminal trial. Of 'orality' he wrote as follows:

This principle dominates the conduct of civil proceedings at all stages both at first instance, before and at the trial, and on appeal, and in all courts both superior and inferior as well as in tribunals . . . Even in instances where written material is produced to the court, as where written pleadings or other documents such as affidavit evidence or the correspondence between the parties, are referred to . . ., the actual hearing of the proceedings in court is conducted orally: there is the oral reading of the relevant written material, the oral arguments, the oral exchanges between the court and the lawyers . . ., the oral evidence at the trial, the oral judgment of the court.[1]

This statement must now be qualified in the light of the changes brought about in 1998 by the promulgation of the Civil Procedure Rules.[2] In particular, considerably less reliance is now placed on the reading aloud to the court of written materials, the contents of which are to be assimilated in advance of the hearing. Nevertheless, in general terms it remains an accurate and succint account of the central features of English legal proceedings, whether civil or criminal.

Orality has consequences both external and internal to the trial process. On the former front it means that '[f]rom beginning to end, the intelligent listener can follow everything'.[3] And in the latter regard it advances the principle of 'immediacy', whereby a 'direct, immediate and dialectical investigation into the relevant facts and the applicable law'[4] is conducted which promotes conditions favourable to the reaching of a correct decision. The principle of orality in combination with the principle of publicity is, for Master Jacob, 'crucial to the proper functioning of the adversary system'.[5]

In short, then, evidence and argument are presented within a relatively confined space in which judge, jurors, witnesses, parties and their legal advisers confront

---

[1] I. H. Jacob, *The Fabric of English Civil Justice* (1987) 19–20.
[2] Civil Procedure Rules 1998, SI 1998/3132.
[3] R. E. Megarry, *Lawyer and Litigant in England* (1962) 167.   [4] Jacob (n 1 above) 20.
[5] Jacob (n 1 above) 19.

one another—and all this within sight and hearing of such members of the public as choose to attend. Nothing bears out the principle of orality better than the rule that the adjudicative *personae* may not change during the trial or absent themselves from any part of the proceedings. A reading of the transcript is never regarded as sufficient to compensate for bodily absence from the courtroom for even part of the hearing. So rigidly is the rule enforced that the death of the judge in mid-trial will require the recommencement of the hearing, with drastic repercussions on the matter of costs in a civil case.[6] In a criminal trial the response to the problem of juror illness or death is slightly different. The hearing is not recommenced with a full complement of jurors: a jury that has been depleted by illness and similar factors is expected to continue with the hearing of the trial (subject to there remaining a minimum of nine members).[7]

Not only are the adjudicative *personae* required to be physically present in the courtroom, they must also attend—and, what is more, must be seen to be attending—to the proceedings. A magistrate, for example, must not be seen to be distracted from hearing the evidence, even if the distraction consists of his reading a law report.[8] Nor must a member of a tribunal appear to doze off intermittently in the course of a hearing, even if a perfectly satisfactory explanation is forthcoming that is consistent with the member having paid full attention.[9] The conduct in these instances has resulted in the invalidation of the proceedings as having been conducted in breach of natural justice. Judges must devote, and must be seen to be devoting, their undivided attention to the case. Otherwise public confidence in the administration of justice would be undermined.

Such cases present an unusual variation on the standard themes of natural justice.[10] They embody elements of both of the limbs of that doctrine, the right to a hearing (*audi alteram partem*) and the rule against bias (*nemo judex in causa sua*). The standard fare of natural justice litigation poses such questions as (for instance) whether the plaintiff was entitled to an oral hearing before a particular tribunal or whether he was entitled to be legally represented. Such issues, raised under the first limb, are quite various. Those raised under the second limb, by contrast, focus on one question: the proper standard to be applied in the scrutiny of tribunals the proceedings of which may have been tainted with bias. Intuitively, there would appear to be some connection between open justice, the subject matter of this work, and natural justice. The latter, indeed, has been described as 'in essence, a skeletal version of the elaborate rules of judicial

---

[6] This has had the consequence that some parties, when embarking on lengthy commercial litigation, have taken out insurance on the judge's life for the expected duration of the trial.

[7] Juries Act 1974, s 16(1).

[8] *R v Marylebone Magistrates' Court, ex p Joseph* The Times, 7 May 1993.

[9] *Red Bank Manufacturing Co Ltd v Meadows* [1992] ICR 204.

[10] See, generally, S. A. de Smith, H. Woolf, and J. Jowell, *Judicial Review of Administrative Action* (5th edn, 1995) chs 9 and 12.

procedure to be found in their fullest form in the Rules of the Supreme Court'.[11] Wherein, precisely, do the similarities and differences lie?

The two forms of justice are alike, above all, in their application to judicial procedures. In the context of open justice that association has already been mentioned.[12] As for natural justice, the observance of the standards laid down in its rules was long required only of bodies which discharged 'judicial' or (on an alternative formulation) 'quasi-judicial' functions. While this limitation has long since been discarded as fallacious, it may well have served to associate the two forms of justice in the legal mind. A subconscious recognition of the link is, perhaps, to be found in some of the textbooks of administrative law. In giving examples of the international recognition of the *audi alteram partem* rule, they cite provisions such as Article 6(1) of the European Convention on Human Rights, which are predominantly expressions of the value of open justice.[13]

Such conflation is, in part, understandable. At root both natural justice and open justice are concerned, though in different ways, with the procedural standards of a fair hearing. One limb of the former, the *audi alteram partem* rule, provides a means whereby the applicant may challenge the outcome of a hearing for reasons which may be described as 'internal' to the conduct of the proceedings (for example, that he was given insufficient notice of the case against him or that he was denied the opportunity to cross-examine witnesses). The rule against bias, too, furnishes him with such a lever—in the form of a test whose perspective is the appearance presented by the hearing. In fact, it was a leading case on the rule against bias which provided the occasion of the pronouncement of a well-known statement: 'it is not merely of some importance but is of fundamental importance that justice should not only be done, but should manifestly and undoubtedly be seen to be done.'[14]

These words, when considered generally and not restricted by the context in which they were delivered, are clearly relevant to the subject matter of the present study. On the specific issue of the application of the relevant test of bias (whether reasonable suspicion, or real likelihood, or some other standard) it would be quite irrelevant whose vantage point is postulated for this purpose. It is noteworthy, however, that one perspective that has been deployed in challenging, for suspicion of bias, the outcome of a criminal trial has been that of 'a reasonable and fair minded person *sitting in the court* and knowing all the relevant facts'.[15] (Emphasis added)

---

[11] P. Cane, *An Introduction to Administrative Law* (3rd edn, 1996) 163.

[12] See Chapter 1, section 5, C, above.

[13] See, for example, H. W. R. Wade, *Administrative Law* (6th edn, 1988) 497. The link is expressed in more muted terms: 'International analogies' in H. W R. Wade and C. Forsyth, *Administrative Law* (7th edn, 1994) 495.

[14] *R v Sussex Justices, ex p McCarthy* [1924] 1 KB 256, 259, per Hewart CJ.

[15] *R v Gough* [1993] AC 646, 660.

Even where the relevant facts are brought to light, it may be difficult to decide whether or not they should be taken as having tainted the hearing in question.[16] Such difficulties are less acute in situations where there is a specific disqualificatory provision.[17] Such provisions apart, the matter will be resolved by reference to the common law rule against bias[18] or the standards of Article 6 of the European Convention on Human Rights.[19] Often the crucial facts emerge only after the conclusion of the hearing. This is strikingly illustrated by the most prominent recent challenge for appearance of bias. In *R v Bow Street Metropolitan Stipendiary Magistrate, ex p Pinochet Ugarte (No 2)* [20] an earlier ruling of the House of Lords (involving extradition proceedings against the former ruler of Chile) was set aside since Lord Hoffmann, who had been a member of the court on the occasion of that ruling, had not disclosed his connection with Amnesty International, one of the parties to the case. The information concerning the link came by an anonymous telephone call to Pinochet's solicitors.[21] Where, on the other hand, the connection between judge and party is through common membership of a secret society, the danger of an unfair hearing is all the greater. It is not surprising, therefore, that there have been proposals requiring members of the judiciary (among others) to record in a public register membership of such organizations as the Freemasons.[22]

It is possible now to discern a closer connection between at least one of the limbs of natural justice, the rule against bias, and open justice. To take the most extreme situation, that a hearing is conducted in secret may be suggestive, in itself, of the existence of bias on the part of the tribunal. At any rate, the means do not exist for discovering otherwise. The same point holds true even of less extreme situations. To refuse disclosure of such information as, for example, the names of the members of the adjudicating panel is to withhold the means of knowing whether, say, one of their number may be affected by some pecuniary or other interest in the case in question. Open justice, then, furnishes a lens through which departures from the standards embodied in at least one limb of natural justice may be perceived.

---

[16] Is it cause for disquiet, for example, that opposing counsel in a criminal trial are cohabiting? In *R v Batt* [1996] Crim LR 910 the Court of Appeal thought it an undesirable situation without deeming it sufficient ground for appeal on the facts of the case.

[17] The Juries Act 1974, Sch 1, disqualifies from jury service the administrative staff of any court. In *R v Salt* [1996] Crim LR 517 the presence on the jury of the son of the court usher was regarded as falling within the mischief of the rule.

[18] For the application of the rule to a variety of situations, in the context of joined appeals, see *Locabail (UK) Ltd v Bayfield Properties Ltd* [2000] 1 All ER 65. In the USA, it is worth noting, the subject of disqualification of judges has assumed far greater importance. See generally R. E. Flamm, *Judicial Disqualification: recusal and disqualification of judges* (1996).

[19] See the ruling of the European Court of Human Rights in *Pullar v UK* (1996) 22 EHRR 391, in which the presence on a (Scottish) jury of an employee of a principal prosecution witness did not violate Art 6.

[20] [1999] 1 All ER 577.   [21] ibid. 582.

[22] Home Affairs Committee, 3rd Report (Freemasonry in the Police and the Judiciary) 1996–97 HC 192 (in two volumes).

Nevertheless, there does exist a clear conceptual distinction between the idea of natural justice and that of open justice. It is possible to imagine a situation in which a person is accorded all the rights that have ever been claimed in the name of natural justice (an oral hearing, a tribunal free of even the slightest suspicion of bias, and so on), and for the hearing nevertheless to take place behind closed doors. Conversely, one could imagine a situation of a hearing being held openly, with full right of access accorded to the public and the press, yet the person whose case is to be heard is denied the most basic elements of a fair hearing (for example, in being denied the right to make representations to the deciding body). The conceptual distinction was implicitly recognized in *R v Denbigh JJ, ex p Williams*.[23] Reference has already been made to this case in the context of the argument of the applicants that the trial had not been conducted in open court, as required by the applicable statutory provision. The applicants submitted, furthermore, that the alleged exclusion of the members of the public from the courtroom had resulted 'in justice not being seen to be done and contrary to natural justice'. While there was at least an arguable case under the first heading (though one that did not, in the event, succeed), Lord Widgery expressly took note of the concession made by counsel in regard to the second heading of the applicants' case: 'there is no case in the books in which it has been said to be a breach of the rules of natural justice to exclude members of the public from the court room'.[24] Any possible link between the concepts of open justice and natural justice, therefore, was not required to be examined by the Divisional Court.

Of course, a legal system which persistently denies to its subjects the basic requirements of natural justice is unlikely to be scrupulous in requiring judicial business to be transacted in public. It may be suitable to conclude this section on a literary note. Throughout Kafka's *The Trial*, the central character, Joseph K., is depicted as being in a state of ignorance of the charges that he has to meet, the identity of the witnesses against him, and even of the composition and seat of the court. The point is also made: 'K. must remember that the proceedings were not public; they could certainly, if the Court considered it necessary, become public, but the Law did not prescribe that they must be made public.'[25]

---

[23] [1974] QB 759. For the facts, see Chapter 1, section 7, above.

[24] ibid. 764. See also *R v Farmer, ex p Hargrave* (1981) 79 LGR 676, in which a ratepayer had objected to the spending of certain sums of money by the council. Furthermore, in the instant proceedings he brought a challenge to the decision of the district auditor to hear *in camera* matters relating to several contracts. The Divisional Court peremptorily rejected the ratepayer's argument 'that the rules of natural justice have been broken, in that the decision [*sc*, to hold the relevant part of the hearing before the district auditor] was made upon private representations which were not conveyed to the applicant' (ibid. 678).

[25] F. Kafka, *The Trial* (1925: Penguin Books edn, 1953) 128.

2. THE DISCIPLINARY RATIONALE OF OPEN JUSTICE

Anyone who peruses the various stages in the *Scott v Scott* litigation, strangely, reaches the final three judgments in the House of Lords before encountering any mention of the purposes served by open justice. Earl Loreburn, indeed, introduces this aspect only in his final paragraph: for him the rationale is 'a danger that a Court may not be so jealous to do right when its proceedings are not subject to full public criticism'.[26] Lord Atkinson conceded that distress was often suffered by parties and witnesses as a consequence of the rule 'but all this is tolerated . . . because it is felt that in public trial is to be found, on the whole, the best security for the pure, impartial, and efficient administration of justice, the best means for winning for it public confidence and respect'.[27] Finally, the judgment of Lord Shaw had a rather different thrust, emphasizing—in overblown terms—the place of open justice as part of the constitutional heritage of a free country.[28] Remarkably for the judiciary of that period, Lord Shaw cited in support the writings of a philosopher (Bentham) and of a constitutional historian (Hallam).[29]

We shall return in due course to a more detailed consideration of Jeremy Bentham's views on the value of open justice. At this stage it is necessary to make some observations on the measured statements made by Earl Loreburn and Lord Atkinson. For they express a commonly held view of the benefit to be derived from exposing judicial proceedings to public scrutiny.

What, then, is the part played by publicity in securing the proper administration of justice? The absence of secrecy is thought, quite generally, to be conducive to the proper discharge of all manner of functions. It appears to take on heightened importance in regard to the transaction of judicial business, where the checks and controls that exist in many areas of government are singularly lacking.[30] The security of tenure of the higher judiciary, at any rate, is second to none. Any criticism of a particular judge or the judiciary as a group is voiced under threat of potential liability for contempt of court (in the form of contempt by scandalizing the court). Criticism, when voiced within Parliament, is privileged but is circumscribed by a strict procedural rule (that a judge may be criticized only on a substantive motion, and not in regard to matters pending adjudication before the courts). On the very few occasions on which a judge has been required to resign,

---

[26] [1913] AC 417, 449.   [27] ibid. 463.

[28] ibid. 484: 'Had [the facts of *Scott v Scott*] occurred in France, I suppose Frenchmen would have said that the age of Louis Quatorze and the practice of lettres de cachet had returned.'

[29] ibid. 477. Hallam's claims appear somewhat exaggerated. The source of the quotation, which is not given by Lord Shaw, is H. Hallam, *Constitutional History of England* Vol I (7th edn, 1854) 230–1: 'Civil liberty, in this kingdom, has two distinct guarantees; [one of which is] the open administration of justice, according to known laws truly interpreted, and fair constructions of evidence, . . .'

[30] Such a common method of enforcing standards of competence as liability in tort for negligent discharge of one's professional functions is not available for use against the judiciary: *Sirros v Moore* [1975] QB 118.

his removal has typically been due to misbehaviour off the bench (being found guilty of a criminal offence, for example) rather than to shortcomings in the discharge of his functions in the courtroom itself. The most recent example of a failing in the execution of judicial duties led to the enforced resignation of Harman J from the bench. He was found to have delayed inexcusably in the delivery of judgment after the conclusion of the hearing phase in a civil case. As far as the parties to the case itself were concerned, the Court of Appeal ruled in *Goose v Wilson Sandford and Co*[31] that the delay, of some twenty months, was so great that a retrial would be ordered. The lapse of time resulted in a number of difficulties, in particular the loss of the advantage of immediacy (the advantage of having had sight and hearing of the witnesses in the case). Generally, errors of law which occur at the trial at first instance are the subject of correction within the judicial system itself, by the appellate courts. Indeed, in this, as in other aspects of a judge's life, the danger of forfeiting the good opinion of his colleagues is a consideration that is more likely to keep him up to the mark than public opinion in general.

Public opinion may go to either of two issues: that the law has been misapplied in a particular case; or that the law, as correctly determined, stands in need of reform. Objections of the former type are to be pursued in the appellate courts, except where the imputation of error is made against the court of final appeal itself. For this purpose there exist procedures for recording the gist of the proceedings in the lower courts.[32] If, by contrast, it is the law itself which is thought to be in need of reform, rarely will it be the case that an inexorable system of open justice will be needed to help substantiate the argument for change.

Moreover, the idea of open justice finds its basic expression in the rule which permits attendance at the trial by members of the public. Yet, in the nature of things, complaint is less likely to be voiced—whether of the manner of conduct of a trial or of the law that required a particular outcome to the case—by the casual onlooker than by such *personae* of the trial as are emotionally involved in the case. No member of the public is likely to have an interest in the outcome which matches that of the losing party (or his family and friends). There are even well-documented instances of the adjudicative *personae* of a case, the members of the jury, giving vent to their dissatisfaction with the outcome, whether by writing articles for the national press[33] or by way of complaint to the Lord Chancellor.[34]

---

[31] The Times 19 February 1998.

[32] The case of *Sweet v Parsley* [1970] AC 132 provides a striking example of one where the hostile publicity surrounding the decision in the lower courts was, perhaps, influential in determining the final outcome of the case in the House of Lords. The appellant had been convicted of being concerned in the management of certain premises which had been used for smoking cannabis resin, an activity of which she was unaware. The decisions of the justices and the Divisional Court holding the offence to be one of strict liability were reversed by the House of Lords.

[33] See The Guardian (23 February 1994) Second Front 2/3, for an article, J. Mullin, 'When truth lies bleeding', written on the basis of an interview with Timothy O'Malley, the foreman of the jury in the Carl Bridgewater case (for the details of which case, see the Appendix).

[34] See, for example, the incident reported in The Times (1 February 1980) 2, where four of the jurors at a recently concluded trial made a complaint to the Lord Chancellor, Lord Hailsham. Judge

For all its limitations, the idea that open justice acts as a check on the judiciary is of long standing. It finds expression in the characteristically vigorous words of Jeremy Bentham which, as we have already noted, were cited by Lord Shaw in *Scott v Scott*: 'Publicity is the very soul of justice, it is the keenest spur to exertion, and the surest of all guards against improbity. It keeps the judge himself, while trying, under trial.'[35]

To Bentham, however, open justice did not perform exactly the same role as it performs in the legal system as we know it. He was highly critical of the independence of the judiciary, at various points in his writings espousing the ideas of popular election and recall of judges.[36] Against such a radically different background the open conduct of trials would serve the function, if no other, of supplying the informational base upon which a person's suitability for continuation in judicial office could be appraised.

The open trial, in Bentham's view, served as a check, not only on the 'unrighteous judge', but also on the dishonest witness. The nature of the discipline exercised over such a person was described in the following terms:

Environed as [such a witness] sees himself by a thousand eyes, contradiction, should he hazard a false tale, will seem ready to rise up in opposition to it from a thousand mouths. Many a known face, and every unknown countenance, presents to him a possible source of detection, from whence the truth he is struggling to suppress may through some unsuspected connexion burst forth to his confusion.[37]

The idea that open justice is conducive to the giving of honest testimony has been expressed by a number of writers. Sir Matthew Hale cited this rationale, together with the check that is exercised over the biased judge, as the very point of holding trials in open court:

[Evidence is given] in the open court, and in the presence of the parties, their attornies, counsel and all by-standers, and before the judge and jury: where each party has liberty of EXCEPTING, either to the competency of the evidence, or the competency or credit of the witnesses, which exceptions are PUBLICLY stated, and by the judges openly allowed or disallowed;—wherein if the judge be PARTIAL, his partiality and injustice will be evident to all by-standers.[38]

Moreover, '[t]he excellency of this OPEN course of evidence' appeared in several particulars, including:

King-Hamilton had criticized the verdict of not guilty returned in regard to several of the accused, describing it as 'remarkably merciful in the face of the evidence'. Lord Hailsham indicated in a letter to the jurors that he would not be drawn into commenting on either the verdict or the judge's remark.

[35] [1913] AC 417, 477.

[36] See G. J. Postema, *Bentham and the Common Law Tradition* (1986) 358–76, especially at 363–4.

[37] J. Bentham, *Rationale of Judicial Evidence*, in J. Bowring (ed), *The Works of Jeremy Bentham* Vol. VI (1843), 355.

[38] M. Hale, *The History of the Common Law of England* (6th edn, 1820) 343–4.

That it is openly, and not in private before a commissioner or two, and a couple of clerks; where, oftentimes witnesses will deliver that, which they will be ashamed to testify publicly.[39]

Wigmore, the leading American work on the law of evidence, also expresses the same viewpoint. It includes a section on publicity (together with sections on the oath and the sanction for perjury) in a sub-heading entitled 'Prophylactic Rules'.[40] Although Wigmore does not base the argument for open justice exclusively on evidential considerations, the effect that publicity will have on the quality of testimony is nevertheless given considerable emphasis:

. . . first, by stimulating the instinctive responsibility to public opinion, symbolised in the audience, and ready to scorn a demonstrated liar; and next, by inducing the fear of exposure of subsequent falsities through disclosure by informed persons who may chance to be present or to hear of the testimony from others present.

The latter part of the quotation presents an unusual, though nevertheless plausible, way in which pressure may come to bear on a witness to tell the truth.[41] As such, it is similar to situations (to be discussed in section 3 below) where the reporting of proceedings simply leads to the emergence of additional persons with relevant evidence, though not necessarily in contradiction of dishonest testimony already before the court.

This is a suitable point at which to consider the claims made by these writers for the value of open justice as a means of controlling the quality of evidence. Such claims appear, on further consideration, to be exaggerated. Above all, the eliciting of the truth from within the stock of evidence already at the court's disposal is the proper function of cross-examination. Apart from the fact that Wigmore seems to assume of a witness that which is controversial and yet to be established ('ready to scorn a demonstrated liar'), there is no reason at all to suppose that a casual spectator in the public gallery would show a greater degree of perception in these matters than would any of the *personae* of the trial. Quite the contrary. Moreover, the rationale of open justice that is proffered by these writers sits uneasily with the fact that compliance with the norm of open conduct of trials is perfectly consistent with a total—and manifest—absence from the courtroom of any member of the public or representative of the press.

There are more fundamental criticisms that can be made of the 'evidential' rationale of open justice. The claims made by Bentham and Wigmore as to the enhanced quality of testimony forthcoming under a system of open justice rest on untested—probably, in the nature of things, untestable—assumptions. In fact, it

---

[39] ibid. 345.   [40] J. H. Wigmore, *Evidence* Vol 6 (Chadbourn Revision, 1976), ch 62.

[41] Wigmore cites some quaint examples of situations where a person, on reading an account of the day's proceedings in a trial, has come forward with vital testimony in contradiction of the evidence of a previous witness. See, for example, *Smyth v Smyth*, n 48, below. Even more remarkable are instances where the source of contradiction of the witness's testimony happens to be attending court as a casual member of the public. See the account given in Wigmore, op cit, section 1834, concerning one of Lord Chancellor Eldon's prosecutions conducted while he was still at the Bar.

has increasingly been seen in modern times how, far from being conducive to the determination of the truth, the examination in open court of particularly sensitive witnesses (children, or adults who have cause to fear reprisals) will have the effect of their inability or refusal to testify at all. Moreover, the norm of open justice applies with undiminished force to aspects of the judicial process where evidence is only occasionally adduced (for example, the sentencing phase of the criminal trial) or where the transaction of business is concerned with points of law or, at most, with inferences that may legitimately be drawn from evidence (that is, in the appellate courts).

The claims made by Sir Matthew Hale, it will be noticed, are more moderately phrased, being concerned predominantly with the role of open justice in dispelling any tendency towards, or suggestion of, judicial bias. However, in his treatment of the effect on both judge and witness, Hale conflates the fact that the courtroom is open to members of the public with the internal aspect of the trial whereby the *personae* directly confront each other.[42] Yet the public nature of the courtroom is only one element in the features of the trial at common law, together with the requirement that the evidence must be produced in the presence of the accused (or, in a civil case, the parties) and of the jury (in a trial on indictment).[43] Although the several elements are all present in the standard trial, the removal of any one of them raises in an acute form the issue of the precise contribution made by each to the giving of truthful testimony.

The disciplinary rationale of open justice is couched principally in terms of the effect on judges and witnesses of exposure to publicity. But there is no reason in principle why publicity should not be viewed as conducive to the proper functioning of any of the *personae* of the trial. In a speech delivered in 1987, Booth J was reported as claiming that the proliferation of private hearings in family cases had been responsible for 'lax and sloppy advocacy'.[44] As is the case with judges, professional esteem is likely to be the most important consideration making for proper discharge of an advocate's functions. For a long time barristers enjoyed immunity from liability in negligence.[45] Statements in some of the cases, to the effect that such immunity was specifically limited to work conducted as an advocate, seemed to accord with the open conduct of judicial business. For it was precisely at the point where tort liability was absent that publicity would be required

---

[42] See A. L.-T. Choo, *Hearsay and Confrontation in Criminal Trials* (1996) for an examination of the element of confrontation in the giving of testimony.

[43] In those situations where some evidential point has been taken out of sight of the accused—for example, an exhibit has been tested in the seclusion of the jury room or (in the case of a summary trial) in the justices' retiring room—a double injustice has been committed, as against the accused and the public. In one such case the dual character of the defect in the trial was clearly, if fleetingly, expressed. The conviction would not stand since evidence had been received in private, in 'breach of the justices' duty to hear the whole case in open court and in the presence of the defendant': *R v Tiverton Justices, ex p Smith* [1981] RTR 280, 284.

[44] The Times (22 May 1987) 3.

[45] From the ruling of the House of Lords in *Rondel v Worsley* [1969] 1 AC 191 until the ruling of the House in *Arthur J S Hall & Co (a Firm) v Simons* [2000] 3 All ER 673.

to supply a significant element of supervision. Precisely how great is the element of control that is supplied by the publicity of an open court is, as always, a matter for conjecture.

It is, perhaps, uncertainty on this score that leads to a slightly different account of the public administration of justice. On this view, the purpose of publicity is not to exert a check on the *personae* of the trial, but simply to inform the public about the law and legal processes generally. In stark contrast to the disciplinary rationale, it would indeed be difficult to deny the purely educative effect of the open conduct of trials. The question should then be asked as to why, of all the possible areas of communal life in which public instruction could be facilitated, the administration of justice should be deemed of special importance. It scarcely needs to be added that the public has always been especially receptive to instruction in legal matters from cases that have a salacious aspect.[46]

3. THE INVESTIGATORY RATIONALE OF OPEN JUSTICE

In the preceding section we considered the effect—or, rather, the surmised effect—on judge and witness of being subject to public scrutiny in the courtroom. In the present section the concern, rather, is with the effect on the public of the knowledge that they gain from the reporting of judicial proceedings in the media. At the outset it is worth noting that, with this line of inquiry, the element of the reporting of trials has been introduced. This is a subject which, in due course, will be examined in its own right.[47] A word of explanation is required at this stage. In considering (in section 2 above) the effect of publicity on the judge and others involved in the conduct of the trial, it would be reasonable to assume that such influence as would be exerted on them by reason of the open conduct of the proceedings would derive principally from those members of the public present in the courtroom. Those learning of the events of the trial through reports in the media, though numerically more significant, do not exert the influence that comes from physical immediacy. In the present section, by contrast, the line of inquiry is reversed, the question now being: what is the effect on the public of the open transaction of court business? Such effects as are deemed to exist will make their influence felt both on those members of the public who actually attend in the courtroom and on those learning at second hand through reports of the trial in the media. However, as will emerge from this and sections 4 to 5 of the present

---

[46] The point was well made by Viscount Buckmaster: 'A woman who has done no wrong at all has to go to the court to disclose in public matters as to which she would rather die of shame than mention them in public. She has to give her evidence before a court that is crowded with vulgar, idle sightseers, who have not gathered for the purpose of seeing justice administered—if they wanted to see justice administered they could go to the Admiralty Court—but who have gathered for the purpose of hearing of unclean matters from the lips of a woman.' J. Johnson (ed), *An Orator of Justice: A Speech Biography of Viscount Buckmaster* (1932) 239.

[47] In Chapters 8 and 9, below.

chapter, the influences that impinge on the public do not depend for their effectiveness on the actual presence of the public. Indeed, in the light of the limited space made available to members of the public in the courtroom, such influences could scarcely make themselves felt on any significant scale if it were otherwise.

One strand in the investigatory aspect of open justice should be identified immediately as following hard on the heels of the material covered in the preceding section. Publicity given to the issues involved in a trial, it has been claimed, may lead to the emergence of additional witnesses. As people learn of the factual issues on which the outcome of the case will turn they realize that they have relevant testimony to contribute. Such testimony may simply be relevant to the issues. It does not necessarily have to be, as the above-quoted extract of Bentham seems to suggest, in refutation of the dishonest evidence tendered by an earlier witness.

Certainly there have been instances where a person attending a trial, or on reading an account of the proceedings in the press, has come forward with vital testimony.[48] But, as a rationale of open justice, this has surely lost much of its force in the modern era. It is difficult to believe that the publicity generated by the reporting of a trial in the media will match in effectiveness the appeals routinely made by the police—not only in the media but also at the place of the crime itself—specifically to that end. Nevertheless, this element seems to continue to figure in discussion of open justice. In *R v Socialist Worker, ex p A-G*,[49] in the course of assessing the benefits to be derived from public knowledge of the names of witnesses, Lord Widgery CJ pronounced:

... very often the only value of the witness's name being given as opposed to it being withheld is that if it is published up and down the country other witnesses may discover that they can help in regard to the case and come forward. That, of course, is not unusual, and if the witnesses' names are not given, it may tend to prevent other witnesses coming forward in that way.[50]

Likewise, the assurance of anonymity granted to the victims of certain sexual offences by the terms of the Sexual Offences (Amendment) Act 1992 may be waived in the interest of producing additional witnesses.[51] Under section 3(1)(a) the judge may direct that the complainant may not remain anonymous if he is satisfied 'that the direction is required for the purpose of inducing persons who are likely to be needed as witnesses at the trial to come forward' and moreover, under section 3(1)(b), that the accused's defence 'is likely to be substantially prejudiced if the direction is not given'.

---

[48] See the account of *Smyth v Smyth* in 1853 (reported in 1 Woodley's Celebrated Trials 115, 140, 144), where, on reading a newspaper report of civil proceedings, a jeweller was able to expose a case of perjury and hence destroy the entire basis of the plaintiff's claim. However, it is noteworthy that this was not a mere chance happening. The perjured testimony related to the date of engraving on items of jewellery that had been left with the jeweller. In the normal course of events, therefore, he would have come to learn of the testimony even in the absence of a newspaper report of the case.

[49] [1975] QB 637.   [50] ibid. 652.

[51] For a detailed account of anonymity protection accorded to complainants in sexual assault cases, see Chapter 5, section 4B, below.

Both these instances involved issues of anonymity. At least the bare facts of the case would be capable of being publicized, shorn of details of the identity of at least one of the *personae* of the trial. It is noteworthy that in the exercise of the discretion granted by statute to permit legitimacy petitions to be heard *in camera*—clearly, a far deeper incursion into the standard of open justice—'the value of publicity in eliciting further evidence'[52] has been placed in the balance as a consideration that weighs in favour of the trial of the issue in open court.[53]

Any publicity whatsoever that is given to a case may have the effect of producing additional witnesses, irrespective of whether the publicity takes the form of reporting of the trial or coverage of entirely different aspects of the case: for example, an account of a recently uncovered crime, or the announcement of a forthcoming prosecution, or post-conviction claims that a miscarriage of justice has taken place.[54] Indeed, the earlier such publicity occurs, the greater its likely utility. The reason is not difficult to imagine. Reports of pre-trial events may well be more useful than reports of the trial proper, since the testimony of a witness who is discovered at this stage might well render unnecessary the holding of a trial, or (at any rate) forestall a situation in which the late emergence of a witness provides a ground for challenging the outcome of a trial that has been concluded. Furthermore, it does not follow that any testimony that is made available as a result of publicity will be admissible at the trial—a point that is illustrated by the background to *A-G v News Group Newspapers plc*.[55] A national newspaper, having decided to fund a private prosecution, gave extensive pre-trial coverage to the identity of the accused and the circumstances of the alleged crime. Such publicity resulted in the newspaper being found guilty of contempt of court in the course of the above-cited case. The law report contains a fleeting reference to the fact that the press coverage led to the emergence of another 'victim' of the same alleged offender.[56] The publication of her story merely served to increase the likelihood of prejudice to the forthcoming trial. Moreover, it is quite clear from even the brief account of her experience at the hands of the accused that her testimony would have been declared inadmissible on the occasion of the private prosecution.

---

[52] *Barritt v A-G* [1971] 1 WLR 1713, 1714.

[53] Note, however, the outcome: 'it was agreed that, in view of the careful and prolonged inquiries that had already been made, it was highly unlikely that any publicity given to the oral evidence would elicit fresh information': ibid. 1714.

[54] A most remarkable example of the role of post-trial publicity in generating new evidence is provided by the case of Sheila Bowler. Mrs Bowler was convicted in 1993 of the murder of her aunt, an elderly and infirm lady whose body was found in a river some considerable distance from the the place where Mrs Bowler had left her. The prosecution case rested largely on the argument that the aunt could not have covered such a distance unaided. The considerable publicity given to the conviction, both in the press and on Channel Four's *Trial and Error*, led to a series of letters from members of the public whose disabled relatives had suddenly shown themselves capable of walking large distances. See A. Devlin and T. Devlin, *Anybody's Nightmare: The Sheila Bowler Story* (1998) 259–62. This evidence was admitted both by the Court of Appeal on a reference from the Home Secretary and at the subsequent re-trial at which Mrs Bowler was found not guilty: ibid. 296 and 333–4.

[55] [1989] QB 110.   [56] ibid. 122.

The need to reach all potential witnesses forms an aspect of the investigatory function that is relevant to the proper functioning of all manner of courts. In contrast, there are courts the tasks of which are entirely investigatory. Their proceedings do not culminate in the making of an order consequent on a finding of guilt or innocence or, in civil cases, liability or immunity from such liability.

The principal example in this context is that of the coroner's inquest. Whether it sits with or without a jury, the inquest has the limited function of the finding of fact in regard to four issues: the identity of the deceased, the place and time of death, and how the deceased came by his death. The Coroners Rules[57] forbid the framing of verdicts in such a way as to appear to determine issues of criminal or civil liability arising from the death under investigation.[58] That it is no part of the function of the inquest to attribute blame had been judicially emphasized.[59] Indeed, it could hardly be otherwise, since the forum does not concede any procedural rights to those whose conduct may be called into question by such judgments.[60] As the Brodrick Committee[61] put it, the purpose of the investigation is to allay rumours or suspicion; to determine the medical cause of death; to draw attention to circumstances which, if left unremedied, might lead to further casualties; to advance medical knowledge; and to preserve the legal interests of the deceased's family, heirs or other interested parties. Coroner's courts, therefore, may be described as 'judicial' in the narrow sense that they hear evidence that is directed to limited, purely investigatory ends.

How far, in view of their limited role, do the standards of open justice apply to a coroner's inquest? The general rule is that inquests are to be held in public,[62] though the Coroners Rules expressly allow for the possibility of the hearing, or any part of it, taking place *in camera* if the coroner so decides in the interest of national security.[63] The position at common law, expressed by Lord Tenterden CJ in *Garnett v Ferrand*,[64] allowed for a range of exceptions at the coroner's discretion.[65] While some of the exceptions mentioned (for example, the prevention of disorder) would carry equal force today, other considerations cited by way of example would be of doubtful weight (for example, the interests of 'decency', the 'preliminary' nature of an inquest, the danger that a possible accused might tamper with witnesses).[66]

---

[57] Coroners Rules 1984, SI 1984/522.   [58] Rule 42.

[59] *R v Coroner for North Humberside and Scunthorpe, ex p Jamieson* [1995] QB 1.

[60] ibid. 24.

[61] Judge Norman Brodrick, *Report of the Committee on Death Certification and Coroners* (Cmnd 4810, 1971).

[62] For an early nineteenth century dispute as to whether inquests should be open to the public, see J. Vernon (ed.), *Re-reading the Constitution* (1996), 129–43. The inquest which was the centre of the dispute was by way of inquiry into the death of a person who had died in the infamous 'Peterloo' massacre of 1819.

[63] Rule 17.   [64] (1827) 6 B&C 611, 108 ER 576.

[65] (1827) 6 B&C 611, 626, 108 ER 576, 582.

[66] Quite apart from legitimate exceptions to the rule of open justice, the place and time of the inquest may be such that the public, or so many of them as is considered proportionate to the interest

Purely investigatory considerations figure, also, in the examination of bank-rupts.[67] In this context, however, private examination has long existed together with the alternative of 'public examination in open court'.[68] The general nature of the proceeding was discussed by Chitty J in the *Re Greys Brewery Co* case.[69] He was at some pains to point out that, if litigation proper were to ensue from the examination, such litigation would undoubtedly take place in public. The nature of the examination was entirely different:

... the person examined is not examined as a witness, and to talk of examination in chief, or cross-examination ... in a case of this kind, is to use terms that are not really applica-ble. What is being done is this: discovery is sought to be obtained which may be useful to the Court in the conduct of the proceedings in the winding-up, ... [70]

In short, the proceedings were not judicial in the strict sense, and therefore the powers exercisable under 'the "Star Chamber" clause'[71] (as it had come to be known) could not work any injustice.

Insolvency proceedings of this kind, though primarily in the interests of the creditors, may have an aspect in particular instances which makes them of legit-imate interest to the general public. A case in point is provided by the resignation of the Home Secretary, Reginald Maudling, in July 1972 in the aftermath of the revelations emerging from the examination of his business colleague, John Poulson. In the same way the proceedings of particular inquests have provided a forum which has elicited information about an organization as secret as the Special Air Service (SAS) regiment.[72] In the case of each type of proceeding, though, it is a specific event—a death, a bankruptcy—which provides the focus of the investigation and which circumscribes the ambit of the inquiry regardless of the presence of wider issues of public concern that may stem from the central event.

In the same way the standard trial is of limited utility as an investigatory vehi-cle. Such trials may sometimes be the occasion on which matters of the gravest concern may be revealed. However, once the trial has concluded, the process of investigation must be taken up in an entirely different setting. Some recent instances may be cited. The most prominent is the inquiry conducted by Lord Justice Scott into the 'Arms for Iraq' affair, which came to light as a result of the collapse of the prosecution of several directors of the firm, Matrix Churchill, on

---

that the surrounding events have stirred, may be denied access to the proceedings. Recall *R v Inner North London Coroner, ex p Chambers*, Chapter 1, section 7, above.

[67] See, further, Chapter 6, section 2, below.

[68] *Bishopsgate Investment Management Ltd v Maxwell* [1993] Ch 1, 21.

[69] (1884) 25 Ch D 400. The case concerned the right of creditors of a company to attend proceed-ings in front of a special examiner, appointed under the Companies Act 1862, s 115, to examine those whom the liquidator believed to be persons able to give information concerning the dealings of the company.

[70] ibid. 403.   [71] ibid. 408.

[72] The most striking instance is provided by the inquest held in Gibraltar in 1988 as a result of the killing of three members of the IRA on 6 March by members of the SAS Regiment.

charges of illegally exporting arms-making equipment to Iraq.[73] Another is the inquiry set in motion by the Secretary of State for Health under the chairmanship of a former Parliamentary Commissioner for Administration, Sir Cecil Clothier, to investigate the circumstances surrounding the murder of a number of children by Nurse Beverly Allitt.[74] In each case matters arising from the trial gave rise to considerable cause for concern: the issue of public interest immunity certificates in unwarranted circumstances in the former; the fact that the nurse's activities could go unsuspected for such a long period in the latter.

In each instance the form of the inquiry was a matter for ministerial discretion. The Allitt hearings were specifically directed to take place in secret. The decision to do so was challenged on behalf of a two-year-old child whom Allitt had been found guilty of attempting to murder. In rejecting the challenge both the judge at first instance and the Court of Appeal ruled that there was no sustainable case to the effect that the Minister had 'acted with perversity' in requiring the investigation to take place in private. It is particularly unfortunate that the application is not officially reported[75] since it appears that it was based, by extension, on the fundamental principle of the criminal justice system of 'evidence being taken in public'.[76] Sir Cecil Clothier, speaking in defence of the form of his inquiry, stated his belief that the chances of determining the truth would be enhanced if he could see the witnesses 'in circumstances where they do not feel threatened'.[77] Lord Justice Scott, on the other hand, stated at the outset his intention to hear in public session as much as possible of the evidence that he would receive.[78] It may be that as a result of the enactment of the Human Rights Act 1998 the courts, with an eye to Article 10 of the European Human Rights Convention, will be more ready to insist on the open conduct of inquiries. Most notably, the decision of the Secretary of State to stipulate a private inquiry procedure in the aftermath of the conviction of Dr Harold Shipman for the murder of numerous patients was successfully challenged by the relatives of the victims.[79] A perusal of these cases

---

[73] For a brief account of the case, see the Appendix.

[74] For an account of the prosecution and its sequel, see the Appendix.

[75] There is a Court of Appeal transcript of July 1993 under the name: *Crampton v Secretary of State for Health*.

[76] It was so put by the solicitor who acted for the families of several of Allitt's victims: The Times (20 May 1993) 4. It emerges from the the transcript of the Court of Appeal that the challenge to the exercise of the Minister's discretion was based largely on the test in *Associated Provincial Picture Houses Ltd v Wednesbury Corporation* [1948] 1 KB 223.

[77] The Times (20 May 1993) 4.

[78] He subsequently published his views on the conduct of inquiries: R. Scott, 'Procedures at Inquiries—The Duty to be Fair' (1995) 111 LQR 596. See especially at 614–15 for a frank recognition of the pressures placed on witnesses, in both courts and inquiries, by giving evidence in public. The claims to be made for private testimony are said to be greater in the case of inquiries on those occasions where, in contrast to courts, witnesses are questioned in order to elicit whether or not they possess any relevant testimony.

[79] *R v Secretary of State for Health, ex p Wagstaff* [2001] 1 WLR 292. It is worth noting that, under the procedure envisaged by the Secretary of State, the inquiry would be open to the relatives, though not to the public. For an account of the Shipman case, see the Appendix.

shows that, with inquiries (as indeed with courts), unsupported assumptions are made as to which form of hearing—whether public or private—best serves the various ends of the investigatory process.[80]

The element of discretion is absent once it is decided to use a formal tribunal of inquiry as the method of investigation. Section 2 of the Tribunals of Inquiry (Evidence) Act 1921 establishes a general rule of openness in regard to that particular mode of investigation 'unless in the opinion of the tribunal it is in the public interest expedient [to exclude the public or "any portion of the public"] for reasons connected with the subject-matter of the inquiry or the nature of the evidence to be given'. Indeed, the approximation of this type of inquiry to standard judicial proceedings is borne out by the application to it, in general terms, of the law of contempt of court.[81]

This concludes the account, in general terms, of the principal justifications of open justice. In the following sections the principal categories of hearing are appraised in the light of these general considerations.

4. CRIMINAL TRIALS

It has already been seen in Chapter 1, on the basis of the principal human rights documents, that open justice is considered to be of the highest importance in the conduct of criminal trials. Jeremy Bentham, in the course of his various pronouncements on the subject, put the matter as follows: 'By publicity, the temple of justice is converted into a school of the first order, where the most important branches of morality are enforced, by the most impressive means . . .'[82]

In essence, then, the open conduct of trials furnishes a means of instruction of the public in moral standards—or, at any rate, such moral standards as are embodied in the (criminal) law. It is important to note that, with this consideration, we encounter a variation on the disciplinary theme of open justice which is far removed from the notion of a public trial as a form of hearing that is adopted in the interests of the accused. The giving of truthful testimony and the curbing of judicial bias (recall section 2 above) are ends which are capable, at the very least, of serving the personal interests of the accused. However, to present a trial as a spectacle for the moral instruction of the community is to eschew all consideration of the interests of the accused and is to make his trial, in both senses of that word, an instrument of public policy.

Certainly, from time to time some defendants seek to turn the public character of the proceedings to their own account by using them as a platform from which to publicize their views.[83] Civil disobedience traditionally functions by the open

---

[80] For a general overview of the issues see J. Peay (ed), *Inquiries after Homicide* (1996).

[81] See, most notably, the Contempt of Court Act 1981, s 20.

[82] J. Bentham, *Draught of a Code for the Organisation of the Judicial Establishment in France* in J. Bowring (ed), *The Works of Jeremy Bentham*, Vol IV (1843), 317.

[83] See, for example, *R v Ipswich Crown Court, ex p Eris* The Times, 23 February 1989.

flouting of the law combined with a readiness to submit to the ensuing punishment, in the hope that the attendant publicity will result in the stirring of the public conscience to press for the abolition of the law or the termination of the policy in question. Not surprisingly, such attempts to distract attention from what are considered to be the true functions of the trial (with its attendant publicity) are held firmly in check.

The topic of publicity in the context of the criminal trial is seldom addressed expressly in theoretical works on criminal justice. Anthony Duff's *Trials and Punishments*, in devoting a few pages to the subject, is an exception.[84] After adverting to the social stigma that inevitably forms part of the punishment for a criminal conviction, Duff reminds his readers that such stigma could largely be eliminated as an inevitable consequence of conviction if trials were held *in camera* and their outcome forbidden to be published. Nevertheless, he argues, there are strong reasons of principle in favour of public trials and verdicts. He adduces, in essence, three reasons.

First, 'the community should be able to see that the law is being properly applied and administered'.[85] This would appear to be a statement of the disciplinary rationale of open justice.

Secondly, 'public convictions may more effectively dissuade actual and potential offenders from crime'.[86] Certainly, the deterrent thrust of the criminal law— to which this point is adverting—works its effect on persons other than the accused through the medium of publicity. Note, however, the limitations of this reason for the open conduct of criminal trials. The deterrent effect of public trial ensues from a finding of guilt combined with the infliction of a particularly severe punishment. Only at that point does publicity play its part as knowledge of the severity of the sentence is spread among the general populace, and especially among would-be malefactors. Yet, only if the ordeal of public trial itself were to be accounted part of the deterrent apparatus of the criminal law would Duff's second reason for open justice carry significant weight. On that basis, however, there would be a significant arbitrary element in that public trial must also be undergone by those whose innocence is eventually proclaimed by the process.

Thirdly, the commission of a crime is an offence against the whole community, which therefore has a legitimate interest in observing the event at which the question whether a transgression has taken place is determined authoritatively. The guilty should be 'publicly condemned', the innocent 'publicly acquitted' and 'freed from suspicion'.[87] But to put the issue in these terms, of course, is to assume an uncontroversial verdict of guilty or not guilty. Even so, do the propositions that the guilty and the innocent should be the object of, respectively, public condemnation and public acquittal not stand on different footings? Certainly, a finding of guilt should be the occasion of publicity. As a general rule this must

---

[84] R. A. Duff, *Trials and Punishments* (1986) 147–8.   [85] ibid. 148.   [86] ibid.
[87] ibid.

unquestionably be so. In Chapter 8, though, an examination will be conducted of the problem of the case that attracts a degree of exposure out of all proportion to the gravity of the crime of which the accused has been convicted. However, to require a person who has been found not guilty to be acquitted publicly is merely to undo—or, rather, to attempt to undo—the damage that has been inflicted on his standing in the community consequent on the publication of his identity as a suspect. Public acquittal is, in many instances, a poor substitute for anonymity until conviction—and no substitute at all in circumstances where a known suspect has been denied so much as the opportunity of establishing his innocence in a contested trial.

There are, quite apart from these three reasons, further considerations that (prima facie, at least) weigh in favour of the open conduct of criminal justice.

For example, there is the entirely legitimate public interest in being informed of the circumstances of the breach of the criminal code. This is distinct from the question of the attribution of guilt or innocence to particular individuals in regard to the infraction—the element emphasized by Duff. Clearly, the two elements will exist side by side in the standard trial format. Occasionally they do not. Where the accused pleads guilty there is all the greater possibility that the public may be denied 'the right inherent in our system of the administration of criminal justice, to know the circumstances of the crime for which an accused is convicted and sentenced'.[88] In circumstances where the information cannot be gleaned from the committal proceedings (either because a hearing did not take place at that stage or because reporting restrictions in regard to them were not lifted), the only authoritative source of information about the circumstances of the crime would be the statement of the facts by the prosecutor in open court as a prelude to the passing of sentence. Information could be derived from other sources (the police, for example) but in other forms it would not come clothed in the various privileges that attach to the reports of court proceedings. In the case of murder there was no cause even for the making of the prosecution's statement in view of the fact that the sentence, life imprisonment, is mandatory. Nevertheless, for the sake of the public interest just mentioned, the Court of Appeal announced by way of Practice Direction that, just as in the case of pleas of guilty to other charges, prosecuting counsel should state the circumstances of the murder in open court before sentence is passed.[89]

Moreover, there is the entirely proper interest that each single member of the public possesses in knowing whether a person with whom he is associating or is minded to associate (whether socially or by way of employment) has a criminal conviction that might have some bearing on the decision whether or not to continue the association. This is a delicate area, where the aforementioned interest must be set against the rehabilitative aims of the criminal justice system. That it

---

[88] *Practice Direction* [1968] 2 All ER 144.

[89] See n 88 above. The Practice Direction is described, in its footnote 4, as 'a sequel to the lack of publicity exemplified in *R v Sokol* The Times, 29 March 1968'.

is, at any rate, an interest that merits weighing in the scales is recognized in the several cases on the question of the anonymity of juvenile defendants.[90] However, it is an interest that is served, not by the open conduct of the trial process itself, but by knowledge of the outcome of trials that end in a verdict of guilty.

5. CRIMINAL TRIALS: ISSUES OF SENTENCE

Although, in one sense, a postscript to the preceding section, the issues relating to sentence merit separate consideration.

If open criminal trials are to be justified on the basis of the legitimate interest of the public in observing the procedures in the course of which alleged transgressions of the most fundamental norms of the community are authoritatively determined, the same rationale would seem to apply with even greater force in the realm of sentencing. In this phase of the criminal process we are exclusively concerned with the guilty, at any rate as far as the official record goes. There is no question, as there is with the trial procedure up to that stage, of the burdens of publicity being inflicted on guilty and innocent alike. One point needs to be emphasized. Our focus of interest is public access to the process of sentencing, not to the carrying out of the sentence. Access to the latter has been uncontroversially denied, with one exception. Capital punishment, until 1868, was inflicted in public.[91] This practice had a certain gruesome logic. If one of the purposes of the open conduct of the criminal trial is to exert a deterrent influence on potential criminals, there are few influences more calculated to achieve that purpose than the public witnessing of the felon's demise. Yet it is worth noting that, even when capital punishment has been carried out within the prison walls (in Britain until its abolition in 1965, and even today in many states of the USA), there has remained an exiguous element of open justice in that facilities have been made available to representatives of the print media to witness the carrying out of the execution.[92]

When one turns, then, to the actual process of sentencing it is apparent that many of the same considerations that were applicable to the trial up to that point

---

[90] See *R v Leicester Crown Court, ex p S (a minor)* [1993] 1 WLR 111, 114; *R v Lee* [1993] 1 WLR 103, 109.

[91] The Capital Punishment Amendment Act 1868, s 2, stipulated that the execution was to take place 'within the walls of the prison in which the offender is confined at the time of the execution'.

[92] The Capital Punishment Amendment Act 1868, s 2, required the presence of certain persons (e.g. the prison surgeon) at the execution. The sheriff and the visiting justices of the prison had a discretion to admit any local justice of the peace, any relatives of the prisoner, or 'other persons as it seems . . . proper to admit within the prison' for the purpose of witnessing the execution. The memoirs of the man who long served as the official hangman record that, initially, representatives of the press were invited to attend. However, from 1888 onwards, as a response to newspaper coverage of some bungled executions, the presence of the press was actively discouraged: A. Pierrepoint, *Executioner: Pierrepoint* (1974) 68–71.

continue to hold force. The taking of evidence for the purposes of sentence is a common feature in some trials.[93] To that extent the open conduct of the sentencing phase is, as we have seen, a spur to the giving of truthful testimony. A further danger in the determination of sentence which publicity may help to avert is, as before, the infiltration of bias on the part of the judge. Such studies as have been conducted in an effort to detect such influences, however, are based inevitably on inter-trial comparisons as between similarly placed defendants.[94]

These are a number of rulings that bear on the open conduct of the sentencing process. Where a guilty plea has been entered, the judge must direct himself openly as to the onus of proof on issues of fact.[95] Where he decides to clarify or amend a sentence, he must do so in open court.[96] Moreover, judges have been urged by the Lord Chief Justice to explain the reasons which led to the sentence passed—in clear recognition that, in itself, openness is of limited value—so as the better to appreciate the way in which the sentence was likely to be received by the public.[97]

While it would be a rare trial where the issues relating to guilt or innocence were entirely heard in secret, it is quite possible that the whole plea in mitigation might be heard *in camera* with the result that the public are denied all basis upon which an unduly lenient sentence, for example, may be judged. In *R v Malvern Justices, ex p Evans*[98] the justices cleared the court of both public and press[99] to hear evidence from the defendant (who had pleaded guilty to driving under the influence of excess alcohol) and her daughter. The testimony related to various intimate aspects of the background to the offence (the defendant's medical history and pending divorce). The court was then reopened for the purpose of pronouncing sentence[100]—one that was markedly more lenient than the norm for that particular crime. The secrecy of the sentencing stage was obtained as a result of the defence solicitor's plea that, without the element of confidentiality, his client would feel utterly unable to adduce the extenuating circumstances. The painful circumstances of marital discord have certainly figured as convincing reasons, in matrimonial cases themselves, for invoking an exception to the rule of open justice. Yet, deprived of the knowledge of what transpired during the plea in mitigation, it is difficult for the member of the public to appraise the quality of the magistrates' reasons for inflicting a light punishment. Little wonder, then,

---

[93] See, generally, M. Wasik, 'Rules of Evidence in the Sentencing Process' (1985) 38 *Current Legal Problems* 187.

[94] For example, see R. Hood, *Race and Sentencing: A Study in the Crown Court* (1992).

[95] *R v Kerrigan* The Times, 30 July 1992.

[96] *R v Dowling* (1989) 88 Cr App R 88. Only in this way 'will all concerned and the public hear the final decision from the judge himself and in his own terms. Only thus will a shorthand note be recorded and available': ibid. 91, per Taylor CJ.

[97] *R v Skinner* The Times, 23 March 1993.   [98] [1988] QB 540.

[99] Note that the application itself to make a plea in mitigation *in camera* should itself be heard in that way: see *R v Ealing Justices, ex p Weafer* (1982) 74 Cr App R 204.

[100] cf. the Official Secrets Act 1920, s 8(4), which stipulates that, as a minimum requirement of an *in camera* official secrets trial, 'the passing of sentence shall in any case take place in public'.

that the validity of the process was challenged by the publishers of the local newspaper, a challenge that was rejected by the Divisional Court on the basis that (however undesirable the *in camera* sitting) the magistrates certainly possessed the legal power so to conduct the relevant part of the hearing.[101]

Before leaving the subject, it would be useful to advert to a rather different aspect of open access to the decision-making procedure in the area of sentencing. The life sentence, whether mandatory or discretionary, causes particular problems in the light of the periodic reviews by the Home Secretary after taking into account the opinions expressed by the trial judge. The procedures put in place by the Criminal Justice Act 1967 in regard to discretionary life prisoners were found to be in violation of Article 5(4) of the European Convention on Human Rights, which guarantees everyone deprived of his liberty the right to take proceedings 'by which the lawfulness of his detention shall be decided speedily by a court'. The adverse judgment of the European Court of Human Rights in *Thynne, Wilson and Gunnell v UK*[102] led to the enactment of section 34 of the Criminal Justice Act 1991, which empowers the Parole Board to grant early release for a prisoner on licence where, inter alia, 'the Board is satisfied that it is no longer necessary for the protection of the public that the prisoner should be confined'.[103] It is noteworthy that the hearing before the Parole Board, for all that its determinations are taken on the basis of its perception of the risk to the public, is held, in private, at the prison where the applicant is confined.

It would only be a matter of time before a similar challenge would be mounted in respect of mandatory life sentences. It materialized finally in *R v Secretary of State for the Home Department, ex p Doody*,[104] where Lord Mustill succinctly described the predicament of the prisoner sentenced mandatorily to life imprisonment for murder:

He never sees the Home Secretary; he has no dialogue with him: he cannot fathom how his mind is working. There is no true tariff, or at least no tariff exposed to public view which might give the prisoner an idea of what to expect . . . The beginnings of an explanation for [the procedure's] unique character might perhaps be found if the executive had still been putting into practice the theory that the tariff sentence for murder is confinement for life, subject only to a wholly discretionary release on licence: although even in such a case I doubt whether in the modern climate of administrative law such an entirely secret process could be justified.[105]

The House of Lords ruled that the prisoner was entitled to be informed of the period recommended by the judge that he should serve and of any other opinion expressed by the judiciary as to the appropriate sentence to be served, and moreover of the Secretary of State's reasons for departing (if he should choose to do so) from such judicial opinions. These and other rights were conceded by their Lordships in the interests of 'fairness'. In this contest between prisoner and

---

[101] See [1988] QB 540, 550. [102] (1991) 13 EHRR 666.
[103] Criminal Justice Act 1991, s 34(4)(b). [104] [1993] 3 WLR 154. [105] ibid. 173.

Secretary of State, however, no account was taken of the public interest in scrutinizing the procedures that regulate the period of incarceration of the most serious offenders against the law.

6. DISCIPLINARY CASES

As we have seen, the procedural guarantee of an open trial is considered particularly important in matters of criminal law. So much is implied, if not clearly expressed, in the leading human rights texts. However, in two areas of state control—the prisons and the armed forces—persons are characteristically subject to a disciplinary code that is largely enforced by 'judicial' machinery which lies outside the regular court system. The content of the disciplinary code will vary from relatively insignificant rules to very serious misconduct. Its overall content, in any event, will be shaped by the needs of the efficient functioning of the particular area of state activity. To take the example of the prisons, some offences listed in the Prison Rules[106] are not criminal *per se*, however desirable the standards of conduct embodied in them might be for the smooth functioning of the prisons. Others, however, are breaches of the criminal law and would have been subject to ordinary criminal process had the prisoner been a free person at the time.

Traditionally, many infractions of the Prison Rules, even those which mirrored offences in the general criminal law, have been dealt with internally under a system of adjudication administered by the prison governor or the relevant Board of Visitors. The argument that they are in this way administering a regime of 'disciplinary law', if accepted at its face value, would have removed matters subject to their jurisdiction entirely from the scope of the guarantees of the European Human Rights Convention in so far as those guarantees apply to criminal trials. However, the European Court of Human Rights has stated in several cases, principally *Engel*[107] (in the context of military disciplinary proceedings) and *Campbell and Fell*[108] (in the context of prison discipline), that the dividing line drawn by national legal systems between the criminal and disciplinary spheres will not be treated as conclusive for the purposes of the Convention. Other factors to be considered are the intrinsic seriousness of the misconduct and the nature and severity of the penalty likely to be incurred as a result of a finding of an infraction of the disciplinary code. If such considerations are sufficiently weighty, they will result in the disregard of the national legal system's classification of the matter as merely 'disciplinary' and the imposition of the full rigour of the Convention's criminal procedure safeguards.

---

[106] The Prison Rules are promulgated pursuant to authority contained in the Prison Act 1952, s 47. Their latest form is the Prison Rules 1999, SI 1999/728.

[107] *Engel v The Netherlands* (No 1) (1979–80) 1 EHRR 647.

[108] *Campbell and Fell v UK* (1985) 7 EHRR 165.

The position of Boards of Visitors as unquestionably beyond the right of public access was defended in various ways. In *R v Secretary of State for the Home Department, ex p Tarrant*[109] the refusal of one such Board, among other things, to allow prisoners the assistance of a 'McKenzie friend' at the disciplinary proceedings was subject to challenge. Webster J, after discussing the role of the 'McKenzie friend' in divorce suits and other proceedings, continued:

A magistrates' court, and the court in which a divorce trial is taking place, is a public court to which all have access; and if a member of the public gives assistance to a party without interfering in the course of the proceedings he does no more than assert his right as a member of the public to come into court and associate with a party to those proceedings. But hearings before boards of visitors are not public hearings at all, and no one has the right to attend them without the invitation or permission of the board of visitors.[110]

The European Court in *Campbell and Fell*, although it identified a number of defects in the mode of conduct of the particular Board of Visitors, found 'sufficient reasons of public order and security' to justify the exclusion of the press and public from the proceedings:

A Board's adjudications are, as befits the character of disciplinary proceedings of this kind, habitually held within the prison precincts and the difficulties over admitting the public to those precincts are obvious. If they were held outside, similar problems would arise as regards the prisoner's transportation to and attendance at the hearing.[111]

Events have moved on apace since the ruling in that case. The institution of Boards of Visitors, combining adjudicatory and supervisory roles within the prison system, became increasingly difficult to defend on general principle. A proposed Prison Disciplinary Tribunal, suggested by the Prior Committee[112] to hear the more serious categories of charge against prison discipline, was to sit within the relevant prison walls and in private. The exclusion of the public was defended in the interests of both security and—surprisingly—the privacy of prisoners.[113] The proposal was never implemented. From April 1992 onwards the adjudicatory role previously exercised by the Board of Visitors has been vested in the prison governor.

7. CIVIL CASES AND ARBITRATION

Many, though by no means all, of the claims that are made for the value of open justice in the criminal law can be reiterated with regard to civil trials. A significant difference is that the enactment of the Civil Procedure Rules 1998 has served to

---

[109] [1985] QB 251.   [110] ibid. 283.   [111] (1985) 7 EHRR 165, para 87.

[112] *Report of the Committee on the Prison Disciplinary System* (Chairman: Peter J Prior) (Cmnd 9641, 1985).

[113] ibid. para 11.69: 'prisoners are entitled to privacy and should not be subject to the prospect that their internal offences will be publicised whether they wish it or not'.

provide a code of instances where all or part of a civil hearing, whether in the High Court or the county court, may take place in private.[114] A perusal of that code reveals a list of circumstances where either there is no dispute, for example, uncontentious matters arising in the administration of trusts, or where the exception to the norm of open justice is well established, such as instances where the case involves matters of national security or publicity would defeat the point of the hearing. Rather more controversial are the terms of the Practice Direction promulgated to supplement the relevant rule.[115] It is difficult to appreciate what interest is served by listing for hearing in private such actions as, for example, an application by a mortgagee for an order for possession of land.

It is not proposed to repeat, with modifications adapted to civil cases, the points that have already been examined at some length in the context of criminal trials. Indeed, in recent years the dividing line between the two forms of proceedings has been blurred on occasion for reasons that are relevant to the subject of open justice. The authorities, to take the most typical instance, decide not to prosecute a person suspected of having committed a rape or murder. The victim (or the victim's estate) brings proceedings in tort against the suspect. The object is not to gain compensation, but rather to gain an official and public determination of the defendant's guilt.

In the context of civil disputes, resort is sometimes had to arbitration as a means of dispute settlement. This is especially so in the context of commercial disputes.[116] However this form of procedure, being regularly conducted in private, is contrary to the principle of open justice.

The referral of disputes to arbitration procedure[117] stems from the wishes of plaintiff and defendant as freely expressed in a prior agreement. Among the frequently cited advantages of this form of dispute resolution, that of the confidentiality of the proceedings ranks highly. Indeed, for standard-form arbitration rules to stipulate that hearings shall take place *in camera* would appear otiose.[118] Since the location of the arbitration hearing is likely to be a private building, neither the public nor the press will enjoy even a presumptive right to attend. The only possibility of disclosure, then, derives from the *personae* of the arbitration

---

[114] Civil Procedure Rules 1998, SI 1998/3132, r 39.2(3).

[115] PD 39, which is conveniently reproduced in *Blackstone's Guide to the Civil Procedure Rules* (1999), 592–5.

[116] Consequently, this preliminary discussion should be supplemented by the examination of arbitration in the sphere of commercial relations in Chapter 6, section 3, below.

[117] Note the hybrid role of the judge-arbitrator, whereby a judge of the Commercial Court is released from his official duties for the purpose of conducting an arbitration: see the Administration of Justice Act 1970, s 4. In such circumstances the personnel of the High Court are employed in discharging a role that is undoubtedly judicial in nature but which, nevertheless, does not fall within the reach of the open justice rule. Certainly, it has been acknowledged that the fact 'that a Judge is a Judge-arbitrator does not mean that his award has the same status as a judgment of the High Court': *Seaworld Ocean Line Co SA v Catseye Maritime Co Ltd* [1989] 1 Lloyd's Rep 30, 32.

[118] See, for example, the United Nations Commission on International Trade Law (UNCITRAL) Arbitration Rules, Art 25(4): 'Hearings shall be held *in camera* unless the parties agree otherwise . . .'

proceedings. However, there is an implied term in arbitration agreements imposing a duty on the parties to respect confidentiality in regard to the award itself, the reasons given by the arbitrator for his award, and all documents that relate to the arbitration. The sole exception encompasses only the first two elements (the award, and the reasons therefor) if disclosure should prove reasonably necessary for the purpose of establishing a party's legal rights against a third person (whether as a defence or by way of a cause of action).[119]

The general availability of arbitration is based on the assumption that the resolution of a large range of disputes is a matter which the parties themselves may legitimately make their private concern. While referral to an arbitrator is characteristic of certain types of civil dispute,[120] it is noteworthy that there is no rule that forbids the referral of criminal matters to this form of adjudication. There is, however, an effective procedural limitation in this respect since, for reasons of public policy, an arbitrator is not competent to impose a fine or term of imprisonment.[121]

8. INFORMAL SETTLEMENT

The norm of open justice applies to the trial proceedings. Voluntary arrangements made by the parties—whether to refer the dispute to an entirely different forum of resolution (as with arbitration), or to compromise an action that would otherwise be tried in the regular courts—escape the presumptive application of the norm. The two principal types of legal proceeding have forms of compromise: out-of-court settlements (in civil actions); plea bargaining (in criminal cases). While not attracting the full rigours of exposure to public scrutiny in all respects, outcomes such as these are sufficiently associated with the standard trial format to be subjected, in part at least, to the demands of publicity. With these preliminary points in mind it is necessary to consider separately the two principal forms of compromise.

The leading work on the settlement of civil disputes states that '[t]here is no magic about compromise. Its foundation is the ordinary law of contract'.[122] The terms of a settlement may be made known to the public, or, alternatively, they may embody an undisclosed sum. Whether the striking of a compromise is

---

[119] See *Hassneh Insurance Co of Israel v Mew* [1993] 2 Lloyd's Rep 243, and *Insurance Co v Lloyd's Syndicate* [1995] 1 Lloyd's Rep 272.

[120] There is (admittedly exiguous) authority to suggest that a judge may, with the consent of all the parties, try a civil case *in camera*: *Malan v Young* (1889) 6 TLR 38.

[121] See M. J. Mustill and S. C. Boyd, *Commercial Arbitration* (2nd edn, 1989), 149–50.

[122] D. Foskett, *The Law and Practice of Compromise* (2nd edn, 1985) 3. Nevertheless, where the litigant's accord is embodied in a court order or judgment (e.g., a consent order), it is arguable that the intervention of the judicial machinery of the state, even in this quite passive form, should suffice to put the terms of the agreement 'in the public domain'.

attended by a duty of disclosure—or, more usually, a duty of confidentiality—is to be determined by reference to the express or implied terms of the contract.[123]

The statement made in open court as part of the process of settlement merits separate consideration. It has long been a familiar feature of the settlement of proceedings for defamation. Its position is somewhat anomalous in that it requires prior judicial approval[124] and, at the same time, it enjoys the advantage of the privilege attaching to the report of judicial proceedings. The basis of the practice is succinctly stated in *Barnet v Crozier*:[125]

Parties to an action do not need the consent of the court to make an effective settlement of their dispute; nor do they need the consent of the court to announce to the world that they have settled it on stated terms. The importance of the making of a statement in open court is, first, that it is likely to come to the attention of the press, who will give to it such attention as its public interest is seen by them to merit and, secondly, since the statement is part of a judicial proceeding, it is made on an occasion of absolute privilege. Thus, the parties to the statement are protected and, moreover, the statement can be reported without the publisher of the report incurring the risk of being sued in respect of it.[126]

In 1990 changes in the relevant rules of court extended the scope of the statement read in open court to encompass the settlement of actions for malicious prosecution and false imprisonment.[127] The scope of the new rule is strictly limited to these two actions together with defamation. Even cognate torts, such as battery, are outside its reach. The only explanation that has been proffered is that malicious prosecution and false imprisonment typically involve a slur on the reputation of the plaintiff, and therein lies the link with defamation. Accordingly, 'in appropriate circumstances a statement in open court making public the vindication, which the plaintiff wished the world to know of, of his or her character and reputation should be able to be publicly announced.'[128]

The inclusion of malicious prosecution in this regard is of particular interest since the statement made in open court may be seen, in that context, as a means of seeking to undo the damage that the plaintiff will have suffered as a result of the adverse publicity incurred in earlier proceedings, albeit a trial which will have concluded with a verdict of not guilty. As with defamation proceedings, leave must be obtained from the judge for the making of the statement. Such guidance

---

[123] Where, however, the judge approves the settlement of a damages claim on behalf of a child or patient, the approval should normally be given in open court: *Beatham v Carlisle Hospitals NHS Trust* The Times, 20 May 1999.

[124] RSC Ord 82, r 5(1). The provision is retained by virtue of the Civil Procedure Rules (n 2 above), Part 50 and Sch 1. For the text of the provision see n 127, below.

[125] [1987] 1 WLR 272.   [126] ibid. 276, per Ralph Gibson LJ.

[127] The applicable provision (RSC Ord 82, r 5(1)) now reads:'Where a party wishes to accept money paid into court in satisfaction of a cause of action for libel or slander, malicious prosecution or false imprisonment, that party may before or after accepting the money apply to a judge sitting in private in accordance with CPR Part 23 for permission to make in open court a statement in terms approved by the judge.'

[128] *Smith v Commisioner of Police of the Metropolis* [1991] 1 All ER 714, 716, per Michael Davis J.

as we possess as to the exercise of the judicial discretion[129] indicates that leave should not, as a rule, be refused where the case is one that has attracted wide-spread publicity. This might be taken as referring only to the civil proceedings. By extension, however, it should also encompass the earlier criminal trial.

In the criminal law the nearest analogous device to settlement out of court of a civil action is provided by the practice of plea bargaining. In its standard form the accused agrees to plead guilty to a less serious charge than the charge that has been brought in the expectation that he will receive a lighter punishment. Alternatively, the accused will agree to plead guilty to only some of a range of charges in return for the prosecution offering no evidence in regard to the remaining charges. Portrayed in this way, plea bargaining sits uneasily between the present section and the subject matter of section 5 of this chapter, namely, matters of sentence in the criminal trial. When the earlier informal exchanges between prosecutor and defence are left out of account, that which transpires in open court can be reduced to the standard process of sentencing consequent on a plea of guilty having been entered. Sentencing is the exclusive preserve of the trial judge, whereas the agreement of the defendant to pay a particular sum of money in consideration of the plaintiff dropping a civil action generally requires no involvement on the part of the judge who is trying the case. Apart from this significant difference between negotiated outcomes in civil and criminal cases, the judge who tries the latter type of case plays a more active part in that he may be approached in private by counsel (whether before or during the trial) with a view to obtaining guidance as to any likely sentence.

Although a long established feature of the American criminal process, plea bargaining became the subject of scholarly and judicial attention in this country only in the late 1960s. An early article on the subject complained that 'very little is known of the informal bargaining processes which go on between prosecution and defence with regard to a negotiated plea of guilty'.[130] Detailed empirical studies on the subject of 'negotiated justice',[131] based on information gathered in and around the Crown Courts, are now available. Such information may well be made available to researchers through the willing co-operation of the prosecuting authorities, defendants, and their legal advisers. But to what extent does the public have a right to know the extent to which plea bargaining is taking place? In other words, how far does the practice fall within the ill-defined norm of open justice?

When, in *R v Turner*,[132] the Court of Appeal first recognized the practice of plea bargaining, it sought to offer guidance to the profession in the form of a number of 'guidelines'. Among these guidelines is to be found a fleeting reminder:

---

[129] *J v R* The Times, 23 February 1984; (1984) 128 Sol J 333.
[130] P. Thomas, 'An Exploration of Plea Bargaining' [1969] Crim LR 69.
[131] To take the best-known of such studies: J. Baldwin and M. McConville, *Negotiated Justice— Pressures on Defendants to Plead Guilty* (1977).
[132] [1970] 2 QB 321.

'It is of course imperative that so far as possible justice must be administered in open court.'[133] But what does that generalized assertion amount to? In terms of the standard requirements of due process, the proper conduct of plea bargaining—at any rate, as laid down in the Court of Appeal's guidelines—occupies an anomalous position. On the one hand, parity of treatment as between prosecution and defence is emphasized: it would clearly be wrong for the judge to hear one side in the absence of the other. On the other hand, there is no requirement that the accused be present at, or even be informed of the contents of, such 'off-stage' discussions. The latter consideration indicates that, both in a physical and a conceptual sense, plea-bargain discussions are not deemed to be part of the trial proper. The discussions take place in 'the judge's room'—a venue distinct from the court's 'chambers', which (as will be seen in Chapter 3) provide a forum in which certain categories of hearing routinely take place. Conceptually, too, if the discussions that take place in the judge's room were considered to be a phase in the trial, there would be a violation of the fundamental principle that the accused has a right to be present at each and every part of that trial.

The confidential character of the discussions in the judge's room may place counsel in a difficult position of striving to maintain the confidences imparted to him while seeking to fulfil his professional duties to his client. In *R v Agar*,[134] a case which did not involve plea bargaining but rather the forestalling of questions that might reveal the identity of a police informer, the Court of Appeal stated:

As this court has repeatedly emphasised, discussions in the judge's room, with the defendant absent, are an expedient of last resort. This appeal demonstrates once again how things can go wrong, and how a real sense of injustice may be engendered in the absent client.[135]

This case was especially noteworthy in that the judge had forbidden disclosure to the accused of even the very fact that proceedings had taken place in the judge's room. In *R v Harper-Taylor and Bakker*,[136] in the course of a consideration of the nature of meetings by counsel in the judge's private room, Mustill LJ conceded that the avowed purpose of such meetings is 'that neither the defendant nor the jury nor the public are there to hear what is going on'. Apart from the infringement of the first principle of the criminal trial, 'that justice is done in public, for all to see and hear', such informal exchanges would tend 'to blur the formal outlines of the trial'. Such informality would create, in particular, two difficulties. First, misunderstandings may well arise as to how far the confidences exchanged in the judge's room are to extend. Moreover, as has already been noted, even if there is no doubt as to the extent of the confidence, the need to preserve it may well jeopardize counsel's duty to his client. Secondly, so much information as is imparted to the accused is gained by him at second hand. There is consequent scope for complaint by him, whether correctly or not, that he was misinformed

---

[133] ibid. 326, per Lord Parker CJ.   [134] [1990] 2 All ER 442.   [135] ibid. 448.
[136] NLJ 18 March 1988.

by his counsel. This difficulty stems from the absence of the accused from part of his 'trial' and goes to illuminate the practical common sense behind the most fundamental component of open justice, the presence of the accused at each and every stage of the proceedings conceptually regarded as the trial.

Quite apart from the possibility of confusion at the point when defence counsel communicates with his client, there is an additional danger that there may be disagreement, even between those present in the judge's room, as to what precisely transpired there. In *R v Smith (Terence)*,[137] following a plea of guilty and the passing of a custodial sentence, counsel for the accused forthwith protested in open court at the passing of a sentence which (he claimed) was at variance with indications given by the judge in his private room. This was followed up by a letter of protest from counsel to the judge and the filing of the instant (successful) appeal. The admonition given by the Court of Appeal, and repeated on several other occasions, warned against informal discussions taking place 'in the absence of a shorthand notetaker, or alternatively, in the absence of some recording device'.[138]

Disquiet concerning the practice of plea bargaining came to a head in 2000, largely as a result of a case where the Crown, by reason of its involvement in the question of a negotiated sentence, was disabled from exercising its right to appeal against an unduly lenient sentence for indecent assault on a number of schoolchildren.[139] This has led to a reconsideration of whether the practice of plea bargaining should be forbidden or whether it should be permitted to continue, in a formal setting only, including a requirement that it should take place in the open.[140]

9. DOMESTIC TRIBUNALS

Section 19 (the Interpretation section) of the Contempt of Court Act 1981 defines the term 'court' to include 'any tribunal or body exercising the judicial power of the State'. This phrase, in a certain sense, defines the principal field of inquiry of this book. The theme is that of the open conduct of trials (whether criminal or civil, or whether staged in the traditional court structure or in administrative tribunals) as part of the machinery of the state. In this section some consideration is given to domestic tribunals which exercise 'adjudicatory' power over certain categories of person.[141]

---

[137] [1990] 1 WLR 1311.   [138] ibid. 1314.

[139] *Attorney-General's Reference (No 44 of 2000), R v Peverett* [2000] 1 Cr App R 416. An important feature of the case was the abuse of trust by the accused, who was headmaster to the children at the time of the offences.

[140] For a recent examination of the whole subject, see P. Darbyshire 'The Mischief of Plea Bargaining and Sentencing Rewards' [2000] Crim LR 895. See, in particular, at 905, where there is a brief reference to the difficulty that plea bargaining does not take place in open court.

[141] See generally B. Harris, *The Law and Practice of Disciplinary and Regulatory Proceeedings* (2nd edn, 1999).

The powers exercisable over sportsmen and professional persons by sporting associations and professional bodies impinge more directly on the livelihood of the persons affected than most rulings that could be given by the court system. Hence the importance, in practical terms, of devoting some space to a consideration of domestic tribunals.[142]

The overriding point to be made is that domestic tribunals are not required to sit in open session when exercising their jurisdiction. It is the rules of the particular association that stipulate how much publicity, if any, is to attend disciplinary hearings and determinations. For example, the Solicitors Disciplinary Tribunal has recently opened its doors after many years of sitting in private.[143]

Of all the various professional bodies, one stands out as particularly deserving of some attention since the disciplinary function is discharged by judges. At the centre of the jurisdiction of the various Inns of Court lie the powers of the Visitors to the individual Inns. These, consisting of three High Court judges, hear appeals from disciplinary tribunals that sit in private.[144] The status of the Visitors has been the subject of some debate, particularly in the context of whether their decisions are subject to judicial review. In *R v Visitors to the Inns of Court, ex p Persaud*,[145] Brooke J in the Divisional Court emphasized that judges, when sitting in the capacity of Visitors, were 'acting as judges and performing judicial duties'.[146] Nevertheless, he continued without any hint of inconsistency, they sat in private (neither in court nor even in chambers) when exercising their visitorial role—a practice that was sanctioned by long-standing custom.[147]

---

[142] See R. Furneaux, *Great Issues in Private Courts* (1964) for an account of some noteworthy cases that have been heard by the disciplinary bodies of the Church of England and the medical and legal professions. The foreword states: 'The title "Private Courts" implies not that the courts are secret, but that they are the tribunals of private associations'. One case which had repercussions well beyond the position of the individual who had been subjected to disciplinary proceedings is that of the barrister, Patrick Marrinan (recounted in ch 8). In the course of the proceedings disturbing practices relating to the administration of telephone tapping came to light, as a result of which a Committee of Privy Councillors was appointed to investigate the subject of interception of communications. As Furneaux notes cryptically, 'At Marrinan's request, the hearing [before the Benchers of Lincoln's Inn] was in public—an unusual innovation': ibid. 126.

[143] The change was effected by the Solicitors (Disciplinary Proceedings) Rules 1994, SI 1994/288, Rule 13(a). This allows for the possibility, in certain circumstances, of a private hearing. See *Addis v Crocker* [1961] 1 QB 11, 30, per Upjohn J, on the reason why the disciplinary hearings of the Law Society were (then) closed to the public: 'Some wholly unfounded charge may be preferred against a solicitor by a disappointed client and the publicity of a hearing followed necessarily by some delay ... might work a serious injustice on the solicitor.'

[144] Code of Conduct of the Bar, Disciplinary Tribunals Regulations, para 11, states:'The hearing before a Disciplinary Tribunal shall be in private unless either: (a) at a preliminary hearing or otherwise it has been directed that it shall be held in public, and this direction has not been over-ruled by the Tribunal; or (b) the defendant has made an application that the hearing shall be in public, and the public interest does not otherwise require.'

[145] Joined with *R v Visitors to the Inns of Court, ex p Calder* [1994] QB 1.

[146] ibid. 18. As the report makes clear, the judgment was prepared by Brooke J but, owing to his absence, was read by Mann LJ.

[147] There was a successful appeal to the Court of Appeal on points which are of no direct concern: ibid., 21. Suffice it to note that the ruling of the Court of Appeal, that High Court judges sitting as Visitors to the Inns of Court sat as a domestic forum of voluntary societies, provided a characterization

It is apparent that, when exercising the jurisdiction of Visitors, the judges have a degree of flexibility and discretion that would be unacceptable in a courtroom setting. In *Re S (A barrister)*[148] the five judges sitting as Visitors to Gray's Inn pronounced: 'Normally when sitting as visitors the judges sit in private, but at the request of the barrister or student concerned may sit in public . . . In this case we were asked by [counsel for the appellant] that the public should be admitted and we acceded to his request.'[149] In *Re H (A Barrister)*[150] the Visitors to Gray's Inn, allowing an appeal from the Disciplinary Tribunal of the Senate, substituted for the original penalty a reprimand without publication of the barrister's name on the ground that 'publication is not necessary either as a warning and deterrent to him or as a marking by the profession of its view of the commission of such an offence [importuning for immoral purposes in a public place] by a barrister'.[151] And finally in our survey of the various procedural formats, it emerges that in *Re T (A Barrister)*[152] the Visitors of Lincoln's Inn heard the appeal itself in private but pronounced their findings in public.[153]

Indeed questions, the answers to which would be regarded as beyond doubt if they were asked in regard to courts proper (for example, on the applicable standard of proof or on the use of evidence that is inadmissible in strict law), are posed from time to time as genuinely doubtful in the context of domestic tribunals.[154] The proceedings of such tribunals, therefore, are 'judicial' only in an attenuated sense of the word.

Nevertheless it is possible to find in this area arguments in favour of both secrecy and confidentiality of proceedings that in large measure reflect arguments that have been deployed to the same ends in regard to the proceedings of courts proper.

Public access to trials is permitted in order to foster confidence in the administration of justice. In the same way, in the case of a professional association, one reason for favouring open disciplinary proceedings is the wish to reassure the public that only the highest standards of probity will be acceptable to the association from its members. In *Bolton v Law Society*[155] the Court of Appeal emphasized that such was indeed the fundamental purpose of disciplinary orders: punitive or deterrent considerations were secondary to the need to maintain the confidence of the public that any solicitor whom they chose to instruct met certain standards of professional honesty and integrity.[156]

---

that was even farther removed than that of the Divisional Court from requiring the open conduct of disciplinary proceedings.

[148] [1970] 1 QB 160.

[149] ibid. 166. A statement attributed to Lord Denman in 1846 characterized the Visitors as a 'a domestic forum but there is a power, certainly exercisable if the request comes from the member of the Inn who has appealed, to sit in public'.

[150] [1981] 1 WLR 1257.   [151] ibid. 1262.   [152] [1982] QB 430.   [153] ibid. 432.

[154] See, for example, *Re a Solicitor* [1993] QB 69.   [155] [1994] 1 WLR 512.

[156] ibid. 518–519.

On the other hand, the disciplinary procedures of the General Medical Council (GMC) have been criticized as unfair in that a doctor could be publicly pilloried (while the person who lodged the complaint remained anonymous vis-à-vis the outside world). Two reforms were suggested. Either the name of the doctor should not be released until such time (if any) as the disciplinary charges are found proved, or a preliminary hearing should take place '*in camera*' on the basis of which a decision would be taken whether or not to send the doctor 'for trial'.[157] The system of screening complaints before they were permitted to be aired in public before the professional conduct committee of the GMC has now been successfully challenged.[158] Compliance with the Human Rights Act 1998, in the judgment of Lightman J, would require greater transparency of procedure, and in particular that complaints should be heard in a public forum 'unless there was some special and sufficient reason to the contrary'.[159]

Much is at stake in the case of investigation of alleged misconduct by a professional person. There is no ready answer to the dilemma of reassuring the public and at the same time exposing individual members of the profession to the harm that inevitably follows from the mere fact that they are under investigation. Yet many of the considerations that underpin the open conduct of civil and criminal proceedings (in particular, the need to show that justice has been done) apply with no less force to the proceedings of domestic tribunals. In regard to the disciplinary jurisdiction exercised by the governing body of many sports, the complaint has been voiced: 'sportsmen who express controversial views are summoned to kangaroo courts, at which the truth or otherwise of their claims is rarely examined. The hearings are held in camera, and the evidence is not published'.[160]

The resulting state of affairs is the opposite to that which attends the adjudications of disciplinary bodies in the professions. The typical sportsman is too well known to escape public knowledge that his conduct has been subject to disciplinary investigation, particularly if an adverse adjudication results in a ban on participation in sporting events. Moreover, rarely is an individual's competence in the sport questioned in the course of the proceedings. As the quotation shows there is, nevertheless, cause for concern about the procedural standards that are observed by such bodies.[161]

---

[157] The Times (15 September 1990) 4.

[158] *R v General Medical Council, ex p Toth* [2000] 1 WLR 2209.

[159] It is difficult to imagine what such reasons might be in the light of the established features of the screening procedure. The evaluation of conflicting evidence was not considered to be the function of the screener. And, in view of the need to safeguard patients, the presumption in favour of letting the complaint go to a full public hearing was treated as particularly strong in regard to a doctor who was continuing to practise.

[160] P. Barnard, 'Free Speech in Sport' The Times (28 August 1992) 12.

[161] Rule 43(a) of the Rules of the Football Association specifically requires the parties before the Tribunal charged with deciding disputes under the Rules to 'preserve and respect the confidentiality of the arbitration proceedings, including the issues in the dispute and the evidence and arguments presented by the parties'. Furthermore, the Commission that is entrusted with the duty to investigate charges of misconduct under Rule 26 has no provision for admitting the public. However, Rule 29

10. PRELIMINARY AND ANCILLARY PROCEDURES

Within the full context of criminal and civil procedure, it is remarkable to note that the requirements of open justice apply within a relatively narrow range.

The recruitment of judges, as far as the quality of justice is concerned, is of the highest importance. Yet it is a process which is conducted entirely in secret. Appointments to the higher echelons of the judiciary are effectively in the hands of one, or at most two, members of the Cabinet: the Lord Chancellor and the Prime Minister. Although the process of appointment has been opened up of late,[162] the changes that have been made fall far short of the procedures in the United States, where the qualifications of nominees to the bench are openly scrutinized before an appointment to the higher US federal courts may be confirmed. Moreover, the point that is of vital interest to the parties to a lawsuit—namely, who will adjudicate their dispute—is a matter of internal administration of the courts. While the allocation of judges from the available pool to try particular cases is a decision that is taken behind closed doors, the equivalent procedure in regard to the composition of the jury is subject to the double safeguard of selection by ballot and in open court.[163]

The recently adopted practice of employing judicial assistants for the purpose of assisting appellate judges has served to create yet another level of pre-trial secrecy. Following the example of their equivalent numbers in other Commonwealth jurisdictions, the task of these assistants is to prepare 'bench memoranda' which summarize the history of the proceedings in the lower courts, identify the key issues in the case, and express a tentative view on the merits of the appeal. Inevitably, they would be supplemented by informal exchanges between the judicial assistants and the members of the court. The contents of the memoranda have never been disclosed to the parties in civil cases, although applicants for leave to appeal in criminal cases have been routinely supplied with copies (with the consequent opportunity to correct the facts set out in them). A ruling of the Court of Appeal has endorsed the practice on non-disclosure to appellants in civil cases, one reason being the inhibiting effect on the drafting of such memoranda that a policy of openness would have.[164]

A similar degree of secrecy attaches to the process of arriving at a decision at the conclusion of the trial.[165] This part of the procedure is invariably conducted

---

states that the Association 'shall be entitled to publish in the public Press . . . reports of its proceedings, acts and resolutions whether the same shall or shall not reflect on the character or conduct of any Club, Official, Player or spectator, and every such Club, Official, Player or spectator, shall be deemed to have assented to such publication'. The contents of these provisions are in the *Football Association Handbook, Season 1999–2000.*

[162] See *Judicial Appointments: The Lord Chancellor's Policies and Procedures* (HMSO, November 1990).

[163] Juries Act 1974, s 11(1).   [164] *Parker v Law Society* [1999] COD 183.

[165] See, further, Chapter 7, below.

in secret, irrespective of whether the decision is in the hands of laymen (jury), lay judges (magistrates) or the professional judiciary. Indeed, the fact that the norm of open justice is deemed not to apply at the very culmination of the trial process lends support to the view that open justice is concerned, above all else, with enhancing the quality of evidence. The rationale that open conduct of trials exercises a disciplinary function over judges simply does not fit with the long-established mode of conducting the decision-taking phase of trials. The safeguard of publicity is removed at the precise moment when it is most needed: where, in the case of a collegiate court, informal exchanges take place with a view to establishing the form of judgment. There have been occasions on which judicial practice at this stage of the proceedings has been divulged to the public. The most notable instance was provided by Woodward and Armstrong's investigation of the US Supreme Court, *The Brethren: Inside the Supreme Court*,[166] which was followed in the United Kingdom by Paterson's *The Law Lords*.[167] The material that formed the basis of these books was obtained, not as of right, but by way of concession or by persistent journalistic investigation.

So much is true of criminal and civil cases alike. To what extent are the preliminary phases in each form of trial conducted in public?

In the realm of criminal procedure there is a certain danger of confusion in the functions of particular officials. Some officials, whose general duties are undoubtedly judicial in nature, are also invested with functions of a rather different character. Circuit judges, for example, are entrusted with the power to issue warrants allowing the police access to 'excluded material' or 'special procedure material' under the Police and Criminal Evidence Act 1984.[168] Magistrates, in addition to exercising summary criminal jurisdiction, may grant 'warrants of further detention' under the same statute to authorize the detention of suspects beyond a period of thirty-six hours (up to a maximum of ninety-six hours).[169] This is in addition to their long-standing powers to issue arrest and search warrants and to grant or refuse applications for bail.

A preliminary comment should be made about these procedures as a whole. There appears to be no expectation that the proceedings that culminate in the grant or refusal of the various orders should be open to the public. There is, in fact, scant authority on the subject. In some respects this is not surprising. The same considerations that require the issue of many such warrants and orders to

---

[166] 1981. The book is an account of the inside workings of the Supreme Court during the years 1969–1976, based on over 200 interviews with the personnel of the Court. The difficulties that the authors encountered in conducting their research are borne out by the flat refusal of the Chief Justice, Warren Burger, to help in any way, and by the fact that nearly all the interviews were conducted on the basis that the authors would protect the identity of the informants.

[167] 1982. It is ch 5 of Paterson's book ('Law Lord Interaction and the Process of Judgement') that most closely approximates to the line of investigation adopted in regard to the US Supreme Court by Woodward and Armstrong.

[168] Police and Criminal Evidence Act 1984, s 9 and Sch 1.

[169] Police and Criminal Evidence Act 1984, ss 43 and 44.

be made in *ex parte* proceedings—namely, the danger that an order will be issued to no avail if the parties to be affected thereby are put on notice—also require the denial of information to the public in general. As we shall see, some such orders may be made either *ex parte* or *inter partes* and the courts have occasionally insisted that, where there are no compelling reasons to adopt the former method, considerations of procedural fairness require the latter to be followed. Whether those same considerations would also require public access to the contest between the parties is rather more debatable.

To consider now the specific issue of the grant of warrants, it appears that the most detailed examination of this process in the light of the demands of open justice is provided by the Supreme Court of Canada, in *A-G of Nova Scotia v MacIntyre*.[170] The applicant journalist in that case had been denied access by court officials to various search warrants (which had been executed) and the informations that had been used to obtain them. He asserted his claim to be permitted to see these materials in right of being a member of the public, not by virtue of his status as a journalist. The Court, by a majority of five to four, granted a declaration upholding the applicant's claim. Clearly, matters were raised in an oblique way since the case concerned, not the right to attend at the warrant-issuing stage, but rather the right of access to the documentation after the event.[171] English authority was cited to the effect that such a right exists only 'when some direct and tangible interest or proprietary right in the documents can be demonstrated'.[172] On the wider issue of the exact nature of the warrant-issuing procedure, it was noted that the usual practice was that warrants are issued in private: the process 'is not adjudicative and is not performed in open Court'.[173] The explanation moved at two distinct levels: in terms of exceptions to open justice (for example, that access at such a stage might endanger the lives of police informers); and that, as properly understood, open justice was concerned with the conduct of the trial proper, and not with the pre-trial procedures.

If the point were to be explicitly raised, it would surely be the latter element that would be advanced in explanation of the private conduct of pre-trial hearings. Public access, it would be argued, is to be limited to the hearing phase, which culminates in a verdict for or against the accused. Proceedings for more limited purposes (whether to authorize prolonged police detention or to grant or refuse bail) are of a different procedural status.

It has been stated that applications for 'warrants of further detention' are to be made on oath and *inter partes* to a magistrates' court, with the decision to be made by at least two magistrates together with a court clerk sitting in private.[174]

---

[170] 132 DLR (3d) 385 (1982).

[171] Note, also, situations in which a decision whether or not to issue a warrant is itself subsequently the object of challenge in (open) court proceedings. See, for example, *R v Chief Metropolitan Stipendiary Magistrate, ex p Choudhury* [1991] 1 QB 429.

[172] 132 DLR (3d) 385 (1982), 398.   [173] ibid. 393.

[174] M. Zander, *The Police and Criminal Evidence Act 1984* (2nd edn, 1990) 84, 95.

This may well be the mode in which such applications are determined as a matter of practice. It is noteworthy, however, that the relevant provisions of the Police and Criminal Evidence Act 1984 are couched in the usual terminology of trial: 'a magistrates' court is satisfied',[175] and 'the court will sit'.[176] And, as a statutory expression, 'the court' usually signifies a judge or judges sitting in open court—though in some contexts (of which, perhaps, this is one) it has been interpreted as meaning a court sitting in chambers.[177]

The disposition of an application for bail, on the other hand, is quite clearly seen as not a judicial matter for the purpose of the open justice rule. A decision whether or not to grant bail, it has been said, 'is not, like a trial, a contest between two parties with the court neutrally holding the ring'.[178] The court, for example, may choose to deny bail even though the police do not object to its being granted. Such hearings, as a matter of practice, are not held in public.[179] On the other hand, a decision whether or not to grant bail has been judged to attract immunity from tort liability: a malicious refusal on the part of the police will not be actionable for misfeasance in public office.[180] Several of the traditional arguments that are deployed in favour of public access to trials proper apply with no less force to bail hearings. Apart from the disciplinary impact exerted by publicity on the bench of magistrates, there is a clear public interest in curtailing the scope for making ill-informed criticism of particular decisions. An unnecessarily severe decision violates the freedom of the suspect, while one that is unduly generous puts the community at risk. In the absence of rights of access, the press have on occasion been reduced to protesting at the decision to grant bail only when the person in question has taken advantage of his freedom to commit another crime of the same type.

To argue that there should perhaps be a presumptive right of access to bail hearings is not to contend that there should be an inflexible rule to that effect. At the very least press access to the proceedings should be offset by the power to impose reporting restrictions (if necessary). Some of the grounds on which bail may be refused to a suspect—for example, previous failure to answer to bail, or substantial grounds for believing that the suspect would interfere with witnesses—would, if published, be highly prejudicial to his trial.

A similar picture appears in the initial stages of civil procedure. As with criminal process, the demands of open justice apply only to the hearing proper. Pre-trial business is routinely conducted in chambers, with the usual consequence that the press and the public are denied admission. Master Jacob argued that this practice

---

[175] Police and Criminal Evidence Act 1984, s 43(1).
[176] Police and Criminal Evidence Act 1984, s 43(5)(b)(ii).
[177] See the authorities in Halsbury, *Laws of England* (4th edn), Vol 10, Title 'Courts', para 725.
[178] B. Harris, *The New Law of Bail* (1978) 18.
[179] See, for example, the account in The Times, 30 October 1993, p. 21, of the hearing before Phillips J of the application by the Maxwell brothers to vary their conditions of bail. Since the hearing took place in chambers, the only information that could be gleaned was that the hearing was an 'application to vary bail conditions'.
[180] *Gizzonio v Chief Constable of Derbyshire* The Times, 29 April 1998.

should be abrogated, drawing attention to the 'strange and perhaps indefensible contrast between the hearing of interlocutory applications for an injunction, in open court in the Chancery Division, and in private in Chambers in the Queen's Bench Division'.[181] The divergence of practice as between the several divisions of the High Court would have been difficult to defend on principle. But what of the more general point that pre-trial business should be transacted in open court? In the normal course of events, it could be said, these matters will culminate in a full trial of the action with the usual consequence of exposure to publicity. However, merely to take the specific form of proceeding identified by Master Jacob, there has been many a case that has been keenly fought at the interlocutory stage but, once the relief sought at that stage has been granted or denied, the parties have not chosen to take the matter further. The specific case of interlocutory hearings aside, it would be difficult to adduce a reason for opening up the whole range of pre-trial procedure to public and press access that did not invite reconsideration of the practice of conducting administration in general behind closed doors.

In one regard, however, there are positive reasons for conducting ancillary and preliminary matters in closed court. The issuing of Mareva injunctions and Anton Piller orders,[182] like the issue of warrants of arrest and search, depends on the element of surprise. Occasionally a glimpse is afforded of the format in which applications for the making of such orders have been disposed. It would seem that the initial application is heard in chambers, though in certain cases (as, for example, in *Commercial Bank of the Near East plc v A, B, C and D*)[183] the judgment may be treated at the discretion of the judge as being given in open court. Thereafter appeal lies to the Court of Appeal, which ensures confidentiality by sitting *in camera*[184] and by granting leave to publish its judgment only after execution of the order (the safeguards adopted, for example, in *Mayer AG v Winter*).[185]

The procedures considered so far in this section are preliminary to the trial proper, whether criminal or civil. It is necessary, finally, to consider a form of

---

[181] Jacob (n 1 above) 23. R. P. Pearson, 'Open Justice' (1986) 130 Sol J 969 stated that 'many matters taken before the Queen's Bench judge in chambers could equally well be heard as Chancery motions' and added that there was a certain amount of 'forum shopping' by counsel seeking to avoid publicity to their clients' affairs by deliberately initiating proceedings in the Queen's Bench. It was anticipated that the anomaly would not survive the introduction of the Civil Procedure Rules 1998, SI 1998/3132: *Hodgson v Imperial Tobacco Ltd* [1998] 2 All ER 673, 686.

[182] To be known, respectively, as 'freezing injunctions' and 'search orders' since the promulgation of the Civil Procedure Rules 1998, SI 1998/3132, Rule 25.1(1)(f) and (h).

[183] [1989] 2 Lloyd's Rep 319, 320.

[184] As will be seen in Chapter 3, section 1, D, the Court of Appeal historically lacks the power to sit in chambers. See, incidentally, *Coca-Cola Co v Gilbey* [1995] 4 All ER 711, where a person who had been made the subject of an Anton Piller order declined to comply with the order out of fear of possible reprisals. At one point in the proceedings it was suggested that the judge should hear the man and his counsel *in camera* so that his fears could be explained. Although declining to adopt this procedure, the judge appeared to accept that such a procedure would be permissible provided that—something the man strenuously opposed—the plaintiff applicants for the order were likewise represented at the closed hearing.

[185] The Times, 13 February 1986.

proceeding which, as the name 'Reference' suggests, is a variation on the standard trial procedure.

The Attorney-General's Reference[186] bears all the apparent features of an appellate hearing. Yet, for all that it resembles an appeal by the prosecution against an acquittal, the verdict of the trial on indictment remains undisturbed irrespective of the outcome of the Reference.[187] The proceedings, therefore, lack an integral element of a function that is truly judicial: the making of an order that affects the rights of the parties. In fact, the implication behind a successful Reference by the Attorney-General is that the accused (or 'the respondent' as he becomes for the purpose of these proceedings) was fortunate to escape conviction. The point of the procedure is to bring a speedy correction to errors of law perpetrated by judges at first instance before they are followed in other cases. In all other respects, save one, the proceedings on an Attorney-General's Reference will resemble an appellate argument on a point of law. The critical difference is that the respondent's identity is not to be disclosed 'during the proceedings on a reference' except where he has consented to its use in this way.[188] Nor shall any mention be made in the reference of the proper name of any person or place that is 'likely to lead to the identification of the respondent'.[189] Moreover, in *A-G for Northern Ireland's Reference (No 1 of 1975)*[190] the House of Lords voiced sympathy with the Attorney-General's submission that the Reference procedure should not be used where there was a danger that the former accused could be identified thereby.[191]

The respondent, as we have pointed out, is not put in jeopardy by the outcome of the Reference proceedings, which consequently have a distinctively abstract air. A hybrid form of procedure is sometimes to be found, in which property is ordered to be destroyed as a result of an adverse ruling though no person (the owner of the goods, to take the most obvious possibility) is at risk of incurring a criminal penalty (by way of imprisonment, fine, or other penalty).[192] Is such a procedure 'judicial' in nature for the purpose of the norm of open justice? The question arose in *Ex parte Norman*.[193] During the course of the First World War certain publications (which were deemed inimical to the pursuit of the war effort)

---

[186] The basis of the procedure is the Criminal Justice Act 1972, s 36. See, generally, J. Jaconelli, 'Attorney-General's References—A Problematic Device' [1981] Crim LR 543.

[187] This is in contrast to Attorney-General's References on sentencing, introduced by the Criminal Justice Act 1988, ss 35 and 36, which (in all but name) are prosecution appeals against unduly lenient sentences.

[188] Criminal Appeal (Reference of Points of Law) Rules 1973, SI 1973/1114, r 6.

[189] ibid. r 3(1).   [190] [1977] AC 105.

[191] ibid. 155. The facts of the case, unlike the typical Reference, were fraught with security issues. It concerned the criminal liability of a soldier on duty in Northern Ireland who had mistakenly shot and killed a person in the belief that he was a fleeing terrorist.

[192] An example is the procedure provided in the Obscene Publications Act 1959, s 3, by virtue of which a magistrate may issue a warrant authorizing search for, and seizure of, obscene materials. These may subsequently be made subject to an order for forfeiture, a number of persons (the author, the owner, etc.) being expressly granted the right to argue before the court to show cause why they should not be forfeited.

[193] (1915) 114 LT 232.

had been seized and, after proceedings *in camera*, an order was made for their destruction. The owners of the documents challenged the ruling of the court of summary jurisdiction (sitting at the Mansion House Justice Room) on the ground that the regulation forming the basis of the order[194] was ultra vires the parent Act, the Defence of the Realm Consolidation Act 1914. The expression used in section 1(5) of the statute, regulating 'the trial of a person for an offence under the regulations', appeared to import the usual feature of trial, namely open access to the public. The Divisional Court, however, ruled that the word 'trial' was not apposite to describe and encompass the procedure there in question. Lush J stated that the applicant had not been 'in the position of a person who has been put upon his trial for an offence';[195] the proceeding had not been an instance of the 'administration of justice'[196] within the meaning laid down by the House of Lords in *Scott v Scott*. The application therefore failed.

This case illustrates well the theme of the present section. The concept of the 'judicial' function is simply too vague to act as a reliable guide to the procedures which should, and should not, be open to public access. Many of the procedural contexts that lie outside the trial proper have simply not formed the subject of challenge by those who have a strong interest in asserting public or press access. Long established practice appears to be decisive of the issue of whether certain procedures should be open or closed. In many situations, even if the norm of openness were presumptively applicable, cogent reasons could be found for departure from the norm in the particular case.

[194] Regulation 51A of the Defence of the Realm (Consolidation) Regulations 1914.
[195] (1915) 114 LT 232, 234.   [196] ibid.

3

The Enforcement of Secrecy

I. THE SECRET TRIAL

A. Introduction

The subject matter of section 1 of this chapter is the various methods whereby trial proceedings may be held in secret. The means that are available fall, broadly, into two categories. The one functions by way of interposing physical obstacles in the way of access to the courtroom. It is typified by the hearing of the trial *in camera* (section 1, C below). In this category should be placed the various ploys (to be considered in section 1, B) whereby a trial that is, in principle, open to the public is staged at such an unusual time or in such an unexpected location that the provision of access to the public is but an empty gesture in the direction of open justice. The other category (examined in sections 1, E and F) comprises restraints which are normative in nature. That is to say, the persons who have been allowed into the courtroom are prohibited by law from disclosing to others what they have seen and heard. In some situations normative constraints may combine with physical barriers to provide a two-fold guarantee of secrecy.

B. Irregularity in the Place or Time of Trial

As was noted in Chapter 1, section 5, A and B, the place and time of trial are matters largely left unregulated by the law. This factor, combined with the occasional connivance of court officials, has rendered possible situations where trials have been open to the public in name only. A publication of the Association of British Editors[1] documents instances of cases being disposed of an hour before the usual times of court sittings, of cases being listed for a specific date and then being surreptitiously rescheduled to an earlier date, and of cases being moved suddenly from one courtroom to another.

Proceedings may be relocated from their natural venue for reasons that are entirely proper. In the United States, for example, a trial may be moved—and also, sometimes, postponed—in order to minimize the impact of prejudicial pretrial publicity. Even in England, where such publicity is tightly curbed by the law of contempt of court, a change in the location of a trial from its natural

---

[1] *How Open is Open Justice?* (1988).

venue may be ordered in the interest of securing a fair trial for the accused. On the other hand, there have been cases where there was not the slightest risk of prejudice (that is, of the type of which the law of contempt would take cognizance), and the hearing has been relocated for no better reason than the defendant's wish to avoid the attendant embarrassing publicity. A criminal trial, in this way, might be scheduled to be heard in a location where the defendant is unknown, so that even the regular listing of the case does not alert the attention of the local media. Even a case that transcends merely local concern may deliberately be relegated for hearing in a backwater.[2]

In section 3 of this chapter we will pursue the issues that have a bearing on the validity (or otherwise) of proceedings that have improperly been held in private. However irregularity in the place or time of trial is not, in itself, sufficient to provide a means of impugning the outcome of the proceedings. That something more is required may be gleaned from the pronouncements of the Judicial Committee of the Privy Council in *McPherson v McPherson*.[3] In this case the appellant challenged the validity of a divorce decree that had been pronounced terminating her marriage to the respondent on the ground that the public had, in effect, been excluded from the hearing of the petition. No order had been made barring access to the public. The case, however, had been heard in the Judges' library in the court building of Edmonton, Alberta, rather than in one of the regular courtrooms.[4] 'It was only a few minutes before the hour appointed', the judgment of the Privy Council states, 'that [the judge] definitely selected the Judges' library as the place for the hearing, and he so informed the Clerk of the Court. The proceedings took place during the luncheon interval, probably as the most convenient hour for all concerned'.[5] This was not at variance with the public listing arrangements in the court building, for such procedures as existed were entirely informal. 'Information on that subject is, it seems, obtained from the orderlies in attendance, and they, apparently, would know as much about a case appointed to be heard or being heard in the Judges' library as about one appointed to be heard elsewhere'.[6]

---

[2] A striking instance is provided by the hearing, during the Abdication crisis of 1936, of Mrs Simpson's divorce petition in Ipswich. This was done on the suggestion of her barrister, Norman Birkett, according to B. Inglis, *Abdication* (1966) 191. However, F. Donaldson, *Edward VIII* (1974) makes the obvious rejoinder that it is difficult to see how a mere unusual choice of trial venue would have the effect of ensuring confidentiality of the proceedings:'[t]he truth seems to be that the London courts were full for more than a year': ibid. 219. Whatever the reason, as Inglis points out at 192, the proceedings between Mr and Mrs Simpson smacked of collusion—an element which was unlikely to be affected in any way by the presence in court of two members of the public, the judge's wife and her friend.

[3] [1936] AC 177.

[4] About the time of the divorce the respondent was Minister of Public Works for the province of Alberta. However, '[t]he suggestion that the procedure adopted . . . is traceable to the fact that the respondent was a Minister of the Crown is one easily made and readily accepted by credulous minds': ibid. 199.

[5] ibid. 198.   [6] ibid. 197.

These facts did not, in themselves, affect the validity of the proceedings. The critical element in the manner of conduct of the hearing was that the Judges' library could be approached from the public corridor only through a pair of swing doors. One door was always fixed in position: the other, though swinging loose, carried the word, 'Private', in bold letters. Although physical access to the library was not barred, the arrangement of the swing doors was 'as effective a bar to the access to the library by an ordinary member of the public finding himself in the public corridor as would be a door actually locked'.[7] The hearing, concluded the Judicial Committee, had not taken place in open court, as it was required to be by the relevant law. The main interest of the case, then, lies in the explicit recognition that misleading public notices may deprive proceedings of their 'open' character. It would follow, *a fortiori*, that physical obstacles have the same effect.[8]

It will be necessary to return to the *McPherson* decision in section 3 of this chapter. Suffice it to note at this stage that the defective hearing rendered the decree of divorce 'voidable' only.[9] In the light of two factors, the lapse of time and the intervention of third-party rights (the husband had remarried), the decree could no longer be impugned and the appeal failed.

In circumstances such as those of *McPherson* one of the parties, at any rate, is sufficiently disgruntled about the conduct of the case to wish to take matters further. Where this element is missing, it may be a matter of chance whether or not the media come to learn of the proceedings. Even when they manage to do so, it will be after the event without any opportunity to observe the conduct of the trial itself. In this regard the Association of British Editors reports one instance where the wife of a judge answered to a charge of drunken driving half an hour before the usual time of commencement of proceedings.[10] In another case—one which, on being uncovered, did attain national publicity—the wife of the then Chancellor of the Exchequer, Mr Nigel Lawson, faced an identical charge and 'appeared unannounced in the dock as the first defendant of the day' without her name even appearing on the day list.[11] The special arrangements made for the hearing of one case in an attempt to avoid publicity resulted in the holding of a special inquiry by Lord Goddard.[12] While Lord Goddard

---

[7] ibid. 198.

[8] In *Storer v British Gas plc* [2000] 2 All ER 440 an employment tribunal hearing was held invalid by virtue of its taking place in the regional chairman's office, to which access was gained through a door with a coded lock. The Court of Appeal deemed it irrelevant that no evidence was adduced to show that any member of the public had actually been prevented from attending the hearing.

[9] However, note the qualification entered, n 3, above, at 203–204: 'Their Lordships would observe, in passing, that they are not in this case dealing with a decree nisi pronounced after a travesty of judicial proceedings – a mere stage trial. The quality of a decree pronounced after such an idle ceremonial may be left to be dealt with when it is produced. Here their Lordships are dealing with a decree pronounced after a serious trial free from every other defect in procedure, . . . To say that such a decree is void would seem to be out of the question.'

[10] *How Open is Open Justice?*, 5.   [11] *How Open is Open Justice?*, 2.

[12] *Inquiry by Lord Goddard: Procedure at a Case Heard before Two Justices at Longton, Stoke-on-Trent* (HMSO, 1945).

pronounced himself entirely satisfied with the judgment of the magistrates (the accused was convicted and bound over for twelve months), his report fails to touch on the wider issues raised by the episode. The facts of the case, involving homosexual acts by a priest, would have led, under the usual conditions of open trial, to a degree of publicity totally disproportionate to the gravity of the offence in the criminal justice system.

As these episodes show, the norm of open justice has led to a paradoxical situation. Public access has traditionally been justified as rendering possible the scrutiny of trials for the detection of possible bias. The attempt, however misguided, to escape the informal, but substantial, element of punishment that derives from the ensuing publicity has led on occasion to the presence of bias, not in the conduct of the trial proper, but in the arrangements made for its secluded hearing.

C. Hearing *in Camera*

In this and the following section attention will be devoted to the two principal modes of conducting hearings in secret which are permitted by law. Although 'in camera' and 'in chambers' are the two principal designations of secret trials (and hence they will be given detailed treatment in turn), expressions such as 'in private'[13] and 'in closed court'[14] are also to be found in the statute book.

A hearing *in camera* is one in which entry to the courtroom is denied to everyone except the *personae* of the trial. The denial of access to the general public may be supplemented, in certain cases, by practical measures aimed at preventing visual or audio surveillance of the courtroom.[15] A hearing *in camera* may be so conducted either under statutory authority or pursuant to the powers deriving from the inherent jurisdiction of the court.[16]

The language of statute may employ the term itself, as in section 5 of the Punishment of Incest Act 1908: 'All proceedings under this Act are to be held in camera'.[17]

---

[13] Administration of Justice Act 1960, s 12(1), where the expression is employed several times.

[14] Army Act 1955, s 94(3), (4) and (5). Note that the term 'in camera' is used in s 94(2). The normal presumptions of statutory interpretation would seem to imply that the use of the two expressions in the same statute signifies that they are not to be taken as exactly equivalent in meaning.

[15] See the account given by the accused of the official secrets trial, *R v Ponting* [1985] Crim LR 318, in C. Ponting, *The Right to Know: The Inside Story of the Belgrano Affair* (1985). (The background to the prosecution is given in the Appendix, below). Part of the hearing on the first and second days of the trial took place *in camera* despite strenuous objection by Ponting's counsel. Ponting's account continues (*The Right to Know* 171): '*Into camera* we go, nonetheless. The glass windows in the doors are boarded up, and for twenty-five minutes the court is swept for bugging devices.' It is worth recalling that the tape recording of court proceedings is prohibited in general terms by section 9 of the Contempt of Court Act 1981 irrespective of whether the proceedings are conducted *in camera* or in open court.

[16] See, generally, I. H. Jacob, 'The Inherent Jurisdiction of the Court' (1970) 23 *Current Legal Problems* 23.

[17] It was repealed by the Criminal Law Amendment Act 1922, s 5.

Alternatively, the statute may set out the meaning of the phrase in some detail, as does section 8(4) of the Official Secrets Act 1920:

... if, in the course of proceedings before a court against any person for an offence under the [Official Secrets Act 1911] or this Act ... application is made by the prosecution ... that all or any portion of the public shall be excluded during any part of the hearing, the court may make an order to that effect, but the passing of sentence shall in any case take place in public.

There is scope for speculation as to the precise meaning, in section 8(4), of the phrase 'any portion of the public'. The presence of the phrase is of some considerable importance because it would seem to indicate the possibility of a middle way, a state of affairs between a court that is fully open and one that is held in secret session. Statutory authority apart, such a form of hearing would seem to be contrary to principle. This is borne out by an incident which occurred in the High Court of Australia in November 1988.[18] The case that was being heard by Deane J was an application by the Commonwealth Government for an injunction to restrain publication of material concerning the activities of the Australian Security Intelligence Organisation. Counsel for the Commonwealth unsuccessfully applied for an *in camera* hearing. It was later drawn to the attention of the judge that lawyers acting for the Government had asked court staff to compile a list of the names of those present in the public gallery. Anyone who refused to identify himself was told that he would not be permitted to remain in the courtroom. Deane J, pronouncing the episode 'a cause for serious concern', ordered the destruction of the list and of any copies that had been made of it.[19]

The episode is of interest in several respects. It has been cited in the present context as indicating the absence of any middle way between a hearing that takes place *in camera* and one held in open court. Even if the situation had occurred in a context where section 8(4) was in force, it is very doubtful—to push the example a little further—whether the exclusion of some persons from the public gallery simply for refusing to give their names[20] could have been defended by reference to the element in section 8(4) that permits the exclusion of 'any portion of the public'. Moreover, by acting on their own initiative in issuing instructions to the court staff, the government's lawyers had interfered with the judge's control over the conduct of the trial. In general terms their misbehaviour was an infringement of the separation of powers. In specifically legal terms it was, arguably, a contempt of court.

---

[18] The incident is recounted in (1989) 63 Australian Law Journal 155–7 (Current Topics).

[19] In the opinion of Deane J, the fact that the government was a party to the proceedings, even if they were only civil proceedings, argued for an accentuated right of the public to be present in the courtroom: ibid. 156.

[20] cf. *Rice v Connolly* [1966] 2 QB 414, where it was affirmed that a person did not commit the crime of obstructing the police in the execution of their duty merely by refusing to comply with a request for identification.

Such issues of general principle aside, it is to the language of statute that one must turn in order to ascertain, in any particular type of case, the preconditions and extent of the jurisdiction to sit *in camera*. The ground that is given in section 8(4), for example, is 'that the publication of any evidence to be given or of any statement to be made in the course of the proceedings would be prejudicial to the national safety'. On occasion it is expressly stated that the statutory jurisdiction is additional to, and does not supersede, that which derives from the inherent powers of the court. Section 8(4), for example, stipulates that it is '[i]n addition and without prejudice to any powers which a court may possess to order the exclusion of the public'. The availability of two alternative bases upon which an *in camera* hearing may take place is particularly useful where there is a significant divergence in the stipulated preconditions. The requirement under the inherent jurisdiction of the court is, quite generally, that 'the interests of justice so require' it.[21] Statute may also impose limits to the phases of the trial which may be conducted *in camera*. It is necessary here to emphasize the proviso to section 8(4): '. . . but the passing of sentence shall in any case take place in public'.[22]

Finally, it remains to consider the form of the hearing in which argument is heard as to the necessity (or otherwise) of conducting a particular phase of the trial *in camera*. It would seem entirely sensible that the trial of this preliminary issue should itself take place in secret. There is a provision to that effect in the Domestic and Appellate Proceedings (Restriction of Publicity) Act 1968[23] (as to the general terms of which, see section 1. D). The form of the preliminary hearing is not generally laid down. It is noteworthy that in one case[24] the Divisional Court ruled that a stipendiary magistrate had been in error in refusing to hear *in camera* an application to have the defendant's address withheld from the public in open court.[25] On principle, therefore, the case is even stronger for hearing in secret the trial of the preliminary issue as to whether or not evidence should be heard *in camera*.

D. Hearing in Chambers

For many purposes there is no need to distinguish between a hearing conducted *in camera* and one held in chambers, the second form of closed hearing known

[21] Jacob (n 16 above) 39.

[22] See also the Domestic and Appellate Proceedings (Restriction of Publicity) Act 1968, s 1(2): 'Without prejudice to the next following subsection, the court hearing the appeal or application shall give its decision and the reason for its decision in public unless there are good and sufficient grounds for giving them in private and in that case the court shall state those grounds in public.'

[23] Section 1(5) states that the application to have the court sit *in camera* under the terms of the Act 'shall be heard in private unless the court otherwise directs'.

[24] *R v Tower Bridge Justices, ex p Osborne* [1988] Crim LR 382.

[25] The application had been made under the Contempt of Court Act 1981, s 11. The purpose of the application was to ensure that the address did not come to the attention of the defendant's husband. The magistrate's refusal to hear the application *in camera* resulted in the defendant's solicitor having to reveal in open court sensitive matters which could have been very detrimental to the defendant.

to the law. Statute sometimes refers to them equally in generic terms: for example, section 12(1) of the Administration of Justice Act 1960, which (as will be seen shortly) restricts the dissemination of information gleaned from 'any court sitting in private'. Judged from the perspective of etymological derivation, there would appear to be little or no difference between the two forms of secret hearing. According to the dictionary, the word 'camera' means a 'vault' or 'large chamber' and, more specifically, a judge's chamber.[26] It is possible, also, that the expression, *in camera*, came to be associated with the procedure of the Star Chamber, *Pro Camera Stellata*, a court whose very name has become a byword for oppressive judicial procedures. If so, the confusion is linguistic only. For whatever shortcomings can be attributed to the Court of Star Chamber, apparently failure to sit in public was not one of them.[27] The promulgation of the Civil Procedure Rules 1998[28] has tended towards even closer assimilation of the two terms. As part of the general approach of the Rules to simplifying procedural language, the phrase 'in private' is required to be used generally. For a number of reasons, however, the long-standing terminology has not been superseded. First, the statutory and other provisions which employ the terms '*in camera*' and 'in chambers' have not been redrafted. Secondly, the whole area of criminal procedure has been left untouched by the Rules. Thirdly, as will be explained shortly, the Court of Appeal recently emphasized in *Hodgson v Imperial Tobacco Ltd*,[29] there are significant differences between the two forms of closed hearing.

Specifically, to say of a judge that he is 'sitting in chambers' is not simply a matter of describing the place where he is discharging his judicial functions. On one occasion, because no regular courtroom was available, a High Court hearing was conducted in a set of barristers' chambers, yet nevertheless, contrary to the usual understanding of what constitutes a chambers hearing, in open court.[30] For, as was said in *Hartmont v Foster*: 'A judge sitting in chambers does not mean that he is sitting in any particular room, but that he is not sitting in open court'.[31] Such a brief explanation comes close to conflating a chambers hearing with one taking place *in camera*. That there are points of difference, however, is implicitly recognized in section 118(2) of the Criminal Justice Act 1988, the provision which governs the hearing of a challenge for cause directed at a potential juror: 'In addition and without prejudice to any powers which the Crown Court may possess to order the exclusion of the public from any

[26] *The Shorter Oxford English Dictionary.*
[27] The Star Chamber was a 'public, and mainly a judicative, thing': K. W. M. Pickthorn, *Early Tudor Government: Henry VIII* (1934), 26. See also A. F. Pollard, 'Council, Star Chamber, and Privy Council under the Tudors' (1922) 37 *English Historical Review* 516, 525: '. . . the star chamber was a public court'.
[28] Civil Procedure Rules 1998, SI 1998/3132.   [29] [1998] 2 All ER 673.
[30] See (1992) 6 *The Lawyer* (Issue 32, 4 August 1992) ('Temple hosts hearing for lack of court').
[31] (1881–2) LR 8 QBD 82, 84.

proceedings a judge of the Crown Court may order that the hearing of a challenge for cause shall be *in camera* or in chambers'.

What, then, are the differences? Proceedings in chambers are less formal. Although the judge may choose to locate a chambers hearing in the usual courtroom, wigs and gowns are not worn. The rights of audience, moreover, differ as between the two forms of hearing. Barristers, as a general rule, enjoy exclusive rights of audience before the High Court. They do not, however, when that Court is sitting in chambers. Those cases that contain an *in camera* phase typically comprise the most serious criminal charges, where the accused will be represented by counsel. The more frequent incidence of chambers hearings, together with their greater informality, has meant that they have furnished the context for exploring the boundaries of the *personae*/public divide, especially the status of the 'McKenzie friend'.[32]

It is the exclusion of members of the public which forms the focus of our concern with hearings in chambers. In this regard matters do stand on a somewhat different footing from hearings conducted *in camera*. That the former are more accurately described as 'private' (in contrast to 'secret') was stressed by Lord Woolf MR in *Hodgson v Imperial Tobacco Ltd*.[33] Contrary to the traditional understanding, the public were not to be excluded entirely from chambers hearings. His Lordship emphasized the fundamental importance of public knowledge of the transaction of judicial business, especially in litigation (such as the instant case) which raised issues of far-reaching concern.[34] Public attendance at chambers hearings was subject to two overriding constraints: the permission of the judge or master who was handling the case; and the limitations of space (a more pressing consideration, of necessity, than in the case of a normal court hearing).[35]

Whether a cause may be heard in chambers, it would appear, depends on whether a positive answer may be given to each of two overriding questions. Does the relevant court have chambers? If so, is the cause properly heard in that form?

[32] It has been held that a litigant in person may be accompanied by a McKenzie friend, even though the hearing is in chambers, provided that the friend did no more than sit quietly and offer assistance: *Re H (a Minor) (Chambers proceedings: McKenzie friend)* The Times, 6 May 1997. This ruling is difficult to reconcile with *R v Bow County Court, ex p Pelling* [1999] 2 All ER 582, affirmed in the Court of Appeal [1999] 4 All ER 751, where the presence of a McKenzie friend was said to be permissible, in general terms, only where the hearing was in public. Where the case was heard in private, however, the same considerations which led to the exclusion of members of the public would also render undesirable the presence of a McKenzie friend. In any event, it was only the litigant in person, not the McKenzie friend, who possessed any right of challenge to a decision of the trial judge concerning the presence of the friend. Where, on the other hand, an individual met the criteria for a right of audience, the judge had no discretion in the matter: *Re H-S (Minors) (Chambers proceedings: Right of audience)* The Times, 25 February 1998.

[33] [1998] 2 All ER 673, 686.

[34] The case concerned the possible liability of the defendant to the plaintiffs, who had contracted cancer after smoking cigarettes manufactured by the defendant.

[35] A five-point summary of the position is given by Lord Woolf MR [1998] 2 All ER 673, 687.

Whether a court may sit in chambers at all is not to be determined, of course, by considerations of the physical structure of the courtroom building. The fact that a judge has available his own chambers within that building does not, in itself, confer on the court in which he sits the power to hear matters 'in chambers'.[36] Certain courts, for obscure historical reasons, do not possess chambers (in the sense of conferring the facility of 'sitting in chambers'). The word 'chambers' when used in this sense, it has been pointed out, appears to have been deployed only in regard to the High Court and the county court.[37] The position of the Divisional Court (in particular) in this respect has been considered uncertain.[38]

It was in the context of courts that clearly lacked the power to sit in chambers that the need for reform was perceived. The leading example here was the Court of Appeal. In *Re Agricultural Industries Ltd*[39] Sir Raymond Evershed MR drew attention to the gap in the forms of hearing available in the court over whose affairs he presided. The matter arose on an appeal from a ruling at first instance where the hearing had taken place in chambers. The facts of the case are rather complex. Briefly, the contributories on the winding up of a company appealed to the Court of Appeal, asking that the proceedings should continue to be conducted in private lest further litigation that they had in mind be prejudicially affected. Evershed MR pointedly declared that 'the Court of Appeal has no power to sit in chambers'.[40] The mere fact that a suit had been heard in chambers at first instance did not, in itself, confer on the Court of Appeal jurisdiction to hear the appeal in private. The only possibility of confidentiality at that level lay in a hearing *in camera*. To gain such a form of hearing, moreover, the case would have to be brought within one or other exception to the general rule in *Scott v Scott*. That is, the litigation in question would have to be shown to be an instance where an open hearing would carry with it the likelihood of the ends of justice being defeated. Faced with such a hurdle, '[c]ounsel for the applicants did not suggest that he could put the matter so high . . .'[41]

In holding out the possibility of an *in camera* appeal hearing, but not a hearing in chambers, Evershed MR was not merely indulging in a verbal quibble. In his half-page coverage of the point it is possible to discern an important difference: '. . . [A]ccording to the Rules of the Supreme Court', said the Master of the Rolls, 'certain matters are referred to the judge in chambers, and they are not heard in public, *whatever be the nature of the particular case*'.[42] (Emphasis added.) Whenever a cause is heard in this way it is not by way of exception to

---

[36] Law Commission, *Report on the Powers of Appeal Courts to Sit in Private and the Restrictions upon Publicity in Domestic Proceedings* (Cmnd 3149, 1966) para 23.

[37] ibid.

[38] The position in regard to the House of Lords was unclear, stated the Law Commission Report: ibid. One possible way of compensating for any shortcoming in this regard, it continued, was to have resort to 'the privilege which it certainly has while sitting as a legislative body to exclude strangers'.

[39] [1952] 1 All ER 1188.   [40] ibid. 1189.   [41] ibid. 1189.   [42] ibid. 1189.

the rule in *Scott v Scott*, but rather because ' "chambers" are a special institution distinct from open court'.[43] It would appear to follow from the institutional distinctiveness of hearings in chambers that a suit must be heard either entirely in that form or not at all.

The peculiar nature of the power to sit in chambers was emphasized when, in the aftermath of a Law Commission Report,[44] the Domestic and Appellate Proceedings (Restriction of Publicity) Act 1968 was enacted. Briefly, the investigation by the Law Commission sprang from a feeling of dissatisfaction at the unduly limited circumstances in which certain courts, among them the Court of Appeal, could sit in private. One of the two principal objects of the statute[45] was to confer a power 'to sit in private'[46] on any court hearing an appeal (or an application for leave to appeal) from a number of listed courts.[47] References to a power to sit 'in private', states section 1(7), are 'references to a power to sit in camera or in chambers'. However, the power that is conferred 'on a court which has no power to sit in chambers is a power to sit in camera only'. Although the Court of Appeal figures clearly in this reform, as a tribunal to and from which appeal may be made, section 1(7) clearly evinces a reluctance to confer the facility of hearings in chambers on courts which, historically, do not already possess it. This stands in marked contrast to *in camera* trial, a mode of proceeding which (as we have seen) is made freely available by statute.

It is now time to address the second of the two main lines of inquiry. On the assumption that a court does have chambers, when is a cause properly heard in that format? Here we encounter an exception to open justice that is defined in extremely loose terms. In *McPherson v McPherson* the Judicial Committee of the Privy Council described the exception as '[a]pplications properly heard in chambers'.[48] But when are such applications 'properly' made? Little guidance is to be derived from section 67 of the Supreme Court Act 1981: 'Business in the High Court shall be heard and disposed of in court except in so far as it may, under this or any other Act, under rules of court *or in accordance with the practice of the court,* be dealt with in chambers'.[49] (Emphasis added.)

Of the three sources of jurisdiction to sit in chambers mentioned by the section, it is necessary to say a few words about the last two. The applicable rules of court were to be found in the Rules of the Supreme Court, Order 32:

---

[43] (Cmnd. 3149, 1966) para 22.   [44] See n 36 above.

[45] The other object was to permit the imposition of restrictions on publicity in certain types of family proceedings.

[46] Domestic and Appellate Proceedings (Restriction of Publicity) Act 1968, s 1(1).

[47] Domestic and Appellate Proceedings (Restriction of Publicity) Act 1968, s 1(4).

[48] [1936] AC 177, 200.

[49] Practice may lead to anomalies that are impossible to defend on any consideration of general principle. See the example cited in I. H. Jacob, *The Fabric of English Civil Justice* (1987) 23, whereby the hearing of an application for an interlocutory injunction would be heard in chambers if lodged in the Queen's Bench Division, but in open court if brought in the Chancery Division.

'Applications and Proceedings in Chambers'. And we have already adverted, in Chapter 2, to the general practice of taking in chambers the range of pre-trial applications. It is quite clear that practice in this area has developed in directions that are at variance with the ideal of open justice. In recent years there has occurred a proliferation of instances of hearings that have been conducted in chambers, the delivery of judgment alone taking place in open court.[50]

Occasionally a concession has been made to the ideal of open justice. Even a matter regulated by Order 32 could be adjourned into open court for hearing, but only at the discretion of the judge if he 'considers that by reason of its importance or for any other reason it should be so heard' (Order 32, rule 13). To take an example, a routine application for summary judgment in *Shell International Petroleum Co Ltd v Transnor (Bermuda) Ltd*[51] was transferred into open court in view of the defendant's allegations of serious misconduct against the plaintiff. Once moved in this way, the matter is treated as in open court, and consequently a reporter may not be removed from the hearing.[52] Similarly, in *Re Crook*[53] the applicant journalist challenged his exclusion from the courtroom[54] as a result of the decision of the judge at two criminal trials to hear in chambers certain matters relating to the disposition of the jury in each case. Dismissing the challenges, Lord Lane CJ warned:

A judge should not adjourn into chambers as a matter of course, but only if he believes that something may be said which makes the determination of that preliminary question in chambers appropriate. If he does sit in chambers, he should be alert to the importance of adjourning into open court if, and as soon as, it emerges that the need to exclude the public is not plainly necessary.'[55]

Even a form of hearing which is routinely conducted in private may be opened up to a legal academic for the limited purpose of gathering material with a view to eventual publication. Small claims hearings in the county courts are traditionally conducted in private, in the district judges' own chambers. The privacy of the hearings is but one way in which such hearings depart from the traditional trial format: others include greater informality, a more inquisitorial role played by the judge, and less reliance on formal legal representation. A recent study of the small claims process was based on the author's admittance to the proceedings, a factor which in itself suggests that the confidentiality of the hearings is

---

[50] Among such instances may be cited *Re T. B.* [1967] 1 Ch 247, where it was recorded (at 248) that the 'application was heard in camera but the judgment was delivered in open court'. In authorizing in principle a settlement of the mental patient's property, Ungoed-Thomas J added that he would 'in due course go into chambers to consider a subsidiary matter and the detailed provisions of the settlement' (at 253).

[51] [1987] 1 Lloyd's Rep 363.   [52] *Hardie and Lane Ltd v Chilton* (1927) 43 TLR 477, 478.
[53] [1992] 2 All ER 687.
[54] The application was brought under the Criminal Justice Act 1988, s 159.
[55] [1992] 2 All ER 687, 693.

not of special importance. Nevertheless, it is significant that the disputes that are referred to in the study are mentioned anonymously.[56]

E. Substantive Legal Restraints

In this and the following section we consider aspects of English law which have been used, or may be used, to enforce courtroom secrecy. Such normative restraints may be employed in their own right or as adjuncts to the physical barriers that have been examined in the preceding sections. The discussion will be limited to emphasizing, in each case, those aspects of the law which are, or would be, particularly relevant to confidentiality of court proceedings.

The action for breach of confidence,[57] to take that first, provides the most general means available in the civil law of enforcing confidentiality. The traditional elements of the action are founded whenever confidential information has been imparted to another (by A to B, for example) in circumstances imposing an obligation of confidence, and B has used the information (most typically, by disclosing it to C) without just cause or excuse in a way that is inconsistent with the obligation. Although it stops short of conferring a general right to privacy, there are indications that, since the enactment of the Human Rights Act 1998, the courts will deploy the action in order to protect such a right in appropriate cases.[58] There has long appeared to be no reason in principle why the action should not lie to enforce the confidentiality of information that has been imparted within a narrow circle for the strictly limited purpose of the trial of a lawsuit. Proceedings for this purpose could be brought in the name of the Attorney-General to secure an injunction restraining publication (or, as the case may be, further publication) of the information in question. In the aftermath of the *Crossman Diaries*[59] and the *Spycatcher*[60] cases this is now a well-established method whereby 'governmental' secrets may be protected (by comparison with the commercial and family confidences that have traditionally formed the standard fare of breach of confidence cases).

One difficulty should be selected for special mention. It is fundamental to this cause of action that the information that is the subject of the litigation is not already 'in the public domain'.[61] Yet trials are generally conducted in open court. There would appear, then, to be minimal scope for successful deployment

---

[56] J. Baldwin, *Small Claims in the County Courts in England and Wales: The Bargain Basement of Civil Justice?* (1997). The author expresses the view that there is no compelling reason why such cases should be heard in private. See especially at 3 and 48–53.

[57] See, generally, F. Gurry, *Breach of Confidence* (1984).

[58] See, in particular, the judgment of the Court of Appeal in *Douglas and Others v Hello! Ltd* [2001] 2 WLR 992.

[59] *A-G v Jonathan Cape Ltd* [1976] QB 752.

[60] *A-G v Guardian Newsapapers Ltd* [1987] 1 WLR 1248, and *A-G v Guardian Newspapers Ltd (No 2)* [1990] 1 AC 109.

[61] Gurry (n 57 above) ch 4, 'The Attributes of Confidentiality'.

of the action for breach of confidence in this particular context.[62] Indeed, the draft Breach of Confidence Bill prepared by the Law Commission in 1980[63] specifically stated that information that was not already 'in the public domain' became so by reason of having been 'orally disclosed in such a way as to be generally available to those present at the proceedings of any court'.[64] The terms of the Bill, therefore, in so far as they dealt with information disclosed during court proceedings, were largely limited to situations where the court sits in closed session.[65]

The Official Secrets Acts 1911–1989[66] have long provided the most important weapon in the criminal law for penalizing the disclosure of government secrets. As with the action for breach of confidence, it is only possible to pick out those aspects which could have a specific bearing on courtroom secrecy. The legislation will be considered in greater detail in Chapter 4, section 4.

Under the 1989 statute criminal liability is imposed on certain classes of person with regard to defined types of document or information.[67] Only the former category concerns us at this point. Those primarily subject to the statute are Crown servants and government contractors. Any person whatever outside these two groups, moreover, may incur criminal liability as a result of unauthorized disclosures by other persons, the offence consisting of the disclosure of information in circumstances where the recipient of the material knows (or has reasonable cause to believe) that it is covered by the Act.[68] In this way a chain of unlawful communications may be established, extending the reach of the criminal law well beyond those occupying positions in central government who form the primary line of liability.

The action for breach of confidence, it has been pointed out, has been used to enforce relations of confidentiality that have arisen in many different spheres of social life. In addition, it may be deployed as a means of checking the dissemination of information that has been imparted in confidence within the courtroom, irrespective of the form of action in the proceedings conducted there. In the same way the Official Secrets Act may be used, whether in the form of a prosecution arising from any sort of factual context or specifically to punish

---

[62] If the dangers ensuing from disclosure are sufficiently grave (for instance, risk to life and limb) the courts will restrain the use even of information that has already reached the public domain. See, especially, *Venables and Another v News Group Newspapers* [2001] 1 All ER 908, where the example is given of information having been placed in the public domain by its appearance on the Internet.

[63] Law Commission Report, *Breach of Confidence* (Cmnd 8388, 1980).

[64] Clause 2(3). It is uncertain whether this means those *actually* present or those who could have been present. If the former, then in the absence of any members of the public or press the information divulged in the course of the trial would still not be in the public domain.

[65] See clause 4(2)–(6).

[66] See, generally, D. G. T. Williams, *Not in the Public Interest: the problem of security in democracy* (1965): P. Birkinshaw, *Reforming the Secret State* (1990).

[67] The types of document and information covered are contained in the Official Secrets Act 1989, ss 1–4.

[68] Official Secrets Act 1989, s 5(2). See also s 5(6).

out-of-court disclosures (irrespective, again, of the nature of the proceedings in question). The former aspect of the official secrets legislation will be examined in the following chapter. It is the latter aspect that concerns us here. Liability, in any event, is based on the juxtaposition of two factors: the nature of the information or document in question; and the position of the accused (whether as the occupier of a particular role which attracts primary liability under the Act or as the recipient of the material from such a person). It is the position of 'Crown servant'[69] that forms the most important role as far as primary liability is concerned. Which of the *personae* of the trial qualify as such? The concept includes such occasional actors in the courtroom scene as police officers and members of the Crown Prosecution Service. Judges, although they are Crown servants in several ways, are not servants of the Crown for the purposes of the definition in the Official Secrets Act 1989.[70] Court reporters,[71] if they qualify as 'government contractors,'[72] would also occupy a position in the front line of liability under the Official Secrets Acts.

It emerges, therefore, that very few of the *personae* of the typical trial—and, in the nature of things, even fewer still of the members of the public—will qualify under either of the two principal classes of person who are subject to the constraints imposed by the Official Secrets Act. Any scope for potential use of the legislation, therefore, as a means of penalizing out-of-court disclosures must rest on the establishment of a chain of unauthorized disclosure under section 5(2) of the Act.

The final area of the law to be sketched is the law of contempt of court. This is an aspect of the law which is not predominantly concerned with the safeguarding of information or confidences. Its central concern, rather, is to maintain the authority of the administration of justice. To quote the definition given by an early monograph on the subject: 'To speak generally, contempt of court may be said to be constituted by any conduct that tends to bring the authority and administration of the law into disrespect or disregard, or to interfere with or prejudice parties litigant or their witnesses during the litigation'.[73]

Interference with the due administration of justice may take a wide variety of forms: disobedience to court orders; commenting on current proceedings in the courts in such a way as to prejudice the proper trial of the issues; casting imputations on the competence and integrity of the judiciary; exacting retaliation on the *personae* of the trial (usually witnesses or jurors) for having played their parts in the trial process. In addition to the hydra-like nature of contempt at

---

[69] Defined in the Official Secrets Act 1989, s 12(1).

[70] ibid. It would appear, however, that they did qualify as such under the Official Secrets Act 1911. See Departmental Committee on section 2 of the Official Secrets Act 1911 (Chairman: Lord Franks) (Cmnd 5104) Appendix 1B, para 2.

[71] In the sense of those employed specifically to make an official record of the proceedings.

[72] Defined in the Official Secrets Act 1989, s 12(2).

[73] J. F. Oswald, *On Contempt of Court* (3rd edn, 1910) 6.

common law, statute has intervened on occasion to declare that certain forms of conduct are to be treated as contempt of court even though the link between the proscribed conduct and jeopardy to the proper administration of justice may be quite tenuous.[74]

The connection between the enforcement of secrecy and the proper administration of justice is typically to be seen where the trial judge makes an order protecting the anonymity of a witness who, without that protection, would be extremely reluctant to testify. The order is flouted by a newspaper's disclosure of the identity, and the issue of the jurisdiction of the court to make the order is raised as a collateral question in determining whether or not the newspaper is liable for committing a contempt of court.

F. The Administration of Justice Act 1960, Section 12

Within the broad heading of contempt of court special attention needs to be drawn to section 12 of the Administration of Justice Act 1960 as a means of enforcing trial secrecy. This rather opaque provision has undergone a few changes in detail since its original enactment. The basic structure, however, remains unchanged.

The principal thrust of the provision, to be found in subsection (1), stipulates that the 'publication of information relating to proceedings before any court sitting in private shall not of itself be contempt of court' with the exception of five listed situations, (a)–(e). Subsection (3) states that references to a 'court' include both judge and tribunal and, quite unusually, 'any person exercising the functions of a court'. Also the non-technical phrase 'in private' is to be taken to 'include references to a court sitting in camera or in chambers'. The use of the term 'in private' is probably to be accounted for by the fact that section 12 applies equally to tribunals, and the more precise wording of 'in camera' and 'in chambers' would appear to be appropriately used of the closed sittings of courts proper. Indeed, one of the leading pronouncements on the scope and effect of the section, *Pickering v Liverpool Daily Post and Echo Newspapers plc*,[75] derived from the publicity attending an application before a Mental Health Review Tribunal.

The terms of section 12 extend to the hearing itself. The judgment of the court or tribunal, whether in full or in summary form, is excepted from the scope of the prohibition unless the court—note, *not* the tribunal—in question expressly exercises a power which it possesses to prohibit even this limited material.

What was the purpose of enacting section 12? In contrast to the areas of law just surveyed in section E, the provision is specifically aimed at penalizing out-of-court disclosure. The scope of the provision is not shaped by the substantive

---

[74] As, most notably, in the Contempt of Court Act 1981, s 8, in penalizing disclosure of the secrets of the jury room. See generally Chapter 7, below.

[75] [1991] 1 All ER 622.

content of the information disclosed (as under the Official Secrets Act), nor by the character of the circumstances in which it was originally imparted to another (as is the case with breach of confidence). Although forming a statutory accretion to the common law of contempt, the section is not concerned—ostensibly, at any rate—with the impact of out-of-court disclosure on the authority of the administration of justice. Rather, the ambit of section 12 is shaped by the place in which the information in question originated. In order to gain a better appreciation of the role played by section 12, it is necessary to refer both to what has already been covered and to material that is to come later in this book. In *Scott v Scott*, it was seen in Chapter 1, there was an acute division of opinion as to the precise effect of an *in camera* direction. Was it no more than an order as to the mode of trial, or could it additionally form the basis for punishing those who revealed the contents of what was said in court behind closed doors? Looking ahead to the topic of jury secrecy in Chapter 7, we can see that there are parallels to be drawn between section 12 of the Administration of Justice Act 1960 and section 8 of the Contempt of Court Act 1981. In regard to both provisions the physical exclusion from, respectively, the seat of trial and the jury room of all save the *personae* of the trial does not suffice to guarantee confidentiality, since even one disclosure from the limited circle could result in the material becoming generally known. Hence the physical separation of persons, in a secret session of the court and in the jury room respectively, has been reinforced by the legal restraints imposed by the two provisions.

The background to section 12 was explained by Sir Jocelyn Simon, the Solicitor-General, in moving the second reading of the Administration of Justice Bill.[76] A report by JUSTICE, entitled *Contempt of Court*,[77] had recently identified the confused state of the law in regard to the disclosure of the content of court proceedings that had taken place in private.[78] Six statements on the subject were quoted by the Committee, five of which sought to state what the legal position was.[79] Among these widely differing statements, proposition (iv) gained cautious support from the Committee's report.[80] It was this proposition which, substantially, formed the basis of the new statutory provision.

As we have seen, section 12 sets out five exceptions to the general rule that out-of-court publication is not in itself to be a contempt. These exceptions will be considered, in turn, at the appropriate places in Chapters 4 to 6. Broadly, the first three relate to the position of children and mental patients as especially vulnerable members of the community. The last two, by contrast, govern matters of national security and secret processes and inventions. In the treatment of state

---

[76] *Hansard*, HC (series 5) vol 625, cols 1698–99 (1 July 1960).

[77] The committee of JUSTICE that produced the report, in 1959, was chaired by Lord Shawcross.

[78] Sir Jocelyn Simon's speech refers to hearings 'in chambers'.

[79] JUSTICE Report, 16–18.

[80] See ibid. 17, for the content of proposition (iv); and at 18 for the committee's tentative endorsement.

secrecy and commercial secrecy, they can clearly be seen as directed at situations where the norm of open trial would defeat the very point of bringing legal proceedings. Of a similar type is an additional exception that was proposed in the draft Right of Privacy Bill prepared by JUSTICE in 1970.[81] If actions for breach of privacy were possible, the pursuit of such claims in open court would simply aggravate the very injury of which the plaintiff would be complaining and hence act as a deterrent against seeking legal redress.

Several matters relating to the scope and effect of section 12 were clarified by the House of Lords in *Pickering v Liverpool Daily Post and Echo Newspapers plc*.[82] The plaintiff had been responsible for a number of violent sexual attacks on women, including the killing of a teenager. Having been detained in a secure mental hospital, he made a series of applications to a Mental Health Review Tribunal in order to secure his release. The question of whether the plaintiff was fit to be released back into the community was one on which the public had the most pressing and legitimate interest. Yet, subject to a number of exceptions, the Mental Health Review Tribunal Rules required the tribunal to sit in private. The confidential nature of the proceedings, in combination with the ruling (overturning earlier authority[83]) that a Mental Health Review Tribunal is a 'court' for the purposes of the legislation, sufficed to bring the case within the broad ambit of section 12 of the Administration of Justice Act.

The House of Lords held that the applicable rule[84] that enjoined secrecy did not confer on the plaintiff a right of action for breach of statutory duty. It is interesting to dwell for a moment on the reason given by Lord Bridge: '. . . publication of unauthorised information about proceedings on a patient's application for discharge to a mental health review tribunal, though it may in one sense be adverse to the patient's interest, is incapable of causing him loss or injury of a kind for which the law awards damages'.[85] This is a frank recognition of the difficulty of categorizing within the established heads of tort liability the violation of a sphere of privacy. Certainly, the proceedings were brought by the mental patient himself, not (as with the great majority of contempt cases) by the Attorney-General. Although much of the material placed in front of the Mental

---

[81] The Bill is appended to its report, *Privacy and the Law*. Clause 10 of the Bill stated: 'In section 12(1) of the Administration of Justice Act 1960 (which provides for the publication of information relating to proceedings in private) there shall be inserted immediately after paragraph (d) the following new paragraph—"(dd) where the court sits in private pursuant to Rules of Court made under the power conferred by section 7 of the Right of Privacy Act 1970."'

Presumably this would have been inserted as an appendage to the present paragragh (d) as being the nearest in scope to the content of that paragraph (which applies to information relating to 'a secret process, discovery or invention').

[82] [1991] 1 All ER 622.

[83] *A-G v Associated Newspapers Group plc* [1989] 1 WLR 322.

[84] Mental Health Review Tribunal Rules 1983, SI 1983/942, 21(5): 'Except in so far as the tribunal may direct, information about proceedings before the tribunal and the names of any persons concerned in the proceedings shall not be made public.'

[85] [1991] 1 All ER 622, 632.

Health Review Tribunal would touch on the state of health of the patient, the thrust of the provisions that required secrecy was to protect the 'privacy' of the tribunal.[86] In one sense, indeed, the private interest of the applicant was co-extensive with the public interest in the proper discharge of the tribunal's functions. His fear was that the publicity generated by his application would lead the tribunal—a factor of which the tribunal itself was aware—to bow to public pressure demanding his continued incarceration.

What exactly were the matters encompassed by section 12's prohibition? The House of Lords, following an earlier ruling of the Court of Appeal,[87] affirmed that extra-curial disclosure in any of the five listed areas (a)–(e) did not *per se* constitute a contempt of court. This liberal interpretation, contrary to the literal reading of section 12(1), stands in marked contrast to the all-encompassing provision that proscribes disclosures from the jury room. Disclosure, emphasized the House of Lords, constituted a contempt in the absence of 'a defence recognised by law'.[88] Some such defences may be implied simply as a matter of common sense: for example, where disclosure is made for the limited and proper purpose of preparing an appeal.[89] Equally, drawing on the ruling of the Court of Appeal in *Re F (a minor)*,[90] there appears to be a defence whereby the passage of time since the private sitting of the court has resulted in a position in which disclosure no longer imperils the interests protected by that form of sitting.[91] While the scope of such a defence would be clear in some situations, for example, the public dissemination of what has hitherto been a secret trade process (under section 12(1)(d)), it is rather more difficult to establish the precise interest that is protected in regard to the affairs of a mental patient. Finally, section 12 of the Administration of Justice Act, falling outside the terms of the strict liability rule, does not benefit from the *bona fide* discussion of public affairs that is protected by section 5 of the Contempt of Court Act 1981.

As regards the substance of the subject matter covered by section 12, the House of Lords held that this encompassed 'the matters which the court has closed its doors to consider . . . [but not] the fact that the court will sit, is sitting or has sat at a certain date, time or place behind closed doors to consider those matters'.[92] This separation of the substance of the hearing from the information about its position in time and space appears an entirely natural way of reading section 12.

---

[86] Incidentally, a private right of action was denied on a number of grounds in *Melton Medes Ltd v Securities and Investment Board* [1995] Ch 137. In particular, s 179 of the Financial Services Act 1986 did not confer a right of action in regard to the non-consensual disclosure of information, whether at the suit of those from whom it was obtained or those to whom the information related.

[87] *Re F (a minor)(publication of information)* [1977] 1 All ER 114.

[88] [1991] 1 All ER 622, 633.

[89] cf. Judicial Proceedings (Regulation of Reports) Act 1926, s 1(4).

[90] See n 87 above, at 137.

[91] cf. the open recognition of this factor in actions for breach of confidence: *A-G v Jonathan Cape Ltd* [1976] 1 QB 752, 771: 'There must, however, be a limit in time after which the confidential character of the information, and the duty of the court to restrain publication, will lapse.'

[92] [1991] 1 All ER 622, 635.

2. THE FRAGMENTATION OF THE COURTROOM

A. Intra-Court Secrecy: General Considerations

The effective conduct of a law suit depends upon the creation and maintenance of a number of barriers in order to restrict the free flow of information that would otherwise pass between the various *personae* of the trial. This is particularly so in the case of law suits that are contested according to the adversarial, in contrast to the inquisitorial, mode of trial. When the word 'barriers' is used in this context we mean a variety of arrangements whereby information that is known to certain participants in the trial sequence is withheld from other such participants. In recent years the development of barriers in the physical sense (for example, in the form of screens) has been increasingly common. In some contexts they merely serve to reinforce the anonymity of witnesses, while in others they avoid the face-to-face confrontation between persons who are known to one another. However, even when no barriers in this sense of the word are erected in the place of trial, the effective functioning of the trial process depends upon the creation of a number of 'zones' of confidentiality. To take one instance, matters that are known to both sides to the suit might be withheld from the judge. Or information may be temporarily kept from the members of the jury or from witnesses waiting to give their testimony, while the same information circulates freely among all other *personae* of the trial.

The subject matter of section 2 of the chapter, then, is the several zones of confidentiality that are created within the courtroom. Their relevance to the theme of this book lies in the consequential need, in some instances, to curtail the right of the public to immediate possession of full information relating to the events of the trial. The danger is that, otherwise, the information in question might leak, via the public and the press, to the very *personae* of the trial from whom the information must be withheld. The incursion into the standard of open justice that results from the creation of the various zones of confidentiality, although incidental, is nevertheless quite considerable. In other instances, however, members of the public stand at an advantage, as compared with the *personae* of the trial, in gaining access to information. Their positions, in this respect, are now inverted. As has already been seen, the secret hearing is characterized by closure to the public only. In the following sections, by contrast, are encountered some situations where, if they are to play their parts to the greatest effect, it is the *personae* of the trial who must be denied information.

B. Adjudication and Conciliation

Adjudication and conciliation are two entirely distinct processes.[93] The former is concerned to establish the parties' legal rights and duties, the latter with getting the parties to settle their differences. That the pre-trial stages of the civil trial have been devoted exclusively to the former has been the subject of considerable criticism. Master Jacob described it as 'a major defect in the fabric of English civil justice as a whole',[94] adding a proposal for court-annexed mediation schemes to be administered by a Master or Registrar as an integral part of the pre-trial process. All that passed between the parties at this stage would be kept secret from the trial judge (if attempts at conciliation should prove fruitless), and also from the public. Clearly, mediation could not function effectively if offers made, and positions surrendered, at that stage could be exploited by the other side if the matter subsequently went to trial.[95] Moreover, the size of any award that was made in the strictly adjudicative part of the trial may be influenced—or, at least, may appear to be influenced—by the knowledge that the judge (or, in the rare case, the jury) gains of the amount that the defendant was willing to pay to the plaintiff by way of out-of-court settlement.

There has long existed a rudimentary mechanism of conciliation, in the form of the facility of making payment into court (with adverse repercussions on the question of costs if the plaintiff rejects the sum and fails to recover at the trial more than the amount paid in). The fact that a Part 36 payment (as it is now known under the Civil Procedure Rules) has been made is not to be disclosed to the trial judge. The prohibition is temporary only, applying only 'until all questions of liability and the amount of money to be awarded have been decided'.[96] It appears to be addressed primarily to the parties to the case. That persons other than the parties are bound by the obligation of non-disclosure appears to emerge from *Re an Action for Negligence (1992 C No 3063)*.[97] In that case (which was decided prior to the Civil Procedure Rules) Knox J deplored the fact that a journal had published not only the fact that the defendants had made a payment into court but also the amount of the payment. Though categorizing such conduct as an 'apparent contempt of court', he did not examine the issue any further since the journal was not represented before him.[98] In a 'familiar

---

[93] This is clearly borne out by the fact that conciliation procedures do not attract the absolute privilege against defamation proceedings enjoyed by judicial and quasi-judicial proceedings : *Tadd v Eastwood* The Times, 28 May 1983, per Hirst J.

[94] I. H. Jacob, *The Fabric of English Civil Justice* (1987) 108–9.

[95] See *Re D (Minors)(Conciliation: Privilege)* [1993] 2 WLR 721, where it was held that statements made by either party in the course of communications with a view to matrimonial conciliation could not be disclosed in proceedings under the Children Act 1989. The judgment of the Master of the Rolls ranged over the role of conciliation in general.

[96] Civil Procedure Rules 1998, SI 1998/3132, r 36.19(2).

[97] The Times, 5 March 1993.

[98] Presumably, it was one of the parties who had supplied the journal with the information about the payment into court in the first place. They *were* represented before him.

judicial exercise' in 'controlled forgetfulness' he would put the matter out of his mind rather than abandon the hearing and waste court time thus far expended. In this way the opportunity was lost for clarifying the legal position of the journal and the parties, and for ascertaining whether the sanction of contempt liability attached to disregard of the prohibition on disclosure.

C. The Exclusion of Witnesses from the Courtroom

Among the various exceptions to open justice that are canvassed in Earl Loreburn's judgment in *Scott v Scott* it is mentioned in passing that 'witnesses may be ordered to withdraw lest they trim their evidence by hearing the evidence of others'.[99] Here, then, is a clear situation in which, in virtue of being a *persona* of the trial, an individual loses his rights as a member of the public. The danger that is sought to be averted is clear enough: that a witness who has been permitted to sit through the testimony of others might be tempted, when it comes to his own turn in the witness box, to adjust his recollection of events in the light of the testimony that he has already heard. Indeed, it has been argued that 'natural justice [is] violated by witnesses being allowed to remain in court and thus in the sight and hearing of other witnesses as they [give] their evidence'.[100] And it is noteworthy that this argument, though unsuccessful, deployed exactly the same basis (of natural justice) on which—as we have seen[101]—exclusions from the courtroom have been challenged.

If there is a real risk that witnesses might adjust their evidence (even subconsciously) in the light of pre-trial conferral or association with other witnesses, exclusion from the courtroom is of only limited effectiveness in dealing with the problem.[102] Clear contradictions between testimony given in court and earlier statements by the same witness are easily detected. Much more difficult to identify are subtle changes in emphasis, for example, in the degree of certainty with which an identification is reported as having been made, as a result of exposure to testimony on the same point from another witness. If, then, exclusion from the courtroom is accepted as a rule with a sound basis, the same reasoning demands, *a fortiori*, a ban on pre-trial discussion of the case between witnesses since such exchanges will be entirely unregulated by the law of evidence and cross-examination by counsel. Logically, too, it should require the imposition of a reporting ban as a routine measure. Otherwise, the witness who must wait outside the courtroom pending his own turn in the witness box might gain access to the forbidden testimony from media reports of the trial.

---

[99] [1913] AC 417, 446.

[100] *Moore v Lambeth County Court Registrar* [1969] 1 WLR 141, 142.

[101] Recall the discussion of *R v Denbigh JJ, ex p Williams* [1974] QB 759 in Chapter 2, section 1, above.

[102] Note carefully the words in the quotation forming the text to n 100, above: '. . . in the *sight* and hearing of other witnesses . . .' (Emphasis added.) These suggest that there is also an element of face-to-face confrontation that is sought to be avoided by exclusion.

The propriety of pre-trial conferral was raised as one of several issues in *R v Dye and Williamson*.[103] Three prosecution witnesses, in a case involving a heroin importing ring, were interviewed on film as if they were giving evidence at the trial. This occurred prior to the trial, but the film was not broadcast until the proceedings were concluded. On appeal against conviction by the defendants it was held that, although there was a material irregularity, the application of the proviso sufficed to sustain the convictions. The staging of the scenario was only one of several elements in the adverse pronouncement of the Court of Appeal,[104] and it is therefore difficult to identify the precise weight that it attached to the episode.

It is now possible to turn to the principal concern of this section. There would appear to be a general rule, at any rate in criminal cases, that the unexamined witness should remain outside the courtroom.[105] Sometimes there is discovered to have been a contravention of the rule, a witness being found to have occupied one of the public seats in an earlier part of the proceedings.[106] Such a situation cannot be avoided entirely since additional witnesses may be called as the trial progresses. Indeed, as was seen in Chapter 2, sections 2 to 3, one rationale of open justice is that the casual on-looker in the courtroom, or the person hearing a report of the proceedings, may realize that he has relevant testimony to contribute. In situations where a person who has been present in court is summoned to give evidence at the last minute, the judge has no discretion to disallow the testimony but it is open to counsel to comment that the witness has been in a position to hear all that has gone before.

In *Moore v Registrar of Lambeth County Court*[107] Edmund Davies LJ, in the course of a general survey of the subject, said that the issue of excluding witnesses was 'purely a matter within the discretion of the court'.[108] This statement is best read in context, as limited to civil cases. Drawing on his practical experience, he recorded his personal preference for the exclusion of witnesses. However, 'I know other judges who take exactly the opposite view; they prefer the witnesses to remain in court so that they may observe their reaction when they hear the evidence of other witnesses'.[109]

Application may be made, in the first place, by any party to a civil case to request the judge to exercise his discretion in favour of exclusion.[110] If a witness refuses to comply with an order to withdraw, this will have consequences for

---

[103] [1992] Crim LR 449. The case is also relevant to issues of televising court proceedings. See Chapter 9, section 1, below.

[104] The others were the potential contempt liability of the television company (averted, it would seem, by its postponement of the transmission), and the failure on the part of the prosecution to inform defence counsel of the episode until after the conclusion of the trial.

[105] See *R v Smith (Joan)* [1968] 2 All ER 115 for the situation where the accused gives evidence. The need to ensure his continuing presence in the courtroom logically requires that he himself should give evidence before any witness that he chooses to call.

[106] *R v Thompson* [1967] Crim LR 62.   [107] [1969] 1 WLR 141.   [108] ibid. 142.

[109] ibid. 142.   [110] *Southey v Nash* (1837) 7 Car & P 632, 173 ER 277.

both the witness himself and for his subsequent testimony. While the testimony continues to be admissible, the witness is in contempt of court.[111]

D. Screens and Similar Devices

A few general observations should be made at the outset. Screens (and other devices of the same nature) may be deployed whether in proceedings held in open court or in the course of a trial held *in camera*. The latter situation may appear rather odd at first sight, until it is recalled that the use of screens and the exclusion of the public from the courtroom serve separate (though sometimes overlapping) purposes. A principal purpose of the use of screens is to secure the greatest possible protection for the anonymity of witnesses. There is still scope for such protection against disclosure of their identity to the *personae* of the trial, even in circumstances where no members of the public may be present. An alternative purpose has no concern whatsoever with anonymity, for the identity of the witness is known only too well to the accused. Rather, the aim of the screening device is to prevent any possible intimidation of the witness that might result from face-to-face confrontation with the accused. However, it could prove impossible, in some circumstances, to separate this 'confrontational' aspect of the subject from the public's right of access to the courtroom. Many witnesses who would be intimidated by eye contact with the accused may likewise shrink under the gaze of known associates of the accused seated in the public gallery. Moreover, where the evidence being given is of an intimate nature, even the presence of disinterested strangers on the public seats is capable of having the same effect on the witness.

The Youth Justice and Criminal Evidence Act 1999 has put on a clear statutory basis the use of screens in addition to that of live television links and videotaped evidence. The last two devices will be dealt with in the following two sections. First, however, it is necessary to preface the discussion of the use of screens with matters that are relevant to all three devices. The three are the principal instances of 'special measures' which may be taken under the Act in regard to 'eligible witnesses'. The only other 'special measure' that is relevant to this work is the power, in certain circumstances, to permit evidence to be given in private.[112] Again, for our purposes, the main category of witnesses eligible for assistance by 'special measures' consists of those the quality of whose evidence 'is likely to be diminished by reason of fear or distress' on account of the behaviour of the accused or his associates.[113] Where the statutory qualifying conditions are not present, resort must be had to the common law. In particular, it

---

[111] *Moore v Lambeth County Court Registrar* [1969] 1 WLR 141, 142 ('. . . the trial judge may well express his grave displeasure over such disobedience . . .').

[112] Under the Youth Justice and Criminal Evidence Act, s 25. See subs (4) for the circumstances in which evidence may be given in private. Strictly, the proceedings would not be held *in camera* since, under subs (3), at least one media representative must be permitted to remain in court.

[113] Youth Justice and Criminal Evidence Act 1999, s 17 (briefly summarized).

may be asked whether such persons as SAS (Special Air Service) commandos or members of the security services would qualify as 'eligible witnesses' since the quality of their evidence is unlikely to be diminished by reason of their experiencing 'fear or distress' in the giving of testimony.

The use of a screen[114] will have the effect of disrupting the standard layout of the courtroom, whereby the dock and the witness box are so placed that their occupants are in full view of each other. Under a typical arrangement screening is effected by removing the witness to a point level with the accused, the introduction of an opaque panel on the side of the dock between them cutting off all possibility of eye contact. This arrangement, it will be appreciated, has the disadvantage of placing the two persons in close physical proximity. Additionally, the introduction of any barrier such as a screen may have the effect of interfering with the acoustics of the courtroom to such an extent that the accused is rendered incapable of following and participating in his own trial.[115]

These preliminary points having been made, the use of screens may be explored further, both in contexts where questions of anonymity are absent and in those where such considerations are present.

Long before the present-day concerns with the legal problems surrounding allegations of child abuse, the issues relating to the proper layout of the courtroom in the trial of such cases were raised in *R v Smellie*.[116] A father was charged with assaulting and ill-treating his daughter. Before the daughter was called to give evidence the accused was ordered to leave his seat and to sit on the stairs by the side of the dock, so that he was out of sight (though not out of hearing) of the witness. The sole ground of appeal against conviction was based on the submission that the whole trial was vitiated by the failure to respect the right of the accused at common law to be within sight and hearing of all the witnesses throughout the proceedings. This point was reinforced by reference to the 'incalculable' effect—to quote defence counsel—on both the jury and the witness of the removal of the defendant from the dock. Coleridge J, giving the judgment of the Court of Appeal in favour of rejecting the argument, stated simply: 'If the judge considers that the presence of the prisoner will intimidate a witness there is nothing to prevent him from securing the ends of justice by removing the former from the presence of the latter'.[117]

It is to be noted, on the other hand, that the witness (who was aged eleven) was not shielded vis-à-vis the public. There is not the slightest indication that her evidence was taken *in camera* or that her identity was sought to be protected from public disclosure.

---

[114] The relevant provision of the Youth Justice and Criminal Evidence Act 1999 is s 23.

[115] In *Stanford v United Kingdom* The Times, 8 March 1994, the petitioner unsuccessfully argued that the loss of sound due to the installation of a screen—in this case, a glass screen placed in front of the dock—was such that he had been denied the right to a fair trial under Art 6 of the European Convention on Human Rights.

[116] (1920) 14 Cr App R 128.   [117] ibid. 130.

The principal authority on the use of screens in order to avoid face-to-face confrontation is *R v X, Y and Z*.[118] Said to be the first case in which such a screen had been erected, it concerned charges of sexual abuse of children to whom the accused were related. The screen prevented the children from seeing—or, indeed, being seen by—the accused. Unlike television links to the courtroom, screens will necessarily have this double impact. Moreover, both at the trial and in the Court of Appeal, orders had been made preventing the publication of any information that might tend to identify the complainants.[119] There was no suggestion that the proceedings were held, even partly, *in camera*.

There were a number of grounds of appeal against conviction. Two of these need not concern us: that the judge had allowed three of the children to take the oath; and that social workers had been permitted to sit beside the children while they gave their testimony. It is the third ground, the prejudice caused to the accused by the use of the screen, which is of particular concern here. The trial judge had warned the jury against the danger of drawing prejudicial inferences from the presence of the screen. Even in the absence of such a warning, said the Lord Chief Justice, neither he nor his colleagues thought that 'any sensible jury could have been prejudiced against any defendant by the existence of this barrier between the witness and the dock'.[120] The appeal was dismissed.

What scope does there exist for impugning the outcome of a trial in which, it is argued, a screen has wrongly been allowed to be used in the courtroom? It was emphasized in *X, Y and Z* that the discretion granted to the trial judge in the matter was to be exercised in the interests of a trial that is 'fair to all, the defendants, the Crown and indeed the witnesses'.[121] In *R v Schaub and Cooper*[122] the Court of Appeal, in view of the charge of multiple rape, endorsed the judge's exercise of discretion in favour of permitting the complainant to give her testimony from behind a screen. It added that, where adult witnesses were concerned, the use of screens was to be taken only as an exceptional step—a view that is unlikely to survive the statutory endorsement of the use of screens for categories of adults by the Youth Justice and Criminal Evidence Act 1999. Quite apart from subsequent challenge in the appellate courts, the question of the possible deployment of a screen could be the subject of a type of *voir dire* examination. In the *X, Y and Z* case, it appears that, ten days before the start of 'the trial proper', in circumstances where (one can only assume) the public had no right of access, the trial judge convened counsel to gain their views as to whether a screen should be used in the trial.[123] Once the trial was under way, representatives of the social services department were not called upon to testify as to the likely effect on the children if no protective screening were provided. In

---

[118] (1990) 91 Cr App R 36.
[119] Under the Children and Young Persons Act 1933, s 39: as to which, see Chapter 5, section 6, B (a), below.
[120] (1990) 91 Cr App R 36, 40.   [121] ibid. 41.   [122] [1994] Crim LR 531.
[123] (1990) 91 Cr App R 36, 39–40.

R v Foster,[124] on an application being made by the accused's step-daughters (aged twenty and fifteen at the time of the proceedings) to give evidence while screened, the trial judge granted the request only after taking evidence from a woman police constable who had talked to the complainants about the coming trial. It is noteworthy that, in both this case and the *X, Y and Z* case, the preliminary question as to whether or not to permit screening of the witnesses was decided on the basis of the questioning of third parties. Nor should this appear surprising. Where the problem is the likely intimidation of a witness by reason of confrontation with the accused, it is difficult to see how an accurate *voir dire* examination of the prospective witness could be conducted without posing the very situation—confrontation, followed by the collapse of the witness—that the process is designed to avert.[125]

The use of screens in order to avoid witness/accused facial confrontation raises issues and problems similar to the deployment of live television links, which will be explored in the following section. A few points of comparison between the two devices are necessary at this stage. Whereas the use of live television links has been authorized by explicit statutory provision, in trials on indictment at any rate, the use of screens emerged simply by way of practice. An initial form of recognition of their existence by central government was in a non-authoritative Home Office circular.[126] Now that the two methods have been available for a while, it emerges from empirical research that the deployment of screens is more frequent. Indeed, it has been thought by some that the 'live' nature of testimony given by a witness who is actually present in the courtroom carries more weight, other things being equal, than evidence conveyed through a television link.[127]

To turn now to the second aspect of this section, a very different use of screens is involved where the threat (whether real or apprehended) to the safety of a witness is such that his identity must be concealed, as much from the *personae* of the trial as from the members of the public seated in the courtroom. So great, indeed, might be the risks involved in testifying in a public forum that the use of a screen may be considered insufficient protection. In the case of the inquest held in Gibraltar in 1988 in connection with the shooting of three members of the Irish Republican Army, the British government demanded, as means of protecting the identity of the members of the SAS called as witnesses, not only

---

[124] [1995] Crim LR 333.

[125] Compare, in this regard, the *voir dire* phase prior to an *in camera* sitting of the court.

[126] Home Office circular 61/1990 (on the use of screens in magistrates' courts).

[127] J. Plotnikoff and R. Woolfson, *Prosecuting Child Abuse: An Evaluation of the Government's Speedy Progress Policy* (1995) 77: 'In our study, most CPS lawyers and law clerks (even those in areas where the TV link was used more frequently) expressed the view that testimony over the TV link lessens the impact of the child's evidence on the jury, and felt this reflected the opinion of many prosecution barristers.'

wooden screens but also special devices fitted to microphones in the witness box which would distort their voices.[128]

Where, as in this case, the presence of a screen is seen as a means of protecting national security and of avoiding jeopardy to sensitive intelligence operations, the scope for possible prejudice to the proceedings will be smaller than in those cases where the use of a screening device in order to avoid confrontation between two persons, witness and accused, who are known to each other suggests that the witness has good reason to fear the accused. Again, there will be cases where these persons are not known to one another but the identity of the witness is sought to be kept from the accused, with the implication that the latter would exact revenge for the giving of the testimony. Indeed, quite apart from the prejudicial impact on the jury resulting from the anonymity–protecting arrangements, the accused might well be prejudiced in a more general way in that he will be denied the right to see, and know the identity of, his accuser. In *R v Taylor (Gary)*[129] the judge acceded to the prosecution's request that the name and address of the witness should not be revealed. This was reinforced by the use of a screen, the accused's view of the witness being available only through a television monitor. The Court of Appeal, upholding the conviction, stated that it would be a rare and exceptional case in which the judge would exercise his discretion in favour of denying to the accused the knowledge of the identity of the prosecution witnesses. It proceeded to state a number of factors to be weighed before such an unusual step could be taken.[130] The *Taylor* case, with its unusual combination of screen and television monitor, forms a suitable bridge to the following section.

E. Live Television Links

For many purposes, a live television link[131] from a witness positioned outside the courtroom serves the same ends as the placing of a screen in front of the witness where he is giving evidence inside the courtroom. The former may simply be seen as a more efficacious means of securing the same ends as the latter. Certainly, there have occurred instances of misconduct—for example, the accused shouting at the witness as she gives her testimony[132]—which would not have occurred (or, at least, would have occurred with a much reduced impact) if a television link had been used in preference to a screen. Where, as in the

---

[128] The Times, (2 July 1988) 1.   [129] The Times, 17 August 1994.

[130] For example, that there must be real grounds for fear of the consequences if the identity were revealed; that the evidence must be sufficiently relevant and important to render it unfair to the Crown to proceed without it; that there would be no undue prejudice to the accused (though some prejudice would be inevitable); and that the creditworthiness of the witness had been fully investigated.

[131] The relevant provision of the Youth Justice and Criminal Evidence Act 1999 is s 24.

[132] See the incident as recounted in *The Guardian* (25 May 1994) 3 ('Impact of "live" evidence on jury counts as priority for prosecution'). The eleven-year-old was required by the judge to give evidence from behind a screen, ruling that she was too old to be allowed to testify by television link.

Taylor case, a television link supplements the use of a screen, it can be used to offset the 'two-way' impact of the screen and allow a person on one side of the barrier a strictly limited and controlled view of the scene on the other side. A variation on this theme is the so-called 'remote TV link', where the sensitivities of the witness are such that he is placed in an entirely different building (albeit one in the locality) to that in which the court is sitting.[133] A very different use of the television link is the situation where the link effects a connection between the courtroom and a witness who is far removed from the courtroom, sometimes on the other side of the world. Whatever the exact form of the link, this departure from the traditional trial procedure means that there is no longer scope for confrontation between the witness and other *personae* of the trial or— to emphasize our principal concern—between the witness and the members of the public who are in attendance.

Where television links have been used as a method of bringing together court and witness, without any need to protect the security of the latter, they are merely an alternative to the moving of the court to the place where the witness is located. As has already been pointed out,[134] occasionally a court will move temporarily to the bedside of a witness who is too ill to be brought to the courtroom in order to testify. In one well-publicized Scottish case, the libel action *Gecas v Scottish Television*,[135] the Court of Session removed to Vilnius in Lithuania in order to hear the testimony of two elderly witnesses who were unable to travel to Scotland to give their evidence.[136] And, in an inversion of the standard situation, it was the plaintiff who remained in Scotland, connected to the court proceedings by the technology in question.

Criminal trials, coroners' inquests, and civil cases form the very different contexts in which live television links have been used or sought to be used.

In regard to criminal cases, section 32 of the Criminal Justice Act 1988 states that a person other than the accused, in a trial on indictment (and in certain other circumstances), may give evidence 'through a live television link' if either the witness is outside the United Kingdom or the witness is under the age of fourteen and the offence charged is one of those listed in section 32(2). In most circumstances the witness will be the alleged victim of the offences there listed, but section 32 is not limited in this way. The leave of the court must be given before evidence may be received pursuant to the section. One of the earliest uses

[133] Under an experimental arrangement at Winchester Crown Court, the witness testifies from a local fire station or NSPCC premises.

[134] In Chapter 1, section 5, A, above.

[135] The plaintiff's cause of action arose out of the defendants' programmes, 'Crimes of War', which had suggested that he had been an accomplice to the mass killings of civilians during the Second World War. The 'overseas' sittings of the court took place in December 1991. There was, in addition, an element of a 'view' since, it was said, the judge would take advantage of the journey to Lithuania to visit the area where the alleged war crimes were perpetrated.

[136] For an account of the case and its background, see R. Hutchinson, *Crimes of War: the Antanas Gecas Affair* (1994), and especially at 173–4 for the making of arrangements for the court to sit in Lithuania.

of the section occurred in March 1992, in a case involving allegations of fraud against two British businessmen. The witness[137] was placed in a transmitting studio in Calgary, Canada, accompanied by an officer of the Royal Canadian Mounted Police. Reception of the signal took place on a monitor, not at the Central Criminal Court where the trial was being held, but at a suite at the Inter-Continental Hotel in Park Lane.[138]

A decade later, legislation extended the use of live television links to preliminary hearings in the criminal process. The conditions were that the accused was being held in custody at the time and that he was able 'to see and hear the court and to be seen and heard by it'.[139] He would then be treated as being present in the court for the purposes of the particular hearing. The arrangement saves time and minimizes security risks, though the departure from the standard procedures is so marked that the parties are entitled to make representations before the court may employ the new facility. And, most recently, the use of a live television link may be used as a 'special measure' under the Youth Justice and Criminal Evidence Act 1999.

In the case of coroners' inquests and civil cases, it is apparent that the courts have considered television links to be so marked a departure from standard trial procedure that they have felt the need to search for some express or implied statutory authorization for their use.

A coroner's inquest, held in May 1992, that investigated the death by 'friendly fire' of several British servicemen during the Gulf War the year before was asked by Mr Geoffrey Robertson QC, acting for the families of the deceased, to set up a satellite link to hear the testimony of the American pilots who had been involved in the incident. The pilots were extremely reluctant to attend the inquest in person. Yet, despite the critical importance of their testimony, the coroner ruled that the provisions which governed his jurisdiction required all witnesses to be examined before him on oath.[140] The use of a satellite link was, therefore, out of the question. In civil cases, on the other hand, inconclusively drafted provisions governing the mode of trial have been held to permit such a method of taking evidence. In *Garcin v Amerindo Investment Advisors Ltd*[141] Morritt J concluded that Order 38, rule 3, of the Rules of the Supreme Court, by virtue of which 'evidence . . . shall be given at the trial in such manner as may be specified' by the court, granted him a discretion to allow a witness in New York to be examined by live television link. He reached this conclusion notwithstanding the requirement in Order 38, rule 1, that facts 'shall be proved, by the examination of . . . witnesses orally and in open court'. His ruling was subsequently approved by the Court of Appeal in *Arab Monetary Fund v Hashim*

---

[137] The witness was unable to attend the trial in person on account of the ill health of a close relative.

[138] The Times, (10 March 1992) 3.   [139] Crime and Disorder Act 1998, s 57(1).

[140] The Times, (16 May l992) 5.   [141] [1991] 4 All ER 655.

(No 7)[142] and, apparently, in *Mannesmann Handel (AG) v Kaunlaren Shipping Co*[143] (which involved an expert witness). The Civil Procedure Rules 1998 now explicitly provide that a witness may be permitted to give evidence 'through a video link or by any other means'[144] notwithstanding the general rule that at trial evidence is to be given 'in public'.[145]

There remain, however, a number of difficulties concerning the nature of testimony given through a live television link.

Consider, for instance, the form of the Lithuanian phase in *Gecas v Scottish Television*. Those members of the local public who chose to attend at that stage were unlikely, in the absence of interpreters, to understand the proceedings of the court. On the other hand, they would understand as a matter of course the testimony of the local witnesses. And, as we have seen, the interchange between the witness and public and between court and public lies at the core of at least one justification of the open conduct of proceedings. The form of the proceedings, certainly, was highly unusual.[146] However, the very fact that there is nowadays much greater flexibility in the possible ways in which courts may sit means that it is all the more important to understand what sort of arrangements are in danger of losing the advantages of open justice.

Many problems are common to the use of any television link but, as we have just noted, particular difficulties are created in the situation where the witness is outside the jurisdiction. Section 32(3) of the Criminal Justice Act 1988 stipulates that a statement made on oath by a witness outside the United Kingdom shall be treated, for the purposes of the law of perjury, as 'having been made in the proceedings in which it is given in evidence'. Such a witness, unlike his counterpart who is linked to the courtroom from an adjoining room or building, is, for the time being, at any rate, outside the reach of the law of perjury and the law of contempt. In the absence of such coercive adjuncts to the giving of truthful testimony, it would seem that evidence is to be admitted from abroad in such a manner only in relatively uncontroversial instances. Certainly, in the *Mannesmann Handel* case Saville J appears to have intimated that, if the witness was one whose veracity was to be challenged, attendance at the courtroom in the traditional manner would be required.

It has been asserted by Dockray that evidence provided by a live television link must 'be regarded as hearsay at common law'.[147] This view is surely untenable if 'hearsay' is to be understood in a strict sense: that is, the witness 'A'

---

[142] [1993] 4 All ER 114, 123.

[143] *The Lawyer*, 20 October 1992 (where the testimony was given from Hong Kong).

[144] Civil Procedure Rules 1998, SI 1998/3132, 32.3.

[145] Civil Procedure Rules 1998, SI 1998/3132, 32.2 (1)(a).

[146] An alternative method of taking the testimony of a witness who is abroad is by way of an order for letters of request. In *Garcin v Amerindo Investment Advisors Ltd* (n 141 above), the defendants opposed the use of the television link, applying instead for an order for letters of request to be directed to the relevant US District Court.

[147] M. Dockray, 'Evidence by Television' (1992) 108 LQR 561, 563.

recounts to the court what 'B' (who is not before the court) told him, the statement from 'B' having been adduced as tending to prove the truth of the facts contained therein. Nevertheless, it is possible to see the general difficulty. Just as 'B' (in the example just given) is not available to be observed while he gives his evidence, so too the intervention of a television link detracts from the direct observation of the witness as he gives his testimony.

Furthermore, Dockray asks, is the evidence that is obtained in this way 'given in open court in London [or wherever the court may be sitting]?'.[148] This question, in fact, conflates two separate issues. Was the evidence given in London? Was it given in open court? As regards the first issue, testimony spoken in a room apart from the courtroom, whether in the same building or on the other side of the world, could be viewed as having been given at the place where the witness is located or where the words are actually received. It is the second issue that is more relevant to this work. How, then, are the demands of open justice—in the form of the requirement that evidence be given 'in open court'—satisfied in such circumstances? The authoritative statements that were discussed in Chapter 1 on the meaning of the phrase 'in open court' were delivered well before the advent of modern technology. To say that an open court is 'a court to which the public have a right to be admitted' is of limited use where the court is divided between two locations. Should the public be given a right, in such circumstances, to attend at the place where the witness is located, or at the main seat of trial, or at both? In situations where the television link is a method of protecting anonymity, there are stronger reasons for denying the public the right of access to the location of the witness and for permitting them entry to the principal seat of trial only. The protection of anonymity aside, however, the disciplinary rationale of open justice would seem to require direct confrontation between the members of the public and the witness while he is giving his testimony. It would seem more natural, though, to confine the public to the 'courtroom' proper, where the other *personae* of the trial are to be found.[149] The following of this practice should not be prejudicial to the rights of public and press to witness the trial spectacle in full. In this regard the relevant provisions of the Criminal Justice Act 1988 and the Youth Justice and Criminal Evidence Act 1999 are silent, devoid of all stipulation that the number and positioning of the television monitors in the courtroom be such that the witness can be seen and heard from the public seats. The silence of the latter statute is all the stranger, since the provision regulating the use of screens expressly stipulates that this barrier may not interrupt

---

[148] There is an analogy here with the conflict of laws problem that typically arises where, for example, defamatory words are uttered in one country but the alleged damage attributable to their publication is sustained in a second country. In which jurisdiction was the tort committed?

[149] It is possible to compare the experience of US courts in conducting 'videotape trials': see section 2, F below.

the view of the screened witness by some of the *personae* of the trial[150]—though, strangely, not the view from the public and press benches.

F. Videotaped Evidence

One step further removed from the live video link is the use of evidence that has been videotaped in advance of the trial. In the United States there have occurred 'videotaped trials', where the entire body of evidence has been conveyed to the jury on pre-recorded videotape. In English law scope for introducing evidence in this format, in the case of child witnesses, was effected in section 54 of the Criminal Justice Act 1991, a long and complex provision that took effect as section 32A of the Criminal Justice Act 1988.[151] This facility, again, is available in general terms under the conditions of the Youth Justice and Criminal Evidence Act 1999.[152] Traditionally, however, such a method of obtaining and recording evidence is alien to English procedural notions. The novelty of the method was raised in *J. Barber & Sons (a firm) v Lloyd's Underwriters*.[153] The plaintiff in proceedings in a US court obtained letters of request addressed to the English court, asking that evidence be taken from four defendants, Lloyd's underwriters, by way of videotape deposition. On an *ex parte* application an order was made to appoint an examiner to take the evidence in this way. A subsequent *inter partes* application to discharge the order was refused by Evans J. The procedure was not so fundamentally at variance with English methods of adducing evidence to a court that it should be disallowed. Indeed, as compared with written depositions, Evans J saw considerable advantage in the procedure since 'courts in this country place great emphasis on the demeanour of witnesses, although opinions may differ as to its value'.[154]

The procedure here permitted marked a limited step in regard to a civil trial being conducted in another jurisdiction. The question needs to be raised of the legitimacy of a criminal trial that is conducted throughout in this mode. The videotape trial—or, to be more precise, 'the pre-recorded videotape trial'—has received a degree of discussion in the United States.[155] It is a trial in which the jury reaches its decision exclusively on the basis of testimony that has been recorded beforehand on videotape. As such, it is different from a trial in which, as just seen, only one segment of evidence has been prepared in this way. Equally, it must be distinguished from an arrangement in which the whole official record of the court proceedings is compiled on videotape.

---

[150] Youth Justice and Criminal Evidence Act 1999, s 23(2).

[151] This provision was amended by the Criminal Procedure and Investigations Act 1996, s 62.

[152] Youth Justice and Criminal Evidence Act 1999, s 27 (for evidence in chief), and s 28 (for cross-examination and re-examination).

[153] [1987] QB 103.   [154] ibid. 106.

[155] See, for example, J. A. Shutkin, 'Videotape Trials : Legal and Practical Implications' (1973) 9 *Columbia Journal of Law and Social Problems* 363.

The taping of the testimony takes place in several locations in the presence of legal counsel and a court officer who is not the trial judge. The filming of sequences of testimony does not necessarily follow the order in which the testimony will finally be presented. The footage, once compiled, is finally reviewed in chambers by the trial judge, again in the presence of counsel. At this point objections are taken on the possible inadmissibility of material. An edited version is then produced that contains only admissible material. The form of the trial is that counsel make their opening statements and closing speeches in the presence of the jury. The intervening stages of the hearing of testimony consist of the replaying of the pre-recorded testimony over television monitors in the courtroom.

This form of trial procedure possesses a number of distinct advantages. Testimony is gathered at times and in locations that are convenient to the witnesses. The delays and adjournments that are characteristic of the traditional trial are avoided. Moreover, inadmissible or prejudicial material will not be heard in the courtroom, since all such matter will have been excised from the tapes that are played to the jury.

Such arrangements, however convenient they might be, are open to a number of objections of principle. One of the most fundamental aspects of open justice, the right of the accused to be present at his own trial, requires that he be permitted to be present when testimony is being taped, and not merely when the tape is being played in front of the jury. The assurance of this right has correspondingly reduced the utility of the pre-recorded videotape trial. The presence of the accused at the recording session gives him the opportunity to confront the witness as he delivers his testimony. More problematic is the issue of witness/jury confrontation and, more specifically the concern of the present work, witness/public confrontation. The latter arrangement could be assured, though at the cost of some inconvenience. It would mean that, prior to each recording session, public notice would need to be issued that such a session was to be held, combined with the setting aside of the requisite amount of seating for public and press.[156] If the presence of the public could be facilitated (even with some difficulty), the provision of witness/jury confrontation would be a nonsense in the light of the intended aims of the pre-recorded videotape trial. It would mean that the jury would have to be empanelled—as it must be in the traditional trial format—before the very first item of evidence is recorded. Moreover, by involving the jury at this stage, it would place them in a position where they would be exposed to testimony twice (first live, then recorded) and, on the first occasion, within hearing of potentially prejudicial or inadmissible information or comment. Finally, it will be recalled, one of the aims served by open conduct of judicial business is the subjecting of the

---

[156] Such arrangement would be at the expense of a vital feature of the traditional trial: that of continuity. Only the most determined member of the public would succeed in following the trial as it moved from location to location in the gathering of evidence. He could, of course, attend at the final showing in front of the jury, but that would lose the element of witness–public confrontation.

judge himself to scrutiny as he manages the conduct of the trial. Yet it is this aspect that is very largely withheld from public scrutiny by the pre-recorded videotape trial. The purpose being to produce an uninterrupted sequence of admissible testimony, objections made by counsel are dealt with in chambers out of sight and hearing of the public.

The pre-recorded videotape trial is the most extreme form of sets of arrangements whereby evidence that is presented to the jury has, in effect, been given at some earlier point in time outside the courtroom. Much of the Anglo-American law of evidence is shaped by the requirement that direct evidence relating to the matters in question should be given in the courtroom itself. In particular, these systems have maintained a long-standing aversion to hearsay evidence. In this way, it is generally impermissible for 'A' to be produced in court to state that 'B' had told him that he ('B') had observed the accused committing the crime charged. The rationale of, and the exceptions to, the hearsay rule are beyond the scope of the present work.[157] From the point of view of open justice, however, the reception of hearsay is objectionable on a number of grounds. Although 'A' is present before the court, 'B' is not. There is no opportunity to cross-examine 'B', nor can the demeanour of 'B' be observed by jury and public while he makes his incriminating statement. In fact, from the point of view of open justice, the admissibility of hearsay evidence is open to more objections of principle than resort to some of the procedural devices that have just been reviewed since these devices lend themselves to minimal confrontation (at least) with the witness.

3. CHALLENGING COURTROOM SECRECY

A. Introduction

Suppose that a trial is improperly held, whether wholly or in part, in private. To what extent may the incorrect procedure be subject to legal challenge? Who is competent to bring such challenges, and in what forms? These questions form the subject matter of the present section of the chapter.

The overriding concern here is with trials from which the public and the press have been excluded in the ways described in section 1, C–D, above. Reference will also be made to proceedings which are held in full public view but where there is, nevertheless, a degree of intra-court secrecy (see, principally, section 2, D). Issues of the correctness (or otherwise) of secret arrangements may be raised as a collateral matter in the course of proceedings that are directed to a different end: for example, as in *Scott v Scott* itself, in order to determine liability for contempt of court. Our concern, however, is with procedures in which the secrecy of trial proceedings is challenged directly.

---

[157] See, generally, A. L.-T. Choo, *Hearsay and Confrontation in Criminal Trials* (1996).

Finally, it will be recalled, the law requires certain types or proceedings—for example, the trial of young offenders—to be conducted in private. If an unauthorized person gains entry to the hearing, what are the consequences for the validity of the trial? Occasional reference will be made to this situation, which (it will be appreciated) is the reverse to that which principally concerns us.

What follows has been divided into two headings: where the challenge is brought by a party to the case that has been improperly heard; and where that issue is raised by persons who are not parties (principally the press).

B. Challenge by a Party

In view of the overriding importance that is attached to the accused being tried in public, this aspect of the subject will be examined first.

Appeal against conviction furnishes the simplest way of correcting an erroneous decision on the part of the trial judge to exclude the press and public. Where an accused has been convicted on indictment, the Court of Appeal traditionally allowed the appeal on any of three grounds:[158] that the verdict was 'unsafe or unsatisfactory'; that a wrong decision was given on 'any question of law'; or that there was a 'material irregularity in the course of the trial'. Even if the point that was raised under any of the three heads was decided in favour of the appellant, the Court of Appeal could apply the proviso (as it was called) and dismiss the appeal on the ground that 'no miscarriage of justice has actually occurred'. These grounds, with their various aspects, were thought to be in need of reform by the Runciman Committee. In accordance with their recommendation, section 2 of the Criminal Appeal Act 1995 substituted a single, more flexible, test: that the Court of Appeal is to allow an appeal against conviction 'if they think that the conviction is unsafe'.[159]

As has been noted, the decision whether or not to hold a phase of a trial *in camera* may be the subject of a *voir dire* examination. However, there appears to be no reported English case in which the exclusion of the public has formed the basis of an appeal against conviction on indictment. The nearest guidance that is available is to be found in the judgment of the Court of Appeal in the *X, Y and Z* case. The deployment of the screen in that case carried a clear risk of prejudice to the accused. The prejudicial impact of shutting off the courtroom from the outside world—whether for complete phases of the trial or during the giving of testimony by a particular witness—is rather more difficult to perceive. Nevertheless, to refuse to grant appellate redress for an erroneous decision to hold part of the trial in secret would appear inconsistent with the great importance that has traditionally been attached to observing the standard of open justice. Of the three headings under which appellate redress could have been obtained under the pre-1995 law, it appears that the phrase 'material irregularity' was most suited to describing the error in question.

[158] Criminal Appeal Act 1968, s 2(1).   [159] Criminal Appeal Act 1995, s 2(1)(a).

Some support for the above conclusions is to be derived from the opinion given by the Judicial Committee of the Privy Council in *Mahlikilili Dhalamini v R*[160] on appeal from the High Court of Swaziland. The Swaziland High Court Proclamation 1938 required proceedings, in the familiar phrase, to take place 'in open court'. At the murder trial in question the administrative officers and native assessors (who sat to aid and assist the judge) had communicated their opinions to the judge in private.[161] Notwithstanding the fact that the decision-taking power was vested in the judge alone, the giving of opinions by the lay members of the court was construed as part of the proceedings of the High Court. It should therefore have taken place 'in open court'. The case, it must be noted, does not furnish a straightforward example of the exclusion of the public. Rather, it concerned the denial of access, both to the public and to the accused, to the lay members' opinions. The fact that they were denied to the accused should be borne in mind as the primary consideration when assessing the following pronouncement of the Judicial Committee on the consequences of the irregularity:

In this country the omission would be a fatal flaw entitling a convicted criminal to have the conviction set aside ... Prima facie, the failure to hold the whole of the proceedings in public must amount to such a disregard of the forms of justice as to lead to substantial and grave injustice within the rule adopted by this Board in dealing with criminal appeals. There may, no doubt, be cases where the guilt of the accused is so apparent that in spite of the disregard of this essential need for publicity this Board would not consider it right to grant leave to appeal.[162]

In some circumstances judicial review provides an alternative means of checking improper secrecy in the conduct of the trial. There are two grounds of challenge that are particularly relevant in the context: procedural ultra vires and breach of natural justice. These will be examined in turn. Some consideration will then be given to the status of judicial decrees that emanate from hearings that are found defective in this way.

When a court derives its jurisdiction from statute, there will be a certain amount of detail in the statute to regulate the composition of the court, the manner of its sitting, and so on. If any such procedural requirements are disregarded, what are the consequences for the ruling of the court?

This question raises a specific instance of a general problem that is familiar to administrative lawyers. The answer that they supply turns on the issue of

---

[160] [1942] AC 583.

[161] There was a suggestion that, when required to give their opinions in public, the native assessors might be constrained to pronounce in favour of the accused, whereas in the privacy of the judge's chambers a more independent line might be taken by them. In so far as this reasoning was advanced in favour of the course of conduct adopted at the trial it was rejected by the Judicial Committee as not providing a reason for departing from the plain words of the proclamation: ibid. 589.

[162] ibid. 590.

whether the statutory requirements are to be classified as 'mandatory' or 'directory'.[163] If the former, the failure to comply will render the ensuing decision invalid. If the latter, such failure will be classified as an irregularity that does not affect the validity of what has been done. Various guidelines have been devised by the courts to determine the category to which particular procedural stipulations are to be assigned. A factor that would tell in favour of mandatory importance is the far-reaching effect upon individuals' rights of the exercise of the power in question. On the other hand, if no substantial prejudice is caused in this regard, if the deviation from the required procedure is of a trivial nature, or if serious inconvenience would be caused to the public by a ruling that the requirements are of mandatory status, they will be found to be of directory importance only.

How, then, is a statutory requirement that proceedings are to take place 'in open court' to be classified? In view of the overriding importance that has been attached to the norm of open justice, the phrase should be interpreted as importing a mandatory requirement. This conclusion has some support in the case law. In *Kenyon v Eastwood*,[164] it will be recalled, without any discussion of the mandatory–directory dichotomy it was held that an order for committal that was not made in 'court' was invalid.

Are statutory requirements that, on the contrary, require seclusion in court proceedings to be treated on an identical basis? Mention has already been made of section 47(2) of the Children and Young Persons Act 1933, with its requirement that juvenile courts (as they were then known) shall sit 'either in a different building or room from that in which sittings of courts other than juvenile courts are held'. In *R v Southwark Juvenile Court, ex p J*,[165] unusually for the type of case in question, the complaint was based on unauthorized exclusion from, rather than improper admittance to, the courtroom. The juvenile's social worker had been excluded from the court during the hearing (though she was allowed, after his conviction, to present a report on him before sentence was passed). The exclusion was successfully challenged in the Divisional Court on the ground that the social worker had been entitled to attend as a person 'directly concerned' in the case within the meaning of section 47(2) of the 1933 Act. The provision was held to be of directory importance only and the violation of its terms did not go to the jurisdiction of the court. Certiorari was nevertheless granted to quash the justices' determination, since 'any fair-minded person who happened to be present at the court at the time and who had seen that [the social worker] was excluded from entering the court during the course of the proceedings might well have come to the conclusion . . . that justice was not seen to be done'.[166]

---

[163] See generally S. A. de Smith, H. Woolf, and J. Jowell, *Judicial Review of Administrative Action* (5th edn, 1995), 265–74.

[164] (1888) 57 LJ QB 455. [165] [1973] 1 WLR 1300.

[166] [1973] 1 WLR 1300, 1303.

In this passage we see once again the idea that there is a possible breach of natural justice when persons are denied entry to the courtroom.[167] Unfortunately, the treatment of both this and the procedural ultra vires point in the case is extremely cursory. Some general observations are in order. Procedural ultra vires is available quite generally as a weapon with which to attack *any* deviation from the requirements of statute irrespective of whether it leads to improper exclusion or improper admission in relation to the courtroom. Breach of natural justice, by contrast, is appropriate only as a possible description of a situation in which persons have been improperly *excluded* from the place of trial. The litigant or accused who has a right to have his case heard in private suffers an undoubted wrong if unauthorized personnel are admitted to the courtroom. The resulting invasion of his privacy, however, is not capable of being captured by even the widest conceptions of natural justice.

There is a further point of comparison to be drawn between the two lines of attack. We have seen that, in the application of the various tests for procedural vires, there is a certain degree of flexibility. By categorizing compliance with the stipulated procedure as of directory importance only, a violation of the procedure does not result in invalidation of the outcome of the trial (or other process under review). If, in contrast, it is breach of natural justice that forms the basis of the challenge, what consequences flow from the finding of a violation? As with issues of procedural vires, it is only possible to extrapolate from the general corpus of administrative law.

There are indications in that corpus that failure to conform to the demands of natural justice will not, in all instances, lead to the conclusion that the ensuing decision is invalid.[168] The 'right to a hearing' aspect of natural justice lends itself particularly to such a flexible approach. Take the standard instance of an application for a licence. If the failure of natural justice, so the argument runs, caused no real prejudice to the applicant (because even a properly conducted hearing would still have resulted in the rejection of his application for the licence), a remedy will not be granted by the courts for what can only be regarded as an error of form. This approach has been cogently criticized on a number of counts.[169] It can only be a matter for speculation whether or not, with the advantage of a properly conducted hearing, there would have been an adverse outcome for the person whose rights were determined by the decision. Any judicial endorsement of laxness in this area, moreover, would send out a clear message to tribunals and other such bodies that there need not be scrupulous regard for procedural standards in those cases where the 'correct' outcome is 'obvious'.[170] Finally, as ever, account must be taken of the maxim that justice must not only be done, it must also be seen to be done.

---

[167] Recall the discussion of this point in Chapter 2, section 1, above.
[168] See P. Cane, *An Introduction to Administrative Law* (3rd edn, 1996) 181–2 and 190–1.
[169] D. H. Clark, 'Natural Justice: Substance and Shadow' (1975) PL 27.
[170] Cane (n 168 above) 182.

These arguments vary in force when transposed to the subject of open justice. On the one hand, it is unlikely that the outcome of a trial would differ according to whether or not a particular phase of the proceedings had been held in private or in public. The possibility that, say, a dishonest witness will be motivated to give truthful testimony once the doors of the courtroom are thrown open to the press and public will surely be quite small compared with—to take once again the standard fare of natural justice litigation in administrative law—the chances of an applicant for a discretionary licence succeeding in convincing a tribunal of the merits of his case once he is permitted to cross-examine adverse witnesses. On the other hand, the recital of the right to open trial in catalogues of human rights powerfully suggests that open trial is to be valued in itself, not merely as a means of advancing some other value.

It would be useful to take stock at this point. Assume that there has been a defective hearing of a trial, in that part or the whole of the proceedings improperly took place *in camera*. If the validity of the outcome is challenged in subsequent litigation, the court that hears the challenge might pursue either of two courses. It might, for a number of reasons, condone the error. It may be persuaded that the form of the hearing made no difference to the outcome or, again, that the error related only to an inconsequential aspect of the trial. Or it might be swayed by evidence that no member of the public or press was actually denied entry to the courtroom or was even deterred from seeking permission to do so— in short, that the 'outcome' from the point of view of the number of spectators would have been no different. Alternatively, the court may conclude that the *in camera* phase in the earlier proceedings in some way vitiates the outcome of the case. The latter conclusion raises, in turn, the question of how far the taint of invalidity extends. The authorities on this point are sparse.

For this purpose it is necessary to return to *McPherson v McPherson*.[171] Earlier in this chapter, that case was explored up to the point where the Judicial Committee had pronounced the proceeding defective as not having taken place in open court. It did not go on to consider whether, in the absence of the failing, any persons would have availed themselves of the right to attend, or indeed whether or not the divorce decree would still have been granted. The Judicial Committee, therefore, proceeded directly to the next issue: the consequences for the validity of the decree. The two options available were to pronounce the tainted outcome either 'void' or merely 'voidable'. The decision went in favour of the latter, but with the rider that 'the time for avoiding [the decree] has long gone by'.[172] Counsel for Mrs McPherson forcefully, but unsuccessfully, advanced the argument that the decree was void. When invited to distinguish the leading case on natural justice, *Dimes v Proprietors of the Grand Junction Canal*[173] (where the financial interest of the Lord Chancellor in the case rendered his decision voidable), he submitted that the decree in the instant case con-

---

[171] [1936] AC 177.   [172] ibid. 203.   [173] (1852) 3 H L Cas 759, 10 ER 301.

cerned, not mere property (as in the *Dimes* case), but 'questions of status in which the public was interested'.[174] The Judicial Committee was willing to leave open the possibility that the term 'void' might be entirely appropriate to characterize the consequences of 'a travesty of judicial proceedings—a mere stage trial'.[175] The present case did not fall into that category, and consequently to pronounce the decree void would be a 'remedy . . . far worse than the disease it was designed to cure'.[176]

It is necessary to refer to *Scott v Scott* once again. The Judicial Committee stated that the decree of nullity pronounced in that suit (as in so many others) remained standing 'on the files of the Court intact'[177] despite the firmly held view of the House of Lords that to hold such suits *in camera* was entirely incorrect. The error in the mode of hearing of the *Scott* case resulted, therefore, in an outcome that was valid: Mr and Mrs Scott were no longer married to each other. At the same time, because the proceedings should not have been heard in private, Mrs Scott and her solicitor could not be judged to be in contempt of court by disclosing the contents of the *in camera* hearing.

There remain a number of difficulties here. There would seem to be a contradiction in the idea that a judicial decree, in *Scott v Scott* a decree of nullity, may be valid despite the presence of a fundamental error in the manner in which the proceedings were conducted. One possible explanation would be to treat the *in camera* order as distinct from the outcome of the trial itself. Yet a hearing that is improperly closed to the public is defective. In view of the overriding importance that is attached to open justice, the result should on principle be open to challenge in the courts. There are, as has been seen, two possible descriptions of the defective decree. The result could be described as 'void' (that is, totally without legal effect) or as 'voidable' (as possessing legal validity until such time, if ever, as it is successfully impugned). As the *Scott* case illustrates, the courts are reluctant to treat a judicial decree as totally ineffective. If the issue arises for litigation years later, there is a danger that—as could easily happen in matrimonial cases—new legal relationships will have been contracted on the basis of the defective judgment of the court.

Often it is not even to the parties' own advantage to raise points concerning the improper exclusion of the public from the trial, since they will share a common interest in maintaining the confidentiality of the proceedings. Certainly, the losing party may capitalize on such faults in the procedure in order to invalidate the outcome and thereby secure an opportunity to relitigate the case. That situation apart, the parties often lack a direct interest in the admission of the public. In order, therefore, to secure the effective monitoring of the standards of open justice, it has proved necessary to grant powers of challenge to persons who, though not themselves parties to the proceedings, nevertheless have a keen

---

[174] [1936] AC 177, 204.   [175] ibid. 203.
[176] ibid. 204.   [177] ibid. 205.

interest in the maintenance of those standards. It is the media who, almost invariably, fulfil that role.

C. Challenge by a Non-Party

The central provision, in this context, is the power conferred by section 159 of the Criminal Justice Act 1988. This created a right of appeal to the Court of Appeal, if it should grant leave to do so, against three categories of order that might be made by the Crown Court:

(a) an order under section 4 or 11 of the Contempt of Court Act 1981 made in relation to a trial on indictment;

(b) any order restricting the access of the public to the whole or any part of a trial on indictment or to any proceedings ancillary to such a trial; and

(c) any order restricting the publication of any report of the whole or any part of a trial on indictment or any such ancillary proceedings; . . .

As the Solicitor-General explained in presenting the relevant clause in Parliament,[178] the new procedure was being introduced in order to comply with obligations under the European Convention on Human Rights. Its scope was confined to trials on indictment. Moreover, it would apply only to trials in which the judge made an order imposing secrecy. It would, therefore, have no application to cases (most typically, prosecutions for rape with their feature of complainant anonymity) where there exists a statutory norm of secrecy—albeit one that could be waived by a judge in the exceptional circumstances of the case before him.[179] The procedure would function by way of appeal, rather than by way of judicial review, so as to preclude debate as to whether or not errors of law were juridictional or not.

The decision of the Court of Appeal is stipulated to be 'final'.[180] It would appear that there is no further appeal, whether on the merits of the appeal, or even on the preliminary decision of the Court of Appeal whether or not to grant leave. The new procedure, inevitably, had to strike a balance between two pressing interests. If challenges lodged under section 159 were to wait their place in the ordinary queue of litigation, the eventual hearing of the challenge might well take on a purely abstract nature. The trial that was subject to a measure of secrecy would probably have concluded. Alternatively, a reporting restriction that was still effective at the time of the hearing of the section 159 application would relate to a trial that was now 'stale news' as far as the media were concerned. On the other hand, any delay to the trial so as to allow a challenge to be argued under the section could be prejudicial to the interests of the accused (not

---

[178] *Hansard*, HC (series 6) vol 135, cols 607–619 (16 June 1988).

[179] For a detailed consideration of secrecy in the context of charges of rape and sexual assaults generally, see Chapter 5, section 4, B, below.

[180] Criminal Justice Act 1988, s 159(1).

to mention the disruption to other persons involved in the trial).[181] The compromise solution was to expedite appeals, but to permit appeal only as far as the Court of Appeal.

The right of appeal is granted in broad terms to any 'person aggrieved'. It was accepted by the Solicitor-General that the media would qualify in this respect. However, it is not confined to them. In *R v Salih; re section 159 of the Criminal Justice Act 1988*[182] the provision was invoked by the accused himself. Basing his defence on a plea of duress, he applied unsuccessfully to the trial judge to have the defence case, at least, heard *in camera*. The Court of Appeal rejected the appeal under section 159, declining jurisdiction on the particular facts. However, it does not appear to have questioned the applicant's standing to bring the case as both defendant and potential witness. The proceedings in the *Salih* case, certainly, were an attempt to invert the purpose for which section 159 was designed. Far from challenging an order that imposed secrecy, Salih was attempting to gain redress against insistence on the open conduct of the proceedings.

The extraordinary nature of section 159 derives from several factors. Consider the typical situation at which the provision was directed. In a trial on indictment the judge wrongfully excludes the public from part of the hearing or wrongfully imposes secrecy on aspects of a trial that is otherwise open to the public. In the event of a conviction, it is unlikely that any of these errors would furnish the accused with grounds for challenging the outcome of the trial. More significantly, even if such grounds were to exist, in many a case the accused would deem it disadvantageous to pursue any channel of redress. The *Salih* application is but one instance of cases where the balance of the accused's interest lies in favour of secrecy. Hence the need for the creation of a ground of appeal in the body that undoubtedly does have the keenest interest in open justice: the media.

4. A JURISPRUDENTIAL POSTSCRIPT: DOES THE ACCUSED HAVE A RIGHT TO A PUBLIC TRIAL?

One of the themes which runs through this work is that many of the requirements of open justice will inevitably prejudice important interests of the accused. The presence of the public and the press at the trial will often result in increased stress for the accused, the invasion of his privacy, and damage to his reputation. Consequently, in most conceivable situations he will have no wish to secure the scrupulous observance of the rules which permit public and media access to the proceedings. Other interested parties, therefore, need to be given

---

[181] The power to order a delay in the trial on indictment is expressly granted to the Court of Appeal: Criminal Justice Act 1988, s 159(5)(a).

[182] *The Times*, 31 December 1994.

the means to challenge the improper exclusion of the public and press. It was in the light of these considerations that section 159 of the Criminal Justice Act 1988 was enacted.

As was seen in Chapter 1, many of the leading human rights documents proclaim that the accused has a fundamental *right* to a public trial. The purpose of the present section is to question the intelligibility of such a notion. A consideration of this 'right' in the context of the two principal theories of rights—the 'will theory' (sometimes known as the 'choice theory') and the 'interest theory' (also called the 'benefit theory')—reveals a number of difficulties.[183]

Public trial, perhaps uniquely among arrangements secured in human rights documents, is not typically preferred by those entitled to it. Many of those who are wicked or unfortunate enough to be facing criminal charges, including those who secure an acquittal, would opt to avoid the stress and ignominy of publicity. They would do so even at the cost of eliminating the possibility—and, in all but a minority of cases, it must surely be a remote possibility—that the publicity might lead (for example) to the discovery of an additional witness who would be able to testify in his favour. This weighing of comparative advantage gains added poignancy in regard to the trial of certain offences which, within the overall framework of the criminal law, are not especially serious. The disgrace that attaches to the charges, however, is such that the damage inflicted on the accused by public knowledge of the proceedings is totally disproportionate to even the maximum sentence allowed by law for the offence.

Yet the accused is given a public trial whether he wants one or not. He has no option in the matter. Now according to the will theory, 'a right exists when the necessary and sufficient condition, of imposing or relaxing the constraint on some person's conduct, is another person's choice to that effect'.[184] But the only element of choice that is accorded to the accused is whether or not to pursue such remedy as the law grants him *if* the conduct of his trial has not complied with the standards of open access. He possesses no *ex ante* power of waiver over his 'right' to be tried in public. This last point is most clearly borne out by a comparison with civil cases, where (as already noted in Chapter 2, section 7) the parties are generally free to refer their dispute to arbitration with its concomitant feature of confidentiality of the proceedings.

The will theory identifies the right-holder as the person who possesses the power to enforce or waive compliance with a duty—the duty, in the case under consideration, to hold trials in public. Who is so placed in the instance of public trial? Under the present position in English law, both the accused and persons aggrieved (by virtue of section 159 of the Criminal Justice Act 1988) possess such a right. Against such a background each may choose to exercise the 'right' in different ways. Typically, the accused will forego redress, while

---

[183] See H. Steiner, *An Essay on Rights* (1994), 57–73, for an account of the two theories of rights, culminating in a defence of the will theory.

[184] ibid. 57–8.

the aggrieved persons (most usually the media) will exercise their right of challenge under section 159. This poses a particular difficulty for the will theory, since most accounts of it are phrased in terms of the right-holder possessing the *exclusive* power of waiver or enforcement over the performance of the relevant duty.

Does the interest theory provide a better explanation of the right to public trial?

According to the interest theory, the right-holder is the person who is intended to benefit from the imposing on others of a duty—the duty, in the present instance, to hold trials in public. The essence of the interest theory is that two elements must be identified in regard to any putative right if the theory is not to lapse into incoherence. Not only must the arrangements that consitute the right be *beneficial*, they must also be beneficial *to the putative right-holder*. It is necessary to examine each of these elements in turn.

It would be fair to say that supporters of the interest theory have not devoted much attention to the question of what truly benefits a person or advances his interests. MacCormick touches on the subject in the course of a paper which is considered to be one of the leading statements of the interest theory position:

It is not necessarily the case that each individual acquiring a right under the law should experience it as a benefit, an advantage, an advancement or protection of his interests. Perhaps there are some people who have been more harmed than benefited by an inheritance.[185] Perhaps in some cases property inherited—e.g. slum properties subject to statutory tenancies at controlled rents—are literally more trouble than they are worth, and, besides, something of an embarrassment to their proprietor. None of that is in any way inconsistent with the proposition that the function of the law is to confer what is considered to be normally an advantage on a certain class by granting to each of its members a certain legal right.[186]

It is, of course, part of the human condition that things which one has desired, or even craved, may not prove ultimately to be beneficial or serve one's true interests. But it is not open to advocates of the interest theory to remain agnostic on the matter of benefit without falling into incoherence. Hence MacCormick's designation of the category of 'what is considered to be normally an advantage'. Yet it is doubtful whether public trial meets even this threshold level. Probably it will only be those who have committed crimes for reasons of civil disobedience who will welcome, as a benefit, the publicity that accompanies the trial proceedings. Moreover, there is reason to question whether public trial is beneficial to the accused in an objective sense. As will be seen in Chapter 5, in common with most civilized systems English law stipulates various degrees of confidentiality in regard to the trial of juveniles. And, within such systems,

---

[185] The passage that immediately preceded this quotation had taken, by way of example, the rights and duties of various persons in a situation of intestate succession to property.

[186] N. MacCormick 'Rights in legislation' in P. M. S. Hacker and J. Raz (ed), *Law, Morality and Society: Essays in Honour of H.L.A. Hart* (1977) 202.

the legal provisions pertaining to children tend to be shaped by an overriding concern for the welfare of the child.

Certainly, every person who is prosecuted has an interest in receiving a trial that is fair: that is, a trial which does not unreasonably expose him to the risk of wrongful conviction. The difficulty is to make sense of the idea of a right to a trial that is public, not simply one that is fair. The most plausible explanation that the interest theory could offer is that the former is invariably guaranteed as the best means of securing the latter. Such an explanation would come at some cost, however. For, in reducing public trial to a merely instrumental position, it would throw into doubt the legitimacy of its inclusion within any catalogue of rights that are supposedly fundamental. Nevertheless, it is the question of the status of public trial as a right, and not the specific issue of its standing as a fundamental right, that has been raised here. Is the explanation that could be proffered by the interest theory, then, entirely convincing?

A principal difficulty that this explanation would encounter is that many human rights documents proclaim the right to a *public* trial. Sometimes, as in the Sixth Amendment to the US Constitution, the right to a public trial is proclaimed independently. More often, however, it is asserted on an equal and independent footing alongside the right to a fair trial.[187] In both situations public trial is being treated as an independent, non-derivative, item in the rights of the accused. Indeed, if it were the fairness of the criminal trial that formed the overriding concern, the approach that would be expected would be the declaration of that value and the protection, by implication, of those arrangements deemed necessary to secure it.[188]

Even if publicity is seen purely as a means to achieve fairness, there is cause to doubt whether there exists a sufficiently strong link between means and ends in this regard. If, throughout the course of history, secret trial has been a favoured weapon of dictatorships, so too has the show trial—the trial that forms the object of excessive, specifically directed, publicity. Even where the background political system could not be described as tyrannical, it is quite clear that the exposure of trial proceedings to an inordinate degree of publicity might have the effect of perverting the testimony of witnesses and the judgment of the court (in particular, by raising expectations of a particular verdict). Moreover, as with all questions of matching means to ends, changes in societal conditions may result in the loosening of a link which might once have been quite strong. As was pointed out in Chapter 2, many of the benefits claimed for public trial by Jeremy

[187] See, in particular, Art 6 (1) of the European Convention on Human Rights; s 11(d) of the Canadian Charter of Rights and Freedoms; Art 10 of the Universal Declaration of Human Rights, and Art 14(1) of the International Covenant on Civil and Political Rights.

[188] Human rights documents commonly specify particular rights of the accused: e.g. the right to the assistance of counsel, the right to cross-examine hostile witnesses. But, in so doing, they are not stating what arrangements are instrumentally related to a fair trial: they are spelling out, though not necessarily in an exhaustive list, what are deemed to be the integral elements of such a trial.

Bentham are achieved today by other means: the peer opinion of fellow judges, routine appeals for witnesses, and the development of legal machinery to challenge faulty verdicts.

The second element in the interest theory analysis focuses on the identification of the putative right-holder. The interest theory cannot simply categorize an alleged right, such as public trial, as beneficial in the abstract: it must be designated as beneficial to a particular person or persons. Who, then, are the intended beneficiaries of public trial? The answer supplied by the human rights documents would appear to be: those who face criminal charges. Yet the traditional justifications—the identification of further witnesses, the rendering of truthful testimony on the part of such witnesses as are already present before the court, the checking of any tendency towards judicial bias—could work to the advantage or disadvantage of the accused. Whether they do so or not involves an inquiry at two distinct levels. First, will any additional witnesses emerging as a result of trial publicity, for instance, testify for or against the accused? Would the judicial bias that is held in check by public scrutiny have worked in his favour or against him? Secondly, where—in any event—does the interest of the accused lie? In favour of an acquittal, irrespective of whether he is guilty or not? Or in favour of the application of due process, the ascertainment of the truth, and, if he is guilty, in his submitting to the punishment pronounced by the court?

A public trial may serve the interests of either the accused or the prosecution in any particular case, if those interests are defined in the narrow sense of securing the desired verdict at the conclusion of the proceedings. Its neutral role in this regard suggests that the true value served by open trial is the proper functioning of the criminal courts as part of the machinery of the state. Indeed, as seen in Chapter 2, some proffered justifications of public trial take no account of the interests of the accused, however those interests might be perceived. Among such utilitarian considerations are, for example, the facilitating of the observation by the public of the administration of justice and the reminding of would-be malefactors within the community of the unpleasant consequences of pursuing the path of crime.[189] Yet it would be absurd to claim that the right to public trial belongs to the public at large. In a very circumscribed sense it may properly be described as a right that inheres in those (of necessity) numerically insignificant members of the public who seek admission to a particular trial.

That the institution of public trial is perceived as an important means of advancing various communitarian goals, such as deterrence of crime and education of the public, is not in itself fatal to its status as a right. The exercise of several undoubted rights incidentally promotes communitarian goals. A good

---

[189] It is worth noting that trial by ordeal took place in public. Indeed, the presence of the public tended to incline the choice in favour of ordeals that rendered an immediate result (for example, trial by cold water, with immediate sinking or otherwise) as compared with trial by hot iron, with its three-day interval in which the hand was bound. See R. Bartlett, *Trial by Fire and Water: The Medieval Judicial Ordeal* (1986) 23.

example is provided by the right to freedom of speech. In addition to the rights-based argument that views freedom of speech as an aspect of self-fulfilment it is also defended, by John Stuart Mill,[190] as being conducive to the discovery of the truth and, by Alexander Meiklejohn,[191] as promoting the effective functioning of representative democracy.

In one regard the interest theory stands at an advantage as compared with its rival. Supporters of the will theory, as has been seen, appear to be embarrassed by the possibility of there being multiple holders of a particular right. The interest theory, in contrast, allows for the possibility that a number of persons or groups may benefit from the creation of a duty. At the same time, it does not slide into a view of rights that equates them with the pursuit of community goals. So, for example, advocates of the interest theory would see no difficulty in the claim that both the accused and the media benefit (if, indeed, the accused can be said to benefit) from the duty to hold trials in public. For the right-holder is the *intended* beneficiary, even though others will also derive incidental benefit. Who, in the case of public trial, is the intended beneficiary, and who merely derives incidental benefit? Even the notion of an 'intended' beneficiary is not free of ambiguity. Does it mean the person or persons with an eye to whose interests (whether real or supposed) the legal institution in question was originally designed? This approach would pose marked difficulties for public trials, since their original purposes were undoubtedly communitarian in nature (being motivated by considerations of deterrence and the need to investigate the circumstances of the crime in a public forum). Alternatively, irrespective of historical considerations, is the intended beneficiary the category of persons who benefit on the soundest possible rationale of the institution of public trial?

There are a number of difficulties, therefore, in applying the standard questions posed by the will and interest theories to the institution of public trial. It may consequently be analysed from two different standpoints. The one starts from the view that there undoubtedly exists a right to such a process. The failure, therefore, on the part of the will and interest theories to explain this right exposes inadequacies in those theories. On the alternative approach, it is not to be assumed that public trial is properly categorized in rights terms. The fact that neither of the two rights theories can give an adequate account of public trial adds weight to the argument that the idea of a *right* to public trial is unintelligible. However valuable the open conduct of trials may be, it can be explained in terms other than those of rights.

From a historical point of view the guarantees of public trial, together with other procedural rights of the accused, were promulgated in the context of the

---

[190] J. S. Mill, *On Liberty* (1859) ch 2.
[191] A. Meiklejohn, *Free Speech and its relation to self-government*, in *Political freedom: the constitutional powers of the people* (1965).

trial of political offences.[192] In that regard the guarantees will have acted as a safeguard of the accused against oppression by government. However, the standard of publicity applies to all trials: to charges of shoplifting as much as to those of sedition. On reflection, there is something strange in the idea of a 'right' to a process where the accused has no element of choice as to whether or not it is followed and, in most conceivable modern situations, the process will damage interests that are no less important to the accused than his interest in avoiding wrongful conviction. Although the right to public trial is one that is frequently proclaimed in human rights documents, scrutiny in the light of the principal theories of rights reveals that the idea is simply incoherent.

---

[192] See the guarantees set out in the Trial of Treasons Act 1696. According to s 2, in particular, a person could not be convicted except on the testimony of two witnesses 'unlesse the Party indicted and arraigned or tryed shall willingly without violence and in open Court confesse the same . . .'

4

Issues Relating to Security

1. INTRODUCTION

This, together with the following two chapters, applies the principles that have been set out in Chapters 1 to 3 to several areas of substantive law. It is necessary, at the outset, to explain in a little more detail the precise scope of the present chapter. The idea of 'security', especially as used in the phrase 'national security', encompasses the protection of the most fundamental institutions of the state from the threat of being undermined by its enemies, whether they be situated within or beyond the country's borders. The substantial part of the chapter, in this way, will be devoted to the traditional concerns of national security: the exercise of wartime emergency powers, the deployment of the armed forces, matters relating to defence and the intelligence services, and so forth.

However, the courts, too, form part of the machinery of the government (in the broader sense of that term). This is clearly borne out by the fact that courts, no less than locations such as army barracks or police stations, are at risk of being the object of terrorist attacks. Indeed, the danger is all the greater since, with the exception of the legislature, courts are unique among 'government' buildings in conceding a presumptive, undifferentiated right of access to members of the public. Apart from their vulnerability to attack as manifestations of governmental authority, the courts also run the risk of being the scene of public disorder. The accused in the more serious criminal cases could exploit the temporary removal to the less strictly controlled environment of the courthouse to attempt escape. Courts are also vulnerable to outbreaks of disorder merely by reason of being places where emotions typically run high. Issues of court security, therefore, will be treated as an integral aspect of the present chapter and will be considered in section 2.

The functioning of the courts may be undermined, not simply by direct and violent assault, but also by way of interference with the *personae* of the proceedings. Those most vulnerable in this respect are witnesses and jurors, the interference being sometimes by way of financial inducement but more often by way of physical threat. The dangers to the integrity of court proceedings which are posed by such conduct are, of course, no less considerable for the threats being made covertly and (in many cases) at some distance removed from the location of the courtroom. Equally, there are persons whose position is such that, even in the absence of a specific threat, their testifying in open court exposes them to the danger of reprisal,

combined—in some instances—with the inability to perform effectively their former duties once their identities are revealed. Persons in this category would typically comprise police informers and members of the intelligence gathering services.
It is in the consideration of the latter group that the connection between witness
protection and national security issues, as they are traditionally understood,
emerges most clearly. Section 3 of the present chapter will examine in general terms
the conflict between the demands of open justice and the problems of securing witnesses against the threat of violence.

The specific issues relating to juror protection, it should be noted, will be
deferred to Chapter 7. Although very similar problems are posed by the phenom-
ena of witness and juror intimidation, it will become apparent in that chapter
that it is not possible effectively to separate matters of juror protection from
wider matters that govern the status of the jury verdict.

2. THE PHYSICAL SECURITY OF THE COURTROOM

The physical security of the courtroom has traditionally been protected by the
power of the judge to punish for contempt committed in the face of the court.
This long-standing jurisdiction has been the subject of criticism. It is claimed,
quite reasonably, that the very judge whose court has been disrupted is least fitted of all to try the issues of liability and punishment. On the other hand, such a
judge will have the advantage of having personally witnessed the disruptive conduct. Moreover, the fact of immediate punishment will act as a more powerful
deterrent of unruly behaviour than any punishment that is meted out after a regular trial of the offenders conducted several months after the events. The merits
and demerits of the present arrangements are not our immediate concern.
However, they do have an incidental consequence that is relevant to our subject.
If the punishment that is inflicted is one that involves confinement to prison, the
culprit is necessarily removed forthwith from the courtroom.

It is quite clear, in addition, that preventive measures may be taken in anticip-
ation of possible disruption. In *Scott v Scott* itself Earl Loreburn stated this need
as a well-established exception to the rule of public access:

Again, the Court may be closed or cleared if such a precaution is necessary for the administration of justice. Tumult or disorder, or the just apprehension of it, would certainly justify the exclusion of all from whom such interruption is expected, and, if discrimination is
impracticable, the exclusion of the public in general.[1]

This power has been substantially reinforced by sections 76 to 78 of the
Criminal Justice Act 1991. In regard to each petty sessions area there may be

---

[1] [1913] AC 417, 445–446. For a statement to the same effect see the then Home Secretary's comment with approval on the ruling in *Re the Sheriff of Surrey* (1860) 2 F and F 236, 240; 175 ER 1039,
1041.

appointed 'court security officers . . ., that is to say, persons whose duty it is to maintain order in any court-house to which they are for the time being assigned . . .'[2] Such officers are invested with the power 'to search any person who is in or is seeking to enter the court-house, and any article in the possession of such a person'.[3] The power of search, in stark contrast to the great majority of police powers, is not premised on any form of 'reasonable suspicion' or 'reasonable cause to suspect'. The only exception in this regard is that the surrender of an article as the condition of entry into the court-house may be required only if the officer 'reasonably believes [it] may jeopardise the maintenance of order in the court-house'.[4] That apart, these provisions dispense even with the need for such officer to demonstrate a subjective state of suspicion, no matter how unreasonable.

Submission to the exercise of powers cast in such wide terms, in short, is a condition of access to the place of trial. The provisions apply equally to both the *personae* of trials being conducted in the court building and to members of the public and representatives of the press. Refusal to submit to a search is, in itself, a valid reason for denial of a right of entry to the building.[5] Court security officers are required to act 'in the execution of [their] duty'.[6] However, in this regard they are unlike police officers in that they do not possess an original jurisdiction whereby they are answerable only to the law. On the contrary, when acting in the execution of his duty a court security officer is required to comply with 'any general or specific instructions which have been given to him . . . by a person in authority'.[7] And, as is to be expected, the persons designated by the statute as being in authority for this purpose are, primarily, 'a justice of the peace, chief clerk or justices' clerk who is exercising any functions in the court-house'.[8]

The provisions were enacted as a consequence of the withdrawal of the police from the task of providing security in the magistrates' courts. The resulting gap may be filled by the appropriate magistrates' court committee, whether by directly employing persons as court security officers or by contracting with others to provide such service.

In those courts where regular police officers bear the burden of maintaining order, the officers will rely on their powers, both statutory and at common law, to prevent or suppress a breach of the peace. The extent of those powers in so far as they have a bearing on court security was clarified in *McConnell v Chief Constable of Greater Manchester Police*.[9] Prior to that ruling there was some doubt as to whether or not a breach of the peace (for the purpose of falling within the scope of the common law power of a constable to arrest without a warrant) could take place on private premises. This could have had a bearing on the powers of the police to remove disruptive spectators from the public seats of a trial. Was the status of the location to be determined by whether the court buildings are

[2] Criminal Justice Act 1991, s 76(1)(a). [3] Criminal Justice Act 1991, s 77(1)(a).
[4] Criminal Justice Act 1991, s 77(1)(b). [5] Criminal Justice Act 1991, s 77(1)(b).
[6] Criminal Justice Act 1991, s 77(1). [7] Criminal Justice Act 1991, s 77(4).
[8] Criminal Justice Act 1991, s 77(5)(a). [9] [1990] 1 WLR 364.

to be considered private property (albeit in the ownership of government) or public property (that is, irrespective of where the legal title to the land is located, by the fact of public access)? The ruling of the Court of Appeal disposes of such difficulties in stating that the constable's power of arrest extends even to breaches of the peace that take place on private premises.

We have already referred to the situation where a member of the public is forcibly excluded from the courtroom as a context in which the limits of the open justice rule could be explored. Tort actions have traditionally provided the context in which the boundaries of many a 'constitutional' right at common law have been determined. Typically, a private individual is subjected to a degree of coercion, however minimal, by a public official. The individual thereupon brings an action in tort, in the course of which the exact limits of the official's powers are necessarily determined by the court. In fact, the situation in which the individual is removed from the court by an official entrusted with the task of maintaining court security has greater potential than most situations for raising the relevant issues. The expulsion of a person already located within the courtroom (in contrast to a denial of entry in the first place), combined with the type of conduct which led to his exclusion, will typically require the use of some force, and at a level that is more than the technical minimum of which the law of tort would take cognizance.

In any tort action that is brought primarily with a view to obtaining compensation for a battery, and only secondarily (if at all) in order to clarify the extent of the exceptions to open justice, there could be problems of identifying the focus of liability. There will be situations where the presiding judicial officer himself takes part in expelling the plaintiff from the courtroom. This is unusual, but the coroner did so act in *Garnett v Ferrand*.[10] In these circumstances any claim for compensation will be defeated by the immunity conferred on the judge of a court of record. Such immunity applies to actions taken in his judicial capacity. More usually nowadays a multitude of tasks, whether relating to security or the general running of the courts, will be discharged by court staff under the general direction of the judiciary.[11] Vicarious liability for tortious exclusion of persons from the courtroom will be borne by their employers (for example, the local police authority in the case of police officers) in accordance with the usual principles of such liability.

At the outset of this work we identified, as one of the elements of open justice, the fundamental idea that the accused has a stronger claim than anyone else to be present at his own trial. Yet in addition to the possibility of disruptive behaviour on his part, his presence at the trial raises a further dimension to the security

---

[10] (1827) 6 B&C 611, 108 ER 576.

[11] See, for example, *Islington London Borough Council v Harridge* The Times, 30 June 1993, in which the Court of Appeal issued a caution to court officials against turning away persons seeking to make an application (in that case, a solicitor seeking an emergency order) 'unless they had the authority of a judge or district judge to do so'.

problem: the danger that he will take advantage of his temporary removal from a remand centre to escape from legal custody. As we have seen, these dangers are such that they have crucially shaped certain proposals for the trial of alleged offences committed while the accused is serving a prison sentence.[12] In the usual courtroom setting an enhanced degree of security may be achieved by an increased police presence, with or without arms, in the precincts of the court. As for the confinement of the accused to the dock, that long-standing feature of the English trial on indictment is thought to add little (if anything) to the security needs of the courtroom,[13] while acting as an impediment to a full view from the public seats.[14] The Runciman Committee was not persuaded on the security point, believing that the dock performed a useful role in that regard and preferring its retention to the alternative possibility of deploying armed police officers in the courtroom.[15]

Disruption of court proceedings by the accused, even where there is no risk of escape from legal custody, raises problems that are all the more acute since, clearly, the interest of the accused in attending his own trial is greater than that of any casual member of the public in observing the proceedings. Sometimes, as with the notorious Chicago Conspiracy trial of 1969–70,[16] the defendant's disruptions are by way of protest against the legitimacy of the tribunal's claim to try him.[17] It is quite clear that a power to exclude the defendant does exist at common law, although the statements on the subject by Stephen[18] indicate that a greater measure of need is required to justify such a step than that required to exclude any member of the public for the same cause. And, by way of mitigation of the effects of exclusion, modern technology would permit the relay to him, at second hand, of the events in the courtroom. In the usual situation where the disruptive defendant is represented by a lawyer, there exist means by which the trial may be continued without toleration of his conduct. More problematic is the case where such a defendant has exercised his right to represent himself. If such a person were to be excluded from the courtroom, in effect he would thenceforth be unrepresented. By way of response to this problem, the Runciman Commission recommended that, if the judge thinks it appropriate, the defendant could continue to be represented by an *amicus curiae*.[19]

---

[12] See the discussion of the prison disciplinary system in Chapter 2, section 6, above.

[13] L. Rosen, 'The Dock—Should it be abolished?' (1966) 29 MLR 289, 299–300.

[14] ibid. 297: '. . . in many criminal courts the dock is a large structure which almost completely obstructs the view of the public and also makes it difficult to hear or follow the course of the trial'.

[15] The Royal Commission on Criminal Justice, Chairman—Viscount Runciman (Cm 2263, 1993) ch 8, para 109, and Recommendation No 261.

[16] Where one of the accused, Bobby Seale, was bound and gagged by way of response to the problem. The background to the case was anti-Vietnam War protests surrounding the Democratic Party national convention in 1969. See, among other accounts, J. Epstein, *The Great Conspiracy Trial: An Essay on Law, Liberty and the Constitution* (1970).

[17] See, generally, G. Zellick, 'The Criminal Trial and the Disruptive Defendant' (1980) 40 MLR 121 and 284 (in two parts).

[18] ibid. 285.   [19] Recommendation No 183.

As an alternative to expulsion from the courtroom there is, in the case of the accused, the possibility of physically restraining him to the extent necessary to allow proceedings to continue. The decision whether or not to place handcuffs on the accused is a matter for the court itself, not the police, to decide.[20] In order to justify this form of restraint, the prosecution must show reasonable grounds for suspecting either that the accused would be violent or that he would attempt escape. Evidence on either of these issues, being necessarily prejudicial to the accused, should be heard in the absence of the jury.[21]

3. SECURITY OF THE PROCEEDINGS: THE PROTECTION OF WITNESSES

At one level, the many problems that are caused for the integrity of the criminal justice system may be confronted by changes in the substantive law so as to render ever more serious the practice of the intimidation of witnesses. The pressure exerted by the law can be brought to bear at two different points, the witness and the intimidator.

Let us take, first of all, the position of the witness. It has long been established that the refusal of the witness to answer a question properly put by counsel may result in liability for contempt committed in the face of the court. The motive of the witness (whether fear or a principled refusal to disclose certain information such as the name of a source) is irrelevant. Where fear is the reason, clearly, we come close to touching the ground already covered in the last chapter, on the subject of the especially vulnerable or sensitive witness.[22] The law's response to the threatened witness has generally been to insist that he gives evidence as required. The reports are replete with cases where the courts have inflicted a custodial sentence on such witnesses.[23] On the other hand, the circumstances are such that the witness, at his own trial, may successfully invoke the defence of duress. In *R v Hudson, R v Taylor*[24] the defendants had been the principal prosecution witnesses against a person charged with wounding. Having changed their story (as a result of which the person so charged was acquitted) they were themselves tried for perjury. Apparently, they had been approached with threats of violence by a group of men, one of whom later turned up in the public gallery prior to their giving evidence on the wounding charges. The Court of Appeal allowed their appeal

---

[20] *R v Cambridge Justices and the Chief Constable of the Cambridgeshire Constabulary, ex p Peacock* [1993] Crim LR 219.

[21] In *R v Vratsides* [1988] Crim LR 251 the conviction was quashed since the reasons were heard in the presence of the jury, who in this way came to know of the accused's previous convictions. However, even if the jury were to remain in ignorance of the reasons for placing handcuffs on the accused, the very fact that he is so restrained would be capable of prejudicing his case. Ideally, in such cases he should be screened from the jury to the extent of concealing the handcuffs.

[22] In particular, Chapter 3, section 2, D.

[23] See, for example, *R v Leonard* (1984) 6 Cr App R (S) 279, and *R v Samuda* (1989) 11 Cr App R (S) 471.

[24] [1971] 2 QB 202.

against conviction for perjury (for which they were granted a conditional discharge for twelve months) and made a number of observations specific to the predicament of the intimidated witness. In particular, the threats to such a person would be no less compelling for the fact that the man in the public gallery would not be in a position to carry them out in the courtroom itself.[25] As for the prosecution argument that the witnesses should have sought police protection instead of giving way to the threat, the Court of Appeal ruled that whether such a course was reasonably available to a witness was an issue which should be left to the jury. After taking into account all relevant considerations, such as the age of the witness, the jury should be directed to decide whether or not the will of the witness had been overborne by reason of the threats.

To turn now to the position of the intimidator, again it has long been clear that at common law such a person is liable whether for threats issued before, or for revenge exacted after, the event. Such offences (contempt of court, perverting the course of justice)[26] have been supplemented by statutory provisions dealing specifically with witness protection. An early example was provided by the Witnesses (Public Inquiries) Protection Act 1892, which (as its name suggests) applies, not to courts, but to proceedings before a Royal Commission or any inquiry conducted by a committee of either House of Parliament.[27] This statute would have supplied an oblique precedent for section 51 of the Criminal Justice and Public Order Act 1994. This lengthy provision, without derogating in any way from the offences at common law that deal with the same mischief,[28] penalizes the intimidation of witnesses and jurors, potential witnesses and jurors, and any person who is (or has been) 'assisting in the investigation of an offence'. The precise details of the range of offences created by section 51 are not directly relevant to the present work. Our concern is the issues of witness intimidation solely in the framework of the norm of open justice. However, it is worth speculating whether or not liability under the section could arise merely by reason of the demeanour of the person seated in the public gallery of the courtroom. In the absence of any overt gesture or spoken word, could demeanour—or even mere presence in the public seats—amount to 'an act which intimidates, and is intended to intimidate'[29] a witness or juror? Moreover, although Earl Loreburn's statement in *Scott v Scott* (quoted in section 2, above) is clearly cast in terms of anticipated physical disorder in the courtroom, could this exception to the principle of open justice be extended to encompass physical intimidation of prosecution witnesses? If so, it would amount to a basis on which to exclude from the courtroom those very members of the public, the accused's associates and family, who have the keenest interest in observing the proceedings.

---

[25] ibid. 207. [26] *A-G v Butterworth* [1963] 1 QB 696.

[27] The Witnesses (Public Inquiries) Protection Act 1892, s 1, explicitly states that it does not apply to 'any inquiry by any court of justice'.

[28] Criminal Justice and Public Order Act 1994, s 51(11).

[29] Criminal Justice and Public Order Act 1994, s 51(1).

The terms of section 51 were supplemented a few years later, by section 54 of the Criminal Procedure and Investigations Act 1996. By way of response to the problems posed by both witness and juror intimidation, this provides a means of quashing an acquittal that has been reached as a consequence of interference with such persons. The provision, which operates (seemingly) by way of exception to the rule against double jeopardy, lays down a procedure for application to the High Court for invalidation of such acquittals. The details of the procedure, and the safeguards placed around it, are not our concern. Several points, nevertheless, are worthy of note. Above all, an important precondition of the use of the process is that a person has been convicted of an 'administration of justice offence' that involves proof of interference or intimidation. Yet, any person who has been frightened into silence in connection with testifying on another charge is very unlikely to prove co-operative with the authorities once the offence charged is an administration of justice crime—still less, when (as is surely envisaged) the person acquitted on the principal charge is tried for a second time. Also, before making an order that invalidates any conviction, the High Court is required, by section 55(3), to allow the acquitted person to make representations—by which is meant 'written representations'—to the Court.

The substantive criminal law, in so far as it penalizes those who threaten witnesses and (in turn) witnesses who bow to such threats, can only be partly effective. Many a witness, on assessing the competing courses of action that are open to him, will conclude that the balance of advantage lies in favour of failing to testify rather than incurring the wrath of the criminal community. The law, then, has needed to be supplemented by a host of administrative arrangements, aimed at reducing the risk to which the witness is exposed.[30] Some of these arrangements have a bearing on the subject of open justice, and therefore require consideration in the context of the present work. In recent years witness support schemes have provided reassurance to those persons, particularly the victims of violent crime, who have been apprehensive or fearful at the prospect of giving evidence in open court. Where those arrangements allow for physical proximity between witness and support worker, they may create the impression that the content of the testimony could be affected by the presence of the worker. As a minimum requirement, therefore, the support worker may not sit by the witness while he is giving his evidence. The Runciman Commission was informed that, in some Crown Court centres, the support worker is required to sit in the public gallery or to absent himself from the courtroom altogether. To confine him to the public seats could be defended as a somewhat extreme measure taken to rebut any suggestion that the support worker is influencing the testimony of the witness. To exclude him from the courtroom entirely is difficult to defend on legal principle. He is entitled, as a member of the public, to occupy any vacant seat in

---

[30] See M. H. Graham, *Witness Intimidation: The Law's Response* (1985) for a general overview of the problem and responses to it in the USA.

the public gallery. On the other hand, since he would not technically qualify as a 'McKenzie friend', he would have to withdraw in the event of the court deciding to sit *in camera*.

How far should there be derogation from the norm of open trial so as to accommodate the special needs of the frightened witness? Some techniques of witness protection are entirely compatible with what is considered to be good practice. Thus, the sequestering of vulnerable witnesses in a specially created area of the court building until it is their turn to give evidence is, in effect, a reinforcement of the standard practice whereby witnesses should wait outside the courtroom lest they hear, and be influenced by, the prior testimony of others. Any more radical method of accommodating the needs of the witness, however, involves a significant departure from the standards of open justice. The accused himself could not be removed from the courtroom in the absence of disruptive behaviour on his part. The same point goes for any members of the public seated in the courtroom, though, arguably, the problem of witness intimidation had not assumed large enough proportions at the time of *Scott v Scott* for it to be addressed as a possible exception to the general rule. It is worth recalling, however, that in *R v Salih*[31] the Court of Appeal declined to allow the procedure created by section 159 of the Criminal Justice Act 1988 to be used as a means of challenging a Crown Court judge's refusal to clear the court by way of response to the fears of a witness.

A measured response to the problem of the frightened witness was adopted in section 23 of the Criminal Justice Act 1988. By virtue of this provision, a statement made by a person in a document is admissible in a criminal trial as a substitute for direct oral evidence if two conditions are met: the statement was made to a police officer; and the person making it 'does not give oral evidence through fear or because he is kept out of the way'. The use to which a statement made in these circumstances can be put is vividly illustrated by *R v Montgomery*,[32] the principal authority on guidelines for the sentencing of the frightened witness. Montgomery had refused to take the oath at the trial of persons charged with violence against the police. The prosecution applied successfully for an earlier statement made by Montgomery that incriminated the accused to be read to the jury. As a result the accused pleaded guilty to one of the charges against him. Montgomery was then sentenced for contempt of court. Subsequently the Court of Appeal reduced his sentence and took the opportunity to pronounce a number of guidelines on the matter of sentencing. A few of these guidelines are relevant to the theme of the present work. There was no rule, said the Court of Appeal, that interference with jurors was to be punished more severely than the threatening of witnesses: the circumstances of each case were to be the decisive factor. Moreover, the effect on the trial of refusal to testify was to be an important consideration in sentencing. This must surely be speculative in the great majority of

[31] The Times, 31 December 1994.   [32] [1995] 2 All ER 28.

cases. Where refusal to testify results in the prosecution withdrawing the case, the effect is reasonably apparent. However, where the case continues and a verdict of not guilty is returned by the jury, it is difficult to know how much the failure of one witness to testify has contributed to this result. Indeed, as the facts of the *Montgomery* case illustrate, the availability of the alternative method of producing evidence conceded by section 23 of the 1988 Act gives scope for argument that the effect on the trial has been minimal.

It must be proved beyond reasonable doubt that the witness is in fear. The trial judge pronounced himself satisfied in this regard, Montgomery and members of his family testifying that they had received a number of threats. More striking for the purpose of the present work is the pointed reference made by the Court of Appeal to the fact that, at the time of his refusal to testify, 'the public gallery was still crowded with relatives of the accused'.[33]

In recent years various steps have been taken to increase the security of witnesses in criminal trials. Many of these steps, such as those contained in the Youth Justice and Criminal Evidence Act 1999, require changes in the physical features of the courtroom. Others function by way of protection of anonymity.[34] Resort to anonymity is particularly appropriate in situations where a person has a well-founded fear for his safety, yet has not received an overt threat from any particular individual. The claim for anonymity can be made in any type of case, irrespective of its subject matter, and by any of the *personae* of the trial. The background to the *Ex p P* case,[35] for example, was an application for housing accommodation. Yet, since the applicants were asylum seekers from Albania, the Court of Appeal readily acceded to the request for anonymity, while reminding itself of the need for the court to exercise vigilance in cases, such as this, where the opposing party acquiesced in the granting of such protection. A well-known instance of the same issue arose in connection with the conduct of the tribunal, set up in January 1998 under the Tribunals of Inquiry (Evidence) Act 1921, to re-examine the events in Northern Ireland on 'Bloody Sunday'.[36] The refusal of the tribunal to grant anonymity protection to the various soldier witnesses was successfully challenged in the courts,[37] in terms which posed the traditional conflict between the interests of the individual witness and the demands of open justice—or rather, here, the proper functioning of an inquisitorial process aimed at finding out the truth of the events on that particular day.

---

[33] [1995] 2 All ER 28, 30.

[34] The most extreme measure available under the Youth Justice and Criminal Evidence Act 1999—that of allowing evidence to be given in private under s 25—in effect confers anonymity only as against the public. The name will still be available to those remaining in the courtroom, including the accused.

[35] The Times, 31 March 1998.

[36] On Sunday, 30 January 1972 a number of civilians were shot dead by soldiers in the course of disturbances arising out of an illegal march in Londonderry.

[37] *R v Lord Saville of Newdigate, ex p A* The Times, 22 June 1999, a decision upheld by the Court of Appeal at [1999] 4 All ER 860.

The Conservative Party, in its manifesto for the General Election of 1997, believed the problem sufficiently grave to promise: 'We will give courts in all cases the discretion to allow witnesses to give evidence anonymously if they believe them to be at risk from reprisal.' A private member's bill which was introduced in the House of Commons in November of the previous year would have gone even further. The Witness Protection Bill 1996 was presented by Irene Adams MP, its initial supporters coming from all shades of political opinion. It stipulated an inflexible rule of anonymity that would have penalized the disclosure of the name, address, picture or other likeness, or 'any other matter likely to lead members of the public to identify' certain persons during 'the relevant period'. The persons so protected encompassed the victim of any offence and also any person reasonably expected to be called upon to give evidence in any criminal trial in the United Kingdom. The Bill, though clearly based on the model already in effect for rape complainants, was lacking in some of the safeguards built into the earlier provision. In particular, no scope was provided for departure from anonymity if the judge believed publicity to be necessary for bringing forward additional witnesses. Strangely, in view of the draconian reach of the Bill, the 'relevant period' terminated at the point of final determination of guilt or innocence of the person accused of the offence—in many cases an inadequate length of time as far as the protection of witnesses is concerned.

The most extreme form of response to the problem, that of clearing the public gallery while the witness is testifying, is occasionally weighed against the conferral of anonymity. In *R v Richards*[38] a principal witness in a murder trial adamantly refused to give evidence unless the gallery were first cleared. The basis for her apprehension was given, at first, as the presence in court of associates of the accused. She later amended this to a statement that she would not otherwise feel comfortable. Rather than holding her in contempt of court, the judge fell in with her wishes. The court was cleared, the girl testified, and the accused was convicted. On the basis of the brief law report, the extreme step of hearing the evidence *in camera* appears to have been taken in preference to a grant of anonymity for two reasons: the age of the witness (she was eighteen years old); and the likelihood that her identity was known in any case to the accused and his circle. The accused subsequently challenged the validity of the conviction on the basis of the impropriety of hearing the evidence *in camera*. The appeal, which was based on both the principle of *Scott v Scott* and Article 6 of the European Human Rights Convention, was rejected.

A consideration of the *Richards* case serves to raise, finally, a fundamental concern about the use of the various techniques of witness protection. Do they compromise the right of the accused to a fair and public trial?[39] Traditionally, the

---

[38] [1999] JP 246, and the note by J. R. Spencer at (1999) 58 CLJ 497.

[39] It is worth noting one of the facets of the inquisitorial procedure that was challenged in *R v Lord Saville of Newdigate, ex p A* (n 37 above). Maurice Kay J, in the Divisional Court, emphasized that, the proceedings being of an inquisitorial nature, the identity of the soldiers would be known to the tribunal and counsel for the tribunal, who was thereby well placed to cross-examine them in full.

accused who has been convicted at the conclusion of a trial which has employed these various techniques will have argued his case on the basis of the various grounds of appeal laid down in the legislation: for example, the present test of whether the conviction is 'unsafe'.[40] Once the standards of the European Convention on Human Rights are superimposed on this test, the question arises as to whether or not the accused was denied a right to a fair and public hearing under Article 6(1) of the Convention. Paragraph (3) of Article 6 spells out what may be taken to be the critical elements of a fair hearing. For our purpose it is paragraph (3)(d) that is most relevant: the right 'to examine or have examined witnesses against him and to obtain the attendance and examination of witnesses on his behalf under the same conditions as witnesses against him'. The terms of the guarantee are less explicitly phrased in the defendant's favour than, for example, the Sixth Amendment to the US Constitution, with its requirement that the accused 'be confronted with the witnesses against him'.

While conceding that matters of the admissibility of evidence are largely the concern of national law, the European Court of Human Rights has laid down guidelines on the openness of criminal trials. Generally, evidence must be adduced in the presence of the accused and at a public hearing with a view to adversarial argument. These requirements were stated in *Delta v France*,[41] a relatively trouble-free case since there was no issue of witness protection and it appears to have been only as a result of administrative failure that the two witnesses against the accused had not been required to attend at his trial. Considerably more difficult are those cases in which some degree of protection of the witness is accorded at the trial. Derogations from the ideal standard of open justice may take place in two possible ways. The witness may be entirely absent from the trial, a written statement from him providing the evidence in question. Alternatively, the witness may be present in the courtroom while giving testimony, but subject to a number of safeguards in the interests of anonymity: for example, by the use of a screen. Each has its merits so far as witness protection is concerned. Equally, each disadvantages the accused in the presentation of his defence. As a rule, the identity of the person who provides a written deposition to the court is not protected. However, he is not available for cross-examination, nor may his demeanour be observed in the act of testifying. In sharp contrast, the witness whose identity is protected by a screen is physically present, is available for cross-examination, and is open to observation—by some persons, at least, in the courtroom—while giving his evidence. Some exploration of the delicate balance of interests was conducted in *X v United Kingdom*,[42] a case which did not reach the European Court since the European Commission of Human Rights was of the opinion that the petitioner's complaints were manifestly ill-founded. The petitioner was convicted, together with others, of the terrorist murder of two soldiers in Belfast. Various press photographers who had been present during the

---

[40] Criminal Appeal Act 1968, s 2(1), as amended by Criminal Appeal Act 1995.
[41] (1993) 16 EHRR 574.   [42] (1993) 15 EHRR CD113.

events in question were allowed to give evidence anonymously since they feared for their safety. (The trial court, it should also be noted, was a 'Diplock Court' sitting without a jury.) In rejecting the petition, the Commission stressed several factors: the witnesses were physically present, they could be seen by the judge and also by the legal representatives of both prosecution and defence. Moreover, the public was not excluded from the proceedings, they could hear all questions and answers passing between counsel and the witnesses. Knowledge of the witnesses' identity was withheld from the accused, the public and the press. In reaching the conclusion that there was no violation of the applicant's rights under Article 6, the Commission stressed that the crucial issue in the case, that of identification, had been a matter on which evidence had been given by witnesses whose identity had not been withheld from the accused or the public.

Again, *X v United Kingdom* is revealed not to have posed the conflict between the various interests in its sharpest possible form. The main item of evidence that incriminated the applicant was given entirely openly by witnesses whose identity was known. The clash between the rights of the accused and the security of the witness occurs head-on in those cases where the testimony of the anonymous witness is the centre-piece of the case for the prosecution. In these cases the European Court has been particularly active in intervening where the evidence of the anonymous witness is either the only evidence upon which the conviction is based or, on an alternative view, it plays a critical role in securing the conviction. It is scarcely surprising that in *Kostovski v Netherlands*[43] the Court concluded that there were breaches of Articles 6(1) and 6(3)(d) since there had been a twofold departure from the ideal standard of open justice: the witnesses were allowed to remain anonymous and they were also not required to attend in person at the trial. The accused was permitted to examine one of the witnesses, but only by way of submitting written questions through the examining magistrate (who also was kept in ignorance of the identities). Added to these considerations was the fact that the testimony of the witnesses, as the Government of the Netherlands conceded, had contributed 'to a decisive extent'[44] to securing the conviction of the accused. While acknowledging that anonymous information may be used in the fight against organized crime, the Court has insisted that the defence be permitted to test the reliability of the testimony either at the trial itself or, at the very least, before the investigating judge. There exists in English procedure no real equivalent to the latter stage of European criminal investigation. In the absence of this stage, it is difficult to resist the conclusion that, as far as English law is concerned, it is at the trial itself that the accused must be permitted to test the credibility of the anonymous witness.

It is noteworthy that, prior to the entry into force of the Human Rights Act 1998, the Court of Appeal ruled in *R v Thomas, R v Flannagan*[45] that the limited jurisdiction to depart from oral evidence pursuant to sections 23–26 of the

---

[43] (1990) 12 EHRR 434.   [44] ibid, para 44.   [45] [1998] Crim LR 887.

Criminal Justice Act 1988 did not violate the European Convention. Article 6(3) is not contravened where documentary evidence is produced from a witness who, for reasons of fear, would not give evidence in open court. Nevertheless, the question must be raised as to whether the result of this decision would be the same since the entry into force of the Human Rights Act, or indeed, in the event of the accused bringing proceedings before the European Court of Human Rights.

4. THE COURTS AND NATIONAL SECURITY

Among the specific areas of conflict between the claims of secrecy and the ideal of open justice that are being reviewed in this and the following two chapters, those issues that are cast in terms of 'national security' are among the most intractable. To insist on the standards of open justice where genuine issues of national security are concerned may have adverse repercussions extending well beyond the concerns of a particular litigant or witness. By its very nature, moreover, national security is an area where judges are less well equipped to adjudicate soundly between the conflicting claims—though there exist statutory contexts in which they are entrusted with that task in the clearest possible terms.[46] Indeed, there is an element of circularity here. It is precisely on account of the open conduct of trials that the sensitive material that would contribute to the formation of an informed judgment by the judiciary is to be withheld from them, thus rendering them even less well placed to perform the task of comparative evaluation. As against such considerations there is the understandable tendency of government to associate national security with matters of party political interest and to attempt to suppress the disclosure of information that is no more than politically embarrassing. There exist several English cases that illustrate these points, but in recent times none has demonstrated the clash of interests as vividly as the *Vanunu* case in Israel, which will be outlined below.

In *Scott v Scott* national security was not mentioned at all as providing an exception to public trial. As far as the common law is concerned, as their Lordships recognized, it would appear to be 'impossible to enumerate or anticipate all possible contingencies'.[47] The failure specifically to anticipate security issues as an exception to open justice was all the more remarkable for the rapidly deteriorating position in Europe even as the *Scott* case was going through the courts. In the period since that case was decided there has evolved a complex array of devices aimed at protecting national security within the trial setting.

A. Removal of the Jurisdiction of the Courts

The simplest and most draconian method of safeguarding national security is to remove the jurisdiction of the courts. The process of decision taking that would

---

[46] As, for example, in the Contempt of Court Act 1981, s 10.   [47] [1913] AC 417, 446.

normally be discharged by judicial bodies is removed into the executive branch of government. Consequently, the presumptive standard of open justice ceases even to be applicable. Typically the circumstances in which such transfer of jurisdiction takes place are those of a state of war or a mass breakdown of law and order—a 'public emergency threatening the life of the nation' (to use the term in Article 15(1) of the European Convention on Human Rights). The characteristic response of government is to intern persons suspected of having enemy sympathies or associations (in wartime) or those involved in terrorist activities (in times of civil disturbance). The most recent occasion on which such methods have been used in the United Kingdom was on the introduction of internment without trial in Northern Ireland in August 1971.[48] But, as that episode illustrates, the circumventing of the standard of open justice (not to mention the other requirements of due process that trial procedure imports) is but one of the motivating factors behind a policy of internment. Some persons who are subject to such process are not even suspected of having broken the criminal law: it is merely politically convenient to incarcerate them. Indeed, very few of those who were imprisoned in this way in Northern Ireland in 1971 were ever charged with any crime.[49]

It will be a truly extraordinary procedure that excludes all possible recourse to the courts. Even the infamous Regulation 18B of the Second World War was the subject of a challenge in *Liversidge v Anderson*.[50] Some strands in the reasoning in the House of Lords' judgments in that case provide an illuminating perspective on the theme of the present section. For the parent legislation that provided the basis for the making of Regulation 18B, namely the Emergency Powers (Defence) Act 1939, expressly provided an *in camera* jurisdiction. Section 6, the operative provision of the statute, appeared so far-reaching that it stipulated that, as long as the 1939 Act remained in force, the operation of the analogous provision in the official secrets legislation—section 8(4) of the Act of 1920 (to which we have already adverted)—'shall be suspended'. The existence of section 6 was put to different uses by the majority and minority judgments. Lord Atkin seized on the section in part of his well-known dissenting judgment in favour of the applicant detainee.[51] It was argued on behalf of the Home Secretary that some of the sources that provided the information on which he had formed his belief about the applicant might be confidential. But, said Lord Atkin, such sources might be withheld from the court, leaving it to form a conclusion on the basis of the material presented before it. Moreover, and more pertinent to our present theme, there existed the power under section 6 whereby the court could hold its hearings *in camera* and prohibit the disclosure of any information derived from such sittings. This was the typical procedure in a spy trial, and his Lordship could not believe 'that proceedings for false imprisonment or for a writ of habeas corpus present more difficulties of this kind than does the trial of a spy'.[52] The majority judgments of the House of

---

[48] See The Sunday Times, 'Insight Team', *Ulster* (1972), ch 15. [49] ibid, 296–7.
[50] [1942] AC 206. [51] ibid. 241–242. [52] ibid. 242.

Lords, however, did not share Lord Atkin's belief in the efficacy of *in camera* hearings. In Viscount Maugham's view such a hearing 'would not prevent confidential matters from leaking out, since such matters would become known to the person detained and to a number of other persons'.[53] Lord Wright, in addition to reiterating the danger of leakage from a secret sitting of the court, drew attention to the fact that 'a hearing in camera, if the public called for full disclosure, would not satisfy the public conscience'.[54]

The exclusion of the jurisdiction of the courts, the most extreme form of response to the call for secrecy, is therefore based on two perceived drawbacks of *in camera* trial: the continuing presence of the accused or applicant as one of the trial *personae*; and the risk that even the possibility of penal consequences will not guarantee that the persons admitted to a closed hearing will refrain from recounting the proceedings to others.

B. Trial *in Camera*

This form of procedure, supplemented (if necessary) by a degree of intra-court secrecy, can be considered to be the measured response to the need for secrecy when courts are confronted with matters of national security. In wartime it is the safeguarding of military and other information which will be paramount. In contrast, under conditions of civil disturbance, such as have prevailed in Northern Ireland in recent years, there will typically be a twofold need: to protect sensitive military and operational information; and to safeguard the identity of vulnerable persons (whether police informers or witnesses generally) from retaliatory attacks as a consequence of having played their role in criminal trials that involve terrorist offences. In recognition of the exigences of such situations, the study of states of emergency that was conducted by the International Commission of Jurists[55] concluded that it was legitimate for a state, should the circumstances warrant it, to derogate from the usual standards of due process so as to permit:

(1) suspension of the right to public trial;
(2) longer delay than normal in proceeding to trial; and
(3) admitting the testimony of prosecution witnesses who do not appear at the trial, 'while making all possible efforts to permit the defence to test the veracity of such testimony and preserving the right to examine all witnesses who do appear'.[56]

The second of these headings is not relevant to this work, and the third has already been examined. It remains, therefore, to consider in detail the *in camera*

---

[53] [1942] AC 206, 221.

[54] ibid. 266. Lord Wright did not address the question why the public should be more content with administrative secrecy than with the same level of secrecy surrounding a judicial process.

[55] *States of Emergency: Their Impact on Human Rights*, a study prepared by the International Commission of Jurists (1983).

[56] ibid. 429.

trial. The essential elements of such a form of hearing were discussed in Chapter 3. In the present context we consider the detailed use of the form of hearing in matters of official secrecy. Before doing so in the context of English law, some mention should be made of a modern Israeli case which, as no other, bears out the tension between the demands of national security and those of a fair trial (or, to be more precise, a trial that is perceived to be fair).

The trial of Mordechai Vanunu[57] took place between August 1987 and March 1988 on three counts, of espionage, treason, and disclosing state secrets. Vanunu was convicted on all counts and sentenced to eighteen years' imprisonment. A former technician at Israel's nuclear research complex at Dimona, he revealed through the *Sunday Times* a number of details about the Dimona plant which sufficed to show that Israel possessed a nuclear capability which placed it among the world's leading nuclear powers. His disclosures, clearly, had significant implications both for the balance of power in the Middle East and within Israel itself, where the work being carried out at Dimona had been kept secret from the people. The story of Mordechai Vanunu is one of high drama and intrigue. The 'cloak and dagger' elements extend well beyond his trial itself, which was conducted *in camera*, encompassing also the manner in which he was brought before the court (international abduction) and his treatment in prison before and after the trial (in particular, his being held under long-term solitary confinement).

Although the wider issues in the Vanunu affair have given cause for much disquiet, it is the manner in which his trial was conducted that is our concern. At a stage some months in advance of the trial 'the Committee for a Public Trial for Mordechai Vanunu' was formed. Its principal (but not sole) aim was to exert pressure on the Israeli authorities for an open hearing of the case.[58] Vanunu's own desire for a public trial was motivated by several considerations. First, his actions had been fired by reasons of personal conscience, and he wished to dispel the public perception of him as a mere traitor. Secondly, he wanted to use his trial as a means of informing the public about the moral issues surrounding the use of nuclear weapons.[59] These variations on the standard themes of open justice were outweighed, in the event, by the reasons adduced by the prosecution for trial behind closed doors. Vanunu might exploit the openness of the proceedings to divulge yet further information in breach of the law: such information, moreover, might be disclosed in the course of testimony by the prosecution's own witnesses, whether officials from Dimona or members of the security and intelligence services (the Shin Bet and the Mossad).

In the event, the entire proceedings before the Jerusalem District Court were held *in camera*.[60] Of the sixty page judgment handed down at the end, only one sentence—'We decided the defendant is guilty on all three counts'—was made

---

[57] *Mordechai Vanunu v The State of Israel* H.C. 172/88. For accounts of the affair as a whole, see T. Gilling and J. McKnight, *Trial and Error: Vanunu and Israel's Nuclear Bomb* (1991), and Y. Cohen, *Nuclear Ambiguity: The Vanunu Affair* (1992).
[58] ibid. 280–1.   [59] ibid. 228.   [60] ibid. 228–30.

public. It was hoped, at one point, that the trial would not take place completely *in camera*, only matters relating to the plant at Dimona and to Vanunu's abduction being heard in secret session. The prosecution did not object to the witnesses for the defence being heard in open court but, if they were to be so heard, they would ask for the accused to be removed from the courtroom while their testimony was being given. What the state feared, in particular, was any direct contact between Vanunu and members of the public of the sort that would permit him to make any form of communication to the outside world.[61] It appears that Vanunu was willing to submit to exclusion from the courtroom if that was the price to be paid for the opportunity of airing in the judicial forum the wider issues of Israel's nuclear capabilities. The judges, however, refused to countenance such an arrangement on the ground that Vanunu's presence throughout his own trial was a more important element of open justice than access to the proceedings by the public. In this way the trial was held entirely *in camera*. That, in itself, did not imply that there was a total ban on disclosure of what had passed in the courtroom. The material that emerged was a result of compromise between prosecution and defence at the conclusion of each day's proceedings after overseeing by the military censors.

What became, in all this, of the various rationales of open justice? If Vanunu received a fair trial, it was not one that was seen to be fair. To appraise the manner of conduct of the trial reliance must be placed on the impressions gleaned by those who, for however short a period in the course of a lengthy case, were allowed admission to the courtroom. The recorded impression of one witness is that the defence was allowed to develop its case at some length and that the court listened with due attention.[62] As to whether the conviction was justified in strict law, that question can be assessed by setting what is known of the episode alongside the substantive provisions of Israeli law. Israel's development of nuclear weaponry was, in a sense, collateral to the strictly trial issues—as, indeed, was the irregular way in which Vanunu was brought before the court.

To return to a consideration of English law, it is quite clear that, in the matter of official secrecy, mere exclusion of public and press may not be deemed sufficient. Other physical features of the courtroom may additionally be changed so as to minimize the possibility of improper surveillance of the proceedings. The windows of the courtroom in both the Vanunu[63] and Ponting prosecutions[64] were boarded up. It is difficult to believe that such measures are routinely carried

---

[61] On an earlier occasion when Vanunu was being held on remand and was taken to court for the purpose of extending the remand period, he held out his hand to waiting reporters on which he had scribbled a note giving the date and place of his abduction.

[62] Cohen (n 57 above) 231.   [63] Cohen (n 57 above) 229.

[64] C. Ponting, *The Right to Know: The Inside Story of the Belgrano Affair* (1985) 171. For the background to the case, see the Appendix. It is all the more strange that this degree of precaution is deemed necessary when it is borne in mind that, in the older court buildings at least, windows have tended to be set high so that no one inside the court can be distracted by what takes place outside. See the feature, 'Silence in Court', The Times, Magazine section, 3 May 1997.

out whenever a court decides to sit in closed session. Yet there is no legal provision which would either demand or preclude such additional precautions, which impinge solely on the physical lay-out of the court.

There are a few safeguards in section 8(4) of the Official Secrets Act 1920. The decision whether to hear material *in camera* is made by the trial judge. This should be contrasted with the situation in regard to employment tribunals, where the relevant provision states that hearings shall take place 'in public' except where a Minister of the Crown has directed the tribunal 'to sit in private on grounds of national security'.[65] It is also stipulated at the end of section 8(4) that 'the passing of sentence shall in any case take place in public'. This proviso is extremely limited, not even encompassing any plea in mitigation made by the accused.[66] Nor does it require the decision of the jury to be pronounced in open court. In this regard there is a violation of the standards of the European Convention on Human Rights. Article 6(1) of the Convention requires that, even in regard to cases that are properly heard in secret, 'Judgment shall be pronounced publicly'.

Cases which raise issues compendiously known as matters of 'national security' are those which may properly deviate from the unswerving demands of open justice. For example, Article 6(1) of the European Convention on Human Rights allows for the exclusion of press and public where such a step is required by, inter alia, 'public order or national security in a democratic society'. Section 8(4) of the Official Secrets Act 1920, which forms our primary focus of interest, is the longest standing of a number of provisions which have been enacted to protect the disclosure of secret information relating to security within the courtroom. Apart from the wartime power granted by section 6 of the Emergency Powers (Defence) Act 1939, there is a limited provision relating to the use of technical information by government contractors for the purpose of producing defence materials: section 4(3) of the Defence Contracts Act 1958.[67] It is possible to discern several similarities in these various provisions. All three sections provide an *in camera*

---

[65] See Industrial Tribunals (Constitution and Rules of Procedure) Regulations 1993, Sch 1, r 8(2). The following subsection, it should be noted, allows the tribunal additionally to sit 'in private' on its own initiative where the evidence is of such a nature that it would be 'against the interests of national security to allow the evidence to be given in public'.

Similarly, the Town and Country Planning Act 1990, s 321(3)–(4), provides that the Secretary of State may direct that, where matters of 'national security' are involved, the evidence to be adduced at a public inquiry 'shall only be heard . . . by such persons or persons of such descriptions as he may specify in [his] direction'.

[66] The dramatic difference once the public is readmitted for the passing of sentence is conveyed in George Blake's autobiography. See G. Blake, *No Other Choice* (1990) 204: 'There was a commotion as the public was now admitted to the gallery. The judge was going to pronounce sentence and this part of the proceedings was no longer in camera.' As emerges from Blake's account—he pleaded guilty—his counsel's plea in mitigation had been heard *in camera*.

[67] Defence Contracts Act 1958, s 4(3) reads: 'Without prejudice to any rule of law enabling a court to sit in camera, the court may make such orders for the exclusion of the public from proceedings under this section, and for prohibiting the publication of any technical information to which section two of this Act applies so far as disclosed or recorded in such proceedings, as appear to the court to be necessary or expedient in the public interest or in the interests of any parties to the proceedings.'

jurisdiction that stands without prejudice to any other power that the court may have to exclude the public and the press. The Emergency Powers Act and the Defence Contracts Act contain supplementary terms that confer a jurisdiction to prohibit the disclosure of information—only 'technical information' in the latter—that is disclosed in the course of the proceedings. In regard to all three sections, criteria are provided in accordance with which the court is to decide on the question of whether or not to go into closed session: prejudice to 'the national safety' in the Official Secrets Act; 'the public safety or the defence of the realm' under the wartime emergencies provision; and 'the public interest' (or, alternatively, 'the interests of any parties to the proceedings') in section 4(3) of the Defence Contracts Act.

A detailed consideration of the Official Secrets Act provision, together with its historical context, is required. We have already noted the surprising omission of the heading of security from the judgments in *Scott v Scott*. Equally surprising is the absence of anything akin to section 8(4) of the Official Secrets Act 1920 from the Official Secrets Act 1911 or from its precursor, the Official Secrets Act 1889. It has been suggested that the belated appearance of the provision was a response to the great importance placed by the House of Lords on public trial in the *Scott* case, the judgments in which were delivered two years after the Official Secrets Act 1911.[68] When much-needed reform of the 1911 statute was enacted in 1989, section 11(4) of the Official Secrets Act of that year carried forward the *in camera* provision, stating that this provision 'shall have effect as if references to offences under [the 1920 Act] included references to offences under any provision of this Act other than section 8(1), (4) or (5)'.

It will be necessary to say something shortly about these exceptions marked out in section 11(4) of the Official Secrets Act 1989. Those apart, there is a clear implication that there exists a close match between the *in camera* jurisdiction of section 8(4) and the trial of offences under the official secrets legislation.[69] But does this understanding reflect the way in which the various sections are drafted? Certainly, section 8(4) is placed within an official secrets statute. It is not, however, expressly confined to the trial of cases that arise under its provisions. The key term of section 8(4), concerning the publication of evidence that 'would be prejudicial to the national safety', may be taken as a compendious method of designating the character of the harm that the various official secrets statutes aim to prevent. Yet, as is well known, the now repealed section 2 of the Official Secrets Act 1911 penalized the disclosure of all manner of information that could not even remotely be regarded as having a bearing on the 'national safety'. Now that section 2 has been sharply pruned in the form of the 1989 Act there would appear

---

[68] M. Friedland, *National Security: The Legal Dimensions* (1980) 46.

[69] See, for example, *A-G v Leveller Magazine Ltd* [1979] AC 440, 451, where Lord Diplock sets out the terms of section 8(4) of the Official Secrets Act 1920 followed by those of section 12(1)(c) of the Administration of Justice Act 1960, and then draws the sweeping conclusion: 'So to report evidence in camera in a prosecution in the Official Secrets Acts would be contempt of court.'

to be a stronger case for arguing that section 8(4) meshes with the newly drafted official secrets offences. For the enactment of the Official Secrets Act 1989 was preceded by a long period of discussion, marked in particular by the deliberations of a Departmental Committee[70] and an abandoned government bill on the subject in 1979,[71] as to what categories of official information truly required the protection of the criminal law against their unauthorized disclosure. Yet it would be difficult to subsume under the one heading of 'prejudicial to the national safety' the various categories of protected information that are delineated in the new statute. Some headings—for example, information obtained as a result of the issue of a warrant under the Interception of Communications Act 1985[72]—may cover both security interests of the state and the privacy interests of the person subject to the surveillance. Some—in particular, the headings that relate to the prevention of crime and the detection and confinement of offenders in general— would be accommodated only by a strained interpretation of 'national safety'. Other headings are defined quite generally, by reference to the 'interests', rather than the safety, of the United Kingdom.

It is clear, then, that section 8(4), with its deployment of the term 'national safety', is too narrow to encompass the variety of interests that are protected by the reformed Official Secrets Act. It will now be made apparent that the section is not even apt to cover all situations raising matters of 'national safety' under that Act. It will be recalled that offences contained in section 8(1), (4) and (5) were excepted from the application of the statutory *in camera* provision to the 1989 statute.[73] A perusal of the excepted provisions reveals that they are predominantly concerned with situations in which persons fail to comply with official directions for the surrender or return of documents the contents of which place them within the ambit of the principal provisions of the statute. It is curious that section 8(4) does not apply to the various offences constituted by disobedience to such directions since the accused could raise, as a collateral question, the issue of whether the document in question is, in truth, one that falls within the protected categories.

On the other hand, the importance of section 8(4) for the new Official Secrets Act is borne out by a detailed consideration of the drafting of the various offences. Typically a disclosure is punishable only if it is 'damaging'—a term which varies in content according to the particular category of protected information. In the context of defence information, for instance, it includes, among others, any disclosure which 'damages the capability of . . . the armed forces of the Crown to carry out their tasks or leads to the loss of life or injury to members of those forces . . .' As the White Paper preceding the legislation stated, the issue of

---

[70] Departmental Committee on Section 2 of the Official Secrets Act 1911 (Chairman: Lord Franks) (Cmnd 5104, 1972).
[71] Protection of Official Information Bill 1979.   [72] Official Secrets Act 1989, s 4(3).
[73] Clause 10(2) of the Protection of Official Information Bill 1979 contained a similar exception (applicable to offences committed under Clause 5 of the Bill).

possible damage would not be permitted to turn on such administrative factors as the level of classification of the information in question and a certificate from the relevant Minister as to the correctness of the classification that had been adopted. On the contrary:

> where it is necessary for the courts to consider the harm likely to arise from the disclosure of particular information, the prosecution should be required to adduce evidence as to that harm and the defence should be free to produce its own evidence in rebuttal. The burden of proof would be on the prosecution, in the normal way.[74]

The free exchange of evidence and argument, envisaged in this way, is facilitated by the possibility of first dismissing all non-*personae* from the courtroom. As was noted in the overview of *in camera* trial in Chapter 3, there will often be a preliminary argument between prosecution and defence as to whether or not such an extraordinary step is warranted.[75] This is an aspect of the subject to which it will be necessary to return shortly. However, in cases where the accused admits to having made the disclosure and the sole issue is whether or not the disclosure was 'damaging' within the terms of the Act, a decision to take *in camera* the various arguments and evidence relevant to that issue may be viewed as, in itself, determinative of that central issue. A word of qualification, however, is necessary. If section 8(4) stood alone, the decision to proceed *in camera* would be prejudicial to the accused, the implication being that in the opinion of the judge, at any rate, any material to be disclosed in that phase of the trial 'would be prejudicial to the national safety'. However, section 8(4) specifically applies 'without prejudice to any powers which a court may possess' in other respects to exclude press and public from the courtroom. As was pointed out in Chapter 3, such a power does exist under the inherent jurisdiction of the court. The power, when derived from that source, may be exercised quite widely—'where the interests of justice so require'.[76] Two points need to be emphasized. First, even if it is the statutory basis that is used for excluding the public in the official secrets prosecution, it would be entirely wrong for the jury to treat that decision of the judge as pre-empting their own conclusion as to whether or not the accused's act of disclosure was damaging within the terms laid down by the legislation. Secondly, such an inference on the part of the jury would be doubly misguided if it were the wider power, under the inherent jurisdiction of the court, that had been used to remove the public.

On those occasions where the Crown Court proposes to sit *in camera* for security reasons (broadly stated), there now exist a number of safeguards to ensure

---

[74] *Reform of Section 2 of the Official Secrets Act 1911* (Cm 408, 1988), para 18.

[75] It is noteworthy that, on occasion, it is the defence that applies for a hearing to be *in camera*. See the charges of conspiracy to kidnap that were dropped by the Director of Public Prosecutions in October 1987: J. Andrews, 'Public Interest and Criminal Proceedings' (1988) 104 LQR 410, 410: '. . . the proceedings were held *in camera*, apparently at the request of the defence. . .'

[76] I. H. Jacob, 'The Inherent Jurisdiction of the Court' 1970 *Current Legal Problems* 23, 39.

that this step is properly taken. Where application is made, whether by prosecution or defendant, for all or part of the trial to be held *in camera* 'for reasons of national security or the protection of the identity of a witness or any other person',[77] notice of the application is required to be displayed prominently within the precincts of the court. The purpose is to alert persons (in particular, the media) of the occasion of a possible challenge to the form of the sitting under section 159 of the Criminal Justice Act 1988.[78] The hearing of the application takes place after the defendant has been arraigned but before the jury is sworn. It takes place *in camera* 'unless the Court orders otherwise'. Though not part of the trial proper, it has been acknowledged that the hearing is required to meet certain standards since it impinges on the 'civil rights and obligations', within the meaning of Article 6(1) of the European Convention on Human Rights, of the media.[79]

It is not unknown for a trial under the Official Secrets Acts to have taken place very largely *in camera*. George Blake, one of the most successful spies of the Cold War era, was sentenced in 1961 to a prison term of forty-two years after one such trial. The justification advanced for the secrecy at the time was the need to recall from the Soviet bloc the agents who had been betrayed by Blake. Another instance is the case of the 'Cyprus Eight' held at the Central Criminal Court in 1985, which resulted in the acquittal of seven of their number and the dropping of charges against the eighth.[80] A more recent example is provided by the case of Michael Smith who, in November 1993, was imprisoned for twenty-five years after having been found guilty of spying for Russia. The trial, which lasted nine weeks, was described as 'mostly held in camera'.[81] In the same year extremely restrictive conditions were placed around a challenge, brought by Captain Carole Maychell of the Intelligence Corps, by way of judicial review and habeas corpus to the conditions under which she was confined pending investigation of alleged breaches of the Official Secrets Act. It is reported that both hearing and judgment took place *in camera*, only 'an edited version' of the judgment being released.[82] The trial in 1984 of MI5 officer, Michael Bettaney, was also described as being held mostly *in camera*.[83] Indeed, when in 1998 Bettaney was released after serving fourteen years in prison, fears were expressed that he remained in a position to damage security since he would still be in possession of sensitive material, including the names of British agents working abroad. The Bettaney case illustrates how, in the case of non-obsolescent security information, the accused remains in a position to inflict further damage even after having served a lengthy term of imprisonment. He remains, of course, subject to the Official Secrets Act and is liable to prosecution in respect of any further disclosures that he makes.

---

[77] Crown Court Rules 1982, SI 1982/1109, r 24(A).   [78] See Chapter 3, section 3, C, above.
[79] *Ex p Guardian Newspapers Ltd* [1999] 1 All ER 65, 75.
[80] For details of the case see R. M. Thomas, *Espionage and Secrecy: The Official Secrets Acts 1911–1989 of the United Kingdom* (1991), 193–6.
[81] The Times (19 November 1993) 5.   [82] The Times (12 February 1993) 3.
[83] The Times (29 May 1998) 3. For some account of the case see Thomas (n 80 above) 57–8.

Finally, it should be noted that occasional instances have been found in which evidence given *in camera* has subsequently been included in the court record. At one stage during the Australian phase of the *Spycatcher* proceedings, the British Cabinet Secretary, Sir Robert Armstrong, corrected in the course of *in camera* testimony a statement that he had previously made in open court. For this reason Powell J acceded to a submission that this particular item should be made part of the public record notwithstanding the confidential context in which it was given.[84]

The exclusion from the trial court of all except the *personae* of the trial is reinforced by two additional points. As is now to be expected, the *in camera* jurisdiction is matched by a provision in the Administration of Justice Act 1960, section 12, that penalizes breaches of courtroom secrecy. The relevant part is section 12 (1)(c): 'where the court sits in private for reasons of national security during that part of the proceedings about which the information in question is published'.[85]

Some measure of the concern that surrounds cases of national security may be gained from an extraordinary statement made by Lord Parker CJ in connection with the trial of Nicholas Prager at Leeds Assizes in June 1971. The judge's attention was drawn to certain newspaper reports concerning the *in camera* phases of the Prager trial, which led him to state that it was 'as damaging for information [of the classified kind] to leak out as it is to have the representatives of the press present and taking their notes at the time'. However, his Lordship went on to stress that merely to speculate in the press as to what took place during the closed sessions of the court was equally reprehensible: 'there is in [the articles in question] a measure of speculation as to what was going on in closed court yesterday and I wish to bring to the notice of the press that that is irregular and a potential contempt of court.'[86]

The existence of the penalty imposed by section 12 has not been considered sufficient in itself to maintain confidentiality in the area of official secrecy. For it has been supplemented by precautionary steps to exclude from the ranks of the trial *personae* those who, undeterred by the penalties imposed by the Administration of Justice Act 1960, might well disclose to others that which has been imparted to them in the course of an *in camera* sitting. This raises the controversial issue of jury vetting.[87] Only part of this question is relevant to our present theme, but it would be useful to recapitulate very briefly before identifying that part. It has long been a fundamental principle that the jury should be chosen at random from the community, subject to the statutory grounds on which particular groups of individuals are disqualified from serving in that capacity. The existence of jury vetting was first conceded by the government as a result of an

---

[84] This episode is recounted in Thomas (n 80 above) 135, n 119.

[85] The choice of the preposition 'about' is strikingly unusual in this context.

[86] 'Hearing in Camera—Newspaper Speculation' NLJ (24 June 1971) 548.

[87] On the subject in general, see L. Lustgarten and I. Leigh, *In from the Cold: National Security and Parliamentary Democracy*, 294–301.

official secrets trial in 1978, known generally as the 'ABC' trial.[88] Its technical basis is the power of the Crown to request a 'stand by' of any member of the panel from which the twelve members of any particular jury will be recruited. In the period since it first came to light 'jury vetting' has formed the basis of a number of appeals. More in point for the present purpose is the fact that the Attorney-General has sought to regularize the practice in the form of guidelines.[89] These stipulate that the correct procedure is for the Crown to exercise 'in open court' its right whether to request the potential juror to stand by or to challenge for cause his suitability to serve.

In what circumstances should the Crown's power be exercised? Apart from the routine checking to ascertain whether persons on the jury panel are disqualified by reason of having a criminal conviction, the guidelines identify two categories of case where extra precautions are said to be necessary. These were defined as: '(a) cases in which national security is involved and part of the evidence is likely to be heard in camera, and (b) terrorist cases'. The categories are not clearly defined in a way that would have been necessary if they had been embodied in legislation. They may, in fact, partly overlap. Each poses its peculiar problems. The former is our principal concern. Here the danger is said to be 'that a juror, either voluntarily or under pressure, may make an improper use of evidence which, because of its sensitivity, has been given in camera'. In regard to the second category, that of 'terrorist cases', the danger is said to be that of a juror whose political views are so extreme as to interfere with his capacity to try the case fairly. Even this category is of some relevance to this work, since, as will be apparent in Chapter 7, it is part of a wider question of the ability of certain types of person to serve as jurors in particular types of trial. Just as the more politically motivated might be excluded from the jury in official secrets cases, so too it has been argued that only those with specialist expertise are capable of trying the issues in cases of complex commercial fraud.

Where the case is one that involves national security, with a likely *in camera* phase, the guidelines state that inquiries extending beyond simply the criminal records may be conducted 'with the records of police Special Branches' and with the 'security services'. Such further investigation, however, may be made only on the authorization of the Attorney-General after an application has been made to him by the Director of Public Prosecutions.

Several points are noteworthy in regard to vetting decisions in 'cases in which national security is involved'. As with all types of case, the decision whether or not to vet, clearly, must be taken before the hearing proper begins. However, the category that we are considering is unique in that it hinges on a decision that will be taken some time later by the trial judge. The question whether or not to hear

---

[88] So named after the initial letters of the names of the three accused: Aubrey, Berry, and Campbell. For an account of the trial, see G. Robertson, *The Justice Game* (1998), ch 5.

[89] These were promulgated in the law reports, at [1988] 3 All ER 1086. See now *Blackstone's Criminal Practice 2001*, Appendix 3.

part of the case *in camera* will be decided by the judge, after hearing argument from both sides in the case. The decision whether to exclude certain persons from the jury is doubly speculative, in that it requires, first, an *in camera* phase in the coming trial and, secondly, the presence of a juror in the courtroom who may not respect the secrecy of that phase. In view of the twofold guess that is required, it would hardly be surprising if the authorities erred on the side of protecting their own interests. Moreover, the methods that are envisaged for use in the guidelines do not fully correspond with the stated aims. The aims, it will be recalled, are to exclude from jury any person who '. . . either voluntarily or under pressure . . . may make an improper use of evidence which . . . has been given in camera'. A search in regard to such a person's political allegiances might disclose whether or not he is the sort of person who might voluntarily render up the evidence in question. It is hard to see how the same search would reveal a person's propensity to disclose the same material as a result of duress or the prospect of financial gain.[90] To anticipate the contents of Chapter 7, this is part of a wider problem of combating improper pressure on jurors (whether to acquit the accused or, as here, to disclose the secrets of an *in camera* hearing). In both respects, as will be seen in that chapter, an element of safeguard may be introduced in confining the identity of the jurors to as small a range of persons as possible, consistently with the requirements of due process. By way of general response to the threat of improper influences being brought to bear on members of the jury, it will be argued that the names of jurors should not routinely be read out in such a way that the information becomes available to anyone who happens to be present in the courtroom.

The practice of 'jury vetting' carries with it the suspicion that the executive may be manipulating the composition of the jury so as to increase the likelihood of its returning a verdict of guilty. The danger is all the greater in view of the understandable tendency of governments to conflate politically embarrassing disclosures with threats to national security. No case bears out that tendency more starkly than the prosecution of Clive Ponting. Yet despite the fact that jury vetting did take place,[91] the jury acquitted Ponting of the charge of divulging material in contravention of section 2 of the Official Secrets Act 1911. It is noteworthy that one person became a member of the jury despite the fact that, prior to the trial, she had publicly called for the discontinuance of the prosecution.[92]

---

[90] Note the Annexe to the Attorney-General's guidelines, 'Recommendations of the Association of Chief Police Officers', which state that the police should check potential jurors for criminal convictions in a number of situations in which either the Director of Public Prosecutions or a Chief Constable deems it is in the interests of justice to do so. One such situation is 'in any case in which it is believed that in a previous related abortive trial an attempt was made to interfere with a juror or jurors': [1988] 3 All ER 1086, 1088.

[91] See Ponting (n 64 above) 169: 'Despite the ostentatious jury vetting, the Crown tells us none of them have shown up on Special Branch files, nor on criminal records'. For further details of the case, see the Appendix.

[92] See T. Healey, *The World's Greatest Trials* (1986) 91: 'It was revealed [after the conclusion of the trial] that one of the jurors, a Ms Lynne Oliver, was a Labour councillor for Islington and had previously voted at a council meeting for the withdrawal of charges against Mr Ponting.'

C. Exclusion of Information from the Courtroom

We saw in the previous section how a standard response to the problem of handling security-sensitive information in the course of legal proceedings is to clear
the courtroom of press and members of the public. Additionally, in circumstances deemed sufficiently grave, certain persons would be excluded even from
the possibility of serving as jurors in the proceedings. An alternative method of
dealing with the problem, to which we now turn, is to permit unimpeded access
to the courtroom but to suppress the disclosure of certain categories of sensitive
information that would otherwise emerge in the normal course of the trial. If (as
may readily be assumed) the information is relevant to the resolution of the issues
in the case, not only is it denied to the press and the public, the denial will also
have the more serious effect of prejudicing the right of one or other party fully to
present its side of the case.

(a) The Problem of Informers

Particularly problematic is the situation regarding informers. Those who supply
information to the authorities, whether for gain or not, often do so on the assumption that their anonymity will be protected. If the information passed on results in
legal proceedings against another person, that person may well claim the right to
investigate the reliability of the informant in a forum such as open court. There
are two interests here that are in direct conflict. Informers almost invariably wish
to remain anonymous: any processes that might result in the loss of that protection will necessarily have an adverse effect on the future supply of information.
On the other hand, the informant may be unreliable, and often the only way of
establishing this is by gaining information which would lead to his identification.
A not untypical case in this regard is *R v Revenue Adjudicator's Office, ex p
Drummond*,[93] where the Inland Revenue successfully resisted proceedings for
judicial review directed at disclosing the identity of one who had informed on the
applicant's financial affairs. The case was easily determined since there was nothing to suggest that the Revenue had treated the informant's information as factual: it had merely suggested lines of inquiry. Far more difficult are criminal cases
which involve the use of a police informer. In addition to the possibility that
sources of information will dry up if informants are not protected, the disclosure
of their identities will create obvious risks for their personal safety and also for the
effectiveness of the fight against crime (the latter being designated as a specific
heading of protected information in the Official Secrets Act 1989).[94] Indeed, counsel in one case stated that professional criminals keep watch from the public gal-
leries of the various Crown Courts in order to learn the identity of police

---

[93] [1996] STC 1312.
[94] Official Secrets Act 1989, s 4(2)(a)(iii), covers disclosure of information which would impede the
prosecution or detection of offences or the arrest or prosecution of suspects.

informers and undercover officers.[95] Although the phrase, 'police informer', is encountered in the law reports (most frequently, in the case law to be examined shortly), it is not a precise term. Many people provide information to the police without being considered to be police informers. The term appears to have special meaning that is derived from its use and interpretation in both case law and the technical literature on policing. The New Zealand Law Commission's *Preliminary Paper No 23* suggested the following definition:

A person is an informer for the purposes of this section if the person has supplied, gratuitously or for reward, information to an enforcement agency, or to a representative of an enforcement agency, concerning the possible or actual commission of an offence in circumstances in which the person has a reasonable expectation that his or her identity will not be disclosed.[96]

Undercover police officers are vulnerable in many of the same ways as police informers, since they associate at a social level with professional criminals and the nature of their work places them outside the immediate protection of their colleagues in the police force. Disclosure of their identity will lead to a loss in their effectiveness as law-enforcement agents, together with possible risk of reprisals from the criminal classes.

The leading authority on non-disclosure of the identity of police informers is *Marks v Beyfus*,[97] a civil action for false imprisonment that arose out of a trial in which the plaintiff had been acquitted. The Director of Public Prosecutions was called as a witness by the plaintiff, who put questions to him concerning the sources of certain information. The DPP declined, on grounds of public policy, either to produce a written statement that had been supplied to him or to give oral testimony concerning the names of his informants. The judge agreed with this position and the plaintiff's case was dismissed since he could not prove a vital element in his case. On appeal Lord Esher MR endorsed the view that a witness could not be asked questions which would disclose either himself or a third party to be an informer. The rule of non-disclosure applied, not only in criminal prosecutions, but also (as there) in a civil action. Lord Esher conceded that the rule, though founded on considerations of 'public policy', was not inflexible. If the trial judge believed that disclosure of the name of the informant was 'necessary or right' in order to establish the innocence of the accused, two aspects of public policy would be in conflict and the interests of the accused would be preferred.[98] The present case being a civil action, the latter aspect was not present to be weighed in the scales.

Certain aspects of the case merit some comment at this stage. After the two other members of the court had delivered their judgments, Lord Esher took the opportunity to add a few lines which clearly based his decision on grounds of

---

[95] See Manchester Evening News (3 April 1992) 1.
[96] *Evidence Law: Privilege* Preliminary Paper No 23 (1994).   [97] (1890) 25 QBD 494.
[98] ibid. 498.

public policy rather than on the personal preferences of the informers whose identity was to be protected. Even if the DPP had been willing to answer the questions put to him, Lord Esher emphasized, the presiding judge ought not to have allowed him to respond.[99] A difficulty that is endemic in the balance struck by the Court of Appeal in this case is that, without knowledge of the background matters (starting, but not concluding, with the informer's name), it would be impossible to know whether or not the identity of the informer had a bearing on the guilt or innocence of the accused.

The exclusionary rule that applies to police informers has also been held to protect from disclosure at trial the location of private premises used as police observation posts.[100] The question is sometimes posed as to the extent of the danger that would justify the maintenance of secrecy in regard to such posts. It has been held that it is not necessary for the prosecution to show that the occupier of the premises used by the police is likely to suffer violence as a result of allowing the use of his property for surveillance purposes. Danger of harassment would suffice.[101]

The system of anonymity lends itself to a number of possible abuses. There are precedents indicating that the name of the informer must be disclosed to defence counsel. It was the refusal to effect even such a limited disclosure, in combination with the trial judge then ruling that the name was not to be disclosed at all, that led to the reversal of the conviction in *R v Vaillencourt*.[102] Clearly, intra-court withholding of the name of the witness may deny the accused the possibility of exploring possible lines of inquiry aimed at showing that the witness is prejudiced against him. Cases have been known to occur where the defence, on learning that an anonymous witness is to be produced, has gone to the expense of employing private detectives in an attempt to ascertain the identity of the witness.[103] A disturbing additional feature is that such private initiatives are available only where the finance is readily available, that is, 'only in serious crime cases'.[104] Whatever the category of offence, it is cause for concern that only certain defendants are in a position to finance initiatives in order to gain information that would routinely be available to all accused under a regime of universal open justice. Moreover, it is unclear whether such initiatives would be entirely legal. By seeking to gain information which has been specifically denied to it, the defence could be viewed as committing a contempt of court. On the other hand, it was clearly established in *Connolly v Dale*[105] that it is a contempt for the police themselves to obstruct attempts by an accused's legal advisers to identify and speak to potential witnesses. This ruling, rendered in the context of witnesses in general, may well be held inapplicable in the case of a witness whose identity is to

---

[99] ibid. 500.
[100] *R v Hewitt and Davis* (1992) 95 Cr App R 81.
[101] *Austin v DPP* (1993) 97 Cr App R 169.
[102] The Times, 12 July 1992.
[103] J. Morton, *Supergrasses and Informers: An Informal History of Undercover Police Work* (1995) 308.
[104] ibid.
[105] [1996] QB 120.

be withheld at the trial. Private inquiries undertaken on the initiative of the defence may lead to suspicions that the witness in question may be harbouring a grudge against the accused. In that event the question would then be raised as to whether the hostility of the witness against the accused would be allowed to be exposed in open court by cross-examination, with the attendant likelihood of this leading to the emergence of material that would point to the identity of the witness.

The high degree of confidentiality granted to the name of informers has created the potential for police corruption. Until the 1970s the senior officer whose duty it was to authorize payment for information did not need to know the identity of the informant. His contact in the police force could simply inform the senior officer that the informant wished to be known by a pseudonym. There was scope, therefore, for two potential abuses. The informant might be in league with a corrupt junior police officer and an agreement made to share the reward money with him. Moreover, there was a temptation for an informant to go beyond the supply of information, and become instead an agent provocateur.[106]

The European Court of Human Rights, when hearing complaints of convictions based on undercover police work, has reiterated the rule that evidence is to be produced in the presence of the accused and at a public hearing with a view to adversarial argument. In *Lüdi v Switzerland*[107] the undercover agent had approached the accused with a view to obtaining drugs from him (in doing so, he also became an agent provocateur). In the interest of retaining his anonymity, and hence his continued usefulness, he had not been called to testify in court. Nevertheless, the fact that the conviction was obtained partly in reliance on written statements supplied by him sufficed to deprive the applicant of a fair trial as guaranteed by Article 6 of the Convention. The European Court acknowledged the legitimate role played by undercover police officers in areas of investigation such as drug offences but added, without specifying how, that it would have been possible to arrange a confrontation between the accused and the agent without jeopardizing the role of the latter. In a sense, of course, the agent was already known to the accused. The only item being withheld from the accused was which of his several 'customers' was in the employment of the police.

An unusual twist to the problem of enforcing security for the informant has arisen in the context of the accused who, having been convicted of an offence, supplies information to the authorities on criminal activity in general. This issue was discussed at some length in the anonymous case, *R v A (Informer: Reduction of Sentence), R v B (Same)*.[108] The Court of Appeal, in the course of reviewing this area of sentencing, emphasized that the element of exposure to personal jeopardy of the informer or his family should be taken into account in determining the sentence to be passed. Personal jeopardy can be minimized, if not entirely

---

[106] Morton (n 103 above) 285–6.   [107] (1993) 15 EHRR 173.
[108] The Times, 1 May 1998.

eliminated, by a regime of anonymity where this aspect of sentence is heard in open court. In *R v M (Sentence)*,[109] in dealing with the sentence to be passed on a convicted drug dealer who had supplied useful information to the authorities, the Lord Chief Justice granted a request of the dealer's counsel that he be referred to in court simply as 'M' in an attempt to forestall what was described loosely as 'parochial trouble' in prison.

In contrast to these cases are situations in which a person's identity is fully known, but he seeks some departure from the standards of open justice on the grounds of possible reprisal. In *Coca-Cola Co v Gilbey*[110] a person whose name appears in the law report had been made the subject of an Anton Piller order. He declined to supply the material required to be disclosed in the order, fearing attacks from his associates. The claim was advanced briefly and without elaboration. The man suggested that Lightman J should hold an *in camera* hearing at which 'the risks could be further elaborated'.[111] The envisaged procedure, strictly, would have been even more confidential than an *in camera* hearing as traditionally understood, since the man applied for exclusion of the plaintiffs and their legal representatives. Alternatively, given the judge's unwillingness to exclude the other side from such a hearing, he suggested that the plaintiffs' lawyers be permitted to be present, on their giving an undertaking not to disclose the material to their clients without the leave of the court. This alternative suggestion was withdrawn when it became apparent to the man that the court could indeed grant such leave. In the end Lightman J ordered compliance with the Anton Piller order. He accepted that the possibility of a risk of violence if disclosure were made was a factor to be taken into account, going to the issue of weight only. However, he went on to reiterate the classic stance of the law that it has taken in cases of witness intimidation. The law should take its course, without surrendering to the possibility of violence, the appropriate response being police protection to the person in fear combined with proceedings for contempt against any person apprehended for threatening violence.

As already stated in section 3, there now exist statutory offences aimed specifically at the problems of witness and juror intimidation. However, the cases just cited demonstrate that there exist situations which, in various ways, fall outside the ambit of the statutory offences. Without having received any intimidatory communication, a person may be only too well aware that to break the code of silence of a criminal fraternity will result in swift reprisal. Also, the man who requested special arrangements in *Coca Cola Co v Gilbey* was neither juror nor witness. The two sentencing cases mentioned just before it provided situations in which information was forthcoming from police informers, though not (as in the classic police informer cases) by way of testimony given in open court. Whether, in the course of time, the informers in those cases would be produced in court to testify against other persons was unclear. The offence created by section 51 of the

---

[109] The Times, 1 March 1994.   [110] [1995] 4 All ER 711.   [111] ibid. 714.

Criminal Justice and Public Order Act 1994 applies to witnesses, and does not encompass police informers as such. Additionally, it requires the making of an overt threat. There is consequent need, as the three cases just discussed illustrate, both for a residual contempt jurisdiction and for safeguards of anonymity so as to encompass instances that do not fall within the terms of the statutory offence.

(b) Public Interest Immunity

A generalized basis for the exclusion of material from the courtroom on the grounds of possible prejudice to the public interest is to be found in the doctrine of Public Interest Immunity (hereinafter PII), formerly known as Crown Privilege. The subject of PII is an aspect of the law of procedure and evidence. When documentary or oral material is sought to be produced, whether by way of pre-trial discovery or in the form of viva voce evidence, its production in this way can be resisted on the ground that its disclosure would be contrary to the public interest. Since the material will be deemed relevant to the disposal of one or more issues in the action, it follows that the party that is denied access in this way suffers a considerable, if not an irreparable, disadvantage in its conduct of the case. Once again, the aim here is not to give a comprehensive account of the subject of PII claims, but rather to draw attention to those aspects which impinge on the open conduct of judicial business.

The starting point of the modern law on the subject is the ruling of the House of Lords in *Duncan v Cammell, Laird & Co Ltd*,[112] a case which arose out of a wartime tragedy. The submarine *Thetis*, while undergoing sea trials, sank with considerable loss of life. The dependants of the men on board brought proceedings for negligence against the shipbuilders, who had obtained from the Admiralty the contract for the construction of the submarine. The defendants were instructed to oppose discovery of the vessel's plans on the basis of Crown Privilege (as it was then known). Without access to this material the plaintiffs would be denied any chance of recovery. Yet, on appeal to the House of Lords, it was held that the courts were to take as conclusive the Minister's certification as to the demands of the public interest. However harsh this decision, the case may well have been decided correctly on its particular facts. The litigation took place in wartime, and production of the plans would have shown that submarines of the *Thetis* design were armed with torpedo tubes which could fire backwards. This information, clearly, would be of considerable advantage to the enemy. It was to forestall the slightest possibility of the enemy gaining access to it that Crown Privilege was successfully claimed.

For this purpose it would be useful to speculate on the course of events had the House of Lords not upheld the Minister's claim. The plans of the *Thetis* would have come into the hands of the trial judge (it being a civil case, there would be no jury), the plaintiffs, and their legal advisers. In the absence of an out-of-court

---

[112] [1942] AC 624.

settlement, the plans would have been produced in court. Unless the court sat *in camera*, some idea of their contents could have been gleaned by those spectators occupying the public seats at the trial. In short, the plans would come into the hands of persons who, unlike the relevant members of the Admiralty and the shipbuilding company, had not been given security clearance.

A particular aspect of this case appears to have been overlooked. One argument advanced by the plaintiffs was that disclosure could not properly be withheld from them since the material had already been disclosed to a tribunal of inquiry charged with investigating the circumstances of the loss of the *Thetis*. The inquiry had been conducted by a High Court judge, Bucknill J, and its findings had already been published.[113] The basis of the plaintiffs' submission, presumably, was that a limited disclosure could safely be permitted under controlled circumstances. If a tribunal of inquiry, why not a court sitting in closed session? To quote counsel's argument, '. . . once a document has been made public it can never be the subject of an objection to produce it on the ground that it should not be made public'.[114] Viscount Simon was not impressed by the argument. Special precautions might have been taken by the tribunal, though he appears to have been unsure on the point ('some portion of the tribunal's sittings may have been secret').[115] In any case, the same conditions of secrecy under which the material had been produced to the inquiry could have been reproduced in the courtroom by going into *in camera* session at any stage when questions of the submarine design were raised.

Viscount Simon, who gave the judgment for the House of Lords, stated in general terms that Crown Privilege could be asserted under two different headings: the contents of the document for which the privilege was being asserted; and, irrespective of the contents of a particular document, the fact that it belonged to a class of material the disclosure of which would be contrary to the public interest. The automatic deference accorded by Viscount Simon to the views of the Minister became increasingly difficult to defend in peacetime, and it was scarcely surprising when, in *Conway v Rimmer*,[116] the House of Lords chose to redefine the judicial duties, when confronted with a claim of Crown Privilege, in terms of striking a balance between the public interest and the private interest of the litigant in securing access to evidence necessary to support his case. Indeed, if the exigencies of war made *Duncan v Cammell, Laird* an easy case in one direction, the facts of *Conway v Rimmer* (which involved an action for malicious prosecution brought by a former police probationer) lay at the other end of the spectrum. Despite the liberalization of the law in the latter case, it is noteworthy that Lord Reid expressly retained the 'class heading' under which Crown Privilege could be successfully asserted.

The decision in *Conway v Rimmer* provides but one aspect of the increasingly critical approach to matters of official secrecy during the 1960s and 1970s. The

---

[113] Cmd 6190, 1940.   [114] [1942] AC 624, 627.   [115] [1942] AC 624, 630.
[116] [1968] AC 910.

bias in favour of executive secrecy under section 2 of the Official Secrets Act 1911 had equally become difficult to justify. Legislative reform in that area, as has been seen, occurred in 1989. Mention has been made here of the Official Secrets Act 1989 for two reasons, in particular. First, whatever one's views on the details of that legislation, it marks an attempt to address with some particularity the problem of identifying which areas of governmental information truly require the sanction of the criminal law against their disclosure. As such, its categories could be pressed into service in the analogous area of identifying matters which should properly be made the subject of a PII claim. Secondly, the 1989 Act itself proceeds on the basis of 'class' claims. That is, regardless of the merits or demerits of disclosure of a particular document, the very fact that it falls within one of the prohibited categories under the statute—that it is a 'damaging disclosure' of, for example, a 'document or other article relating to defence'[117] or 'document or other article relating to international relations'[118]—suffices to found criminal liability. It was in the light of the class-based status of the protected categories under the new Official Secrets Act that calls have been made, unsuccessfully, for the addition of a 'public interest' defence to the terms of the Act. That is, even if a particular occasion of disclosure happened to fall within one of the prohibited categories, it should be open to the accused to argue that the material actually disclosed did not jeopardize the public interest. Such calls were resisted by the government when drafting the new statute.[119]

Several criticisms can be made of the class contents basis for PII. Should the contents of the particular document, not the class to which it belongs, not be the decisive consideration on questions of possible disclosure? What factors, indeed, determine membership of a class? Can a document belong to more than one class? Suppose, for example, that a document related to international co-operation on matters of the environment. Would it be classified as one that relates to 'international relations' merely by virtue of the fact that it emanated from discussions with other nations? Nevertheless, there does appear to be one category where the class-based claim for privilege appears intelligible, if rather wide-ranging. It has often been argued that civil servants will be less candid in the tendering of advice to Ministers if they are aware that such advice could, at some future point, be disclosed to the public. In the interest of the proper functioning of the civil service, therefore, it could be argued that policy advice as a category—whatever the area of government to which the advice relates—should be kept confidential. This argument has been credited with varying degrees of force by the courts when assessing claims to PII. Passing note should be made of the fact that, in this context, it is the maintenance of confidentiality which is argued to be conducive to the tendering of candid advice. This is in marked contrast to the conduct of judicial business, where, of course, it is openness which is traditionally cast in this role.

---

[117] Official Secrets Act 1989, s 2(1).　　　　[118] Official Secrets Act 1989, s 3(1)(a).

[119] For a statement of reasons see *Reform of Section 2 of the Official Secrets Act 1911* (Cm 408, 1988), para 60.

As always in the area of official secrecy, there is the danger that the national interest will be confused with the party political interest of the government of the day. This is illustrated by the events of the Matrix Churchill trial,[120] where the refusal of the trial judge to uphold the claims to PII led directly to the collapse of the prosecution. The resulting pressure on the government was such that it announced that a senior judge, Lord Justice Scott, would conduct an inquiry into the affair. The Scott inquiry report,[121] as was to be expected, devoted some considerable attention to the circumstances under which PII claims could legitimately be made. Much has been written on the Scott Report and its sequel.[122] The aim here is to direct attention to the practice of PII in the context of open justice.

Clearly, the difficulty is posed by the conflict between two claims: that of the public interest; and that of the right of the litigant to gain access to all material relevant to bringing or defending a law suit. There is a heightened tension in criminal cases, such as the Matrix Churchill trial, where PII is claimed in respect of material which the accused has reason to believe necessary for his defence. Indeed, there has been some question as to whether authority exists at all for making PII claims in criminal cases, and if so, whether it could be asserted on a class basis. The government relied heavily on *R v Governor of Brixton Prison, ex p Osman (No 1)*[123] as providing the basis for the potential use of PII claims in criminal cases. However, the case is weak authority for the point. Although Mann LJ expressed the view that, on principle, PII was equally applicable in the criminal area, his pronouncement to that effect cannot be regarded as part of the *ratio decidendi* since the case concerned a contested application for extradition.

Nevertheless, there are authorities which would appear to support the contention that PII was not limited to civil actions. It is surprising that no mention is made of the earlier ruling of the House of Lords in *R v Lewes JJ, ex p Home Secretary*,[124] which concerned applications for certain material in the possession of the Gaming Board in order to support proceedings for criminal libel already commenced by the applicant. The courts proceeded to dispose of the issue on the merits, holding that in the circumstances the material in question should not be disclosed. Certainly, the asserted claim to PII was not made in the actual context of a criminal trial: unusually, the applicant sought the material in order to provide support for his private prosecution. Nevertheless, there is no indication in the judgments that PII was limited simply to civil cases. Moreover, the contention that PII has no possible application in criminal prosecutions is difficult to reconcile with the long-standing line of cases barring access to knowledge of the identity of police informers. One could argue about whether such cases are properly categorized under the PII heading. To repeat one of the themes of the current

---

[120] For details of the prosecution, see the Appendix under the heading 'Arms to Iraq case'.

[121] *Report of the Inquiry into the Export of Defence Equipment and Dual-Use Goods to Iraq and Related Prosecutions* (Chairman: Sir Richard Scott) HC (1995–96) 115.

[122] See especially A. Tomkins, *The Constitution After Scott: Government Unwrapped* (1998).

[123] [1992] 1 All ER 108.   [124] [1973] AC 388.

chapter, the identity of police informers is safeguarded as much to protect their personal safety as to advance the public interest in general. There are certain features of the police informer cases that are markedly different from the standard instances of PII: in particular, the claim is not made by a Minister on each occasion of a police informer coming before the courts. On the other hand, there are statements in *Marks v Beyfus* that the DPP could not choose whether or not to answer the questions put to him.[125] The absence of discretion on the matter accords well with the view expressed in certain quarters that the assertion of PII is a matter of duty, not discretion.[126]

Once PII is seen to be applicable in the area of criminal law, various procedures can be deployed in order to keep to a minimum the disadvantage to the accused arising from a successful claim of immunity. Lord Justice Scott recommended that 'class' claims should not be deployed in criminal cases. The contents of a particular document would have to be shown to be in need of protection: their membership of a class which merited protection would not suffice. The Scott Report did not even advocate the balancing exercise that is adopted as a matter of course in civil cases. Once a document was shown to be of possible assistance to the accused, it was to be disclosed. There is authority, at any rate, that in criminal cases the judge must always inspect the document in question.[127] In addition, *ex parte* applications to the court to rule against admission are to be adopted only in very limited circumstances as being 'contrary to the general principle of open justice in criminal trials'.[128] The Court of Appeal has subsequently ruled, however, that *ex parte* hearings on PII matters do not violate the right to a fair trial, as guaranteed by Article 6 of the European Convention on Human Rights.[129] In reaching this conclusion, great reliance is placed on the judge to hold the balance between the public interest and the procedural rights of the accused. Suggestions have been advanced in recent cases that the accused should, at least, be represented by 'special counsel' at hearings from which he is excluded.[130] These pleas have been without success. Such safeguards as exist now go part way towards minimizing the inevitable tension between the rights of the accused and the public interest, but they cannot totally eliminate it.

---

[125] (1890) 25 QBD 494, 498, 500.

[126] On the other hand, an informer will generally be permitted to waive his anonymity in order to bring legal proceedings to recover, for example, money allegedly owed to him by the police for having supplied information to them: *Savage v Chief Constable of Hampshire* [1997] 1 WLR 1061.

[127] *R v Trevor Douglas K* (1993) 97 Cr App R 342, 346. It follows that a decision of the prosecution to withhold relevant evidence on public interest grounds without even notifying the trial judge is improper. In *Rowe and Davis v UK* (2000) 30 EHRR 1 the European Court of Human Rights ruled that this resulted in a violation of the right to a fair trial as guaranteed by Art 6 of the European Convention. In *R v Davis, Rowe and Johnson* The Times, 24 April 2000 the court stated that it would hear in chambers the prosecution's PII application.

[128] *R v Keane* [1994] 2 All ER 478, 483.

[129] *R v Smith (Joe)* The Times, 20 December 2000. To the same effect see the judgment of the European Court of Human Rights in *Jasper v UK* (2000) 30 EHRR 441.

[130] The cases in n 127, above.

In terms of the perspective of open justice, there exist three possible levels of disclosure.

First, the judge may decide not to inspect the document concerned. This may occur because there is automatic deference accorded to the Minister's certificate—the position adopted in the *Thetis* case, but now discarded. Alternatively, the ground may simply be that the applicant has failed to make out a case for inspection of the document. There are modern cases, such as *Air Canada v Secretary of State for Trade*,[131] where inspection has not taken place.

Secondly, the judge may decide to view the material with a view to weighing the conflicting claims of the interests of the litigant and the public interest. Such examination will take place in private, without the advantage of the submissions of counsel. The status of the context in which the material is inspected by the judge alone is rather difficult to identify. It is noteworthy that in the leading American case, which arose out of the Watergate scandal, the US Supreme Court categorized the inspection process as taking place *in camera*:

Absent a claim of need to protect military, diplomatic or sensitive national security secrets, we find it difficult to accept the argument that even the very important interest in confidentiality of presidential communications is significantly diminished by production of such material for *in camera* inspection with all the protection that a district court will be obliged to provide.[132]

If the PII claim is upheld, the only person outside the government department concerned who will have seen the document will be the judge. It is highly unlikely that this very limited disclosure will lead to public dissemination of the contents. However, it is necessary to bear in mind that claims to PII can be asserted in all manner of court and tribunal, and are not confined to the limited ranks of the senior judiciary.[133]

It is the third situation that presents scope for widespread access to the sensitive information concerned: that is, where the document is inspected by the judge, who rejects the claim advanced on the basis of the public interest. In those circumstances, presumptively the material is made available to the parties concerned in the case together with all others happening to be present in court when the contents of the documents are read out. The question is then raised as to whether or not such orders as can be imposed to prevent disclosure would be effective to maintain security while, at the same time, not putting the national interest in jeopardy.

When, as now, the ministerial certificate is not treated as conclusive, the question arises as to the procedural context in which the trial judge is to determine the issue of balance between the public interest and the private interest of the litigant

---

[131] [1983] 2 AC 394.   [132] *US v Nixon* 418 US 683 (1974), 706.
[133] In *Balfour v Foreign and Commonwealth Office* [1994] 2 All ER 588, for example, the claim was raised before an employment tribunal.

seeking access to the material in question. Under the law as derived from *Duncan v Cammell, Laird* the relevant Minister, as the political head of the department concerned, was required personally to see and consider the contents of the document in dispute. Since this process would take place within the executive reaches of government, there would be no presumption of openness of the sort that applies, initially at least, where judicial processes are concerned. Once the process of consideration is removed into the judicial branch, as it now stands, the question is posed as to the conditions under which the examination takes place. Such inspection, presumably in private and without benefit of representations from counsel, took place in *Conway v Rimmer*.[134] Whether such inspection takes place as a matter of course (as is now the rule in criminal cases) or as part of a balancing exercise (in some, but by no means all, civil cases), the status of the phase in the trial at which inspection takes place is uncertain.

Finally, attention should be drawn to the observations on the subject in an article by Lord Simon of Glaisdale (as he eventually became).[135] Although published in 1955, in the era immediately following the *Thetis* case, its conclusions are still worth considering today. The subject of Crown privilege, he argues, is often approached as if there were two situations: that the document in question is so sensitive that it must be withheld from the court under all circumstances; and that the contents of the document are so innocuous that it may be made available, through proceedings in open court, to the whole world. Yet there must surely be a range of possible situations in between these two extremes. As Simon argues, outside the most pressing matters of national security, where the document must be withheld from all, there is much to be said for devising arrangements whereby the degree of access to the document will reflect the sensitivity of the information that it contains and its importance to the parties before the court.[136] Under one such set of arrangements, the document would be released to the parties (or to the other side, in cases where the Crown is a party) on condition that it was not to be disclosed other than in closed court. Failure to comply with this condition would be punishable as a contempt of court. This suggestion is inspired by the example of section 8(4) of the Official Secrets Act 1920. It will be recalled that the condition applicable before the court may sit *in camera* by virtue of this provision is that 'the publication of any evidence to be given or of any statement to be made in the course of the proceedings would be prejudicial to the national safety'. The case for adapting this provision can only have been fortified by the enactment, five years after the article, of section 12 of the Administration of Justice Act 1960 and its explicit

---

[134] [1968] AC 910, 996–997.
[135] J. E. S. Simon, 'Evidence excluded by Considerations of State Interest' (1955) CLJ 62.
[136] ibid. 76–8.

power to punish as contempt of court certain categories of disclosure from a 'court sitting in private'.[137]

Under a slightly less stringent alternative, the document could be disclosed to third parties only for the purposes of the proceedings or pursuant to an order of the court. But once disclosure is permitted in the courtroom, even one that is sitting in private, disclosure may emanate from any of those remaining within its confines. The prohibition, therefore, would need to encompass not only the parties, but also the judge himself, legal representatives, and members of the jury.

As the Matrix Churchill case illustrates, the occasion of a criminal prosecution can provide a glimpse into the workings of government. Open justice, in this context, furnishes primarily a means of exercising a check on government rather than on the conduct of the trial judge and other *personae* of the trial. There is little scope for the latter except in clearcut situations in which the judge declines to inspect the material in question. Even where private examination of the contentious document takes place, no information is conceded to the public as to the correctness or otherwise of the decision of the judge to refuse disclosure.

---

[137] See Chapter 3, section 1, F, above. The Administration of Justice Act 1960, s 12(1)(c), may not be entirely appropriate for this purpose as it stands, since it extends to the situation where the court sits in private for the somewhat extreme reason of 'national security'. Section 12(1)(e) is expressed more openly: 'where the court (having power to do so) expressly forbids the publication of . . . information of the description which is published'.

5

Privacy and the Family

1. PRIVACY AND THE PROTECTION OF THE VULNERABLE

Article 6(1) of the European Convention on Human Rights, while proclaiming the right to a fair and public hearing, allows a number of exceptions. The press and public may be excluded from all or part of a trial when, among other reasons, 'the interests of juveniles or the protection of the private life of the parties so require, or to the extent strictly necessary in the opinion of the court in special circumstances where publicity would prejudice the interests of justice'. These exceptions delineate, in broad terms, the themes of the present chapter.

The first theme is the safeguarding of the privacy interests of the parties to litigation. Such interests frequently involve, but are by no means confined to, the family life or the sexual behaviour of the parties. In so far as the exposure of the intimate details of such behaviour tends to evoke a prurient interest among members of the public, it has been a concern for public morality rather than for the privacy of litigants that has, on occasion, furnished the basis for curtailing the open conduct of trials.[1]

The second theme is the need to ensure that the publicity that attaches to trial proceedings should not act as a deterrent to the vindication of private rights or the administration of criminal justice. It will be appreciated that there is a significant measure of overlap between this and the first theme. It is precisely because a court appearance will result in the disclosure of information that a person would prefer to keep secret that he or she is often unwilling to seek legal redress.

The law has equally been concerned to protect particularly vulnerable persons (mental patients, wards of court, and children in general) whose affairs may require judicial resolution. The concern to afford such protection forms the third theme of the present chapter.

Various devices have been deployed in order to protect the interests under consideration. Despite the fact that Article 6(1) of the European Convention appears to permit the most drastic means available for their protection, namely secret proceedings, the response of the English courts has varied from the use of private hearings to permitting unencumbered public access but subject to enforced anonymity and reporting restrictions.

---

[1] The European Convention on Human Rights, Art 6 (1), also permits the exclusion of the public from a trial 'in the interest of morals'.

There might appear to be a strong similarity between some of the matters covered in the present chapter and the question of protecting witnesses and jurors from intimidation (covered, respectively, in Chapters 4 and 7). There is, however, a fundamental difference. The making of an undisguised threat is the typical means of intimidating a witness or juror.[2] Such conduct is consequently amenable to criminal sanction.[3] Open justice, certainly, facilitates the making of such threats by making public the identity of the witness or juror. Yet seldom, if at all, in these instances does open justice in itself act as an intimidatory factor. Where, on the other hand, events in a person's private life may be disclosed and reported as a consequence of court proceedings, it is open justice *itself* which creates the problem. The witness who, as a result of an overt threat, refuses to testify has, at any rate, the possibility of resorting to duress as a possible defence to any charges arising out of failure to give evidence. Those who refuse to testify because they find the public nature of the proceedings intimidating are denied the possibility of raising such a defence. This is borne out by *R v Rodger*,[4] where the accused sought to avoid conviction for escaping from prison on the basis that the condition of incarceration had given rise to suicidal feelings. The Court of Appeal, in upholding the conviction, ruled that the causative feature in a defence of duress must be extraneous to the accused.

Some general introductory remarks should be made about the scope of each of the themes of this chapter.

The relevant pronouncements of the House of Lords in *Scott v Scott* amount to little more than repetitions of the, by then, well-established exceptions to open justice. Some years prior to that ruling, for example, in *Nagle-Gillman v Christopher*,[5] Jessel MR stated that the High Court did not possess the jurisdiction to hear cases in private, even if the parties so wished. Only in four situations could a private hearing take place: cases involving 'lunatics'; those involving 'wards of Court'; those where a public trial would defeat the very purpose of bringing the action; and those suits where the old Ecclesiastical Courts had traditionally heard cases in private, and that practice had been continued. The case itself formed a straightforward Chancery action relating to the trusts of a marriage settlement, in which the trustees claimed that the wife was acting under the undue influence of the plaintiff husband. The plea that the wife's testimony should be heard in private, on account of its sensitive nature, was rejected as not falling within any of the four stated exceptions to the rule of public trial.

The third theme of this chapter is concerned with the interests of the most vulnerable members of society when their affairs come before the court. The legal system has traditionally been concerned with the protection of, not only children,

---

[2] However, in the case of persons whose position is intrinsically fraught with risk—police informers, or members of the security forces—the mere exposure of their identity puts them at risk without the making of an overt threat.

[3] In forms such as the Criminal Justice and Public Order Act 1994, s 51.

[4] [1998] 1 Cr App R 143.   [5] (1876–77) 4 Ch D 173.

but also persons suffering from mental illness or severe mental impairment. In these respects an exception to the norm of open justice is founded simply on the basis of the status of a party before the court. The fact that a person is a child (to take the standard example) is treated as sufficient, in itself, to justify proceedings being subject to a degree of privacy that they would not otherwise be offered. The exception to open justice founded on the paternalistic role of the courts in regard to vulnerable persons is of long standing. It is not surprising, therefore, that the pronouncements of the House of Lords in *Scott v Scott* advert to this aspect of the subject. The basis of the exception was explained in different ways by their Lordships. Viscount Haldane said:

In the two cases of wards of Court and of lunatics the Court is really sitting primarily to guard the interests of the ward or the lunatic. Its jurisdiction is in this respect parental and administrative, and the disposal of controverted questions is an incident only in the jurisdiction. It may often be necessary, in order to attain its primary object, that the Court should exclude the public.[6]

The Earl of Halsbury stated simply that these two instances did not form part of 'the public administration of justice'.[7] And Lord Shaw pronounced that the two exceptions:

depend upon the familiar principle that the jurisdiction over wards and lunatics is exercised by the judges as representing His Majesty as parens patriae. The affairs are truly private affairs; the transactions are transactions truly intra familiam; and it has long been recognised that an appeal for the protection of the Court in the case of such persons does not involve the consequence of placing in the light of publicity their truly domestic affairs.[8]

Some initial criticisms can be made at this point of the various ways in which their Lordships sought to justify this exception to the standard of open justice. Viscount Haldane's pronouncement in *Scott v Scott* that in the 'two cases of wards of Court and of lunatics' the jurisdiction of the court is essentially 'administrative' is not entirely accurate. The proceedings are, on any view, essentially judicial in nature, even though they might not be fully adversarial in character. Equally, Lord Shaw's statement that wardship and related matters are 'truly domestic affairs' simply expresses the exception in a different way. Certainly, the courts have been anxious to protect the privacy of the ward and the ward's family. In this sense the relevant affairs are, descriptively, private: that is, they are respected as confidential. However, in the prescriptive sense of the term 'privacy', the need to protect confidentiality in these areas requires justification on the basis of general principle. Indeed, in *Scott v Scott* itself, notwithstanding the delicate matters involved in the case, the House of Lords gave full effect to the general standard of open justice for the simple reason that the proceedings affected matters of 'status', in regard to which 'the public has a general interest which the parties cannot exclude'.[9]

---

[6] [1913] AC 417, 437.   [7] [1913] AC 417, 442.   [8] [1913] AC 417, 483.
[9] [1913] AC 417, 436.

In areas of law relating to the family there is debate as to whether the classic form of trial dispute is entirely appropriate. Such judicial procedures that exist are heavily overlaid with mechanisms for reconciliation. Moreover, even where judicial procedures are used, they do not typically conform to the standard adversarial method of trial. There is no doubt, too, that in 'family matters', as generally conceived, there appears to have been a greater willingness to depart from the standard of open justice. There are a number of explanations for this tendency. In the majority of cases concerning children, the court is anxious to avoid any judgment that is not actuated by the best interests of the child. Even in family cases that do not involve children, procedures tend to be more flexible and less formal than in ordinary litigation, partly out of concern for the more sensitive nature of the issues, and partly in the interests of effecting a reconciliation between the parties. It is scarcely surprising, therefore, that the proposals for the creation of a 'Family Court', with a general jurisdiction over all aspects of family law, should attach importance to informality in the conduct of such a court's proceedings. One such proposal recommended that hearings in the envisaged Family Court should take place in chambers in all cases 'which the public interest did not decisively demand should be conducted in open court'.[10]

The first theme, that of privacy, has a number of distinct elements. The norm of open justice, clearly, is inimical to the protection of privacy. By pursuing their dispute in the forum of a court, the parties inevitably place themselves in a situation in which their privacy is compromised. Traditionally, the response of the law has been that the private interests of the parties must be subordinated to the overriding need, for the reasons surveyed in Chapter 2, to ensure that justice is dispensed in public. Sometimes, however, limitations have been placed on the disclosure of material beyond the circle of the parties themselves out of deference to the privacy of one of their number. For example, one factor that weighed with the House of Lords in *Harman v Home Office* against permitting further disclosure of documents obtained on discovery was the fact that the process of discovery 'constitutes a very serious invasion of the the privacy and confidentiality of a litigant's affairs'.[11] Equally, a number of exceptions to the standard of open justice have been formed out of deference to interests which may be categorized loosely as privacy interests. As Lord Shaw recognized in *Scott v Scott*, the refusal to expose vulnerable persons to courtroom publicity may be justified on the basis of according them a limited privacy interest. Moreover, even persons other than children and the mentally ill may be accorded limited privacy rights when they face the prospect of becoming involved in court proceedings—a situation typified in the rape complainant's right to anonymity.

There are, finally, a number of objections of principle that can be advanced against each of these three grounds for departing from the standard of open trial.

---

[10] *Report of the Committee on One-Parent Families*: chairman Sir Morris Finer (Cmnd 5629, 1974), Vol 1, para 4. 408.

[11] [1982] 1 All ER 532, 540, per Lord Keith.

The need to monitor the performance of the judiciary is no less insistent in family matters than in other aspects of the law. In so far as the subject matter of the present chapter encompasses the criminal law, there is a heightened requirement that the conduct of the trial should be open to public scrutiny. And, irrespective of whether the proceedings be civil or criminal in nature, the prophylactic role of openness in regard to the truthfulness of witnesses' testimony applies with equal force here as elsewhere. On the other hand, it is equally recognized that, if publicity acts as a significant deterrent to the seeking of redress, an equally important value—that of unimpeded resort to the courts—is jeopardized. Striking an acceptable balance between these competing values is an extremely difficult task.

The organization of the chapter is as follows. Section 2 examines the protection of privacy in the context of the judicial process. Section 3 considers the response to parties who refuse to play their part in court in the absence of some guarantee of confidentiality. In section 4 these (admittedly overlapping) themes are examined in the context of three specific areas. In section 5 attention shifts to family law. The treatment here will be selective only, concentrating on the dissolution and annulment of marriage, since a consideration of open justice in the context of every form of matrimonial proceeding would be prohibitively long.[12] The vulnerable, and the treatment of their affairs by the courts, are considered in section 6. And, in the concluding section of the chapter, the characteristic modes of trial of juveniles prompt further criticism of the idea that the accused has a right to a public trial.[13]

2. CURTAILING COURT PUBLICITY IN THE INTERESTS OF PRIVACY

It is necessary, at the outset, to make some remarks about the concept of privacy and its legal protection. Those interests which are properly asserted as aspects of 'privacy' have been the subject of much theoretical literature. The starting point of the present chapter is a conception of privacy which is based on the person's right to control the dissemination of personal information.[14] It is generally recognized that English law has not traditionally offered legal protection to privacy, as understood in this sense. Such protection as has been afforded has been both fragmentary and parasitic on the protection given to proprietary and other interests through the law of tort (in particular, through such actions as trespass and defamation). The frank recognition of the Court of Appeal in *Kaye v Robertson*[15] that there exists such a gap in legal protection has been the starting point of a

---

[12] There is a very detailed, if slightly dated, account in *Review of Access to and Reporting of Family Proceedings* (A Consultation Paper, Lord Chancellor's Department, August 1993).

[13] See Chapter 3, section 4, above, for initial criticism of this idea.

[14] It is one conception offered by a leading American commentator on the subject. A. Westin, *Privacy and the Law* (1967) 7: 'Privacy is the claim of individuals, groups, or institutions to determine for themselves when, how and to what extent information about them is communicated to others.'

[15] [1991] FSR 62.

renewed investigation of the subject, in the form of a committee chaired by Sir David Calcutt.[16]

It is only possible to speculate, on the basis of the various Right to Privacy bills that have been unsuccessfully introduced in Parliament over the past thirty years, as to the likely scope of a statutory right to privacy. However, it is clear that, had any of them been enacted, they would have had a minimal impact on the problem of loss of privacy consequent on appearance in court. The primary concern of the bills was to curtail the practice of secret surveillance of persons or property—most usually, in the form of the taking of intimate photographs or the recording of private conversations. These areas of concern are far removed from any possible change to the norm of open conduct of court proceedings. The place of trial, being a public forum, is one which offers little scope for secret surveillance. Equally, material disclosed in court is a matter of public record. And it has been argued, in a seminal article on the law of privacy in the United States, that the dissemination of matters of public record (such as dates of birth or marriage) does not found an action for violation of privacy.[17]

It is possible, however, to discern in the various reports on the subject of privacy an increasing concern with the adverse consequences for the individual of being embroiled in judicial proceedings.

The earliest detailed examination is the report published in 1970 by the organization, JUSTICE. Entitled *Privacy and the Law*, it appends a draft Right of Privacy Bill. The report contained no specific recommendation on the loss of privacy consequent on court proceedings. Even if (which is very unlikely) the open conduct of such proceedings had been construed as violative of privacy as defined in the Right of Privacy Bill, Clause 3(f) furnished a defence to any possible action founded on violation of privacy that 'the defendant acted under authority conferred upon him by statute or by any other rule of law'. Clearly, the terms of this defence would have encompassed situations in which the gist of the action was that disclosure had been made of material properly revealed in open court.

The *Report of the Committee on Privacy* chaired by Sir Kenneth Younger,[18] only two years later, did express some concern on the subject of trial publicity, raising the issue of whether there might not be grounds for restraining 'the present haphazard way' in which minor court proceedings were reported.[19] A consideration of this particular problem will be deferred until Chapter 8. Suffice it to note at this stage that the Younger Committee saw no reason for changing the present legal position in this regard. However, it thought that magistrates could

---

[16] *Report of the Committee on Privacy and Related Matters* (Cm 1102, 1990), and *Review of Press Self-Regulation* (Cm 2135, 1993).

[17] W. L. Prosser, 'Privacy' (1960) 48 *California Law Review* 383, 396. For a critique of the notions of 'public' and 'private' as rigid categories, see E. Paton-Simpson, 'Private Circles and Public Squares: Invasion of Privacy by the Publication of Private Facts' (1998) 61 MLR 318, especially at 329–331 on the subject of trial-generated publicity.

[18] Cmnd 5012, 1972.   [19] ibid. paras 169–76.

issue a request to the press, in particularly sensitive cases, not to disclose the identity of an offender.

Finally, the Calcutt Committee had a block of recommendations, the implementation of some of which would have had marked consequences for the open conduct of criminal trials. It suggested amendments to the legislation on non-identification of minors, in the interests of consistency and certainty. It proposed that the anonymity extended to rape complainants should also encompass the complainants (whether female or male) in regard to various other sex crimes—a reform that was implemented by the Sexual Offences (Amendment) Act 1992. Finally, and most radically, the Committee proposed that, in any criminal proceedings, the court should be empowered to prohibit the publication of the name and address of any person against whom the offence is alleged to have been committed, or any other matter likely to lead to his identification. The basis of the exercise of the power would be the court's belief that such steps were necessary to protect the person's mental or physical health, or his personal security or that of his home. This far-reaching third proposal encompasses two distinct interests. The one is the victim's interest in being secure against possible violence. This overlaps with the general problem of providing protection for those who have testified against the accused (covered in the last chapter), and would result in a double layer of protection to the witness who also happened to be the victim of the crime. Entirely distinct is the type of interest that is defined by reference to the mental health of the victim. In so far as the victim's mental equilibrium is disturbed by considerations other than fear of retaliation by the accused or his associates, the interest is properly categorized in privacy terms.

The immediate consequence of the recommendations of the Calcutt Committee was the creation of the Press Complaints Commission. One of the first tasks of the Commission was the promulgation of a Code of Practice. Clause 3(i) of the present Code enunciates the general principle, in terms evocative of Article 8 of the European Convention on Human Rights: 'Everyone is entitled to respect for his or her private and family life, home, health and correspondence. A publication will be expected to justify intrusions into any individual's private life without consent.'

Particular provisions of the Code of Practice were specifically drafted with an eye to mitigating the adverse effects of open justice. Several of these clauses will, undoubtedly, have to be read alongside the relevant legal prohibitions. Clause 12 stipulates that the press must not identify the victims of sexual assaults or publish material likely to contribute to their identification 'unless there is adequate justification and, by law, they are free to do so'. This provision, on its face, scarcely seems to advance the level of privacy protection beyond that already afforded by the law. Clause 7, by contrast, requires the press, 'even where the law does not prohibit it', not to identify children under the age of 16 'who are involved in cases concerning sexual offences, whether as victims or as witnesses'.

A more far-reaching provision of the Code, Clause 10, states that the press 'must avoid identifying relatives or friends of persons convicted or accused of crime without their consent'. This clearly extends far beyond the protection of the *personae* of the trial. The terms of the prohibition are not even defined by reference to any trial. It is possible, however, to envisage situations in which identifying a familial or other relationship between the defendant and a particularly prominent individual could be a matter of legitimate public concern. Take an example that has already been mentioned: the case of Mrs Lawson, wife of the then Chancellor of the Exchequer.[20] Public knowledge of the identity of her husband would have considerable bearing on the question of whether or not she might have received preferential treatment in dealing with her case. In this way, knowledge of the relationship would serve to support one of the traditional rationales of open justice: namely, that sufficient information should be available so as to reach an informed judgment as to whether or not the administration of justice has been conducted fairly. In this type of situation, therefore, establishing a familial link is indeed relevant to the question of whether the law is being applied even-handedly. Paradoxically, however, had her case been treated like any other charge of the same character, it would have been rather more difficult to establish that the familial relationship was one that should be known to the public. The only possible public interest in knowing the relationship would have been an entirely speculative one (in showing, perhaps, the strains under which the families of Cabinet Ministers live).

In the light of these hesitant moves towards the creation of a statutory right to privacy, there are two overriding issues that need to be addressed where privacy encounters the demands of open justice. First, if a right to privacy were to be created in any of the forms that have been proposed, what should be the appropriate method of hearing actions based on violation of that right? Secondly, irrespective of the nature of the litigation, to what extent should there be departure from the ideals of open justice to accommodate the privacy interests of one or more parties?

As regards the first matter, there would appear to be a strong case for invasion of privacy suits to be less than fully open. It would appear entirely contradictory to concede a right to privacy, while simultaneously requiring vindication of that right in a forum which serves to increase both the likelihood and the degree of dissemination of the material in question. The outcome of any particular proceedings, of course, would be uncertain. Consequently, where they result in rejection of the plaintiff's claim for violation of privacy, the argument for openness would apply with undiminished force. The better approach, therefore, would appear to be one in which reporting would be prohibited pending the outcome of the action. At the moment, there being no actionable right to privacy, such law suits as have been brought to assert privacy interests have been based on a variety of legal claims. Prominent in this regard is the action for breach of confidence. The inconsistency of permitting such actions while, on the other hand, exposing the plaintiff to the full force of trial publicity was illustrated by *Stephens v Avery*.[21]

---

[20] See Chapter 3, section 1, B, above.   [21] [1988] Ch 449.

This case was founded on the plaintiff's distress at disclosure by the defendant confidee of the fact that the plaintiff had had a lesbian relationship with a third party. The background facts were, indeed, described by Lord Browne-Wilkinson V-C as 'lurid'. In the initial stages of the litigation there appears to have been some measure of confidentiality, if only because the proceedings were initially before a Master on an application by the defendants to strike out the statement of claim. The secrecy at this stage of the case will have been determined not so much out of concern for the plaintiff's privacy as by the standard format for hearing such applications. Thereafter, the appeal against the Master's refusal to strike out was heard by the Court of Appeal in chambers. Paradoxically, the decision of the Court of Appeal itself, upholding the plaintiff's right to have her confidences respected, was given in open court.

There are two aspects of the case which might justify the open nature of Lord Browne-Wilkinson's judgment. First, damage had already been done, and on a considerable scale, since the second defendant, a national newspaper, had carried details of the disclosure in its columns. Further publication, therefore, would cause only marginal harm which would not suffice to override the general principle in favour of open justice. Different considerations should apply where disclosure has not yet taken place, and the plaintiff is seeking to restrain publication by way of injunction. Secondly, an unusual aspect of the case is to be found in the fact that the plaintiff's lesbian relationship had been with a married woman, whose husband unlawfully killed her. The plaintiff had not been called at the husband's trial, and consequently her identity had not been placed in the public domain at that point. Nevertheless, it can be appreciated that the disclosure by the defendants merely made public one aspect of an earlier trial that arguably should have emerged at the time.

The JUSTICE report's draft Right of Privacy Bill, had it been implemented, would have avoided the open hearing of breach of privacy actions. Clause 7(b) would have conferred on the Lord Chancellor the power to make rules for the conduct of violation of privacy suits, including the specific power to make provision for the hearing of such actions 'or of any interlocutory proceedings therein or any appeal therefrom otherwise than in open Court'. Clause 10 would have complemented this provision by adding to the terms of section 12(1) of the Administration of Justice Act 1960 a provision relating to situations in which a court would sit in private pursuant to the powers conferred by Clause 7. The draft Bill, therefore, would have conferred the highest form of protection available to the plaintiff: trial *in camera* or in chambers. It is only possible to speculate as to the scope of any rules that would have been promulgated under Clause 7(b). It is unlikely that they would have required a private sitting of the court in all forms of action created by the proposed legislation. In particular, the Right of Privacy Bill, had it been enacted, would have encompassed forms of conduct (for example, unauthorized appropriation of the plaintiff's name or likeness for another's gain) which would not appear to require confidentiality in the mode of trial of the action. Rather less defensible, however, was the conclusion of the Committee that exclusion of the press and public was to be the appropriate method of protecting the privacy of the plaintiff. That there are other methods of securing the same end—methods less invasive of the ideal of open justice—appears not to have been considered by the Committee. In belated recognition of the absurdity of unhindered public access to breach of confidence hearings, the Civil Procedure Rules 1998 similarly list, among suits that may be heard in private, those involving 'confidential information (including information relating to personal financial matters) [where] publicity would damage that confidentiality'.[22]

The second matter concerns the extent to which, irrespective of the nature of the suit, there should be departure from the ideals of open justice to accommodate the privacy interests of the parties. This question is capable of arising irrespective of whether or not there is an actionable right to privacy. It is difficult to extract any firm principle, as an examination of the cases shows.

In *H v Ministry of Defence*[23] a civil suit was brought by the plaintiff, identified simply as 'a 27 year old serviceman', in respect of negligent medical treatment which had resulted in a penectomy with consequent psychological trauma. The problem posed by open justice was here presented in its clearest form. A person suffering from medical and psychological trauma would be fully entitled to seek medical assistance in the full realization that patient–doctor confidences would be respected. However, once he sought legal redress, he would fall within the orbit of the presumption of open justice. This particular case was argued up to the Court of Appeal on the question of whether jury trial was permissible in the circumstances. Lord Donaldson MR dealt with the anonymity point very briefly at the outset of his judgment, stating that an order had been made prohibiting the naming or other identification of the plaintiff. In addition, only such reference to the extent of the medical condition as was necessary would be made.

A number of points are noteworthy. As it was a civil case, the press did not possess statutory standing to contest the making of the order. Moreover, the medical condition itself was subject to well-established norms of confidentiality as far as the question of its treatment was concerned. It would appear correct, therefore, that there should be a similar degree of privacy once legal redress was pursued in respect of the infliction of the injury.

In contrast, *Birmingham Post and Mail Ltd v Birmingham City Council*[24] concerned an order made against an individual under section 37 of the Public Health (Control of Disease) Act 1984. The subject of the order was allegedly suffering from tuberculosis, a notifiable disease within the terms of that statute, and one where professional practice, as well as legislation, required breach of doctor–patient confidentiality. The council had applied *ex parte* to a local magistrate for the making of the order. Though declining to hear the application *in camera* or in

---

[22] Civil Procedure Rules 1998, SI 1998/3132, r 39.2(3)(c).   [23] [1991] 2 QB 103.
[24] The Times, 25 November 1993.

chambers, the magistrate made an order under section 11 of the Contempt of Court Act 1981 that prohibited in perpetuity the disclosure of the patient's name. The argument for disclosure was advanced in the above-named proceedings by a newspaper, basing its claim on the interest of local residents in the relevant area of Birmingham in knowing whether a person suffering from such an easily communicable disease was living nearby. Clearly, there are analogies to be drawn with one of the rationales of open justice in criminal proceedings: namely, the interest in knowing whether a person suspected of crime is present in the neighbourhood. The consideration to be weighed against this interest was, not that would-be litigants might be deterred from seeking redress in the courts (the procedure under the Public Health Act was initiated by the council), but rather that persons who suspected that they might have contracted such an embarrassing disease would be reluctant to seek medical assistance. In the event, the court ruled that to allow publication of the patient's name and address would not be fair: the order under the Public Health Act had been made *ex parte*, and therefore without giving him full opportunity to contest the council's application. However, once all opportunity to challenge that order had been exhausted, it was no longer legitimate to withhold the patient's identity under section 11, whether as a means of protecting his privacy or in order to spare his embarrassment.

R v Westminster City Council, ex p Castelli[25] is similar to *H v Ministry of Defence*, in that the confidentiality issue was argued as part of the substantive application for redress. Here, the application was by way of judicial review against the defendant council for its failure to house the applicants who, being HIV positive, were in priority need under the legislation. Unlike *H v Ministry of Defence*, however, counsel were instructed both as *amicus curiae* and to represent a newspaper interest. The implication from the judgment of Latham J is that, for that reason alone, the ruling on the point in the *H* case was to be viewed as having been given *per incuriam*. Consistently with the *Birmingham* case, it was held that considerations of privacy and embarrassment did not in themselves justify the grant of an order under section 11 of the Contempt of Court Act. In the particular circumstances it was inferred that publicity had not deterred the applicants since the trial of the full application for judicial review had commenced. As will be seen in regard to blackmail cases and cases of sexual assault, however, account must also be taken of similarly placed individuals who might be deterred from seeking legal redress. Latham J confessed to having no secure information on the question of how many such persons there might be, and left open the possibility that any one of them could be allowed to adduce evidence to the effect that anonymity was necessary to the proper interests of justice. One possible rationalization of this case is that HIV is not a notifiable disease under the Public Health (Control of Disease) Act 1984,[26] whereas tuberculosis is (in certain circumstances) so notifiable. Also apparent

[25] [1996] 1 FLR 534.
[26] There is some academic dispute on this point: see I. M. Kennedy and A. Grubb, *Medical Law: Text with Materials* (2nd edn, 1994), 83–4.

from this case is a reluctance to adopt a general rule on privacy. Latham J envisaged that each similarly placed applicant would be reduced to arguing for confidentiality on the facts of his own situation. However, there is a strong argument in favour of a general rule so that those contemplating legal action will be able to anticipate with some confidence how their claims for anonymity protection are likely to be received by the court.

3. MITIGATING THE DETERRENT EFFECT OF COURT PUBLICITY

On occasion, an argument in favour of departing from the standard of open justice that might have been framed in terms of protecting the privacy interests of one or other of the parties before the court is couched, instead, in terms of the need to prevent exposure to publicity from deterring persons from seeking redress or giving testimony in the courts. The protection of privacy and the avoidance of deterrence, though potentially overlapping in particular contexts, provide different bases for departing from the open conduct of trials. Considerations of privacy are capable of objective determination. Those associated with deterrence, by contrast, raise a host of questions. Should the courts defer to the needs of the person of above-average sensitivity? Or should the standard be objective? How, in any event, are the courts to gauge whether or not the particular individual (whether party to the case or witness) reaches the applicable standard?

There are a number of pronouncements on the subject in *Scott v Scott* itself. These are to be treated with a little caution since they were expressed obiter. The facts of the case did not pose the problem in its straightforward form. There was no suggestion that Mrs Scott would have withdrawn her petition or refused to testify unless she had been permitted to give the critical evidence in a closed session of the court. On the contrary, her subsequent action in effecting an (admittedly limited) disclosure of the *in camera* phase of the hearing would suggest a certain resolve on her part to set clear the record of her marriage. Nevertheless, the various members of the House of Lords felt the need to address the matter. Lord Shaw, at one extreme, counselled against making concessions for the litigant:

One's experience shews that the reluctance to intrude one's private affairs upon public notice induces many citizens to forgo their just claims. It is no doubt true that many of such cases might have been brought before tribunals if only the tribunals were secret. But the concession to these feelings would, in my opinion, tend to bring about those very dangers to liberty in general, and to society at large, against which publicity tends to keep us secure.[27]

Other opinions were more sympathetic to the stress likely to be caused by appearance in court. Earl Loreburn said:

[27] [1913] AC 417, 485.

... if the Court is satisfied that to insist upon publicity would in the circumstances reasonably deter a party from seeking redress, or interfere with the effective trial of the cause, in my opinion an order for hearing or partial hearing in camera may lawfully be made. But I cannot think that it may be made as a matter of course, though my own view is that the power ought to be liberally exercised, because justice will be frustrated or declined if the Court is made a place of moral torture.[28]

Viscount Haldane was rather more strict on the conditions that would justify departure from the norm of open justice:

He who maintains that by no other means than by [a secret hearing] can justice be done may apply for an unusual procedure. But he must make out his case strictly, and bring it up to the standard which the underlying principle requires.[29]

A typical case, though one presented in an unusual format, is *R v Chancellor of the Chichester Consistory Court, ex p News Group Newspapers Ltd*.[30] This represented an unsuccessful challenge to an order of the Chancellor of the Consistory Court which directed the exclusion of the press and public from the hearing.[31] The subject matter was the trial of disciplinary charges against a clergyman alleging that he had committed adultery with two parishioners. The intimate or embarrassing nature of the evidence, in itself, did not give rise to a power of exclusion. However, it might form the basis of a proper exclusion order in circumstances where a witness would otherwise be unable or unwilling to give evidence. The tearfulness of at least one of the parishioners appeared to satisfy this standard.

It is difficult to extract any consistent line of authority from the case law. Some areas have the benefit of a statutory provision or a consistent line of practice for dealing with the relevant category of case. In cases which are not regulated in this way, the question falls to be decided on the basis of judicial discretion. Often it can only be a matter for conjecture whether a party will abandon an action or a witness will decline to testify in the absence of some guarantee of privacy. The most extreme instance in this regard is *B (orse P) v A-G*[32] where a mother who had brought legitimacy applications on behalf of two infants categorically assured the judge that she would withdraw the applications unless the press and public were excluded from the court. The judge, while conceding that such a stance was perfectly reasonable, formed the view that he had no power to order the exclusion.

---

[28] [1913] AC 417, 446.   [29] [1913] AC 417, 438.
[30] [1992] COD 48.
[31] The Ecclesiastical Jurisdiction Measure 1963, s 28(f), furnished the basis of the order: 'the chancellor, if satisfied that it is in the interests of justice to do so, may give directions that during any part of the proceedings such persons or classes of persons including the assessors as the court may determine shall be excluded'.
[32] [1966] 2 WLR 58.

4. PRIVACY AND DETERRENCE: THREE PROBLEMATIC ASPECTS

In this section, consideration will be given to three aspects of publicity that has been generated as a consequence of trial proceedings. Each of the three presents a situation in which the interests of privacy and/or the avoidance of deterrence have been advanced—whether successfully or not—as a ground for imposing temporary or permanent restraints on disclosures that would ensue from appearance in court as a witness or accused.

First, there is the question whether it is proper to extend anonymity to the accused until such time, if any, as the trial concludes with a verdict of guilty. There are arguments, founded on the presumption of innocence, which suggest that such protection should be afforded.

Secondly, the emphasis will shift to the victim, and the question will be raised as to whether the victims of certain types of alleged offence—blackmail and rape figure most prominently in this regard—should be allowed a guarantee of anonymity. In contrast to considerations founded on the presumption of innocence, the guarantees in this second area, if they are to be effective, must confer lifelong anonymity. In rape and blackmail trials, the victim is very commonly the principal witness against the accused. This type of trial, consequently, poses but one aspect of a wider question: whether the victim of any newsworthy crime whatsoever should be shielded from trial-generated publicity. Nevertheless, the situation in the the aforementioned cases is distinguishable from the generality of criminal trials since the complainant is typically concerned to avoid the publication of matters of an intimate nature.

Thirdly, to return to the position of the accused, to what extent should rehabilitative considerations permit a person who has served his allotted sentence a degree of exemption from public knowledge of a previous conviction?

A. Anonymity and the Presumption of Innocence

The issue has come before the English courts in *R v Dover Justices, ex p Dover District Council*.[33] A council environmental health officer had brought proceedings against a restaurant owner, who applied successfully to the magistrates for the making of two orders: that neither he nor his business be identified before the end of the proceedings; and that there should be no disclosure—at any time, it would seem—of any charges of which he was acquitted. The validity of the orders was challenged by the district council in whose name the prosecution was brought. Neill LJ ruled that there could be no conceivable justification for restricting the reporting of charges of which a person was acquitted. The

---

[33] [1992] Crim LR 371: and see H. Scheer, 'Publicity and the Presumption of Innocence' (1993) CLJ 37.

rationale of this ruling was, presumably, that such a verdict would undo any damage inflicted on the reputation of the accused by the initiation of the proceedings. His Lordship thought, however, that, in appropriate circumstances, there might be some basis for imposing a temporary order which would restrain publicity until the defendant had fully developed his case. Equally, he left open the possibility that it might be permissible to restrain the reporting of evidence which was ruled inadmissible by the court.[34]

The ruling represents a tentative and cursory treatment of some difficult matters. The presumption of innocence, as it is understood in the common law, is a doctrine directed solely at the evidential burden to be discharged by the prosecution before a conviction may be obtained. Whether a constitutionally guaranteed presumption of innocence would require acceptance of the argument unsuccessfully advanced in the *Dover* case was investigated, against the background of the Canadian Charter of Rights and Freedoms, in *Re Regina v Several Unnamed Persons*.[35] The charges of gross indecency in that case had led to a great deal of local interest. The defendants sought to restrain publication of their names on two grounds: that knowledge of their identity would lead to prejudicial pre-trial publicity; and that publication of their names was at variance with the presumption of innocence. Added to the latter ground was a privacy interest based on the suffering that would be caused by publicity to the families of the defendants. The Ontario High Court, in rejecting the application, pronounced:

> . . . if one were to accept the applicants' argument in this case, it would follow logically that, subject to the exercise of some judicial discretion, the more serious the alleged criminal act, or the higher the standing or reputation of the accused in the community, the more such accused should be protected from publicity and, therefore, it would follow many serious criminal trials should be either privately or secretly conducted, or the identity of the accused not disclosed.[36]

An interesting exercise in anonymity for the sake of the unconvicted accused was provided by the terms of section 17 of New Zealand's Criminal Justice Amendment Act 1975.[37] This stipulated a rule of anonymity 'unless and until [the accused] is found guilty of the offence with which he is charged'. Escape from the rule was permitted only by court order, the accused being permitted under section 45B(2) to apply to the court for such an order. The application was to be granted only if, in the light of five listed factors (which included rather openendedly 'any other relevant matters'), the court was satisfied that the interest in not having the information released was offset by either the interests of the general public or the interest of any particular individual who would otherwise be suspected of having committed the offence concerned. This last consideration,

---

[34] In summary trials, in contrast to trials on indictment, there is no equivalent to the *voir dire* phase to determine matters of admissibility in the absence of the jury.

[35] (1984) 4 DLR (4th) 310.   [36] ibid. 313.

[37] See, generally, R. Munday, 'Name Suppression: an adjunct to the presumption of innocence and to mitigation of sentence' [1991] Crim LR 681 and 753 (in two parts), especially at 683, n 26.

the need to protect persons who might wrongly be identified as the accused in a criminal case, has been met on several occasions as providing a reason—though not figuring as one of the central rationales—for open justice. More familiar is one of the five reasons listed: 'the likelihood of further evidence relating to the proceedings being offered by members of the public if publication is permitted'.

Issues analogous to the presumption of innocence arise even in the context of civil cases, where the loss of a law suit that will be fully reported may inflict harm on a party's commercial standing. The decision of the Court of Appeal in *R v Legal Aid Board, ex p Kaim Todner (a firm)*[38] draws together many of the themes of the present chapter. The applicants sought judicial review of a decision of the Legal Aid Board that had terminated their franchise at a branch office. At first instance the firm applied unsuccessfully for an order enforcing anonymity, the order to be lifted should the application for judicial review fail. Before the Court of Appeal they made an additional application: that their anonymity be retained irrespective of the outcome of the appeal. Clearly, only the former was founded on 'presumption of innocence' considerations. Their submission was that incalculable damage would be inflicted on their business reputation if the reasons given by the Legal Aid Board were to be publicized. In dismissing the appeal, the Court of Appeal emphasized two points. First, the applicants were in no special position, as compared with other categories of litigant, merely by virtue of being a firm of solicitors. This was in spite of the fact that, in addition to the general damage that would ensue from newspaper coverage, their reputation within the profession would also suffer from the likely precedent-setting nature of the case.[39] Secondly, in contrast to the position of the accused or witnesses, the plaintiffs had freely chosen to bring matters to court.

The latter point is not convincing since the rape victim, too, exercises a choice whether to file a complaint which may ultimately lead to a courtroom appearance. Indeed, as between these two situations, there are points to be made on both sides. The effect of publicity in deterring individuals from becoming embroiled in court proceedings, it could be argued, is particularly to be avoided where an alleged crime has been committed. On the other hand, any civil action may cease, as many do, on an out-of-court settlement being reached even before the first day of the hearing.

On occasion the argument is heard in the courts that anonymity for the defendant is necessary to secure the anonymity of other *personae* of the trial, most typically the rape victim or the identity of any children involved in the proceedings. This 'parasitic' basis for confidentiality is entirely distinct in character from that founded on the presumption of innocence. In particular, the logic of this form of argument requires that the accused should remain anonymous even if—some would say, especially if—they are convicted. It is not surprising, therefore, that

---

[38] [1998] 3 All ER 541.

[39] In the manner akin to the barrister singled out for the important ruling on alleged negligence in *Rondel v Worsley* [1969] 1 AC 191.

the courts have been particularly reluctant to accept this basis for anonymity. In *Ex p Godwin*,[40] the defendants were charged with having committed a number of indecent assaults on two children. The prosecution successfully applied for an order under section 39 of the Children and Young Persons Act 1933 directing that no report should be published identifying the children named in the indictment. The judge also acceded to a request to suppress the names of the defendants, on the basis that both they and the children formed part of a close-knit community and disclosure in regard to the former posed a risk that the identity of the children could be ascertained. The second part of the order was successfully challenged by the press under section 159 of the Criminal Justice Act 1988.[41] The irony in many of these cases is that, where there is a family link between the defendant and the child victim, naming of the former will usually give a clear indication of the identity of the latter. Therefore, the more serious the breach of trust, the more likely the defendant's identity will be protected.

B. Blackmail and Rape[42]

Prosecutions in respect of blackmail and rape are conducted in open court, subject to protection being afforded to the identity of the complainant.

The term 'blackmail' is the common word for an offence which is given its technical definition in statute. A person is guilty of the offence 'if, with a view to gain for himself or another or with intent to cause loss to another, he makes any unwarranted demand with menaces'.[43] Although the popular perception of the crime sees the 'menace' as consisting of a threat to divulge information which the victim would pay to remain private, it is clear that the offence is not limited in this way. Nevertheless, it is only those aspects of the crime that accord with the public perception of it that raise issues of possible confidentiality. The following account, therefore, will be limited in that way.

There are indications that it had long been standard practice in such cases that the name of the victim should not be divulged in court. It is difficult to identify the point at which informal protection of anonymity was extended to blackmail victims in the hope that they would confide in the police. In the course of a blackmail case conducted at the Old Bailey in 1936, prosecuting counsel is reported as having stated: 'it is customary in these Courts that anyone prosecuting in these sorts

---

[40] [1992] QB 190.

[41] Compare *Ex p Crook* [1995] 1 All ER 537, where the judge did not specifically prohibit the publication of the identity of the accused, while recognizing—correctly, in the view of the Court of Appeal— that in the circumstances of the case such publication would have the effect of identifying the children.

[42] It should be stressed immediately that, when the term 'rape' is used in this section, sometimes it will be referring only to the crime of rape in the technical sense, and sometimes (depending on the period) as indicating charges of sexual assault (of which rape is now only one) where complainant anonymity is conferred.

[43] Theft Act 1968, s 21.

of cases should not have his or her name disclosed, because it always causes a great deal of unpleasant publicity.'[44] The exact status of such a practice appears to have been unclear. It may be that, only with the less deferential style of journalism that has characterized more recent decades, has it become necessary to indicate the precise status of the custom and the consequences attaching to failure to abide by it.

The basis of anonymity protection was squarely confronted in *R v Socialist Worker Printers and Publishers Ltd, ex p A-G*.[45] The Attorney-General applied to commit the respondents for contempt of court on the ground that they had flouted a direction given by a judge that the blackmail victims' names should be withheld and that they should be referred to only as 'Mr Y' and 'Mr Z'—a direction which defence counsel had not challenged. There was some dispute as to the status of the direction, the validity of which was central to the liability of the respondents. In this, as in earlier cases, there appears to have been no developed discussion of the level of confidentiality that would be deemed appropriate to the proper administration of justice. The respondents, invoking the traditional authorities in favour of open access to the courts, argued that the trial judge had no authority to give the direction in favour of anonymity. Lord Widgery CJ responded that there was a fundamental difference between a secret hearing and one which, as in the present case, had been open to the public subject to anonymity being granted to the victims. His Lordship believed that the arrangements at the blackmail trial were the appropriate level of response. Without developing the point, he stated that it would be 'disastrous' if blackmail charges were to be heard *in camera*, though (as he immediately conceded) there were distinct parallels to be drawn between such charges and trials involving some secret industrial process, where *in camera* proceedings are conceded as a matter of course.[46] Although he did not seek to justify the difference in the mode of hearing between the two types of case, the fundamental basis of distinction may be that secret processes are litigated in civil suits, where the demands of open justice are less insistent than in criminal trials.

Again, in *John Fairfax Group Pty Ltd v The Local Court of New South Wales*[47] the magistrates had ordered the victims of extortion to be known only by pseudonyms. It was held that the media did not have standing in the local court to contest the order. Moreover, even if they had such standing, the ruling was held to be perfectly correct. Mahoney JA ruled: 'the principle that the courts are to be open and that the media may publish what is done in them is not an end in itself. The principle is adopted because it is judged to be the means by which other and more fundamental goods will be achieved'.[48]

---

[44] M. Hepworth, *Blackmail: publicity and secrecy in everyday life* (1975) 24.
[45] [1975] QB 637.   [46] ibid. 651.
[47] (1992) 66 Australian Law Journal 308 (New South Wales Court of Appeal, 4 September 1991).
[48] ibid. 309.

One point that was pressed on the court in the *Socialist Worker* case was the lack of parity of treatment as between alleged victims of blackmail and rape. It was argued that, if the latter was denied anonymity, so too should the former. Lord Widgery suggested that, in the context of rape, the matter was more properly dealt with by Parliament—as, indeed, it shortly was. The legislative initiatives in the area of rape will be examined next. For the moment it is necessary to consider Lord Widgery's assertion that 'there are . . . significant differences between the complainant in blackmail and in rape respectively'.[49] As in rape cases, the rationale of granting anonymity to the blackmail victim demands that the anonymity protection is not limited to the trial itself. It must encompass both the pre-trial and post-trial phases. Unlike rape charges, however, the need for anonymity in blackmail cases can scarcely be questioned. By the very fact of making the threats in question, the alleged blackmailer has shown that the victim places the highest possible value on retaining his secret. The response of rape complainants, on the other hand, has varied. Most have insisted on their right to remain anonymous. A significant minority, however, have waived the entitlement in favour of promoting other objectives.

Even as regards the precise mode of protection of anonymity, there appears to be a divergence between blackmail and rape. In trials of the latter offence it is common for the woman to be known and referred to in court by her real name. The media, however, are prohibited from reporting the name or any detail likely to lead to her identity being disclosed. The victim of a blackmailer, by contrast, is allowed anonymity even within the courtroom itself. The standard practice is that, when called to the witness box to testify, the victim is allowed to write his name on a piece of paper with the result that the press and public present in the court are denied this knowledge.[50]

A theme common to both blackmail and rape, as just indicated, is that the period of protection of anonymity must, in order to be effective, predate the commencement of the trial. The present situation with regard to rape is that protection is afforded from the time when an allegation is made.[51] Under an earlier provision, anonymity protection ran only from the point when the accused was charged (and, hence, at some point after he had been apprehended).[52] This gap in protection was clearly exposed in the so-called 'Vicarage rape case' of March 1986, where the identity of the victim of an especially brutal attack, the daughter of a vicar, was revealed in the media while the police were still conducting their investigations.[53]

---

[49] [1975] QB 637, 653.

[50] There is a clear statement about the practice in the *Socialist Worker* case: [1975] QB 637, 644. Where the victim is a well-known figure, even this will not suffice to maintain his anonymity. It was, perhaps, because the two men concerned in that case were such figures that their identities were apparent to those present in the court.

[51] Sexual Offences (Amendment) Act 1992, s 1(1).

[52] Sexual Offences (Amendment) Act 1976, s 4(1).

[53] Compare a regime of anonymity based on the presumption of innocence, which logically would be required to run from the moment when, under present arrangements, the accused is publicly identified—whether by way of arrest or charge, or even by 'being wanted for questioning'.

To turn specifically to the issue of rape anonymity, it is necessary to draw attention to some recent developments concerning the scope of the concept of rape and its mode of trial which will have a distinct bearing on the issues of anonymity.

First, the long-standing rule that in law a husband could not be guilty of the rape of his wife has been abolished.[54] This raises difficulties in the situation where husband and wife have the same surname since anonymity conferred on the wife, in order to be effective, must extend to the husband.

Secondly, as in other areas of the criminal law, those persons whose complaints have not resulted in a criminal prosecution are increasingly turning to the use of the civil law in order to secure public recognition that the defendant did commit a criminal offence. There have also been cases where a civil action has been successfully brought against a man who has already been convicted and sentenced in regard to a sexual assault. The civil action poses distinct problems since it is not, as such, covered by the anonymity provisions applicable to prosecutions. Nevertheless, provided that recourse is initially had to the criminal process, the terms of the statute would seem wide enough to encompass a situation where no prosecution is brought by the authorities, and the complainant then resorts to civil law.[55] The plaintiff in such a case would also derive some measure of protection from the Code of Practice of the Press Complaints Commission. Clause 12, as already noted, forbids the press from identifying the victims of sexual assault unless it is legally permissible and there exists 'adequate justification' for doing so. However, even in the absence of specific legislation, it would be possible for a civil court to grant anonymity to the plaintiff on the general ground that she would be otherwise deterred from seeking legal redress.

Thirdly, that anonymity should apply only to rape was increasingly seen as an absurd limitation. Women who were the alleged victims of equally serious sexual assaults, it was cogently argued, were entitled to a measure of protection equal to that conferred on the rape complainant.[56] When Parliament finally responded, the reforms went even further and granted a right to anonymity in regard to a range of sexual offences, some of which can be perpetrated on men.[57] Consequently, from this point onwards the discussion will be directed to these offences in general, though rape will remain the archetypal offence within this category.

These preliminary points having been made, there are three possible approaches to the question of anonymity, each of which is reflected in a particular phase of the history of rape trials.

---

[54] *R v R* [1992] 1 AC 599.

[55] The Sexual Offences (Amendment) Act 1992, s 1(1), starts the anonymity protection from the point where 'an allegation has been made that an offence to which this Act applies has been committed.'

[56] As argued by J. Spencer and B. Markesinis, 'Sex victims twice over' The Times, (18 November 1987) 12.

[57] Sexual Offences (Amendment) Act 1992, s 2(1).

One possibility is to confer no legal right to anonymity, whether on the complainant or the accused. This, as we have seen, was the law at the time of the *Socialist Worker* case, and it remained so until the enactment of the Sexual Offences (Amendment) Act 1976 as a result of the recommendations of the Heilbron Committee the previous year.[58] On a second approach, the accused and complainant could be treated equally in a different respect, in both benefiting from a right to anonymity. This was the situation from 1976[59] until 1988.[60] Thirdly, the complainant alone could be given the right to be anonymous. This has been the position since 1988.[61]

The clear justification advanced in favour of complainant anonymity is that, without such protection, women would be more reluctant to report instances of rape or any other form of sexual assault. The assurance that her identity will not be available for reporting in the media means that any trial that may take place will, to that extent, be less of an ordeal for her. Furthermore, anonymity protection has been supplemented, since the 1976 Act, by prohibitions on wide-ranging examination of the complainant's sexual history. By way of additional protection, applications by the prosecution to adduce evidence about the sexual behaviour of the complainant are now to be heard 'in private' and, remarkably, in the complainant's absence.[62] Once the argument for complainant anonymity is accepted, it naturally raises the question whether similar protection should be afforded to the accused. It is universally accepted that, at the very least, the man's name should be released if he is found guilty. However, there is a persuasive body of opinion that, pending such an outcome, he should receive the same protection as the woman. Instances may be cited of cases where the accused has been found not guilty, yet—in marked contrast to the position of the complainant—his identity has been disclosed on a national scale. There have also been cases in which men awaiting trial for rape, overwhelmed by the prospect of their coming ordeal (including the attendant publicity), have committed suicide. It is very difficult, of course, to identify the precise role played by the prospect of trial publicity in these situations. In one inquest into such a death, the East Sussex Coroner voiced a plea for a change in the law, so as to allow anonymity for the accused pending the outcome of the trial.[63] Such arguments, as already noted, proved persuasive with Parliament in the period between 1976 and 1988.

The difficulty in appraising such arguments stems from identifying the appropriate point of comparison. Those who oppose anonymity for the man would argue that, in no other crime, does the accused have such protection. Those who argue for such protection in the specific context of charges of sexual assault,

---

[58] Report of the Advisory Group on the Law of Rape (Cmnd 6352, 1975).

[59] Sexual Offences (Amendment) Act 1976, ss 4 and 6.

[60] Criminal Justice Act 1988, s 158(5).

[61] The change was effected by the Criminal Justice Act 1988, s 158(5): 'Section 6 (anonymity of defendants in rape etc. cases) shall cease to have effect.'

[62] Youth Justice and Criminal Evidence Act 1999, s 43(1).   [63] The Times (27 August 1998) 6.

therefore, must show why a verdict of not guilty does not clear the reputation of the accused to the extent that it does in the context of other charges. Otherwise, the argument for defendant anonymity must be cast in general terms for all crimes equally, in the way considered earlier in this chapter. It is possible to avoid this consequence by arguing that the case for defendant anonymity in the area under consideration does not rest on the lack of efficacy of not guilty verdicts in clearing the defendant's name. It rests, rather, on the need for parity of treatment as between complainant and accused. Trials of sexual assault charges, it could be argued, are unusual in setting the word of the complainant against that of the accused, in the absence of any testimony by a third party. Apart from the question whether they are untypical in this regard, the proposition would appear to be correct only in situations—to take the instance of rape—where it is agreed that intercourse took place and the only issue is on the question of consent.

Even under a regime of complainant anonymity, there is a possibility of disclosure of identity, whether voluntary or forced. These will now be considered in turn.

The option of the complainant voluntarily waiving her right to anonymity was not available under the changes introduced in 1976. A statutory defence is now expressly provided whereby the person charged can prove that 'the publication or programme in which the matter appeared was one in respect of which [the complainant] had given written consent to the appearance of matter of that description'.[64] Authorization, therefore, need not be in general terms: it may be conceded only for the purpose of a particular article or programme. Moreover, a valuable safeguard is provided whereby the written consent does not provide a defence if it is proved that 'any person interfered unreasonably with the peace or comfort of the person giving the consent, with intent to obtain it'.[65] It is noteworthy that the term 'peace or comfort' is also to be found in the legislation that safeguards the position of the residential occupier. Under the Protection from Eviction Act 1977 it is a criminal offence for any person, with a view (broadly) to forcing the occupier to leave, to do acts 'calculated to interfere with the peace or comfort of the residential occupier'.[66] The act of interference with the rape complainant's peace or comfort does not, in itself, found criminal liability. It merely furnishes a possible basis for challenging the position of a publisher who purports to have acted pursuant to the consent of such complainant. For the question whether the statutory conditions had been breached in obtaining the 'consent' could be raised as a collateral issue in any prosecution brought against any person charged with disclosing the identity of the complainant.

Notable instances have occurred in which complainants have consented to the disclosure of their identities. In one prominent case, an elderly former magistrate, Mrs Muriel Harvey, who was raped on Christmas Day 1992 while walking home

---

[64] Sexual Offences (Amendment) Act 1992, s 5(2).
[65] Sexual Offences (Amendment) Act 1992, s 5(3).
[66] Protection from Eviction Act 1977, s 1(3).

after midnight mass, exercised her right in this regard. She did so in the belief that public knowledge that she was the victim of the attack might encourage witnesses to come forward. Alternatively, she thought, the publication of her identity might lead the rapist to boast to others of what he had done. The case also illustrates well the possibility that, in the absence of a tightly drawn consent, disclosure may take place on a far wider basis than is necessary for the purpose for which it was made. The story was originally carried, together with a photograph, in the woman's local newspaper, *The Shropshire Star*. That was the most effective forum for the purpose of eliciting information from members of the local community. It eventually reached the national press, where it took the form of a human interest story illustrating the victim's courage and resolution.[67] In one respect the decision to waive the right to anonymity in this case was an easier one to make than for most women. There was no suggestion that the woman's assailant was known to her. If the matter came to trial, therefore, it would be very unlikely that she would have to undergo the examination of her sexual history to which younger complainants have been subjected in such cases. On the other hand, by putting her name in the public domain, she acknowledged that she had created the risk of a second, calculated attack by the same man.

The decision to waive anonymity can be taken at any time, and for any reason. It can take place before or after any trial, nor need it be motivated by any of the standard arguments in favour of open justice. In November 1999 a notable example of post-trial waiver occurred when a thirty-four-year-old woman, Allison Brown, revealed that she had been the complainant in the recently concluded trial of the pop star, Gary Glitter (whose real name is Paul Gadd). Although the defendant was acquitted of having sexually abused Ms. Brown,[68] he was sentenced to a term of imprisonment for possession of child pornography. The complainant stated at the time that her decision to reveal her identity was motivated by a wish to encourage other victims of sexual abuse to report the crime in preference to suffering in silence. Doubtless, too, her communication had the effect of casting doubt on the correctness of the verdict on the sexual abuse charge. As is to be expected, whatever the message and the reasons behind it, a photograph and a real name do more to reinforce its contents than a disembodied communication.

The option of waiver does create possible difficulties for the media in that they might erroneously believe that the victim's option to waive the right has been exercised. Associated Newspapers, the owners of the *Evening Standard*, were fined £750, with costs, for naming the victim in the first instance of marital rape.[69] The newspaper's editor stated that the article had been written on the mistaken assumption that the woman had waived her right to anonymity.[70]

[67] The Times (1 January 1993) 5.
[68] It was disclosed to the jury that the complainant had sold to a newspaper the rights to her story, the contract containing a prejudicial element that the amount to be paid for the story would vary according to the outcome of the trial.
[69] *R v R* (n 54, above).   [70] The Times (1 April 1992) 6.

Certain feminist writers have argued that rape victims should not resort to anonymity protection. They contend that anonymity, whether formal or informal, merely serves to perpetuate the view that a stigma attaches to any woman who has been the victim of a rape. Such a view holds that a policy of openness would be a more healthy situation, while conceding that the decision whether or not to avail herself of anonymity should be left with the woman concerned. The specifically feminist element in the argument has diminished somewhat since the Sexual Offences (Amendment) Act 1992 extended the range of sexual offences subject to anonymity to offences that can be committed against men. Moreover, the offence of rape has undergone recent redefinition. It can now be committed by a man in regard to either a woman or another man, the crime being expressed in gender-neutral terms.[71]

Apart from voluntary waiver, there exists a discretionary power in the trial judge to refuse anonymity on the basis of a number of grounds. Particularly noteworthy is the factor identified in section 3(1) of the Sexual Offences (Amendment) Act 1992: that disclosure is required 'for the purpose of inducing persons who are likely to be needed as witnesses at the trial to come forward' and, moreover, that the conduct of the accused's defence at the trial is 'likely to be substantially prejudiced if the direction is not given'. The linking of these requirements, which are cumulative, suggests that the witnesses who would not have come forward under a system of anonymity might do so for the benefit of the accused once the complainant's name is released. As we have just seen in the case of the retired magistrate, the complainant's personal decision to allow the release of her name may be motivated by the desire to bring forward witnesses who would identify a particular individual and eventually testify against him. It is also noteworthy that, alone among the rationales of open justice surveyed in Chapter 2, the production of further witnesses counts as an argument in favour of disclosure. No mention is made—perhaps not surprisingly—of the proper functioning of the court itself. Nor does the statute advert to the likely impact of anonymity, or its loss, on the veracity of the witnesses already available to testify at the trial.

There is an additional provision which confers a power to make an order lifting anonymity protection in circumstances in which the accused, having been found guilty, sets in motion the machinery of appeal.[72] The making of an order is within the jurisdiction of 'the appellate court', and the preconditions broadly reflect, *mutatis mutandis*, those found in section 3(1).

An alternative ground for dispensing with anonymity focuses on the position of the media. The conditions required to be satisfied are that anonymity imposes

---

[71] Criminal Justice and Public Order Act 1994, s 142. See E. J. Kramer, 'When Men are Victims: Applying Rape Shield Laws to Male Same-Sex Rape' (1998) 73 *New York University Law Review* 293 for a discussion of the differing purposes served by laws protective of the complainant as between same-sex and opposite-sex rape. Heterosexual male complainants fear being categorized as homosexual, while those who are homosexual fear being revealed as such in the very public arena of the trial court.

[72] Sexual Offences (Amendment) Act 1992, s 3(4).

'a substantial and unreasonable restriction upon the reporting of proceedings at the trial' and that it is 'in the public interest to remove or relax the restriction'.[73] Although no clear guidance is given as to the meaning of these conditions, it is categorically stated that the relaxation of anonymity is not to take place 'by reason only of the outcome of the trial'.[74] The wording is to be noted. It suggests that the verdict may well be a relevant consideration though it is not to be taken as, in itself, decisive on the matter. It raises the vexed problem of whether an initial grant of anonymity should be lost as a consequence of the verdict. As already noted, one possible approach is that an initially anonymous accused could be identified on a guilty verdict being returned. In the same way, the law could be framed in such a way that the media would be permitted to name the complainant as a consequence of a finding that the accused is not guilty.

While the first of these approaches was, at one time, implemented in English law, the second has been considered as a possible reform. It gained some airing as a result of two trials, each originating from the academic world. In the first case, in October 1993, a history student at King's College London, Austen Donnellan, was acquitted of the rape of a fellow student. Intercourse, which took place after a party, was admitted: the sole issue was on the question of consent.[75] In the second, in 1997, Professor John Cottingham of Reading University was found not guilty of the indecent assault of two young women.[76] Both cases attracted a measure of media attention significantly greater than the norm for the type of trial, and on grounds that had no bearing on the legal merits of the cases. Factors that undoubtedly pushed the Donnellan case into prominence were the light that it shed on student life and the fact that Donnellan's tutor, who did much to support his cause, was Conrad Russell, a leading Liberal Democrat peer and son of Bertrand Russell. It was suggested that, by way of attempt to 'compensate' the men concerned, in such cases the name of the complainant should be revealed. In several respects, however, the suggestion was misguided. No person is compensated for unwelcome publicity merely by subjecting his accuser to the same measure of exposure. Its only possible basis is that any woman who is minded to make a complaint would have to enter into her calculations the possibility of the revelation of her identity at the conclusion of any trial that were to be held.

There can be little doubt that there is also a 'punitive' element in the proposal for disclosure of the complainant's name as a consequence of a verdict of not guilty. The clear implication is that the charges were falsely brought. It should be noted, however, that there are other methods available for pursuing those who have been responsible for bringing unwarranted charges before the courts. These were pointed out by Mr Michael Howard, Home Secretary at the time, in the

[73] Sexual Offences (Amendment) Act 1992, s 3(2).
[74] Sexual Offences (Amendment) Act 1992, s 3(3).
[75] The issues raised by the case were discussed in The Times (20 October 1993) 1, 3, together with the report of the verdict.
[76] The verdict, together with the background to the case, is reported in The Times (22 July 1997) 1, 3.

course of a Parliamentary written answer.[77] Emphasizing that complainants could subsequently be prosecuted for perjury or attempting to pervert the course of justice, his written answer went on to state that, in the event of such prosecutions being brought, the protection of anonymity would be lost. A number of points, however, should be made about the cogency of this reply. Mr Howard could equally have added that those who are indirectly responsible for initiating legal process by giving false testimony to the police may be sued for malicious prosecution.[78] But this tort action, like the charge of perjury, is difficult to bring successfully. Moreover, there is no clear basis for Mr Howard's assertion that, in the event of such proceedings successfully being brought, the woman's name could be released. The legislation, on its face, seems quite clear in conferring a lifetime assurance of anonymity. There is, however, at least one case in which a woman who admitted to having made a false complaint of rape (although not against any named individual) was deprived of her anonymity.[79]

A survey of these difficulties, therefore, appears to make all the more attractive the facility of releasing the complainant's name. However, it has been strongly resisted. Presumably, in the unlikely event of such a proposal being accepted, disclosure would not inevitably follow on a verdict of not guilty. The trial judge would be entrusted with a residuary discretion of the sort that he already holds under section 3 of the 1992 Act. If this proposal were to be seriously considered, as a matter of consistency the same rule must surely apply to the complainant in a blackmail case. Clearly, the possibility of disclosure at the end of the trial in either type of case must act as a significant deterrent to the lodging of complaints with the police in the first instance. In fact, the proposal would be even more damaging to the complainant than the regime of openness that applied prior to 1976. In that period the name of the alleged rape victim was known as a matter of course, and rape trials were no different in this regard to any other criminal trial. Where, however, the name of the complainant is released consequent on a verdict of not guilty, there is a clear implication that she brought false charges and is being 'punished' for having done so. Yet a verdict of not guilty does not normally carry with it the imputation that any prosecution witness, even the principal such witness, gave dishonest testimony. The tribunal may feel that, on balance, the accused is guilty of the offence charged, while returning a verdict of not guilty since it feels that the burden of proof beyond reasonable doubt has not been met.

If the rape complainant who chooses to bring civil proceedings is to be granted a statutory right to anonymity similar to that conferred in criminal trials, analogous questions would be raised to those just considered. Should the plaintiff (as

[77] *Hansard*, HC (series 6) vol 237, col 1029 (18 February 1994).

[78] *Martin v Watson* [1996] AC 74.

[79] The conviction for wasting police time was reported on the front page of The Times, 30 October 1999, together with two sketches of the woman by a courtroom artist. A strange twist to the case is that the woman fabricated the story by way of response to an actual rape two years earlier which she had not reported.

the complainant would now become) be deprived of anonymity as a consequence of losing the case? Should the defendant be accorded anonymity, and, if so, should he lose that protection in the event of an award of damages against him? Such issues also arise in other forms of civil case where the veracity of an allegation of rape is central to the dispute. The matter was presented in a most unusual format in a case heard by the High Court in Newcastle. The woman, without reporting the matter to the police, had made a number of allegations of rape against the plaintiff. The outcome of the plaintiff's successful action for defamation was, not only an award of substantial damages, but also the making of an order lifting the defendant's anonymity.[80] Whatever the form taken by the civil proceedings, there are some points of difference between these and criminal cases. Such differences might, at first glance, seem to favour a situation in which plaintiff and defendant alike would start out with anonymity protection, but with judgment for the one side carrying with it the consequence of loss of anonymity for the other. In particular, the burden of proof in civil cases—on a balance of probabilities—is more evenly poised than the criminal standard. However, in addition to the overriding need to protect from disclosure the name of the complainant, there is a formidable disincentive to the frivolous commencement of civil proceedings, in the shape of the rule that the losing side may be responsible for all the costs.

The trial of rape and associated crimes vividly illustrates certain features of anonymity protection. First, several of the proposals are based on a tacit recognition of the fact that publicity, alongside the more traditional modes of sentence, is in fact a form of 'punishment'— especially where the exposure to publicity is the outcome of a considered decision of the court. Secondly, this area, perhaps more than most, exposes the potential for the incremental growth of anonymity. The complainant is first accorded this safeguard. Then, as a result of trials in which the defendant has been subject to an inordinate degree of publicity, the case is advanced for granting him a similar degree of anonymity (at any rate, pending the outcome of the trial). The first stage of anonymity, then, is justified on a long-standing exception to open justice: if publicity deters people from reporting crime or vindicating their private law rights in the courts, then there must be a departure from the general standard of openness in that particular type of case. The move to the second stage, to protect the anonymity of the accused, is not taken on the basis of considerations of open justice. The accused, by virtue of being charged and facing trial, is deprived of all choice as to whether or not he is exposed to publicity. Its basis, rather, is that of parity of treatment as between complainant and accused.

As we noted at the outset, the extension of the concept of rape to the situation between husband and wife has brought into sharp relief a number of questions.

---

[80] The Times (8 February 2000) 1, mentions that at the conclusion of the case there was a formal application by both the plaintiff and the press for the making of such an order.

Some issues turn on the wisdom of procedural and evidential rules which might have the effect of undermining the marital relationship. For example, should the wife be compellable as a witness against her husband? Of greater concern to the subject matter of the present work is the question whether or not there might be arguments for defendant anonymity in cases of marital rape that do not apply in rape charges generally. The Law Commission Report *Rape within Marriage*[81] concluded that there were.[82] The husband, it felt, should have the advantage of anonymity so as to forestall the damage that would be caused by public investigation in court of the history of the marriage. But such damage will inevitably be inflicted, unless the further step is taken of holding these cases *in camera*. Enhanced protection for the anonymity of the wife, however, was advanced as the main consideration in favour of conferring like protection on the accused husband. Logically it requires, as the Law Commission conceded, that the latter's name be withheld even in the event of a conviction. Although it has the advantage that derives from a fixed rule, it is an extremely blunt means of dealing with the problem. Situations of rape cover a spectrum of possibilities: the random attack by a complete stranger; 'date rape'; or rape carried out by an unmarried partner or by a husband. The closer the previous relationship between the two persons, the greater the danger of identifying the woman through release of the man's name. And, in the particular case of husband and wife, they will very commonly have the same surname. On the other hand, the fact that the accused is, or was at the time of the incident, married to the complainant could be withheld in media reports of the case in order to forestall the possibility of 'jigsaw identification' of the woman.[83]

It is noteworthy that another factor identified in favour of the Law Commission's recommendation was the need to protect the children of the family.[84] This appears to be a rather weaker argument than that founded on the parasitic safeguarding of the wife's anonymity. There might be no children of the marriage. But even if there are, in common with other relatives of an accused, they will inevitably suffer as a result of publicity given to the trial and its outcome, regardless of the particular nature of the offence charged. The Law Commission Report does not adduce any reason why rape should be different in this regard. Moreover, any considerations which might require the protection of children at a certain stage in their emotional development will inevitably lose their force as the children grow older.

Although much can be said of the respective positions of complainant and accused in regard to anonymity, it should not be forgotten that, in some rape trials, a witness may give testimony of an intimate and delicate nature. This was

---

[81] Law Com. No. 205 (HC 167, 1992).   [82] ibid. para 4.42.

[83] Jigsaw identification occurs when different items of information about a case are reported in different newspapers. Each is innocuous yet, when taken together, they lead members of the public to draw a conclusion about the identity of the person whose anonymity is protected.

[84] ibid. para 4.43.

shown in the Donnellan case, where a fellow student who had had intercourse with the accused testified from her personal experience that she believed him unlikely to indulge in forced sexual relations. Her name was openly available and was published in the course of media accounts of the trial. It is not apparent from such reports whether or not she sought an anonymity order, or, indeed, whether she refused to avail herself of any protection in this regard that might have been offered to her. It could be argued that such a witness is in a fundamentally different position since, unlike the complainant, she is not being required to recall the details of a sexual assault. Yet she, too, is required to testify in public on matters of an intimate nature.

The sexual privacy of witnesses is a subject that has not received much attention. This is strange since one of the common arguments deployed against the anonymity of the accused in a rape case is that publication of his identity may well induce other women who have not hitherto reported sexual attacks by him to come forward with a view to giving evidence on the present charge. This argument is weak on a number of counts. The approach of the law of evidence would be that such evidence, in general, has no bearing on the question of the guilt or innocence of the accused in the case being tried. In fact, such testimony is likely to have a prejudicial effect on the accused and to have little bearing on the question whether he did rape or sexually assault the woman in the present case. Only exceptionally (for example, in order to show a particular pattern or method) would the evidence of other women be admissible.[85] However, in the exceptional case where the testimony of other women would be admissible, their role would simply be that of a witness. They would enjoy no automatic right, as does the complainant, to anonymity. Instead, they would be reduced to seeking the exercise of the court's discretion on the basis that, without an anonymity order, they would feel unable to testify in open court. As already noted, section 3(1) of the Sexual Offences (Amendment) Act 1992 does permit displacement of anonymity where that is necessary 'for the purpose of inducing persons who are likely to be needed as witnesses at the trial to come forward'. This provision does not appear suitably drafted to encompass the position of witnesses who may have previously been subject to sexual assaults by the accused. As a matter of interpretation, the word 'witness' in this context would mean a person whose testimony would have a direct bearing on the guilt or innocence of the accused in the instant proceedings.

Trial in open court is the standard mode of trial in rape cases. The complainant passes under her actual name as far as the court proceedings themselves are concerned, although she remains anonymous as far as the general public is concerned. Although this mode is not invariable, the exceptions to the rule are

[85] A case in point is the trial of William Kennedy Smith in Florida in 1991, for the details of which see the Appendix. Smith was found not guilty. But the jury was not informed of the fact that three other women had accused him of sexual assault in circumstances similar to those alleged by the complainant: A. McColgan, *The Case for taking the Date out of Rape* (1996) 85.

sufficiently limited that a woman who is considering the consequences of reporting an attack can reckon on the support of this protection. There can, however,
be departure from the norm in the direction of lesser, or greater, protection for
the complainant. Mention has already been made of the limited circumstances in
which disclosure of her identity might be required against her express wishes.
Alternatively, anonymity may be supplemented by a requirement that the public
and the press should absent themselves from the court while the complainant is
giving testimony. This has not commended itself as a general rule. However,
instances have been found in which, as a response to the pressures clearly being
experienced by the complainant in the witness box, the judge has ordered the
clearing of the court. For example, during a trial at Liverpool Crown Court in
1992, a woman collapsed while giving evidence of having been indecently
assaulted during the course of a medical examination. The judge ordered the
public to be removed from the courtroom for the time being.[86] Clearly, this further step cannot be expected by a complainant as a general rule. Equally, it is not
ruled out as a possibility. The exclusion of the press and public as a matter of
course from cases of this type is reckoned to be an excessive response to the problem of protecting the complainant. For example, an employment tribunal, purportedly acting pursuant to its general discretionary power to avoid formality,
had excluded the public and press from a hearing in which allegations of sexual
misconduct were made. Brooke J granted a declaration by way of judicial review
that the tribunal had acted ultra vires in making this order. The proper response,
he added, was to make an unambiguous order prohibiting identification of the
people involved.[87]

The complainant in a rape case has no status other than as a witness. Almost
invariably she is the only witness. Her failure to testify once called into the court
could, in principle, be visited with the same contempt sanction as has been
inflicted on those witnesses who withdraw as a result of overt intimidation. In
two respects, indeed, her legal position is weaker than such witnesses. Her testimony will be indispensable to the prosecution case, and she will be unable to
plead duress.

Finally, it is worth noting one possible mode of conduct of rape trials that has
recently gained some prominence. Any defendant may waive his right to legal
representation and represent himself in court. Where the defendant in a rape case
conducts his own defence and proceeds to engage in a lengthy cross-examination
of the complainant, the exercise of the option of representing oneself may also be
a covert means of intimidating the woman. Such a situation occurred in 1996,
when the defendant, Ralston Edwards, was sentenced to life imprisonment after
a trial in which he spent six days questioning the complainant, attired (it appears)
in the same clothes as he wore during the attack. The woman, Julia Mason,

---

[86] Manchester Evening News (6 October 1992) 7.
[87] *R v Southampton Industrial Tribunal, ex p INS News Group Ltd* The Times, 22 April 1995.

waived her right to anonymity for the express purpose of advancing her campaign for a change in the law.[88] Defendants who choose to represent themselves have lost their right personally to cross-examine victims of the alleged crime if the victims are children.[89] In the same way, it was argued, defendants in rape cases should be denied the right to conduct the cross-examination of the complainant. When the law was changed to conform with this proposal, its terms encompassed charges which involved any form of bodily injury or threat.[90] Yet the intimidatory nature of cross-examination could equally have been reduced by permitting such questioning only if conducted through the medium of a video link. It would eliminate any effect that the accused sought to achieve by dressing in the same clothes as those worn at the time of the offence (since these would not be visible on the television monitor). Altogether, it might be considered a sufficient safeguard to justify the retention of the right of the accused to conduct the cross-examination in person.

C. Open Justice and Rehabilitation

There is an inevitable tension between the norm of open justice and the ideal of rehabilitation of offenders. Once the punishment consequent upon conviction has been served, a person should be entitled to resume his or her place in the community without further unwarranted repercussions stemming from public knowledge of past convictions. Yet those who have served their sentence may reoffend.[91] Equally, those who secure an acquittal may nonetheless have been guilty of the crime charged. In both these respects the public may legitimately claim an entitlement to be informed of the identity and whereabouts of persons who have passed through the criminal justice system.[92]

Nowhere is the tension between the claims of the community and the rehabilitative ideal more evident than in the question, posed in recent years, as to whether the identity of convicted paedophiles should be disclosed to those living in the area in which they have settled once released from prison. The enactment of the Sex Offenders Act 1997 places the initial burden with the police, who are required to be notified by persons convicted (or, in certain circumstances, persons who have been acquitted) of the various sexual offences listed in Part I of the Act. How the police use such information was the subject of discussion in *R v Chief Constable of North Wales Police, ex p AB*.[93] A challenge was brought by judicial

---

[88] The Times (15 March 1997) 6.   [89] Criminal Justice Act 1991, s 55(7).

[90] Youth Justice and Criminal Evidence Act 1999, ss 34 and 35.

[91] The fact of a previous conviction could, in some circumstances, legitimately constitute an element in reasonable suspicion for the purposes of furnishing grounds for arrest: *McArdle v Egan* [1933] All ER Rep 611, 614.

[92] See, generally, B. Hebenton and T. Thomas, *Criminal Records: State, citizen and the politics of protection* (1993), especially chs 5 and 6 on the disclosure of criminal records outside the criminal justice system.

[93] [1997] 4 All ER 691, DC; [1998] 3 All ER 310, CA.

review to the decision of the Wrexham police to inform the owner of a caravan site of the presence on the site of a married couple newly released from prison after serving sentences for serious sexual offences against children. In rejecting the application, the Divisional Court stated that the police were right to pass on the information where there was a risk of the convicted person re-offending. Each situation was to be considered on its own facts, balancing the dangers posed by the offender against the vulnerability of those persons at risk from him, together with the impact of disclosure on the former offender. The Court of Appeal dismissed the appeal against this decision. Lord Woolf recorded the fact that the couple had been referred to as 'AB' and 'CD' in both courts, so as to protect their identities until the conclusion of the proceedings in the Court of Appeal.[94] His judgment retains that designation, despite the fact that *The Times* report of the ruling of the Court of Appeal refers to the couple by name ('Thorpe').[95] Indeed, one day after the giving of judgment by the Court of Appeal, *The Times* carried a photograph of the couple.[96] The result of bringing the action, therefore, was not only a vindication of the police action in informing the caravan site owner but also (as so very often happens) a focusing of attention on the applicants that would not have occurred in the absence of the litigation.

One significant consideration in the case, at any rate before the Divisional Court, was the fact that 'the applicants' convictions and sentences, formally announced in open court, were information in the public domain and as such subject to no duty of confidence in the hands of the police'. [97] That, in itself, did not suffice to dispose of the matter, since the police were in a position to construct the link between those convictions and the persons resident on the caravan site. There was a presumption, based on 'a fundamental rule of good public administration', that such information should not be passed on by the police unless there was a specific justification for so doing. As this judgment well illustrates, the idea that information has been placed in the public domain does not embody the notion that the information may thereafter be disclosed by any person whatsoever for any purpose.

Previous convictions, even of those who have not re-offended and are very unlikely to do so, can be publicized again for a number of reasons. Sometimes, the fresh disclosure takes place in a court, for example, where there is an attempt to discredit a witness by revealing his previous convictions. Here again it is open justice, in combination with the rules on cross-examination, that creates (or, where there is reporting of the case, exacerbates) the problem. Often, however, disclosure of a long-distant conviction occurs in private, being required by the questions listed on a job application or insurance proposal form. Hence the proposal that, after the lapse of a certain period of time without re-offending, a person should be entitled to act as if the conviction in question had never taken place.

---

[94] [1998] 3 All ER 310, 313.   [95] The Times, 23 March 1998.
[96] The Times (19 March 1998) 5. Judgment was given by the Court of Appeal on 18 March 1998.
[97] [1997] 4 All ER 691, 701.

The controlled use of material that is a matter of public record has been embodied in the Rehabilitation of Offenders Act 1974, which is largely based on the recommendations of the report by JUSTICE of two years earlier, *Living it Down*.

The point at which a person with a conviction was to be treated as rehabilitated could be left for determination in a number of ways. One possibility considered by JUSTICE was to leave the precise point to be determined by a judicial tribunal to which persons seeking the status could have resort. However, the report acknowledges by implication that the public sitting of such a tribunal would merely aggravate the problem to which the applicant would be seeking a solution.[98] Alternatively, rules could be laid down—as they were in the 1974 Act—stipulating that the new status was to be conferred after the lapse of a certain number of years. The report also acknowledged that convictions may be disseminated for all manner of reasons—in the law reports because they raise important points of law, or even in the memoirs of retired police officers. It recommended that there should be a prohibition on persons reviving long-forgotten cases, years after they were tried, for other than educational, scientific, or professional purposes.[99]

The reforms enacted in the Rehabilitation of Offenders Act 1974 were undoubtedly valuable, though ultimately they can supply only a partial solution to the problem. JUSTICE recommended the creation of a new statutory offence: that of the unauthorized publication of any official record of the previous convictions of any rehabilitated person.[100] However, this cannot deal with the situation where the information is gleaned from newspaper coverage of the trial and conviction, nor with that in which the chain of information originates from a person who was present at the trial. The proceedings of criminal courts are matters of public record and, as such, are available to everyone.

In situations where a person has changed his name and identity since the trial, these particulars do not form part of the public record. There may consequently be grounds for establishing a violation of privacy in situations where information is published that constructs a link between a particular individual and a concluded trial. This is well illustrated by the facts and the ruling of the court in the Californian case, *Melvin v Reid*.[101] The action was a suit for violation of privacy brought by a former prostitute who, some years earlier, had been acquitted in a murder trial which gained considerable publicity. The plaintiff had subsequently married and moved to a different part of the country, where her background was unknown to the local community. The defendants released a film chronicling the events of the trial together with disclosure of the present name and address of the woman. Several points about the case are worthy of note. The film company was not seeking to 'relitigate' the case by suggesting that she was guilty of the murder in question. Nor did the substance of the complaint reside in the retelling of the

---

[98] *Living it Down*, para 44.
[99] *Living it Down*, paras 64–67.
[100] *Living it Down*, Recommendation (11).
[101] 112 Cal App 285 (1931), 297 Pac 91.

story of the trial. Rather, it lay in linking the *personae* of that earlier case with the current identity of the plaintiff. Marks J explained: 'the use of the incidents from the life of appellant in the moving picture is in itself not actionable. These incidents appeared in the records of her trial for murder, which is a public record, open to perusal of all . . . Had respondents, in the story of [the film], stopped with the use of those incidents from the life of appellant which were spread upon the record of her trial, no right of action would have accrued.' However, 'if any right of action exists, it arises from the use of [her] true name in connection with the true incidents from her life'.[102] In the light of the plaintiff's acquittal, the issue in the privacy action was not rehabilitation as it is technically understood. The gist of her complaint was the defendants' disruption of her 'rehabilitation' from her former existence as a prostitute. The defendants were judged liable in having gone beyond that record and by publicizing her present identity.

5. DIVORCE AND ANNULMENT OF MARRIAGE

The discussion now turns to the specifically familial aspects of the chapter, although it will be apparent that some of the subject matter already covered will be reworked in the specific context of the proceedings taken to annul or terminate marriage.

Before dealing with the main theme of this section, it will be useful to mention some of the requirements of the marriage ceremony itself. For, by analogy to open trial, the law has insisted in modern times on conditions of openness at the point when the parties enter into marriage. The clandestine marriage, at times a significant feature of British social history, was contracted for a number of reasons: a wish to avoid the requirements of parental consent; a desire to contract a bigamous relationship; or simply a concern for privacy in itself.[103] Such marriages were eventually prohibited by Lord Hardwicke's Marriage Act 1753. The avoidance of secret marriages, moreover, has been achieved by steps going well beyond a mere requirement that marriages take place in public. As has been seen in regard to trials,[104] it is possible to comply with the requirement of public trial at a formal level only. A trial might take place in such an unusual place or at such an unexpected time that there is only a nominal compliance with the requirement of public access. In the case of marriages, however, the possibility of mere nominal compliance has been partly averted by the requirement of the prior publication of banns, on a number of occasions prior to the ceremony, in the church where the wedding is to be solemnized.

The Marriage Act 1949 requires register offices to perform ceremonies 'with open doors',[105] and a similar requirement applies in regard to certain religious

---

[102] 297 Pac 91, 93.
[103] R. B. Outhwaite, *Clandestine Marriage in England 1500–1850* (1995), especially ch 3.
[104] See Chapter 3, section 1, B, above.   [105] Marriage Act 1949, s 45 (1).

ceremonies of marriage.[106] The necessity of openness does not apply to every form of marriage (Jewish and Quaker ceremonies are exempt). This statute was amended by the Marriage Act 1994 so as to allow civil marriages to take place, quite generally, on premises that had been approved for the purpose by local authorities. The change was effected by way of inserting an additional provision into the earlier statute. In particular, the Secretary of State is empowered to impose conditions 'so as to secure that members of the public are permitted to attend any marriage solemnized on approved premises'.[107] The terms of this power, in securing that 'members of the public are permitted to attend', appear to impose conditions that would be equivalent to the standard expressed by the words, 'with open doors'. Indeed, the latter phrase would appear to express the same idea as that conveyed by the word 'open' in the familiar term, 'in open court'.[108]

As for the dissolution and annulment of marriage, reservations may be expressed as to whether the judicial format is entirely appropriate for deciding the relevant matters. The latest changes in the law, embodied in the Family Law Act 1996, place considerable store by mediation in addition to denying petitioners the opportunity to obtain a divorce on the basis of proof of fault.[109] The concentration in the ensuing discussion on what is predominantly old law, therefore, calls for some explanation. There are three reasons for this emphasis. First, over a considerable period divorce proceedings were unique in being a form of civil case where even a hint of scandal suggested by an appearance in court would blight a promising career. Secondly, some of the cases concerning parties and witnesses intimidated by the public nature of the hearings retain their relevance today, even though the particular form of proceeding has now largely disappeared. Thirdly, however unusual resort to a contested divorce hearing may now be, the possibility of its use remains.

As long as the judicial format is retained, challenges may be brought on the basis of violations of the procedural standards essential to judicial proceedings.[110] One of those standards is, of course, that the tribunal sits in public—a requirement that has puzzled those who have been subjected to the consequent loss of privacy. An empirical study of hearings of undefended divorces at various county courts during 1973[111] noted that some of the petitioners who were

---

[106] Marriage Act 1949, s 44 (2).   [107] Marriage Act 1949, s 46B.

[108] However, there appears to be no case law interpreting the phrase, 'with open doors'. According to S. M. Cretney and J. M. Masson, *Principles of Family Law* (6th edn, 1997) 33, the validity of a marriage which took place under conditions falling short of this requirement would probably not be affected.

[109] For a general survey of the changes contained in the new measure, see M. La Follette and R. Purdie, *A Guide to the Family Law Act 1996* (1996).

[110] In *Stone v Stone* [1949] P 165 the Court of Appeal, in invalidating the trial of a divorce petition, stated: '. . . a decree made in a judge's private room is not a valid decree. It is voidable because it offends against the fundamental rule that the hearing of a case, and the whole of the hearing, must take place in open court' (at 168).

[111] E. Elston, J. Fuller, and M. Murch, 'Judicial Hearings of Undefended Divorce Petitions' (1975) 38 MLR 609.

interviewed had not even realized that the hearing was open to the public. Two-thirds of those interviewed, mainly those relying on adultery or behaviour in order to obtain a divorce, were embarrassed or, at the very least, disliked relating intimate details in the setting of an open court. By way of possible justification for the public form of the hearing, the authors of the study cited the following: to ascertain that it has been proved that the marriage had irretrievably broken down; to be satisfied about proposed arrangements for any dependent children; and, exceptionally, to see that no unnecessary hardship would result from the granting of a decree.[112] These would appear to be reasons that would be equally applicable to a system of divorce, such as that envisaged by the Family Law Act 1996, which seeks to move entirely away from notions of fault. Investigation of these matters would certainly appear to require the holding of some form of hearing. That the hearing should take a public form is rather more difficult to justify. Since the proceedings are not defended, there is no adversarial element of the sort which has traditionally been viewed as justifying determination of the issues in public. Moreover, few of the people interviewed in the study could appreciate why the proceedings were held in public, in comparison with the important ancillary matters which were routinely heard in chambers.

The leading case of *Scott v Scott* was, of course, decided in the context of matrimonial causes. Its significance needs to be seen against the background of the major change in the jurisdiction over marriage effected by the Divorce and Matrimonial Causes Act 1857. Prior to this Act there existed a secret method of gathering evidence before the Ecclesiastical Courts which had jurisdiction in these matters. Witnesses were questioned in secret by the Registrar, at which time the parties were not permitted to be present. Examination of witnesses both orally and in open court did not commence until 1854, three years before the new system came into force. The new procedures brought with them the disadvantage of modern court hearings with their attendant publicity, a problem exacerbated by the prurient interest in the cases which were typically litigated in the divorce courts. The long-standing dissatisfaction with this state of affairs culminated, as will be seen shortly, in the imposition of reporting restrictions by the Judicial Proceedings (Regulation of Reports) Act 1926.

The ruling in *Scott v Scott* was preceded by *A v A*,[113] a case which was markedly indulgent to the claims of secrecy. The wife's suit for restitution of conjugal rights was met by the respondent's prayer for judicial separation on the basis of the wife's cruelty. The respondent wished the matter to be heard *in camera*, the petitioner objecting to such a procedure. The Judge Ordinary had to decide whether he possessed the power to hear the case *in camera* and, if so,

---

[112] E. Elston, J. Fuller, and M. Murch, 'Judicial Hearings of Undefended Divorce Petitions' (1975) 38 MLR 609, 634.
[113] (1875) LR 3 P and M 230.

whether he should exercise his discretion in favour of such a hearing. The respondent succeeded on both points, the judge believing himself empowered to sit in secret by virtue of the practices of the old Ecclesiastical Courts. In *Scott v Scott* the decision in *A v A* was subject to considerable criticism, being described in the headnote as 'overruled'. Viscount Haldane believed the critical provision of the Divorce Act 1857 to be section 46, by virtue of which '. . . the witnesses in all proceedings before the Court were, where their attendance could be had, to be sworn and examined orally in open Court . . .,' with the result that the court was to conduct its business '. . . on the general principles as regards publicity which regulated the other Courts of justice in this country'.[114] Furthermore, the procedure in the old Ecclesiastical Courts was so different '. . . that the modern distinction between hearing in camera and hearing in open Court obviously had nothing approaching to the importance which it possesses to-day'.[115]

The general rule of open justice, therefore, applies in proceedings to dissolve marriage. As has already been noted, the ruling in *Scott v Scott* was superseded, on its particular facts, by section 48(2) of the Matrimonial Causes Act 1973. This expressly provides for a hearing *in camera* in nullity suits 'on the question of sexual capacity'.[116] Two points are worthy of note. The provision is very narrowly drawn, not even applying to the related ground of nullity for wilful refusal to consummate the marriage. Also, the judge may direct that the evidence be heard in open court if satisfied that it is 'in the interests of justice' to do so.

When the matter was raised in the immediate aftermath of *Scott v Scott*, open justice was sometimes abandoned in favour of the emotional needs of a party. In *Moosbrugger v Moosbrugger*[117] the courts were again confronted with such a case. The case concerned cross-suits for divorce between husband and wife. The wife's testimony proving scarcely audible, the judge ordered the clearing of the public gallery. The only indications in the law report that such a step might prove necessary were two pronouncements by the wife, and one by her counsel, that the whole case was 'horrible'. Strangely, even though this step would have prevented the presence of the press, it did not (as can be seen) have the effect of preserving the anonymity of the parties—at any rate, as far as the law reports were concerned. The judge stated briefly that he possessed the power to hear the wife's testimony in private 'notwithstanding' the recent decision in *Scott v Scott*. In *Cleland v Cleland*,[118] on very similar facts, Bargrave Deane J[119] went even further and heard the wife's evidence in his private room, partly because the wife felt that it would be impossible to give her evidence in open court, and partly because open disclosure of the evidence would be contrary to 'the interests of public

---

[114] [1913] AC 417, 434.   [115] [1913] AC 417, 433.

[116] One wonders exactly how one of the commonly cited rationales of open justice—the production of further witnesses—could be said to apply to the factual dispute that is in issue here.

[117] (1913) 29 TLR 658.   [118] (1914) 109 LT 744.

[119] It will be recalled that he was the judge who heard the contempt proceedings at first instance in *Scott v Scott* itself.

morality'. In contrast to the *Moosbrugger* case, Bargrave Deane J's decision was taken on the basis of a perusal of the papers, his conclusion being that it was 'about as horrible a case as I ever came across in my somewhat long experience'.[120] He appears, indeed, to have imposed on himself limitations as stringent as those eventually imposed by the Judicial Proceedings (Regulation of Reports) Act 1926 on those engaged in reporting the proceedings ('I am unable in giving judgment in open court to state the facts proved before me').[121]

To some extent, the decisions on the facts in these cases may be justified by reason of the failure to enact any measure to curb the uncontrolled press reporting of divorce cases. This reform came eventually in the form of the Judicial Proceedings (Regulation of Reports) Act 1926. The presence on the statute book of such a measure at the time of the *Cleland* ruling would have undermined any case for a secret hearing based on the supposed threat to public morality. Its presence may well help to explain later reluctance to order the removal of the press and the public. One example is *E v E*,[122] a divorce suit in which the wife charged her husband with having committed sodomy on her. While being cross-examined by counsel for the husband, the wife complained that she felt unable to continue giving evidence in the presence of so many people. Cairns J ruled that he did not have power to hear her evidence *in camera*, since Parliament had expressly empowered such a hearing in nullity suits, and then only on the question of sexual capacity. In contrast to the above cases, he appears to have been unmoved by any residuary consideration that, in the circumstances, the witness was unable to continue with her testimony. In the event the problem was resolved, as the brief law report notes, since every member of the public present in the court withdrew voluntarily.[123] In those cases where the spectators do not prove so accommodating, it can result in a party being required to give evidence on sensitive and painful matters before a courtroom full of strangers. In one such case in 1988 involving a leading person in the entertainment industry, the degree of interest was such that 'Court full' signs were prominently displayed in the corridor outside the courtroom, and Judge Callman, who heard the case, stated publicly that it was tragic that 'this husband and wife had to face this costly suit in the glare of publicity'.[124]

Throughout the second half of the nineteenth century and for much of the twentieth century, the open conduct of divorce proceedings had two noteworthy social aspects.

The mere fact of being cited in a divorce case, usually as co-respondent, often resulted in social ostracism and the ruin of a promising career. Perhaps the most famous example is provided by the case (in 1890) of the leading Irish politician, Charles Stewart Parnell. There was no doubt, at any rate, that Parnell had indeed

---

[120] (1914) 109 LT 744, 745.   [121] ibid.   [122] (1963) 107 Sol J 813.
[123] In situations where, in effect, the perpetrating of a sexual assault provides the ground on which the divorce is being sought, some protection of anonymity may be gained from the Sexual Offences (Amendment) Act 1992.
[124] Sunday Times (17 July 1988) A11. The petitioner was the actress, Jenny Seagrove.

committed adultery. However, a finding of adultery, even when obtained on the flimsiest evidence, could destroy a political career. A prominent instance in this regard is the case of Sir Charles Dilke, who was cited as co-respondent in the Crawford divorce suit brought in 1886. Remarkably, under the law at that time the petitioner husband was able to gain a divorce merely on the basis of a confession of adultery made by his wife. The allegation of adultery with Mrs Crawford was strongly denied by Dilke, and it is generally acknowledged among modern historians that he was innocent of the charge.[125]

Moreover, regardless of the position in society occupied by those whose affairs were the subject of investigation in the divorce courts, any salacious material emerging from such tribunals would provide ready copy for certain types of newspaper. In this regard the fault lay with the substantive law of divorce, in requiring proof of adultery and (where proceedings were brought by the wife) adultery in combination with some aggravating factor. The gradual extension of the grounds on which a divorce could be granted has, in itself, diminished the attraction of divorce proceedings as a source of salacious amusement. Additionally, the enacting of the Judicial Proceedings (Regulation of Reports) Act 1926 severely curtailed the reporting of the details of cases in the divorce courts.

The period from 1857, when the Divorce Act was passed, until 1926 was marked by a number of widely publicized divorce cases, the reports of which caused both amusement and scandal. One of the better known cases of this type was the trial in 1886 of the petition and cross-petition brought by Lord and Lady Colin Campbell. After a nineteen-day hearing the jury decided that neither husband nor wife had been guilty of adultery. The interest in the case was such that barriers had to be put up in the building in order to hold in check the throng of spectators trying to gain entry to the public gallery.[126] The proceedings which are traditionally regarded as having given the impetus for a change in the law were those in *Russell v Russell*.[127] This case, which involved a divorce petition brought by a husband on the ground of his wife's alleged adultery, was of the sort that would attract a certain prurient interest. The wife denied adultery, claiming that the child to which she had given birth was her husband's. The central issue in the case was whether the child could have been fathered by the husband in the light of the sexual practices that they had followed. The case was taken on appeal to the House of Lords, where Lord Dunedin stated that he regretted having to go into details which might shock listeners, adding in an obvious aside to *Scott v Scott*: 'I regret whole-heartedly that, according to a recent decision of this House, cases such as the present may not be tried in camera.'[128] And in a lesser known

---

[125] The repercussions for Dilke's career are vividly borne out by the title of a modern biography: D. Nicholls, *The Lost Prime Minister* (1995). See especially ch 11.

[126] There is an account of the case in H. Wyndham, *The Mayfair Calendar: Some Society Causes Célèbres* (1925) 39–58.

[127] [1924] AC 687.

[128] [1924] AC 687, 722.

case of the same era, *Sneyd v Sneyd*,[129] the facts were described by the judge as embodying 'incidents of degradation and of abuse of all the ordinary conventions of society and disregard of what we conceive to be the elementary rules of morality which make the whole set of circumstances unwholesome and repugnant . . .'.[130]

Any attempt to curb the open reporting of cases in the divorce courts, as expected, was opposed on the basis of the overriding requirement of the public transaction of court business. In particular, attempts to require the divorce court to sit *in camera* were successfully resisted. Moreover, public knowledge of the proceedings of the divorce court was sought to be justified on the ground that it would deter potentially errant spouses from engaging in conduct that would lead to disgrace and ridicule in the popular press. In a curious inversion of the priorities of the present chapter, publicity was to be seen as a good thing in itself. For every reported case that tended to undermine public morality (by providing the newly literate working classes with salacious information about the conduct of those perceived to be their social superiors) there would surely be several instances of married couples who were held together by the prospect of their intimate details being made available for the public entertainment.[131] In the end, however, the impetus in favour of reform proved irresistible. Moving the second reading of the private member's bill that became the 1926 Act, its promoter stated that, as long ago as 1859, Queen Victoria had written to the then Lord Chancellor, Lord Campbell, expressing her apprehension about the publication of many of the proceedings that were coming before the new divorce court.[132] The extraordinary nature of the measure is, perhaps, reflected in the fact that the criminal offences created by the measure require the consent of the Attorney-General before a prosecution may be brought.

Apart from the provisions of the 1926 Act which are specifically confined to matrimonial causes, section 1(1)(a) prohibits, in relation to any judicial proceedings whatsoever, the printing or publishing of any indecent matter or indecent medical details 'the publication of which would be calculated to injure public morals'.

The principal matrimonial causes covered by the Act are proceedings for dissolution and annulment of marriage. In regard to the enumerated causes it is forbidden to publish (or even to print) any particulars other than: (i) the names, addresses and occupations of the parties and witnesses; (ii) a concise statement of the charges, defences and counter-charges in support of which evidence has been given; (iii) submissions on any point of law arising in the proceedings and the decision of the court thereon; and (iv) the summing-up of the judge, the findings

---

[129] (1925–26) 42 TLR 106 and 247.   [130] (1925–26) 42 TLR 247, 248.

[131] For detailed examinations of the background to the 1926 Act, see G. Savage, 'Erotic Stories and Public Decency: Newspaper Reporting of Divorce Proceedings in England' (1998) 41 *Historical Journal* 511; and S. M. Cretney, *Law, Law Reform and the Family* (1998), ch 4.

[132] *Hansard*, HC (series 5) vol 194, col 733 (16 April 1926).

of the jury (if any), the judgment of the court and the observations made by the judge in passing judgment.[133]

The third exception can be seen as being aimed at facilitating the process of law reporting. It is to be read in the light of a further provision which provides that the restrictions contained in the Act do not encompass '. . . the printing or publishing of any matter in any separate volume or part of any bona fide series of law reports . . .'.[134] The fourth exception has the effect of narrowing considerably the extent of the protection that is afforded to privacy, since in any contested case the judge will conduct a full survey of the evidence which has been presented. Nevertheless, the enactment of the 1926 Act meant that no longer could there occur the detailed reporting of the intimate evidence given by witnesses. To that extent the checking function exercised by publicity over the veracity of the witness was removed. Somewhat superfluously, it was stipulated that the four excepted categories could not be taken as permitting the publication of any indecent matter that was forbidden by section 1(1)(a) of the Act. A perusal of the debates illustrates that the motivating factor behind the introduction of reporting restrictions was, not a desire to protect the privacy of the litigating parties, but rather a fear as to the consequences for the ordinary newspaper reader of exposure to such material. This is borne out by express mention in the parliamentary debates of the standards of obscenity as laid down in the leading case on the subject, *R v Hicklin*.[135]

The Act also had the (unintended) effect of limiting the damage that would otherwise be inflicted on the reputation of third parties whose names might be mentioned in the course of a divorce hearing. In *Windeatt v Windeatt*,[136] a woman was held to have been correctly refused permission to intervene as a party to a divorce suit brought by a wife. The latter's petition for divorce was based on a long-standing association (though not one that was adulterous) between the woman and the husband. The Court of Appeal pointed out that, in the light of the limitations imposed by the 1926 Act, the woman's connection with the case would become known ' . . . only to such people as happened to be present in court . . .' at the relevant time—a matter to which the court could not give 'any very great consideration'.[137]

Where, as in *Argyll v Argyll*,[138] an attempt is made to suppress publication of marital confidences exchanged between parties who are no longer married, the plaintiff may gain some assistance from the Judicial Proceedings (Regulation of Reports) Act. Although the plaintiff in that case, the Duchess of Argyll, based her case on a number of grounds, she was able to derive some support from the 1926 Act. Two features, in particular, emerge from the decision. First, the statute is one of those pieces of criminal legislation that allow of possible civil enforcement in the hands of those who will be damaged by the breach of its terms. Secondly, the structure of the statute made it quite clear that it was not solely concerned

---

[133] Judicial Proceedings (Regulation of Reports) Act 1926, s 1(1)(b).
[134] Judicial Proceedings (Regulation of Reports) Act 1926, s 1(4).   [135] (1868) LR 3 QB 360.
[136] [1962] 1 WLR 527.   [137] [1962] 1 WLR 527, 533.   [138] [1967] Ch 302.

with the protection of public morals. It also extended to protecting the reputation of those who might be drawn into the proceedings in the divorce court.[139]

Although rarely the subject of discussion nowadays, the 1926 Act figured prominently in proceedings brought in 1996 by two Filipina women advancing the claims of their respective sons to the title of the late Baron Moynihan.[140] The case, as such, was not a contested divorce. However, the question of who took the late Baron Moynihan's title turned on whether an earlier divorce of the Baron from his fourth Filipina wife was fraudulently obtained. Sir Stephen Brown, President of the Family Division, ruled that the proceedings fell within the spirit of the 1926 Act and therefore restricted reporting within the limits imposed by that statute until judgment was given. Nevertheless, the press were allowed to report the essential features of the case, as given in the opening speech by counsel for the Queen's Proctor. This was facilitated by an indication from the Attorney-General that he would be reluctant to institute criminal proceedings against newspapers which, by reason of oversight, broke the terms of the 1926 Act.[141]

In those situations where well-known figures bring or defend divorce proceedings, the court hearing may well afford information about the figure that is at variance with the impression that the public has hitherto held. Perhaps the element that underlies the irregular mode of holding of the divorce petition in *McPherson v McPherson*[142]—the husband, it will be recalled, was a prominent Canadian politician—was an attempt to forestall public access to embarrassing details that might emerge in the course of the hearing. In 1997 the public sympathy felt for Earl Spencer, the brother of Princess Diana, in the aftermath of his speech at the Princess's funeral, substantially diminished within several months with the reporting from a South African court of the acrimonious divorce proceedings between the Earl and his estranged wife. The details which emerged from the Cape Town courtroom—cataloguing the Earl's extra-marital affairs and Lady Spencer's eating and alcohol disorders—could not have been reported under the Judicial Proceedings (Regulation of Reports) Act 1926.

In neither of these cases was there any suggestion that the proceedings were, or might be, misreported. However, where it is alleged that the proceedings and outcome of a divorce suit had been misreported to the disadvantage of one of the parties, that party may have grounds for suing the newspaper for defamation. In *Time Inc v Firestone*[143] the wife's complaint against the defendant magazine was

---

[139] [1967] Ch 302, 342: 'in Divorce Courts in particular, reputations were apt to be disproportionately and, perhaps, quite unjustifiably besmirched and, even more, innocent persons were apt to have their most intimate relationships publicly exposed. Even children might suffer cruelly from their parents' divorce proceedings without there being an injury at all to public morals. Such suffering can, of course, occur in other courts but it is notorious that it was in Divorce Court proceedings that such suffering was most widespread.'

[140] *Moynihan v Moynihan* [1997] 1 FLR 59. See also the ruling of the House of Lords' Committee for Privileges: The Times (28 March 1997) 40.

[141] As reported at [1997] 1 FLR 59, 62.   [142] [1936] AC 177. See Chapter 3, section 1, B, above.

[143] 424 US 448 (1976).

to the effect that her husband was granted a divorce on the grounds of her extreme cruelty and adultery. In fact, the reason pronounced by the court for granting the decree was simply that neither party had evinced 'the least suscepti- bility to domestication'. The magazine appealed against the award of damages on the ground that the plaintiff was a 'public figure' and, therefore, was entitled to a lesser degree of protection in accordance with the well-established ruling on the law of defamation in *New York Times Co v Sullivan*.[144] The majority of the US Supreme Court rejected the contention that Mrs Firestone was to be consid- ered a public person. Part of the reasoning of the Court concentrates on her posi- tion in the social circles of Florida. More relevant to the concerns of this book is the question of whether or not her appearance before a public court could, in any way, contribute to the argument that she was a public figure. In the view of the Supreme Court this was an irrelevant consideration. Mrs Firestone's appearance before the divorce court was not voluntary: it was required by virtue of the fact that the legal system compelled parties to resort to a judicial forum in order to gain a dissolution of their marriage. Moreover, repeating a point that has often been made, the Court emphasized that the mere fact of a public controversy did not mean that the controversy was of legitimate interest to the public.

6. PROTECTION OF VULNERABLE PERSONS

A. Mental Impairment

The long-standing practice of according confidentiality to the mentally impaired was recognized in section 12(1) of the Administration of Justice Act 1960. That provision, as we have seen, lists five subsections designating areas in which dis- closure of information relating to judicial proceedings is a contempt of court. According to subsection 12(1)(b), one of those areas is: 'Where the proceedings are brought under Part VIII of the Mental Health Act 1959, or under any provi- sion of that Act authorising an application or reference to be made to a Mental Health Review Tribunal or to a county court.'

In regard to the mentally impaired, it is the work of Mental Health Review Tribunals which poses the most acute conflict between the claims of privacy and the requirements of open justice. The purpose of such Tribunals is to hear appeals from persons subject to compulsory detention under the Mental Health Act and to determine whether the illness of the detainee is of such a nature and degree as to justify continued detention in hospital. A variety of considerations may be advanced in favour of the secrecy or openness of a Tribunal hearing. As far as the patient is concerned, the balance of advantage may lie in favour of

---

[144] 376 US 254 (1964). Under the ruling, a public official or public figure is prevented from suing in respect of a defamatory falsehood unless the statement was made with 'actual malice': i.e. in the knowledge that it was false or in reckless disregard to whether it was false or not.

secrecy in order to minimize the stigmatizing effect of mental illness. On the other hand, the patient's liberty interest may be better served by a hearing where the proceedings of the Tribunal will come under open scrutiny. Moreover, since the Tribunals have the power to order the release into the community of people who may prove to be dangerous, the public can claim a plausible interest in being assured that these bodies have as much regard for the public safety as they have for the rights of the patient.[145]

The legislation decisively favours confidentiality of proceedings. The Mental Health Act 1983 empowered the Lord Chancellor to make rules, among other things, to enable Tribunals 'to exclude members of the public, or any specified class of members of the public, from any proceedings of the tribunal, or to prohibit the publication of reports of any such proceedings or the names of any persons concerned in such proceedings'.[146] According to the promulgated rules, Tribunals are required to sit in private unless two conditions are satisfied: the patient asks for a public hearing; and the Tribunal is satisfied that such a form of hearing 'would not be contrary to the interests of the patient'.[147] This is reinforced by a provision which states that, except in so far as the Tribunal directs, any information before the Tribunal and the names of any persons concerned in the proceedings shall not be made public.[148]

The provisions emphasize that formality should be avoided and the Tribunal should conduct hearings in the most suitable manner 'bearing in mind the health and interests of the patient'.[149] In practice, hearings are informal, often taking place on hospital premises rather than in a location specifically set aside for the purpose. There are, nevertheless, a number of safeguards. The Tribunal is required to give at least fourteen days' notice of the time and place of the hearing, a lesser period being permissible only with the consent of all the parties.[150] Any member of the Council on Tribunals, the body charged with overseeing the performance of tribunals in general, may attend provided that he takes no part in the proceedings. Equally, where a Tribunal refuses a request for a public hearing (or, alternatively, decides that a hitherto public hearing shall thenceforth be conducted in private) it is charged with the duty of recording its reasons in writing and informing the patient of the same.[151] On the other hand, the flexibility of procedure permits withholding from the patient, out of concern for his wider interests, evidence and other material which, as a matter of procedural fairness, he should be entitled to see.

---

[145] Mention has already been made of *Pickering v Liverpool Daily Post and Echo Newspapers plc* [1991] 1 All ER 622. Note, in particular, the issue in *R v Canons Park Mental Health Review Tribunal, ex p A* [1994] 2 All ER 659, as to whether a person with a psychopathic disorder has a right to be discharged if the condition is not likely to be alleviated by further hospital treatment.

[146] Mental Health Act 1983, s 78(1)(e).

[147] Mental Health Review Tribunal Rules 1983, SI 1983/942, r 21(1).

[148] Mental Health Review Tribunal Rules, r 21(5).

[149] Mental Health Review Tribunal Rules, r 22(1).

[150] Mental Health Review Tribunal Rules, r 20.

[151] Mental Health Review Tribunal Rules, r 21(6) and 21(2).

Professor Gostin, the leading commentator on mental health law, has criticized the position of Mental Health Review Tribunals as 'fraught with secrecy'.[152] Writing in the mid-1970s, Gostin noted that in the previous ten years there had been only one public hearing of a Mental Health Review Tribunal, in Broadmoor Hospital. Such a location, as has been noted, is entirely usual. Yet since reporters cannot enter such institutions as a matter of course, the very location of the hearing acts as an informal barrier to publicity of the hearing. In the absence of some means of notifying the public and press, any application made by the patient for an open hearing, even if it is conceded, may turn out to be devoid of any real substance. Gostin's opinion is that the views of the patient should be decisive on the question of whether the hearing should be public or private. That so little regard is paid to the views of the patient leads him to suspect that it is as much the privacy of others involved in a hearing (the doctor, for example) that is protected by the secret arrangements that he criticizes.

The applicant before a Mental Health Review Tribunal, at any rate, is capable of understanding the consequences of a decision in favour of opening the proceedings to members of the public, although, on account of his illness, he may lack true capacity to consent to their being opened.[153] The situation of the detainee under the Mental Health Act may be contrasted with the person who is the subject of an application to court for the withdrawal of life support. The procedure for the hearing of such applications is governed by a Practice Note,[154] which stipulates that the case should 'normally' be heard in chambers but with judgment being given in open court. In this way there is a reversal of the standard presumption: the proceedings are to be held in private, except where there is some compelling interest in their being held in open court. Also, in the event of there being an appeal against the original decision—as there was, for example, in *Frenchay Healthcare NHS Trust v S*[155]—presumably the Court of Appeal, and in turn the House of Lords, must hear the appeal in private.

The person who is the subject of such a process cannot appreciate, and will never be in a position to appreciate, the comparative advantages of publicity and confidentiality of the proceedings. To that extent it could be argued that the privacy interests that are secured by a secret hearing are those of others involved in the case (the doctors, the family). Whatever the conditions under which the hearing takes place, the Practice Note requires judgment to be given in open court. This aspect serves two purposes. First, it avoids the disturbing situation where not the slightest part of the case is rendered open to public scrutiny. Secondly, it

---

[152] L. O. Gostin, *A Human Condition* Vol 1 (1975) 90.

[153] The question of 'capacity to consent' is a matter of general concern in the modern law of mental health. See, in particular, the issues in *R v Bournewood Community and Mental Health NHS Trust, ex p L* [1998] 3 All ER 289.

[154] *Practice Note (persistent vegetative state: withdrawal of treatment)* [1994] 2 All ER 413.

[155] [1994] 2 All ER 403.

provides an opening through which the reporting of cases in the law reports, for the purpose of providing legal guidance to others, can take place.[156]

B. Children and Young Persons

(a) Appearance in Court

The primacy of the privacy interest of children and young persons[157] in cases where either they or their affairs come before the courts forms a clear and long established exception to the open administration of justice. The exception has even survived the liberalization of access to hearings in chambers marked by the ruling in *Hodgson v Imperial Tobacco Ltd*.[158] In *Clibbery v Allan*[159] Munby J emphasized that in matters of open access the Family Division stood, in principle, on the same footing as the Queen's Bench and Chancery Divisions. Certainly, there might be express statutory provisions that forbade disclosure in some Family Division proceedings: for example, section 12 of the Administration of Justice Act 1960, or the Judicial Proceedings (Regulation of Reports) Act 1926. Apart from these and any proceedings that involved children, cases in the Family Division were subject to no greater requirements of confidentiality than cases in any other division of the High Court.[160]

Such is the protective role of the courts in regard to children that practices that would be regarded as the violation of an undoubted right of an adult litigant are sought to be justified on the basis of such role. Even the most basic element in open justice, the right to attend trial proceedings as an interested party, has been denied on this paternalistic basis. For example, in *Re W (a Minor) (Secure accommodation order: Attendance at court)*,[161] Ewbank J held that a court which was hearing an application for a secure accommodation order could allow the child to be present, but could equally refuse permission if it deemed attendance not to be in his best interests. It is scarcely surprising, then, if similar restrictions apply to the child in roles such as a witness or spectator of the trial.

---

[156] This element in the delivery of judgment in open court has been recognized in the work of the Court of Protection, a court which is concerned with managing the property and affairs of the mentally impaired. See *Re W* [1970] 2 All ER 502, 509.

[157] It should be noted at the outset that the following pages paint with a broad brush. Different terms, with different age limits, are used in various parts of the law to designate the category of the young.

[158] [1998] 2 All ER 673.

[159] [2001] 2 FCR 577. The case arose out of a dispute between Ivan Allan, the racehorse trainer, and his former partner, Miss Clibbery, who, having unsuccessfully brought proceedings against Mr Allan, was keen to publicize the lack of legal protection for cohabitant women.

[160] The ruling was swiftly criticized by the Solicitors' Family Law Association on the ground that the freedom of parties to disclose material about cases to the media would jeopardize the chances of resolving family disputes in a conciliatory manner: *New Law Journal* (29 June 2001) 955. Although the judgment was thought to be expressed in excessively broad terms, it was upheld by the Court of Appeal: The Times, 5 February 2002.

[161] The Times, 13 July 1994.

The Children and Young Persons Act 1933 expresses a number of standards relevant to the status and protection of children, whether as *personae* of the trial or as members of the public. Their presence in the courtroom is forbidden, except when they are required as a witness 'or otherwise for the purposes of justice' or while the court itself consents to their presence.[162] The prohibition is unexceptionable since the child spectator is extremely unlikely to perform the monitoring function in regard to the conduct of trials that has traditionally been assigned to members of the public. Equally, the presence in court of younger children, in particular, is likely to detract from the solemnity of the proceedings. Whether a hearing would be vitiated by the improper presence of a child, in contravention of this provision, probably admits of a negative answer. The provision exists for the benefit of the child, and it is difficult to see how the improper presence of any person—in contrast to the circumstance of improper exclusion[163]—would taint the validity of the hearing.

When the child is a witness, there is a power to exclude from the courtroom all save the *personae* of the trial while he is giving testimony. The power exists only '. . . in relation to an offence against, or any conduct contrary to, decency or morality . . .'[164] On those occasions when the power is exercised, the court is not sitting *in camera* since there is a saving provision which forbids 'the exclusion of bona fide representatives of a newspaper or news agency'. There is, however, a statutory suggestion that even this newspaper presence could, in certain circumstances, be eliminated since the facility of sitting *in camera* under the general law is expressly preserved.[165]

The legal provisions are supplemented by the extra-legal standards of the Code of Practice of the Press Complaints Commission. Clause 7 stipulates that, even where it is permissible by law, the press should not identify children under the age of sixteen who have been involved in the trial of sexual offences, whether as victims or as witnesses. In those cases where the child is the victim, 'the adult'—by which is presumably meant the accused—may be identified. At the same time, however, the report must not reveal any detail that might imply the relationship between the adult and child. In particular, the word 'incest' must be avoided where it might lead to the identification of the child. The terms of Clause 7 are badly drafted and somewhat repetitive. For example, the provision does not specify by whom the child might be identified. Clearly, the publication of even some sparse details might permit identification by a few individuals, while still leaving every other reader of the newspaper in the dark. This is to be compared with the statutory prohibition in regard to the complainants of the offences listed in the Sexual Offences (Amendment) Act 1992, where the test is identification by 'members of the public'.

---

[162] Children and Young Persons Act 1933, s 36; as amended by the Access to Justice Act 1999, s 73(1).
[163] See Chapter 3, section 3, B, above.
[164] Children and Young Persons Act 1933, s 37 (1).
[165] Children and Young Persons Act 1933, s 37 (2).

It is the situation where the child is the accused that is the most problematic. Indeed, the age-range of persons subject to these problems has been increased. There was a long-standing rule that a child between the ages of ten and fourteen was to be presumed 'doli incapax' (incapable of criminal responsibility)—a presumption that could be rebutted only by clear evidence that the child knew that his action was seriously wrong.[166] This has now been changed by statute.[167] There are significant departures, too, from the standard trial format in youth justice. The approach to the accused minor is shaped by an overriding concern for his welfare, in which the determination of guilt or innocence is but one factor. Trial may take place either in the Youth Court or the Crown Court, according to the gravity of the charge. These merit separate consideration.

The Children Act 1908 first established different courts for the trial of juveniles. The system has evolved piecemeal, culminating in the modern system of Youth Courts established by the Criminal Justice Act 1991.[168]

Admission to juvenile courts was tightly controlled by section 47(2) of the Children and Young Persons Act 1933, a provision which now applies in respect of Youth Courts. Unusually, such courts are closely regulated as to both location and time of hearing.[169] The categories of person who may be present at the sitting of the court are closely defined. Apart from the *personae* of the trial, *bona fide* representatives of newspapers or news agencies have a right to be present, all other persons needing special authorization from the court.[170] In terms of clarity, this provision is to be preferred to provisions which simply state, for example, that the proceedings are to take place 'without publicity'.[171]

The admittance of representatives of the press to the Youth Court is qualified by severe reporting restrictions contained in section 49 of the 1933 Act. The restrictions apply irrespective of whether the child or young person is the accused or a witness in the proceedings.[172] Briefly, no newspaper report shall reveal such particulars as the name, address, or school of the defendant in question. The court has power to waive the restrictions in certain situations. One, rather open-ended, situation arises where it is 'appropriate to do so for the purpose of avoiding injustice to the child or young person'.[173] Clearly, in this context the usual considerations in favour of open justice must be balanced against the harm caused to the child or young person as a result of the ensuing publicity. Rather

---

[166] The rule was reiterated by the House of Lords as recently as its decision in *C (A Minor) v DPP* [1996] AC 1.

[167] Crime and Disorder Act 1998, s 34.

[168] See C. Ball, K. McCormac, and N. Stone, *Young Offenders: Law, Policy and Practice* (1995).

[169] See Chapter 1, sections 5, A and B, above.

[170] Children and Young Persons Act 1933, s 47(2).

[171] This is the expression used in the Juvenile Delinquents Act 1970, s 12(1), of Canada—an expression that has been taken by the Canadian Supreme Court as being tantamount to a hearing *in camera*: *C. B. v The Queen* (1982) 127 DLR (3d) 482.

[172] Children and Young Persons Act 1933, s 49(4).

[173] Children and Young Persons Act 1933, s 49(5)(a).

more specific is the situation where a child or young person, charged with or convicted of specified serious offences, is unlawfully at large and publicity is required for the purpose of apprehending him.[174]

Where a juvenile is tried on indictment, the legal position as regards openness of access is fundamentally different. The proceedings are open to the press and public in the same way as with the trial of an adult. There is no provision analogous to section 47(2) of the Children and Young Persons Act 1933. Moreover, the initial rule is in favour of freedom of reporting, but with the significant difference that the court may direct that the identifying features mentioned above (name, address, school, etc.) may not be reported. The difficulty for any trial judge is to know how to exericise the discretion conferred by section 39 of the 1933 Act, since the provision does not furnish any guidance on when it is appropriate for the court to make or lift a reporting restriction. Moreover, there is some doubt as to whether the exercise of the discretion in any particular case is open to challenge by way of judicial review.[175] It is clear, at any rate, that the exercise of the discretion is partly shaped by the various rationales of open justice. To this extent, therefore, the subject was touched on in Chapter 2, where reference was made to *R v Leicester Crown Court, ex p S*[176] and *R v Lee.*[177]

The traditional arguments in favour of open justice do not apply with unmitigated force where juveniles are concerned. It has been held that there must exist good reasons for naming the defendant.[178] Naming could not take place, for example, because a severe sentence inflicted on a named individual would carry greater deterrent impact than in regard to an anonymous person.[179] In stark contrast to the Youth Court provision (section 49), the applicable conditions of which the court must be satisfied before allowing reporting are not set out in detail in section 39. In one instance the judge ordered the disclosure of the identity of two youths convicted of a particularly brutal rape of a thirteen-year-old girl. One consideration in favour of disclosure was the fact that the girl, since reporting her complaint, had been subject to abuse in the area surrounding her home and consequently had felt unable to live there. It appears that one aim of publicizing the names of the accused was to channel the feelings of the local community 'in the appropriate direction'.[180]

---

[174] Children and Young Persons Act 1933, s 49(5)(b) and (6).

[175] The issue turns on whether or not an order made under s 39 is a matter 'relating to trial on indictment' under the Supreme Court Act 1981, s 29(3). Since such matters are excluded from the supervisory jurisdiction of the High Court, judicial review of a s 39 order would be possible only consequent on a finding that such an order is not one 'relating to trial on indictment'. For a recent authority see *R v Crown Court at Winchester, ex p B (a minor)* [1999] 4 All ER 53.

[176] [1993] 1 WLR 111.   [177] [1993] 1 WLR 103.

[178] *R v Central Criminal Court, ex p S and P* [1999] Crim LR 159.

[179] *R v Inner London Crown Court, ex p Barnes (Anthony)* The Times, 7 August 1995; also reported as *R v Inner London Crown Court, ex p B* [1996] COD 17.

[180] The Times (4 March 1993) 3.

The enactment of the Youth Justice and Criminal Evidence Act 1999 has largely superseded section 39, which now applies to non-criminal proceedings.[181] The new statute does not apply to Youth Courts. Otherwise it furnishes a comprehensive power to restrict the reporting of information that is 'likely to lead members of the public to identify' any person under the age of eighteen who is concerned in any criminal proceedings—whether as defendant, witness, or victim.[182] This is supplemented by a restriction on reporting where a criminal investigation has begun in regard to an offence where a person under the age of eighteen is merely 'involved' in the offence.[183] While the courts are empowered to dispense with the restrictions in any particular case, no clear guidance is given as to the grounds on which a dispensing order may be made. It is interesting to note that such an order may not be made in regard to the trial itself 'by reason only of the fact that the proceedings have been determined in any way'.[184] Otherwise, resort must continue to be made to the body of case law on the exercise of discretion under section 39 of the Children and Young Persons Act 1933.

It is noteworthy that, in the treatment of juvenile offenders, there are safeguards against publicity which correspond to some of the safeguards that have been unsuccessfully claimed for adults. If a trial ends in a verdict of not guilty, it is quite possible that reporting restrictions may never be lifted. Where the proceedings, by contrast, culminate in a finding of guilt, the name of the offender will usually be disclosed in the more serious cases. When the juvenile has been convicted of a relatively minor offence, the curb on publicity will facilitate the process of rehabilitation which, as far as adult offenders are concerned, is rendered all the more difficult by reason of the publicity accompanying the trial.

Finally, something should be said about public access to, and the reporting of, civil cases in which childen are involved.

Once the focus of attention is removed from criminal to civil cases, some of the traditional arguments for public access—in particular, notions of deterrence—are no longer applicable. It is not surprising, therefore, that the claims of open justice are permitted to give way more readily to the claims of confidentiality. A remarkable instance of resort to argument on general principle in this area is provided by *Re P-B (a minor) (child cases: hearings in open court)*.[185] The father of a five-year-old boy applied for a residence order. He unsuccessfully asked for the proceedings to be heard in open court, his standing to bring the challenge undoubtedly deriving from his position as the child's father. It is worth emphasizing, moreover, that an anonymous person—a 'Mr G', described simply as a member of the public—was also joined as an intervenor in the proceedings. The

---

[181] Youth Justice and Criminal Evidence Act 1999, Sch 2, para 2(1).

[182] Youth Justice and Criminal Evidence Act 1999, s 45.

[183] Youth Justice and Criminal Evidence Act 1999, s 44.

[184] Youth Justice and Criminal Evidence Act 1999, s 45(5). This would mean that the return of a verdict of guilty would not, in itself, justify the lifting of reporting restrictions.

[185] [1997] 1 All ER 58.

judge at first instance refused the application, and the father appealed to the Court of Appeal. The mischief of secret justice in this particular context was summarized in the father's skeleton argument.[186] This was to no avail since, according to the Court of Appeal, the Family Proceedings Rules 1991 were quite clear. These stipulated that the particular type of application was to be heard in chambers, unless the judge hearing the case chose to direct otherwise.[187] He had seen no reason to depart from the the general rule, and the exercise of his discre-. tion would be left undisturbed.[188]

Section 39 of the Children and Young Persons Act 1933, as it originally stood, stipulated that it applied in any proceedings against, or involving any conduct contrary to, 'decency or morality'. Section 57(1) of the Children and Young Persons Act 1963 effected the removal of the words: 'which arise out of any offence against, or any conduct contrary to, decency or morality'. At a stroke, therefore, the scope of section 39 was extended, not only to all criminal cases irrespective of whether or not they involved conduct contrary to decency or morality, but also to civil cases. The details identifying the child may not be published if the court so directs. A notable example of the court exercising its discretion in favour of openness occurred in *R v Cambridge and Huntingdon Health Authority, ex p B (No 2)*.[189] The background to the case involved an application for judicial review brought on behalf of 'child B' against the defendant Health Authority for refusing to provide the child with medical treatment for her condition. The refusal was based on the cost of the treatment together with the poor prospects for its success. The interest generated in the story was such that the child's father was in a position to raise finance for her medical care by collaborating with the media in giving them the full details of the case and its background. In the above judgment the Court of Appeal, against the objections of the Official Solicitor (who doubted whether identification was really necessary for the envisaged purpose), took the common view that a full account with name and photographs would have greater impact on the public than an anonymous story.[190]

(b) Wardship and Similar Proceedings

The protective role of the court in regard to minors finds its clearest expression in regard to wards of court.[191] The wardship jurisdiction of the court is of ancient

---

[186] ibid. 63. Many of the considerations listed there are shaped by the peculiar circumstances of the father in that case as a litigant in person.

[187] Family Proceedings Rules 1991, SI 1991/1247, r 4(16) (7).

[188] In *B v UK, P v UK* The Times, 15 May 2001, the European Court of Human Rights ruled that the English practice of private hearing of disputes concerning the residence arrangements of the children of divorced parents was compatible with both Art 6 and Art 10 of the European Convention on Human Rights. This outcome was scarcely surprising in the light of the exception to Art 6(1) where 'the interests of juveniles' are involved.

[189] [1996] 1 FLR 375.

[190] For the background to the case see S. Barclay, *Jaymee: The Story of Child B* (1996). The argument before the Court of Appeal, and its ruling, is discussed at 154.

[191] See generally N. V. Lowe and R. A. H. White, *Wards of Court* (2nd edn, 1986).

origin. Often described as 'paternal' or 'administrative', it is the jurisdiction by virtue of which the court, acting on behalf of the Crown, acts as guardian of all non-adults. The subject is complex, but for the purposes of the present work it can be divided into two aspects. Our central concern, of course, is the confidentiality of wardship proceedings. To what extent is the public denied access to the court which adjudicates on these issues? Which matters, if any, may be reported from the hearing before that court? As elsewhere, the examination of these questions involves the relevant part of section 12 of the Administration of Justice Act 1960. However, there is a different strand to the subject which consists of a body of law that protects the ward from harmful publicity irrespective of whether the information that is disseminated derives from wardship proceedings or not. The protection of the ward from 'extra-curial publicity' (as we shall call the second aspect) furnishes the child with a rudimentary form of privacy protection. Both aspects of the subject derive from the same starting point: that publicity, irrespective of its source, can be harmful to the child. It will be convenient to deal, first, with the extra-curial aspect of the subject.

The most widely known case in this category is that of Mary Bell. In 1968, when only eleven years old, she was convicted of the manslaughter (by reason of diminished responsiblity) of two children.[192] The trial, as was usual for a child facing such a serious charge, took place in the Assize Court. It was not, it is worth noting, subject to an anonymity order.[193] Mary Bell was released from prison on licence in 1980 and, having changed her name, has been living in a number of secret locations together with a man whom she subsequently married and a daughter who was born in 1984. In the year of her birth the daughter, by way of response to a forthcoming publication about Mary Bell, was made a ward of court. An order was made forbidding the publication of any matters that might lead to the identification of the ward herself or her parents.[194] The form of legal process in this case has since been known as the making of a 'Mary Bell order', although it is merely a dramatic example of a type of order that has been in use for the protection of the ward from harmful publicity. There are several noteworthy aspects about the case. The protection afforded to the ward, in order to be effective, must similarly extend to her mother and father. This, incidentally, is yet another example of a familial relationship where the safeguarding of the child requires a similar measure of protection for others in the family circle. Moreover, the privacy afforded to the family circle by the order is limited in point of time, since it will terminate (at the very latest) on the daughter reaching the age of majority.

---

[192] For an account of the case and the many issues that it raises, see G. Sereny, *The Case of Mary Bell: A Portrait of a Child who Murdered* (1972).

[193] ibid. 75. The trial judge, Cusack J, invited the opinions of counsel for both Mary Bell and her co-accused before allowing publication of their names. They expressed no objection for two reasons. Their identities were already generally known in Scotswood, the district of Newcastle upon Tyne where the crimes took place. And suspicion might fall on other children unless the identity of the accused was published in reports of the trial.

[194] *Re X (A Minor) (Wardship: Injunction)* [1984] 1 WLR 1422.

The extra-curial jurisdiction rests on the making of an order of the court. This was recognized by Balcombe J's judgment in that case,[195] and also by the Court of Appeal in *Re M and N (minors) (wardship: publication of information)*.[196] Any protection that extended beyond the terms of section 12 of the Administration of Justice Act had to be by way of express prohibition of the court. Such order, moreover, would be binding on the world at large, not simply those represented before the court in the particular proceedings. In making the order, the welfare of the child is to be balanced against the public interest in publication. The form that the public interest takes will vary according to the circumstances. Most usually, it is freedom of speech that is the interest to be weighed against the interests of the child.[197]

To turn to the secrecy of wardship proceedings themselves, these depart from the classic trial model. This is borne out by several of the features of the court when exercising the wardship jurisdiction. Evidence is given on affidavit, supplemented by oral evidence at the hearing. The judge may see one party in the absence of the other. The normal rules of evidence do not apply, and it has been said that an inflexible rule against hearsay is inconsistent with the paternalistic nature of the jurisdiction.[198] All these departures from the standard safeguards of litigation are justified in the name of seeking out the course of conduct that is best for the child. It is scarcely surprising, therefore, that they are accompanied by another significant departure from the classic adjudicative model, in that they are invariably heard in private.

Prior to 1960 the wardship jurisdiction was clearly established as an exception to the rule of open justice. It was, as we have seen, the subject of several observations in *Scott v Scott* itself. The difficulty was how to deal with publications that breached the confidentiality of wardship proceedings. The issue was avoided in *Re Martindale*,[199] a case which was described in the newspaper that carried the disclosure as involving 'a rarely romantic story' of a clandestine marriage between the ward and a young poet. The contempt was judged unintentional and, in any event, not a serious one. Some guidance was afforded by *Re Beaujeu's application for writ of attachment against Cudlipp*,[200] which concerned inaccurate information of wardship proceedings published by the *Daily Herald*. The wards' mother argued that the editor was in contempt of court in publishing the item. In rejecting her argument, Wynn-Parry J recognized that (the inaccuracy aside) it would prima facie be a contempt of court to publish an account of proceedings held in chambers relating to an infant. However, the newspaper had acted in good faith, the item being supplied to it by a reputable news agency. Moreover, it would not be a contempt to publish simply the order made at the

---

[195] ibid. 1425.   [196] [1989] 3 WLR 1136.
[197] As, for example, in *R v Central Independent Television plc* [1994] 3 WLR 20.
[198] *Re K (Infants)* [1965] AC 201, 242, per Lord Devlin.   [199] [1894] 3 Ch 193.
[200] [1949] 1 Ch 230.

conclusion of the proceedings, unless the judge stipulated that such order should not be published.[201]

The legal situation was clarified somewhat by the relevant parts of section 12 of the Administration of Justice Act 1960. As already stated, this provision stipulates that, in the five listed types of case, it is a contempt of court to publish information from the private sitting of any court. Heading (a), the one that is here in point, has undergone some change since it was first enacted in order to reflect subsequent legislation on the care of children. As it now stands, it encompasses: proceedings relating to the exercise of the inherent jurisdiction of the High Court with respect to minors; those brought under the Children Act 1989; and those that relate wholly or mainly to the maintenance or upbringing of a minor.

The wording of section 12(1)(a), seemingly absolute in its terms, was held by the Court of Appeal to import a requirement of knowledge in *Re F (orse A) (A Minor) (Publication of Information)*.[202] Two newspapers, the *Daily Telegraph* and the *Slough Evening Mail* had published material concerning the circumstances in which a fifteen-year-old girl had been made a ward of court. The staff of the newspapers made inquiries and were informed, wrongly, that she was no longer a ward. In the circumstances the newspapers were not guilty of contempt of court since they were unaware that the information that they published related to wardship proceedings. Indeed, in the light of the secrecy surrounding the wardship court, the press were in no position to check whether their story did or did not encompass such material.

On the other hand, there remains a discretion on the part of the judge sitting in the wardship court to authorize release of material to outside bodies. Resort must be had to that judge for the purpose of exercising the discretion, it has been stressed, even for the most innocuous purposes. Disclosure of evidential documents to outside parties—including medical experts and other professionals for the purpose of seeking specialist assistance for the hearing of the case—may be a contempt if done without the prior leave of the court.[203] The point was emphasized by Waite J in *Re X, Y and Z (Wardship: Disclosure of Material)*:[204] 'The privilege of confidentiality is that of the court, not of the child, and the primary purpose of that privilege is to protect the court in the exercise of its paternal functions.'[205] Among the various cases where disclosure has been permitted, there are some which touch on some of the themes of the present work. In *Re F (Minors) (Wardship: Police Investigation)*[206] the Court of Appeal endorsed the judge's decision to release to the police the judgment in the wardship case, together with affidavits and other material that had been produced to the court, despite the adverse impact that such disclosure might have on the frankness of conduct of

[201] [1949] 1 Ch 230, 235.   [202] [1976] 3 WLR 813.
[203] *Practice Direction* [1987] 3 All ER 640.   [204] [1992] 1 FLR 84.
[205] ibid. 86. The inquiry into the allegations of child abuse in Cleveland formed the background to this case. For an account see *Report of the Inquiry into Child Abuse in Cleveland 1987* (Cm 413, 1988).
[206] [1988] 3 WLR 818.

future wardship proceedings.[207] Whatever the merits of the point, it is interesting to note here yet another untested assumption as to the circumstances—secrecy or candour—which promote optimum witness performance.

The very high priority that is accorded to protecting children from publicity was reflected in the ruling of the Court of Appeal in *Re R (Minor) (Court of Appeal: Order against identification)*[208] which laid down that all orders emanating from that Court that related to children would contain a restriction on identification of the child irrespective of whether a specific order had been given in the particular case. Nevertheless, it is possible to identify situations in which the courts have adjusted the degree of protection for the child to the extent that is only just necessary in the particular circumstances. In that case, for example, the hearing took place in open court notwithstanding its having taken place in chambers at first instance. It was said to be especially important that there should be open access to hearings in appellate courts. In *Re G (Minors) (Celebrities: Publicity)*[209] an order that prohibited the publication of even the bare outcome of the case was held to be excessive in the circumstances, even though there existed a statutory jurisdiction to do so[210] and it might appear warranted by a case dealing with a dispute between well-known personalities. Finally, in *Re F (orse A) (A Minor) (Publication of Information)* Geoffrey Lane LJ stated that the embargo on publication was not necessarily perpetual and would extend only as long as necessary to protect the interests that were served by confidentiality.[211]

It is worth mentioning, finally, an anomalous former practice in regard to applications to attach or to commit for contempt of court. Such cases are heard in open court, and properly so in view of the penal consequences flowing from a successful application. However, in cases involving wards of court, the applications were heard in chambers. This practice was rightly criticized by the JUSTICE Report on Contempt of Court, which stated that the contempt power did not form part of the paternal jurisdiction of the court in regard to wards.[212] The anomaly continued until it was brought to the attention of the public by a newspaper reporter who, while in the precincts of the Royal Courts of Justice, happened to observe a man emerging in confinement from such a private hearing.[213] There was a consequent change in the law, requiring such cases to be heard in open court together with the release of the name of the person committed, the nature of the

---

[207] Incidentally, it has been suggested that to take a professional person's testimony *in camera* is, in certain circumstances, a suitable way of reconciling the need of the court to gain access to all relevant evidence with the desirability of respecting the client confidentiality of such persons as medical practitioners. See P. Westen, 'Compulsory Process II' (1975–76) 74 *Michigan Law Review* 191, 248, n 198.

[208] The Times, 9 December 1998.   [209] [1999] 1 FLR 409.

[210] Administration of Justice Act 1960, s 12(2).

[211] [1976] 3 WLR 813, 841. For other authorities, see Lowe and White, *Wards of Court* (n 191 above) 92.

[212] JUSTICE Report, *Contempt of Court* (1959), 21–3.

[213] The incident, which occurred in 1965, is recounted in H. P. Levy, *The Press Council: History, Procedure and Cases* (1967) 271.

contempt, and the length of the period of committal. Yet, in *Re C (a Minor)*,[214] an order for committal arising out of wardship proceedings was made in violation of these requirements, as laid down by the Rules of the Supreme Court.[215] In the event, the Court of Appeal ruled that such an irregularity could be corrected under a further provision of the same Rules.[216] In a demonstration of scant regard for the value of open justice, the Court of Appeal confessed to having difficulty in appreciating why the original order had given rise to any injustice.

7. THE LIMITS OF PUBLIC TRIAL: JUVENILE JUSTICE

The manner of conduct of criminal proceedings against minors illuminates, as no other area does, the limitations of the values served by public trial. In this concluding section of the chapter, therefore, we will continue the critique of the right to public trial that was conducted at the end of Chapter 3.

The United Nations Standard Minimum Rules for the Administration of Juvenile Justice emphasize that 'the well-being' of the juvenile offender must be a prominent feature of the criminal justice system.[217] In particular, the offender's privacy is to be respected at all stages 'in order to avoid harm being caused to her or him by undue publicity or by the process of labelling'. 'In principle', it is added, 'no information that may lead to the identification of a juvenile offender shall be published.'[218] Such international standards reflect the approach taken by civilized national legal systems, which recognize that the traditional trial procedure is inappropriate where juveniles are concerned.[219] Witnesses before the *Committee on Children and Young Persons*,[220] which reported in 1960, urged that the then system of juvenile courts should be replaced by tribunals that were 'non-judicial or quasi-judicial' in nature.[221] Although the system of juvenile courts that the Committee was investigating was less formal and less public than the adult court, in the opinion of some witnesses the proceedings were still conducted with too little regard to the interests of the juvenile. Notwithstanding the limitations on the categories of persons permitted to attend sittings of juvenile courts, it was thought that proceedings were often conducted in the presence of too many people. The Committee agreed that, ideally, proceedings in a juvenile court 'should be as private as possible', adding that 'if too many people are present they change the character of the court'.[222]

---

[214] The Times, 16 November 1988.   [215] RSC Order 52, r 6(2).   [216] RSC Order 2, r 1.
[217] Rule 5.1.   [218] Rules 8.1 and 8.2.
[219] In *McKerry v Teesdale and Wear Valley Justices* [2000] Crim LR 594, the Divisional Court had recourse to the United Nations Standard Minimum Rules for the Administration of Juvenile Justice, in addition to other international texts, as background sources of law in adjudicating on the propriety of revealing a juvenile offender's identity.
[220] Cmnd 1191, 1960. Chairman: Viscount Ingleby.   [221] ibid. para 69.
[222] ibid. para 188.

Such points are readily conceded in regard to the trial of most charges. They have proved more difficult to accept in the context of the most serious charges brought against children. Such trials, as has been seen, have long taken place in an adult court.[223] A recent example was the proceedings in 1993 against the two boys, Robert Thompson and Jon Venables, for the abduction and murder of two-year-old James Bulger. The two boys were tried and found guilty at the Crown Court. The form of the trial, among other things, was challenged before the European Court of Human Rights.[224] It was not surprising, in view of the mode of trial prevalent in Europe, that the judgment of the European Court condemned by a large margin the public character of the hearing at the Crown Court,[225] with the consequent need to change the practice governing the trial of young defendants.[226]

Few cases illustrate so vividly the paradoxes in the institution of public trial. The core of the applicants' case was based on the fact that they had been subject to a public trial—one of the very rights secured in Article 6 of the Convention. Yet, by a margin of sixteen to one, the judges of the Human Rights Court found that the applicants had consequently been denied a trial that was fair. More remarkably still, five of the judges were also of the opinion that the trial procedure amounted to 'inhuman or degrading treatment or punishment' within the meaning of Article 3 of the Convention.[227] Certain features of Crown Court trial had been modified out of deference to the age of the two accused. They were shown the courtroom before the trial, and judicial procedure explained to them; their legal advisers were placed in close proximity so as to facilitate consultation and to minimize feelings of isolation; and the court sat over shorter than usual periods. Nevertheless, the Court of Human Rights ruled that the trial process must have appeared bewildering to the petitioners, such that their ability effectively to organize their defence must have been impaired.

An accused of any age, clearly, is denied a fair trial if he is unable effectively to participate in the process because, for example, the acoustics of the courtroom are poor, or because he is not accorded the services of an interpreter even though he is not fluent in the language of the proceedings. Rather less clear is the situation in which it is contended that an accused's defence is impaired solely by reason of the stress that accompanies the public character of the trial. To be tried for

---

[223] On the arrangements in Scotland, see K. McK. Norrie, *Children's Hearings in Scotland* (1997).

[224] For details of the case, see the Appendix. Note, in addition, the subsequent case brought by the two boys to assure their continuing anonymity—a step the necessity for which (it has been argued) was increased by the decision of the judge at the Crown Court to permit disclosure of their identities.

[225] *T v UK, V v UK* (2000) 30 EHRR 121.

[226] The changes were promulgated by Lord Bingham CJ in a Practice Note, *Crown Court—Trial of children and young persons—Procedure* [2000] 2 All ER 285. In particular, para 14 states that only a restricted number of persons should be allowed admission to the trial, to be limited perhaps to those with 'an immediate and direct interest' in its outcome. The court would rule on any controversy relating to the right of any particular person to attend.

[227] They were in a minority on this point, twelve judges ruling that Art 3 had not been breached in this regard.

a serious offence is stressful for any accused, irrespective of his age. The public nature of the process serves only to magnify the ordeal. By way of reduction of the stress for younger defendants, the Human Rights Court indicated that their trials should take place in accordance with 'a modified procedure providing for selected attendance rights and judicious reporting'.[228] Yet, such conditions would prove totally unacceptable in the trial of adult offenders. What of the supposed advantages of publicity for the accused, regardless of age? Under the proposed conditions, would judges become slipshod, and witnesses unreliable? Certainly, in many respects there are substantial differences in the legal position of children and adults. Their common theme, however, is that they entail a degree of compulsion of children (or with respect to children) that would be considered inappropriate and paternalistic if applied to adults. The justification for the difference is that the former lack the degree of maturity required to take responsibility for their own decisions. What is remarkable about trial procedures is that each group—adults and children—is alike subject to compulsion. The compulsion is in regard to different arrangements—publicity and privacy, respectively. That the safeguards of publicity should be so readily abandoned where the younger accused are concerned would suggest that the advantages that they confer are so marginal that they can readily be sacrificed for the sake of other aspects of the younger accused's well-being.

[228] (2000) 30 EHRR 121, para 87.

6

Secrecy and Commercial Litigation

1. OPEN JUSTICE IN COMMERCIAL COURTS

As one might expect, the issue of open justice in the commercial environment does not provoke the passionate debate that is encountered in other areas of law.[1] The question of secrecy and the judicial process is, nevertheless, of considerable significance in this field of legal practice. Some of the issues raised in this chapter reflect themes of general importance in this work, whereas other matters are exclusively relevant to the business environment.

As a general principle courts dealing with commercial disputes are required to sit in public, as reflected in Rule 39.2 of the Civil Procedure Rules 1998.[2] However, many commercial courts are classified as specialized courts for the purposes of Part 49 of the Civil Procedure Rules with the consequence that matters of procedure are often dealt with in discrete Practice Directions. The basic rule, therefore, is that the Civil Procedure Rules apply unless excluded by specific provision in the relevant Practice Direction.

Public access is the rule in the Commercial Court of the Queen's Bench Division[3] and the Companies Court within the Chancery Division. The Mercantile List Courts in various major commercial centres follow suit.[4] So does the county court (which deals with minor commercial disputes).[5] Other specialist courts that administer justice in commercial litigation, such as the Admiralty Court,[6] the Patents Court in the Chancery Division[7] and the Restrictive Trade Practices Court,[8] hold their proceedings in public. Official referees conducted

---

[1] For general discussion see J Hull, *Commercial Secrecy: Law and Practice* (1998), 12.20–12.36.

[2] SI 1998/3132 (as amended). Note also Rule 32.2 (witnesses' evidence to be given in open court).

[3] *Commercial Court Guide* (August 1999) para 17 and *Statement in Open Court: Commercial Law Guide* [1999] 4 All ER 471 where Longmore J produces useful information on the *Guide*.

[4] For relevant *Practice Directions* affecting the Mercantile Lists see, for example, [1992] 1 WLR 726, [1996] 1 WLR 1210 and [1997] 1 WLR 219.

[5] County court procedure is now also governed by the Civil Procedure Rules: see Civil Procedure Rules 1998, SI 1998/3132, Rule 2.1(a).

[6] This court is based in the Queen's Bench Division and adopts its procedural practices: see *Practice Direction (Admiralty Court: Practice)* [1996] 1 WLR 127.

[7] One exception to this rule is to be found in the practice of dealing with summonses by telephone: see *Practice Direction (Patents Court: Revised Procedure)* [1998] 1 WLR 1414 para 35. This procedure cannot be used on a point of general public importance.

[8] See Restrictive Practices Court Act 1976, s 6(6), which permits public or private sittings, though the former are the norm: Restrictive Practices Court Rules 1976, SI 1976/1897, r. 15. It would appear that proceedings will be held *in camera* if this is necessary to protect national security, to preserve secrets or confidences, or to guard against substantial injury to a business.

their business in public and that practice has carried over to their successor, the Construction and Technology Court.[9] And, quite generally, the Court of Appeal (Civil Division) hears in open court both applications for leave to appeal[10] and substantive appeals.[11]

The general rule also applies to international judicial bodies. The European Court of Justice and the Court of First Instance, both of which are frequently required to rule in matters of commercial dispute where there is a European Community dimension, sit in public.[12] On the other hand, the dispute settlement procedures of the World Trade Organization are conducted on a confidential basis.[13] This may well be due to the fact that the procedures of the World Trade Organization are more akin to arbitration than adversarial litigation.

The same general rule applies in regard to tribunals.[14] Members of the public are allowed to attend both hearings of employment tribunals[15] and appeals heard before the Employment Appeals Tribunal,[16] unless those tribunals direct to the contrary.[17] Hearings of VAT tribunals are held in public unless the tribunal decides to exclude the public in a particular case.[18] The same is true of the

[9] TCC claims may be dealt with either in the county court or the High Court.

[10] See *Practice Note* [1999] 1 All ER 186, para 39.

[11] See *Practice Direction, Court of Appeal (Civil Division)* [1999] 1 WLR 1027, paras 2.3.1 and 13.1.

[12] Protocol on the Statute of the Court of Justice, Arts 28 and 34. Deliberations of the judges are to be kept confidential: Arts 32, 9 and 12. The Court of First Instance applies similar rules: Council Decision 1988 Art 46 ([1989] OJ C215/1). For discussion of this issue see (1986) *New Law Journal* 1182. Reasoned opinions of the Advocate General are delivered in open court: EU Treaty, Art 222 (ex 166) and Case C-17/98 *Emesa Sugar (Free Zone) NV v Aruba* The Times 29 February 2000. This policy of openness does not extend to giving access to preliminary documentation relating to reasoned opinions of the Advocate General or decisions of the Commission (for example, in competition matters). For discussion see Case T-309/97 *Bavarian Lager Company Ltd v Commission* [1999] 3 CMLR 544 and Case T-92/98 *Interporc Im-und Export Gmbh v Commission* [2000] 1 CMLR 181.

[13] See A. H. Qureshi, *International Economic Law* (1999) ch 13, for a full discussion of the issue of confidentiality in the context of dispute settlement in the World Trade Organization.

[14] The Council on Tribunals has attempted to regulate the position and, indeed, its members are often allowed to attend those tribunals that sit in private.

[15] Employment Tribunals (Constitution and Rules of Procedure) Regulations 1993, SI 1993/2687, r 8(2), *Storer v British Gas* [2000] 2 All ER 440, and *R v Secretary of the Central Office of Employment Tribunals (England and Wales), ex p Public Concern at Work* The Times, 9 May 2000 (register on decisions kept at Central Office on tribunal cases to be fully comprehensive and open to public inspection). For general background discussion, see J. McIlroy, *Industrial Tribunals* (1983) 164.

[16] The EAT can restrict reporting of cases involving allegations of sexual misconduct or where details of the health of a disabled person might be disclosed: Employment Tribunals Act 1996, ss 31 and 32. See generally *Cahm v Ward & Goldstone Ltd* [1979] ICR 574 and *Milne & Lyall v Waldren* [1980] ICR 138.

[17] The tribunal can conduct the hearing in private in cases where national security is at stake: Employment Tribunals Act 1996, s 10. A power to limit reporting of cases exists where there are allegations of sexual misconduct: see Employment Tribunals Act 1996, s 11(6), and *R v London (North) Industrial Tribunal, ex p Associated Newspapers Ltd* [1998] ICR 1212. There has been dispute as to whether corporate bodies may enjoy the protection of this provision: compare *M v Vincent* [1998] ICR 73 with *Leicester University v A* [1999] ICR 701. Reporting restrictions can also be imposed in disability cases to protect details of the health of the complainant: Employment Tribunals Act 1996, s 12.

[18] See VAT Tribunal Rules 1986, SI 1986/590, r 24(1), and the discussion in *McNicholas Construction Co Ltd v Customs and Excise* [1998] *Simon's Tax Intelligence* 1391.

General Commissioners[19] and Special Commissioners,[20] though the hearing in this form of an appeal against assessment to tax may lead to the disclosure of the private financial affairs of the taxpayer.

By contrast, tribunals which are set up under self-regulatory regimes tend to hear disputes in private. Thus, the Financial Services and Markets Tribunal, which penalizes breaches of conduct by participants in the investment market, can conduct its business either in public or in private.[21] The Panel on Take-overs and Mergers, which exercises a regulatory jurisdiction in regard to take-overs, stages its hearings in private. Its rulings, nevertheless, are well publicized.[22] Although take-overs are the subject of statutory and common law rules, the prime task of the Panel is the enforcement of the extra-legal Take-over Code (which originated in 1968). In addition to issuing 'sanctions', in the form of reprimands and demands that certain forms of conduct should cease, the Panel can issue requests for additional information and even waive breaches of the Code. Its status, therefore, is 'judicial' in a very attenuated sense only.[23]

2. INVESTIGATORY PROCESSES

In the commercial area it would be misleading to view the process of the administration of justice exclusively in terms of the work of courts or tribunals. Other bodies, even if they are not recognized as judicial in name,[24] can play a significant role in the administration of commercial justice, whether by providing investigatory input into subsequent legal rulings or by reaching conclusions on issues of fact which may lead, in turn, to legal action.

[19] General Commissioners (Jurisdiction and Procedure) Regulations 1994, SI 1994/1812.

[20] Special Commissioners (Jurisdiction and Procedure) Regulations 1994, SI 1994/1811.

[21] The Tribunal was established pursuant to the Financial Services and Markets Act 2000. Under Sch 13, the Lord Chancellor is empowered to make rules regulating the hearing, and para 9(b) allows for hearings to take place in private 'in such circumstances as may be specified in the rules'. It is anticipated, however, that the Tribunal will be required by Art 6 of the European Convention on Human Rights to hold a public hearing unless either the situation falls within one of the exceptions to Art 6 or the person whose rights and obligations are being determined waives the right to a public hearing: L. Minghella in M. Blair, L. Minghella, M. Taylor, M. Threipland and G. Walker, *Blackstone's Guide to the Financial Services and Markets Act 2000* (2001) 131.

[22] See *R v Panel on Take-overs and Mergers, ex p Guinness plc* [1989] BCLC 255, 263. Take-over Panel hearings are not open to the public, but key rulings, in which the public has a legitimate interest, are publicized. *The Journal of Business Law* regularly reports such rulings. The unreported decision in *Graff v Shawcross, Macdonald and Frazer* (Queen's Bench Division, 10 October 1980), noted by D. Chaikin at (1981) 2 *Company Lawyer* 33 is also of interest in dealing with the legal problems which may arise when details of Take-over Panel rulings are disseminated.

[23] On the status of the Panel, see *R v Panel on Take-overs and Mergers, ex p Datafin plc* [1987] QB 815, 824–826.

[24] For example, the fact that, strictly speaking, company inspections are outside the administration of justice may be gleaned from the unreported case of *Re Countyglen plc* (HC of Ireland, 28 October 1994), where Murphy J of the High Court of Ireland ruled that the provision in the Irish Constitution requiring the administration of justice to take place in public (Art 34.1) did not apply to such inspections.

An example of the first category is to be found in the examination processes in cases of insolvency. Under these procedures, bankrupts or officers of insolvent companies can be required to offer explanations for the cause of the insolvency. The evidence gleaned from these inquiries might lead to criminal prosecution or the imposition of civil sanctions. The application of the rules of contempt of court reinforces the status of these investigations, especially their mandatory character as far as the duty to respond to questions is concerned. There are two types of insolvency examination. The process known as public examination was much feared by bankrupts because it represented a form of ritual humiliation. As a result of criticism in particular high profile cases and wider concerns about its use, the public examination is now rare in bankruptcy cases,[25] but it is still permitted where the official receiver successfully applies for such an examination to be held.[26] Public examinations of officers of companies undergoing compulsory liquidation were intended to be more widely used when the Insolvency Act 1986 was enacted,[27] but that hope has not materialized. Private examinations are much more commonly used.[28] Such investigations are usually conducted well away from the public gaze[29] and often involve little more than the completion of a questionnaire.

The second category of investigatory process worth examining in the light of the requirements of open justice is that of official inquiries.[30] A Department of Trade and Industry (DTI) investigation has much in common with the aforementioned examination procedures in that it may be characterized as primarily investigatory in nature rather than as a form of adjudication.[31] But it differs from them in one crucial respect. The inspectors produce a report which, by virtue of section 437 of the Companies Act 1985, may be published if the Secretary of State so directs. That report can destroy an individual's professional reputation and can lead to formal sanctions such as disqualification as a company director. It is at the discretion of the Secretary of State whether or not to publish a report, but that discretion must be exercised in accordance with established public law principles. Thus in *R v Secretary of State for Trade and Industry, ex p Lonrho plc*[32] a

---

[25] See the Insolvency Act 1976, s 6.   [26] Under the Insolvency Act 1986, s 290.

[27] Under the Insolvency Act 1986, s 133.

[28] Pursuant to the Insolvency Act 1986, ss 236 and 366.

[29] Insolvency Rules 1986, SI 1986/1925, r 9.4(2).

[30] The Bingham investigation into the collapse of BCCI and the role of the Bank of England was conducted largely in private, though a major report was produced on completion of the inquiry: *An Inquiry into the Supervision of the Bank of Credit and Commerce International*, HMSO 1992. For comment see L Blom-Cooper, 'Bingham and the BCCI Affair' *The Financial Times* 5 August 1991. The Board of Banking Supervision's investigation into the collapse of Barings involved the collecting of information, disclosure of which was tightly controlled by the terms of the Banking Act 1987, s 82. However, once such information had been exhibited in director disqualification proceedings, it might be regarded as in the public domain: *Barings plc (in liquidation) v Coopers and Lybrand* [2000] 1 WLR 2353.

[31] Nevertheless, the rules of natural justice apply to ensure that the process is conducted fairly: *Re Pergamon Press Ltd* [1971] Ch 388 and *Maxwell v DTI* [1974] 1 QB 523.

[32] [1989] 1 WLR 525. The DTI inspectors' report was officially published in 1990, though not before it was carried in a special mid-week issue of *The Observer* dated 30 March 1989.

decision to delay publication of a report pending a decision of the authorities on whether to institute a prosecution was held not to be unreasonable.

There are different types of DTI investigation. Some take the form of informal and discreet inquiries,[33] whereas others may be characterized as formal interrogations under oath[34] which are protected by the law of contempt in the event of obstruction.[35] Such investigations are held in private and the evidence given by the witnesses is subjected to a degree of confidentiality.[36] The law governing these investigations was reviewed in *Re Mirror Group Newspapers plc*.[37] In this case a person who was being interviewed by DTI inspectors refused to sign a confidentiality undertaking and also complained that the investigation was being conducted in an oppressive manner. The inspectors argued that his behaviour constituted obstruction and therefore amounted to contempt. Sir Richard Scott V-C disagreed and, in reaching that conclusion, reviewed the legal nature of the investigation procedure. He confirmed the well-established principle[38] that DTI investigations were to be held in private. Privacy was necessary to protect the reputation of individuals while the inquiry was being conducted. However, within the constraints imposed by privacy, some flexibility was allowed to inspectors.[39] They could, of necessity, admit shorthand writers. As it was expected that the evidence given would remain confidential until the report was published, inspectors were not required to extract confidentiality undertakings from witnesses and failure to give such an undertaking did not amount to contempt. Moreover, there was sympathy expressed for the amount of questioning which the witness in that case was expected to undergo and the court indicated that the scope of the inquiry should in future be refined. However, once the scope of the inquiry was more focused, the examinee was obliged to answer.

---

[33] Some DTI investigations, notably those carried out pursuant to the Companies Act 1985, s 447, have always been conducted in secret in view of the potential effect that they may have on share prices and the securities market. Note here *Application for Permission: 'R'* [2001] EWHC Admin. 571. The fact that such an inquiry is being held often finds its way into the press, only to be met by a 'no comment' response by the authorities. For a rare incident where the authorities were more forthcoming see 'Burton Investigation Clothed in Secrecy' *The Financial Times*, 13 January 1988.

[34] Under the Companies Act 1985, s 434(3).   [35] Companies Act 1985, s 436.

[36] For a comprehensive account of this aspect of DTI investigations, see A. Lidbetter, *Company Investigations and Public Law* (1999) 5.5. Note also that statements given to the police during the course of a fraud investigation should remain confidential unless read out in open court: see *Bunn v BBC* [1998] 3 All ER 552. The DTI is anxious to ensure that inspectors' reports remain private until finalized. This is partly due to the desire to protect the confidentiality of witnesses' evidence and partly to allow parties an opportunity to comment on the draft report. The DTI accordingly responded to the leaking of a draft report by issuing a public rebuke: see DTI Press Notice P/2001/95 for full details.

[37] [1999] 3 WLR 583.

[38] *Hearts of Oak Assurance Co Ltd v A-G* [1932] AC 392. This aspect of the procedure was noted by Lord Denning MR in *Re Pergamon Press Ltd* [1971] Ch 388, 399, and in *Maxwell v DTI* [1974] 1 QB 523, 533.

[39] *Re Gaumont-British Picture Corporation Ltd* [1940] Ch 506.

3. COMMERCIAL ARBITRATION

Arbitration proceedings, as already pointed out in Chapter 2, section 7, are a commonly used method of resolving commercial disputes, and are normally held in private.[40] Indeed, this is one of the great attractions of this mode of dispute resolution and the reason why arbitration clauses are standard features of major commercial contracts. In this way the norm that justice is to be administered in public is subordinated to the freedom of contract of the parties in dispute. In *Oxford Shipping Co Ltd v Nippon Yusen Kaisha, The Eastern Saga*,[41] Leggatt J explained the position as follows:

The concept of private arbitrations derives simply from the fact that the parties have agreed to submit to arbitration particular disputes arising between them and only between them. It is implicit in this that strangers shall be excluded from the hearing and the conduct of the arbitration.[42]

His Lordship ruled in this case that an arbitrator had no power to hear separate, but identical, disputes concurrently, as this was not within the terms of the arbitration agreements. This presumption in favour of confidentiality, which may be expressed in terms of an implied term in the contract, was reiterated by the Court of Appeal in *Ali Shipping Corp v Shipyard Trogir*[43] in the context of the disclosure of material arising in one arbitration in later arbitration hearings. The essentially contractual feature of arbitrations has been left undisturbed by the attempt to provide a more developed regulatory framework in the Arbitration Act 1996. It is stated at the outset of the statute that it is founded on the principle that 'the parties should be free to agree how their disputes are resolved, subject only to such safeguards as are necessary in the public interest',[44] while later provisions clearly indicate the primacy of the arbitration agreement over the legislation in many matters, including procedural issues.[45]

It is necessary to qualify in several respects the statement that arbitrations are private affairs. Publicity may be incurred if one of the parties fails to respect the award of the arbitrator or the award is challenged on a point of law before the High Court. In the latter instance an arbitrator may be called upon to give evidence of what transpired before him.[46] There may be other situations where a

---

[40] The fact that arbitrations are conducted in private is implicit in *Haigh v Haigh* (1861) LJCh 420 and *Advance Specialist Treatment Engineering Ltd v Cleveland Structural Engineering (Hong Kong) Ltd* [2000] 1 WLR 558 (on the subject of access to arbitration claims). Privacy may be expressly stipulated for, but in any case it is likely that there is an implied term in an arbitration clause that the arbitration is to be conducted in private: see the discussion in (1993) 67 *Australian Law Journal* 630.

[41] [1984] 2 Lloyd's Rep 373.   [42] ibid. 379.

[43] [1999] 1 WLR 314. See also *Dolling-Baker v Merrett* [1990] 1 WLR 1205. The High Court of Australia took a much more restricted view of the concept of confidentiality in arbitrations in *Esso Australia Resources Ltd v Plowman* (1995) 183 CLR 10.

[44] Arbitration Act 1996, s 1(b).   [45] Arbitration Act 1996, ss 4(2) and 34(1).

[46] On this point see *Duke of Buccleuch and Queensbury v Metropolitan Board of Works* (1871–2) LR 5 HL 418. Arbitration applications to the court may be heard in chambers unless it is a substantive

party to an arbitration agreement in a contract may disregard that method of dispute settlement and opt instead for a court hearing in public. Under section 9 of the Arbitration Act 1996 (formerly section 4 of the Arbitration Act 1950) the court would normally stay such proceedings, but it does have a discretion to refuse to do this. Two illustrations of such refusal are furnished by partnership law.[47] In *Radford v Hair*[48] a partnership agreement between surveyors contained a clause to the effect that disputes between the parties were to be settled by arbitration. The particular dispute involved contested allegations of fraud against one of the partners, who preferred the matter to be aired in open court. Pennycuick V-C refused to stay the proceedings on the ground that a man's professional reputation was at stake. Support was drawn from the comments of Pollock B in *Minife v Railway Passengers Assurance Co* to the effect that: '. . . where fraud is imputed . . . it would be difficult to say that the plaintiff ought not to have the opportunity of clearing himself from so grave a personal imputation in open court'.[49]

This principle was further extended in *Turner v Fenton*[50] where the allegations were of professional incompetence, rather than fraud. Again, Warner J held that the partner (a solicitor) who was the target of these allegations was entitled to have his day in court to rebut the charges. These cases clearly illustrate how publicity may be actively sought by a person who is confident that he will be able to refute in a public forum allegations which have so far had a limited, but damaging, circulation.

4. OPEN JUSTICE IN COMMERCIAL LITIGATION: THE GENERAL RULE EXEMPLIFIED

It is clear that virtually all bodies charged with adjudication (as opposed to investigation) in commercial matters conduct their hearings in public. It is now appropriate to examine the operation of that rule in specific contexts. The two areas of company law and insolvency law will be chosen for this purpose. These are central topics in any commercial environment and the rules here are clear, having been embodied in three Practice Directions.

Matters of company law are dealt with either by the Companies Court in the Chancery Division or by the county court. Company proceedings fall under Part

---

appeal hearing or a matter dealing with a point of law, in which case the hearing may be in open court: see *Practice Note (Arbitration: New Procedure)* [1997] 1 WLR 391 and *Hiscox v Outhwaite* The Times, 7 March 1991, reported on appeal at [1992] 1 AC 562.

[47] For general discussion see D. Milman and T. Flanagan, *Modern Partnership Law* (1983) 114.

[48] [1971] Ch 758.

[49] (1881) 44 LT 552, 554. It may well be that the target of such an allegation prefers to have the matter resolved under the arbitration facility, in which case the court will be happy to respect that preference: *Cunningham-Reid v Buchanan-Jardine* [1988] 1 WLR 678.

[50] [1982] 1 WLR 52.

49 of the Civil Procedure Rules 1998: that is, the general rule embodied in Rule 39.2 does not apply if specific procedural regulations are laid down in Practice Directions. These are to be found in a 1999 Practice Direction[51] issued by Sir Richard Scott V-C, who identifies the most common forms of application and petition. For example, it is stated in paragraph 7(3) of this Practice Direction that petitions to reduce a company's share capital (which can be contested, but rarely so) are to be heard in open court.

The *Practice Direction (Insolvency Proceedings)*[52] is equally explicit on the public form of hearing. The concept of insolvency proceedings encompasses proceedings involving insolvent companies as well as bankrupt individuals. As far as the former are concerned, the mandatory nature of the obligation to advertise winding up petitions is reinforced on pain of the petition being dismissed.[53] Paragraph 5 then lists twelve types of application to be heard in public. These include applications for the appointment of a provisional liquidator and petitions for the appointment of an administrator. Winding up petitions (whether opposed or not) must be heard in public. It is significant, and paradoxical, that applications to restrain the advertisement of a winding up petition are to be heard in public unless the court directs otherwise. Public examinations of company officers are, by definition, to be heard in public. The position of private examinations, which is not dealt with by the Practice Direction, is less clear. They are not technically held *in camera* but there are limitations on who can attend. Basically, the creditors alone may do so, subject to a right of objection on the part of the person who has applied for the examination.[54] Rule 9.5(2) of the Insolvency Rules 1986 states that the file of the examination is open to inspection by creditors and by others if the leave of the court is obtained. Bankruptcy cases are regulated by paragraph 9 of the Practice Direction. Again, public examinations are highlighted for hearing in open court, as are opposed applications to discharge a bankrupt. The making of a bankruptcy order is clearly a matter for the public

---

[51] *Practice Direction: Applications under the Companies Act 1985 and the Insurance Companies Act 1982* [1999] BCC 741. Applications for the appointment of a provisional liquidator may be heard *in camera*: *Practice Direction (Companies Court: Provisional Liquidator)* [1997] 1 WLR 3.

[52] *Practice Direction (Insolvency Proceedings)* [2000] BCC 927. This replaces, among others, *Practice Direction (No 1 of 1995): Insolvency Appeals; Individuals* [1995] BCC 1129. Publicity has always been viewed as an important element in the bankruptcy procedure. In the eighteenth and early nineteenth centuries, when the bankruptcy commissioners administered cases, the fact that they sat in public was regarded as a safeguard against malpractice. See the comments of Lord Eldon in *Ex p King* (1805) 11 Ves Jun 417, 426–427, 32 ER 1148, 1152.

[53] This point had already been made in *Practice Direction (Companies Court: Winding Up)* [1996] 1 WLR 1255. As to what constitutes advertisement, see *Secretary of State v North West Holdings* [1998] BCC 997.

[54] See Insolvency Rules 1986, SI 1986/1925, r 9(4). In Ireland, notwithstanding Art 34.1 of the Constitution (which requires justice to be administered in public), private examinations of company officers can indeed be held in private: see *Re Redbreast Preserving Co Ltd* (1956) 91 ILTR 12, a case that must now be read with some caution in the light of *O'Donoghue v Ireland* [2000] 2 IR 168. There has been considerable use in Ireland of what is known as a 'private sitting', at which the public have no general right of admittance. See, for example, the arrangements procedure under Part IV of the Bankruptcy Act 1988 and, in particular, s 99. Note also the Bankruptcy Act 1988, s 134.

domain in view of the importance for members of the business community of knowing whether they are dealing with a bankrupt. Dissemination of the names of those who had been declared bankrupt used to be imperfect, with the result that commercial credit agencies did good business in searching court records. This practice was viewed uncomfortably by the courts.[55] However, the fact that a person has been declared bankrupt is a matter of genuine public concern has been reflected by the setting up of a register of bankrupts which is open to public access.[56]

Company law and Insolvency law overlap in the increasingly important area of director disqualification. A separate Practice Direction[57] has laid down the new post-Civil Procedure Rule procedures, though these need to be read alongside procedures established by delegated legislation. These regulations establish the principle of public access to director disqualification proceedings.[58] This is limited by paragraph 13.4 of the Practice Direction which assumes that *Carecraft* proceedings[59]—essentially, a summary procedure which is based upon an agreed schedule of facts relating to the conduct of the director, and in that respect resembles a plea bargain—are to be conducted in private. Nevertheless, as with other proceedings conducted in secret, paragraph 13.5 emphasizes that the final order (at least) is to be given in public. Instead of pursuing a director through the courts, there is an alternative system of taking a binding undertaking from him not to act as a director. But, again, the disqualification will appear in the public register kept for this purpose under the Company Directors Disqualification Act 1986.[60]

5. EXCEPTIONS TO THE GENERAL RULE

Some of the following headings are unique to commercial litigation, while others take the form of variations on themes that have been encountered in earlier chapters. The inclusion of the latter group may be justified on the basis that, in the commercial context, there are aspects which are significantly different from the norm and which therefore merit a more detailed consideration.

---

[55] *Re Austintel* [1997] 1 WLR 616, where the judge at first instance refused a request by a commercial searcher for the multiple copying of court records pursuant to the Insolvency Rules 1986, r 7.28. The Court of Appeal, though clearly unhappy with the state of the law, decided not to interfere with this exercise of judicial discretion, which r 7.28 specifically described as 'final'.

[56] Insolvency (Amendment) Rules 1999, SI 1999/359.

[57] *Practice Direction (Disqualification Proceedings)* [1999] BCC 717.

[58] Insolvent Companies (Disqualification of Unfit Directors) Proceedings Rules 1987, SI 1987/2023, r 7(2).

[59] So named after the disqualification procedure developed by Ferris J in *Re Carecraft Construction Co Ltd* [1994] 1 WLR 172.

[60] Insolvency Act 2000, Sch 4, para 13.

A. Settlement Out of Court

Negotiated settlements of legal claims are the most common way in which commercial disputes are resolved.[61] The terms of such settlements are often kept secret. It is, however, open to the parties to publicize the compromise. This often happens where the facts of the litigation have attracted much public comment and it is in the interests of all parties to ensure that the fact that they have reached an amicable compromise is well known. In the *Opren* (Benoxaprofen) litigation,[62] which involved the question of the safety of a widely used drug, the terms of the final settlement of the claim were read out in open court by Hirst J.[63] A variation on this theme is the so-called Tomlin order[64] by which a piece of litigation is settled and the settlement is embodied in the form of a court order. This type of judicially sanctioned secrecy is a common feature of commercial litigation and reinforces the binding nature of the settlement.

B. Hearings in Chambers

It was pointed out in Chapter 3 that when a judge sits in chambers this does not necessarily mean that he is sitting in his private quarters in the court building. It means, rather, that he is not sitting 'in open court'.[65] Many commercial cases, especially those of an interlocutory nature, are disposed of by judges in chambers.[66] This is partly for reasons of convenience and partly to encourage openness between parties by conducting the hearing in the informal setting of the judge's room. The decision whether to attach any publicity to such rulings is within the discretion of the judge concerned, though the parties can, if they wish, invite the judge to sit in public. Generally speaking, however, for reasons of practicality linked to space restraints, the public are denied access to hearings in chambers. Often there is no report of the decisions reached.[67] However, rulings given in the

---

[61] If the parties leave their settlement until after the judge has issued his draft judgment, the judge may in the interests of public policy deliver that judgment in open court: *Prudential Assurance Co Ltd v McBains Cooper (a firm)* [2000] 1 WLR 2000.

[62] For some account of the case, see G. G. Howells (ed), *Product Liability Insurance and the Pharmaceutical Industry: An Anglo-American Comparison* (1991), especially at 32–4 and 49.

[63] For the procedures used in the settlement of the Opren claims see The Independent 10 December 1987, The Independent 15 January 1988 (sub nom *Davies v Eli Lilly & Co*) The Times 4 February 1988 (sub nom *Randall v Eli Lilly & Co*) and The Independent 30 March 1988.

[64] So named after the form of order devised by Tomlin J in *Practice Note* [1927] WN 290.

[65] *Hartmont v Foster* (1881) 8 QBD 82. For modern explanations see *Forbes v Smith* [1998] 1 All ER 973 and *Hodgson v Imperial Tobacco* [1998] 1 WLR 1056.

[66] Authority for this in the High Court is provided by the Supreme Court Act 1981, s 67. Mortgage repossession cases are specifically set aside for chambers hearings in order, it would seem, to avoid embarrassment to the mortgagor.

[67] See the note of guidance by Hewart CJ in [1932] WN (Misc) 185 and *Vernazza v Barburriza Ltd* [1937] 4 All ER 364. Where transcripts are produced the court will jealously protect their confidential nature if the proceedings are such as to require privacy: *S v S (Judgment in Chambers: Disclosure)* [1997] 1 WLR 1621. Another option where there is a need for confidentiality is to allow the case to be reported subject to the condition that the identity of the parties is not disclosed: *X v Y* [1990] 1 QB 220, 221; *A Company Ltd v Republic of X* The Times, 9 April 1990.

privacy of chambers are not confidential and can, unless otherwise directed, be publicized—an important application of the principle of open justice recently underlined by the Court of Appeal in *Hodgson v Imperial Tobacco Ltd*.[68] It is, of course, possible for a judge to decide that a matter normally disposed of in chambers be dealt with in open court in any particular case.

An interesting development in recent years has been the increased willingness of judges who have disposed of a case in private chambers to deliver their judgments in open court and thereby place them in the public domain. This practice is usually adopted where the litigation is of general importance to commercial practitioners[69] or where rumours of the outcome could lead to investors taking up false market positions. An example of the latter situation is furnished by *British and Commonwealth Holdings v Quadrex Holdings Inc*.[70] Hirst J had given summary judgment for the plaintiff (B & C) in chambers in an action for breach of contract and had ordered an interim payment of £75 million to be made by the defendant (Quadrex), which had no arguable defence to the plaintiff's action. Moreover, the judge had decided to make public his reasons for giving summary judgment. Quadrex appealed against the decision to publicize the ruling but the Court of Appeal,[71] after a hearing *in camera*, supported the exercise of discretion by Hirst J. Both of the companies concerned were listed on the Stock Exchange and, in view of the size of the payment, ill-informed speculation could lead to the creation of a false market in the companies' shares. As Lord Donaldson MR put it:

where you are dealing with very large sums of money in relation to public companies and the information is truly price sensitive, there is a public interest in ensuring that there is no false market, both in the interests of those who hold shares and might wish to sell them and in the interests of those who might be contemplating purchasing, on the basis of incomplete information.[72]

The discretion of the trial judge in these matters was paramount, although the Court of Appeal did indicate that the possibility of some judicious editing of the published material could have been considered. Having lost the argument on

---

[68] [1998] 2 All ER 673. See also *Forbes v Smith* [1998] 1 All ER 973.

[69] For examples see *Mail Newspapers Ltd v Insert Media Ltd* The Times, 21 April 1987; *Meadows Insurance Co Ltd v Insurance Corporation of Ireland Ltd* The Times, 3 June 1988; *Securities and Investments Board v Pantell SA* [1989] 3 WLR 698; *Al-Nakib Investments (Jersey) Ltd v Longcroft* [1990] 1 WLR 1390; *Owens Bank Ltd v Bracco* The Times, 29 August 1990; *Tudor Grange Holdings Ltd v Citibank NA* The Times, 30 April 1991; and *Melton Medes Ltd v Securities and Investments Board* [1995] 2 WLR 247.

[70] The Times, 8 December 1988.

[71] This decision is reported as *British and Commonwealth Holdings v Quadrex Holdings Inc (No 2)* The Times, 8 December 1988.

[72] See The Times 8 December 1988 and pp. 3–4 of the transcript of this judgment, which does not appear to be fully reported. The price-sensitive nature of judgments must also be borne in mind. See the procedures here for release of judgments: *Practice Direction (Court of Appeal, Civil Division)* [1999] 1 WLR 1027, para 9.1.1.

the secrecy point, the defendants met with more success when the substantive issue came to be considered by the Court of Appeal.[73]

Another significant decision in this context is that of Steyn J in *Shell International Petroleum Co Ltd v Transnor (Bermuda) Ltd*,[74] a case where summary judgment was being sought under the Rules of the Supreme Court, Order 14.[75] This case was originally set down for a hearing in chambers but Steyn J concluded that, as there were issues of public interest at stake, it should be heard in open court (as opposed to the judgment merely being read out in open court). Supporters of the principle of open justice welcomed this ruling.[76]

C. Disguising the Identity of Litigants to Protect Commercial Interests

There is no principle of law protecting a party to litigation from the inevitable injury to business or professional reputation caused by involvement in a disputed case. That fact was confirmed, in the specific context of the legal profession, by the Court of Appeal in *R v Legal Aid Board, ex p Kaim Todner (a firm)*.[77] However, if the litigation involves serious allegations being made against one of the parties, the mere fact that such charges have been voiced may do such damage to the commercial credibility of the target of the allegations that there is a case for dealing with the litigation in secret until the matter is resolved. This may be a particularly relevant consideration where a company is involved, since collateral damage can be inflicted on its shareholders, creditors and employees, none of whom may be directly connected with the litigation. Thus, although there is a general rule to the effect that winding-up petitions must be advertised,[78] the court can restrain advertisement in a borderline case to prevent a run on the company.[79] This limitation on open justice has also been applied in cases involving petitions by the Secretary of State to wind up a company in the public interest. By their very nature such petitions do not involve simple questions of liability but, rather, more diffuse matters of consumer protection.[80] This power to restrain the usual publicity generated by a winding-up petition can also be exercised where there is an outstanding petition for an administration order under Part II of the

---

[73] [1989] 3 WLR 723.

[74] [1987] 1 Lloyd's Rep 363. An appeal to the Court of Appeal, on another point, was dismissed: The Times, 24 April 1987.

[75] Now Civil Procedure Rules 1998, SI 1998/3132, r 24.

[76] (1988) 7 *Civil Justice Quarterly* 89.

[77] [1998] 3 WLR 925. See also *Trustor AB v Smallbone* [2000] 1 All ER 811. For a similar expression of the need to maintain the principle of open justice in the context of the Lloyd's litigation saga, see *Hallam-Eames v Merrett Syndicates Ltd* The Times, 16 June 1995. The background to the Lloyd's saga is explained in A. Raphael, *Ultimate risk, the inside story of the Lloyd's catastrophe* (1994).

[78] See Insolvency Rules 1986, SI 1986/1925, r 4.11.

[79] Or where the presentation of the petition might constitute an abuse of process, in that it was presented for an ulterior purpose: *Re A Company* [1894] 2 Ch 349, and *Re A Company* [1986] BCLC 127.

[80] For examples see *Re Companies (Nos 007923 and 007924 of 1994)* [1995] 1 WLR 953.

Insolvency Act 1986[81] or even in cases where there is merely an undertaking to present such a petition.[82] Such a departure from the normal rule may be necessary to promote a possible rescue of the company.

An interesting authority in this context is the ruling of Browne-Wilkinson V-C in *Re London and Norwich Investment Services Ltd.*[83] Here the DTI had, in the public interest, presented a winding-up petition against an investment company, and a provisional liquidator had been appointed to protect the assets of the company pending the hearing of that petition. All of these proceedings had been conducted *in camera* because the company had intimated that it would contest the case. It became apparent to Browne-Wilkinson V-C that the company's resistance was futile and accordingly he decreed that the veil of secrecy be lifted. He declared:

Hearings in closed court are contrary to the public interest and should only take place if it is clear that there is a contrary public interest overbearing the need for public justice. I can no longer see any need for hearings in closed court. I have therefore given judgment in open court.[84]

Another decision worthy of note here is *R v Secretary of State for Trade and Industry, ex p R*,[85] which concerned the question whether the Financial Services Act 1986 applied to investment business carried on before the statute came into force (that is, prior to 18 December 1986). 'R', who was described in the financial press as a 'well-known City figure' under investigation by DTI inspectors,[86] argued (among other points) that the legislation did not empower the inspectors to investigate his business affairs before the relevant date. As this was a test case, the court agreed that the identity of 'R' should be kept secret until a ruling on the scope of the Act had been given. This appeared to be a sensible precaution because 'R' might have been successful. It is difficult, however, to reconcile the anonymity ruling with general principle.

The practice grew up in the 1980s in connection with shareholder petitions under section 459 of the Companies Act 1985 and its predecessor provision, alleging unfair prejudice by controllers of companies, to list the action as '*Re A Company*' (with added reference to a petition number). This convention causes difficulties for commentators trying to grapple with this burgeoning jurisdiction.[87] The reason for adopting anonymity in reporting seems to have been to

---

[81] See *Re A Company (No 00192 of 1988)* [1989] BCLC 9. On the full trial of this case (reported in *Re Manlon Trading Ltd* (1988) 4 BCC 455) Harman J stressed that there must be either an outstanding administration order petition or at least a firm undertaking to present such a petition before the court will restrain the advertisement of the winding up petition.

[82] *Re A Company (001448 of 1989)* [1989] BCLC 715.   [83] [1988] BCLC 226.

[84] ibid. 230.   [85] [1989] 1 WLR 372.   [86] The Financial Times (21 November 1988).

[87] One problem is that the case might be reported as *Re A Company (petition number)* in one set of law reports, only to be included in another report without the benefit of anonymity. The Law Commission Report No 246, *Shareholder Remedies* (Cm 3769, 1997), paras 4.54–4.56, called for clarification of procedures on advertising petitions under the Companies Act 1985, s 459. In Ireland the comparable shareholder protection jurisdiction, the Companies Act 1963, s 205, confers anonymity, but this is specifically provided for by sub-s (9). For an example of the provision at work, see *Re R Ltd* [1989] ILRM 757.

protect the company from damage to its business reputation pending the resolution of the matter. Certainly, it has little to do with protecting share prices on the market as the overwhelming majority of such companies are private and not listed on the Stock Exchange. The impression of recent years, however, is that more section 459 cases are being reported by reference to the names of the parties.[88]

D. Protecting Confidential Information

Cases can be heard *in camera* where the litigation might result in the disclosure of confidential information: for example, details of a secret industrial process or other commercially sensitive information. As in several other situations where the court sits in private, section 12 of the Administration of Justice Act 1960 now stipulates that disclosure of what passed in secret is punishable as a contempt of court. The relevant provision here is subsection 1(d), which states: 'where the information relates to a secret process, discovery or invention which is in issue in the proceedings'. An interesting illustration of a closed sitting of the court in the interests of commercial secrecy is furnished by *Badische Anilin Und Soda Fabrik v Levinstein*,[89] a patent infringement case, where Pearson J allowed details of the process in question to be disclosed in court while it sat *in camera*. Although the remainder of the proceedings were open to the public, the shorthand writer's notes which disclosed the secret process were placed under tight control by the court. A further illustration of this exception at work is provided by the hearing before Whitford J of an application under section 23 of the Patents Act 1949[90] for extension of *Illinois Tool Works Inc's Patent*.[91] Here the judge allowed certain financial data relating to the global trading position of the applicant to be kept secret from all but the judge and the Comptroller General on the grounds that the disclosure was not strictly necessary to establish a case for extension. However, Whitford J, after adverting to the basic norm established in *Scott v Scott*,[92] added:

I think it is of particular importance to adhere to the strict rule in cases concerning petitions for extensions of letters patent for very often the public interest is the issue which is really of vital importance in cases of this kind and the public has a right in general to know exactly what is taking place upon the hearing of a petition for an extension.[93]

The court enjoys considerable flexibility in protecting the integrity of confidential or secret information and can order, for example, limited disclosure to legal representatives subject to undertakings that the information divulged will not be allowed to enter the public domain. As the Court of Appeal emphasized in

---

[88] Likewise, all the pre-1980 cases under the equivalent provisions to section 459 were reported under the name of the company.

[89] (1883) 24 ChD 156.   [90] As amended by the Patents Act 1977, s 132 and Sch 6.
[91] [1975] FSR 37.   [92] [1913] AC 417.   [93] [1975] FSR 37, 38.

Warner-Lambert Co v Glaxo Laboratories,[94] it is better to deal with particular cases on an individual basis rather than by laying down general guidelines as to what should (or should not) be disclosed. As so often in this subject, it is difficult for the court to balance the competing needs of the parties to maintain secrecy against the ideal that judicial matters should be heard in public.

E. Preventing Prejudice to Associated Proceedings

Commercial law is an area where civil and criminal proceedings may often go hand in hand. Celebrated recent instances of misconduct of corporate affairs include: the notorious Guinness share support scheme;[95] the Barlow Clowes investment collapse in 1988;[96] the insolvency in 1990 of Polly Peck (Holdings) Ltd, the holding company for over 200 companies worldwide; and the unprecedented Bank of Commerce and Credit International (BCCI) fraud that led to the presenting of a winding-up petition in 1991. In such situations it is open to a judge hearing a civil case to allow a degree of secrecy in the manner of conduct of the proceedings or, indeed, to place restrictions on the reporting of the case to prevent undue prejudice to the defendant who may also be facing criminal prosecution. The danger here is that excessive publicity might lead to potential jurors being prejudiced.[97] In the Guinness saga one of the defendants apparently sought to have a civil action[98] heard in secret to prevent embarrassment, but Hoffmann J rejected the request.[99] A subsequent attempt to secure reporting restrictions on this litigation also proved unsuccessful.[100] A different conclusion was reached in *Re DPR Futures Ltd*,[101] where civil and criminal proceedings against the directors of an investment company were running simultaneously. Millett J (as he then was) decreed that the civil case should not be brought to trial until the related criminal proceedings had been concluded and that, in the meantime, any interlocutory proceedings in the civil action should be heard *in camera*. There was support for this solution in the form of one particular judgment in the protracted

[94] [1975] RPC 354. This case was heard *in camera* by the Court of Appeal but judgment was read in open court. See also *Colley v Hart* (1890) 7 RPC 101 and *Reddaway & Co Ltd v Flynn* (1913) 30 RPC 16. See also the guidelines of the Court of Appeal in *Lilly Icos Ltd v Pfizer Ltd (No 2)*, The Times, 28 January 2002.

[95] For details of the episode, see the Appendix, below.

[96] For the difficulties facing the courts in dealing with concurrent criminal and civil proceedings see *Barlow Clowes Gilt Managers v Clowes* The Times, 2 February 1990.

[97] This section, therefore, illustrates the application of the general principles discussed in Chapter 8, section 6, below.

[98] This was the action in *Guinness plc v Saunders* [1990] 2 AC 663 which eventually reached the House of Lords.

[99] See The Financial Times 2 April 1987 ('Men and Matters'). The Court of Appeal took a similar view: see The Independent, 27 April 1988.

[100] See *Re Saunders* The Times, 8 February 1990. The manner in which Saunders was prosecuted on the basis of evidence gleaned from DTI investigations without the benefit of the right of silence resulted in the UK being taken to the European Court of Human Rights in *Saunders v UK* (1997) 23 EHRR 313, and ultimately to changes in the use of such evidence by the prosecuting authorities.

[101] [1989] BCLC 634.

Guinness litigation.[102] A full stay on all the civil proceedings was not necessary to protect the directors against the risk of their criminal trial being prejudiced. Of equal importance was the need to protect the interests of the numerous small investors who had a stake in the outcome of the civil proceedings.

The general approach was extended by Cooke J in New Zealand in *Skope Enterprises Ltd v Consumer Council* [103] to justify the hearing *in camera* of a civil cases where one of the parties was also the defendant in subsequent and associated *civil* proceedings. This extraordinary step was taken on the basis that either party could request trial of the issues by a jury—a method of trial which remained a distinct possibility since, as yet, neither side had abandoned that option.

F. Preventing the Frustration of a Remedy

A plaintiff in a civil action may have, as the basis of his claim, a desire to prevent the publication of certain confidential commercial information by the defendant. As already indicated in Chapter 5, if that plaintiff had to submit the hearing of his case to public scrutiny, any victory in those proceedings would be of a pyrrhic nature. The courts have been quick to grasp the realities of the situation here. Early English authority for this is provided by the Court of Appeal decision in *Mellor v Thompson*,[104] where Lord Halsbury LC thought it was within the power of the court so to proceed. In *Skope Enterprises Ltd v Consumer Council*[105] Cooke J cited this as an additional justification for hearing *in camera* the application before him.

The clearest example of this ground being used to justify secrecy in commercial law is provided by the decision of the Court of Appeal in *R v Chief Registrar of Friendly Societies, ex p New Cross Building Society*.[106] The background to the case was the decision of the Chief Registrar to remove certain strategic powers from a building society because of concerns about its financial position. Had this revocation order not been lifted, grave damage would have been inflicted on the standing of that society in the eyes of the public. The hearing of the society's application to lift the order was held before Webster J *in camera*, and the revocation order was lifted. It was restored by the Court of Appeal, who held that the Chief Registrar had acted correctly. The Court of Appeal did indicate that it had been proper to draw a veil of secrecy over the earlier proceedings because publicity prior to the resolution of the case would have been harmful to the society. However, the need for secrecy no longer applied as the society had indicated that it was not intending to maintain its legal action. Sir John Donaldson MR reiterated the importance of the public administration of justice:

---

[102] This is the unreported judgment of Browne-Wilkinson V-C in *Guinness Ltd v Saunders* (ChD 15 April 1987), which was followed by Millett J (as he then was) in *Re DPR Futures* [1989] BCLC 634 at 645–646.

[103] [1973] 2 NZLR 399.   [104] (1885) 31 Ch D 55.   [105] [1973] 2 NZLR 399.

[106] [1984] 2 WLR 370: see the note by J. Vaughan in (1985) 5 *The Company Lawyer* 224. For the background to the Registrar's order, see Cmnd 9033.

It is fundamental to British justice as we know it, and as our forebears have known it, that the Queen's courts are open to all. And when I say that they are open to all, I do not limit this to those who have business in the courts. The judges administer justice in the Queen's name on behalf of the whole community. No one is more entitled than a member of the general public to see for himself that justice is done.[107]

The Master of the Rolls acknowledged that there were exceptions to this principle. Embarrassment, in itself, was no justification for a hearing *in camera*, but in this case 'a public hearing would effectively have deprived the society of the relief to which in law and justice it was or might be entitled'. His Lordship displayed an acute insight into the commercial realities when he acknowledged:

Building societies, like banks, are always subject to the risk of abnormal levels of withdrawal due to a loss of confidence upon the part of their customers. However, building societies are much more vulnerable than banks for, by the very nature of their business, they are compelled to borrow short and lend long.[108]

An interesting aspect of the judgment of the Court of Appeal was that it was prepared to confront the commercial difficulties posed by maintaining secrecy. For instance, Sir John Donaldson MR acknowledged that a depositor who had paid money into the society at a time when these secret proceedings were in progress would have a genuine grievance. This could be averted by requiring the society to pay into court any deposits received during this period. A precedent existed for such a solution.[109] Had the case been won by the building society, the question of how it would be reported would have arisen. Reporting would be necessary in the interests of justice as important points of statutory interpretation were involved. The best solution here, according to the Master of the Rolls, would be to protect its identity by reporting the case as '*Re A Building Society*'.[110]

G. Serving the Interests of Justice

This is a catch-all category that could be used to embrace cases not covered by the previous headings. Reference may be made here to the 'overriding objective of enabling the court to deal with cases justly' expressed as the aim of the Civil Procedure Rules 1998.[111] The irony, of course, is that, in order to serve the interests of justice in a particular case, a hallowed general principle of justice—that of public access—will have to be discarded. In *Re Green*,[112] the Court of Appeal allowed the hearing *in camera* of an application by a trustee in bankruptcy for the private examination of a witness under what was formerly section 25(1) of the

---

[107] [1984] 2 WLR 370, 377.

[108] [1984] 2 WLR 370, 377–378. Similar reasoning might also explain why the petition to place a bank in administration was conducted in secret: see *Re Chancery plc* [1991] BCC 171, and the note by D. Milman in (1991) 12 *The Company Lawyer* 103.

[109] [1984] 2 WLR 370, 378 and 417. For an earlier authority see *R v Registar of Building Societies, ex p a Building Society* [1960] 1 WLR 669.

[110] As in *R v Registrar of Building Societies, ex p a Building Society*, above.

[111] Civil Procedure Rules 1998, SI 1998/3132, r 1.1(1).   [112] [1958] 1 WLR 405.

Bankruptcy Act 1914.[113] The justification for this course, which was couched in terms of 'the interests of justice', seems to have been to prevent the premature disclosure to the witness of the trustee's report, resulting in the undermining of the very purpose of the examination. A similar conclusion was reached by the Divisional Court in *Re Poulson (A Bankrupt), ex p Granada Television Ltd v Maudling*,[114] where it was held that the county court registrar could place a 'stop order' on transcripts arising from the private examination of a witness (a leading politician of the day, Reginald Maudling) conducted under section 25 of the Bankruptcy Act 1914. Such a restriction forbade the filing for inspection by others of the material subject to the 'stop order'. The existence of the order, it was conceded, was not specifically provided for in the legislation. Its use was justifiable, however, in the interests of maintaining the utility of the private examination procedure, which was primarily aimed at discovering the location of the bankrupt's assets. By analogy with trade secrets litigation, Walton J emphasized that 'the normal rules [of public access] have to be displaced in view of the overriding necessity to produce a just end result'.[115]

This particular ground was also exploited by Powell J in the Supreme Court of New South Wales in *General Motors—Holden's Ltd v David Syme & Co Ltd*,[116] a breach of confidence action, the hearing of which was conducted in secret. The judge, who must have been influenced by the plaintiff's statement that it would abandon its claim altogether rather than have the case heard in public, went to great lengths to justify his decision:

I believe it to be of fundamental importance to the administration of justice that the public be kept informed of the principles upon which the court, from time to time, acts, and, in particular, of reasons why, in any particular case, the court has thought it proper that, in order that it might do justice, it is necessary to depart from the general principle that the courts administer justice in public.[117]

H. Furthering the Demands of Public Policy

To permit an exception to the norm of publicity on vague public policy grounds is infinitely more controversial. Until recently there was little clear authority on this point in English law. Perhaps the best example that has come to light is an anonymous case that progressed as far as the Court of Appeal in total secrecy.[118] The case concerned possible money laundering. A plaintiff had secured an order against a bank in respect of funds which it alleged had been misappropriated from it by some third party. The order required the bank to disclose certain information to the plaintiff. The bank, unknown to the plaintiff and the judge who had made the disclosure order, had already made suspected money laundering reports to the

---

[113] See now Insolvency Act 1986, s 366.

[114] [1976] 1 WLR 1023. For discussion, see the Cork Committee on *Insolvency Law and Practice* (Cmnd 8558, 1982) para 309.

[115] [1976] 1 WLR 1023, 1033.   [116] [1985] FSR 413.   [117] ibid. 418.

[118] See A. Zuckerman, 'A Case of Secretive and Opaque Justice?' The Times (8 February 2000) 15.

National Criminal Intelligence Services pursuant to a legal requirement. Apparently, if the bank complied with the court order to disclose, it would commit an offence of 'tipping off' contrary to section 93D of the Criminal Justice Act 1988.[119] In view of its dilemma the bank sought guidance as to its responsibilities from the courts. On the application for directions the plaintiff was given no notice of the proceedings. Rimer J lifted the disclosure order, and in later proceedings Jacob J refused to reinstate it. The proceedings appear to have been conducted under circumstances of the utmost secrecy, with the plaintiff being left in the dark. On appeal to the Court of Appeal, the plaintiff was again denied the usual rights of a party to litigation. Although the Court of Appeal upheld the practice of secrecy in this case, it clearly had concerns that the interests of all affected parties be protected. The judgment was published in order to offer guidance to financial institutions caught in this dilemma in the future,[120] though the names of the parties were kept secret. Lord Woolf, after commenting on the importance of the principle of open justice and the requirement that the parties should have a fair opportunity to respond to the case made against them, declared:

Without seeking to diminish the importance of these principles and the interests of the individual that they are designed to protect, it has to be accepted that their importance cannot always be paramount. There are situations where the interests of the individual have to give way to the interests of the public . . . it is for the courts to decide how conflicts between these interests are reconciled.[121]

A further development in this increasingly important area of the law for banks came with the ruling of the Court of Appeal in *Bank of Scotland v A Ltd*.[122] A bank was caught in a dilemma between paying out on a customer's account and thereby possibly being held liable to a third party as constructive trustee, and not paying out and thereby running the risk of contravening the anti-tipping off money laundering legislation. The Court of Appeal held that it could seek the confidential guidance of the court by applying in private for an interim direction as to the most appropriate course of action to take. This was, however, to be regarded as guidance of last resort and was not meant to be a substitute for the bank's use of its own sense of commercial responsibility.

In offshore jurisdictions the demands of public policy have taken a very different form. The courts of the Cayman Islands, for example, have recognized that the requirements of state policy—in this case the overriding economic need to promote the jurisdiction as an offshore banking centre—may be cited as an additional justification for conducting commercial litigation in private. In *Re S*,[123] petitioners for the winding up of a company sought an order that the hearing of their petition should take place *in camera*, on the ground that an open hearing would result in certain information about their financial affairs entering into the public domain and consequently coming to the attention of the tax authorities in

---

[119] Inserted by the Criminal Justice Act 1993, s 32.   [120] See *C v S* [1999] 2 All ER 343.
[121] ibid. 348.   [122] [2001] 1 WLR 751.   [123] 1986 PCC 241.

their home country. Their argument rested on the strict laws of secrecy applicable in the Cayman Islands, and the fact that the petitioners had been persuaded, by the presence of those rules, to invest there. Summerfield CJ in the Grand Court held that, although this was not covered by any of the established exceptions to the rule in *Scott v Scott*,[124] the case would be heard in chambers. Indeed, it is possible to find examples in offshore jurisdictions where legislation specifically prescribes secrecy. The statute of the Cook Islands regulating international trusts provides for hearings *in camera* and the requirement of the leave of the court before the proceedings may be publicized.[125]

All judicial proceedings, other than criminal proceedings relating to international trusts shall, unless ordered otherwise, be heard in camera and no details of the proceedings shall be published by any person without the leave of the Court or person presiding.

In a significant ruling in favour of publication,[126] the High Court of the Cook Islands agreed that secrecy and confidentiality formed the cornerstone of the offshore financial centre. However, it would be very strange if those most affected by the statute and the manner of its interpretation (potential investors and their advisers in the legal and accountancy professions) were to be denied knowledge of a ruling of the highest domestic court of the Islands. It therefore decreed that the judgment should be published both at home and overseas.

6. A CONCLUDING COMMENT

To depart from the standard of the public administration of justice where the interests of public policy are involved is unique to commercial litigation. Such litigation can often be staged in a number of possible jurisdictions. The prospect of complete confidentiality may well attract international business to one forum in preference to another, with consequences for the foreign earnings of the countries concerned. As for the other exceptions to the open administration of commercial justice, many of these reflect in large measure considerations that have already been encountered in this work, especially in the preceding chapter. Certainly, it may be difficult, both in theoretical and practical terms, to identify whether companies possess a 'privacy' interest (of the sort that was discussed in Chapter 5)[127] that can be weighed against the demands of open justice. Nonetheless, the need not to deter recourse to the courts may perform for companies the same function that the concept of privacy and the avoidance of embarrassment does for individual litigants—in combination with the economic interests of those groups (employees, shareholders) whose fortunes are inextricably linked to the survival of particular companies.

---

[124] [1913] AC 417.   [125] International Trusts Act 1984, s 23 (2).
[126] 515 *South Orange Grove Owners Association and Others v Orange Grove Partners and Others (No 1)* (1995) Plaint No 208/94.
[127] See this issue in a different context in *R v Broadcasting Standards Commission, ex p BBC* [2000] 3 All ER 989.

7

Jury Secrecy

1. PUBLIC TRIAL AND JURY SECRECY

At the culmination of the criminal trial on indictment lies the collective decision of the jury, and, in the case of many summary trials, the collective decision of the lay magistrates. In civil cases that are taken to appellate level there is the collegiate judgment of the court on the outcome of the appeal. The process of arriving at such decisions poses special problems in the context of open justice and requires the treatment of a separate chapter. In principle, all three areas that have just been mentioned—the jury, the lay magistracy, and the appellate judiciary—could give rise to issues of the same kind. However, it is the collegiate decision-taking of the jury that has generated most discussion together with a certain amount of litigation. Accordingly, it is the jury which provides the main focus of the present chapter, occasional reference being made to analogous issues in the other decision-taking contexts.

A few preliminary points may be made by way of comparison and contrast. In the case of the jury and the magistracy the process of reaching a decision is formally conducted, the deliberations taking place in a part of the court building that is specifically set aside for the purpose (the jury room, the justices' retiring room). This stands in marked contrast to the equivalent process when conducted in the higher judiciary, where the exchange of views on the outcome of an appeal is entirely informal and is by no means confined to the physical limits of the court building. Again, all three areas have traditionally stood on the same footing, alike subject to a practice of secrecy. The practice has been relaxed occasionally in regard to the higher judiciary for the sake of academic research.[1] In regard to the jury, however, the conditions of *de facto* secrecy in which their deliberations take place have been substantially reinforced, in section 8 of the Contempt of Court Act 1981, by an unqualified legal obligation to maintain the confidences of the jury room.

Whether one is speaking of the period before or since the enactment of section 8, the most striking aspect of the conditions of jury deliberation—and the same point could also be made for the other two areas of decision-taking that have just been mentioned—is their secrecy.[2] At the culmination of the trial process the

---

[1] As, most notably, in the empirical research conducted into the workings of the House of Lords that was published in A. Paterson, *The Law Lords* (1984).

[2] The two principal works on the English jury, which both predate the enactment of s 8, devote little space to jury secrecy. See P. Devlin, *Trial by Jury* (1956) 46–8: W.R. Cornish, *The Jury* (1968) 22.

hitherto insistent demands of openness suddenly give way to equally insistent requirements of confidentiality. The stark contrast has been sanctioned by long-standing practice. It has but rarely been defended on principle. Sissela Bok is an exception. In her book *Secrets*[3] she adverts to a number of circumstances in which there may be good grounds for respecting collective secrecy. Even where such secrecy is justifiable, however, some measure of accountability is necessary. She continues:

> The difference it makes is illustrated by the comparison between the practice of secrecy in two types of court proceedings: jury deliberations, and the secret tribunal or Star Chamber trial. Jury members are selected so as to be representative and without evident personal bias in a case. Their task is to arrive at a joint decision about an individual's innocence or guilt. Secrecy for their deliberations protects the members from attempts to influence them, increasing the likelihood of a fair decision; and it allows the resolution of difficult conflicts even when the evidence is ambiguous, generating a degree of confidence in the final result that might otherwise be unattainable. Full publicity to every aspect of the deliberations might cast doubt on the most careful of decisions. The secrecy, moreover, is terminated as soon as a decision has been reached, and the verdict itself is open to public scrutiny and to appeal.
>
> No such safeguards have accompanied the many secret police systems that have plagued humanity. They have permitted secret probes and accusations, secret verdicts and punishments.[4]

Secret accusations and secret verdicts and punishments, however, have scant relevance to the subject of jury secrecy. The points in the passage that do have some bearing on that subject identify two arguments in favour of secrecy. First, there is the need to combat outside pressure that might be applied to a juror in an attempt to corrupt his judgment. This, as will be seen later in the chapter, is a most important consideration. Secondly, jury secrecy confers a measure of public confidence on the verdict which might well be lacking under a more open system of deliberation.

The latter argument is, on reflection, quite extraordinary since it turns on their heads several of the traditional rationales of open justice. Secrecy, far from engendering suspicion in the minds of the public, now becomes a factor making for public confidence in the outcome of the trial. Yet many of the failings that public trial is deemed to avert may taint the proceedings at the stage of jury deliberation. Jurors may prove to be prejudiced, racist, credulous, or even (especially in the case of complex commercial trials) incapable of understanding the issues. They may reach their verdict on the basis of procedures that defy all standards of rationality. In one murder trial, *R v Young (Stephen)*,[5] several members of the jury resorted to the use of a Ouija board. The only element of publicity that might act as a deterrent against the manifestation of such failings on the part of a juror

---

[3] S. Bok, *Secrets: On the Ethics of Concealment and Revelation* (1986).   [4] ibid. 110–11.
[5] [1995] QB 324.

is the exposure to the views and criticisms of his fellow jurors, who, for all that the public is allowed to know, may share the same failings. Even if jurors are beyond all possible reproach in the discharge of their duties, this again is a matter of which there can be no public knowledge.

Such considerations, historically, have had little (if any) bearing on the practice of jury deliberation. The idea fundamental to jury decision is its collective nature. Whatever doubts and reservations there may have been in the jury room, these are hidden behind the verdict that is announced. The jury's decision is inscrutable. Jurors do not give reasons for, nor are they required to justify or defend, their decision. Until 1967, moreover, their decisions were invariably unanimous.

Several features of jury deliberation have had the incidental effect of reinforcing the confidentiality of their deliberations. Most notably, there is the tightest possible control over their contact with the outside world while they ponder their verdict in the jury room and (in the case of lengthier deliberations) in the course of their stay overnight in hotel accommodation. In the case of the lay magistracy, likewise, every effort is made to ensure that the retiring room is occupied by no more than one bench of magistrates at a time, lest the verdict in one case be affected by exposure to the course of deliberations in the other.[6] The secluded nature of the jury room has been vividly borne out by the obstacle that it has created to the recruitment of deaf jurors. Even if they are able to follow the proceedings in the courtroom, in cases where their condition is alleviated only by the use of an interpreter the presence of a thirteenth person in the jury room (even for such a limited purpose as this) is arguably irregular at common law. What, for this purpose, is the rationale of the seclusionary rule? If the difficulty is that of maintaining the confidentiality of what passed in the jury room, it has been pointed out that interpreters for the deaf receive specific training to maintain the confidences which they come across in the course of their work.[7] If, on the other hand, the danger is that a person extraneous to the decision-making forum might influence the course of the jury's deliberations (or, at any rate, the deaf juror's perception of the issues), the problem is aggravated by the lack of knowledge of the course of the jurors' discussions. In any event, the matter has now been put on an (it must be said) uncertain statutory footing.[8]

---

[6] This point is emphasized in an account of how magistrates reach their decision: see D. Edmunds, 'Consider Your Verdict,' The Times (2 January 1996) 30. As is to be expected, the same advantages are cited for the seclusion of the retiring room as for the secrecy of the jury room: 'The retiring room enables . . . a discussion to be carried out by magistrates in complete privacy, with the freedom of expression and independent thought that such privacy brings.'

[7] See the article in The Times (21 January 1994) 6. A deaf juror had been barred from sitting as such by a judge at King's Lynn Crown Court. The judge was reported to the Lord Chancellor by Lord Ashley, who has long championed the cause of deaf people.

[8] In the form of the Criminal Justice and Public Order Act 1994, s 41. This provides that, on a referral by the appropriate court officer, a person suffering from a relevant 'physical disability' shall be brought before the judge, who shall affirm the jury summons 'unless he is of the opinion that the person will not, on account of his disability, be capable of acting effectively as a juror'.

The physical seclusion of the jury, once directed by the judge to consider their verdict, has been relaxed by statutory provisions which, as a concession to complex trials, permit the court to allow the jury to separate. The continuing intellectual isolation of the jury under such circumstances has been emphasized by the Court of Appeal. In *R v Oliver*,[9] in the course of recounting the directions that were to be given to the jury on its being permitted to separate, it was stated that jurors could talk about the case only with their fellow jurors, and then solely when engaged in formal deliberation in the jury room. In many ways these restrictions are unexceptionable. If the jury has been designated as the decision-taking forum for the verdict, acting exclusively on the basis of material heard in the courtroom, it follows that no person outside its membership should have, or be reasonably suspected of having, any voice in the discussions that precede their decision. Any failing in that regard may properly be viewed as grounds for impugning the verdict.[10] The effect of section 8 of the Contempt of Court Act has been to extend the obligation of confidentiality indefinitely beyond the conclusion of the jury's deliberations.

In this aura of secrecy, therefore, all the more striking have been occasions on which the appellate courts have insisted that matters which passed in secret in the jury room should have been transacted in open court. In *R v Stewart (Angela)*, *R v Sappleton (Marcia)*,[11] the Court of Appeal quashed the convictions of the accused for knowingly importing cannabis on the ground that the trial judge had erroneously allowed the jury's request to be provided in the jury room with a set of weighing scales. The cannabis in question had been carried in holdalls that had been fitted with false compartments. The accused denied all knowledge of the existence of the compartments or of their contents: they also denied even being aware of the increased weight of the holdalls so fitted. It was a reasonable inference that the holdalls (which, as exhibits, were properly allowed to the jury) had been weighed under various conditions in the jury room. Such experiments were irregular, as amounting to the introduction of new material in the trial in the absence of counsel and the accused.[12]

---

[9] The Times, 6 December 1995. In fact, the trial was being conducted when the relevant statutory provision, the Criminal Justice and Public Order Act 1994, s 43, came into force.

[10] This contrasts sharply with the flexibility of practice followed by members of the appellate courts. See, for example, the incident recalled by Professor P.S. Atiyah in 'An Autobiographical Fragment' in G. Wilson (ed), *Frontiers of Legal Scholarship: Twenty-Five Years of Warwick Law School* (1995), ch 3, 37: 'When *Parry v Cleaver* reached the House of Lords I happened to see Lord Wilberforce at a . . . dinner, and I asked him about the case. He told me that the other four law lords had already written their speeches, and that two were in favour of allowing the appeal, and two for dismissing it, so that his would be the deciding vote. I thought this would be my chance to influence the development of the law, so I gave Lord Wilberforce the benefit of my views. It would be agreeable to record that I persuaded Lord Wilberforce to decide against the injured plaintiff, but in fact he decided the other way.'

[11] [1989] Crim LR 653.

[12] See, also, *R v Higgins* The Times, 16 February 1989, where a conviction for carrying an offensive weapon was quashed because the jury had experimented with the weapon in the jury room. Furthermore, such a potentially dangerous item should not have been released to the jury.

In contrast, incidental aids that could not be used as the basis of experiments by the jury could properly be supplied to them: for example, a ruler, a tape measure,[13] or a magnifying glass. Electronically recorded material has occasioned some dispute. Tape recordings of police interviews with the accused have been properly taken by the jury on retiring on the same basis as any other exhibit.[14] Although the judge has an overriding discretion, it might be better practice for an open court to be reassembled and for the jury to rehear the tape under such conditions.[15] Video recordings of evidence pose special problems, a particular hazard of a replay of such evidence being the jury's failure to view the item in the context of the whole body of evidence that had been presented in court. A number of safeguards have been laid down by the Court of Appeal, including an express requirement that the replay (if it should prove necessary) take place in open court in the presence of the judge, counsel and accused.[16]

Accordingly, there is a dividing line to be drawn—although in some cases it is difficult to know precisely at what point it is to be drawn—between matters which are to be protected by the confidentiality of the jury room and those which must be taken in open court. Briefly, issues of evidence are the province of the latter, while those of inference and decision-taking are the subject of the former. The rule that the adducing of material on the basis of which the verdict might be given is to take place in open court serves primarily to protect the interests of the parties to the trial.[17] Any item that might properly form the basis of the verdict must be handled in a context in which it may be the object of critical scrutiny by counsel and, ultimately, the subject of guiding comment in the judge's direction to the jury.

A procedural requirement, therefore, that protects the interests of the parties before the court will also, if only incidentally, safeguard the status of the public as observers of the proceedings. Yet, as we have intimated, the various possible rationales of open justice that were proffered in Chapter 2 have no small difficulty in accommodating the confidentiality of jury deliberations. Perhaps the dichotomy between open hearing and closed deliberation is best rationalized by focusing on the conditions under which evidence is produced and tested. This is a point which is wider than the traditional claim that a witness who is required to give his account of events in front of representatives of the public and the press is more likely, other things being equal, to prove a reliable witness than if he is

---

[13] The subject of explicit decision in *R v Maggs* The Times, 2 March 1990. The Court of Appeal added that obiter statements in *R v Stewart (Angela)* (n 11 above) 8, that such items as a ruler or a magnifying glass were impermissible had been expressed too widely.

[14] *R v Emmerson* The Times, 5 December 1990.

[15] *R v Riaz, R v Burke* The Times, 22 November 1991.

[16] *R v Rawlings, R v Broadbent* (1994) *NLJ Practitioner* (25 November) 1626. Caution has also been urged in regard to a transcript of the video evidence of a complainant, which (subject to stringent safeguards) may be supplied to a jury on retirement: *R v Coshall* The Times, 17 February 1995.

[17] The point is borne out, in regard to lay magistrates, by *R v Tiverton JJ, ex p Smith* [1981] RTR 280.

allowed to testify in secret. Rather, it is based on the supposition that the public have the right to be informed of the issues in the trial (of which, of course, the evidence forms a substantial component), the arguments constructed by counsel around these issues, and the judge's conduct in managing the proceedings. However, the public (like the parties themselves) are to be denied access to the jury's process of inference and reasoning that leads from the raw forensic material to the verdict.

2. SECTION 8 AND ITS ANTECEDENTS

Prior to the enactment of section 8 of the Contempt of Court Act 1981 there was scant authority on the subject of jury secrecy. Then, as now, disclosures might be deployed for two different ends: by an unsuccessful party in the trial in an effort to impugn the verdict; or by the media and others concerned to shed light on the workings of the jury in general or on how it approached its task in a particularly newsworthy case. Such disclosures, irrespective of their motivation, were condemned in the most uncompromising terms. In one case,[18] it was alleged, the conviction had been secured on the basis of a juror's dissemination to his fellows in the jury room of strictly inadmissible evidence, the accused's previous convictions. Dismissing the appeal against conviction, Lord Parker CJ said: 'It has for long been a rule of practice, based on public policy, that the court should not inquire, by taking evidence from jurymen, what did occur in either the jury-box or the jury-room.'[19]

Again, after the conviction of the infamous poisoner, Armstrong,[20] certain newspapers claimed to have inside knowledge of the jury's views of the evidence in the case. It was not entirely certain that the published accounts were accurate. The material disclosed, if true, did cast some doubts on at least one juror's understanding of the nature of the verdict for which he was casting his vote.[21] Lord Hewart CJ issued a warning in the following terms:

It may be that some jurymen are not aware that the inestimable value of their verdict is created only by its unanimity, and does not depend upon the process by which they believe that they arrived at it . . . If one juryman might communicate with the public upon the evidence and the verdict so might his colleagues also, and if they all took this dangerous course differences of individual opinion might be made manifest which, at the least, could not fail

---

[18] *R v Thompson* (1962) 46 Cr App R 72.					[19] ibid. 75–6.
[20] *R v Armstrong* [1922] 2 KB 555.
[21] J. Mortimer (ed) *Famous Trials* (1984) 340, gives the contents of the disclosure: 'Apparently, when the jury retired, the foreman asked each juror to write his verdict on a piece of paper. Eleven voted for a verdict of guilty, while the twelfth wrote down 'Not proven'. When the foreman read out the result, the twelfth juror explained himself in the following terms: '. . . you know what "Not proven" means. I really believe the man is guilty'. The foreman inferred from this that they had reached a unanimous verdict and simply added: 'We have heard enough of the case, and we needn't discuss it any more. Let's have a quiet smoke before we go back into Court.'

to diminish the confidence that the public rightly has in the general propriety of criminal verdicts.[22]

Stern admonitions sufficed no longer in *A-G v New Statesman and Nation Publishing Co*,[23] where an attempt was made to punish those responsible for disseminating jury secrets. The background to this attempt was a high profile trial, in which the former leader of the Liberal Party was indicted with others for conspiracy to murder. All the accused were acquitted. The editor of the *New Statesman*, feeling that a number of matters raised in the course of the trial required further investigation, commissioned a series of articles. One juror in the trial, it so happened, was willing to impart the considerations that had weighed with the twelve in deciding on their verdict. The information supplied by him was published in the third of the journal's articles on the trial, and on that basis the Attorney-General applied for an order for contempt of court against the defendant company as the publishers of the *New Statesman*.

A significant body of case law on contempt is concerned with publications that might be prejudicial to pending or imminent criminal proceedings. Clearly, the publication of the jury room secrets is not of this order since, *ex hypothesi*, the trial will have concluded. Rather, the Attorney-General based his case on the damage that he alleged had been inflicted on the administration of justice as an ongoing process. Leakages from the jury room would put at risk the 'finality' of verdicts and undermine public confidence in the correctness of such verdicts. Moreover, persons summoned in future for jury service would hesitate to play that role to the full if they were aware that what they said and how they voted in the jury room would not be treated as matters of the utmost confidentiality. Jury secrecy, therefore, served to protect two distinct interests: the integrity of the criminal justice system itself; and the security of individual jurors. The latter forms yet another aspect of the problem of protecting the *personae* of the trial against retribution for the proper discharge of their responsibilities. The noticeable point of difference is that the juror is protected as a matter of course, whereas the use of a device, such as a screen, to protect an apprehensive witness is the outcome of a decision that is taken in the light of the specific needs of the case. The two interests that formed the basis of the Attorney-General's case are not entirely separate. Reluctant and fearful jurors, if present in any significant number in the machinery of criminal justice, will eventually undermine the system. However, for the purposes of this chapter they will be treated as distinct focuses of concern.

Lord Widgery CJ, giving judgment in the *New Statesman* case, felt that the publication under consideration did not 'justify the title of contempt of court'.[24] His recital of the authorities amounted to little more than a disapproving overview of earlier occasions of disquiet arising from jury room disclosures. Even so, his Lordship felt, certain categories of disclosure were entirely permissible—'where serious research is being carried out',[25] or 'from a study of them it would not be

---

[22] [1922] 2 KB 555, 568.   [23] [1981] QB 1.   [24] ibid. 11.   [25] ibid. 7.

possible to identify the persons concerned in the trials'[26]—or even commendable (where 'jury secrets were revealed in the main for the laudable purpose of informing would-be jurors what to expect when summoned for jury service').[27]

No such qualifications were written into section 8 of the Contempt of Court Act. That provision makes it a contempt of court to obtain or disclose, or even to solicit (regardless, it would appear, of whether or not the solicitation proves successful), 'any particulars of statements made, opinions expressed, arguments advanced or votes cast by members of a jury in the course of their deliberations in any legal proceedings'. The only safeguard built into the section is the requirement of the consent of the Attorney-General to the institution of the proceedings, which, alternatively, may be brought on the motion of 'a court having jurisdiction to deal with it [sc. the contempt of court]'.[28]

To the blanket rule against disclosure of the forbidden particulars there are two limited exceptions. No offence is committed if, in the case in question, the particulars are disclosed 'for the purpose of enabling the jury to arrive at their verdict, or in connection with the delivery of that verdict'.[29] In the absence of such an exception, an absurd situation would ensue in which the court and its officials would be guilty of instigating a breach of section 8 in the routine execution of their duties. Nor is an offence committed if, in later proceedings, the particulars are disclosed by way of evidence of an offence 'alleged to have been committed in relation to the jury' in the earlier case.[30] The offences most likely to have been intended by this phrase are those aimed at protecting the integrity of the jury's judgment against bribes and intimidation. Such offences—whether in the generalized form of contempt of court or in the specific, but antiquated, form of embracery—are unlikely to require investigation of the course of jury deliberations in the earlier case since liability is incurred irrespective of the effect of the improper approach on the juror's judgment.[31]

This is a suitable point at which to consider more closely the terms of the prohibition imposed by section 8.

The section applies, in the first place, to 'statements made, opinions expressed' and 'arguments advanced' by 'members of a jury'. The inclusion of these matters in the ban is remarkable in that, in large measure, they will reflect the statements, opinions and arguments that were fully aired in open court. There would be something fundamentally amiss if the jury room discussions did not substantially reflect the issues as they were debated in the courtroom itself. Certainly, in the informal atmosphere of the jury room a more forthright approach is likely ('The

---

[26] [1981] QB 1, 11.   [27] ibid.   [28] Contempt of Court Act 1981, s 8(3).
[29] Contempt of Court Act 1981, s 8(2)(a).   [30] Contempt of Court Act 1981, s 8(2)(b).
[31] P. H. Winfield, *History of Conspiracy and Abuse of Legal Procedure* (1921) 161 defines embracery as 'the actual or attempted corrupt or forcible influencing of jurors'. In more detailed terms: 'Any attempt to corrupt or influence or instruct a jury in the cause beforehand, or in any way to incline them to be more favourable to one side than the other, by money, promises, letters, threats, or persuasions, except only by the strength of the evidence and the arguments of counsel in open Court at the trial, is an act of embracery.'

witness, Smith, was obviously lying'). Nevertheless, the point continues to hold: the very same arguments which could have been reported with impunity when expressed in open court bear the possibility of criminal sanction when conveyed from the jury room.[32]

The final item in the proscribed list is the particulars of 'votes' cast 'by members of a jury'. Does that mean the votes of individual jurors ('Jones voted throughout for a verdict of guilty')? Or does it refer to the collective vote ('We were divided 7–5 in favour of a verdict of not guilty for the first half-hour')? Or, again, does it encompass both kinds of disclosure? This point of interpretation, narrow though it would seem, goes to the rationale of section 8.

If the provision is directed against the disclosure of the votes of individual jurors—note that it does refer to the votes cast by 'members' of a jury—it should be perceived to that extent as a means of protecting the juror in the fearless and disinterested discharge of his duty.

If, on the other hand, the provision is to be taken (whether exclusively or in part) as referring to the vote of the jury as a collegiate body, the rule is all the more astonishing. For, subject to a major exception to be discussed in the following paragraph, the final configuration of votes is actually known. The cutting edge of this aspect of section 8, then, would appear to be the laying of a cloak of secrecy on all the collective votes of the jury with the exception of the final vote which registers the verdict. This interpretation of the section, as covering the whole series of inconclusive votes, gains support from the first of the two exceptions to section 8 that were mentioned above. For, if section 8 were limited to maintaining the confidentiality of the final vote only, there would be no point in specifically excepting from its scope—as subsection (2)(a) does—the disclosure of particulars 'for the purpose of enabling the jury *to arrive at* their verdict' (Emphasis added). On this view, therefore, with what mischief does section 8 deal? In the absence of the provision there might be disclosed a series of votes the earlier ones of which might have been far removed from the verdict and vote which was finally recorded. (But, even under a regime of secrecy, the length of time taken by the jury in reaching its verdict is suggestive of the existence of a strong faction of dissent to the final verdict, though a faction that is eventually overcome.) Or, again, the possibility of disclosure might lead to the public learning of a pact struck between the members of the jury as to how they would cast their votes. Such a pact may not necessarily be a corrupt arrangement: it might develop, for example, as a response to pressures to avoid an inconclusive trial. At the same time, however, if it results in certain jurors casting their votes in a way

---

[32] Section 8 carries no defence of prior disclosure—a defence that was suggested in some quarters, but rejected by the government, in connection with the reform of the official secrets law. See *Reform of Section 2 of the Official Secrets Act 1911* (Cm 408, June 1988), paras 62–64. The argument there presented against such a defence is also applicable, with some variation, to the subject of jury secrets: that second (and later) disclosures may go to confirming the truth of the first account and therefore prove harmful in their own right.

that is inconsistent with their true convictions about the case, it will not show the jury system in the best possible light.

It is now necessary to consider one type of situation where the prohibition of the disclosure of votes could be viewed as serving a legitimate purpose. Where the accused has been acquitted by a majority verdict, the bond of confidentiality off-sets the change brought about by the introduction of such verdicts and avoids the public stigma of a second-rate acquittal that would otherwise attach to such an outcome to the trial. Certainly, this is not the avowed purpose of section 8, which (in any case) applies irrespective of whether the verdict in question was unani-mous or by a majority. And it is noteworthy that neither the provision which first permitted the taking of majority verdicts[33] nor any of the subsequent statutes relating to the jury contains an express prohibition of disclosure of the fact of a not guilty verdict having been reached by majority decision.[34] Such an outcome to a particular trial, of course, may be inferred (probably correctly) by the outside world from the mere fact of a majority direction having been given by the trial judge. But such assurance of confidentiality as is to be found lies, not in section 8 (since it excepts disclosures made in connection with the delivery of the jury's ver-dict), but rather in the judge's exhortation to reach a unanimous verdict (if that is at all possible) and in the form and order of the questions to be put to the foreman of the jury at the conclusion of their deliberations.[35]

It could be said to be a fair inference from the above analysis that the purpose of section 8 is to preserve public confidence in regard to the adjudication of issues of fact. The premise that underlies the provision is indeed a pessimistic one: namely, that disclosures under the headings of 'opinions expressed' and 'argu-ments advanced' would redound to the discredit of trial by jury. Yet, even if this gloomy premise is shared, section 8 is both under-inclusive and over-inclusive. In the former regard, any misrepresentation of what transpired in the jury room could well have a deleterious effect on public confidence in the standards of crim-inal justice. However damaging they might be, pure fabrications (for example, that the verdict was reached on the toss of a coin) would not fall within the scope of section 8. In order to constitute (at the very least) an attempt to commit the offence, there must be some intent to disclose the secrets of the jury room, even

---

[33] Criminal Justice Act 1967, s 13.

[34] Such a prohibition could perhaps be garnered by applying *expressio unius exclusio alterius* rea-soning to the Juries Act 1974, s 17(3), which substantially reproduces the Criminal Justice Act 1967, s 13(2): 'The Crown Court shall not accept a verdict of guilty by virtue of subsection (1) above [i.e. the majority verdict provision] unless the foreman of the jury has stated in open court the number of jurors who respectively agreed to and dissented from the verdict.'

[35] For the proper form see *Practice Direction (Crime: Majority Verdicts)* [1967] 1 WLR 1198, in particular paras 2 and 3. The latter stipulates the questions to be asked: '(i) Have at least 10 . . . of you agreed upon your verdict? If "Yes", (ii) What is your verdict? Please only answer "Guilty" or "Not Guilty". (iii) (a) If "Not Guilty"—accept the verdict without more ado. (b) If "Guilty"—Is it the ver-dict of you all or by a majority? (iv) If "Guilty" by a majority—How many of you agreed to the ver-dict and how many dissented?'

though one that was encumbered by a faulty memory.[36] There are, too, several considerations that point to an over-broad provision. Even though section 8 was conceived as catching disclosures from the criminal jury, there is nothing in the wording of the Contempt of Court Act that expressly so limits it. The jury which is occasionally called upon to serve in civil trials is equally subject to the scope of section 8, as would the coroner's jury. Section 8, moreover, embodies no qualification that would except disclosures taking place after a given lapse of time since the trial in question. It penalizes in equal terms disclosures which would bolster faith in the criminal justice system and those which would be destructive of public confidence.

The ambit of section 8 has been the subject of interpretation by the House of Lords in *A-G v Associated Newspapers Ltd*.[37] The background to those proceedings consisted of a serious fraud case, *R v Natwest Investment Bank* (more popularly known as the 'Blue Arrow' trial). On 5 July 1992, a few months after the conclusion of the proceedings, the *Mail on Sunday* published an article containing details—some of them discreditable—about the course of deliberations in the trial. The route by which the particulars came into the hands of the *Mail on Sunday* was not entirely clear. It was conceded by the appellants (the publishers and editor of the newspaper, together with a journalist on its staff) that the details in the article comprised the matters covered by section 8. Their case in the Divisional Court and in the House of Lords, to which lay a direct appeal, rested on the construction of the word 'disclose'. It is a contempt of court, says section 8, to 'obtain', 'disclose' or 'solicit' any of the prohibited particulars. The appellants had not solicited the material: they had not been involved in the initial breach of the confidences of the jury room, the material only later coming into their hands.[38] Their actions, even at this remove, could have been interpreted as 'obtaining' the information. However, the thrust of the Attorney-General's case lay in the verb that was the focus of interpretation: that the newspaper had 'disclosed' the information to the world at large. Was that word apt to describe the newspaper's actions? Or, as the appellants contended, did it encompass only the initial disclosure from juror to non-juror?

The central difficulty for the Attorney-General lay in the absence of a chain of legal liability for jury room disclosures. Such a chain is to be found, for example, in the Official Secrets Act 1989. Section 5(2) imposes liability, in general terms, on those who, having received information that falls within any of the categories protected by the Act, proceed to disclose it without lawful authority. The absence of an equivalent provision from the Contempt of Court Act 1981 did not prove fatal to the Attorney-General's case: on the contrary, the word 'disclose' on its natural meaning described the actions of the appellants. Liability, together with

---

[36] For an unusual instance of the application of the criminal law to such fabrications, see the Official Secrets Act 1989, s 1(2), which encompasses *purported* disclosures relating to security or intelligence by members or ex-members of the security and intelligence services.

[37] [1994] 2 AC 238.   [38] The circumstances of the initial breach are set out ibid. 253–254.

fines totalling £60,000, was affirmed. The judgment of the House of Lords, given by Lord Lowry, did not simply turn on the meaning of the critical word. In the light of the *Mail on Sunday*'s particular interest in the 'Blue Arrow' trial, his Lordship did touch on the wider issues surrounding the issue of jury secrecy. We will have occasion, therefore, to return to the case later in this chapter.

When considering the term 'votes', as used in section 8, we noted that there were two possible interpretations of that word which corresponded, in turn, to two different rationales of jury secrecy. Since those rationales form the basis of the next two sections it is worth recalling them in summary form. First (section 3), there is the need to safeguard the integrity of the criminal justice system. Secondly (section 4), there is a vital interest in encouraging the individual juror to speak his mind freely in the jury room and to secure him thereafter against possible reprisals from a convicted accused or his associates. The two interests, though not entirely distinct, will be treated separately for the sake of analytical clarity.

3. PROTECTING THE ADMINISTRATION OF JUSTICE

The defence of the rule of jury secrecy—at any rate, when specifically directed to the general health of the criminal justice system—is frequently expressed in terms of the need to safeguard the 'finality' of the jury's verdict. The term is to be found both in the academic literature on the subject and in the judgments of the courts, most notably in the *New Statesman* case.[39] But what exactly is this quality of 'finality' in the name of which jury secrecy is defended? Is it synonymous with the 'inscrutability' of the jury's verdict? Is 'finality' an attribute which is capable of being realized only in regard to findings of fact, in contrast to rulings on points of law? Is it a phenomenon the presence of which—as would appear to be so from the present-day use of the term—is consistent with majority jury verdicts but inconsistent with disclosure of the course of jury deliberations?

It is possible to isolate several distinct strands in the use of the concept.

In the first place, the term 'finality' may be used perfectly sensibly to deal with the following problem. The jury in a given case returns a verdict. It might be a majority verdict or one reached unanimously. If it is the latter, for example, the jurors are asked in the time-honoured way whether it is the verdict of them all. To this they assent. Subsequently an individual juror,[40] or even (as in one case) the whole jury[41] returns to state that the verdict that had been announced and then

---

[39] See [1981] QB 1, 6, where part of the Attorney-General's case is summarized in the claim that disclosure of what happened in the jury room will tend 'to imperil the finality of jury verdicts and thereby diminish public confidence in the general correctness and propriety of such verdicts'. Note, also, the frequent use of the word in *Solicitor-General v Radio New Zealand Ltd* [1994] 1 NZLR 48, especially at 53–54: for example, the statement at 54 that the 'finality argument goes to the core of how the jury system functions'.

[40] *R v Roads* [1967] 2 QB 108.

[41] *Boston v W. S. Bagshaw & Sons* [1966] 1 WLR 1135.

recorded by the court is not the verdict that they had intended. Such submissions are not entertained by the appellate courts,[42] irrespective of whether the jury verdict was pronounced in criminal or civil proceedings. In the name of 'finality' of decision-taking the verdict stands as recorded[43]—a rule that has been held to survive the entry into force of the Human Rights Act 1998.[44]

Consider, now, a variation on the same theme. This time the initiative is taken by the accused, who attempts to impugn his conviction, not by way of appeal against that verdict, but by way of separate civil proceedings. This stratagem has taken various forms: by commencing proceedings for negligence against the defence barrister,[45] or by suing the police for assault in regard to the obtaining of an allegedly invalid confession which had been ruled admissible by the trial judge.[46] There exist several well-established doctrines (issue estoppel, most notably) in the name of which the courts will reject such attempts. Whatever the merits or demerits of such doctrines they serve, in a more complete manner, the same cause of securing 'finality' of verdicts.

All legal systems have need of a line beyond which issues of liability, guilt or innocence, are to be treated—at any rate, as far as the court structure is concerned—as conclusively determined: *interest reipublicae ut sit finis litium* (it is in the common interest that there should be an end to litigation). 'Finality', in this context, is secured by stipulating that certain avenues, and only those avenues, are to be available for challenging the decision of the trial court. It is apparent from the scope of section 8 of the Contempt of Court Act that it is not concerned with safeguarding particular verdicts from challenge by way of subsequent legal process. The means to this end (such as issue estoppel) existed long before 1981. Rather, section 8 strives to maintain the authority of particular verdicts—and, through them, the authority of jury trial in general—in the eyes of the public.

At this point it is necessary to set out two competing conceptions of how such authority is to be gained and protected. The one approach closely identifies the jury's verdict with the truth in the case. It is pithily expressed, in the context of jury unanimity, in the following way: 'the requirement of unanimity (found, for instance, in England and America) is based on the more or less unconscious assumption that the objective truth must always be subjectively convincing, and that, inversely, the identity of subjective convictions is the criterion of objective truth.'[47]

---

[42] Compare the 'enrolled bill rule', under which the courts will not inquire into the validity of an instrument that bears the outward insignia of a correctly enacted Act of Parliament.

[43] In *Boston v W. S. Bagshaw & Sons* [1966] 1 WLR 1135, 1136, Lord Denning MR adduced a further reason which is, in part, reflected in section 4 of the present chapter, and is particularly borne out by the facts of *A-G v Judd* The Times, 15 August 1994: 'to protect the jury themselves [*sic*] and to prevent them being exposed to pressure or inducement to explain or alter their views.'

[44] *R v Lewis* The Times, 26 April 2001.   [45] *Rondel v Worsley* [1969] 1 AC 191.

[46] *McIlkenny v Chief Constable of West Midlands* [1980] QB 283.

[47] *The Sociology of Georg Simmel* (translated and edited by K. H. Wolff: 1950).

This conception holds that the public interest is best served by accepting jury verdicts, subject to appeal to the higher courts, as final and correct. Even if, in the occasional criminal case, the wrong outcome is shown to have been reached or a dubious line of reasoning adopted by the jury to reach what may well have been the correct result, the uncovering of such cases will harm the public interest in the long run by leading to a loss of faith in the criminal justice system as a whole. A minor theme of this approach (although one that is only implicit in it) is that in many cases it is difficult or impossible to demonstrate to the public's satisfaction what is the 'right' or 'wrong' outcome. Far better, in such cases, to accept as correct whatever verdict is returned by the jury.

The rival conception need not detain us long since it is one which, generally stated, we have already encountered in Chapter 2 as supplying a rationale of public trial. Other things being equal, the various actors in the trial are more likely to discharge their roles properly if exposed to the searchlight of publicity—in short, the disciplinary rationale of open justice. (Note that the stage of jury deliberation is distinct in that there is no scope for a policy of openness advancing the investigatory rationale of open justice.) Furthermore, the availability of as much information as possible about a trial and its mode of conduct will provide the basis for an informed discussion of whether or not the correct outcome was reached, even if the case in question is continually re-argued in this form down the years.

An erroneous outcome that leads to the conviction of an innocent person is considered far more grave than one which results in a guilty person going free. Much disquiet is occasioned whenever instances of miscarriage of justice are brought to light. It is noteworthy, however, that the two principal cases which involved breaches of jury secrecy, *New Statesman* and *Associated Newspapers*, arose out of criminal proceedings which had culminated in decisions favourable to the accused. The outcome in the former was entirely the result of the jury's deliberations, while in the latter the same result was reached by a variety of routes: one defendant was acquitted by jury decision, others were found not guilty by judicial direction, and the convictions of the remainder were quashed by the Court of Appeal. The danger is that persons who are acquitted as a result of (what is revealed to be) dubious jury reasoning—like those declared not guilty on a majority verdict—will have the status of a second-rate acquittal.

In this context mention should be made of the controversy occasioned by the publication of *Easing the Passing*. The book forms an account by Lord Devlin of a sensational murder trial, that of Dr John Bodkin Adams, over which he had presided nearly thirty years earlier.[48] At the time of its publication reservations were expressed about the propriety of a judge taking advantage in this way of the central role that he had played in the trial drama. Such accounts are regarded as

---

[48] The book was published in 1985. References in this chapter will be made to the new edition, that was published in the following year with a postscript added by the author.

unproblematic when published by police officers and lawyers who have played a part in the investigation and trial. They are to be treated very differently when they appear under the name of one who, whether as juror or judge, had direct or indirect responsibility for the outcome of the trial. When emerging from such quarters, these accounts may cast doubt on the correctness of the verdict in a way which the memoirs of police officers and advocates (unless they contain new information) would not. Lord Devlin, however, appears to have been alert to the risk that his book could reduce to the level of a second-class acquittal the verdict of not guilty that was pronounced against the accused. The first edition was published a mere two years after the death of Dr Adams[49]—which might suggest that publication was waiting on that event. Moreover, Devlin goes to considerable pains to meet the charge of having 'tampered with the verdict' by citing passages in the body of the book where he endorsed the jury's decision as 'unquestionably a true verdict'.[50]

It was in the name of a conception of the public interest that the *Mail on Sunday* took the decision to publish the secrets of the jury room in the 'Blue Arrow' trial. To quote from the agreed statement of facts and issues in *Associated Newspapers*:

The appellants published the particulars included in the article because they sincerely believed that those particulars made an important contribution to the public debate about whether serious fraud trials ought to be conducted before a jury, and because the appellants believed that any interference with such publication would be a breach of article 10 of the European Convention on Human Rights [the right to freedom of expression].[51]

The claim that the article contributed to an important public debate about the limitations of jury trial could go only to the purity of the appellants' motive. In regard to the substantial area of the Contempt of Court Act 1981 that is governed by 'the strict liability rule'[52] there is available a defence of discussion of public affairs. This provides that a published comment on current proceedings is not to be treated as a contempt of court provided that two requirements are satisfied: that the risk of prejudice to the particular proceedings is merely incidental; and that the discussion is conducted 'in good faith' in regard to 'public affairs or other matters of general public interest'.[53] The defence is not available for use in proceedings such as the *Associated Newspapers* case since section 8 defines an area of contempt liability outside the scope of 'the strict liability' rule. The defence is typically pleaded when some matter of general public interest and concern (as in one case, the practice of 'mercy killing' by physicians[54]) is debated by a newspaper against the background of a current trial where that very matter is in issue. In the context of jury secrecy the topic that is of public interest and concern is the

---

[49] This point is emphasized, but without elaboration, at 221.
[50] At 219–220 (in the postscript).   [51] [1994] 2 AC 238, 254–255.
[52] Defined in the Contempt of Court Act 1981, s 1.   [53] Contempt of Court Act 1981, s 5.
[54] *A-G v English* [1983] 1 AC 116.

essentially introspective one of probing how well certain parts of the machinery of justice match up to the demands that have been placed on them.

In view of the absence of a defence under English law it is not surprising that the appellants cited Article 10 of the European Human Rights Convention. Since the penalty exacted on the *Mail on Sunday* would constitute a violation of the right to freedom of expression guaranteed by Article 10, paragraph 1, the application of the standards of the Convention would soon pass to the question whether section 8 could be redeemed under the second paragraph as a restriction that is 'prescribed by law and . . . necessary in a democratic society'—to take the countervailing interest that is most clearly in point—'for maintaining the authority and impartiality of the judiciary'. It will be readily apparent that the word 'judiciary' is not appropriate to describe the situation at present under consideration. The true intent of the treaty is borne out in the French text of the Convention, which is designated as equally authentic with the English text. This refers to the '*pouvoir judiciaire*', a phrase of altogether wider import which was construed by the European Court of Human Rights in *Sunday Times v UK*[55] as extending to 'the machinery of justice or the judicial branch of government as well as the judges in their official capacity'.[56] The Court in that case observed that the particular heading had been listed in the drafting of Article 10(2) as a concession to the peculiarly common law doctrine of contempt of court. However, the heading redeems only the general aims of the law of contempt, and not necessarily in every point of detail.[57] The authority of 'the judicial branch of government', the Court said, consists of several aspects: these include the feature that 'the public at large have respect for and confidence in the courts' capacity to fulfil [their] function'.[58] Whether that respect and confidence would be best fostered by secrecy or publicity was a question that was left open.

We have spent some time exploring two conceptions of how public confidence in the jury system is best nurtured: whether by a policy of openness or by a regime of enforced secrecy. The tacit assumption underpinning a rule of jury secrecy is to the effect that knowledge of what passes in the jury room would reflect badly on the institution of trial by jury in general and on the verdicts reached in certain trials in particular. But, even if one shares that gloomy assumption, does the forbidding of disclosure serve any substantial purpose? For as long as the media have existed they have shown an interest in the correctness (or otherwise) of the outcome of particular trials. It is now common to read articles or see television programmes which, after going over the ground of famous cases, leave the distinct impression that a faulty verdict was reached.[59] Where the accused is still alive and, even more so, when he is still serving a prison sentence, these articles and programmes are of more than historical or speculative interest. If the accounts

---

[55] (1979–80) 2 EHRR 245. [56] ibid. para 55. [57] ibid. para 60.
[58] ibid. para 55.
[59] See, for instance, M. Young and P. Hill, *Rough Justice* (1983) for a collection of such cases which had originally formed the subject of a series on BBC television.

given of the trials are believed to be accurate and impartial—and, as we shall see in Chapter 8, those accounts which are not run the risk of forfeiting certain immunities—they carry an implication that the jury in the trial reached a perverse verdict. Such an outcome may not necessarily be due to defective jury reasoning. The fault may lie at some earlier point in the process of criminal investigation (for example, in the lack of safeguards governing the admissibility of certain types of evidence). Wherever the fault is located, there are two possible approaches to the re-arguing of decided cases. One view of such exercises is that they are mischievous, as tending to undermine public confidence in the criminal justice system. Alternatively, they might be viewed as serving an important function. However, even on the former approach, the forbidding of disclosures by ex-jurors will serve little, if anything, to remove the deleterious impact of such exercises. Either the raw material for the investigation can be amassed from the period prior to the point at which the jury retires or (if the fault is believed to be that of the jury) it is possible to surmise from primary knowledge or secondary sources of the hearing phase what the correct verdict should have been.

4. PROTECTING THE INDIVIDUAL JUROR

It has already been emphasized that there is an inevitable link between the subject matter of this and the preceding section. Protecting the individual juror against threats (or inducements) is but one aspect of protecting the integrity of the criminal justice system. The most extreme manifestation of this concern has been found in the institution of the 'Diplock courts' in Northern Ireland, under which trial by jury has simply been abolished for the hearing of what are referred to as 'scheduled offences'.[60]

In Great Britain, too, the intimidation of jurors—like the intimidation of witnesses—has been perceived as a problem of ever-growing seriousness in recent years. As long ago as 1967 it was the perception of the scale of the problem that was responsible for the introduction of majority verdicts, the first of a series of stages in what some regard as the 'subversion of the jury'.[61] It has been argued that 'it was not clear that this possibility [of intimidation of jurors by professional criminals] was any greater than it had been in the past'.[62] A more serious objection is that, irrespective of the size of the problem, it was a peculiarly blunt solution. There are available, as will be seen, other ways of safeguarding the jury from possible threats. The effect of the introduction of majority verdicts was that (subject to some safeguards) a guilty verdict could be returned over the dissent of

---

[60] So called since they were listed in Sch 1 of the Northern Ireland (Emergency Provisions) Act 1991. Broadly speaking, they comprise offences that were connected to a terrorist presence in the province.
[61] H. Harman and J. Griffith, *Justice Deserted: The Subversion of the Jury* (1979).
[62] ibid. 14.

as many as two jurors. But the dissenting jurors might not necessarily have been intimidated or corrupted: they may simply have had genuine reservations about the guilt of the accused.

There have been occasions where persons who have taken reprisals against a juror for discharging the duties of his office have been punished for contempt of court. Whoever the person might be—a convicted accused or, in some cases, an employer annoyed at the temporary loss of the juror's services[63]—such conduct has been penalized on the same principle as was applied for the protection of witnesses in *A-G v Butterworth*.[64] In one such case, *A-G v Judd*,[65] the convicted accused had combined a breach of section 8 (in the form of seeking details of the voting in the jury room) with intimidating conduct towards the juror (by instructing her to write to the judge who had presided at his trial, informing him that she had been mistaken about the guilt of the accused). As the details of this case could well have borne out, several of the matters covered by section 8 are protected against disclosure as much for the safety of individual jurors as to safeguard the reputation of the criminal justice system. Certain types of 'opinions expressed' and 'arguments advanced', if made generally known, would reflect no discredit on the conduct of the jury. However, if attributed to an individual juror, they might expose him to the possibility of reprisal by the accused or his associates.

Given the theme of the present work, the substantive law of juror intimidation is of marginal interest. Our concern is the extent to which departure from the ideal of open justice may be defended by reference to the need to protect jurors from threats. In this regard secrecy is available as a safeguard against the possible undermining of the jury, just as openness (to refer back to Chapter 2) is a safeguard against possible lapses by the trial judge or potential dishonesty on the part of a witness. Indeed, in at least one respect the prophylactic aspect is of much greater importance than the punitive aspect of juror intimidation. There have occurred courtroom situations where, owing to the presence and bearing of the accused's associates in the public gallery, a threatening atmosphere has hung over the trial even in the absence of overt person-to-person approaches. In *R v Brown, R v Slaughter*,[66] the accused unsuccessfully sought to mount a challenge to their convictions on the basis of the jurors (who had retired) having communicated their anxieties ('We were frightened. You can cut the atmosphere with a knife') to the jury bailiff.[67] Such cases demonstrate the seriousness of the

---

[63] See, for example, the incident recounted in The Times (27 February 1993) 3. A pub manager was fined £500 for attacking and then dismissing an employee who had been absent from work for jury service. Sentencing him, Judge Halnan said that, had he not offered to re-engage the employee, he would have been sentenced to a substantial term of imprisonment. This episode, incidentally, bears out two further aspects of the subject of open justice. The juror-employee could not be identified in the newspaper report, and the contempt hearing took place at 'a special late-night sitting' at Southwark Crown Court.

[64] [1963] 1 QB 696.   [65] The Times, 15 August 1994.   [66] The Times, 25 October 1989.

[67] The bailiff simply asked 'Why?' before communicating the jury's fears to the judge. That one word did not amount to a discussion of the merits of the case with the bailiff, and therefore was not a material irregularity.

problem.[68] Equally, they illustrate the limitations of statutory measures that have been enacted to protect the *personae* of the trial. Section 51 of the Criminal Justice and Public Order Act 1994, which has already been encountered in the context of witness protection in Chapter 4, section 3, is equally applicable to jurors (whether past, present, or potential). This provision, again, applies in addition to any common law offence of juror intimidation.[69] The core of the section consists of the doing of an intimidatory 'act', among other things, where such 'act is done in the presence of [the juror] and directed at him directly'.[70] The mere presence of known associates of the accused in the precincts of the court would not qualify as an 'act' for such purposes. Something more would be required. Yet it is doubtful whether anything falling short of an overt threat— for example, glowering at a juror—would be covered by the terms of section 51. Again, as in the case of interference with witnesses, the provisions of the 1994 Act have been supplemented by section 54 of the Criminal Procedure and Investigations Act 1996 in creating a procedure for the quashing of acquittals tainted by juror intimidation. The outlines of this procedure, so far as relevant, were sketched in Chapter 4. However, there is one point, unique to juror intimidation, that has some bearing on matters of secrecy. Before making an order that quashes an acquittal, the High Court is required by section 55 of the 1996 Act to be satisfied as to certain conditions. The first of these is that 'but for the interference or intimidation, the acquitted person would not have been acquitted'. This is a sensible requirement, though one that inevitably involves a degree of speculation. In the particular case of threats to one or more jurors, inquiry into whether or not the requirement has been met would logically necessitate investigation into the pattern of voting in the jury room.

There are two possible responses to the implicit threat that may emanate from eye contact between the juror and a known associate of the accused. Each corresponds, in essence, to the responses that have been encountered in earlier chapters of this book.

The first method is to arrange the physical features of the court so as to avoid confrontation between the individuals in question. A new design of the Crown Court places the jury box underneath the public gallery, and provides that the points of access to these two parts of the courtroom would be by means of two different entrances.[71] Clearly, this solution is one that is effective only in the long

---

[68] See the account in The Times (25 July 1988) 5. The article recites that in 1987 jury protection cost Scotland Yard 3,588 man days of work, and that for the first six months of 1988 the figure had risen to 5,862 man days.

[69] Criminal Justice and Public Order Act 1994, s 51(11).

[70] Criminal Justice and Public Order Act 1994, s 51(3).

[71] For a detailed account of measures that have been proposed for the protection of jurors as part of a return to jury trial for scheduled offences in Northern Ireland see S. C. Greer and A. White, *Abolishing the Diplock Courts: The Case for Restoring Jury Trial to Scheduled Offences in Northern Ireland* (1986) 74–6. The Royal Commission on Criminal Justice (chairman: Viscount Runciman) also recommended that, so far as practicable, the waiting and refreshment areas for jurors should be

run and is dependent on the speed of the various building programmes for Crown Court centres. It is a variation on the arrangement whereby a witness will give evidence while screened from sight by members of the public. As compared with the situation of the witness, it possesses at least one advantage: that the juror has always played his part in the case under conditions of *de facto* secrecy, and little appears to be gained by subjecting the jury to the attention of the public gallery while they listen to the evidence and assimilate the issues in the case.[72]

Such arrangements could be deployed as an alternative, or as an addition, to a second method: a policy of juror anonymity. This would be a marked departure from the present practice whereby the names of the members of the jury are available to all since they are read out in open court before they take the oath. For some time the nearest legal authority in point was the ruling of the Divisional Court in *R v Felixstowe Justices, ex p Leigh*,[73] which appeared to suggest that at common law the anonymous adjudication of cases is illegal. Successful challenges were brought by *The Observer* against the policy of not disclosing the names of magistrates who sat to try particular cases within the jurisdiction of the benches of Felixstowe, Ipswich and Woodbridge. The clerk to the justices defended the policy by reference to instances where, under a practice of disclosure, magistrates had been subjected to abusive communications as a result of their decisions in particular cases. As members of the local community, they were especially vulnerable in this regard. Moreover, each bench being a collegiate body that arrived at a collective decision, there should be no call to single out any particular member of a bench for mention by name. Since there was no statutory provision directly in point, the court decided the issue by reference to the general principle that justice is to be administered openly. Indeed, reference was made in passing to the practice whereby jurors are 'known persons'.[74]

It would appear that the interest in the name of which we are seeking to argue the case for juror anonymity has been found, in the context of the magistracy at any rate, not sufficiently compelling. Nevertheless, the diversity of treatment of jurors and magistrates is defensible on general principle. The involvement of the individual juror in the criminal justice system is both under compulsion of law and limited to the specific case. The discharge of the office of magistrate, on the other hand, is voluntarily assumed and of a continuing nature. Although general studies of the magistracy (its foibles, strengths and weaknesses) are carried out, the focus of interest at the local level will naturally be the performance of individual magistrates. Moreover, there is a sense in which the anonymity of the

---

set apart from areas of the court building to which members of the public have access. (recommendation no 260).

[72] Mere observation of the jury, even at this relatively passive stage of the proceedings, may give cause to question a juror's lack of impartiality. The Times (13 August 1993) 19, recounts that the previous day a juror had been dismissed from hearing the trial of a complex fraud case in New York 'because her body language with the prosecution counsel was claimed to render her less than impartial'. She was alleged to have shown bias by smiling at the principal lawyer for the prosecution.

[73] [1987] QB 582.   [74] ibid. 595.

individual juror fits well with the idea of the random selection from the community of the jury's membership.

At what point in the assembling of a jury should anonymity attach? Particular groups of twelve are chosen at random from the jury panel. There is a statutory provision that allows access to the information contained on the panel.[75] It is submitted that, at this point in the process, a policy of openness should be retained.[76] The twelve who are to try a particular case are then required to be selected from the panel by ballot in open court.[77] No vital interest, it is suggested, is served by the announcement of their names so that they can be heard in the public gallery. Their disclosure to the accused, on the other hand, is necessary for the purpose of the possible exercise by him of the right to challenge for cause.[78] It might be thought that such limited disclosure is enough to subvert the scheme of juror anonymity by introducing a possible leak into the system. Once the accused and his representatives are privy to the information, it is also potentially available to the accused's friends and associates. However, as we have noted, this is not the premise upon which *in camera* hearings are held. As an irreducible minimum, such a hearing must take place in the presence of the accused so that he may be informed of the case that he has to meet.

Further light has subsequently been cast on these issues by the ruling in *R v Comerford*.[79] This is a case which draws together several of the strands in the present work. The defendant's initial trial for drugs offences was stopped, and the jury discharged, after the judge received information in chambers on an *ex parte* application by the prosecution. At the time no reasons were communicated to the defence, but it subsequently emerged that there had been an attempt to interfere with the jury. In particular, a person had been observed in the public gallery making a written note of the jurors' names as they were being sworn in.[80] A second hearing was arranged, on this occasion with police protection of the jury. This time, however, the names of the jurors were not disclosed in open court and they were known in court simply by number. The defendant, having been convicted, unsuccessfully challenged the outcome on the basis of both this practice and the failure to involve the defence in the question of whether or not

---

[75] Juries Act 1974, s 5(2), grants the right to any 'party to proceedings' in which a jury may be required to try an issue. Section 5(4) provides that the court, 'if it thinks fit', may afford to 'any person' the same right even though that person would not qualify under section 5(2). As was first intimated in Chapter 4, section 4, B, above, these provisions explain in part why the practice of 'jury vetting' is lawful. In gaining access to the names on the jury panel, and thereafter investigating the background of those persons, the prosecuting authorities are simply availing themselves of their statutory rights under section 5.

[76] Clearly, the risk of an improper approach under these circumstances will vary according to the ratio between the size of a given panel and the standard jury size.

[77] Juries Act 1974, s 11(1).

[78] The availability of full information on the basis of which to exercise this right is all the more important with the removal from the defence of the right of peremptory challenge: Criminal Justice Act 1988, s 118(1).

[79] [1998] 1 All ER 823.   [80] ibid. 829.

to discontinue the first trial. To deal with the latter point first, the Court of Appeal acknowledged that the ideal procedure was an application made *inter partes* but conceded that there could be departure from this ideal if the trial judge was sufficiently impressed by the exigencies of the situation. On the principal ground of appeal, it was simply held that there was no provision in the Juries Act which required the public announcement of the names of the jurors.

There are some disconcerting features about this ruling. In contrast to the proposal outlined above, the names of the jurors were withheld from the accused as much as from the members of the public present in the courtroom. In this respect the denial of information to the accused was more far-reaching than under the standard form of *in camera* hearing. The Court of Appeal drew some reassurance from the fact that the trial judge had intended to preserve the accused's right of challenge, and from his counsel's omission to contend that he would have exercised this right if the names of the jurors had been known to him. However, as his counsel is reported as conceding, 'a name may ring a bell when a face does not'.[81] Therefore, one cannot readily assume from the lack of challenge to any particular juror that no such basis for challenge existed in the case.[82]

Quite generally, jurors have an interest in privacy that partly overlaps, and also partly transcends, the value of the proper administration of justice. This idea is reflected in the judgment of the High Court of New Zealand in *Solicitor-General v Radio New Zealand Ltd*.[83] The case concerned approaches made by an employee of the defendant, with a view to conducting interviews, to nine of the jurors who had served in a murder trial nearly a year earlier. Interest in the case had been rekindled by the discovery of the body of one of the two victims. The defendant company broadcast extracts from the interviews, in one of which the particular juror voiced doubts as to whether he and his colleagues had been right in returning a verdict of guilty. There appears to have been little, if any, violation of the secrecy of the jury room itself in the course of the interviews and transmissions. Nevertheless, the defendant, even with the protection of the freedom of expression guarantee of the New Zealand Bill of Rights Act 1990, was judged to be in contempt of court. Not only did its conduct imperil the 'finality' of the verdict (conduct that was described as an 'endeavour to prolong the life of the jury'),[84] it was also implicated in a breach of the jurors' privacy. The identities of the jurors had somehow become known to the defendant, notwithstanding a statutory provision that (except by leave of the court and for certain limited purposes only) the jury list or panel was to be confidential to the court registrar and his staff.[85] The jurors' own expectations in this regard were borne out by the

---

[81] [1998] 1 All ER 823, 826.

[82] The Court of Appeal added: 'Had the appellant's decision to exercise his right of challenge depended on knowing the names of the jurors, he could have exercised his right to ascertain the names of all the jurors forming the relevant panel, and we have no doubt that the judge would have been willing to hear, and if necessary rule on, any challenge made after inspecting the names of the panel, . . .': ibid. 832.

[83] [1994] 1 NZLR 48.   [84] ibid. 54.   [85] Juries Act 1981, s 9(6).

surprise and annoyance that most of them displayed on being approached by the defendant's employee and being asked to reconsider the case in the light of the recent find.

The difference in outcome as between this and the *New Statesman* case is worthy of note. In the latter there was held to have been no contempt even though the incursion into the confidences of the jury room was direct and substantial. It is difficult to resist the conclusion that, in the *Radio New Zealand* case, the element of interference with the jurors' privacy added significantly to such undermining of the criminal justice system as was caused by the conduct of the defendant. Discharging the office of juror is a thankless task, even in the absence of threats from professional criminals.[86] The maintenance of juror anonymity is available as a means of lessening the burden of the office without jeopardizing the values served by open justice.

5. PROBLEMS OF JURY RESEARCH

It is now time to take stock of section 8 in the general context of the problems of conducting research into the strengths and weaknesses of trial by jury.

Despite the wide-ranging terms of section 8, there are several matters which it does not encompass: a person's generalized reminiscences of several experiences of jury service; his views about the desirability or otherwise of a prosecution having been brought in a particular case in which he served as a juror; and his expressions of doubt as to whether he and his colleagues returned the correct verdict.[87] Instances have now occurred of publications by ex-jurors which, in each of these ways, fall outside the prohibitions of section 8.[88] Furthermore, the essential precondition of liability is that the matters disclosed were ventilated 'in the course of [the jurors'] deliberations'. In this way a trial that has been aborted will not even have reached the critical phase, and a juror—so far as section 8, at least, is concerned—may speak freely.[89] Nor will every stage from the retiring of the jury to

---

[86] So much so that juror personation is perceived to be a growing problem. See S. Enright, 'Britain's reluctant jurors' NLJ (29 July 1988) 538.

[87] C. J. Miller, *Contempt of Court* (2nd edn, 1989) 405.

[88] For example, a juror in the Bulger trial (see the Appendix) criticized the decision to try the two eleven-year-olds accused in an adult court, condemning the trial as a 'process of public retribution': The Observer (14 May 1995) 3. Recall, also, the public statements made by the foreman of the jury, Mr Tim O'Malley, in the Carl Bridgewater case (see the Appendix) that, in retrospect, the jury was wrong to convict the four accused: J. Mullin, ' When truth lies bleeding' The Guardian (23 February 1994) Second Front, 2/3: and P. Foot, *Murder at the farm: who killed Carl Bridgewater?* (1997), 302–3.

[89] The foreman of the jury in an aborted criminal trial arising out of the mode of conduct of a takeover bid by Guinness plc for Distillers plc made several outspoken comments. Mrs Edna Wijeratna was not wholly critical of the conduct of the trial in a letter that she sent to *The Financial Times* in March 1992. Contrary to widespread fears about the suitability of jury trial in complex financial cases, she reported that the jurors had not found the issues in the case unduly difficult to follow. See 'Juror speaks out' NLJ (6 March 1992) 302. The background to the Guinness litigation is set out in the Appendix.

the delivery of its verdict necessarily be considered an aspect of the 'deliberations'. It was in the course of an overnight stay in a hotel that the notorious Ouija board incident occurred in *R v Young (Stephen)*.[90] The jury's deliberations being in suspense until their return to the jury room the following morning, the Court of Appeal felt that it could inquire into the incident without itself being in breach of section 8 of the Contempt of Court Act.

Where section 8 does apply, it does so irrespective of the identity or motives of the person who seeks to breach the confidentiality of the jury's deliberations. The force of this axiomatic principle of the criminal law was illustrated, in *R v Young (Stephen)*, by the Court of Appeal's reminder to itself of the danger that it too could find itself in breach of the provision. Apart from the media and academic researchers, the parties to a case could find themselves in danger of violating section 8. It was well established, even before 1981, that the Court of Appeal would not entertain a disclosure from the jury room in judging whether a verdict was unsafe or unsatisfactory.[91] The enactment of section 8 has served only to confirm that rule.[92]

Within the constraints imposed by the present law various methods have been devised for conducting (of necessity) limited research into the jury and how it works. The 'sound-shape system' designed by Robertshaw and Greenhough monitors the cadences of jurors' discussion without tracking the words themselves.[93] Its particular strength is to monitor the extent of the contributions made by different types of juror (as designated by age or gender) and the way in which factions emerge within the twelve and the manner of their interaction. An alternative method, used by McConville with the co-operation of the Lord Chancellor's Department, draws together a 'shadow jury' on the same basis as real jurors are recruited from the electoral register.[94] Taking advantage of their entitlement to attend trials as members of the public, they sit through the entire proceedings of a trial and hear exactly the same material as the real jury. At the conclusion of the hearing, however, they consider their 'verdict' in a room where their deliberations are fully observed. McConville felt at the conclusion of the experiment that there must be a high degree of correspondence between the course of proceedings in real and shadow juries since, in four out of five trials shadowed in this way, an identical result was returned by both 'juries'.

Traditionally, the jury has deliberated under conditions of *de facto* secrecy, nor is it being suggested that they should do otherwise. On the enactment of section 8, a level of *de jure* secrecy was superimposed—in much the same way (as we have seen) that the *de facto* confidentiality of private sittings of the court has been buttressed by the legal prohibitions imposed by section 12 of the Administration

---

[90] [1995] QB 324.   [91] *R v Thompson* (n 18 above).

[92] *R v Chionye* (1989) 89 Cr App R 285.

[93] P. Robertshaw and M. Greenhough, 'The Jury Sound-Shape Project: Harbinger of Things to Come?' (1993) 6 *International Journal for the Semiotics of Law* 305.

[94] M. McConville, 'Shadowing the Jury' NLJ (22 November 1991) 1588.

of Justice Act 1960. In this regard it is noteworthy that a Bill that was aimed at reforming section 8 would have retained, subject to significant exceptions, the legal prohibition that was effected by that section. The Courts (Research) Bill 1990[95] was a private member's measure introduced in the House of Commons by Dr Michael Woodcock MP. Like so many such bills, it advanced no further in the legislative process. It consisted of two principal provisions. Clause 1, being concerned with the televising of the courts, will be deferred for consideration until Chapter 9. Clause 2 is directly relevant to our present subject and must be set out at length:

(1) Section 8 of the Contempt of Court Act 1981 shall have effect subject to this section.

(2) Rules of court may provide, in relation to all or any class of legal proceedings, that authority may be given by any judge or other person specified in the rules to conduct research, in a manner approved by the person giving authority, into any specified matters affecting trial by jury, and may also make provision for amending or revoking such authority.

(3) It is a contempt of court to disclose in any report (howsoever described), made in the course of or arising out of research conducted following an authority given pursuant to rules made under subsection (2), any fact or opinion relating to any matter occurring, or alleged to have occurred, in the course of the deliberation of a jury in any legal proceedings, in such manner as to identify the particular case, or any party or witness or circumstances, or to enable any of them to be identified.[96]

This suggested revision of section 8 embodied two elements. The first was that any disclosure that failed to respect the anonymity of particular proceedings ran the danger of incurring contempt liability. The anonymity of party and witness, too, would be protected—though surely only *ex abundanti cautela*. Strangely, however, that of the individual juror was not. The second was the requirement of prior licensing, whether by judge or other designated person, of the conduct of the research. The two elements were to be cumulative: even if a disclosure were to protect the various identities listed in subclause (3), it would still fall foul of the law if the required prior authorization had not been obtained.

The thrust of the Bill, with its emphasis throughout on 'research', was the breach of the confidences of the jury room in a systematic way, in contrast to the haphazardly received, and possibly one-sided, account that came into the public domain in (for example) the *Associated Newspapers* case. That disclosure must be of the fruits of 'research' would appear to embody, in itself, a balanced account of the findings. Hence there would be inbuilt safeguards analogous to

---

[95] Ordered to be Printed, 5 December 1990.

[96] Subclause (4) went on to stipulate that, as long as an authorization granted under sub-cl (2) was in force, the actions or omissions of any person purporting to act pursuant to such authorization, together with responding to requests for information from such person, were protected from liability for contempt of court. There were to be two exceptions: where the actions or omissions took place 'in bad faith'; and where the person, knowingly or recklessly, divulged any of the items of information prohibited by sub-cl (3).

those of fairness and accuracy that are central to the reporting of proceedings that take place in open court.

What form would such 'research' take? Presumably, a provision such as sub-clause (3) could not be taken as authorizing the presence of the researcher in the jury room itself. Such a state of affairs, as at present, would taint the validity of the verdict. There would appear, then, to be two possibilities. One would be the introduction in the jury room of audio recording equipment (combined, possibly, with its video recording equivalent). The other would be the systematic questioning of jurors as soon as possible after the conclusion of the trial in the hope that memories of what transpired in the jury room would not have begun to fade.[97] While it is commonplace to hear of the need for jury research, rarely is there any indication of the form that it is to take once the barrier created by section 8 has been partly or wholly removed. Consider, for example, the pronouncements of the Royal Commission on Criminal Justice chaired by Viscount Runciman.[98] In the body of its report it refers to the disqualification on jury service by reason of having a criminal record of certain defined types, and then proceeds to wonder aloud what sort of role is played by the juror who has previously undergone criminal conviction.[99] Is it different from that of the average juror? And, if so, in what way? Again, at the very beginning of the report there is a call for the reform of section 8 so that data might be gathered with a view to considering the following matters: whether there should be a literacy requirement demanded of jurors; whether the age limit for jury service should be raised; and whether the procedures governing majority verdicts should be changed.[100] Some of these issues relate to the functioning of the jury as a collective body. More commonly, however, they bear on the performance of individual jurors: are certain categories of juror impeded (by age, illiteracy, previous contact with the criminal justice system) from proper performance of the duties of that position? Quite clearly, to research such questions adequately would require very detailed knowledge of the course of deliberations in particular trials.

So much for the issue of 'research'. The other focal point in clause 2 of the Woodcock Bill is the person—'any judge or other person specified'—who would be empowered to authorize the necessary intrusion into the confidentiality of the jury room. Any impression that it is the presiding judge at the trial who is so intended would be dispelled by the decision in *R v McCluskey*.[101] After verdict and sentence such a judge is devoid of jurisdiction. It is the consent of the Court of Appeal that is required.[102]

---

[97] Incidentally, would former jurors have been obliged to submit to such questioning? Would it have been treated as another aspect of jury service?

[98] Cm 2263.   [99] ibid, ch 8 ('The Trial'), paras 58 and 59: and, also, recommendation no 218.

[100] ibid, ch 1, para 8: and, also, recommendation no 1.   [101] (1994) 98 Cr App R 216.

[102] *R v Young (Stephen)* [1995] QB 324.

The approach exemplified in the Woodcock Bill, if implemented, would have fallen between the two extremes of a blanket criminal prohibition and the complete absence of any prohibition. Clearly, where qualifying conditions are imposed before access may be obtained to the secrets of the jury room, questions will arise as to the precise meaning of those conditions. Comparison can be made with the situation in the United States, where post-trial interviews with jurors are commonplace.[103] In this respect, as with the televising of the hearing phase, material that has been obtained under the more open system of the United States is available for public dissemination in Britain and countries that place greater store by the secrecy of the jury room.[104]

From time to time, even in Britain, a person publishes an account of his or her experience as a juror. A perusal of these accounts illustrates that, even within the constraints imposed by section 8, a great deal of information about the working of the jury is being made public, even though some such publications are not sufficiently structured to qualify as 'research'. It is quite clear, also, that these accounts do take care to observe the spirit, if not the letter, of section 8. For example, in one account published in *The Times*[105] the author did not identify either the defendant or the venue, indicating only that the charge was one of indecent assault.[106] Although a unanimous verdict of not guilty was returned, the account did disclose that, at the outset of their deliberations, those jurors who supported this decision were 'in a tiny minority'—a phrase not sufficiently specific to fall foul of the prohibition imposed by section 8 on the revelation of 'votes cast'. A rather different account, one that covers the full trial of a kidnapping case, was given in *The Juryman's Tale*[107] by a professional journalist who had been summoned for jury service. This case was identified by name and venue. However, references to the other jurors (whose background, occupation, hobbies etc. are given in some detail) are anonymous. The page immediately following the title page states succinctly: 'The names of the jurors in the case *R v Korkolis* have been changed.' The account of the jury deliberations records that an initial sounding of opinions 'was absolutely inconclusive'.[108] Although, as was publicly known,

---

[103] See, for example, J. Mitford, *The Trial of Dr Spock* (1969) 220–35, for an account of the jury's deliberations by three of the jurors in the trial of Dr Spock. The famous writer on child rearing was convicted together with several co-defendants of conspiring to incite violation of the draft law in protest against the Vietnam war. S. J. Adler, *The Jury: Disorder in the Courts* (1994) is a journalist's probing of the American jury on the basis of interviews conducted with the jurors in a cross-sample of six cases. A radically different type of study is the collection of theoretical essays in R. Hastie (ed), *Inside the Juror: The Psychology of Juror Decision Making* (1993).

[104] Particular mention should be made of a documentary, called *Innocence Lost*, broadcast on BBC2 in May 1994. This consisted in part of interviews with jurors who had tried a child sexual abuse case in North Carolina in 1992. Several of the jury complained of pressures from fellow jurors to return a verdict of guilty, and felt that the evidence did not warrant such a conclusion.

[105] C. Kane, 'BritPop in the jury room' The Times (10 June 1998) 18.

[106] In view of the nature of the charge, the Sexual Offences (Amendment) Act 1992 prohibited disclosure of the identity of the complainant.

[107] T. Grove, *The Juryman's Tale* (1998).   [108] ibid. 178.

the judge indicated that he would accept a majority verdict, some sixteen hours of discussion concluded in a unanimous verdict of guilty on every count.

As these publications vividly illustrate, there is still much material to be gleaned about the workings of the jury system even within the constraints imposed by section 8 of the Contempt of Court Act 1981.

8

The Reporting of Judicial Proceedings

1. RECORDING AND REPORTING

This chapter examines various matters relating to the reporting of trials, in particular the privileges against liability under the civil and the criminal law that are conceded in order to facilitate such reporting. It should be noted, at the outset, that the term 'reporting' can be used in various senses in order to describe markedly different activities.

The first—the sense in which it is used throughout the greater part of this chapter—refers to the process of disseminating as many particulars of the trial as might be of possible interest to those who were not present in the courtroom. In this regard the focus is predominantly, though not exclusively, on the position of the mass media. The second sense is concerned with the recording of the trial for the official purpose of establishing an authoritative account of the proceedings. Apart from matters of public record, such an account may well prove of immediate value in recording possible defects in the conduct of the trial for the purposes of lodging an appeal. Thirdly, there is an intermediate sense in which the term is used: that of law reporting, by which cases of possible value as precedents are drawn together in various series of law reports. The overwhelming emphasis in this regard is on recording and disseminating the decisions of the higher courts.

It is necessary, at this point, to give a brief account of reporting in the second and third senses since these functions cannot be entirely separated from a discussion of reporting in the first sense.

The compilation of an authoritative record of the words spoken in a trial is a task which is undertaken as a matter of course. On the rare occasion when there is a failure in this regard, the consequences for the administration of justice are potentially very serious. In many criminal cases, for example, appeals against conviction are based on the allegedly faulty terms of the summing-up to the jury. Yet if there is no authoritative record of the summing-up, and moreover there is disagreement as to what was said on that occasion, the consequence in certain circumstances may be the quashing of a conviction. Such was the outcome in regard to one of the two accused in *R v Payne, R v Spillane*.[1] The shorthand writer who was present in court at the point of the summing-up to the jury was not specifically trained in the needs of trial recording, with the result that the record of that phase of the proceedings was totally inadequate (consisting of a mere

---

[1] [1971] 3 All ER 1146.

three pages for a summing-up that lasted for an hour). The Court of Appeal took the opportunity to stress that it is the judge's duty to ensure adequate recording, whether (as usual) through a competent shorthand writer, or by an 'adequate mechanical recording', or by means of the judge's own note.

Not only must there be a reliable and authoritative record of the trial proceedings, the demands of due process require also that the record be readily available to the parties in the case. In constitutional terms this was expressed by the US Supreme Court in *Griffin v Illinois*.[2] It was a violation of the Fourteenth Amendment, the Court ruled, for a state to deny a free transcript of the trial proceedings to an indigent defendant who wished to appeal against conviction, especially since the state required a transcript to be furnished as a precondition to lodging a challenge to the conviction.

Reporting in the third sense of the term contains an element of chance. In order for a case to be reported in this way it must be selected, often from a multitude of available cases, for inclusion in a series of law reports. Law reporting for the internal purposes of the legal profession was an activity that was established well before the advent of the modern mass media.[3] It was placed on a more regular basis in 1870 with the creation of the Incorporated Council of Law Reporting for England and Wales.[4] The slight value that is attached to unreported cases means that the omission of a particular case from the principal series of reports will detract from any potential value possessed by the case by way of precedent. Instances may also be found of belated reporting of cases whose importance for the development of particular legal doctrines was perceived only some considerable time after the delivery of judgment.[5]

The function of law reporting is the dissemination of the judgment given at the conclusion of the proceedings (or, to be more precise, the proceedings at a particular level of the court structure). For nearly all practical purposes the essential points in the preceding stages (in particular, findings on disputes of fact) are summarized in the judgment. There are indications that the pronouncement of judgment in public is a precondition of the possibility of the case being reported in this sense of the term. For example, in *St Martins Property Investments Ltd v Philips Electronics (UK) Ltd*[6] Rattee J heard in chambers an appeal from the decision of a district judge. He proceeded to give judgment in open court, having been asked by the Treasury Solicitor (the Crown being a party to the proceedings) to do so since the case raised a novel point in the interpretation of the Rules of the

---

[2] 351 US 12 (1956).

[3] See generally L. W. Abbott, *Law Reporting in England 1485–1585* (1973).

[4] Considerable detail on the purposes of the institution is to be found in its contested application for charitable status: *Incorporated Council of Law Reporting for England and Wales v A-G* [1972] Ch 73.

[5] For example, the judgment in *Dorchester Finance Co Ltd v Stebbing* was reported in [1989] BCLC 498, twelve years after it was delivered in 1977. The ruling of Romer J in *Re Thomas Mortimer Ltd* in 1925 appeared only years later, both at [1964] 3 WLR 427 and as an appendage to the report of *Re Yeovil Glove Co Ltd* [1965] Ch 148, 186–192.

[6] [1995] 1 All ER 378.

Supreme Court.[7] The journalistic reporting of trials is facilitated by the grant of legal immunities that require, among other things, that the matters reported were conducted in public. It may be that the pronouncement in open court of judgment in proceedings that were conducted in private takes place with a view to conferring a similar measure of protection on law reporters. Equally, it will amount to formally placing the judgment in the public domain.

The importance of law reporting, and furthermore of making an official record of the exact course of trial proceedings, has been recognized in exempting these processes from general rules of law. The prohibition imposed by the Judicial Proceedings (Regulation of Reports) Act 1926 on the reporting of certain matters does not apply to any 'transcript of evidence' or to 'the printing or publishing of any matter in any separate volume or part of any bona fide series of law reports which does not form part of any other publication and consists solely of reports of proceedings in courts of law'.[8] Equally, the use of tape recorders in court, though prohibited in general, is permitted for 'the making or use of sound recordings for purposes of official transcripts of proceedings'.[9] The impermissibility of the use of such devices on the part of members of the public and the press has meant that, in the case of the lengthier documents read out in court, they must rely on the co-operation of one of the parties to the action to gain sight of the text.[10]

The central role played by the doctrine of precedent would appear to require that the reports of decided cases be available on equal terms to all persons interested, even if such reports be abbreviated so as to focus attention on the relevant points of law. This takes place as a matter of course so far as the decisions of the higher courts are concerned. It has not always been so in regard to the decisions of specialist tribunals.[11] Proceedings before the General and Special Commissioners, previously held in private, have now been rendered public. The loss of privacy for the appellant taxpayer has been offset by the availability to taxpayers in general and their professional advisers of a series of decisions which, while technically non-binding, provide some indication of the way in which particular classes of appeal are decided.

2. SOME GENERAL CONSIDERATIONS ON PRIVILEGE

It should be noted, at the outset, that the landmark decision of *Scott v Scott*[12] was itself rendered in the context of a dispute about the 'reporting' of judicial

---

[7] ibid. 379.   [8] Judicial Proceedings (Regulation of Reports) Act 1926, s 1(4).

[9] Contempt of Court Act 1981, s 9(4).

[10] It was the furnishing of such a text that gave rise to the problems in *Home Office v Harman* [1982] 1 All ER 532.

[11] See A. Nicol 'Immigrants: not so much what they tell as what they can't remember' The Times (25 October 1982) 10, on the subject of immigration law. 'Few judgments and even fewer administrative appeals are reported; immigration specialists trade private transcripts like rare stamps.'

[12] [1913] AC 417.

proceedings. Mrs Scott, it will be recalled, sought to vindicate her reputation in the eyes of her husband's relatives by reporting to them parts of her nullity suit. This was far removed from reporting in the sense in which we mean it to be understood in the greater part of this chapter. Mrs Scott was not a representative of the press: she was the petitioner in the case, one of the *personae* of the trial. The recipients of the 'report' were not simply people who found it more convenient to read an account of the case than to attend in person: they would have been barred from attendance by reason of the decision to hold the proceedings *in camera*. Most remarkably, the 'report' was not compiled by Mrs Scott; it took the form of the court transcript, which both she and her solicitor arranged to be seen by those for whom it was not intended.

The *Scott* case vividly illustrates the potential links between the several aspects of reporting as identified in the previous section. It is not difficult to imagine why it was in the particular form of making available the official transcript that Mrs Scott decided to effect her 'report' of the proceedings. The transcript would be viewed as a definitive record which, unlike any account of her own making, could not be challenged for possible bias. For most jounalistic purposes such a report would clearly be too long and technical (even if it were available) to be suitable for use as a direct means of informing the public. Nevertheless, as one of the judgments of the House of Lords in *Scott v Scott* made very clear, any 'report' of proceedings that took place in secret—irrespective of its form—would be published without the benefit of the standard immunities from liability in defamation and contempt of court.[13]

'Reports' of trials take many diverse forms. They may appear as books written by one of the participants in the proceedings, such as the presiding judge[14] or the accused.[15] More usually, however, trial reporting has been the preserve of the mass media. But even accounts of trials that are published in newspapers may be supplied on an exclusive basis by one of the *personae* of the trial. The most problematic situation is that where the account is furnished, for payment, by a witness. Most usually, the exclusive account given by a witness will partly replicate, and partly extend beyond, the evidence that he gave in open court. Only in the former respect, of course, are such accounts protected by privilege. However, the newspaper account that is limited to reproducing what was said in court scarcely justifies the payments that such accounts command. This explains the considerable concern to which the practice of payment to witnesses

---

[13] [1913] AC 417, 452, per Lord Atkinson.

[14] As, most notably, in Lord Devlin's account of the trial of Dr John Bodkin Adams: P. Devlin, *Easing the Passing* (1986).

[15] As in J. Caunt, *An Editor on Trial* (1947), an account of *R v Caunt*. This was a prosecution for seditious libel arising out of an allegedly racist piece published by Caunt in the *Morecambe and Heysham Visitor*. The book consists of the official shorthand transcript of the trial, which attracted a great deal of interest both in the UK and abroad, together with a brief account of the background to the prosecution.

has given rise.[16] The danger is that witnesses might be tempted to withhold testimony from the court (thus making it available for exclusive use by the newspaper concerned). Or they might embellish and render more sensational evidence that they have already given. An approach to the witness prior to the trial may also lead to the evidence being 'rehearsed'. Particularly suspect is the common arrangement whereby the sum payable to the witness varies according to the outcome of the trial, a verdict of guilty attracting a larger fee.[17] At present, the matter is regulated by the Press Complaints Commission's Code of Practice, whereby payment to witnesses or potential witnesses is not to be made 'except where the material concerned ought to be published in the public interest and there is an overriding need to make or promise to make a payment for this to be done'.[18] The drafting of this rule appears to concede that payment, no less than publicity, may act as a means of eliciting additional testimony from witnesses.

From this point onward, our concern is with reporting in the traditional sense, as an activity conducted by the mass media on the basis of accounts compiled by their own staff. It is worth making some general observations about the conflicting considerations that are present in this activity. Public access to the courtroom has been stressed as one of the central facets of open justice. A derivative aspect of that principle requires that accounts of the proceedings should be available to those who did not attend in person. The difficulty, however, is that reports of what was said in court may themselves act as a vehicle by which additional wrongs are committed. A report of a defamatory statement made by (for example) a witness will be actionable, on general principle, as a republication of the statement. The importance of the defamation privilege attaching to trial reports is amply borne out by comparison of the distribution figures of even the smaller newspapers with the typical numbers of persons gathered together in the courtroom to hear the words of the witness at first hand. Likewise, a published report of matters disclosed in the trial of X may prejudice the position of Y, against whom legal proceedings are due to commence in the near future.

Defamation and contempt of court are our predominant concerns. However, any trial involving speech that may be actionable as a tort or punishable as a crime is, in principle, in need of a similar reporting privilege. Such an example is provided by incitement to racial hatred. This crime has undergone three statutory formulations.[19] In the last two forms it has been accompanied by an extensive

---

[16] See, for example, the Second Report of the National Heritage Committee, Session 1996–97: *Press Activity Affecting Court Cases*.

[17] Various arrangements were made for the payment of five witnesses in the case of Rosemary West (see the Appendix for details of the case). The existence of the arrangements was unsuccessfully advanced as a ground of appeal against conviction: *R v West* [1996] 2 Cr App R 374, and B. Masters, *'She must have known': The Trial of Rosemary West* (1997) 365 and 372.

[18] Press Complaints Commission Code of Practice, para 16 (i).

[19] As the Race Relations Act 1965, s 6; the Race Relations Act 1976, s 70; and the cluster of offences contained in Part III of the Public Order Act 1986.

reporting privilege. In its present form the terms of the privilege stipulate: 'Nothing in this Part applies to a fair and accurate report of proceedings publicly heard before a court or tribunal exercising judicial authority where the report is published contemporaneously, as soon as publication is reasonably practicable and lawful.'[20]

As will shortly be seen, this provision closely follows the drafting of the equivalent privileges in the spheres of defamation and contempt. The problem in all these areas of the law is not simply that the reporting of trial proceedings substantially increases the number of persons to whose notice the offending words are brought. Those, whether *personae* of the trial or members of the public, who are present in the courtroom during the trial are also in danger of succumbing to the allegedly harmful effects of the words that form the subject matter of the prosecution. They, too, may be depraved and corrupted (in the case of allegedly obscene literature) or stirred to racial hatred (in being directly exposed to racially inflammatory material). Those present in the courtroom, whether as active participants or passive spectators, are deemed susceptible to the effect of words which, if published outside the courtroom, would be actionable as defamatory. Damage will be done to reputations as a result of words spoken by witnesses, counsel and others. This will be so even if (as in all but a small minority of cases) defamatory imputations do not form the subject matter of the trial itself, and even if (as will be apparent from the judgment or verdict) the slurs cast by a witness's testimony or the damaging claims made by counsel are rejected by the tribunal.

This explains the central importance of the immunity attaching to words written or spoken in the course of judicial proceedings.[21] It is possible to refer to this simply as the 'intra-court' defamation privilege, so as to differentiate it from the 'extra-court' privilege that comes into play once the words are reported to those who were not present in the courtroom. Statements made in the course of a trial, as on several other occasions identified by law, are the subject of absolute privilege:[22] that is, the privilege is retained even though the maker of the defamatory statement can be shown to have acted as he did, knowing full well that his statement was false and calculated to injure the plaintiff's reputation. The rationale of absolute privilege is based on public policy: that the issues in a trial cannot be fully explored unless the *personae* are free to speak uninhibited by fear of even the remotest risk of exposure to liability for defamation. Quite apart from the 'chilling effect' that it would exert on words spoken by the *personae* of the trial, the availability of defamation proceedings could provide a route whereby matters decided at the trial could be opened up once again for litigation.

---

[20] Public Order Act 1986, s 26(2).

[21] In certain respects, it should be noted, the making of defamatory allegations may carry adverse consequences that are internal to the trial. For example, an accused who casts imputations on the integrity of prosecution witnesses may be thereby exposed to the possibility that the jury may be allowed to hear of his previous convictions.

[22] See, generally, Gatley on *Libel and Slander* (9th edn, 1998), 282ff.

The details of the intra-court defamation privilege need not concern us. However, some of its features need to be identified for the purpose of comparison with our principal concern, the extra-court or reporting privilege.

As may be gathered from its basic purpose, it is irrelevant whether the defamatory statement is made in proceedings conducted in private or in open court or, for that matter, in the course of some pre-trial stage (for example, in the text of the pleadings or answers to interrogatories).[23] As regards the pre-trial stages, however, there must be a sufficiently proximate link with possible court proceedings.[24] Nor does the privilege depend on the context of a formal contested hearing: it attaches to statements made in the course of *ex parte* proceedings as much as those conducted *inter partes*. Equally, it is applicable as a matter of principle (though there is no decided case on the point) to statements uttered in the privacy of the jury room.

There must, nonetheless, be firm limits to the scope of an absolute privilege. Not everything that is said in the courtroom will be protected. For example, gratuitous interjections by a witness in the course of responding to a question would probably not be privileged.[25] The structured character of trial proceedings lends itself to the ready identification of extraneous matters as compared with the nearest analogous situation, that of proceedings in Parliament. If publication of a defamatory statement in a courtroom setting is not a sufficient condition of immunity from suit, equally, it is not a necessary condition. The rationale of the privilege, as we have seen, requires that it extends to statements made for the proper initiation of judicial proceedings, provided that publication is not made to persons having no business in the conduct of the proceedings.

Finally, the privilege also extends to the conduct of quasi-judicial businesss by bodies, such as tribunals, whose functions and procedures approximate sufficiently closely to the role and methods of the courts.[26] There is no reason to repeat here the earlier discussion on the identification of bodies that are 'judicial'

[23] In *Taylor v Serious Fraud Office* [1998] 4 All ER 801 it was held that documents disclosed by the prosecution to the defence could not be used as a basis of a libel action. Apart from the immunity point, aimed at encouraging freedom of speech, there was an important policy, based on privacy, that compulsory disclosure of documents by way of discovery should take place only for the limited purpose of contesting the particular case.

[24] Such a link was held to be absent in *Waple v Surrey County Council* [1998] 1 All ER 624, where the communication was made by a local government officer seeking to recover maintenance contributions pursuant to powers granted them in the Children Act 1989. Equally, in *Daniels v Griffiths* The Times, 2 December 1997, a communication to the Parole Board was held not to be absolutely privileged, notwithstanding the similarity between the work of the Board and the sentencing function of the criminal courts.

[25] Gatley (n 22 above) para 13.11. This was clearly borne out by a case where a newspaper reported the gratuitous comment, made just after the adjournment of the proceedings: *Hughes v Western Australian* (1940) 43 WALR 12. The report of the interjection, that the solicitor for the opposite side was 'the biggest racketeer in Perth' was not privileged.

[26] A process aimed at conciliation does not qualify for absolute privilege: *Tadd v Eastwood* The Times 28 May 1983. Hirst J ruled that, while some forms of arbitration would attract absolute privilege, proceedings aimed at conciliation would not conclude in a judicial determination.

in nature.[27] Suffice it to note that, in a case that involved the disciplinary hearing by a professional association, the fact that the committee was required to conduct all its proceedings in private was used, unsuccessfully, as the basis of a submission that the committee's findings were not protected by the privilege attaching to judicial proceedings.[28]

The consideration of the 'intra-court' defamation privilege prompts the question whether there also exists an 'intra-court contempt privilege'. Statements made in the courtroom are capable of prejudicing the outcome of the trial, in the same way that they may damage the reputation of particular individuals. As between the two areas of defamation and contempt, however, there is a fundamental difference of approach. In common with the stance taken by English law towards prejudicial material published outside the courtroom, the overwhelming emphasis is on the process of prevention. Principal among the techniques of prevention is the *voir dire* hearing. This is a phase of the trial (sometimes known as a 'trial within a trial') in which issues of the admissibility of prejudicial items of evidence, such as confessions or previous convictions, are tested. The *voir dire* is conducted in the absence of the jury and combined with reporting restrictions, the point being that the material should not come to the jury's attention if the ruling should go against admissibility.

As regards the extra-court privilege that forms our principal concern, at common law there has long existed an immunity against liability for defamation in the reporting of judicial proceedings.[29] The rationale of the privilege is traditionally based on the right of the public to attend in person at the trial in question. In *McDougall v Knight*[30] Lord Halsbury LC put the matter thus:

> ... the ground on which the privilege of accurately reporting what takes place in a court of justice is based is that judicial proceedings are in this country public, and that the publication of what takes place there, even though matters defamatory to an individual may thus obtain wider circulation than they otherwise would, is allowed because such publication is merely enlarging the area of the court, and communicating to all that which all had the right to know.[31]

The idea of a courtroom that has been 'enlarged' by the act of reporting is, in many respects, a fiction. For example, the privilege at common law is qualified only, and therefore defeasible on proof of malice on the part of the person who published the report. Yet the recipients of such reports, had they themselves been seated in the public gallery, would have heard words that were cloaked in the protection of absolute privilege.

The extent to which reports of foreign court proceedings are covered by the common law privilege merits particular attention since it has provided an illuminating

---

[27] See Chapter 1, section 5, C, above.   [28] *Addis v Crocker* [1961] 1 QB 11.
[29] See D. A. Elder, *The Fair Report Privilege* (1988) for a detailed treatment of the American aspects of this subject (including the privileged reporting of bodies apart from courts).
[30] (1889) 14 App Cas 194.   [31] ibid. 200.

point for reconsideration of the purposes served by public trial. The matter came before Pearson J in *Webb v Times Publishing Co Ltd*[32] in the context of a report published in *The Times* of criminal proceedings conducted against a British subject in a Swiss court. The former wife of the accused, Hume, argued that the report defamed her. The basis of her claim was as follows. Some years earlier, Hume had been acquitted by a British court of the murder of one Setty. The plaintiff, who at that time was married to Hume, testified in his favour and stated (among other things) that she had never met Setty. In the course of the proceedings before the Swiss court, Hume claimed that a child born to him and the plaintiff during their marriage had been fathered by Setty. It was the reporting of this allegation by the defendants that formed the gist of the plaintiff's claim, in that it implied both that she had had an adulterous relationship and that she had committed perjury in the proceedings before the British court.

The defendants pleaded that their report of the trial proceedings in Switzerland was protected, at common law, by qualified privilege. In the absence of any decisive authority in regard to reports of trials conducted abroad, Pearson J sought to derive the applicable rule from a consideration of general principle. For this purpose, five different aspects of the reporting privilege were identified.[33]

First, courts are open to the public. The reports of their proceedings should consequently be freely available. Secondly, the administration of justice is a matter of legitimate public concern. In this regard the press performs the valuable function of setting before the public the material on the basis of which it may monitor the standards of performance of the courts. Thirdly, it is beneficial that the public receive education in matters relating to the administration of the legal system. Fourthly, persons affected by the reporting of a particular trial may well be better off with fair and accurate reports than with inaccurate rumours circulating about the case. Fifthly, the advantages to the public were to be balanced against the injury suffered by the person defamed.

What is immediately striking about this account is the explicit, though qualified, recognition in the last two considerations of the interests of the person whose reputation risks being damaged by the institution of public trial. The fourth consideration is of limited significance since, in the *Webb* case as in so many other cases, the burden of the plaintiff's complaint was precisely that the trial report was fair and accurate: the grievance related to the substance of what was said in court, not to the manner of its reporting. Indeed, an account that is partial or inaccurate may well be more favourable to the plaintiff, depending (of course) on the exact words spoken at the trial.

The force of the considerations listed by Pearson J is inevitably diminished when applied to reports of the proceedings of a foreign court, as compared with the proceedings of its English counterpart. The procedures of a Swiss court, for example, are unlikely to be better organized as a result of their exposure to a

---

[32] [1960] 2 QB 535.   [33] ibid. 559–562.

British audience. Equally, such an audience is likely to have, at the very most, only a passing interest in the way in which justice is administered in other countries. Surprisingly, however, there is no explicit recognition, among the first three considerations, of the possibility that the material unfolded in a foreign courtroom may have a direct bearing on the accountability of the British government for its actions. A case very much in point is the opening episode in the series of *Spycatcher* cases, litigated in New South Wales, Australia, and followed with great interest in the United Kingdom.[34] Equally in point is the case of the inquest proceedings conducted in Gibraltar consequent on the killing by the SAS of three members of the IRA in March 1988. At the other extreme, there are cases which have received a great deal of interest, despite their having no bearing whatsoever on the public affairs of the United Kingdom. Rather, it is the identity of the accused, whether he be a famous sportsman (O. J. Simpson) or scion of prominent political dynasty (William Kennedy Smith),[35] that has provided the focus of attention—facilitated, in some cases, by the availability of television footage from a jurisdiction that permits such a form of reporting.

Applying the five considerations that he had identified to the case before him, Pearson J ruled that the defendants were in the circumstances protected by privilege. The test, he stated, is that '[o]ne has to look for a legitimate and proper interest as contrasted with an interest which is due to idle curiosity or a desire for gossip'.[36] The presence of such a legitimate interest was established by the fact that the accused in the Swiss trial was a British subject and that his statements in the course of those proceedings tended to cast doubt on the correctness of his acquittal for the murder of Setty. At first sight, the suggestion that the plaintiff had committed adultery would appear to be a matter of no proper concern to the public and therefore not covered by the privilege. In the circumstances, however, it appeared to provide Hume with a motive for murdering Setty and therefore was inextricably linked with a matter of undoubted concern to the British public.

The reasoning of the court in *Webb v Times Publishing Co Ltd*, as we have seen, explicitly recognizes that there are legitimate private interests that may well be compromised by a thoroughgoing attachment to public trial, and that there may be instances where the private interests should prevail. Why, then, is a similar approach not taken to the reporting privilege as regards the proceedings of English courts? Pearson J addressed the matter in this way:

As regards English proceedings, it is desirable to have a simple rule, and it is not unreasonable to say that all persons living in England have a real interest in, and are concerned with, anything that happens in any part of the country in the administration of their law in any of their courts.[37]

---

[34] *A-G v Heinemann Publishers* [1989] 2 FSR 349.
[35] See the Appendix for brief summaries of these two cases.   [36] [1960] 2 QB 535, 569.
[37] [1960] 2 QB 535, 562.

Although neither point is developed, there are two reasons for the simple, unequivocal rule in regard to the reporting of English proceedings. It would be difficult for news organizations to anticipate how any court that eventually tried the defamation issue would strike the balance between public good and private interest. This is rather more convincing than the second reason that attributes to all persons residing in England a genuine interest in the business transacted in any English court. Certainly, they possess an interest in—by which is meant they have a legitimate concern for—the standard of performance of every such court. Yet the same could not be said of the subject matter of the disputes that come before such courts.

The question needs to be asked whether the privileges granted to the media in reporting trial matters tilt the scales excessively in favour of the public interest. An uncompromising standard of open justice is capable of doing untold damage to the reputations of those who, in two different ways, figure in the business of the courts.

First, such persons may be the object of only a passing mention in the course of a trial. This is borne out by the *Webb* case, where the libel action was founded on the reporting of matters which were far from central to the issues before the Swiss court. More recently, a respected Member of Parliament, Mr Greville Janner, was the subject of allegations concerning sex abuse in the trial of one Beck. Mr Janner complained bitterly of the legal arrangements that made such an attack possible: 'Surely it must be wrong for people who have no part in a trial to be opened to venomous and preposterous attacks with no remedy, with no recompense and, above all, with no right of reply.'[38]

Secondly, and more usually, adverse publicity stems from an appearance in the courts as an accused. Publicity has been identified as one of the 'social consequences' of conviction[39]—it could equally have been identified as a consequence of appearing as an accused—the degree of publicity varying according to the seriousness of the crime, the presence of any unique or bizarre features in the case, and the social standing of the accused. However, unlike the instances in the first category, the accused (like any party to a case) has the opportunity, within the trial setting, of refuting any imputations on his character.

From time to time disquiet has been expressed about the possible unfairness of a system that permits unrestrained reporting in the media of criminal convictions, particularly those lying at the lower end of the scale of seriousness. In Chapter 5 consideration was given to the arguments in favour of anonymity for the accused until such time (if any) as he is convicted. Proposed as an adjunct of the presumption of innocence, the logic of this suggestion would require its application to every criminal charge. In the present context, however, publicity is seen as an undoubted form of punishment. In contrast to the argument based on the

---

[38] The Times (4 December 1991) 5.
[39] J. P. Martin and D. Webster, *The Social Consequences of Conviction* (1971) ch 3.

presumption of innocence, the force of the view that publicity is an element of punishment varies according to the gravity of the offence of which a person has been declared guilty. While public knowledge will add little to a lengthy custodial sentence, in the case of minor offences of a disgraceful nature the element of publicity is likely to be experienced as a form of 'punishment' out of all proportion to even the maximum sentence allowed by law for the offence. Hence the proposal that there be controls over the reporting of convictions for minor offences (however defined). Before examining the merits and demerits of such a proposal, it is necessary to make a few points by way of further clarification.

We have isolated two potential rationales of the anonymity of the accused: as a possible requirement of the presumption of innocence; and as a means of exerting control over the punitive element, following on from conviction, that consists of public knowledge of the fact of an adverse finding on the part of the court. The second, no less than the first, would require as a matter of logic that there should be an enforced regime of anonymity during the trial itself, and even in the pre-trial period. Indeed, if any legal system were to be persuaded of the merits of both arguments for the anonymity of the accused, it would result in a possible situation where the identity of a person who has been before the criminal courts might never be disclosed. During the trial itself anonymity would be ensured, both as an adjunct of the presumption of innocence and in order to reserve the court's position on the question of possible punishment. After the conclusion of the trial, disclosure of the accused's identity would be impermissible even following a verdict of guilty if the crime in question qualified as one of the minor offences where publicity acts as a disproportionately large element in the punishment.

It is necessary, also, to emphasize that we are concerned with publicity alone. For there have been cases where a minor conviction has, purely by chance, come to the attention of the accused's employer—a fact that has resulted in the dismissal of the employee. A striking instance occurred in the late 1980s, when a school teacher was convicted in a magistrates' court of possessing cannabis. She was granted a conditional discharge in view of her explanation that she cultivated the cannabis plant for her private use as a sedative. A journalist who happened to be present at the hearing published the story. The teacher's employers, who (it appears) would not otherwise have learned of the conviction, required her to resign.[40] Again, it is to be noted, the case fell at the lower end of the scale of criminal offences. Any conviction for a serious crime would result in a custodial sentence, with obvious consequences for the person's continued availability to the employer. Whether a conviction for a lesser offence should be permitted to have further repercussions for the convicted person's job is a matter of the law of employment.

These points having been clarified, it is possible to find instances when government committees have considered the possibility of recommending a measure of

[40] *New Society* (19 February 1988) 4.

secrecy for criminal convictions. The Younger Report on Privacy[41] dismissed the suggestion for a number of reasons. It reiterated several arguments in favour of open justice, concentrating on those grouped around the values served by public knowledge of the identity of the accused and the outcome of the trial (as protecting the accused if he is acquitted and as safeguarding the reputation of others who, in the absence of firm knowledge, may be suspected of having been prosecuted). As for the possibility of shielding defendants in 'minor cases' from possible publicity, the Committee was taxed with the difficulties that such a category would create and the anomalies that could be inherent in its mode of operation. For example, would it be the maximum possible sentence, or the sentence actually imposed, that would furnish the criterion of whether publicity would be permissible? On most conceivable definitions the implementation of the suggestion would cast a protective pall over a considerable amount of the criminal business coming before the magistrates' courts. The Committee did concede, however, that there existed a problem in regard to cases, 'probably not numerous', where 'the public revelation of the offender's identity might involve a risk of severe mental disturbance to him or members of his family'.[42] The responsibility in those situations, it continued, would lie with the magistrates to ask the press not to publish the identity of the offender, failure to comply with the request furnishing grounds for complaint to the Press Council (the defunct body equivalent to the Press Complaints Commission).

This treatment of the problem would be unsatisfactory for two reasons. First, the potential scope for anonymity is greatly increased once one takes into account, not merely the risk of mental disturbance to the accused, but also the risk to any of his family. Secondly, in addition to the fundamental drawback to the jurisdiction of the Press Council that (like the present Press Complaints Commission) it was not empowered to grant specifically legal redress, its role in the area of privacy is even less useful since, with the publication of its 'adjudications', the degree of exposure suffered by the complainant would be increased.

Several years later the Royal Commission on the Press[43] returned to the issue. Some of its members hoped that it would be possible for the press—under the aegis of the Press Council again—voluntarily to refrain from the naming of defendants in magistrates' courts.[44] Being divided on the matter, the Commission confined itself to urging the government to appoint another committee to investigate the question of anonymity against the background of the claims of the public to be informed by the media about the identity of persons coming into contact with the magistrates' courts.[45]

The Royal Commission received a submission on the question from Dr Marjorie Jones who, in a book on the subject,[46] had recommended that—contrary to the

---

[41] *Report of the Committee on Privacy*: chairman Sir Kenneth Younger (Cmnd 5012, 1972) paras 169–176.

[42] ibid. para 176.   [43] Cmnd 6810, 1977.   [44] ibid. para 19.21.   [45] ibid. para 19.22.

[46] M. Jones, *Justice and Journalism* (1974).

views of the Younger Committee—three groups of persons charged with minor offences be entitled to the protection of anonymity. The groups were: those against whom proceedings had not been determined; those pronounced not guilty; and those found guilty who were then subjected only to an order of absolute or conditional discharge or were merely put on probation.[47] The first category appears to be advanced by Dr Jones in its own right, but (as we have seen) it is the inevitable concomitant of the second category. Each possesses the disadvantage that, by focusing on the verdict (of guilty) entered at the conclusion of the trial, it will tend to concentrate the mind of the public on that pronouncement alone. This will be to the detriment of attention to the course of the evidence, a full consideration of which (in some cases, at least) could create the justified impression among the public that the accused was convicted on rather flimsy grounds.

As with the proposals of the Younger Committee, Jones's approach would leave the question of the enforcement of the proposed limitations with journalists' own sense of restraint. They would remain free to depart from these informal restraints 'when they feel it right to do so',[48] an unwarranted departure providing the basis for complaint to the then Press Council. However attractive Dr Jones's scheme, therefore, there is considerable reason to doubt whether it would work in the form advanced by her. Not only would it rely on voluntary self-enforcement, it would also deploy a wholly subjective basis for departure from the general norm of silence, combined with a form of 'redress' the resort to which would result in yet more publicity for the conviction in question.

3. THE DEFAMATION REPORTING PRIVILEGE

Having made some observations in the preceding section about the tensions inherent in the free reporting of trial proceedings, especially those of a criminal nature, it is now necessary to examine in closer detail the extent of the privilege attaching to reports in the matter of defamation.

Some general points must first, however, be made. Although the privilege encompasses defamation in general, most typically the actionable publication is in written form, or in some oral form that is treated by the law as equivalent to written form, and therefore the term 'libel' will be used interchangeably with 'defamation'. An interesting question is the untested issue of how far the privilege carries over into other areas of the law that serve purposes similar to the law of defamation. One such area is that of malicious falsehood. The high costs incurred in defamation proceedings, combined with the unavailability of legal aid for bringing or defending such proceedings, led at one point to increasing resort to malicious falsehood as a means of seeking to restore one's reputation.[49]

---

[47] M. Jones, *Justice and Journalism* (1974) 163–4.   [48] ibid. 165.
[49] This practice was sanctioned by the Court of Appeal in *Joyce v Sengupta* [1993] 1 All ER 897.

As we shall note, it may be that—except where statutory language may fairly be read as barring such a possibility—the underlying rationale of the defamation privilege will be read as conferring privilege against possible liability in the related tort of malicious falsehood.

The special status granted to reports of court proceedings held in public (and, moreover, to parliamentary reports) was recognized in exempting such reports from the scope of the wide-sweeping injunctions against publication granted by Millett J in the *Spycatcher* proceedings. The terms of the order were that the defendant newspapers were not to publish any information obtained by Peter Wright as a member of the British Security Service:[50]

Provided that . . .

(2) no breach of this Order shall be constituted by the disclosure of [*sic*] publication of any material disclosed in open Court in the Supreme Court of New South Wales unless prohibited by the Judge there sitting or which, after the trial there in action no 4382 of 1985 is not prohibited from publication

(3) that no breach of this Order shall be constituted by a fair and accurate report of proceedings in (A) either House of Parliament in the United Kingdom whose publication is permitted by that House; or (B) a court of the United Kingdom sitting in public.

From a historical perspective it is not surprising that, with the rise of newspaper publication in eighteenth century Britain, the question whether newspapers enjoyed any immunity against defamation in the course of reporting court proceedings should quickly be presented.[51] In *Curry v Walter*[52] the defendant, the editor of *The Times*, was sued in regard to the entirely faithful record published in the newspaper's columns of proceedings in the Court of King's Bench. The plaintiff, a magistrate, had refused a licence for an inn. The refusal was unsuccessfully challenged in the King's Bench on the ground that the plaintiff's motive was corrupt. In reporting those proceedings, Eyre Ch J directed the jury in the libel case, the defendant was entitled to give a true account of what was said in a court of justice that was open to all to hear.

Two aspects of this landmark case are of special note. First, it is unusual in being concerned with imputations cast on the presiding judge or magistrate. In that respect, however, it accords well with one traditional rationale of open justice: that of ensuring that the judge himself is kept accountable. Secondly, it bears out the point that many a judicial failing (whether actual or alleged) is the subject of possible correction *within* the court structure itself—although, of course, we possess no means of knowing whether the Court of King's Bench was correct in dismissing the challenge to the original determination.

---

[50] The terms of the injunctions are set out in *A-G v Guardian Newspapers Ltd* [1987] 3 All ER 316, 319.

[51] On the style of reporting see J. Oldham, 'Law Reporting in the London Newspapers, 1756–1786' (1987) 31 *American Journal of Legal History* 177.

[52] 1 Bos and Pul 525, 126 ER 1046.

The common law privilege was not clearly defined. That there existed a number of gaps in the scope of this privilege was borne out, in particular, by the ruling in *Ashmore v Borthwick*.[53] In this case the libel privilege was held not to protect the report of a claim made by a prosecuting solicitor in his opening address that was not substantiated by the evidence produced in the course of the trial. The effect of this case would clearly be to discourage day-by-day reporting of trial proceedings until it became clear which allegations made by the lawyers would eventually be substantiated. It was fitting, therefore, that the defendant in that case, Sir Algernon Borthwick, should take advantage of his position as a Member of Parliament to sponsor through Parliament the Bill which became the Law of Libel Amendment Act 1888. Section 3 provided a statutory privilege for the reporting of cases:

a fair and accurate report in any newspaper of proceedings publicly heard before any court exercising judicial authority shall, if published contemporaneously with such proceedings, be privileged: provided that nothing in this section shall authorise the publication of any blasphemous or indecent matter.

The effect of the proviso relating to the publication of 'any blasphemous or indecent matter' is rather obscure. Its aim may well have been to prevent the dissemination of salacious material under the cover of the reporting of court proceedings. As has been seen in Chapter 5, this period was marked by growing concern at the unhealthy level of interest shown by the less reputable newspapers in the daily business of the divorce courts. Whatever the sanction attached by section 3 to the inclusion of the offending matter, the proviso was superseded by the enactment of the Judicial Proceedings (Regulation of Reports) Act 1926, under which it became unlawful to print or publish any indecent material 'being matter or details the publication of which would be calculated to injure public morals'.[54]

Section 3 has now been repealed and replaced by section 14(1) of the Defamation Act 1996. In essence, this is a modernized version of the earlier provision. It states simply: 'a fair and accurate report of proceedings in public before a court to which this section applies, if published contemporaneously with the proceedings, is absolutely privileged'.

The proviso relating to blasphemous and indecent matter is removed. The limitation to newspapers, which required statutory definition and (with technological progress) extension to the non-print media,[55] has also now gone. The defence applies primarily to reports of proceedings of any 'court' in the United Kingdom, a term which is defined to include 'any tribunal or body exercising the judicial power of the State'.[56] In line with the United Kingdom's membership of the principal

---

[53] (1885) 2 TLR 209. See also Jones (n 46 above) 62–3.

[54] Judicial Proceedings (Regulation of Reports) Act 1926, s 1(1)(a).

[55] Defamation Act 1952, s 9(2).

[56] Defamation Act 1996, s 14(3). cf. the Defamation Act 1952, s 8, which stipulated that s 3 of the Law of Libel Amendment Act 1888 'shall apply and apply only to courts exercising judicial authority within the United Kingdom'.

European organizations, the privilege also encompasses the proceedings of the European Court of Justice and the European Court of Human Rights.[57]

Mention should also be made of those reports of court proceedings that are protected by qualified privilege. Unlike the foregoing categories, their protected status can be removed on proof of malice. Section 15 of the 1996 Act, in combination with Schedule 1 thereto, confers such lesser protection on a variety of reports and statements. Most relevant to our theme are the items: '[a] fair and accurate report of proceedings in public before a court anywhere in the world'; and '[a] notice or advertisement published by or on the authority of a court, or of a judge or officer of a court, anywhere in the world'.

A noteworthy qualification to the protection extended to the material listed in Schedule 1 is to be found in section 15(3). The protection conferred by qualified privilege is inapplicable to 'the publication to the public, or a section of the public, of matter which is not of public benefit'. The terms of the privilege conferred by section 15, as already noted, extend to reports of proceedings 'before a court anywhere in the world'—a phrase which, on its face, includes the United Kingdom. As a matter of practice, any person sued in respect of a report of a trial conducted in the United Kingdom would be loath to rely on section 15 when a stronger defence would be available under section 14. Accordingly, section 15 is likely to be deployed only in regard to reports of foreign cases. To what extent has this new provision overtaken and superseded the ruling in *Webb v Times Publishing Co Ltd*? In that case, it will be recalled, the application of the five criteria identified by Pearson J led to the conclusion that the defendant's publication was protected by qualified privilege. Now, by contrast, the reporting of foreign trials is protected in this way, subject to the conditions (of fairness, accuracy, etc.) listed in Schedule 1, provided that section 15(3) does not come into play. There are several striking features about this subsection. First, it applies to a publication 'to the public or a section of the public'. This contrasts sharply with the element of defamation that requires mere publication of the material in question. Therefore, the wider dissemination of the material that constitutes publication to the public, or a section thereof, is required to meet the standard of public 'concern' or ' benefit'. Any lesser dissemination is not required to meet this standard in order to qualify as an occasion of qualified privilege. Secondly, if section 15 will be deployed predominantly in regard to the reporting of foreign court proceedings, which country's yardstick is to supply the applicable standard of public concern or benefit: the United Kingdom, or the country providing the seat of the trial? The better view may well be that, in partial continuance of the ruling in *Webb*, it is the former which will prevail in the (not unlikely) event of a divergence between the two.

As already stated, there is nothing in the words of section 15 and Schedule 1 of the Defamation Act 1996 that would make these inapplicable to the reports of the

---

[57] Rather less obviously, the proceedings of various international criminal tribunals are also privileged.

United Kingdom courts. Section 15(4)(b) states that nothing in the section is to be 'construed . . . as limiting or abridging any privilege subsisting apart from this section'. This would seem to preserve, not only the privilege conferred by the immediately preceding section, but also that which has long been available at common law. In view of this multiplicity of sources of privilege, it would be useful to compare their principal features.

The main point of contrast between the privileges conferred by section 14, on the one hand, and those available at common law and under section 15, on the other, lies in the fact that the last two can be defeated if the report is shown to have been made with malice. Indeed, the presence of malice has a particular bearing on the recent use of the tort of malicious falsehood, which, as already noted, fulfils many of the same purposes as the law of defamation. What would be the scope for extending the immunities enjoyed by reports of judicial proceedings to actions for malicious falsehood? The difficulty with the statutory forms of privilege is that their wording—not to mention their location in statutes devoted to defamation—appears to restrict them to proceedings for libel and slander only. The common law privilege, on the other hand, might well be so available, since it is not stated in canonical form and lies open to development in accordance with what may be perceived to be its basic rationale: the facilitation of the vicarious presence of the public. Yet it must also be borne in mind that the common law privilege, being qualified, is defeasible on proof of malice—which is also an element of the tort of malicious falsehood.

A second respect in which the various defences differ is on the question whether, in order to be privileged, the report must be published 'contemporaneously' with the proceedings covered. The defences group differently in this regard: section 14 is the odd one out, being alone in requiring this element. Contemporaneous report is required as the *quid pro quo* for the protection afforded by absolute privilege. Although that section—unlike its predecessor in the Law of Libel Amendment Act 1888—is not specifically designated as available only to newspapers, as a matter of practice it is the media that benefit most from its protection. Section 14, moreover, specifically addresses the difficulty posed by the issuing of orders that impose delays on reporting. Where reporting is required to be postponed pursuant to an order made under section 4(2) of the Contempt of Court Act 1981, the report is treated as published contemporaneously 'if it is published as soon as practicable after publication is permitted'.[58] As a matter of common sense, it could scarcely be otherwise. It would inflict a double disadvantage on the media if their reporting of a case were ordered to be postponed and, as a result of compliance with the order, they found that they had lost the benefit of a reporting privilege on the sole ground that the report was not published contemporaneously with the proceedings.

---

[58] Defamation Act 1996, s 14(2).

In many respects, however, the terms of the various privileges are identical, requiring that the report be fair and accurate and that the proceedings should have taken place in public. This is not the place to give a detailed account of these requirements. It is appropriate only to emphasize those aspects that have a particular bearing on the themes of this book.

Take the element of accuracy. In the first section of this chapter we considered, in general terms, the process of making an official recording of the words spoken at the trial. This activity takes on a heightened importance where, as in the present context, rendering an accurate report is a vital element in gaining the protection of privilege for one's account. The events in *R v Brighton County Court, ex p Westminster Press Ltd*[59] illustrate the difficulties that can occur in the absence of an accessible and authoritative account of the trial that has been reported. The applicants, owners of a local newspaper, published a report together with a feature article about an unsuccessful suit for assault and false imprisonment. The plaintiff in that suit brought proceedings for libel against the newspaper owners, who entered a defence that the items in question were protected by reporting privilege. In the absence of an official transcript, the judge who tried the reported proceedings stated that he would furnish his own notes only in response to a joint request from the parties to that case. The plaintiff being unwilling to join in making such a request, the defendants in the libel proceedings were driven to bringing an application for judicial review to compel the judge to produce a record of the case over which he had presided. The application was unsuccessful. The only legal duty of any relevance was that of a judge to furnish a note of the proceedings for the limited purpose of pursuing an appeal.[60]

On the issue of fairness, there has been a certain amount of case law, which it would serve no useful purpose to expound here.[61] A number of points about the issue of fairness, nevertheless, do require emphasis.

To begin with, it is the report of the trial itself which must be fair in order to be privileged. The decision to select one case rather than another for reporting is not, in itself, one that the law requires to be taken fairly. Whenever selectivity is required (because of considerations such as the constraints of space), grievance will be felt by those defendants whose cases have been selected for reporting. Indeed, Dr Jones records that, during the 1920s, editors of provincial newspapers were unduly sensitive to charges of bias in their selection of cases and responded to such charges by developing the practice of publishing an account of every case heard in the local courts.[62] Clearly, the larger the catchment area the greater the difficulty in following this practice, which in any event was impossible for the national newspapers to adopt. The inevitable result was that cases would be selected for report on the basis of news interest alone. Even now, however, it is not always so. There are instances where local newspapers, by way of response to

---

[59] [1990] 2 All ER 732.   [60] Under the County Courts Act 1984, s 80.
[61] See Gatley (n 22 above) para 13.34.   [62] Jones (n 46 above) 86–7.

a serious social problem, have systematically reported convictions in respect of certain offences. Prominent in this regard is the 'Gallery of Shame' carried from time to time by the *Manchester Evening News*. This is a list of the names and addresses, together with the sentences passed, of persons who have recently been convicted in the local courts of a particular category of crime. In some instances this information is accompanied by photographs of the accused.[63] The column was started in regard to convictions for drunken driving.[64] After several years it was extended to 'kerb crawling'. The first group of men to be so 'named and shamed' in this new initiative[65] underwent the additional disgrace of having their names carried in *The Times*.[66]

Alternatively, the element of unfairness may relate to the reporting of an unfair allegation made within the trial itself. When such a slur is cast, it is not actionable since it is covered by the intra-court privilege. If reported, the damage is magnified considerably since it reaches a significantly greater audience. The problem has reached such proportions now that it has been addressed by the legislature. The traditional response to a defamatory remark made in Parliament, namely a challenge to the Member of Parliament to repeat the allegation on an occasion that is not covered by privilege, is not apt for use in the context of defamation in the course of a trial. The issue of such an invitation, where the trial is in a criminal matter and has not yet been concluded, is likely to be construed as a possible contempt of court on the part of the person issuing the challenge. Moreover, rarely will a participant in a trial have the degree of access to the media that is enjoyed by a Member of Parliament. Also, in those instances where the defamatory remark emanates from an accused who is convicted, conditions of incarceration will naturally limit still further his avenues for repeating the allegation in question.

It should be added that there exist disciplinary restraints on the casting of imputations on persons in court under cover of defamation privilege. In recognition of the extremely damaging effects of such imputations, the Code of Conduct of the Bar of England and Wales imposes a number of restrictions on the conduct of barristers while conducting proceedings in court. A member of the Bar must, if possible, avoid 'the naming in open Court of third parties whose character would thereby be impugned'.[67] Nor may counsel put questions or make statements which are calculated to 'vilify' or 'insult' either a witness or

---

[63] The taking of these photographs in an area which might be construed as part of the precincts of the court is, however, fraught with legal difficulty. See Chapter 9, section 2, below.

[64] This particular 'Gallery of Shame' is used especially over the Christmas and New Year periods. For examples, see Manchester Evening News (18 December 1996) 16, and (27 December 1996) 14: and Manchester Evening News (29 December 1999) 13.

[65] See Manchester Evening News (25 August 2000) 11.

[66] The Times may have acted independently on this occasion since its report, in the issue of 23 August 2000, at p. 3, predates the report of the Manchester Evening News by two days. An unfortunate member of that first group had his photograph carried in The Times in addition to the Manchester Evening News.

[67] Code of Conduct, para 610(f).

'some other person'.[68] Equally, a barrister must not, in the course of a speech, impugn a witness whom he has had the opportunity to cross-examine, unless in the course of such cross-examination the witness has had the opportunity to respond to such allegation.[69] Such rules of professional conduct afford little by way of consolation to the person whose reputation and standing have been damaged by their violation. A fundamental difficulty stems from counsel's general obligation to act in accordance with his client's instructions. The Royal Commission on Criminal Justice[70] heard evidence of particularly distressing cases in which, during the course of pleas in mitigation, the accused had made hurtful allegations about other persons, most usually the victim. The hurt was greatly increased when the allegations came to be reported in the media.

Parliament responded to the problem, in the Criminal Procedure and Investigations Act 1996, by imposing restrictions on the free reporting of such allegations. The jurisdiction to curb reports is limited to allegations made in the course of submissions made during the sentencing phase, whether in the trial court or on the hearing of an appeal.[71] There is no power to restrict reporting if the slur has already been cast in the course of the preceding trial or during 'any other proceedings relating to the offence'.[72] As far as this provision is concerned, therefore, the reporting of the substantive trial may not be curbed. The allegation must be 'derogatory to a person's character' by suggesting that he has been engaged in conduct that is 'criminal, immoral or improper'. Moreover, there must be substantial grounds for believing that the slur is false or, at any rate, 'irrelevant to the sentence'.[73] The court may make either an interim or full order. A particularly remarkable feature of the latter is that it ceases to have effect after twelve months from the date of its making.[74] In any event, the making of such orders has been added to the range of orders made subject to possible challenge under section 159 of the Criminal Justice Act 1988, where it has been made in relation to a trial on indictment.[75]

The most interesting aspect of this jurisdiction is its interplay with liability for defamation. One possible approach to the problem of unwarranted slurs cast at the sentencing phase would be the removal of the protection of privilege, at any rate as far as the media are concerned. The approach taken by the legislature, however, was the creation of a number of criminal offences.[76] If a newspaper were to fall foul of these offences, that would not, in itself, result in exposure to possible libel proceedings, since the report in question would remain a report of proceedings held in open court. The choice of the word 'derogatory' rather than

---

[68] Code of Conduct, para 610(e).   [69] Code of Conduct, para 610(g).
[70] Cm 2263, 1993, ch 8.
[71] Criminal Procedure and Investigations Act 1996, s 58(1), (2).
[72] Criminal Procedure and Investigations Act 1996, s 58(5).
[73] Criminal Procedure and Investigations Act 1996, s 58(4).
[74] Criminal Procedure and Investigations Act 1996, s 58(8)(c).
[75] Criminal Procedure and Investigations Act 1996, s 61(6).
[76] Contained in the Criminal Procedure and Investigations Act 1996, s 60.

defamatory is striking, and could eventually attract an amount of technical case law to rival the latter term. The chosen term could, indeed, prove wider than the concept of defamation. Whatever their rival merits, to base this jurisdiction on the familiar terminology of libel and slander would be difficult to reconcile with the limited duration of orders made with a view to protecting the reputation of the person attacked.

4. PUBLIC ACCESS TO TRIAL DOCUMENTATION

This chapter has been concerned, thus far, with the recording and reporting of trials as a whole. Sometimes, however, the focus of interest of a member of the public is not the whole trial but a particular document which has figured in the proceedings. The document might be one which comes into existence only for the purposes of the case (the pleadings, for example). Or it may be a hitherto confidential file, whether from the public or private sector, the contents of which are disclosed in court on account of their relevance to the case.

Access to trial documentation is a subject that may be approached at several levels. The records of the major courts in the United Kingdom, as one form of public record, are subject to the Public Records Acts 1958 and 1967.[77] These statutes grant a general right of access to public records, but only when they are considered to be of historical significance. The normal lapse of time before records may be made available to the public is thirty years. The Lord Chancellor, furthermore, is made responsible for the public records of every court of record or magistrates' court which are not deposited in the Public Record Office.[78]

Our focus of interest, however, is the right to see documents emanating from current trials. The matter of contemporaneous access to official files is the province of 'freedom of information' systems. Increasingly, measures have either been implemented or proposed in a number of jurisdictions whereby citizens are granted access to information held by government. That is, individuals have an enforceable right to be supplied with the information, rather than being provided with a defence under the law if they should happen to gain access to it. In at least one respect there is a close parallel between open justice and freedom of information schemes. Just as any member of the public may enter the courtroom without giving an account of his reason for doing so, the person who lodges an application under a freedom of information statute need advance no special justification for seeking access to the information in question. At first sight, documentation held by courts, as part of the structure of government, might be viewed as falling within the scope of any freedom of information scheme. However, as a general rule, the courts have been treated as falling outside the proper scope of such a right of access. The New Zealand Official Information Act 1982, for example,

---

[77] Public Records Act 1958, 1st Sch, para 4 (1).   [78] Public Records Act 1958, s 8 (1).

grants to individuals the right to request 'official information' from a Minister of the Crown, a 'Department' or an 'organisation'.[79] Yet the last two terms are expressly stated not to include a court, or (in relation to its judicial functions) a tribunal.[80] This approach is followed in the United Kingdom's Freedom of Information Act 2000, which, in general terms, grants a right of access to information held by a 'public authority'.[81] This is subject to a number of exceptions, categorized as 'exempt information'. One prominent class of exempt information comprises documents filed with a court for the purpose of particular legal proceedings (such as pleadings) and documents drawn up by the court's administrative staff or the court itself for the purpose of disposing of individual cases (for example, memoranda prepared by judicial assistants or draft judgments).[82]

It is clear, in any event, that the situation in regard to trials falls well short of the statutory provision applicable to public planning inquiries. Such inquiries provide a quasi-judicial forum in which matters of both private interest and public concern alike are investigated. They are governed by a clear provision that, subject to some closely defined exceptions, the oral evidence at inquiries shall be heard 'in public' and, moreover, that 'documentary evidence shall be open to public inspection'.[83]

Two recent trends in civil and criminal procedure have accentuated the problem of access to trial documentation. First, there has been a movement away from the recital by counsel of the contents of documents in open court. In the interests of speed and efficiency, these papers are increasingly read by the judge in private in advance of the hearing. Members of the public present in court are, to the extent to which this takes place, denied knowledge of elements in the case. Secondly, there have been increasing obligations imposed on the prosecution to make material available to the defence prior to the trial by way of a process analogous to discovery in civil cases. The greater this obligation, the greater the possibility of disclosure to the world at large of the contents of previously confidential documents.

The wider obligations to make material available to the accused stem from the Criminal Procedure and Investigations Act 1996. It consequently proved necessary to state with some precision the uses to which the disclosed material might be put.[84] Any transgression of the statutory limits is a contempt of court.[85] Particularly noteworthy, however, is the release of the accused's obligation of

---

[79] Official Information Act 1982, s 12(1).
[80] Official Information Act 1982, s 2(6)(a) and (b).   [81] Freedom of Information Act 2000, s 1.
[82] Freedom of Information Act 2000, s 32(1). Note, also, the category of exempt information defined in s 21 (information which is 'reasonably accessible to the applicant' otherwise than by lodging a request under the Freedom of Information Act itself). Even if s 32(1) had not expressly removed court-held information from the scope of the Act, s 21 might have been taken to encompass matters that could have been gleaned by attending in court as a spectator. (It should be added that the Act will be brought into effect gradually, over a maximum period of five years.)
[83] Town and Country Planning Act 1990, s 321(2).
[84] Criminal Procedure and Investigations Act 1996, s 17.
[85] Criminal Procedure and Investigations Act 1996, s 18(1).

confidence in regard to an 'object' to the extent that 'it has been displayed to the public in open court', and in regard to 'information' to the extent, again, that 'it has been communicated to the public in open court'.[86]

The problems of disclosure of documents obtained at the pre-trial stage had already been explored, in the context of civil law, in *Home Office v Harman*.[87] Miss Harman was a solicitor acting on behalf of a client who had challenged the legality of his confinement in the 'control unit' in Hull Prison. In the course of that action, discovery was obtained of a large number of documents in the possession of the Home Office. (In regard to some of these, it is worth noting, the Home Office made an unsuccessful application for public interest immunity from disclosure.) The contents of some 800 pages were subsequently read aloud by counsel at the hearing of the action. Between the hearing phase and delivery of judgment by Tudor Evans J, Miss Harman quite properly retained the documents. However, she showed them on a number of occasions to a journalist who was researching an article for a national newspaper on the subject of the control unit. This disclosure was ruled to be a contempt of court by Park J, and also by a unanimous Court of Appeal. The House of Lords, by a three to two majority, dismissed Miss Harman's appeal.

Lords Scarman and Simon, in the minority, were impressed by the inconsistency implicit in a contempt finding. The offence was committed by handing over to the journalist the bundle of disclosed documents, but no liability would have been incurred by making available to the journalist the same information when recorded in the transcript of the proceedings by virtue of having been read out in open court. The majority, on the other hand, attached considerable weight to the understanding that material obtained by way of discovery was made available to the other side only for the purposes of pursuing the particular suit. Interestingly, both sides categorized the dispute in terms of the contradiction between open trial and the privacy interests of the litigants—a topic that was covered in Chapter 5. Lord Keith stated that discovery 'constitutes a very serious invasion of the privacy and confidentiality of a litigant's affairs'[88] while Lord Scarman acknowledged 'the general right of the citizen to privacy, which includes a right to keep his own documents to himself'.[89] To take one particular point, Lord Keith reasoned that, if full public disclosure were to become the possible consequence of discovery, there would be an increased temptation on the part of litigants to destroy or suppress the existence of documents whose contents they did not wish to be disclosed. In this respect there is a clear analogy to be drawn with the question of the extent to which the lack of anonymity offered to the rape complainant acted as a deterrent to the reporting of this category of crime.

---

[86] Criminal Procedure and Investigations Act 1996, s 17(3). It is noteworthy that the phrase 'to the public' is used in addition to the traditional term 'in open court'. This would seem to suggest that disclosure in a court attended by no—or even few—members of the public would not suffice to come within the terms of the exception.

[87] [1983] 1 AC 280.   [88] ibid. 308.   [89] ibid. 312.

There were some attempts to integrate the issues in this case with the wider considerations of open justice. Stated briefly, Miss Harman's case was that confidentiality for documents read in open court is lost since the public is 'notionally present' at any trial and 'anyone might have come in and noted down the contents of any discovered document which is read out'.[90] Lord Diplock went so far as to quote Jeremy Bentham on the value of open trial, in particular his familiar assertion that publicity 'keeps the judge himself, while trying, under trial [i.e. accountable]'.[91] Yet it is rather difficult to fit the issues in *Home Office v Harman*, or the issues raised by discovery in general, into the traditional rationales of open justice. Clearly, no witness (whether actual or potential) was involved. Moreover, it is impossible to see how the question of access to the Home Office files had any potential bearing on the mode of conduct of the hearing before Tudor Evans J. There was no suspicion of misconduct on his part that needed to be kept in check. The criticisms being made were in respect of the Home Office's management of the controversial control unit. Indeed, the only allusion to judicial lapse lay in a suggestion by Lord Diplock that it is incumbent on a judge to read documentation in advance of the hearing, if at all possible, rather than to rely on counsel reading the material aloud to him. Yet this is unsatisfactory as a consideration since, as we have already seen,[92] the practice of reciting the contents of documents in open court has been described as a valuable feature of the English trial in that it allows the bystander to follow the hearing from start to finish. His capacity to do so would be severely impaired if documents important to the understanding of the case were not read in this way, and moreover, if he were to be denied access in other ways to their contents.

Miss Harman responded to her defeat in the House of Lords by bringing an individual petition under the European Convention on Human Rights.[93] The petition concluded with a 'friendly settlement' before the European Commission, by which the British Government undertook to change the law so that it would no longer be a contempt of court to publicize material contained in documents disclosed pursuant to discovery once the material had been read out in open court.[94] A new order of the Supreme Court, Order 24, rule 14A, was introduced:

Any undertaking, whether express or implied, not to use a document for any purposes other than those of the proceedings in which it is disclosed shall cease to apply to such document after it has been read to or by the Court, or referred to, in open Court, unless the Court for special reasons has otherwise ordered on the application of a party or of the person to whom the document belongs.

There are several noteworthy points concerning the new rule. The express or implied understanding to treat as confidential material that has been obtained as

---

[90] ibid. 308.   [91] ibid. 303.   [92] See Chapter 2, section 1, above.
[93] *Harman v UK* Application No 10038/82. The decision declaring the petition admissible is reported at (1985) 7 EHRR 146.
[94] The text of the friendly settlement is set out in the judgment in *Bibby Bulk Carriers Ltd v Cansulex Ltd* [1989] QB 155, 159.

a result of discovery would cease to have effect after the relevant document has been read in open court. More remarkably, the terms of the new order would become applicable even if the document had not been read aloud in this way. The mere reading *by* the court, or reference *to* it in open court, would suffice to raise the presumption of release from the rule of non-disclosure. The terms of the new order were discussed by Hirst J in *Bibby Bulk Carriers Ltd v Cansulex*[95] where the plaintiffs made an application to be released from their implied undertaking. The application was refused for a number of reasons. Not only were the documents in question confidential, they also contained commercially sensitive information which could prejudice the defendants. Hirst J stressed the importance placed by the House of Lords in the *Harman* case on the adoption of practices that would not discourage full and frank disclosure of documents on discovery. Moreover, one particular point that is of interest to our general theme is the importance that his Lordship seemed to attach to the question of how many members of the public were in court at the relevant time:

This document unquestionably started off as a confidential document . . . Although it was read out in open court and quoted in the transcript (albeit with no list of the attenders) there is no evidence as to the extent, if any, of public attendance at the trial, nor of the dissemination of the transcript. The Lloyd's List report is quite general in its description of the allegations against Cansulex (all of which were of a kind naturally to be expected in this kind of litigation) and contained no quotation from, nor even a reference to, the document itself.[96]

In short, one of the considerations deemed relevant was the extent, if any, of actual public attendance at the hearing. The mere reading of the document 'in open court' was not, in itself, sufficient to deprive it of its confidentiality.

The Civil Procedure Rules 1998,[97] while following the general pattern of Order 24, rule 14A, differ from it in several respects. The relevant provision, Rule 31.22, departs from reliance on the concept of an undertaking, whether express or implied. It stipulates simply that a disclosed document may be used only for the purpose of the proceedings in which it has been disclosed. To this there are three exceptions. The first two turn on the presence of consent: namely, where the court itself grants permission; or where there is the combined consent of the owner of the document and the person who disclosed it to the court. For our purposes the third exception is the most important: that is, where 'the document has been read to or by the court, or referred to, at a hearing which has been held in public'. Especially noteworthy is the choice of the term 'in public' in preference to the more usual 'in open court'. This appears to be an embodiment in the Civil Procedure Rules of the approach taken by Hirst J in the above-quoted passage. Moreover, in a significant qualification to the third exception, the court may make an order either restricting or prohibiting the use of any document which falls within its terms.[98]

---

[95] [1989] QB 155.   [96] ibid. 165.   [97] Civil Procedure Rules 1998, SI 1998/3132.
[98] An application for the making of such an order may be made either by a party or by any person to whom the document belongs: r 31.22 (3).

Documents produced by way of discovery are at risk of further disclosure since, apart from their being read or referred to in open court, they are placed in the hands of the other party to the case. The risk of such disclosure is present to a much smaller degree as regards documents that are filed in court, since the custody of the files rests with the court officials and the acquiescence of these officials is required before a person may gain access to them. The disputes that have arisen fall into two categories: those where an official has (arguably, wrongly) granted access, and proceedings are then commenced in order to restrict further dissemination of their contents; and those where officials (improperly, it is maintained) deny all access.

The former situation is illustrated by *A-G v Limbrick*,[99] where the plaintiff unsuccessfully sought an order to restrain further use of the released document, and by the application for committal for contempt in *Dobson v Hastings*.[100] The respondents in the latter case were the editor and publishers of the *Daily Telegraph*, which had carried in its columns material that had been filed in court in connection with proceedings brought to disqualify five directors or ex-directors of a public limited company. The five included the two applicants in the case and Sir Edward du Cann, a former Chairman of the Conservative Party—a factor which undoubtedly added an extra element to the commercial aspects of the case. The material in question was a report submitted to the High Court by the official receiver in connection with the disqualification proceedings, which had not as yet been heard. A journalist employed by the *Daily Telegraph* had obtained the report by openly approaching the court offices. She was presented with the file and, although knowing that the leave of the court was required, she understandably thought this to be a mere formality in view of the fact that she had been given the material. When subsequently the court registrar contacted the newspaper's office, again there was some misunderstanding, as a consequence of which the newspaper felt that there was no possible legal impediment to publishing (as it did) two articles on the basis of the information gleaned from the file.

Nicholls VC exonerated the respondents from any liability for what had happened. He emphasized: 'a court file is not a publicly available register. It is a file maintained by the court for the proper conduct of proceedings . . . Non-parties have a right of access to the extent, but only to the extent, provided in the rules'.[101] The applicable rules stipulated that a person who was not a party to the case could inspect the official receiver's report only with the leave of the court.[102] To publish the contents of the report without such leave, knowing that permission was necessary, would be contempt, as would the use of deception in order to obtain the requisite leave. That, however, was not the situation as far as the journalist was concerned. It would be a contempt, however, for the editor of the newspaper thenceforth to publish unused material from the journalist's notes.

---

[99] The Times, 28 March 1996.   [100] [1992] Ch 394.   [101] ibid. 401–402.
[102] RSC, Ord. 63, rr 4 and 4A.

Finally, it went 'without saying' that there would be no possible contempt liability in publishing the contents of the report 'once the report has been used in open court'.[103]

It is noteworthy that, in contrast to *Scott v Scott* (where the approach to the court offices had taken place after the hearing), the relevant proceedings had not yet taken place against the five directors. To be set against this were several elements in the case that were favourable to the defendants. The case against the men (again, in contrast to *Scott*) would not be heard *in camera*. Nor was there, despite the commercial nature of the background case, any issue of trade secrecy. Above all, disqualification proceedings would be heard by a judge sitting without a jury. Like Mrs Scott and her solicitor, the journalist did not resort to trickery in order to gain access to the document. She proceeded on the perfectly understandable basis that, if the report had been truly confidential, the court officials would not have allowed her access to it. Although *Scott v Scott* was not cited in *Dobson v Hastings*, the cases can be reconciled by reference to a rule of court, applicable only in the latter case, that limited access to material filed in court. The relevant rule appeared to apply irrespective of whether the hearing for disqualification had taken place when application was made for leave, nor did it mention any possible sanction for failure to comply with its terms. In any event, where (as on these facts) the document was obtained and published before the hearing, the link with the classic objectives of open trial is extremely tenuous.

By contrast, there is the type of case where access is denied and the propriety of the refusal forms the subject matter of litigation. This is exemplified by *Ex p Creditnet Ltd*,[104] which concerned the question of general access to the list of winding-up petitions stored in the Liverpool District Registry of the High Court. The applicable rule, rule 7.28 of the Insolvency Rules 1986, stipulated that the courts records 'shall be open to inspection by any person' while providing that, if the registrar was not satisfied as to the 'propriety of the purpose for which inspection is required', he should refuse it subject to appeal to the judge. The terms of this rule are at variance with the standard approach in open justice, in inquiring into the propriety of the reasons why a person seeks to gain access to court proceedings. Parker J ruled, not surprisingly, that generalized access would undermine the balance struck by the rules between safeguarding the company and, on the other hand, that of its creditors or any other parties proposing to have dealings with the company.[105] This decision is to be compared with the application for judicial review in *R v Secretary of the Central Office of the Employment Tribunals (England and Wales), ex p Public Concern at Work*.[106] Here the point in contention was the true scope of a statutory instrument that regulated a register, one

---

[103] [1992] Ch 394, 410.   [104] [1996] 1 WLR 1291.

[105] In *Re Austintel Ltd* [1997] BCC 362 the Court of Appeal ruled that it did not have jurisdiction to hear an appeal from the decision at first instance. Nevertheless, Ward LJ at 366–369 made some general observations on the propriety of granting access to the particular court records.

[106] The Times, 9 May 2000.

that was 'open to the inspection of any person', listing details of cases decided by employment tribunals. On its natural interpretation, the terms of the statutory instrument required sufficient details to be entered in the register that a member of the public would be able to glean the gist of the applicant's complaint in any particular case. The argument for this measure of access to the records, it was held, was strengthened by the fact that members of the public would have been entitled to attend the tribunal hearing in person, notwithstanding the ensuing embarrassment and lack of privacy for the parties.

In the absence of a particular rule of court or statutory provision, there must be recourse to considerations of general principle to resolve the dispute. This was the situation in *Gio Personal Investment Services Ltd v Liverpool and London Steamship Protection and Indemnity Association Ltd (FAI General Insurance Co Ltd Intervening).*[107] FAI General Insurance intervened in the action between 'Gio' and 'Liverpool and London', which raised points of relevance to a separate action that FAI was currrently defending. Its purpose in so doing was to gain access to counsel's written opening statement (in lieu of an opening speech) together with the documents referred to therein. FAI therefore counted for this purpose as members of the public only. Walker J, in rejecting the application, dismissed as spurious FAI's claim as founded on the traditional role of the public in observing the processes of justice: 'this application has nothing whatever to do with the public interest: it is to do with the commercial interests of FAI and references to the confessed desire to understand the nature of the case being put forward are in effect mere window dressing.'[108]

The Court of Appeal, after ruling that the matter of disclosure was not covered by the Rules of the Supreme Court, fell back on a consideration of the application in the light of the inherent jurisdiction of the court to regulate its own procedures. The case thus came to be viewed in the light of open justice and its rationale. On this basis the written opening statement by counsel, together with the skeleton argument, stood on a different footing from documents referred to in those texts. Historically, members of the public had never enjoyed a right of access to documents simply by reason of the fact that they had been referred to in open court. The other material being sought, however, had assumed the role previously played by the opening speech by counsel in explaining the issues in the case. To the extent that this explanation was now embodied in written form that was read and assimilated by the judge in the privacy of his room, an important part of the judicial process was no longer taking place in open court. Consequently any member of the public, such as FAI, would be entitled to apply for a written copy of this material.

---

[107] [1999] 1 WLR 984.   [108] ibid. 988.

5. PRELIMINARY HEARINGS AND OPEN JUSTICE

The trial on indictment has traditionally been preceded by some form of preliminary hearing. The purpose and scope of such hearings has varied over time. Committal proceedings, now largely defunct,[109] are the form of hearing that has predominated in modern legal history. Their purpose was to ascertain whether the prosecution case was sufficiently strong to justify putting the accused on trial. The process of sending the case from the examining magistrates to the Crown Court is now achieved through the largely perfunctory committal for trial without consideration of the evidence. Side by side with the decline of the formal committal stage there has been an increase in the use of the 'preparatory hearing' or, as it is sometimes known, the 'pre-trial hearing'. In its original form the preparatory hearing was introduced by the Criminal Justice Act 1987 for use in complex cases of commercial fraud. It was thereafter extended, by the Criminal Procedure and Investigations Act 1996, to encompass complex cases generally.

The status of committal proceedings in magistrates' courts, when judged against the general principles of open justice, is somewhat equivocal. The proceedings are essentially preliminary to the trial on indictment, the sole issue to be determined by the magistrates being whether to send the accused for trial or to dismiss the case for lack of sufficient evidence. Moreover, if one hallmark of a judicial function is the element of finality,[110] this is an element that is absent from the committal stage. The decision of the magistrates not to send the case for trial is no barrier to the prosecution deciding to prefer new charges in respect of the same offence. The issue of double jeopardy simply does not arise in these circumstances.[111]

Committal proceedings only evolved gradually into some semblance of a judicial form.[112] Increasingly, in the course of the eighteenth century, the preliminary examination was held in public. Even where such examination was transacted by the justice in his own house, the proceedings had a public character.[113] Writing in 1885, Maitland expressed the view that the place of preliminary examination could not be considered an 'open court' since the public could be excluded if the magistrate thought that this would best serve the ends of justice.[114] The conclusion that the proceedings did not take place in open court would appear, however, to be a mistaken inference from the mere fact that the general rule admitted of exceptions.

---

[109] They no longer exist for indictable-only offences: see the Crime and Disorder Act 1998, s 51.

[110] Recall the discussion in Chapter 1, section 5, C, above.

[111] See M. L. Friedland, *Double Jeopardy* (1969) 37, n 1, for English and Canadian authorities. See also *R v Manchester City Stipendiary Magistrate, ex p Snelson* [1977] 1 WLR 911, 913, where it is stated that 'all the authorities show that no question of autrefois acquit arises' by reason of the previous discharge of the accused at the committal stage.

[112] J. M. Beattie, *Crime and the Courts in England 1660–1800* (1986) 274–81.   [113] ibid. 279.

[114] F. W. Maitland, *Justice and Police* (1885) 129.

The critical phase in the modern development of committal proceedings came with the trial for murder in 1957 of Dr John Bodkin Adams. The presiding judge at the trial, Lord Devlin, subsequently published an unorthodox—and, in the view of some—improper 'report' of the trial in the form of a book-length examination of the case. This includes a brief account of the committal stage in the proceedings, set against a discussion of the role of committal in that particular era.[115] Although magistrates would sit in public for such purposes, it was recognized that they had the power to hear a witness in private if an application were made to hear his testimony in that form.[116] In the Adams case an objection was raised to certain evidence on the ground of admissibility. Clearly, if the evidence were heard, and at the subsequent trial the judge declared it inadmissible, the damage would already have been done to the accused. The extent of that damage would be considerably increased in view of the worldwide publicity that the case had attracted. The magistrates were in a quandary as to how to deal with the evidence. At first, they heard it in private. Then, having heard it, they decided that it should be given in public. The Lord Chief Justice, Lord Goddard, subsequently communicated to Lord Devlin his view that the evidence should have been heard *in camera*, and in the course of his summing-up Lord Devlin took the opportunity to express his belief that any defence application to hear *in camera* evidence of doubtful admissibility should readily be granted. His pronouncement, continues Devlin's account, 'led directly to the statute that now restricts the reporting of committal proceedings and indirectly to their present moribund state'.[117] This is an oblique reference to the Criminal Justice Act 1967, a statute passed in belated response to the report of a Departmental Committee chaired by Lord Tucker.[118] The central provision, section 3, rendered it unlawful to publish reports of committal proceedings unless the accused himself requested removal of the restrictions.

The imposition of reporting restrictions in this way was heavily criticized by the Press Council, both in evidence to the Tucker Committee and when, some ten years later, the government indicated that it proposed to legislate in the way recommended by that Committee. The Press Council argued that to admit members of the public, while imposing restrictions on the reporting power of the press, would leave with the chance individuals who might be in attendance the important role of monitoring the standards of justice applied by the examining magistrates. Indeed, one incident from that era furnishes an unusual variation on one of the traditional themes of open justice: that of the emergence of additional witnesses as a result of publicity given to a case. In May 1967 a man charged with robbery with violence was committed for trial. At the commencement of the trial prosecuting counsel informed the court that the charges were being dropped. As a result of publicity given to the committal proceedings, another individual had

---

[115] P. Devlin, *Easing the Passing* (1986) ch 4.   [116] ibid. 28.   [117] ibid. 37.
[118] *Proceedings before Examining Justices* (Cmnd 479, 1958).

come forward and confessed to the offence, adding that he did not want the person charged to bear the responsibility for what he himself had done.[119] Of course, the part played by the publicizing of the committal stage in this case can be a matter for speculation only. It may be that the real culprit would have come forward in any event. Equally, the spur to his conscience could have been supplied by publicizing the arrest, the charge, or the trial proceedings themselves.

At the outset of this section a number of observations were made casting doubt on the essentially judicial nature of committal proceedings. The manner of their conduct has varied quite considerably over the course of time. Without giving a full account of their present mode of conduct, it is possible to identify certain of their current features which do not lend themselves to a characterization of them as judicial in character. Committal proceedings, above all, are not the only preliminary to a trial on indictment: there exist other methods, most notably the preferment of a bill of indictment by a High Court judge or by means of serving a notice of transfer. Even when committal proceedings do take place, the evidence is documentary in nature, none being tendered by the defence. The explanation for this one-sided treatment of the case is that the object of the procedure is to exclude cases where no reasonable jury could convict the accused. The result is that many committal stages are perfunctory only, with the accused keeping his case in reserve for the Crown Court.

Yet committal proceedings do retain certain characteristics in common with the full trial of the case. The most basic elements of open justice are retained: the accused is entitled to be present, as are the public and the press. The justices are statutorily required to sit 'in open court' subject to two exceptions: where there is an express provision to the contrary; and where it appears to them that 'the ends of justice would not be served' by their so sitting.[120] Moreover, except where the defendant's disorderly conduct renders it impracticable, he is entitled to be present at the giving of evidence and his legal representative is entitled to question any witness.[121]

The press are subject to a number of considerable restrictions in the reporting of the proceedings. It is, in general terms, unlawful to publish a report of committal proceedings other than those items listed in section 8(4) of the Magistrates' Courts Act 1980. These comprise such outline matters as the names of the magistrates, witnesses and parties, the offence that is charged, the outcome of the proceedings, and such incidental questions as arrangements for bail and legal aid. These restrictions apply automatically, unless lifted in the ways that will be discussed shortly. There are strong reasons of principle why this should be so. In the relatively few instances in which the committal stage is more than a formality, any account that would emerge of the process would, of necessity, be favourable to the prosecution. Not only is the whole process directed to the issue of whether

---

[119] H. P. Levy, *The Press Council: History, Procedure and Cases* (1967) 433–4.
[120] Magistrates' Courts Act 1980, s 4(2).
[121] Magistrates' Courts Act 1980, ss 4(3) and 4(4).

or not the prosecution has met a threshold justifying the trial on indictment, there may be several critical elements (most notably, challenges to the admissibility of evidence) that would be dealt with in a *voir dire* phase of a Crown Court trial.

There remain three situations in which reporting is unrestrained by law. The first is uncontroversial: where the accused has been committed for trial on indictment, and the trial has been concluded. The effect, then, is merely to impose a delay rather than a complete ban on reporting. The release from the restrictions in this way, however, is likely to prove of limited value, since any matter ventilated in the course of contested committal proceedings would also emerge in the course of the trial on indictment.

The second may equally be viewed as unexceptional. Where the accused has been discharged by the examining magistrates for want of evidence, reporting may take place forthwith. Since no trial on indictment is to take place in this situation, it would seem appropriate that the media should be entitled to report this stage at least. However, on an alternative view, the defendant's brush with the criminal process system should not be publicized. If the case against him is so weak as not to justify sending it further in the criminal justice system, it could be argued that it is an unwarranted violation of his privacy to expose him to the consequent publicity. On the other hand, the very fact that the examining magistrates deemed the case against him to be so weak might suggest that any publicity would not besmirch his name. Moreover, publicity would exercise its normal limited function in this aspect, as in other aspects, of the court system in subjecting the judiciary to some rudimentary form of check.

The third of the situations in which reporting may take place is the most interesting. This applies where reporting restrictions are lifted at the request of the accused. Such a situation is especially remarkable, since it is one in which the accused exercises a measure of choice over the degree of publicity which is to attend his appearance in the criminal justice system. Indeed, the wishes of the accused also determine whether a full scale committal takes place with consideration of the evidence, or whether to allow this stage to take place expeditiously in a matter of minutes under the new form of committal. There are a number of reasons why, as a matter of tactics, the accused might choose to exercise the decision in favour of lifting restrictions. The attendant publicity might, for example, bring his case to the attention of a possible witness who would testify in his favour. This traditional rationale of open justice carries particular strength in the context of committal proceedings in view of the fact that the trial is yet to take place.

The role of the wishes of the accused has been rather more problematic in those situations where there is more than one accused and there is a division of opinion between them as to whether or not reporting restrictions should be lifted. The facts in *R v Leeds Justices, ex p Sykes*,[122] in addition to illustrating this difficulty, demonstrate how publicity may be sought for reasons which are, perhaps,

---

[122] [1983] 1 All ER 460.

peripheral to the trial itself but which nevertheless bear on other matters of public concern. Five men had been charged with conspiracy to rob, and at the committal stage two of the co-accused applied to have reporting restrictions lifted by way of protest against the way in which the police had decided to bring the charges. The applicant opposed this move, for the more traditional reason that he feared prejudice to his coming trial. He successfully applied for judicial review of the magistrates' decision to lift reporting restrictions. The Divisional Court emphasized that the burden of proof lay on those who wished restrictions to be lifted. In the circumstances, publicizing a grievance against the police was less important than averting possible prejudice to a coming trial.

Committal proceedings no longer occupy their previously prominent position in the criminal justice system. Nevertheless, they may create tensions within that system on those few occasions when a case does attract an intense degree of publicity. An example in point is the trial of Rosemary West.[123] Committal proceedings in this case commenced in February 1995 in the Dursley Magistrates' Court in Gloucestershire. The purpose of contesting the proceedings at this stage was to make the submission that it would be an abuse of process for a trial to be held at all. This was largely, the defence argued, on account of the lapse of time since the murders with which the accused was charged. Moreover, the measure of adverse publicity which the case had received would render a fair trial impossible. No precedent was cited to the examining magistrate for the proposition that such a person, rather than the trial judge, possessed the power to stop a trial on these grounds. Whatever the substance of the point, defence tactics dictated that a formal committal hearing should take place as the forum in which these points could be addressed as early as possible. On the other hand, it followed from the nature of the last point that the accused would not apply for reporting restrictions to be lifted. The various accounts of the committal stages of the case that have since been published[124] provide practical examples of the point (made above) that reporting restrictions cease to apply at the conclusion of the eventual trial.

Rarely does an obscure magistrates' court, the daily business of which is the most minor of offences, play host to proceedings that have gained worldwide notoriety. During Rosemary West's committal proceedings only a dozen places were available for the press in the courtroom itself, the proceedings being carried to other representatives of the press by means of an audio link.[125] Since reporting restrictions were not lifted, the British newspapers were confined to reporting only the basic details mentioned above. The foreign press, however, was not limited in this way, although any material published abroad would impose a duty on the British distributors to see that British contempt limitations were observed.[126]

---

[123] For the background to the case, see the Appendix.
[124] See, for example, B. Masters, '*She must have Known*': *The Trial of Rosemary West* (1997) ch 9.
[125] The Times (6 February 1995) 8.
[126] See *R v Griffiths, ex p A-G* [1957] 2 QB 192 for the dangers of failure to exert control over material published abroad which is then distributed in the UK.

In contrast to committal proceedings, it is quite clear that preparatory hearings form an integral part of the trial itself.[127] This would suffice to render such hearings open to the public. Indeed, the reporting restrictions that can be imposed on a preparatory hearing[128] would have no point if the situation were otherwise. As with committal proceedings, the restrictions may be lifted at the behest of the accused and, in the event of there being more than one accused with a division of opinion between them, the court is to decide the dispute 'in the interests of justice.'[129] Preparatory hearings encompass, in part, matters that would fall to be determined in the course of a typical trial as part of a *voir dire* phase (issues as to the admissibility of evidence, or disputed questions of law). In part, also, they embody one of the traditional functions of committal proceedings: to ascertain whether there is sufficient evidence to justify sending the accused for trial on indictment. For it remains open to the accused to apply to the Crown Court, whether orally or in writing, for the charge to be dismissed on the ground that the evidence disclosed could not properly form the basis of a conviction.[130]

6. CONTEMPT LIABILITY AND THE POSTPONEMENT OF TRIAL REPORTS

In the area of contempt, as in defamation, protection is afforded in respect of the contemporaneous and fair reporting of cases. The contempt privilege differs, in some significant respects, from its counterpart in the law of defamation. Publication without the cover of this privilege results in criminal liability on the part of the publisher of the report. Moreover, in view of the nature of the law of contempt of court, the privilege is of particular value in reporting criminal cases, rather than (as with the defamation privilege) the reporting of any kind of legal proceeding. Indeed, the element of contemporaneity is especially significant in the contempt privilege, since the danger of prejudice to particular proceedings (with consequent exposure to contempt liability) arises only where the publication is made at or about the same time as the case that is being reported. Publications after the event are scarcely capable of exercising a prejudicial effect on the case.

The statutory form of the privilege is to be found in section 4(1) of the Contempt of Court Act 1981: 'Subject to this section a person is not guilty of contempt of court under the strict liability rule in respect of a fair and accurate report of legal proceedings held in public, published contemporaneously and in good faith.'

Inaccurate reporting, with consequent exposure to possible contempt liability, can arise most commonly through a journalist's knowledge of matters relating to

---

[127] Criminal Justice Act 1987, s 8(1). [128] Set out in the Criminal Justice Act 1987, s 11.
[129] Criminal Justice Act 1987, ss 11(2) and 11(3). [130] Criminal Justice Act 1987, s 6.

a case which do not emerge in the trial itself. Lapse of memory results in his reporting those matters as if they had emerged in the course of the trial proceedings. For example, in *A-G v BBC*[131] the BBC was found to be in contempt of court for broadcasting material which was inadmissible in the trial that was being covered. The journalist who supplied the report happened to know the material from sources other than the trial. In view of the fact that four of the jurors saw the relevant programme, the BBC was ordered to pay a substantial fine. There was a particular danger of faulty recall in the days of full-scale committal proceedings. In *R v Evening Standard Co Ltd*[132] contempt liability was incurred because the journalist who supplied the report erroneously attributed to the trial some material that he had heard at the committal stage, but which had been ruled inadmissible at the trial itself.

As these cases illustrate, the emphasis of the English criminal trial on the exclusionary rules of evidence raises the issue of reporting restrictions in its simplest form. The evidential rules on admissibility strictly control the flow of information to the jury. If the law of evidence requires that certain items of information are to be withheld from the jury, the logic of exclusion requires that they should not reach the jury even by an indirect route. Not only, therefore, is the material not to be communicated to them in the courtroom itself, precautions are to be taken lest it reaches them through the media. The scope for such leakage is increased in situations where argument has taken place in court as to whether or not the jury should be allowed to hear the material in question. There might, for example, be dispute as to whether a confession has been given voluntarily by the accused. The determination of this point will typically involve argument on issues of fact, and (in some cases) points of law. The possibility that there will be a ruling against admissibility means that the argument on the relevant matters takes place out of sight and hearing of the jury. If the ruling goes in favour of inadmissibility, nothing more is to be heard on the matter. The format for dealing with these matters, as already mentioned, is the holding of a *voir dire*. The public and press remain present throughout this stage of the proceedings, subject to the proviso that any report emanating from these quarters that comes to the attention of any of the jurors before they have delivered a verdict may well involve those responsible in liability for contempt of court.[133]

In contrast to such instances of 'intra-trial' reporting restriction, there are various situations of 'inter-trial' restriction. The latter arise through the risk of prejudice to a criminal trial through the unrestricted reporting of earlier proceedings, whether criminal or civil. There would appear to be three standard situations. First, there might be a civil action (to recover misappropriated property, perhaps), followed by a criminal trial arising out of the same facts. Secondly, a single

---

[131] [1992] COD 264.   [132] [1954] 1 QB 578.
[133] *A-G v Leveller Magazine Ltd* [1979] 1 All ER 745, 750.

accused might face two indictments, to be heard sequentially.[134] Thirdly, there could be several trials of a number of defendants in regard to a series of connected events where, again, the trials will not take place contemporaneously.

There exist early indications that the courts recognized the danger of prejudice to particular proceedings in the mere reporting of an earlier trial. Sometimes informal arrangements were made in order to maintain secrecy. For example, in *R v Gordon, Hickson and ors*[135] applications were made for leave to appeal against convictions for robbery on the basis of the availability of new evidence. A person who was awaiting trial on a separate matter had been found who was willing to testify that he (together with four other men who were not the appellants) had committed the robbery. The possibility of prejudice to the man's trial, which was to take place that very week, was averted by the man's name being given to the court registrar without it being mentioned in public. In the earlier case of *R v Clement*[136] resort was had to the alternative expedient of making an order that postponed the reporting of the trial.

The jurisdiction to order a stay on reporting trial was put on a statutory basis by section 4(2) of the Contempt of Court Act 1981, which provides:

In any such proceedings the court may, where it appears necessary for avoiding a substantial risk of prejudice to the administration of justice in those proceedings, or in any other proceedings pending or imminent, order that the publication of any report of the proceedings, or any part of the proceedings, be postponed for such period as the court thinks necessary for that purpose.

By virtue of section 159 of the Criminal Justice Act 1988, orders made under section 4(2) were made subject to possible challenge to the Court of Appeal. The function of the Court of Appeal, in that event, is to form its own view of the material. It therefore possesses full power to confirm, overturn or vary the order that is subject to complaint.[137] It is possible to have three perspectives on the question whether or not to impose an order under section 4(2): that of the prosecution; that of the accused (of whom there is sometimes more that one, with the consequent possibility of a division of opinion); and that of the media. The position of the media was strengthened by the inclusion of orders made under section 4(2) in the list of orders that are subject to challenge in the Court of Appeal by virtue of section 159 of the Criminal Justice Act 1988. The duty of the prosecution, it has been decided, is to contribute to the issues in an objective and unpartisan spirit, especially in cases where there is an absence of a media representation

---

[134] This situation is exemplified by the trial of general medical practitioner, Dr Harold Shipman, in 1999–2000. For further details, see the Appendix. As a consequence of the publicity surrounding the trial and conviction, which went unrestrained by reporting restrictions, it proved impossible to give Dr Shipman a fair trial for the murder of a second group of patients.

[135] (1913) 8 Cr App R 237.   [136] (1821) 4 B & Ald 218, 106 ER 918.

[137] *R v Beck, ex p Daily Telegraph plc* [1993] 2 All ER 177, 180, per Farquarson LJ: '... in applying the subsection we, as the Court of Appeal, can exercise our own discretion. It is not a case of reviewing the exercise of the learned judge's discretion with the limitations imposed on the Court of Appeal in such circumstances.'

and where, consequently, it falls to the prosecution to furnish the court with the only perspective in opposition to that of the accused.[138]

The speed of modern communications has served to accentuate the difficulties of reconciling freedom to report with the prevention of prejudice. The technology of modern transmission is such that material disclosed in the courtroom can be disseminated within a few seconds by radio, television, computer link or over news agency wires. This imposes a corresponding obligation on those who seek such an order from the trial judge. The time factor is also significant in regard to the jurisdiction conferred by section 159 of the Criminal Justice Act 1988 to challenge the making of such orders. Where the delay imposed by court order is extremely short—it has been as short as one night[139]—the matter will usually be moot by the time the appeal against the order is heard in the Court of Appeal. There are indications that, in this regard, the courts will not follow their usual disinclination to rule on hypothetical points. As Lord Lane CJ said: 'Section 159 would not be an effective remedy if orders wrongly made could not be reversed simply because they had ceased to operate.'[140]

A detailed examination of the wording of section 4(2) is necessary.

The section confers a power to postpone reports. It does so, moreover, only in regard to 'legal proceedings held in public'. It is worth noting that the hallowed phrase, 'in open court', is not used. Although the terms of section 4(2) do not refer specifically to trial proceedings, the provision does not extend to aspects of the criminal process that might take place in public: for example, the making of an arrest.[141] It must surely follow that a preliminary stage in the criminal process that does not even occur in public—for example, the laying of an information—would not fall within the scope of the section. At any rate, judicial doubt has been expressed on the point.[142]

The ambit of section 4(2) extends to both 'those proceedings' and 'any other proceedings pending or imminent'. To take the former, why might a judge restrain reporting of the instant trial in circumstances where there is no prospect of a further trial arising out of the same events? There are two possible reasons: in order to maintain the secrecy of the *voir dire*; or as a pre-emptive strike against the possibility of unfair or inaccurate reporting. It has been held that to impose a reporting delay merely in order to avoid inconveniencing the jury is not a proper use of section 4(2). In *Re Central Independent Television plc*[143] the Court of Appeal was confronted with a situation where the trial judge had imposed such an order that would restrict radio and television coverage of a fraud trial[144] just prior

---

[138] *Ex p News Group Newspapers Ltd* The Times, 21 May 1999.
[139] See *Re Central Independent Television plc* [1999] 1 All ER 347, 349.
[140] *ibid.*, 351.
[141] *R v Rhuddlan JJ, ex p HTV Ltd* [1986] Crim LR 329.
[142] *R v Clerkenwell Magistrates' Court, ex p Telegraph plc* [1993] 2 All ER 183, 186.
[143] [1991] 1 All ER 347.
[144] Incidentally, that the order, by being limited in this way, discriminated in favour of the print media was another point that was cursorily dealt with: ibid. 350.

to the jury retiring to a hotel prior to considering its verdict. Three television and radio companies successfully challenged the order. Two reasons were given for upholding their right to report immediately. Any possible prejudice could be averted by denying the jury access to radio and television contact in the hotel. Also, there was nothing so far in the reporting of the trial which would suggest that any reports broadcast at this stage would be other than fair and accurate.

The latter consideration, however, could be a matter of conjecture only. The possibility of prejudicial material emerging at this late stage in more sensational trials is far from remote. During the course of the trial of Beverly Allitt,[145] representatives from various media organizations were required to appear before Latham J at Nottingham Crown Court to give an account of their publication of material while the jury was still considering its verdict. The material in question included articles on Munchausen Syndrome by Proxy, the condition from which the accused was suffering. These articles were potentially prejudicial to the trial, since Latham J had expressly disallowed any reference to the defendant's medical condition at the very outset of the proceedings. More prejudicial still was a national newspaper leader that described Nurse Allitt as a psychopath and stated that the hospital ward on which she worked had been turned into a 'slaughter house'. Latham J made arrangements to ensure that the jury would not have access to this material. However, in contrast to the *Central Independent Television* case, he expressed reluctance to restrict in general terms the reading and viewing of material available to the jury since that would only add to their strain.[146]

A frequent consideration is the feasibility of resort to alternative means of reconciling free reporting and fair trial. Sometimes, as in the *Central Independent Television* case, the alternative means—sequestration of the jury—is preferred. Sometimes, as in *Ex p Telegraph plc*,[147] it is not. In this case the full range of alternative means was considered and rejected: reversal of the original decision as to separate trials; change of venue; and postponement of subsequent trials so as to negate the effect of publicity.[148] The case is particularly instructive in the formation of the groupings of those who opposed the restriction and those who supported it. Some of the defendants contested the reporting restriction on the (now familiar) ground that publicity would encourage other persons to come forward with important testimony.[149] In this regard, naturally, they had the support of the media. Other defendants—those who would be tried in the final phase—argued that the judge's order was not wide enough and should encompass reporting of any of the proceedings in the first trial until the conclusion of the final trial.[150]

The questions to be asked by the judge in determining whether to make an order under section 4(2) were set out by Lindsay J in *MGN Pension Trustees Ltd v Bank of America National Trust and Savings Association*.[151] First, is there a

---

[145] For an account of the case, see the Appendix.   [146] The Times (19 May 1993) 5.
[147] [1993] 2 All ER 971.   [148] ibid. 976.   [149] ibid. 977.   [150] ibid. 974.
[151] [1995] 2 All ER 355.

substantial risk of prejudice to the administration of justice in the criminal trials? Secondly, if so, does it appear to be necessary, in order to avoid that risk, that some order should be made postponing publication of trial reports? Thirdly, if so, ought the court in its discretion to make any order?[152] The tests have subsequently been refined by the Court of Appeal, in the light of the European Convention on Human Rights, in *R v Sherwood, ex p The Telegraph Group plc*.[153] Recognizing that the jurisdiction under section 4(2) must hold the critical balance between freedom of the press and fair trial, the court emphasized that, under the third test, the degree of risk to a later trial might be regarded as tolerable and as a lesser evil than the imposition of a reporting restriction.

There exists no inherent power to control the reporting of trial proceedings co-existent with the power conferred by section 4(2) of the Contempt of Court Act 1981.[154] This stands in marked contrast to the jurisdiction to sit *in camera*, where statutory facilities exist alongside the inherent power of the court to sit in secret.

It is necessary, finally, to give some consideration to the position of temporary reporting restrictions in the light of the values served by open justice. As we have seen, reporting privileges are conceded to the media on the basis of the idea that, through them, the public is 'notionally present'. Where reporting restrictions are placed on aspects of a trial, the notional presence is (to that extent) postponed until some time after the events covered by the restriction. As far as many of the traditional claims made for the value of open justice are concerned, a temporary postponement of reporting may not prove completely antithetical to these values. Witnesses may still emerge as a result of reading a non-contemporaneous report. Those witnesses who are already before the court will give their testimony in the realization that, later rather than sooner, it may be available to the general public. On the other hand, the specific interest of the media is in favour of the immediate reporting of news before it becomes stale. The trial the reporting of which is ordered to be deferred is more likely (other things being equal) to be the trial that goes completely unreported. In this respect there is a link between the commercial interests of the media in being permitted to publish immediate reports and the wider values served by open justice.

---

[152] It has been noted that the courts tend to merge the two questions of necessity and exercise of discretion: *Ex p Telegraph plc* [1993] 2 All ER 971, 975.

[153] The Times, 12 June 2001.

[154] *Re Belfast Telegraph Newspapers Ltd's Application* [1997] NI 309. The order had been made for the purpose of protecting the identity, and safety, of a person appearing before the magistrates' court on a charge of indecent assault.

9

The Broadcasting of Judicial Proceedings

1. PHOTOGRAPHY, TELEVISION, AND THE CRIMINAL PROCESS

It is already commonplace in some legal systems for court hearings, under controlled conditions, to be open to radio and television coverage. In some countries the applicable conditions are such that material is produced in sufficient abundance to maintain in existence a regular programme, or even a whole network, devoted to the broadcast of trial proceedings. Respective examples are: *Un giorno in pretura* (A Day in Court), the programme run by the RAI, the Italian state broadcasting service; and 'Court TV', a 24-hour cable network that commenced operations in the United States in 1991.

The example of such jurisdictions has prompted the call for the admission to the English courtroom of audio-visual technology with a view to the transmission of the proceedings. In part, too, the calls have been reinforced by the recognition that such technology has superseded the print media as the prime source of public instruction on matters of general concern. Such proposals for change as have been advanced have been in favour of permitting the televising of court proceedings, and it is this aspect of the subject that forms the principal (though not exclusive) focus of the present chapter. Clearly, it raises wider problems than the mere radio coverage of trials. In these respects there may emerge a development parallel to the coverage of proceedings in Parliament. For a long period even after the advent of modern technology the public gained knowledge of the business of Parliament only through the intermediary of the print journalist. This state of affairs was changed, first by permitting the radio broadcast of debates, and then, following that intermediate stage, by allowing television cameras into the debating chambers.[1] The lead in regard to television coverage was taken by the House of Lords. A Select Committee of that House produced a report on the subject in July 1984, which paved the way towards a period of experimental transmission which began in January of the following year. The House of Commons was more cautious, the equivalent experimental scheme being approved in February 1988. The first pictures were broadcast live, on the occasion of the state opening of Parliament, on 21 November 1989.[2]

[1] See, generally, Erskine May's *Parliamentary Practice* (22nd edn, 1997) 229–30, on the arrangements regulating the broadcasting of parliamentary proceedings.

[2] The devolution legislation is silent on the matter, neither requiring nor precluding access to the deliberations of the assemblies on the part of the audio-visual media. The Scotland Act 1998, s 22(2) and Sch 3, para 3(1), states that the standing orders of the Scottish Parliament 'shall include a provision

The example of Parliament will be of only limited value in furnishing solutions to the various problems that would beset any move to admit television cameras to the courtroom. There is but one national legislature: there is consequently no problem in the legislative area analogous to that of selecting, from the multitude of trials that are available for coverage, those which are to be broadcast. The requirements of democratic accountability, moreover, argue for the greatest possible dissemination of knowledge of how the business of the legislature is transacted and of the performance of individual legislators. However, one of the themes of the present work, it has been stressed, is that the values that are served by open justice are not secured in the highest possible measure by the greatest degree of publicity. Finally, those who are elected to legislative assemblies have freely consented to be public figures in a way which the *personae* of the trial have not. A word of qualification, however, is necessary. These observations on the respective positions of legislature and courts apply with the greatest force in those jurisdictions, such as the United Kingdom, where the judiciary and the role of prosecutor are appointed offices. Their force is somewhat diminished in countries, such as the United States, where the lower ranks of the judiciary and the office of prosecutor are elective positions.

It is necessary to preface this account of audio-visual technology and the courts with some general observations on the extent to which legal controls may be exerted over the recording or broadcast of a person's visual image and voice. To what extent can these processes amount to a crime or a civil wrong, whether generally or in the particular context of the trial process?

As a matter of general law, the mere taking of the photograph of another person, even in the absence of that person's consent, is not a legal wrong. Nor is the act of publication of the photograph.[3] No matter how reprehensible the conduct has been in securing the photograph, something more is required in order to found liability.[4] For example, there might be a defamatory imputation in the content of the photograph. Alternatively, control over the use of the photograph might be exercised through the assertion of ownership rights in the form of copyright.[5] Apart from the strictly legal position, the taking of photographs is prohibited in certain circumstances by the Code of Practice of the Press Complaints

---

requiring the proceedings of the Parliament to be held in public, except in such circumstances as the standing orders may provide'. The Government of Wales Act 1998, s 70(1), says that the standing orders of the Welsh Assembly must include provision 'for all proceedings of the Assembly itself to be held in public'. The Northern Ireland Act 1998, s 41(3) and Sch 6, para 2(1), states that the standing orders of the Northern Ireland Assembly 'shall include provision requiring the proceedings of the Assembly to be held in public, except in such circumstances as the standing orders may provide'.

[3] *Sports and General Press Agency v Our Dogs Publishing Co Ltd* [1916] 2 KB 880.

[4] See *Kaye v Robertson* [1991] FSR 62 for a judicial struggle to bring within the categories of legal redress outrageous conduct on the part of a press photographer and his colleague.

[5] For a limited right of control, in the case of photographs or films that have been commissioned for domestic purposes, see the Copyright, Designs and Patents Act 1988, s 85.

Commission.[6] Equally, no wrong is committed simply by recording another's voice into a sound system, or by subsequently publishing that recording to others. Such proposals as are advanced for prohibiting such activities tend to be made in the context of surreptitious surveillance. Not only do they have no bearing on the open recording and transmission of trial proceedings, it is also paradoxical that the only general prohibition on the use of photography should penalize the taking of photographs in a public place: namely, the place of trial. For, in the particular context of the courtroom, there exist two statutory prohibitions which present legal barriers to the television coverage of trials: section 41 of the Criminal Justice Act 1925, in regard to the taking of photographs; and section 9 of the Contempt of Court Act 1981, in regard to sound recording. These sections will be considered in detail in section 2, below. They should first be set alongside the more specific provisions which secure the privacy of particular classes of person caught up in the trial process by forbidding (among other things) the publication of such persons' photograph or other likeness.

We may recall from Chapter 5, in the first place, the anonymity protection extended to victims of the various offences listed in section 2(1) of the Sexual Offences (Amendment) Act 1992. As part of the scheme of protection, section 1(1) of the Act covers, among other things, any 'still or moving picture' of a person alleged to be a victim of any of the offences there listed. The prohibition extends to such pictures, wherever they are taken. It encompasses, not the taking of the picture, but its embodiment in a written publication or television transmission, under certain defined circumstances, where such dissemination of the picture 'is likely to lead members of the public to identify that person as the person against whom the offence is alleged to have been committed'. In the area of the criminal law covered by the 1992 Act, therefore, there is a dual level of protection to the complainant: against the taking of photographs within court, and in their dissemination (irrespective of where they are taken) in such a way as to identify him or her as a complainant in respect of any of the crimes listed.

Again, it will be recalled, there is specific protection of children who are *personae* of particular trials. Section 39(1) of the Children and Young Persons Act 1933 provided a general anonymity protection in regard to children involved in any proceedings, whether as defendant or witness. Subsection (1)(b) expressly stipulated that 'no picture shall be published in any newspaper as being . . . a picture of any child or young person so concerned in the proceedings . . .'. Section 49 of the 1933 Act was cast in identical terms. Several points are worthy of note about these provisions. Again, unlike section 41 of the Criminal Justice Act 1925, they are not limited to photographs or sketches made in the courtroom. Moreover, the critical term is a 'picture', which may be sufficiently general to

---

[6] Of the sixteen provisions of the present Code of Practice, no fewer than six explicitly refer to photography (cls 1, 3, 4, 6, 9, and 11). An additional four implicitly include photographs, in regulating intrusion into grief and shock (cl 5) and the identification of certain categories of person (cls 7, 10, and 12).

encompass by implication the concepts of photograph, portrait and sketch which are deployed in section 41. Equally wide-ranging is section 97 of the Children Act 1989, which guarantees a measure of privacy for children involved in certain types of legal proceedings.[7] Liability is imposed for publishing material intended to, or likely to, identify such a child. For this purpose section 97 (5) defines 'material' to include 'any picture or representation'. That the term 'publish' includes 'broadcast . . . by television' would suffice to encompass moving pictures. It is also reasonably clear from the word 'representation' that it would include such a matter as pencil sketches. As will be seen later in this chapter, those jurisdictions which permit television access to the courtroom have taken care, in the applicable rules, to protect children and young persons from such exposure.

It is necessary to emphasize that the provisions set out above regulate actual trials. Hypothetical trials of particular individuals, whether alive or dead, are relatively free of legal regulation. Occasionally, television seeks to investigate an issue of liability by staging a 'mock trial' of a person who has never been subject to actual criminal process. The absence of such process may be due to a number of reasons: failure to apprehend the person; his death before proceedings could be brought; or a lack of sufficient evidence to bring the prosecution during his lifetime. A noteworthy instance of failure to arrest is the case of Lord Lucan, who for many years has been sought by the police in connection with the murder of his family's nanny. In the same vein, Sir Roger Hollis, the former head of MI5, was placed on 'trial' by London Weekend Television in the spring of 1988 and was judged, contrary to persistent allegations, not to have been a Soviet spy. Occasionally a case is subjected to a mixed procedure: part documentary account of the background, part reconstruction of the trial itself, and part decision at large on the merits of the case. On 6 February 1995, the case of paratrooper Lee Clegg was subjected to this type of process by *Panorama*. While serving in Northern Ireland in 1990, Private Clegg shot and killed a joyrider who drove through a military checkpoint and was erroneously assumed to be a paramilitary. Clegg was convicted of murder and sentenced to life imprisonment. In the television programme witnesses were summoned and professional counsel employed to argue both sides. At the end of the 'hearing' a studio audience carefully selected for its political balance was asked to vote, not on the correctness of the actual trial verdict, but on the question whether Private Clegg should be released.[8] Such reconstructions could raise issues of contempt of court if conducted in regard to a living person of whom there is a possibility of imminent prosecution. That apart, the televising of the 'proceedings' does not breach any criminal law. Although it may make for more vivid spectacle to conduct such investigations in the form of a trial, such a format is not fundamentally different

---

[7] Initially limited to proceedings before a magistrates' court, the provision has subsequently been extended: Access to Justice Act 1999, s 72(1).

[8] They voted for his release by a margin of 56 to 44. In March 1999, after a retrial obtained on the basis of fresh ballistic evidence, Clegg was acquitted by the High Court.

to any other form of reporting which canvasses the arguments for and against the likely guilt or innocence of the individual concerned.

As long as radio and television have existed, they have been used to effect sound or visual reconstructions of actual trial proceedings. Sometimes the trial in question has only recently concluded.[9] Most commonly the proceedings are sufficiently far removed in time that the use of the transcript must be supplemented by background explanations of the context in which the trial took place.[10] Such reconstructions, it emerged, were far from being harmless entertainment combined with some rudimentary instruction in criminal procedure. The programmes caused distress in those instances where there were still living relatives of the accused or of the victim.[11] Sometimes the accused himself, having been acquitted, had disappeared from view. If, as was sometimes suspected, he had changed his identity in the hope of being rehabilitated, the transmission of the programme was likely to expose him in his new social circle.[12] Certainly, the possibility of producing such programmmes exists even without the admission of the audio-visual technology to the courtroom. Once photographic reproduction of the courtroom scene is permitted, however, the possibility is eliminated of accommodating the conflicting interests by the use of fictitious names in the reconstruction.[13]

It is possible to gain an occasional glimpse of the problems of television coverage of contemporaneous trials when the media have aimed to give reconstructions which are near in time to the events portrayed. Particular difficulties are presented when the reconstruction is, in effect, a form of reporting of the day's events in the case. A striking example was provided by Channel Four's reconstruction of the courtroom events in the leading official secrets case *R v Ponting*.[14] In the event, the day's proceedings were recounted nightly by newsreaders who, in traditional fashion, did not assume individual roles of the *personae* of the trial. However, the original plans were to the effect that a limited reconstruction of the courtroom scene should take place, with experienced actors taking the role of counsel, judge, etc.[15] In particular, the actors would be seen to be reading 'their parts' and would be strictly forbidden to imbue them with characterisation or dramatic inflection. Each reconstruction would last only half an hour, as compared with the full day's proceedings of some five hours. On the other hand, it was envisaged that the actors' lines would be taken directly from the transcript of the trial. This limited

---

[9] A recent case in point is BBC2's transmission in March 2000, a bare two months after the conclusion of the case, of a reconstruction of the libel action unsuccessfully brought by former MP, Neil Hamilton, against Mohamed Al Fayed. The programme, entitled *Justice in Wonderland*, was compiled on the basis of 7,500 pages of court transcript. The case, incidentally, involved a point of law on parliamentary privilege that was appealed up to the House of Lords: *Hamilton v Al Fayed* [2000] 2 All ER 224.

[10] S. Shale, 'Listening to the Law: Famous Trials on BBC Radio 1934–1989' (1996) 59 MLR 813.

[11] ibid. 825.   [12] ibid. 828.

[13] A device that the BBC was most reluctant to use in any event: ibid. 836.

[14] The background to the case is set out in the Appendix.

[15] See C. Ponting, *The Right to Know: The Inside Story of the Belgrano Affair* (1985) 170.

reproduction was prohibited by the trial judge, McCowan J, who issued an order under section 4 (2) of the Contempt of Court Act 1981 in the following terms: 'That a report of any part of the proceedings in the form proposed by Channel Four in their nightly half-hour *Court Report* be postponed until after the jury has given its verdict in this case or until further order.'[16]

The order, not being open to challenge under English law, became the object of proceedings before the European Commission of Human Rights in *Hodgson, Woolf Productions Ltd and the National Union of Journalists v United Kingdom*.[17] The applicants argued that they had been denied a fair hearing of their 'civil right', within the meaning of Article 6 of the Convention, to report matters stated in open court. In the opinion of the Commission, the form of the report envisaged by the applicants could not properly be described as a right which was 'civil' for the purposes of Article 6. The applicants based their case, in the alternative, on the freedom of expression guarantee of Article 10. Again, although there was an interference with the applicants' freedom of expression, the judge's order could be defended under one of the exceptions listed in paragraph 2 of Article 10, in 'maintaining the authority and impartiality of the judiciary' in the sense explained by the Court of Human Rights in the *Sunday Times* case.[18]

It should be noted that the thrust of the objection was to both the timing and the form of the representation that was envisaged. While the criminal trial was still incomplete, there was a danger that the jury might be influenced by the television reconstructions of the day's events. In principle such a possibility could be averted by jury sequestration, but this is an extreme response which adds considerably to the burdens of jury service. As to the matter of form, television coverage of the actual trial would have the advantage of verisimilitude as compared with the use of intermediaries to portray the proceedings. On the other hand, the dramatic reconstruction of courtroom scenes by the use of actors will have a significant advantage in situations where anonymity of such persons as witnesses is to be preserved. Vulnerable persons may not be content with an arrangement which does no more than obscure the television image of their face. Indeed, outside the courtroom setting it is not uncommon for a person's story to be narrated by an actor in the interests of the highest possible degree of confidentiality.

Yet another attempt at television reconstruction of the events in a current proceeding of considerable public interest was thwarted on the application of the Attorney-General in *A-G v Channel Four Television Co*.[19] The television company was seeking to broadcast, in a one-and-a-half hour programme entitled *Court Report*, an abbreviated version of the appeal hearing of *R v Callaghan* (far better known as the 'Birmingham Six' case). The script of the programme was to be taken from the official shorthand transcript of the proceedings, actors taking

---

[16] The terms of the order are set out in (1988) 10 EHRR 503, 504.   [17] (1988) 10 EHRR 503.
[18] *Sunday Times v UK* (1979–80) 2 EHRR 245.
[19] The Times, 18 December 1987: The Independent, 9 December 1987.

the part of witnesses, counsel, and members of the court. The Court of Appeal, in granting the injunction against transmission, was concerned that there would inevitably be a very considerably condensed version presented of what had happened in the courtroom. Moreover, no matter how well-intentioned the actors might be, they would inevitably create an impression among viewers of the programme about the degree of reliability of key witnesses in the proceedings. In subtle ways such as by eye movement or voice inflection, it might be possible for an actor playing the part of a witness in a reconstruction of a trial to suggest that the witness was more, or less, reliable than he appeared in the courtroom. There seems, indeed, to have been no indication that the actors themselves deemed it part of their duty to attend in the courtroom itself, entire reliance being placed on the 'script' furnished by the official shorthand writer. In short, therefore, the Court of Appeal dismissed the analogy sought to be drawn by counsel for the television company between television reconstructions and ordinary press reports in the newspapers. Since the question of the reliability of witnesses was central to the outcome of the criminal proceedings, the transmission that was envisaged would be likely to undermine public confidence in the administration of justice. It is noteworthy that, in reaching this decision, the Court of Appeal declined to ask for a preview of the programme. This decision is, perhaps, not entirely surprising in the circumstances. Unless the members of the Court of Appeal had themselves attended the hearing of the 'Birmingham Six' appeal, they would lack the basis for the making of an informed judgment as to whether or not the reconstruction distorted the events at that hearing.

Equally important was the fact that the programme, had it been transmitted, would have reached the public while the appeal hearing of the 'Birmingham Six' was still in progress. This, too, bodes ill for judicial sympathy for television transmission, since in contempt proceedings the general thrust of the law has been to allow a far greater degree of discussion once cases have reached the appellate level, on the basis that judges sitting in the Court of Appeal and the House of Lords are far less likely to have their views of the case swayed by media reports than are members of the trial jury. In the circumstances, the Court of Appeal reasoned that broadcast of the programme before the conclusion of the hearing might create an impression with the defendants that the Court's exposure to the programme would have exerted some influence on its judgment.

The hypothetical trial or the trial that is re-enacted in dramatic form, therefore, provides some insight into the problems that would be confronted by the televising of current trials. It is to current trials that the remainder of this section is devoted.

The stages that precede and follow an actual trial are relatively free of constraints from the point of view of audio-visual coverage. A television programme may take as its theme the entire sweep of pre-trial inquiries by the police, together with post-trial consequences. The first occasion of such comprehensive coverage was the filming by ITV of the inquiry into the murder of

Mohammed Rafia, camera crews covering the whole process from the discovery of the body through to the stage where the convicted killers were imprisoned.[20] The relative freedom with which filming may take place of both pre-trial and post-trial stages in the criminal process has been borne out in a number of cases. To take the process of arrest, the Divisional Court ruled in *R v Rhuddlan Justices, ex p HTV Ltd*[21] that the filming of an actual arrest did not count as 'legal proceedings held in public' for the purposes of section 4 of the Contempt of Court Act 1981. Indeed, it is often a matter of mere chance as to whether an arrest is carried out in public or in private. The magistrates therefore possessed no jurisdiction to make an order under section 4(2) of the Act. However, there is a danger that the transmission of the film of such an arrest—like the publication of a photograph of the accused—at any time while proceedings are 'active'[22] against the person filmed may amount to a contempt of court. Where the interests of children are involved, there may be additional obstacles to television transmission. In one such case a television company's planned programme about a police operation which led to the arrest and conviction of a paedophile was temporarily disrupted by an action brought on behalf of the man's five-year-old child. In the event the television company was held to be taking the requisite precautions to protect the child from publicity, though it had to fend off a claim that the broadcast material should obscure the man's face.[23]

A general obstacle that will confront those seeking to impose restraints on pre-trial media coverage is that of finding a suitable cause of action. Most commonly, it will be argued that there is a risk of prejudice to a fair trial for the accused, resulting in possible contempt liability on the part of those who published the material in question. These considerations apart, it will often prove difficult to identify some legal wrong. The difficulties were clearly illustrated on the facts in *R v Marylebone Magistrates' Court, ex p Amdrell Ltd t/a 'Get Stuffed'*.[24] Search warrants had been obtained in regard to the applicants' business premises. Unusually, during the process of execution of the warrants the police were accompanied by film crews, who remained outside while search and seizure were taking place. The firm unsuccessfully applied for judicial review of the search warrants on the ground that the police had failed to inform the magistrates, when applying for the warrants, that there would be a media presence. Such non-disclosure, the Divisional Court held, was irrelevant to the obtaining of a warrant since the manner of its execution was an operational matter within the exclusive control of the police.

These considerations were sufficient to dispose of the application. However, the Divisional Court did stress the possibility that the public mode of executing

---

[20] For the background see The Guardian (18 July 1990) 23.   [21] [1986] Crim LR 329.

[22] In the sense used in the Contempt of Court Act 1981, s 2 (3) and Sch 1.

[23] *R v Central Independent Television plc* [1994] 3 WLR 20.

[24] The Times, 17 September 1998.

warrants might impinge on several important values, not least of which was the need to secure a fair trial for any possible defendants. Two matters, in particular, are worth stressing in regard to this case. First, counsel for the police identified certain advantages in there being a media presence, which correspond remarkably to the classic claims made for open trial: the prompting of further witnesses to come forward; reassurance to the public that the police were acting effectively and responsibly; and deterrence of possible future crime. Secondly, the report is curiously silent as to when, if at all, the footage was broadcast. However, in criticizing the procedures, the Divisional Court mentioned that the media would naturally wish to publish without delay the footage that it had obtained.

Broadcast interviews with persons who are subsequently charged with a criminal offence, as in *R v Savundra*,[25] run the risk of incurring liability for contempt of court. Alternatively, the attention of a particular programme might be focused specifically on the testimony of particular witnesses, who are invited to contribute that testimony informally before television cameras in advance of the trial. This formed one of the points in issue in *R v Dye and Williamson*,[26] the background to which was a filmed interview of three prosecution witnesses in a case involving a heroin importation ring. The form of the interview gave the impression that the witnesses were giving evidence at the actual trial. A point that is particularly relevant to the theme of the present chapter is that the filming occurred prior to the trial, but the footage was broadcast only when the trial was over. The Court of Appeal upheld the convictions of the accused despite the fact that it noted a number of irregularities in such conduct. In both the *Savundra* and *Dye and Williamson* cases a particular danger was the widespread dissemination of material that was unduly favourable to the prosecution, there being no formal representation of other points of view. The risk of prejudice was especially acute in the former case, the interview being broadcast before Savundra was charged and tried. Certainly, in both these cases the very same prejudicial material might have been conveyed in the print media. However, the wider audience reached by television, together with the more vivid representation of the material through that medium, combined to accentuate the degree of possible prejudice.

The mere publication of photographs—and, even more so, the broadcasting of film footage—concerning an accused who is awaiting trial may amount to a contempt of court without even being accompanied by any form of interview. The prejudicial effect of such exposure is clear in those cases where a central issue is that of mistaken identity. In *R v Daily Mirror, ex p Smith*[27] the publication of a photograph on the morning of an identification parade resulted in contempt liability being incurred by the *Daily Mirror*.[28] Nor need the photograph be published in the media for issues of such liability to arise. In *Connolly v*

---

[25] [1968] 3 All ER 439.   [26] [1992] Crim LR 449.   [27] [1927] 1 KB 845.
[28] *R v Evening Standard Company Ltd, ex p Attorney-General* The Times, 2 November 1976, is almost identical. The headline that accompanied the photograph of the well-known leader of the Young Liberals, Peter Hain, ran: 'Hain: he's no bank robber.'

Dale[29] an inquiry agent acting for a man charged with murder had shown a photograph of the man to the residents of a hostel in the hope of securing corroboration for his alibi defence. The detective who was in charge of the investigation sought to obstruct these inquiries, but in doing so he was held to be in contempt of court. In reaching this conclusion the Divisional Court acknowledged that the detective's motives were entirely proper, since he was concerned about the possibility of prejudice to any identity parade that used the members of staff of the hostel. Even where issues of alibi are absent from a case, it is clear that the publication of a photograph of the accused taken in prejudicial circumstances (for example, in an aggressive posture) can constitute contempt. This occurred in *A-G v News Group Newspapers Ltd*,[30] where a newspaper was fined £5,000 for publishing such a photograph of one of the co-accused, combined with an emotive headline concerning the injuries allegedly sustained by the victim at the hands of the accused. Even in cases where there is no possible issue of identification and the published photograph itself bears no prejudicial aspect, the conjunction of a photograph with prejudicial written material may have the effect of increasing the likelihood of tainting an imminent trial. For the presence of the photograph will undoubtedly reinforce the effect of the printed material in the minds of potential jurors.[31] That the publication of pictorial images is fraught with potential difficulties is readily apparent. They are far more valuable than lengthy descriptions of appearance in leading to the identification and arrest of a suspect. However, they have considerable potential for prejudicing any subsequent trial where issues of identification are at stake.[32]

One of the issues that has figured prominently in some contempt cases is whether material that is admittedly capable of exerting a prejudicial effect will have lost its force because the lapse of time between the publication and the trial is such that it may have been forgotten by any potential juror who was exposed to the material. On the particular facts of *A-G v News Group Newspapers Ltd* this argument would not have been available since the material (which had been printed owing to a misunderstanding between the court reporter and the editorial staff) was published on the second day of the trial. There are cases, however, where the argument has been advanced with some plausibility.[33] In such cases the

---

[29] [1996] QB 120.   [30] (1984) 6 Cr App Rep (S) 418.

[31] See *A-G v News Group Newspapers plc* [1989] QB 110, where, at 122, there is a fleeting reference to the publication of a photograph of the accused alongside a prejudicial caption.

[32] The American constitutional lawyer, John Hart Ely, recounts such an incident from his student days in London. 'When Scotland Yard was seeking John Henry Cole for attacking and robbing a number of women, they requested the press not to publish photographs of him on the ground that such publication might undercut the value of identification testimony given subsequently at the trial. Disregard of such a request subjects a paper to a real threat of a contempt citation. Nonetheless the *News of the World* (6 million circulation) printed Cole's picture. Two days later Cole was recognised and captured, although the *Police Gazette* had run his picture for weeks without result.' J. H. Ely, *On Constitutional Ground* (1996) 158.

[33] For an analysis of the factors to be weighed when this argument is advanced, see *A-G v Independent Television News* [1995] 2 All ER 370 and *A-G v MGN* [1997] 1 All ER 456.

publication of a photograph to accompany the prejudicial material may well serve to reinforce in the mind of a potential juror the link between the material and the person eventually tried. This appears to have been the basis of the decision in *R v Thomson Newspapers, ex p A-G*,[34] although the exact role played by the photograph that accompanied the prejudicial caption is difficult to extract from the short judgment. Admittedly, transposing these factors from still photographs published in the print media to film footage broadcast on the television networks may prove problematic. For while the latter has the potential for reaching a far wider audience than that attained by any single newspaper, it is likely to be deemed more transitory in nature than still photographs.

The post-trial stages are free of problems of liability for contempt of court. The extent of the difficulty in finding legal weapons with which to suppress the dissemination of material gathered during this phase is illustrated by *Secretary of State for the Home Department v Central Broadcasting Ltd*.[35] The case involved an unsuccessful attempt to prohibit the broadcast of an interview of a notorious serial killer, Dennis Nilsen. Since the case was fought only on the interlocutory point, the legal basis for the decision is difficult to extract. The tape in question had been gained irregularly, in breach of Home Office policy relating to the broadcast of interviews with convicted prisoners. Breach of contract and breach of copyright were both unsuccessfully invoked by the Secretary of State. The latter argument, indeed, was also advanced by Central Broadcasting, who submitted that, since it owned the copyright under section 9(2)(a) of the Copyright, Designs and Patents Act 1988, it possessed the right to copy and broadcast the tape. Not only were these causes of action inapplicable in the circumstances, Aldous J thought that the material positively served a public benefit in showing how ordinary and intelligent a killer such as Nilsen might appear to be. This conclusion, founded on an actual viewing of the footage by the judge, demonstrates an advantage in film coverage over still photography and adds a most unusual further element to the advantages of public knowledge of the criminal justice system that were explored in Chapter 2.

Of further note was the argument advanced by the Secretary of State based on the likely renewal of feelings of distress among relatives of the killer's victims. This consideration has already been encountered earlier in this chapter. The repetition of the events of the trial, whatever legitimate interests it might serve, would rekindle the distress that the relatives endured in the actual courtroom. The likely retort would be the response that the Court of Appeal found entirely convincing in the instant case: that anyone likely to suffer such distress could choose not to view the programme, particularly if warning announcements were to be made prior to transmission.

---

[34] [1968] 1 All ER 268.
[35] The Times, 27 January 1993, per Aldous J; The Times, 28 January 1993, CA.

It is scarcely surprising that in the United States, with its greater experience of television coverage of trials, the issue has been raised as to whether cameras should be permitted access to prisons for the purpose of televising executions.[36] Several state legislatures have seen unsuccessful attempts to enact legislation that would permit the simultaneous broadcast of the event, whether with or without the condemned person's consent. The issues raised by the possibility of a modern equivalent to the public hangings of former times were explored in 1991, in *KQED v Vasquez*.[37] The plaintiff, a California television station, brought proceedings in the federal courts against the warden of San Quentin Prison in order to be allowed to position cameras in the witness seats of a forthcoming execution. In accordance with the reasoning that has been deployed in regard to trials, KQED argued that the form of coverage envisaged was fundamentally no different to the long-standing tradition of press attendance, admittedly in small and controlled numbers, at executions. In reply, the governor, reflecting an ever-present concern in regard to access to prisons, cited security reasons as a compelling factor against allowing television coverage. Schnacke J rejected the television company's case on several bases. 'The press', he said, 'has a right of access to whatever the public has a right to, but no *special* access.' The judge went on to cite a host of reasons, based on security considerations, against allowing television coverage. There was a risk that it would result in exposure of the identities of prison personnel, together with the potentially inflammatory effect on inmates of the prison, who would already be disturbed by the mere knowledge that the execution was taking place in the prison.

Once executions ceased to be public, selected individuals were allowed behind prison walls, both in Britain and the United States, for the formal purpose of witnessing the fact that the law had run its course. Attendance was permitted, in particular, to a limited number of representatives of the print media. Nevertheless, many American states imposed 'reporting restrictions' that forbade publication of any of the details of the execution. It is not surprising that, in view of the extremely limited numbers permitted access to the execution chamber, there should emerge a movement in favour of televising the event.[38] Of the three arguments advanced in favour of television access,[39] two reflect general themes which have been seen to permeate the rationales of open justice. One is that the public

---

[36] See generally W. Lesser, *Pictures at an Execution* (1993), and J. D. Bessler, *Death in the Dark: Midnight Executions in America* (1997) ch 7.

[37] 18 Media L.Rep (BNA) 2323 (N.D. Cal. 1991) (No C90-1383RHS).

[38] The scale of the crime can be such that special arrangements are made for the observation of the execution without the event being carried on the networks. A case in point was the execution in June 2001 of Timothy McVeigh for the bombing of a federal building in Oklahoma City in 1995. With the death of 168 people and the injury of hundreds more, a two-tier level of witnessing of the execution was arranged. It was personally observed by ten survivors, selected by lot, and was followed on closed-circuit television, at a site 600 miles away, by 300 others who had been affected by the explosion. McVeigh's trial in 1997 had similarly been relayed by television to the survivors and the families of the victims.

[39] Bessler (n 36 above) 182–4.

have a right to observe processes carried out by government in their name. The other stresses the potential deterrent value of witnessing the process of infliction of punishment. A third reason, in an unusual twist to the theme of public scrutiny of criminal justice, looks to the emergence of a tide of opinion in favour of abolition of capital punishment once the public is confronted on television with the stark reality of the process. The subject of televised executions, it can be appreciated, provides an interesting, if rather grim, variation on the standard themes of open justice.

2. CAMERAS AND TAPE-RECORDERS IN THE COURTROOM

The principal legal obstacle to the televising of the courts is section 41 of the Criminal Justice Act 1925. By virtue of this provision no person 'shall take or attempt to take in any court any photograph, or with a view to publication make or attempt to make in any court any portrait or sketch, of any person being a judge of a court or a juror or a witness in or a party to any proceedings before the court, whether civil or criminal; . . .'.

Section 41 entered English law as part of a general criminal justice measure which was dominated by other considerations.[40] It appears at the time to have been quite uncontroversial, and gained only a passing mention by the Home Secretary, Sir William Joynson-Hicks, in speaking in the second reading debate on the Bill: 'There is a small Clause to prevent photographs of the parties being taken in Court. Everybody has suffered for a long time by prisoners in the dock and witnesses being pilloried by having their photographs taken, and this is to prevent that happening'.[41]

No instances were cited by the Home Secretary, notwithstanding the existence of photographic techniques since the middle of the preceding century. Equally, there is nothing in this passage that indicates any special mischief brought about by photographs in court as opposed to other contexts. Nevertheless, there are well-documented instances of courtroom photography in the immediately preceding years. In 1910 Dr Crippen was photographed together with his mistress, Ethel Le Neve, in Bow Street Magistrates' Court shortly after his arrest. The photograph is taken at ground level and in close proximity to its principal subjects. A more dramatic moment was captured in March 1912, when Frederick Seddon was being sentenced to death for murder at the Old Bailey. Published the following day in the *Daily Mirror*, there is every reason to suppose that the photograph was taken illicitly since it looks down on the well of the courtroom, possibly from the public seats. The moment of the passing of the death sentence held a macabre fascination. It is the subject of an unknown photograph taken in 1922

---

[40] See M. Dockray, 'Courts on Television' (1988) 51 MLR 593, 594–7, for some account of the background to the drafting of the measure.

[41] *Hansard*, HC (series 5) vol 183, col 1599 (11 May 1925).

of Avory J wearing the Black Cap while passing sentence on one Thomas Allaway. The judge appears to have 'posed' for the camera on this occasion, the photograph being taken at an upward angle from a point just in front of his seat.[42]

No equivalent provision to section 41 has ever been enacted for Scotland. The present legal position, however, is generally understood as being similar to that under English law. The taking of photographs within the precincts of the courts is forbidden, regardless of whether proceedings are thereby disrupted.[43] The absence of an express statutory prohibition, as will be seen, has facilitated a certain flexibility of approach in Scotland. Yet there are recorded instances of courtroom photography in Scotland, no less than in England, in the pre-1925 years. From the same period as the above-mentioned English cases there is an extant photograph of one of the most famous of Scottish trials: the prosecution in 1909 of Oscar Slater for a particularly brutal murder.[44] The photograph of the High Court of Justiciary in Edinburgh is taken at ground level, the centre-piece being Slater himself wedged between two police officers. That a photograph of this trial should have been made available was particularly unfortunate since the case against Slater turned on identification evidence—evidence that turned out to be defective.[45]

The sensational murder trial has always proved a popular subject for courtroom photography, the likely market for the product outweighing the risk of incurring any legal penalty. Scenes from two of the most notorious murder trials of the twentieth century have been captured on film. Widely reproduced in the American press was the illicit photograph taken as the foreman of the jury announced the verdict of guilty against Bruno Hauptmann in the Lindbergh kidnapping case in New Jersey in 1935. A 35mm Contax had been smuggled into the courtroom, despite the judge's threat of a six-month prison sentence for anyone found in possession of a camera in the court.[46] Also, during the trial in May 1981 of Peter Sutcliffe (the so-called 'Yorkshire Ripper') the representative of a German magazine was able to take a secret photograph inside the courtroom. It appears that, when the relevant issue of the magazine was produced to the judge, the only sanction that he was able to inflict was an order forbidding the London editor of the magazine from attending the remainder of the trial—an unusual

---

[42] The photograph is preserved in the Mary Evans Picture Library, London.

[43] See B. McKain, A. Bonnington, and G. Watt, *Scots Law for Journalists* (6th edn, 1995), 124–8.

[44] The photograph is reproduced opposite p. xxvii of *The Trial of Oscar Slater* in the *Notable Scottish Trials* series.

[45] See the Appendix for some interesting aspects of the case and its sequel that bear on the subject of open justice.

[46] The photograph is reproduced in A. Rothstein, *Photojournalism* (3rd edn, 1974), 213. The account of the trial in A. Scaduto, *Scapegoat: The Lonesome Death of Bruno Richard Hauptmann* (1976) contains a number of scenes from the courtroom, including a dramatic waving of the arm by prosecuting counsel as he cross-examined Hauptmann.

variation on the standard theme of ordering the exclusion from the court of those who 'disrupt' the proceedings.[47]

As these instances demonstrate, the same technological advances that facilitate the unobtrusive recording on film of trial proceedings—and, in that respect, lend support to the case for the authorized entry of the audio-visual media to the courtroom—also open up the possibility of the taking of 'stolen' photographs. Certainly, the photograph that is taken contrary to the express prohibition of the law detracts from the administration of justice. However, the publication of the split-second of the trial that is caught on film is very unlikely to pose any of the hazards that beset the televising of the proceedings. It would be difficult, for example, for any still pictorial image—be it photograph or sketch—to create an impression that will be biased in favour of one side or the other. It is only a selective publishing of the verbal, in contrast to the pictorial, side of the proceedings that is capable of exerting such an effect.

The terms of section 41 of the Criminal Justice Act 1925 now merit closer examination.

The overriding point to be made about section 41 is that it is applicable only to courts. An inquiry presided over by a judge and approximating to a judicial format is outside the scope of the section. To take the most prominent recent example, the Scott inquiry into the 'Arms to Iraq' episode[48] fell outside the prohibition and so the question of admitting audio-visual equipment to the hearing was within the discretion of the chairman. When Lord Justice Scott was asked, at his first press conference, about the possibility of admitting such technology to the inquiry, he replied that the precedents were against it—an unfortunate conclusion since the inquiry covered matters of the highest importance and included the examination of the Prime Minister, Margaret Thatcher, by counsel to the inquiry. In sharp contrast was the conduct of a royal commission chaired by Sir Louis Blom-Cooper in Antigua in 1990. This was charged with the task of investigating the responsibility of local politicians for traffic in arms, and its proceedings were transmitted in full each evening on both radio and television.

There does appear to be some doubt as to whether the House of Lords, sitting as a judicial body, would be caught by the terms of section 41. While undoubtedly a court for the great majority of purposes—including disqualification of its members for possible bias[49]—the judges who sit to hear cases are also members of a legislative body which has taken the decision to admit television cameras to cover its proceedings. It was perhaps on this basis that on 24 March 1999 the senior law lord, Lord Browne-Wilkinson, gave a short summary in the chamber of the House of Lords, before television cameras, of the decision that he and six

---

[47] The incident is recounted in D. Cassell, *The Photographer and the Law* (3rd edn, 1997) 82.

[48] For details of the 'Arms to Iraq' cases and their sequel, see the Appendix.

[49] See, most recently, *R v Bow Street Metropolitan Stipendiary Magistrate, ex p Pinochet Ugarde (No 2)* [1999] 1 All ER 577.

colleagues had just reached in *R v Bow Street Metropolitan Stipendiary Magistrate, ex p Pinochet Ugarte (No 3)*.[50]

Equally, it is clear that section 41 does not prohibit the photographing or sketching of court buildings *per se*—in the way that, for example, the Official Secrets Act forbids the making of sketches of 'prohibited places'.[51] When the buildings are not in use for the transaction of judicial business, the section is not applicable.[52] It would appear, therefore, that it does not apply even during short intermissions, such as adjournments. The mistaken supposition that the ban applies outside court hours has been given as the reason why the fine architecture and interior of Britain's oldest court buildings have seldom been caught on film.[53]

Section 41 encompasses civil and criminal trials alike. Subsection (2)(a) stipulates that the word 'court' means 'any court of justice, including the court of a coroner'. Tribunals are not included in the prohibition. The omission was surely one of oversight only—understandably so in view of the limited use of the tribunal forum in the 1920s. The word 'judge' is defined as including a registrar but, somewhat unnecessarily, as also extending to a 'recorder . . . magistrate, justice and coroner'. There are, it will be seen, a number of objections that can be made to the televising of criminal proceedings—the presumption of innocence, and rehabilitative considerations in the event of a conviction—that are largely absent from civil cases and coroners' inquests. Yet the prohibition applies with equal force in regard to each type of hearing. In regard to the last-mentioned judicial officer, a documentary series about the work of such officials, entitled 'The Coroner', which was broadcast by Channel Four in early 1999 was debarred by section 41 from filming any inquest.[54] It is also noteworthy that the first occasion of television coverage in regard to a judicial proceeding in Australia centred on a coroner's inquest. The question of the attribution of blame in the course of the inquest, which took place in 1981, ensured that the proceedings attracted a very considerable degree of public interest.[55] The background was the infamous 'dingo' case. The previous year a baby had disappeared from a camping area. The parents, Lindy and Michael Chamberlain, claimed that it had been taken by a

[50] [1999] 2 All ER 97.

[51] Official Secrets Act 1911, s 1. Although this provision encompasses the making of any 'sketch, plan, model, or note', strangely it does not cover the taking of photographs.

[52] In this respect it is worth noting the highly unusual circumstances of *R v Loveridge* The Times, 3 May 2001. The accused were secretly filmed by the police while confined in the cell area of a magistrates' court. The footage was used against them, being compared with pictures taken earlier on closed-circuit television cameras. The Court of Appeal took the view that the action of the police contravened the Criminal Justice Act 1925, s 41, even though the accused were not being tried at the time of filming.

[53] See The Times, Magazine Section (3 May 1997): 'Silence in Court.'

[54] A surviving photograph from the pre-1925 era captures the scene at a coroner's court. M. Gilbert, *Churchill: A Photographic Portrait* (1999), photograph 83, shows Winston Churchill giving evidence at the Sidney Street inquest on 18 January 1911. Churchill, as Home Secretary, had directed a controversial operation which resulted in the death of two anarchists trapped by the police in Sidney Street, London.

[55] See G. Nettheim, 'Cameras in the Courtroom' (1981) 55 *Australian Law Journal* 855.

wild animal, a dingo. The inquest, held in Alice Springs, culminated in the coroner reading his 13-page findings before television cameras.[56] He justified this extraordinary step as an attempt to dispel the suspicions which had fallen on the baby's parents, though it is to be noted that the inquest proceedings themselves were not televised.[57]

The prohibition imposed by section 41 applies equally to both *personae* of the trial and members of the public and representatives of the press. On the other hand, the ban on the making of portraits or sketches is limited to drawings that are made of judges, jurors, witnesses, and parties to the proceedings before the court. Solicitors and counsel, in particular, are outside the ambit of this part of section 41: so too, it would seem, are friends, family, and associates of the parties who are present in the courtroom. As is implicit in the criminal law, the consent of the 'victim' will not afford a defence to the person charged with contravening the section. It has been tentatively suggested, however, that the presiding judge may be able to authorize photography in court in certain exceptional circumstances.[58] In the course of the famous A6 murder trial of James Hanratty in 1962 at Bedford Assizes, Gorman J gave express permission to photograph or film him, on one occasion only, while he was leaving the court building to go to the judges' lodgings.[59] The idea that judicial permission would exonerate from liability under section 41 is difficult to reconcile either with general principle or with the wording of the provision. It is also at odds with the position taken by the judiciary in regard to penetrating the secrecy of the jury room. As was noted in Chapter 7, the appellate courts have regarded the terms of section 8 of the Contempt of Court Act 1981 as binding on themselves as much as on journalists, parties, and their legal advisers. Indeed, section 41 can be taken as protecting the interests of the administration of justice in general, rather than the privacy rights of the various persons of whom photographs and sketches may not be made. It is noteworthy, nevertheless, that the forbidden material need not be accompanied by captions identifying their subjects as the *personae* of trial proceedings. The mere publication of their likenesses suffices to bring the material within the scope of section 41, irrespective of the presence of any accompanying matter that would serve to identify them as jurors or witnesses, let alone material that would link them with proceedings in a particular case.

---

[56] See Lindy Chamberlain's autobiographical account, *Through My Eyes* (1991), 156–7, for the coroner's explanation.

[57] This tentative venture in television coverage, however, did not succeed in achieving the coroner's objective. Lindy and Michael Chamberlain were tried and convicted of the child's murder, although their convictions were subsequently quashed. So great was the interest of the world's media in the trial, held in the Supreme Court in Darwin, that their representatives had to be accommodated in a separate room, linked up to the courtroom by a closed circuit television system. For the judge's explanation to the jury of the presence of cameras, see ibid. 242–3. (The story of the case is also represented in a 1988 film, starring Meryl Streep, called *A Cry in the Dark*.)

[58] M. Dockray, 'Cameras at the door of the court' NLJ (20 April 1990) 548, 549.

[59] D. Cassell, *The Photographer and the Law* (3rd edn, 1997) 82.

This last observation is necessitated by the differential treatment of photographs and sketches. There is an absolute prohibition on the taking of photographs in court. Any picture taken of persons in the courtroom would probably also catch sufficient additional detail to identify it as a courtroom scene. The ban on the making of portraits or sketches, in contrast, applies only if they are made 'with a view to publication'. The difference may be explained and justified on the ground that the taking of photographs is the more disruptive of the two activities. The drawing of sketches may be done with a minimum of fuss. The difference is no longer justified, however, if television recording is to be equated with the taking of photographs. Modern technology permits the unobtrusive recording on cinefilm of the whole of a trial. In fact, there is a double disparity in the terms of section 41: as between photographs and sketches; and as between those sketches that are made with a view to publication and those that are not. There is no restriction on the making of sketches that do not have that end in view. If, however, they are drawn for the purpose of publication, they must be made from memory outside the court. It is this uneasy compromise that has permitted the rise in the trade of the courtroom artist, whose work has so often been used to illustrate evening news reports of current trials. Some courtroom artists, such as Priscilla Coleman, Julia Quenzler, and Richard Cole (who have served as principal artists for, respectively, ITN, the BBC, and Channel Four) are now well-known practitioners of this particular genre.[60] Their method of working is to sit in the courtroom, memorize the scene, and leave the building in order to draw the actual sketch. Transmission of the finished product is then effected by placing the drawing in front of a television camera situated somewhere near the court building. In this way the processes of sketching and televising take place well away from the courtroom. The procedure that is imposed on artists by section 41 may appear rather strange. It could be argued that they should be permitted to sketch in the courtroom itself, just as the traditional reporter is permitted to make notes on a notepad. The possible disadvantages of allowing such a change were borne out by the trial in France during 1987 of Klaus Barbie on charges of crimes against humanity, where the profusion of courtroom artists was such as to detract from the solemnity of the proceedings.[61] The drawing of courtroom sketches did not appear to have occasioned sufficient annoyance to warrant specific mention by Sir William Joynson-Hicks in the course of his explanation of the provision that became section 41. In any event, there are in existence drawings of nineteenth-century trials that were published at the time in *Punch*.[62]

---

[60] On occasion they have exhibited collections of their work.

[61] The scale of the problem was such that one lawyer in the case is reported as having opened his address to the court with the words: 'This is not a court of law. This is an art class'. *The Lawyer* (3 July 1990) 17.

[62] See E. S. Turner, *May it please your Lordship* (1971) for three such sketches: 'An Interesting Trial for Murder' opposite p. 129; 'An Old Bailey Trial, 1881' and 'The Lord Chancellor's Court at Lincoln's Inn Hall' opposite p. 193.

The very fact that the work of such artists is permitted at all detracts from one possible service performed by section 41: the protection of witnesses and jurors from identification and possible intimidation. In those increasing numbers of trials that have been characterized by anonymity for such persons, the implication is that the plain words of section 41 must be read subject to the the the overriding need to protect their identities.[63] Concerns are raised from time to time about the propriety of photographing witnesses outside the precincts of the court building. Even where no issue of witness anonymity or national security is involved, the degree of interference with the person's comfort is such that, on occasion, it has elicited a judicial order prohibiting the use of the photograph. For example, during the trial of Rosemary West[64] one person called as a witness was the defendant's step-daughter, Anne Marie West. Her testimony was interrupted by a stay in hospital. On discharge from hospital, she was photographed while emerging from the building on the way to returning to the courtroom. This situation fell outside the terms of both section 41 and the Press Complaints Commission's Code of Practice.[65] The trial judge, Mantell J, made an order prohibiting the use of the photograph or of any news item which would identify the hospital where Anne Marie West had been treated.[66]

Even in the absence of security considerations, the mere knowledge that an artist is present in the courtroom may detract from the business of the trial. Julia Quenzler, extrapolating from her experience of jurisdictions where both sketching and television recording are permitted, has stated her belief that the way in which individuals present themselves will change if they believe that their image is being recorded at the relevant time.[67] Her views, if correct, are of considerable importance for the question of whether television cameras should be permitted in the courtroom. Moreover, they indicate a strong basis for defending the present position in regard to the making of sketches in the English courtroom. If the artist cannot be identified as such, and is present in the same way as any other member of the public, it will be impossible for any of the *personae* of the trial to ascertain whether his or her image is being memorised with a view to the subsequent drawing of a sketch.

---

[63] See the interview with Priscilla Coleman: The Times (12 September 1988) 17. It emerges that she is not allowed to draw the members of the jury in any event. Moreover, in the course of covering the inquest in Gibraltar in 1988 into the shooting by the SAS of three IRA terrorists, she drew only a corner of the curtained witness box, with coroner and lawyers looking towards it, when the commander of the SAS unit was giving evidence anonymously.

[64] For a brief account of the case see the Appendix.

[65] Code of Practice, cl 9, specifically mentions hospitals, requiring photographers to obtain permission to enter non-public areas and stipulating that the privacy provision of the Code (cl 3) is 'particularly relevant to inquiries about individuals in hospitals or similar institutions'.

[66] B. Masters, *'She Must Have Known': The Trial of Rosemary West* (1997) 325. As the passage goes on to comment, it did not emerge in the courtroom how any photographer had been in a position to know the hospital in which the witness was being treated.

[67] *The Lawyer* (3 July 1990) 17.

Although section 41 encompasses the taking of still photographs, it is not entirely clear that it is appropriately drafted so as to include the recording or transmission of proceedings by television. Even if such technology had been available in 1925 (it was not until 1936 that the first television service was launched by the BBC) it would certainly not have developed its potential to such a stage that it would have been within the contemplation of the mischief that Parliament sought to correct when enacting the section. It could be argued that, since cinefilm consists of a series of single photographic images, the wording of section 41 is suitably drafted to include within the prohibition the televised recording of trials. Those who are obviously trying to bring photographic equipment of any type into the court building will be prevented from doing so. Consequently, it might be thought that a factual situation could not be presented in which the point of law would be resolved. Even so, there has long existed the potential for clarifying this particular point. Since the scope of the prohibition on photographs extends to the 'precincts of the building' and also encompasses photographs of persons while in the course of entering or leaving the building, the legality of film footage taken in this context could easily present itself for decision by the courts. In any event, it is noteworthy that the only measure that has been initiated with a view to facilitating the televising of trials sought to amend section 41. The Courts (Research) Bill 1990, as was noted in Chapter 7, failed to get a second reading in the House of Commons. Had it been enacted into law, it would have created two new subsections, (1A) and (1B), to section 41(1) of the Criminal Justice Act 1925. Consequently section 41(1) would have read in such a way that nothing 'shall affect any broadcasting of court or tribunal proceedings, or any publication of or relating to any report of court or tribunal proceedings including material derived from or created for the purposes of any such broadcast'. This mode of drafting, it is to be noted, would have left in place the prohibition on still photography. Clearly, in view of the omission of tribunals from the 1925 provision, the inclusion of such bodies in the text of the Bill was unnecessary. Its sponsor, Michael Woodcock MP, informed the House of Commons that it was not the intention of his measure to make television in court a permanent feature, but rather to allow controlled experiments with a view to testing the arguments for and against television transmission.

Two important preconditions had to be satisfied before exemption from liability would be gained under the proposed measure. First, arrangements for the broadcast in question and for the prior collecting of material must be carried out in accordance with rules made for the purpose by the appropriate authority. Such arrangements were expressed to include 'any question of obtaining or dispensing with consents', though the Bill was not specific in stating whose consent was necessary. Secondly, the exemption from section 41 furnished by the new provision would apply only to 'proceedings broadcast by television for the purposes of research or used for such purposes'. This condition would have raised difficult issues of interpretation of the meaning of 'research'. It is difficult to avoid the conclusion that the concept was simply carried over from the other main provision of the Bill, where the idea of jury research is eminently plausible as a consideration weighing in favour of access to the secrets of the jury room.

That section 41 does function as a barrier to the televising of court proceedings was the outcome of the judgment in an unusual case: *Re St Andrew's Heddington*.[68] The Salisbury Consistory Court was faced with a dispute as to whether a valuable silver tankard, which belonged to the parish of Heddington, should be sold in order to finance urgently needed repairs to the parish church. Shortly before the hearing, permission was sought to record the proceedings of the Consistory Court, extracts from which would eventually appear on BBC television in a series about village life.[69] The Chancellor, Judge Ellison, regarded the matter as taken outside his discretion by the terms of section 41—a ruling which, incidentally, is at variance with the view that the presiding judge possesses an inherent power to permit photography in limited circumstances. A church, he said, was normally to be considered a public building. However, when used for the purpose of the holding of a Consistory Court—'which is not a private church tribunal but one of the courts of the realm'[70]—it was brought within the ambit of section 41. This would appear to be an important qualification, which would not have the effect of making section 41 applicable on the occasion of discharge of every 'judicial' function. What did the Chancellor mean by this description? It was a reference, presumably, to the basis of the Consistory Court's jurisdiction in a Measure of the Church of England, equivalent to an Act of Parliament. A paradoxical situation is thereby revealed. If an institution is a regular court of the realm, there is a presumptive right of access on the part of members of the public. However, section 41 is equally drawn into play so as to forbid particular visual representations of the proceedings. If, on the other hand, the institution is not such a court, members of the public do not have the right to attend. Yet those who do gain admittance are not restrained by the terms of section 41. In any event, the judge regarded it as beyond argument that the filming of the court's proceedings would contravene section 41. The purpose of the provision, he said, was 'clearly to afford necessary privacy to judges and others concerned from unwelcome intrusions . . . Justice could not be properly administered if judges or witnesses suffered the pressures, embarrassment and discomfort of being photographed whilst playing their particular role in

---

[68] [1977] 3 WLR 286.

[69] The media have not always shown such deference to the proceedings before a Consistory Court. In *R v Chancellor of the Chichester Consistory Court, ex p News Group Newspapers Ltd* [1992] COD 48, it was reported that the press and television had 'openly flouted' s 41 in regard to the particular hearing, which involved a disciplinary case against a vicar for having committed adultery with two of his parishioners.

[70] [1977] 3 WLR 286, 290. On the rules relating to when the proceedings must take place in open court see G. H. Newsom and G. L. Newsom, *Faculty Jurisdiction of the Church of England* (2nd edn, 1993) 79–80.

court with the expectation that every sign, mood, mannerism or observation should later be displayed on the public media.'[71]

The case also contributes to our understanding of the physical ambit of section 41. Some guidance is already afforded on the point by section 41(2)(c). This provides that a photograph or sketch shall be deemed to have been taken in court 'if it is taken or made in the court-room or in the building or in the precincts of the building in which the court is held, or if it is a photograph, portrait or sketch taken or made of the person while he is entering or leaving the court-room or any such building or precincts as aforesaid'. Judge Ellison expressed some doubts as to the precise ambit of the statutory phrase: 'the precincts of the building in which the court is held.'[72] For that particular purpose he ruled that the precincts extended as far as the 'curtilage' of the building. Any further exploration of the term in the context of that case would probably not have furnished general guidance, since a Consistory Court generally sits in a church, not in a purpose-built court building. Two points merit emphasis at this stage. It is quite clear that the phrasing of section 41 is cast in terms of the trial process being conducted in a specific building, whether or not one exclusively devoted to that purpose. This exposes a possible lacuna in the legislation since, on those occasions when a 'view' is being conducted, the extent of the area subject to the prohibition is far less clear. The same point may also be made in regard to the situations when the court is obliged to move from its usual seat in order to receive the testimony of a bed-ridden witness. Yet, on general principle, the same considerations which lead to bans on photography in a court building also point to similar prohibitions on those rare occasions when the court sits in other locations.[73] Moreover, if the term 'precincts' is to be equated with the curtilage of the building in which the trial is taking place, the effect is to substitute one unclear expression for another. That the word 'curtilage' is not free of considerable ambiguity has been demonstrated from other contexts in which the word has been used.[74] A number of points emerge from an analysis of the term: that there is no single test applicable to all the contexts in which 'curtilage' is used;[75] that the central characteristic is that of 'integrality' with a building;[76] and that the size, and—most remarkably for our purposes—the type of building in question may be important considerations in determining the ambit of the curtilage.[77]

Clearly, there is scope for argument as to the exact ambit of the 'precincts' of a court building. In order to clarify the position the Phillimore Report on

---

[71] [1977] 3 WLR 286, 289–290.

[72] It is worth recalling that the term 'the precincts of the Court' is also used in the Crown Court Rules 1982, SI 1982/1109, r 24A(2), for the purpose of stipulating where a notice must be displayed of an intention to apply for an order that all or part of a trial be held *in camera*.

[73] The situation when the court sits temporarily in a hospital, the witness being too ill to be removed to the regular courtroom, would be covered by the relevant provisions of the Code of Practice of the Press Complaints Commission. See especially cl 9.

[74] N. Stanley, 'Curtilage—a pernicious lack of certainty' [1996] Conv 352.   [75] ibid. 355.

[76] ibid. 356–7.   [77] ibid. 364.

Contempt of Court recommended that a map or plan should be displayed, wherever practicable, in the court premises indicating the boundaries of such precincts.[78] This measure, in order to be useful, would need to be based on an authoritative judicial ruling since it would seek to clarify a point of interpretation in an Act of Parliament. There is potential for legal dispute, especially in the light of the possibilities opened up by the long-range camera, as to the precise point at which a photograph is deemed to have been 'taken or made' for the purposes of section 41(2)(c) of the 1925 Act. Is it the point where the photographer stands? Or is it the place where the subject of the photograph is located?

The aim of section 41 could be said to create a 'safe zone'[79] around the transaction of judicial business. Clearly, in the light of the rationale of the measure, an extended scope should be given to the meaning of the 'precincts' of the court. The Recorder of London, Sir James Miskin, in an unreported case, ruled that the word included all the streets surrounding the court.[80] On the other hand, it is recorded that the former Lord Chancellor, Lord Gardiner, while in legal practice, once successfully defended a photographer charged with having contravened section 41 by submitting that a photograph taken of a prisoner arriving on the footway outside the doors of the court at Bow Street was not one taken within the 'precincts' of the court.[81] More remarkably, the same writer attributes to Avory and Darling JJ the extraordinary view that 'the precincts of the court' also include the steps of the hotel where the judge was staying while on circuit.[82] There is something to be said for prohibiting photographs taken in such a location in the light of terrorist attempts on the lives of any figures considered as representative of the British state. The identification of the location of judges' lodgings by means of photographs is capable of posing a serious threat to the security of the judiciary. Whether section 41 is suitably drafted to ward off these threats is another matter.

Although section 41 prohibits the taking of photographs within the specific area covered by subsection (2)(c), the same activity may still be punishable as interfering with the administration of justice even when taking place outside the forbidden area. A case in point is *R v Runting*.[83] The appellant had taken photographs of one defendant, and attempted to do the same in regard to his co-defendant, as they came down the steps of the court building during their trial on charges of living on immoral earnings. For the next two minutes the photographer ran after the two

[78] *Report of the Committee on Contempt of Court* (Cmnd. 5794, 1974) para 41.

[79] Anonymous, 'Privacy, Photography, and the Press' (1998) 111 *Harvard Law Review* 1086, 1091.

[80] The Independent (29 January 1988) 3. This report adds that the City of London Police have threatened to arrest any photographer taking photographs in those adjoining streets. Again, The Independent (3 February 1988) 2 reports that a freelance photographer, Renee Schulz, was arrested and charged with contempt of court for allegedly photographing a witness near the Old Bailey. He was also ordered to hand over the film. The incident, nevertheless, is reported as having taken place 'some distance from the court building'.

[81] C. H. Rolph, NLJ (16 March 1990) 382; and NLJ (13 December 1991) 1716.

[82] To Avory J in NLJ (16 March 1990) 382; to Darling J in NLJ (13 December 1991) 1716.

[83] (1989) 89 Cr App R 243.

defendants trying to take photographs, despite the fact that the co-defendant was doing everything possible to cover his face and escape. The chase took all three well away from the court building and towards a nearby underground railway station. In that respect, therefore, the physical confines protected by section 41 were not longer relevant. Nevertheless, the Court of Appeal emphasized the importance of not intimidating persons (such as witnesses or the accused) who had business to perform in court: any such interference could result in an unwillingness to perform their respective functions. There was, in addition to this need, the importance of maintaining the authority and dignity of the court system. The Court of Appeal, in quashing the photographer's conviction, viewed his actions as falling short of contempt of court. Despite their reprehensible nature, something more (for example, snatching away the newspaper which was shielding the co-defendant from public view) would be required.

Insofar as section 41 strives to protect images of an accused from public disclosure, it can be supplemented by the practice of covering his head with a blanket on the way into the court building. Although the criminal defendant is not specifically mentioned in subsection (1)(a), he could certainly be construed as 'a party to any proceedings'. There is scope for argument that taking a photograph, within the prohibited areas, of an accused covered in this way could still qualify as an offence under section 41. Certainly, in so far as the practice of covering the head has some point, it has been reported as being that of 'protecting the person's identity before trial'.[84]

In view of the limited protective role served by section 41, it is ironic that the provision has been considered to raise difficulties in regard to the implementation of security measures which are now commonly found in and around public and large commercial buildings. It has been suggested that the use of closed circuit television cameras in order to monitor movements into and around the court building may, paradoxically, be a contravention of that provision.[85] There is a difference in principle between security cameras and cameras that are present in the court building with a view to publication of the material recorded. Yet both function by way of taking a succession of still photographs. Consequently, it is not a difference that the terms of section 41, as it stands, are capable of reflecting.[86]

Another respect in which section 41 may inhibit what are considered to be entirely proper uses of modern video technology lies in the use of live television links in order to connect a witness with the proceedings in the courtroom. The

---

[84] C. H. Rolph, NLJ (13 December 1991) 1716.

[85] M. Dockray, 'Cameras at the door of the court' NLJ (20 April 1990) 548.

[86] This stands in contrast to Scots law, as reflected in a particular incident in the Dundee District Court. In March 1999 a security camera was installed in that court on account of incidents of vandalism in the public seats. It was originally mounted in the wrong position, pointing towards the dock. Even when repositioned so as to cover the public benches, lawyers acting for certain defendants objected to the presence of a camera anywhere in the courtroom. The District Court Manager retained it on the basis of a letter from the Lord President that the prohibition in Scots law does not apply to security cameras.

issues relating to the consequent 'fragmentation' of the courtroom were discussed in detail in Chapter 3. A difficulty that has been held over until now is the question, which has been raised by Dockray, as to whether the use of certain types of live video link might contravene section 41.[87] If there is such an inconsistency, the difficulty can be avoided by holding that later statutory provisions permitting these links, such as section 32 of the Criminal Justice Act 1988, have impliedly repealed *pro tanto* section 41. It should be added, though, that a similarly convenient conclusion could not be drawn where the provision authorizing the use of a live video link is located in a mere statutory instrument. But is there an inconsistency between section 41 of the 1925 Act and the provisions authorizing video links? Once again, the question is raised as to whether section 41 must be read as limited to still photographs, or whether it can be taken as encompassing more modern technology. Even if section 41 is given the wider interpretation, there is scope for doubting the validity of Dockray's conclusion. He argues that any arrangement whereby the witness could see those in the courtroom would fall foul of section 41, although there would be no difficulty with a situation where the link enabled those in the court to see the witness. This conclusion appears to be based on the view that only the former arrangement could be construed as admitting television into the courtroom. Such a view appears to be based on the assumption that only the seat of the trial (where the judge, parties, counsel, etc. are located) can count as the 'court' for this purpose. There is a plausible alternative interpretation, under which the 'court' could be regarded as encompassing both its principal seat and any annexe where, for the time being, a witness is giving his testimony.[88]

A variation on this problem is to be found in those arrangements where it is the accused who is connected with the courtroom by means of a live video link. The special difficulty in this type of case stems from the possible infringement of what we have seen to be the most basic aspect of open justice: the right of the accused to be present at his own trial. A cautious approach was adopted in the Crime and Disorder Act 1998, in permitting live television links to the court from the prison or other institution in which the accused is confined. The facility is limited to pre-trial hearings only; the court is to hear representations from the parties before directing that 'the accused shall be treated as being present in the court' for the purpose of compliance with the standards of open justice; and it is a basic requirement that the accused is able to see and hear the court, and to be seen and heard by it.[89]

Yet another set of arrangements may fall foul of section 41. That is where the media interest in a case is so intense that a closed circuit television system is

---

[87] M. Dockray, 'Evidence by Television' (1992) 109 LQR 561, 562–3.

[88] Dockray's conclusion would also lead to the unacceptable conclusion that it would result in confrontation in only one direction: that is to say, the witness is able to confront those seated in the court building, but these people would be invisible to the witness as he gave his testimony.

[89] Crime and Disorder Act 1998, s 57.

installed so that the media may follow the proceedings in an adjoining room in the court building.[90] In this, as in the other two situations just discussed, the technology is not installed with a view to permitting subsequent publication of the footage. On one view, therefore, the arrangement has been thought to be permissible. The legality of the situation was pondered in September 1999 in the course of the laying out of the Bow Street Magistrates' Court for the hearing of the application for the extradition of General Pinochet, the former dictator of Chile. Senior judges were reported as having concluded that the construction of closed circuit television links to two adjoining courtrooms was not illegal, provided that two conditions were met: that the material would not be recorded; and that it would be shown only within the precincts of the court.[91]

This concludes our discussion of section 41. It is now necessary to give some account of the other legal barrier to audio-visual recording: section 9 of the Contempt of Court Act 1981. This stipulates that it is a contempt to use a tape recorder in court, at any rate without the leave—which presumably means the *prior* leave—of the court.[92] Equally, it is punishable as a contempt to publish 'a recording of legal proceedings' made in such a way 'by playing it in the hearing of the public or any section of the public'.[93] Under the former provision, leave may be granted or refused outright or may be granted 'subject to such conditions as the court thinks proper with respect to the use of any recording made pursuant to the leave'.[94] The issues surrounding the use of tape recorders were addressed in the Report of the Phillimore Committee on Contempt of Court. The Committee thought that tape recordings were to be made only with the consent of the trial judge and should be used solely for educational purposes or for broadcasting when the proceedings had become of historical interest. Its principal objection to the general use of tape recorders was that they 'produce a more dramatic but not necessarily more accurate record of what occurred in court'.[95]

A Practice Direction has been handed down which indicates the factors to be borne in mind when application is made for the permission of the court.[96] One consideration that was to weigh in favour of giving permission was the reasonable need of the applicant, whether as a litigant or as 'a person connected with the press or broadcasting'. The need of a mere onlooker from the public gallery was deemed not sufficiently pressing to be worthy of consideration in this regard. The other two considerations listed were capable of inclining the decision of the court towards refusal. One was the possibility that the proceedings might be disturbed by the use of a recorder or that witnesses or 'other participants' might be distracted or worried by the presence of the device. The other was the risk that the

---

[90] As, for example, in the criminal proceedings brought in Australia against Lindy and Michael Chamberlain (n 57 above).

[91] The Times (28 September 1999) 11.   [92] Contempt of Court Act 1981, s 9(1)(a).

[93] Contempt of Court Act 1981, s 9(1)(b).   [94] Contempt of Court Act 1981, s 9(2).

[95] *Report of the Committee on Contempt of Court* (Cmnd 5794, 1974) para 42.

[96] *Practice Direction: (Tape Recorders)* [1981] 1 WLR 1526.

contents of the recording would be communicated to a witness who had been required to absent himself from the court prior to the giving of his own testimony. However, the Practice Direction emphasized that the court should always bear in mind the possibility, apart from granting or refusing permission outright, of giving permission subject to various conditions. The possibility of 'leaking' the material recorded to a witness awaiting his turn outside the courtroom could be averted by attaching appropriate conditions to a grant of permission.

The prohibition imposed by section 9 is categorically stated as not applying to 'the making or use of sound recordings for purposes of official transcripts of proceedings'.[97] It is also made clear that any private person who is granted permission may not offer his recording as either an official transcript of the proceedings or as a rival to the official record.

A striking instance of the grant of permission, prior to both the Contempt of Court Act and the promulgation of the Practice Direction, was the obscenity prosecution, *R v Anderson*.[98] As a subsequently published account of the trial relates,[99] permission was sought by a freelance film producer to tape the entire proceedings of the trial. This was granted except in respect of the judge's summing-up, which inexplicably fell outside the scope of the permission. The result was a series of 130 half-hour tapes which facilitated both the written account of the trial and, several years later, a television reconstruction of the proceedings.

Section 9 would have been amended in the following way by Clause 1 (2) of the Courts (Research) Bill:

In section 9 of the Contempt of Court Act 1981, the following subsection shall be inserted after subsection (1)—

'(1A) Nothing in subsection (1)(b) shall apply to any broadcast or related publication pursuant to arrangements which are carried out as envisaged in section 41(1A) of the Criminal Justice Act 1925'.

Yet it is far from clear that section 9 would necessarily form a legal obstacle to the sound broadcasting of trials, whether in itself or as an adjunct to television broadcasting. The live transmission by radio of the trial proceedings, since it would not involve any act of recording, would not necessarily contravene the section.

3. THE SCOTTISH EXPERIMENT

It has already been noted that section 41 of the Criminal Justice Act 1925 does not apply in Scotland. That, in itself, does not preclude all possibility of incurring contempt liability as a consequence of the taking of photographs in the environs

---

[97] Contempt of Court Act 1981, s 9(4).   [98] [1972] 1 QB 304.
[99] T. Palmer, *The Trials of Oz* (1971) 10.

of court buildings.[100] Nevertheless, there was no statutory bar to the making of a number of programmes that have involved the filming of courtroom sequences. Most notably, a series of five documentaries was compiled and broadcast by the BBC in 1994 under the series name, *The Trial*. These covered a number of Scottish trials (in particular, trials for attempted murder and attempted armed robbery). Rather less well known were two Scottish programmes which televised civil and criminal proceedings in February and March of the same year.[101] The permission of Lord Hope, the Lord President, was obtained for this experiment. On 6 August 1992 he handed down practice directions to provide ground rules under which filming could take place in the Court of Session and the High Court of Justiciary.[102] In regard to the latter, the Lord Justice General additionally promulgated a more detailed set of rules concerning criminal trials. For the purposes of the Sheriff Courts, the sheriffs principal published a similar set of directions.[103] The aim of these standards was to protect both the administration of justice and the interests of all concerned in the trials. They have the status of standing directions, being in place (until revoked or amended) to regulate all applications that are made to televise Scottish proceedings.[104] They could provide useful precedents if a similar development were to occur in England and Wales.

The most important condition imposed by the Lord President was the requirement that the filming of a criminal trial would be permitted only on condition that no material would be broadcast until the proceedings had been completed. The reason given was the risks to the administration of justice. These same factors were deemed to apply to civil proceedings at first instance despite the general absence of a jury in civil cases: the danger appears to have been in 'the televising of current proceedings while witnesses are giving their evidence'.[105] Once they reached the appellate level, both civil and criminal cases could, in principle, be subject to television coverage provided that lighting arrangements were satisfactory and provided also that the presiding judge gave his consent. Such consent, it was envisaged, could be made subject to such conditions as the judge deemed necessary. From time to time, the trial judge was empowered to revoke or qualify an initial grant of consent in the light of unfolding circumstances.

Another limitation of great practical significance was the need to obtain the consent of all those who were to be filmed, irrespective of whether they were to be named in the transmitted material. In general terms, the possibility of withholding consent is an important safeguard for those who are reluctant to be filmed while they play their part in the trial. At the same time, the difficulty of obtaining the necessary consents is a significant stumbling block to the television

---

[100] See generally McKain, Bonnington and Watt (n 43 above) 121–4.

[101] For brief accounts of these programmes see notes in *SCOLAG Journal* (March 1994) 41, and (April 1994) 59.

[102] They are set out in 1992 SLT (News) 249.   [103] 1992 SLT (News) 332.

[104] Since *The Trial* a number of applications have been made to televise proceedings in Scotland, though only for the limited purpose of compiling documentaries.

[105] Lord Hope's Practice Directions, para (d).

company seeking access to a trial. As has already been emphasized, in English law no legal wrong is committed by photographing a person against that person's wishes. Any requirement of obtaining that person's consent before he may be photographed in the trial setting, therefore, is a significant additional element. Some rules of television coverage allow an individual veto, others permit individual wishes to be overriden. Whenever consent is in issue, what is invariably meant is the *prior* consent of the person concerned.

Under Lord Hope's guidelines, the requirement of consent applied to all *personae* of the trial, including even the shorthand writers and the clerk of the court. The presiding judge would thus enjoy a twofold consent power, in regard to the proceedings as a whole, and in his personal capacity as one of the *personae* of the trial. As in so many areas of this subject, the guidelines are particularly solicitous of the needs of witnesses and jurors. Witnesses were to be approached by post, indicating their consent by signing and returning a form the contents of which had been approved by the Lord Justice General. If witnesses declined to be filmed, their refusal was to be conclusive and they were not to be approached with a view to 'negotiating the conditions on which they would give their consent'. Perhaps this is a euphemism for the offering of monetary compensation for the granting of a consent which had initially been withheld. If so, it raises an interesting variation on the theme of media payment to witnesses for the obtaining of their 'stories'. If a witness did grant his consent, it could be withdrawn any time up to twenty-four hours after the conclusion of his evidence. The provisions with regard to the jury were somewhat different. Here each juror would possess an individual veto, the consent of all members being necessary before the filming of even one of their number.

A number of matters could neither be recorded nor transmitted. Many of these are entirely unexceptionable: any part of the proceedings from which members of the public were excluded; conversations between the accused or the parties and their legal representatives; and any close-up view that would reveal the contents of any books or papers of the judge, the clerk of the court, or legal representatives. The prohibition also extended to unempanelled jurors where the shot enabled identification of any such juror. Two further prohibitions merit special attention. There could be no view of any member of the public seated in the public gallery if such a view enabled his identity to be revealed. Most remarkable of all, there was to be no filming of the precincts of the court building itself, unless permission was given by the Lord Justice General in accordance with the existing guidelines for filming in Parliament House.[106] This forms the only concession to the security needs of the court building itself, in contrast to the needs of particular individuals.

The executive producer of *The Trial*, Mr Nicholas Catliff, has spoken publicly of his experience of filming under the constraints imposed by Lord Hope's rules.

---

[106] The seat of the Court of Session and the High Court of Justiciary.

The series took almost two years to make. Of the trials initially identified for coverage in the High Court, there was a success rate of less than 1 per cent. The eventual cost averaged out at a very high £180,000 per hour. The principal difficulty identified by the producer was the obtaining of the necessary chain of consents. Even where the consent of witnesses had been obtained, the judge himself would usually veto filming. On one occasion the judicial veto was interposed a mere half hour before the trial started.

A little-noted sequel to the experiment was the marketing of five videos by the BBC. Although offered for sale under the rubric, 'Videos for Education and Training', the tone of the advertisements tends toward the dramatic. With the exception of one video that takes as its focus the daily routine of a procurator fiscal, the collection concentrates on the depiction of criminal trials and, in the case of three videos, trials in which the charge is some form of violent crime. The caption for one cassette, after naming the accused and reciting the charge (attempted armed robbery), asks:'Is he [the accused] just an innocent abroad or a cool and convincing liar?' Apart from the implicit invitation in this question to challenge the accuracy of the verdict reached by the court, the question may reasonably asked as to what precise educational value such videos possess. More important still, it raises a dimension to the televising debate which has not been addressed. Some measure of control may be exercised over transmission of court proceedings over the television networks. More problematic would be the exercise of controls over the sale of the footage in video format. Even if this were to be subjected to suitable rules of coverage, there could be no effective control over the recording of transmissions on to home video recorders and the subsequent use of the tapes.[107]

Lord Hope's guidelines could have been put to a most extraordinary use—a use that could not even have been conceived at the time of their pronouncement. In December 1988 an aeroplane in the early stage of a transatlantic flight exploded over the town of Lockerbie in Scotland. This resulted in the deaths of everyone on board, and of several persons on the ground. The explosion was caused by a bomb placed on board, which was suspected to be the work of two Libyan nationals. Diplomatic negotiations led to the emergence of a compromise by virtue of which the two suspects were handed over for trial at Camp Zeist, in the Netherlands. The applicable legal rules, it was agreed, would be those of Scots law, with the marked difference that there would be three Scottish judges instead of a jury. The trial eventually opened in May 2000, and concluded early the following year with the conviction of one of the men.

---

[107] Some idea of the difficulty of finding suitable methods of control may be gleaned from *R v Brentwood Borough Council, ex p Peck* The Times, 18 December 1997. A closed-circuit television camera operated quite properly by a local authority in a public place happened to record the applicant in the act of attempting suicide. The footage was displayed in a local newspaper and on television, to the embarrassment of the applicant since he was recognized by friends and neighbours. On application for judicial review, it was held that the authority had not acted irrationally under the Criminal Justice and Public Order Act 1994, s 163, which provides the legislative basis for local authorities' use of such cameras.

The promulgation of Lord Hope's guidelines opened the proceedings to the possibility of television access. The absence of a jury to be protected, together with the gravity of the charge, made the case—it was argued—one where the opportunity of television coverage should be seized.[108] Nevertheless, the BBC's application for permission to conduct a live transmission of the trial was rejected,[109] as was its appeal against that decision.[110] Neither of the accused would give his consent to this form of coverage. In itself, this would suffice to dispose of the matter. Lord Macfadyen, in the High Court of Justiciary, went on to rule that the onus lay on the applicant broadcaster to show that televising would not pose a risk to the administration of justice. It was not for the prosecution or the accused to show that there was such a threat. The BBC had failed, in the circumstances, to discharge the burden of proof. A renewed attempt by the BBC also proved unsuccessful.[111] On this occasion the challenge was based, partly on the differential treatment of the BBC as compared with the families of the victims, and partly on the duty of the Lord Advocate under the Scotland Act 1998 to comply with the obligations of the European Convention on Human Rights. The basis of the first ground was the facility accorded the families in being permitted to follow the case by means of television link on four sites some distance removed from the courtroom itself. It was clear, however, that this merely amounted to an extension of the seating area that forms part of every courtroom.[112] In particular, the signal was encrypted so that interception would prove fruitless, and the tapes were destroyed at the conclusion of each day's proceedings. As regards the second ground, the arrangements for restricted transmission had been made by the court itself, though admittedly against the background of earlier discussions between the office of the Lord Advocate and the US Department of Justice.

4. THE REPORT OF THE BAR COUNCIL: A CRITIQUE

In May 1989 a working party of the Public Affairs Committee of the General Council of the Bar published a report, *Televising the Courts*. The Committee, chaired by Mr Jonathan Caplan, rendered a unanimous report which was strongly in favour of the televising of the courts. Its principal recommendation was that the legal barriers should be removed forthwith so as to pave the way for an experimental period of televising. Broadly, the Committee's pro-televising stance was supported by several overriding considerations: the importance of television as a source of instruction in the modern age; the successful precedents

---

[108] D. Hogan and P. Mason, 'Let the people see the Lockerbie trial' The Times (9 February 1999) 35.
[109] The Times (3 February 2000) 9.
[110] *BBC Petitioners (No 1)* 2000 SLT 845 (High Court of Justiciary).
[111] *BBC Petitioners (No 2)* 2000 SLT 860 (High Court of Justiciary).
[112] It is interesting to note the submission of the BBC, as part of its argument that the families were not seated in the courtroom itself, that any acts committed on any of the four sites would not be amenable to the contempt jurisdiction of the court.

(in the view of the Committee) from other jurisdictions; and the fact that modern technology now made possible the smooth and unobtrusive filming that was unimaginable in earlier years.

Before considering how the Caplan Committee envisaged that the procedure relating to television coverage would function, it is necessary to offer an account of its less controversial recommendations. Principal among these was its concession that certain matters should be absolutely excepted from being televised.[113] There would be no coverage of any proceedings held in private, or where an order had been made under the Contempt of Court Act 1981.[114] This is unexceptionable: it would be very remarkable if the television camera were to gain access to material which, at present, is placed even beyond the reach of the print media. Equally, the demands of client-lawyer privilege justify the exception in favour of conferences between such persons and documentation in the possession of counsel or solicitors. In addition, there would be no filming of a witness whose identity was 'protected by law' or of a person the exposure of whom would be 'liable to endanger the safety of that person' (for example, a police informer). On the other hand, no visual coverage of jurors was to be permitted despite their being on view—in the traditionally designed Crown Court, at least—to anyone seated in the public gallery.

Far more controversial is the Committee's dismissal, without giving reasons, of each of four possible rules of coverage. These will now be considered in detail.[115]

First, the Caplan Committee rejected the rule that televising be permitted only 'with the consent of all the parties'. But what precisely is meant by a 'party', especially in the context of criminal trials? Would it include the victim of a crime? If, as is often the case, the victim is also called as a witness, considerable problems could arise. As a party to the proceedings, the victim would be denied, under the Caplan proposals, a veto on televising. As a witness, however, he may well protest that he is unable to give evidence properly in the presence of television cameras. In such a situation, the court may well be confronted with the difficult task of appraising the full extent of the inability of the witness/party without, at the same time, indirectly conceding him a veto which the rules of coverage have expressly denied him. Even under present arrangements, the point has been taken that exposure to modern video technology may embody an element of stress which the court should recognize as being greater than the giving of testimony in the traditional format. In Chapter 3, it will be recalled, one element of the fragmentation of the courtroom was identified as the giving of evidence in some permanent form that subsequently was not given *viva voce* by the witness at the trial. One such case was *J. Barber and Sons v Lloyd's Underwriters*,[116] in which an

---

[113] Caplan Committee, 43.

[114] This phrase is unclear, but is probably to be taken as encompassing orders made under the Contempt of Court Act 1981, s 4(2).

[115] Caplan Committee, 44.　　　　　　　　　[116] [1987] QB 103.

English court was asked to supply a video tape examination of witnesses for the purposes of proceedings in California. Evans J heard submissions from the persons whose testimony was sought to be recorded in this way that 'the presence of a camera would oppress them and cause additional stress'.[117] The submission was rejected on the ground that any additional stress would not suffice to outweigh 'the value and convenience' of providing the video evidence. It is possible to appreciate the scale of the conceivable difficulties that could be encountered under a system of televised court proceedings. The material produced in the case just cited would provide evidence for the Californian court that was necessary to enable it to judge a particular law suit. Moreover, there would be no wider dissemination of the material than the confines of one American courtroom. Contrast that with a situation where the presence of television cameras would not be relevant to the conclusion of the matter before the court and, furthermore, the person exposed to the cameras would be subject to a far wider dissemination of his image and testimony.

Under an extensive consent rule any individual participant in the trial would possess a power of veto, not simply over coverage of himself, but as to coverage of the proceedings as a whole. This is a form suggested by the Canadian writer, David Lepofsky.[118] Largely inspired by Lepofsky's scepticism about the value of televising trials, this approach would require unanimous consent on the part of all the *personae* of the case before television coverage would be permitted. As such, it would be radically different from a *de facto* veto exercisable by (for example) a key witness, whose refusal to be televised would render pointless the coverage of the trial as a whole.

Furthermore, the issue of consent itself is problematic. The very fact that it is considered as a precondition of the televising of proceedings implies—correctly—that television coverage of a trial is, qualitatively and quantitatively, a different form of exposure from the traditional forms in the print media. Consent already figures in the existing law as a means whereby the complainant of a sexual assault may waive his or her right to anonymity. In this context it has hitherto posed no difficulties. The complainant's name is not already in the public domain, nor will it be in the absence of the exercise of the right of waiver. However, in most trials the names of parties (however they be defined) will not be similarly protected, and it would not be difficult to foresee the types of pressure to which they might be exposed in order to obtain their consent to the televising of the case. It is only necessary to glance at the difficulties posed by the notion of consent to medical treatment to gain some insight into the full range of problems that could arise in this area. A witness or party might argue after the event, for example, that he or she did not truly consent to the repeated replaying of the

---

[117] ibid. 105.
[118] M. D. Lepofsky, 'Cameras in the Courtroom—Not Without My Consent' (1996) 6 *National Journal of Constitutional Law* 161.

footage of his testimony on prime-time television. If such objections are well founded, one of the essential preconditions of television access would turn out not to have been satisfied.

Secondly, the Caplan Committee was opposed to the rule that televising should be permitted only if conducted 'gavel to gavel'. This is a technical term which is also used in the context of the televising of the legislature. It signifies the entire coverage of the proceedings of the body in question while it is in session. It is not to be confused with live transmission of the proceedings, though, as a matter of practice, the former may entail the latter. It would be difficult to envisage some five hours' 'gavel to gavel' coverage of the day's proceedings being transmitted other than on daytime television. The absence of a 'gavel to gavel' requirement would mean that a television company could select scenes for broadcast from a current trial. In this regard the Committee's proposal most closely accords with the present practice whereby members of the public may choose to attend particular phases of the trial. Moreover, to impose an 'all or nothing' requirement on television executives would give rise to a number of difficulties. In a trial of any length it would signify such a deep incursion into the available transmission time that it would act as a powerful deterrent against the use of the new facility.

The conclusion of the Committee on this point, therefore, is eminently sensible. If there were to be a 'gavel to gavel' requirement, the question should be asked as to what legal sanction could be imposed for failure to comply with it. Moreover, any selective editing of highlights that were to give a distorted impression of the proceedings could lose the privileges that protect fair and accurate trial reports. It is especially noteworthy that the Committee was prepared, in this respect, to allow the greatest degree of freedom to the broadcasters, since it was adamant that the court should not exercise any control whatsoever over the editing of the material.[119]

A third possibility that was rejected after due consideration was that transmission should be permitted only when the proceedings had been concluded. This limitation, presumably, would apply only in regard to the conclusion of proceedings at a particular level of the court hierarchy. It would not be necessary, in other words, to await the outcome of any potential appeal to the Court of Appeal or the House of Lords. The difficulty in regard to a delay until the outcome of the proceedings was known would be the danger that any transmission of the trial footage would not be viewed as contemporaneous for the purpose of the privileges attaching to trial reports.

Fourthly, in regard to criminal trials, the Committee rejected the suggestion that no televising should be permitted unless and until a conviction was obtained. This limitation is identical to the third possibility, with the exception that a verdict of not guilty would result in a permanent ban on the broadcasting of the proceedings. It simply reflects, in the context of television transmission, the idea that

---

[119] Caplan Committee, 45.

the presumption of innocence requires some limitation on trial publicity until such time, if any, as a verdict of guilty is entered against the accused.

The starting point of the Committee's recommendations was that 'there should be a clear presumption in favour of allowing broadcasting'.[120] In the light of this, it would be important to know what considerations might be taken as rebutting that presumption. In this regard the Committee was guided by the Rules of Coverage operative in New York. Several of these Rules merely replicate situations which, irrespective of television access, would be attended by a degree of confidentiality. Among these are cases where coverage would cause harm to any participant (for example, a child), or where it would interfere with law enforcement measures, or—most simply of all—where reporting would be specifically prohibited by some other legal provision.

Another consideration, of a different type, which would rebut the initial presumption was 'the physical structure of the courtroom available'. This is a rather strange exception since, characteristically, a case may be assigned to be heard in any of a number of available courtrooms, or even in a building which is not specifically set aside for the hearing of trials. What may have been intended is the idea that the public seating available in the courtroom would not be commensurate with the degree of interest that the proceedings had engendered. We have already noted the briefly reported case of *R v Inner North London Coroner, ex p Chambers*,[121] in which these matters were touched upon. There are several lines of inquiry surrounding the issue. First, is the adequacy of the courtroom in this regard to be judged by considerations of the public interest, or those of the interest shown by the public? It is a trite observation that not all that interests the public is of genuine public concern. Secondly, could the physical inadequacies of the courtroom, in terms of the inadequate number of public seats, be taken as a strong factor in favour of the grant of permission to allow television access? Thirdly, is it only contested trials that are to be the subject of possible television coverage? The point is worth emphasizing, since the inquest in *Ex p Chambers* appears to be the only reported example of a challenge brought on the basis of the physical inadequacies of the intended seat of the proceedings in the light of the extent of the interest shown by the public in the case.

To turn now to the procedural aspects, the Caplan Committee envisaged that there would be no entitlement as of right to televise any particular trial. An application would have to be made in advance to the judge, which would then form the subject of an oral hearing.[122] Although, as we have seen, a party (however defined) would not have a right of veto over the televising of the trial, he or she would be entitled to make representations at the oral hearing.

It is necessary, first, to advert to the problems in the situation where more than one television company applied for access to the same trial. Two possible solutions

---

[120] Caplan Committee, 41.   [121] (1983) 127 Sol J 445.   [122] Caplan Committee, 41.

are canvassed in the Report.[123] An independent contractor could be appointed, under the control of the Lord Chancellor's Department, to compile and supply the material to all interested television companies. Alternatively, permission could be given to only one company—it was envisaged, the first company to make an application—but on condition that it shared the material with the other companies that were seeking access.

As regards the form of the advance hearing, the question whether it would be open to the public and representatives of the print media was not addressed. This is a strange omission in the light of the subject matter of the Report. The costs of the hearing, it was envisaged, would be paid by the broadcaster who made the application 'save in exceptional circumstances'. Alternative arrangements would have to be made for the sharing of costs in the situation where more than one company had been interested in access, but (as indicated above) permission was given to only one such company on condition that it shared the material with the others. The precise status of the preliminary hearing was not explored. Perhaps the nearest equivalent in the present law is to be found in the 'preparatory hearing', which takes place before the jury is sworn in serious fraud prosecutions and in long and complex cases generally.[124]

In the event of a refusal of the application, there would be a right of appeal available to the applicant similar to that granted under section 159 of the Criminal Justice Act 1988. Remarkably, the parties (or the defendant, in a criminal case) would not be granted a similar right of appeal against a decision to allow television coverage. The disparity between the two situations is not even noticed by the Report. The supposed analogy with section 159, moreover, is only partly founded. That section confers a right of appeal on any 'person aggrieved' by the decision of the trial judge. If section 159 were to be taken as the model of the granting of appeal rights in this area, a range of persons could be taken as having *locus standi* to challenge the decision of the judge. The analogy with section 159 is, perhaps, misconceived in another respect. It may be that the operative provisions would function as rules: that is, unless another party could bring the case within the scope of one or more of the exceptions, the television company making the application would be entitled as of right to gain access to the trial. If, on the other hand, the judge (and the Court of Appeal, in the event of a challenge to a refusal of permission) were to be given an element of discretion, it would be difficult to challenge successfully the initial decision. The matter might be left entirely to the discretion of the trial judge, in the same way that decisions taken by him at present on issues such as the place of trial are extremely difficult to review.

Apart from the pre-trial procedures regulating the issue, it must surely be the case that the existence of these procedures would be without prejudice to the

---

[123] Caplan Committee, 40.

[124] In regard to the latter the relevant law is to be found in the Criminal Procedure and Investigations Act 1996, ss 28–38.

channels of appeal regularly available to the convicted accused. He would not be debarred from challenging a conviction on the basis that the trial verdict was to be deemed unsafe as a result of television coverage. Such forms of *ex post facto* challenge would be shaped by the extent of the applicable rules of coverage. For example, if the rules permitted transmission of material prior to the conclusion of the trial, the verdict might be challenged on the basis of the exposure of members of the jury to, for example, distorted nightly summaries of the day's proceedings. If, on the other hand, transmission in this period were prohibited, the accused would have to focus his arguments more narrowly: for instance, on the effect of the presence of television cameras on the behaviour of witnesses and jurors. If he were unable to use infraction of the relevant provisions as a direct means of attacking the verdict, there would remain the possibility of basing some other cause of action on breach of the rules.[125]

Even if the initial decision were taken to permit television coverage, the Caplan Committee envisaged that the judge would retain an overriding discretion to exclude television coverage at any subsequent stage. The passage in the Report that deals with exclusion in mid-hearing envisages a number of situations which might justify such a decision.[126] Some of these amount to a reiteration of circumstances which would be taken as justifying a decision to refuse television coverage in the first place. Among these are such factors as the safety of a witness or the inability of a witness to give proper testimony in the presence of such coverage. The judge, if he were to be denied this power, would not be well equipped to deal with possible unexpected changes in the course of events as the trial unfolds. An entirely different set of considerations relates, not to the integrity of the trial proceedings, but rather to the misconduct of the television company that has gained the permission. If the company were to use the material for an 'improper purpose' or if the rules of coverage were breached, the revocation of permission would be available, in effect, as a possible sanction. On principle, such misconduct should be dealt with exclusively as a matter of contempt of court. But some forms of misconduct—for example, the failure of the television company whose cameras are admitted to the courtroom to respect pooling arrangements made to share the material obtained—would seem far removed from protecting the administration of justice as it is traditionally conceived. Moreover, a suspension of all televising in such circumstances would smack of injustice as punishing all for the misdeeds of one.

The Committee envisaged that a mid-hearing suspension of television coverage would be the subject of a right of appeal on the part of the media. In this context the decision not to accord similar rights to other persons involved in the trial does seem rather more sensible. However, the suggestion that a revocation decision should be the subject of a right of appeal in the same way that an initial

---

[125] See, however, *R v Horseferry Road Justices, ex p Independent Broadcasting Authority* [1987] 1 QB 54 for the difficulties of finding such a cause of action.

[126] Caplan Committee, 42–3.

refusal of permission would be appealable, makes rather less sense, especially in the light of the Committee's concern that the trial 'should not be delayed to allow for such an appeal'.[127] Yet either the proceedings must be stayed in order to allow the appeal to proceed or any appeal which is not accompanied by a stay in the proceedings will run the risk of becoming a moot exercise.

The Caplan Committee wondered whether, with the introduction of television facilities, it would be difficult to retain the ban on the use of still photography. It is submitted that such a prohibition should, nevertheless, be retained. The very factors that the Committee identified as smoothing the path for the filming of trials—more compact cameras, their unobtrusive positioning, the absence of the need for intensive lighting—also show how easy it would be to conduct unauthorised filming of the trial.

Finally, as noted at the outset of this section, the Committee envisaged an experimental period prior to the regular admission of TV cameras under the above-mentioned rules. The precise nature of the experiment was not explained. Perhaps trials that formed part of the experiment would be subject to close scrutiny after the event, with extensive interviews of the *personae* involved. Of course, there is no possibility of conducting a controlled experiment where the trial is conducted first with, and then without, television coverage. And, as regards the questioning of jurors, there would be the ever-present risk that researchers and jurors would stray into the prohibited areas covered by section 8 of the Contempt of Court Act 1981.

5. TELEVISING TRIALS AND INDIVIDUAL RIGHTS: THE UNITED STATES EXPERIENCE

One possible approach to the issue of televising of court proceedings is to debate the merits and demerits of this form of coverage, and then to forbid or permit it in the light of the resulting balance of advantage. Alternatively, against the background of an appropriate constitutional system, the peremptory force of rights will be deployed. The overriding consideration will then be whether the contents of the particular catalogue of human rights, as authoritatively construed, preclude such debate since they either permit or forbid the televising of trials. Before proceeding to examine the case law, it would be useful to make some general observations on this aspect of the subject.

There exists ample scope for conducting the debate about the televising of trials in the language of constitutional rights. In favour of this form of reporting may be deployed the traditional rights of free speech and public trial. Against access by television may be cited the overriding value of fair trial. While the claims of the first two are to be resolved purely as matters of interpretation of the

[127] Caplan Committee, 43.

relevant human rights text, the question whether television coverage poses a threat to the fairness of trial proceedings will inevitably rest largely on controversial social science evidence concerning the ways, if any, in which the *personae* of the trial behave differently once television access is permitted. These do not, however, exhaust the categories of rights-based arguments. The unfortunate accused whose trial is selected for televised coverage may argue that he has been disadvantaged as compared with those defendants who escape such enhanced publicity. To deny ingress to television cameras could be viewed as discriminatory in a different respect, as between the print and electronic media. Finally, where prosecution and defence are united in their opposition to the entry of cameras, the television company that is denied the opportunity of putting the case to the contrary will have to cast around for some procedural right that gives it standing to argue the point.

Many constitutional charters, of course, were promulgated before the advent of such modern technology. That the technology was not even within the contemplation of the draftsmen of these documents is not conclusive against the possibility of a constitutional right of access. Analogies may be drawn, for example, with the situation under the Fourth Amendment to the US Constitution, where the guarantees against unreasonable search and seizure have been held applicable, not only to physical invasion of premises, but also to electronic surveillance in the form of telephone tapping. To deploy the explanation advanced by Ronald Dworkin, the Fourth Amendment guarantee embodies a *concept* of unreasonable search and seizure, which is open to the reception of various *conceptions* in the light of changed circumstances.[128] So, too, with access to the courtroom. The promulgation of the Sixth Amendment guarantee of public trial in an era of personal attendance at trials, together with exiguous coverage in the few journals then in existence, would not be conclusive against a constitutional right vested in the audio-visual media.

Any explanation of television access in the language of constitutional rights, however, would encounter a number of difficulties. Some legal systems that permit such access to the courtroom do so subject to the consent of the trial judge and, in some instances, subject to a veto by any of the trial *personae*. It would surely be a strange constitutional right that could be peremptorily defeated by the exercise of will of another person. It is easier, in this respect, for a person whose trial has been exposed to mass publicity to argue that the process has resulted in the violation of one of his rights. Often, as will be seen in the context of American case law, the claim takes the form that the defendant, by reason of the presence of television cameras, was denied a fair trial.

On those occasions where the trial has resulted in acquittal, some other form of redress must be sought. For this purpose it is necessary to refer to a jurisdiction other than the United States. In the Italian case, *Giannini v RAI*,[129] the legality of

[128] R. Dworkin, *Taking Rights Seriously* (1977) 132–7.   [129] Tribunale di Roma, 5 July 1989.

televising a trial without the consent of the accused was explored by means of a civil action. The accused, having been acquitted of a relatively minor charge, claimed damages against the defendant television company for injury to his reputation inflicted by the broadcast of the proceedings (which took place some six months later). In rejecting the claim, the court stated that the mere fact that a criminal trial takes place in public did not exonerate the RAI from liability. The absence of the consent of the plaintiff was an important factor,[130] which could be overriden only if the transmission served some social and cultural purpose. The latter requirement would not amount to much of a safeguard, since the value was found to reside in the light that the trial cast on the problems of social existence— a value which, with a little imagination, could be found to be present in almost any type of litigation.

There are situations where the attendant publicity reaches such a scale of intensity that it results in violation of the right of the accused to a fair trial. Despite the more indulgent approach in the United States towards media discussion of pending trials, the degree of publicity has on occasion been held to have crossed the threshold of prejudice and has resulted in the quashing of a conviction, most notably in *Sheppard v Maxwell*.[131] In that case a medical practitioner was belatedly indicted for the murder of his wife. The case attracted massive media interest, including extensive television and radio coverage. Indeed, the exposure on the audio-visual media was most prominent in regard to the inquest proceedings. The manner of conduct of the case can be gleaned from the following description in the judgment of the US Supreme Court:

> [The inquest] was staged . . . in a school gymnasium; . . . In the front of the room was a long table occupied by reporters, television and radio personnel, and broadcasting equipment. The hearing was broadcast with live microphones placed at the Coroner's seat and the witness stand. A swarm of reporters and photographers attended. Sheppard was brought into the room by police who searched him in full view of several hundred spectators.[132]

As this extract reveals, the attendance of radio and television personnel at the hearing was simply one component in the 'Roman Carnival' atmosphere in which the proceedings were conducted. Many aspects of the process would have been prejudicial to the accused quite independently of the coverage of the proceedings by the audio-visual media.

In the previous year the US Supreme Court, in *Estes v Texas*,[133] was required to confront the constitutionality of televising trials. The issue, again, was not presented in a clear-cut form, since the trial took place against the background of massive prejudicial publicity. The live televising was limited to the prosecution's

---

[130] The RAI argued that the plaintiff must have known of the filming of his trial, since he could not have been oblivious to the presence in court of cameras and similar equipment. His failure to voice an objection at the time must therefore be taken as tacit consent. The plaintiff retorted that, after a night in the cells, he was in no condition to notice these things. The court ruled in favour of the plaintiff on this point, holding that consent must be express and unequivocal.

[131] 384 US 333 (1966).   [132] ibid. 339.   [133] 381 US 532 (1965).

closing speech and the delivery of the jury's verdict. There was scrupulous protection for witnesses and jurors, who could not be televised without their consent. In the light of the restraint exercised at the trial itself, it was the conduct of the pre-trial hearing that formed a significant element in the appeal. And it is ironic that the intrusion of television cameras took place at a hearing the principal purpose of which was to decide whether or not to allow cameras admission to the trial.

Estes, a well-known financier, was prosecuted on charges of fraud. He appealed against his conviction on the ground that the broadcasting of his trial deprived him of due process under the Fourteenth Amendment to the Constitution. A sharply divided court decided by a bare majority in favour of the appellant. Clark J, giving the judgment of the court, reviewed many of the traditional arguments for and against televising that have subsequently been aired. In particular, he emphasized that it is not the function of a trial to educate the public, and that there was a great danger that the public would simply equate trial proceedings on television with other forms of entertainment regularly received through that medium. His conclusion was that the appellant had been prejudiced by the television coverage of the proceedings. As for the point that no such prejudice had specifically been identified, the concurring judgment of Warren CJ retorted: 'I cannot agree with those who say that a televised trial deprives a defendant of a fair trial only if "actual prejudice" can be shown. The prejudice of television may be so subtle that it escapes the ordinary methods of proof, but it would gradually erode our fundamental conception of trial.'[134]

The ruling, incidentally, contains a number of pronouncements on the requirements of public trial. For example:

[The] prohibition [of televising] does not conflict with the constitutional guarantee of a public trial, because a trial is public, in the constitutional sense, when a courtroom has facilities for a reasonable number of the public to observe the proceedings, which facilities are not so small as to render the openness negligible and not so large as to distract the trial participants from their proper function, when the public is free to use those facilities, and when all those who attend the trial are free to report what they observed at the proceedings . . .[135]

In *Chandler v Florida*[136] the media interest was generated by the fact that the accused were serving police officers in Miami Beach at the time of their arrest on burglary charges. The original provision in the state law of Florida had required the consent of all parties before televising could take place. In view of the fact that such unanimity had rarely been forthcoming it had been replaced by a revised provision, in force at the time of the trial, which permitted television access over the objections entered by the accused. The verdict of guilty was challenged on the ground that the accused, on account of the television coverage, had been denied due process. There were elements in such coverage that could undoubtedly have

---

[134] ibid. 578.   [135] ibid. 584, per Warren CJ.   [136] 449 US 560 (1981).

been viewed as prejudicial to the defence case. The grant of permission to televise was not accompanied by sequestration of the jury. Moreover, the three-minute clip of the trial that was transmitted was devoted entirely to the case for the prosecution. However, the accused based their argument on the submission that broadcast coverage was inherently a denial of due process. The Supreme Court unanimously rejected their application for a new trial. In reaching this conclusion the Court was persuaded by two factors: the absence of empirical data establishing that the mere presence of the broadcasting media exerts a prejudicial effect on the proceedings; and the value, within a federal system, of allowing individual states the freedom to experiment with new institutions. This ruling, of course, was difficult to reconcile with the *Estes* judgment. Stewart and White JJ believed that the Court should have specifically overruled the earlier judgment. In merely distinguishing *Estes*, the majority in the *Chandler* case took advantage of the difficulty of extracting a majority ruling from the earlier case. Harlan J in particular, concurring with Clark J, seemed to emphasize the peculiarities of the *Estes* case, as involving 'a heavily publicised and highly sensational affair'.

It is ironic, in the light of this ruling, that the Supreme Court views the televising of its proceedings as being inconsistent with the dignity of its proceedings. The ban on television cameras is maintained despite the absence of witnesses. Moreover, the far-reaching effects of the Supreme Court's power of constitutional review would appear to render it more suitable than any other court in the United States to be opened to this form of reporting.[137]

In view of the constitutional permissibility of televising trials, what are the typical rules of coverage? Those of the state of North Carolina may be taken for this purpose.[138]

These rules encompass equally coverage by television, motion picture and still photography, and—in the case of audio technology—tape recorders and microphones for broadcasting. They are, in large measure, concerned with limitations designed to prevent intrusion, whether by the technology itself or its personnel, on the smooth running of court proceedings.

The rules encompass 'public judicial proceedings' in 'the appellate and trial courts' of the state. Nevertheless, certain categories of person are expressly excepted from the scope of the rules. Apart from the specific case of the members of the jury, coverage of whom is absolutely forbidden, these may be divided into three categories. First, reflecting traditional concern for the welfare of children, it is not possible to televise minors. Secondly, there is a group of exceptions encompassing persons whose safety would be threatened by knowledge of their identity

---

[137] Oral arguments are recorded, for the purpose of transcription, as a matter of course. This takes place under the supervision of the Court itself. Counsel are forbidden to bring their own recording devices.

[138] West's North Carolina Rules of Court—General Rules of Practice for the Superior and District Courts Supplemental to the Rules of Civil Procedure, Rule 15 ('Electronic Media and Still Photography Coverage of Public Judicial Proceedings').

and role: police informers, undercover agents, and relocated witnesses. Thirdly, the privacy interest of the victims of 'sex crimes' is reflected in their being excepted from coverage. It is noticeable that the last exception encompasses, not only the victims themselves, but also their families.

A different set of provisions, defined by subject matter, forms an additional group of exceptions. In many respects these would overlap with the exception relating to minors that was just mentioned: adoption proceedings, juvenile proceedings and child custody proceedings. A further cluster have, as their basis, the idea that publicity would destroy the very point of bringing the proceedings: motions to suppress evidence, for example, and also cases involving trade secrets. Uncontroversially, *in camera* hearings may not be subject to broadcasting. Nor, in the interests of lawyer–client privilege, may there be audio recording or broadcast of exchanges between client and counsel or between opposing counsel or between counsel and judge. A surprising category of exceptions, on the other hand, covers divorce and alimony proceedings.

A striking provision governs the subsequent use of material that has been regularly recorded. No photographs or video or audio recording of a trial 'shall be admissible as evidence in the proceeding out of which it arose, any proceeding subsequent and collateral thereto, or upon any retrial or appeal of such proceedings'. In one respect this is very surprising since video and audio footage would compare favourably with the official shorthand transcript as a faithful record of the trial. For the purpose of appellate correction of errors of law in the first instance trial, the printed record will suffice. However, where judicial misconduct is alleged on the basis of the manner of conduct of the trial, only a video or audio record of the proceedings is likely to be full enough to bring out the signs of bias. This will be considered in greater detail in section 6, below.

Apart from these specific prohibitions, the judge or (as the case may be) the presiding judge is invested with an overriding discretion to prohibit or terminate television coverage, whether in the courtroom itself or 'the corridors immediately adjacent thereto'. The possibility of the judge being enmeshed in discussions with, and representations from, a number of media organizations is obviated by the designation of certain bodies in the state as official representatives of the various media interests. It is expressly stipulated that such designated persons shall be the only ones 'authorized to speak for the media to the presiding judge concerning the coverage of any judicial proceedings'.

The British public were brought up sharply against the American experience of televised trial in the form of two well-publicized proceedings within the space of two years. These were the trial in 1995, in California, of Orenthal James Simpson, and that in 1997, in Massachusetts, of Louise Woodward.[139] The personal circumstances of the two accused could scarcely have been more different. O. J. Simpson was an American celebrity, a black who had overcome adversity to

---

[139] For details of the two cases, see the Appendix.

pursue a successful career as a football player and a minor film star. Louise Woodward was a teenager, a British subject who had been gaining her first experience of life overseas by working in America. The only factors linking their cases were the gravity of the charge—homicide—and (in the view of many who followed the proceedings) the inconclusive nature of the outcomes.

Neither of the relevant state rules required the consent of the accused to the presence of television cameras. The provision applicable to O. J. Simpson, Rule 980 of the California Rules of Court, as then drafted, was a very spare provision which was largely directed to questions of lighting and the pooling of footage between media agencies. An amended Rule 980, taking effect on 1 January 1997, set out no fewer than nineteen factors to be taken into consideration by a judge in ruling on a request to televise a trial.[140] At a conference held at Southampton Institute in February 1999, Louise Woodward complained that television accounts of the trial gave a distorted impression since much of the technical medical testimony was not carried on the networks. However, she did derive some incidental benefit from the televising of the proceedings. Many of the persons with the closest ties to her, in her home village of Elton in Cheshire, were not required to travel to the United States in order to be able to follow the proceedings. Moreover, the trust fund that was established in Cheshire in order to defray her legal expenses undoubtedly received contributions from those who, in the absence of television coverage, would not have been moved to contribute.

6. ARCHIVAL PURPOSES

Certain types of case are so far removed from the ordinary, or the work of a tribunal is so unusual, that the call for audio-visual recording is almost irresistible. For example, photographs were taken of the various stages in the proceedings of the Nuremberg War Crimes Tribunal and these are easily accessible in the various published accounts of the work of the Tribunal. A trial in the same vein was that of Adolf Eichmann in Israel in 1961 for his part in the Holocaust. At the outset of the trial, the Israeli Attorney-General applied to the court for permission to record the public phases of the trial on videotape with soundtracks, with a view to the dissemination of the tape in both cinema and television networks in Israel and abroad.[141]

An interesting point about the application in the Eichmann case was the absence of a specific legal rule on the subject of photography and televising, with the result that the question fell to be decided from first principle. Defence counsel advanced two arguments against allowing television coverage. First, broadcast accounts of a trial were likely to be distorted, the presiding judges themselves

---

[140] California Rules of Court, Rule 980(e), para (3).
[141] *The Trial of Adolf Eichmann: Report of Proceedings in the District Court of Jerusalem* (Ministry of Justice, Israel, 1992) 1–2.

adding that the footage could also be put to uses inconsistent with the dignity of the court. However, if this were to occur, the court could withdraw its permission to televise—an option that would clearly be foreclosed once the trial was concluded. Secondly, witnesses, knowing that their image would be broadcast to a worldwide audience, would either 'play-act' or be too timid to tell the truth. Those dangers, the court felt, were fundamentally no different from the usual trial context of testifying before spectators and representatives of the print media. In the course of reaching these conclusions, the judges cited Bentham's classic writings on trial publicity and also the observations on open justice made by Lord Halsbury LC in *MacDougall v Knight*.[142] The latter was a curious choice since the case itself did not involve a trial report published in the media. Rather, the contentious account consisted of a pamphlet that purported to be a verbatim report of the judgment given in an earlier law suit between the same parties, and the question was whether that judgment gave a complete and accurate account of the issues in the trial. The Israeli Attorney-General, anticipating one of the problems that (as we have seen) beset television coverage, attached to his application a contract between the government of Israel and an American broadcasting company under which the latter had been conceded the exclusive right to record the trial 'subject to the rules of court'. In the event the court deemed it unnecessary to consider the terms of this token of the prosecution's optimism that permission to televise would be granted.

Trials, whether conducted in a national or international forum, of persons accused of complicity in the genocidal activities of the Nazis pose unique claims for the televising of the proceedings. The broadcast of such cases, it can be argued, will act as a powerful weapon against those who deny that the Holocaust took place. In this context mention should be made of the strange compromise struck over the trial of Klaus Barbie in Lyons in 1987. Robert Badinter, the French Minister of Justice who secured Barbie's extradition to France, decreed that the trial should be filmed, but with the proviso that the footage should not be shown for thirty years.[143]

A more topical example is provided by the work of the United Nations International Criminal Tribunal for the former Yugoslavia (hereinafter 'the ICTY'), which was established in 1993. At an early stage of its existence the ICTY decided to arrange for audio-visual recording of its public proceedings on a 'gavel to gavel' basis. The process of recording is conducted by the staff of the Tribunal itself—an option which was adopted in preference to three other possibilities. To allow external cameras from any television station that wished to record the trials would result in disruption through a multiplicity of equipment. The second possibility, that of granting exclusive rights to one television company, was dismissed on the ground that disappointed companies would feel aggrieved by their

---

[142] (1889) 14 AC 194.
[143] See A. Finkielkraut, *Remembering in Vain: The Klaus Barbie Trial and Crimes against Humanity* (1989) 69–70.

exclusion. Curiously, the possibility of granting such rights to one company on condition that it shared the material with other interested companies, as suggested by the Caplan Report, does not appear to have been considered a viable possibility. Perhaps it was not feasible in view of the international nature of the interest that would be shown in the footage, combined with the difficulty of enforcing sharing agreements across national frontiers. The third possibility, under which the ICTY would perform all functions of editing and mixing, was also rejected on the ground that the exclusion of an independent element at this stage would expose the ICTY to the charge of selectivity and bias in the material that it chose to release to the world's media. In the event, the ICTY's near immediate release of footage allows the possibility of live coverage. However the slight delay, of thirty minutes, permits the possibility of amendment in those cases where there has been a slip of the tongue or a protected person's identity has inadvertently been disclosed. Anonymity is protected by the Tribunal going into closed session (in which event, no coverage is permitted) or by continuing in public, with continued audio-visual recording, but with the identity of the witness protected by the scrambling of his face and the distortion of his voice.

The ICTY was motivated by several considerations in permitting such extensive coverage. Above all, it was conscious of its obligations to the international community which had been responsible for its creation. That apart, it was moved partly by the need for the creation of an audio-visual archive, and partly by the desire to allow instant access by a much wider audience than would have been able to attend in person. Reservations, however, must be expressed concerning the consideration that the judgments of the ICTY were to be 'a deterrent for the generations to come'[144]—an assumption that appears to proceed on the basis of an inevitable finding of guilt.

The overriding concern of those who argue for television coverage of trials is to increase the circle of spectators of the trial scene. However, recording in this form could take place routinely as a means of facilitating scrutiny of the conduct of the proceedings. It occasionally happens that a ground of appeal against conviction is based, not so much on straightforward errors of law, but rather on allegations of judicial misconduct in the manner of conduct of the case.[145] Whenever this ground of appeal is advanced, it can prove difficult to convey the particulars of the allegation merely on the basis of the shorthand record of what was said in the trial at first instance. In *R v Wood*[146] one of the grounds of appeal was based on such factors as expressions of impatience by the trial judge: the raising of eyebrows, sighing, and the shrugging of shoulders. The Court of Appeal ruled that they should not act on such particulars unless they were agreed between counsel

---

[144] Mr Christian Chartier, Head of Public Information, United Nations International Criminal Tribunal for the former Yugoslavia, in a paper delivered at a conference at Southampton Institute, February 1999.

[145] See A. Samuels, 'Judicial Misconduct in the Criminal Trial' [1982] Crim LR 221.

[146] (1996) 1 Cr App R 207.

or supported by evidence. In these circumstances the necessity for counsel to give evidence would bring into play the rule that a barrister who gave evidence in a trial could no longer act as counsel in the same case. Again, in *R v Ahmed*[147] the Court of Appeal dismissed an appeal against a conviction for arson where the ground of appeal was the extent and manner of the interventions made by the judge. Glidewell LJ, while warning against the undesirability of critical interventions, admitted that the Court of Appeal was in no position to judge, from the transcript alone, the manner in which they had been made (for example, whether they conveyed impatience with defence counsel or a preconceived view of the case). By far the most notorious case in this regard is that of Craig and Bentley. Derek Bentley was executed in the early 1950s after a trial which, in the intervening years, had attracted a great deal of criticism for the way in which it had been conducted by the then Lord Chief Justice, Lord Goddard.[148] Finally, in 1998, on a reference by the newly established Criminal Cases Review Commission, the Court of Appeal pronounced that Bentley had been denied a fair trial and his conviction was consequently unsafe.[149] In reaching this conclusion the Court of Appeal relied predominantly on a verbatim transcript of the trial. One aspect that could not be caught by the transcript, but would be conveyed on film, was the highly prejudicial manner of Lord Goddard's charge to the jury. In particular, he put on the co-defendant's knuckleduster in order to show the jury how it worked—a matter of no relevance to the proceedings since it was not the murder weapon.[150]

Video recordings of trial proceedings would clearly circumvent these difficulties of proof. However, recordings made for this purpose would have to be made as a matter of course and irrespective of the wishes of the parties, but (of course) without the prospect of television transmission.

7. A CONCLUDING COMMENT

It is clear beyond dispute that the inclination of the Caplan Report lay in favour of the maximum freedom to televise trial proceedings. The years between the publication of the Report and the transmission of *The Trial* formed a period in which there was a marked willingness among the most senior English judges to consider the admission of television cameras into the courtroom. That period, by common consent, ended with the trial of O. J. Simpson. It was this trial that was responsible for confronting the English judiciary with the dreadful prospect of intrusive media intervention in the process of criminal justice, with commentaries not only on the performance of the trial participants but also on such matters as their dress and appearance. However, it would clearly be unfair to

---

[147] The Times, 9 March 1995. [148] For further details of the case, see the Appendix.
[149] *R v Bentley* [1999] Crim LR 330.
[150] M. J. Trow, *'Let Him Have It, Chris': The Murder of Derek Bentley* (1990) 120–1 and 138.

extrapolate from the experience of that trial to the likely conduct of English criminal cases in the event that cameras were allowed into the courtroom. The media in the United States, under the protection of the First Amendment, are free to comment on pending or imminent trials in ways that would undoubtedly constitute contempt of court under English law. Yet it has never been seriously suggested that—apart from the necessary changes to section 41 of the Criminal Justice Act 1925—the law of contempt should be abolished or substantially changed as a consequence of television coverage. In the public relations battle that is waged between prosecution and defence in the United States, the possibility of the televising of the proceedings is a tactical weapon in the hands of the trial attorney. Professor Alan Dershowitz, who has been part of the defence team in a number of high profile American trials, has stated: 'One of the hardest decisions faced by a defense lawyer is whether to support or to oppose the televising of the trial.'[151] The televising of trials in the United States is but one aspect of a generally more open attitude towards investigation of the courts. Witnesses and jurors, and in some cases the judges themselves, feel free to approach, or to respond to approaches from, the mass media. An especially pertinent example is provided by the research conducted by Paul Thaler on the impact of the presence of television cameras on those involved in a well-known New York case.[152] The case in question was the prosecution of Joel Steinberg for the murder of his six-year-old daughter in 1988. As the contents of the book reveal, Thaler published the results of his interviews with all the leading participants in the case: not only counsel, witnesses, and jurors, but also—more remarkably still—the accused and the presiding judge. The trial took place soon after the cautious and (in the American context) belated admission of cameras into the New York courts. Thaler's aim was to identify how the presence of cameras affected the behaviour and modes of thinking of all concerned. No definitive conclusion is offered by him. In stark contrast to the reports 'which exude a type of statistical certainty' the work presents 'a viewpoint that takes into account the ambiguity that is integral to the human experience'.[153]

In the United Kingdom, quite apart from legal prohibitions such as that contained in section 8 of the Contempt of Court Act 1981, there are unspoken norms of self-restraint that would forbid such research. It will be appreciated, therefore, that the effect of television on the conduct of trials is even more difficult to ascertain than the effects of allowing, first spectators, then the media, to the seat of trial. In view of the absence of reliable empirical evidence, the question whether or not to permit televised coverage is best approached in the light of the traditional

---

[151] A. M. Dershowitz, *Reasonable Doubts: The O. J. Simpson Case and the Criminal Justice System* (1996), 145. The passage continues: 'Sometimes that decision is made with no input from counsel, but often the court will ask the prosecutor and defense counsel to take a position on this issue.'

[152] P. Thaler, *The Watchful Eye: American Justice in the Age of the Television Trial* (1994).

[153] ibid. xv.

rationales of open justice. Would the ends of open justice be advanced, or jeopardized, by the introduction of the camera? Clearly, television possesses very considerable scope for instruction of the public in matters of law and legal procedures. In some regards, the effect of the camera is likely to prove neutral (for example, on the standard of conduct of the trial judge or the veracity of witnesses). The consequences for the accused, on the other hand, are likely to be disproportionate to any gain (if there be any gain) in these areas. If he is acquitted, television coverage will have greatly exacerbated his ordeal. If he is convicted, his rehabilitation will be all the more difficult to achieve. For these reasons, if for no other, it is submitted that the English judiciary have been right in opposing the introduction of television cameras into the criminal courtroom. It may be that, as part of a number of measures designed to render the judiciary less remote, television access will be permitted to civil cases, at least. If so, the experience gained in Scotland may well prove useful in shaping arrangements south of the border.[154]

[154] Television coverage was permitted of the appeal of the Libyan who was convicted of the Lokerbie bombing (see p. 332, above). The proceedings, which commenced in January 2002 before a panel of five Scottish judges, were carried on BBC: *News 24*.

Coda

The ideal of open justice may be simply stated. An accused is subject to a fairer process, other things being equal, if certain fundamental conditions of his trial are satisfied. Those conditions are: that he is physically present at the place of trial; that witnesses who testify against him must also be present in the court-room; that the identity of such witnesses should be known to him; that there should be no physical or technological barrier between him and the witness (whether by way of screen, video link, or voice distortion device). And, to take the principal concern of this work, such confrontation is to take place before such members of the public who choose to attend the proceedings, and such representatives of the media as choose to report them. The same requirements, though in more muted terms, are also deemed intrinsic to the fairness of conduct of civil actions. The insistence on the requirements of openness, however, has attached to the 'hearing' phase alone of the trial process. Access to the deliberations of the decision-taking body, in particular the jury, has not historically formed part of the concept of open justice.

These procedural arrangements may be considered, in themselves, to be the integral elements of a fair trial. That is to say, any trial that does not observe these standards is, in itself, unfair. Or they may be viewed as means for the attainment of other ends. On the latter view, there may properly be departures from the standard procedures in particular situations—typified by the examination of vulnerable witnesses (children, or the victims of sexual assault)—where it is felt that the procedures do not serve their primary purpose of promoting the emergence of the truth about the case.

The latter categorization, especially, raises the issues of an empirical nature which underpin the subject of open justice. Other things being equal, is a witness more likely to tell the truth if confronted face to face with the accused? Is the truth more likely to emerge if the witness testifies in front of casual members of the public or representatives of the media? Is the competence or the integrity of judge or juror likely to be affected by the withholding of his name? Certainly, there are instances where witnesses, confronted by the prospect of an open court, have simply refused to testify. But, when they are not reduced to silence in this way, it is very difficult to determine whether the veracity of their statements is enhanced, diminished, or simply left unaffected, by the public forum in which the testimony is presented. The lack of scientifically reliable data on the performance of the *personae* of the trial under different conditions is most keenly felt in the context of the question whether or not to permit televised coverage of trials.

The lack of reliable information on these questions should not be surprising. It would be difficult to construct controlled experiments which would test the propensity of the truth to emerge from the same person when placed in different procedural settings. For the stresses imposed by appearance in court, even in the absence of additional factors such as facing one's assailant or having one's private life subject to minute examination, are considerable.

Prior to the advent of the print and other media, the requirements of open justice could be identified uncontroversially. The recording techniques made available by them have created different forms in which access to trial proceedings may be achieved. The possible use of such techniques now requires more careful thought about the precise scope and rationale of open justice.

Consider three hypothetical situations where the public and press may be denied entry to the courtroom. In the first situation, transcripts of the proceedings made by the court personnel would be made available free of charge to anyone who cares to collect one. Under the second set of arrangements the press and public, though barred from access to the place of trial, may sit in an adjoining building where they may follow the proceedings which are relayed to them by video link. The third arrangement would be one where the only access to the proceedings is made available by video tape, copies which are distributed to members of the public free of charge.

One difficulty with the first arrangement is the absence of any certain, independent knowledge that the written word accurately reflects the course of the proceedings. In this regard the third possibility has an advantage over the others in that it encompasses the visual element, though it may not do so entirely accurately. The element of independent report may be present or absent, depending on whether the task of compiling the video record is entrusted to court officials or an independent organization. Modern technology has the potential to convey knowledge of the trial to a worldwide audience. Yet, at the same time, the interposition of any medium between the *personae* of the trial and the rest of the world diminishes the effect of open justice. The medium may falsify, whether deliberately or inadvertently, the reality of the courtroom. Moreover, how important an element is the eye contact deriving from actual physical presence in the same room of the accused, judge, jurors, witnesses, and members of the public? Can this element be reproduced, or compensated, by the secure knowledge of the *personae* that their demeanour will be observed, though after the event, by a considerably larger number of persons than those capable of squeezing into the confines of the courtroom?

Developments in reporting technology have taken place while the severity of sentences has generally diminished. For the accused whose trial ends in conviction, therefore, the element of public access to the proceedings has varied in significance. In the era before the print media, with its routinely savage punishments, public knowledge was unlikely to bulk large in the ordeal of a condemned prisoner. With the reduction of the level of sentences from the draconian levels of former times, and with the greater facility for worldwide communication of trial events, the element has assumed a proportionately greater aspect of the 'punishment' endured by persons accused before the courts. To 'name and shame' individuals is increasingly seen to be a proper function of bodies apart from the criminal courts.

Obviously, it is the trial that has a salacious or unusual interest that is more likely than any other to be both observed at first hand and reported in the media. It would be naive to suppose that the observers are motivated, even in part, by the wish to observe the administration of justice. Indeed, on one of the rationales of open justice, those trials that generate a prurient interest, and consequently attract the greatest attention, should be the most fairly administered of all. Yet there have been deeply disconcerting practices in the conduct of rape trials—practices that have been discontinued, not as a result of popular pressure, but rather as a consequence of the critical writings of professionals.

The well-documented instances, in recent years, of miscarriages of justice have largely been traced to failings of process outside the courtroom itself. Lack of safeguards on matters such as the admissibility of confessions and duties of disclosure by the prosecution have meant, in some cases, that the outcome of the trial itself was all but a foregone conclusion. This surely demonstrates that, as a means of ensuring the rectitude of criminal procedure as a whole, the part played by the open conduct of trials is relatively small.

The idea of trial as public spectacle is very deeply rooted in the legal procedures of mankind. That it should be so has been seen, in modern times, as being to the advantage of the accused. It may serve to expose bias against the accused, but it is also capable of working to the advantage of the prosecution. In any event, whatever the outcome of the proceedings, it renders infinitely more difficult the post-trial assimilation of the accused into society. Perhaps the time has come for a re-assessment in view of the crude and unpredicable nature of trial-generated publicity.

Appendix

The following cases illustrate several points of general relevance to the theme of this book. Many of them have not been reported in the law reports. Even in those instances where a law report is available, the report does not contain the requisite details. For ease of reference, therefore, brief summaries are provided here. The cases are designated in their most familiar form, most usually by the name of the accused, though sometimes under the name of the victim.

1. BEVERLY ALLITT

Nurse Beverly Allitt was tried at Nottingham Crown Court in early 1993. The principal charge was the murder of four patients on the children's ward at Grantham Hospital. She was found guilty on all these counts, together with a number of counts of attempted murder and grievous bodily harm. Sentence was set by Latham J at thirteen life sentences. The case attracted considerable attention by virtue of the fact that Allitt was suffering from Munchausen Syndrome by Proxy. At the conclusion of the trial, a non-statutory inquiry was appointed by the Secretary of State for Health to investigate how the events of the case were allowed to occur and to draw any lessons from the episode. Despite the existence of a power under section 84 of the National Health Service Act 1977 to set up a formal inquiry, the Secretary of State decided to establish a form of inquiry that lacked powers to compel the attendance of witnesses and to demand the production of documents. This decision was unsuccessfully challenged by way of judicial review in the unreported case, *Crampton v Secretary of State for Health* (CA, 9 July 1993, Transcript No 824 of 1993).

2. ARMS TO IRAQ CASE

In fact, this is a group of cases, the most famous of which is the prosecution of three directors of the firm, Matrix Churchill, in 1992. The background was an embargo on the sale of military equipment to Iraq, which Matrix Churchill were accused of having breached by exporting machine tools. The defendants' case rested on the fact that both the security services and the government were fully aware of the nature of the company's exports to Iraq. The latter, in the person of the Minister for Trade, Alan Clark MP, had encouraged the firm, in its application for export licences, to stress the peaceful uses to which the exports could be put. A central feature of the trial was the resort to public interest immunity (PII) certificates in order to deny the defence access to government papers establishing collusion in the exports. The case against the directors collapsed in November 1992 after the trial judge, Judge Smedley, examined the evidence for which PII was claimed and allowed much of it to be disclosed. Lord Justice Scott was subsequently entrusted with the conduct of an inquiry into the issues raised by the case. Geoffrey Robertson, one of the defence counsel, gives an account of the trial in *The Justice Game* (1998) ch 15.

3. CARL BRIDGEWATER

Schoolboy Carl Bridgewater was murdered while on his newspaper delivery round in 1978. A year later, at Stafford Crown Court, four men were convicted of his murder: Vincent Hickey, Michael Hickey, James Robinson, and Patrick Molloy. The convictions were obtained largely as a result of a confession given by Molloy, which he subsequently retracted as having been made under duress. Molloy himself died in prison a few years later, but a campaign was started by the mother of one of the other three to clear their names. Notable aspects of the campaign were: the publication of a book about the case, *Murder at the Farm* (1986) by journalist Paul Foot; a feature entitled *Bad Company*, broadcast by the BBC in 1993; and the subsequent announcement by the foreman of the jury, Timothy O'Malley, of his belief, in the light of disclosures since the trial, that the men were innocent of the charge. Eventually, in February 1997, on a reference from the Home Secretary, the Crown conceded before the Court of Appeal that the convictions could not be sustained and the three men were released on unconditional bail. In July of the same year the Court of Appeal formally quashed the convictions.

4. JAMES BULGER

The abduction and murder of two-year-old James Bulger early in 1993 by Robert Thompson and Jon Venables gave rise to intense public outrage.[1] The case was highly unusual on account of the age of the accused, who were both ten years old at the time. At their trial, held later the same year at Preston Crown Court, the two boys were found guilty and ordered to be detained during Her Majesty's pleasure. Known only as 'Child A' and 'Child B' during the trial, their identities were released by the judge at the conclusion of the proceedings.[2] Over the following years a number of cases were brought in which aspects of the criminal justice system were challenged. In particular, the staging of the trial in an adult

---

[1] For an account of the case, see David James Smith, *The Sleep of Reason: The James Bulger Case* (1994).

[2] See ibid. 193, 223, and 226–7, for passages on the making of the initial anonymity order and the later order permitting identification of the accused.

forum was the subject of an application under the European Convention on Human Rights: *T v United Kingdom, V v United Kingdom*.[3] Other cases concerned the tariff: the level at which it should be set, the role of the Home Secretary in setting it, and the question whether the family of the victim could challenge a tariff that was arguably set too low. Controversy continued on the question of whether Thompson and Venables would continue to pose a threat to others. Fears for their own physical safety after release led them to sue successfully for an injunction, based on breach of confidence, restraining disclosure of their identity and whereabouts: *Venables and Another v News Group Newspapers and Others*.[4] After hearings in June 2001 before the Parole Board (which, following its usual practice, did not release the identities of the three members of the panel who conducted the hearings), Thompson and Venables were released on licence. The decision of the Crown Court judge to permit their identities to be disclosed has been questioned in the light of the most recent developments. Taken, in part, in order to facilitate debate on the highly unusual circumstances of the crime, the decision had the effect of fanning interest in the case and increasing the exposure of Thompson and Venables to acts of revenge. There are indications that, in the light of this case, courts are less inclined to reveal the identities of juveniles who have been found guilty of horrific crimes.[5]

5. CHRISTOPHER CRAIG AND DEREK BENTLEY

Craig and Bentley, respectively sixteen and nineteen years old at the time, were trapped by the police during the course of a robbery in 1952. Craig, who had a weapon, shot and killed one of the officers. He could not be sentenced to death on account of his age at the time. Bentley, who was unarmed, was hanged on the basis that he had called out to Craig 'Let him have it, Chris'—a cry that gave the name to both a book[6] and a film[7] of the case. The proceedings were the subject of intense controversy for a number of years thereafter. Disturbing features were Bentley's youth and low mental age, and the ambiguous nature of his exhortation to Craig. In addition, the manner of handling of the trial, by Lord Goddard, was the subject of much criticism. Eventually, after years of lobbying, the case was referred to the Court of Appeal: *R v Bentley*.[8] Bentley's conviction was declared unsafe since he had been denied a fair trial.

---

[3] (2000) 30 EHRR 121.   [4] [2001] 1 All ER 908.
[5] See The Times (26 June 2001) 1 ('Bulger fears stop judge naming boys').
[6] M. J. Trow, *'Let Him Have It, Chris': The Murder of Derek Bentley* (1990).
[7] *Let Him Have It* (1991).   [8] [1999] Crim LR 330.

6. THE GUINNESS LITIGATION

This series of cases arose out of one of the most prominent corporate scandals of the 1980s. In 1985 Guinness and Argos launched rival take-over bids for Distillers. Since both bidders were offering their own shares in exchange for shares in Distillers, it was important that the price of the bidders' shares did not fall as this would diminish their appeal to Distillers' shareholders. Certain members of the Guinness board allegedly initiated a share support operation by secretly buying Guinness shares with the aid of the company's funds. This was a breach of a long-standing provision in the Companies Acts. When the matter came to light a number of charges were brought against four persons, including the chief executive of Guinness, Ernest Saunders. An investigation was conducted concurrently by the Department of Trade and Industry, and related civil proceedings were brought against leading officers of Guinness.[9] That different types of legal proceeding were taking place at the same time caused the accused concern that their trials might be prejudiced by reports of the other cases. There were also fears that the jury in the criminal proceedings might not understand the complex financial data in the case. The prosecution relied heavily on evidence obtained by the Department of Trade and Industry inspectors from company officers who were not accorded the right to remain silent. Although this was regarded as acceptable under English law, it was found to contravene Article 6 of the European Convention on Human Rights.[10] More than a decade after the 113-day trial, allegations emerged that there had been an attempt to solicit sums of money purportedly on behalf of a member of the jury.[11] This may furnish additional grounds for overturning the convictions since, although known to the Serious Fraud Office (which handled the prosecution case), it was not reported to the judge at the time. Accounts of the take-over battle that led to these developments are Jonathan Guinness, *Requiem for a Family Business* (1997) and Nick Kochan and Hugh Pym, *The Guinness Affair, Anatomy of a Scandal* (1987).

7. WILLIAM KENNEDY SMITH

In Florida in December 1991 there took place the trial, on a charge of rape, of William Kennedy Smith, a younger member of the Kennedy family and nephew of Senator Edward Kennedy (who was called to testify in the case). The accused was acquitted. The case is a prominent instance of a charge of 'date rape' since the complainant, Patricia Bowman, admitted that intercourse had taken place, the

[9] See, for example, *Guinness plc v Saunders* [1990] 2 AC 663.
[10] *Saunders v United Kingdom* (1997) 23 EHRR 313.
[11] The Times (29 June 2001) 1. There was no suggestion that any of the defendants was involved in the attempt.

sole dispute being on the issue of consent. The proceedings were televised, Miss Bowman's face being obscured by a dot on the television screen. She subsequently waived her anonymity for the purposes of a television interview. Apart from the involvement of members of America's most prominent family, the trial raised two matters of particular interest to the themes of this book. Payment to witnesses was in issue since a friend of Miss Bowman, who had been in the vicinity and testified for her, was revealed in cross-examination to have been paid a substantial sum for her story by a television company. Also, the prosecution was notified of the testimony of three women who claimed that between 1983 and 1988 they had been sexually assaulted by the accused. The judge refused the prosecution's request to call them as witnesses since their testimony did not demonstrate a pattern of behaviour on the part of the accused.

8. CLIVE PONTING

Clive Ponting, a civil servant at the Ministry of Defence, was prosecuted in 1985 at the Central Criminal Court under section 2 of the Official Secrets Act 1911. The background to the case was the conflict, three years earlier, between Britain and Argentina over possession of the Falkland Islands. A central point in the conflict was the sinking of the Argentine warship, *General Belgrano*. The decision to authorize the attack proved controversial since the warship posed no immediate threat to British vessels, and the revulsion at the considerable loss of life ended all possibility of a peaceful resolution of the dispute. After the conclusion of the conflict, pressure was exerted on the government to explain the circumstances of the sinking of the *General Belgrano*. Ponting, believing that Parliament was being misled by the answers that were given, disclosed the relevant Ministry of Defence documents to an MP who had been pressing the government for an explanation. This disclosure, though made in good faith, was a breach of the Official Secrets Act. The verdict of not guilty in *R v Ponting*[12] may be characterized as the jury asserting its historical role of acquitting an accused who is guilty according to the letter of the law by way of protest against an oppressive prosecution. Ponting published an account of his conduct and trial in *The Right to Know: The Inside Story of the Belgrano Affair* (1985).

9. HAROLD SHIPMAN

Dr Harold Shipman, a general medical practitioner in Hyde, Greater Manchester, practised serial killing on an enormous scale. Estimates of the total number of his victims, however, have varied considerably. There have been three

---

[12] [1985] Crim LR 318.

forums in which his activities have been investigated. He was convicted in January 2000 at Preston Crown Court of the murder of fifteen of his patients. A coroner's inquest concluded that he unlawfully killed twenty-five more. In the aftermath of the trial the Secretary of State for Health announced that he was using his general powers under section 2 of the National Health Service Act 1977 to set up an independent inquiry, which would take evidence in private. A successful action for judicial review was brought by the relatives of the victims and by various media organizations, as a result of which the decision to hold the inquiry in private was quashed: *R v Secretary of State for Health, ex p Wagstaff, R v Secretary of State for Health, ex p Associated Newspapers Ltd.*[13] The inquiry consequently sat in public. Chaired by a High Court judge, Dame Janet Smith, it began sitting on 20 June 2001. Expected to last two years, the inquiry is charged with examining the deaths of 459 of Shipman's patients.

10. O. J. SIMPSON

The trial in 1995 of Orenthal James Simpson for the murder of his ex-wife, Nicole Brown Simpson, and her friend, Ronald Goldman, was one of the most widely publicized of modern cases. The issues in the case sharply divided America, because (among other things) the evidence in the course of the trial revealed racial prejudice among the Los Angeles police. The proceedings were televised, though the presiding judge, Judge Ito, threatened several times to suspend television coverage and did so on one occasion when a camera closed up on the accused while writing a note to his lawyers. Not only were the names of the jurors publicized, but also how they voted and what factors swayed them in their decision. These revelations have added to the speculation ever since as to whether, in acquitting Simpson, the jury reached the correct verdict. A civil suit, again tried by a jury, brought against Simpson shortly afterwards reached a different conclusion from the criminal trial: Simpson was found liable for the two deaths and was ordered to pay damages of $33.5 million. Several of the participants in the criminal proceedings subsequently published accounts of the trial: for example, Christopher Darden, one of the team of prosecutors, with Jess Walter, *In Contempt* (1996); Robert L. Shapiro, a defence attorney, with Larkin Warren, *The Search for Justice: A Defense Attorney's Brief on the O. J. Simpson Case* (1996); and Alan Dershowitz (who was employed for the defence with a view to conducting an appeal in the event of a conviction) in *Reasonable Doubts: The O. J. Simpson Case and the Criminal Justice System* (1996).

---

[13] [2001] 1 WLR 292.

11. OSCAR SLATER

The conviction of Oscar Slater for murder in 1909 is one of the best-known examples of a miscarriage of justice under Scots law. The trial is also noteworthy in having attracted the attention of Sir Arthur Conan Doyle, who in 1912 published a booklet entitled *The Case of Oscar Slater*. The work, based on the transcripts of the trial together with interviews with the witnesses, drew the attention of the public to the flimsy and contradictory nature of the case for the prosecution. So persuasive did the booklet prove that a commission of inquiry was established to review the case. It is worth noting that the commission sat *in camera*.[14] However, it was not until 1928 that Slater secured his release. Apparently, Sir Arthur Conan Doyle came to know of the case in two ways: by reading a report of the trial, and by being contacted independently by lawyers acting for Slater.[15] The former provides an unusual variation on one of the rationales of the free reporting of trials.

12. ROSEMARY WEST

The suicide, while awaiting trial, of her husband, Frederick West, resulted in Rosemary West facing charges alone relating to the murder of a number of young women. The case attracted worldwide interest on account of the number of victims, the element of sexual perversion in the killings, and the fact that the bodies were disposed of at the house, in Cromwell Street, Gloucester, that was the Wests' home for the greater part of their marriage. The trial, in autumn 1995, resulted in Rosemary West being convicted on all ten charges of murder. Both the contested committal proceedings (held in Dursley magistrates' court) and the subsequent appeal against conviction (*R v West*)[16] were used to explore a number of issues, chief among which was the question of the propriety of payments to witnesses. Among several accounts of the case see, in particular, Brian Masters, *'She Must Have Known': The Trial of Rosemary West* (1997).

13. LOUISE WOODWARD

Louise Woodward was a nanny employed by an American couple, Sunil and Deborah Eappen. In February 1997 the family's baby, Matthew, was admitted to hospital in Boston and was found to have severe head injuries. When the baby died several days later, Woodward was charged with murder. Her trial under the law of Massachusetts, which took place later in the same year, was broadcast not

---

[14] M. Booth, *The Doctor, the Detective and Arthur Conan Doyle: A Biography of Arthur Conan Doyle* (1997) 272.
[15] ibid. 270.   [16] [1996] 2 Cr App R 374.

only in the United Kingdom but also in other parts of the world. The jury returned a verdict that she was guilty of murder in the second degree, but this was peremptorily reduced by the trial judge, Judge Zobel, to one of involuntary manslaughter without any further reference to the jury or any reconvening of the court. Since he also reduced the sentence to the period that Louise Woodward had already spent in confinement—279 days—she was freed immediately. The Supreme Judicial Court of Massachusetts, on appeal by the Eappen family, affirmed that Judge Zobel had been entitled to take these courses of action.

Index